WITHDRAWN

Teaching Speech

McGraw-Hill Series in Speech

Glen E. Mills, *Consulting Editor in General Speech*
John J. O'Neill, *Consulting Editor in Speech Pathology*

Teaching Speech

Fourth Edition

DUDLEY

LOREN REID , 1905-

Professor of Speech and Dramatic Art
University of Missouri, Columbia

Illinois Central College
Learning Resouce Center

McGRAW-HILL BOOK COMPANY

New York, St. Louis, San Francisco, Düsseldorf, Johannesburg,
Kuala Lumpur, London, Mexico, Montreal, New Delhi, Panama,
Rio de Janeiro, Singapore, Sydney, Toronto

41146

TEACHING SPEECH

Library of Congress Catalog Card Number 79-136193
07-051785-1

1234567890MAMM7987654321

This book was set in Press Roman by Creative Book Services,
division of McGregor & Werner, Incorporated, and printed on permanent
paper and bound by The Maple Press Company.
The designer was Creative Book Services. The editor was Robert Fry.
Loretta Palma supervised production.

contents

3   The Classroom Extended

4   The Profession of Teaching

5   Appendixes

foreword

This book is for the beginning teacher. I have always had a special concern for the beginner, because I have been one so many years of my life. I had little formal preparation for teaching: my adviser simply said, on a momentous occasion, "Someday you may want to teach school," and worked out a program in which a psychology course counted as curriculum, a history course as philosophy, a literature course as method.

One day the telephone rang in the hall of my college residence at Grinnell; the superintendent of a western high school was on the wire. "Could you join our staff next year and perhaps direct the school paper?" he said. "Yes," I replied, "that would be right down my line." "And could you also take over the debate team?" he continued. "I would like to," I answered. "And how about giving us a hand with assembly programs?" "That will be no problem," I responded. "Well," he said, "we'll consider it settled." Then a long pause: "By the way, can you teach English?"

How can one forget the first class he ever taught? September came, and I found myself, a beginner, standing before thirty enrollees in sophomore English. At the back of the room the superintendent himself was standing. He had been startled by my young looking face. "Do you expect you will have trouble with discipline?" he had asked me that morning—a little worried, I felt. "I don't think so," I said. He came to my first class anyway.

On the station platform of my home town the day before, I had had a conversation with the ticket agent. "I taught once," said the station-master. "One thing about teaching—it gives you self-confidence." I didn't feel self-confident as I stood in front of this class. I began by telling a few stories, and the class relaxed. The superintendent and I also relaxed. After a while I asked the pupils to go to the board and work on some drills. I remember wondering whether they would actually obey me or just sit there in defiance. I had never had any experience in ordering people about. They quickly and quietly went to the board, and the superintendent departed.

After two years I entered graduate school, first at the University of Chicago, and later at the State University of Iowa, and began a fearful program of study. I enrolled in phonetics, vocal anatomy, and rhetoric, studying alongside students who were mature and sophisticated. I took acoustics with physics majors, psycho-physics with psychology majors, abnormal psychology with dormant psychiatrists, linguistics with doctoral candidates deeply imbedded in ancient tongues. In speech pathology, my first patient had a defective *s* that I could not even hear, much less correct. What little I did know seemed trifling and unimportant; my professors always pushed me into new fields, thus keeping me at beginner's status. In my final week of graduate study the registrar notified my adviser that I did not even have an undergraduate major in speech, and therefore should not have been allowed on the campus in the first place. That ripe statistic always struck me as the beginning of wisdom.

Eventually I achieved an advanced degree, and was ready to resume teaching. By then the depression was full upon the country—and me. Banks were locked up, farm mortgages were foreclosed, wages and salaries were down. I went to Kansas City to be interviewed for a speech position in a large high school. The preceding day machine gun bullets had swept Union Station Plaza as gangsters attempted to deliver their buddies from the prohibition agents. Life seemed rugged indeed. The superintendent of the city schools, a friendly, jolly-eyed man with a white mustache and beard, liked my credentials. Finally he said, "Of course you are also prepared to teach dramatics and direct plays." I thought of the men selling apples in the streets. "Of course," I answered. I went home and put aside my books on British oratory and rhetoric, and compiled a collection about acting and directing. I conferred with friends who taught stage lighting and stagecraft, and made a lapful of sketches. Is there no end to the field of speech? I was again back in grade one.

I skip a few years, and visualize a class of another sort: a course in the teaching of speech, at Syracuse University. I was now a dual professor of speech and education, a teaching supervisor. I wore two hats: in me were embodied both content and technique. I had had *Actual* Teaching Experience. One could almost put that into a college catalog, like a degree: M.A., Ph.D., A.T.E. For this class I outlined sure-fire, never-fail units. These materials having been digested, the students went into the public schools to begin their practice teaching. For teaching, like law and medicine, has both an art and a practice. When the students returned they wore long, disappointed faces. "These ideas may work for you, but they don't for us," they complained. "Come visit our classes, and tell us what is wrong."

That brought me up short, and made me a beginner again. What one student may achieve through intuition, another may accomplish only after precept and formalization. My students did not appear to learn much from lectures or outside readings: they prospered most when we visualized an assignment in detail, with illustration and example. If we studied, for instance, problems in the teaching of oral reading, and discussed classroom activities and techniques, demonstrating useful procedures and locating difficulties and pitfalls, student teachers were fairly likely to evolve interesting lesson plans that could be tried out on students with a degree of success.

I must not, however, underestimate another sort of training that goes underneath and beyond these early classroom experiences. I was reared in a Missouri newspaper family and grew up in a newspaper office. As editor my father enjoyed a wide correspondence with well-known state and national figures. He was keenly interested in public speaking, and often, as a member of the local speakers' committee, he was able to persuade well-known people to come to our small Missouri town and speak at the annual homecoming picnic. Often, too, they appeared on chautauqua and lyceum circuits. I had a chance to hear William Jennings Bryan, Thomas R. Marshall, William Joel Stone, and James A. Reed. Marshall was Woodrow Wilson's Vice-President, and Stone and Reed were nationally prominent Missouri senators. I also heard Charles M. Hay, Joshua W. Alexander, and A. M. Dockery, much less well known today, along with scores of other speakers whose names even I have forgotten. As my father and his friends were well-informed, their discussions of the various speakers and their messages were usually as stimulating as the addresses themselves.

On the dramatic side my heritage is less distinguished but certainly distinctive. I got to see *Uncle Tom's Cabin* half a dozen times, and a hundred tent shows. They came on their own, and as a part of the chautauquas and lyceums. As art they ranked somewhere between Apache knife throwers and Swiss bell ringers, but they left an imprint of sorts. Entertainments like these were a part of the growing-up of every midwestern boy before and during World War I. They were doubly and triply a part of mine, because, being in a newspaper family, I had free passes to everything.

One day when I was a high school sophomore the superintendent announced tryouts for an oratorical contest. I carried the news home to my father and mother, with a thought of trying out, and I see now why they seconded the notion so readily. After all, this was the way Bryan had made his start. Father got out a well-thumbed copy of Ingersoll's orations—there was no reason for starting with anything less than the best—and inside of two hours we had worked out a ten-minute cutting of his tribute to Thomas Paine. By midnight I learned half of it. In the next three years I delivered it in twenty or more contests. I also did some debating, starting in the parlor with jousts with my brother on the horse versus the cow, and moving up through woman suffrage, prohibition, the League of Nations, and the World Court. I am glad to report that my generation of high school and college debaters settled these issues, removing them for all time from the lists of debate topics.

So when I stood before that first class in a South Dakota high school, and later faced my first students at the State University of Iowa, I at least had a certain mass of subject matter experience behind me. Most beginning teachers can make the same statement. If they have been even mildly attentive to TV, they have heard all the great speakers of today worth hearing. Perhaps a few of these speakers they have heard in the flesh, in their home towns or on their college campuses. They have had a world of opportunities to participate in speaking contests and in debates, on radio and TV shows and in plays. They have had a wide variety of experiences in their speech and drama courses. They have walked the hot coals of stage fright and have survived more or less whole. They have learned the necessity for preparation, and have realized, small bit by small bit, that the principles on which the communicative arts are founded make strong, solid sense.

All sorts of observations, therefore, have gone into the writing of this book. Wherever I thought an example would illuminate a point, I have put it in. Wherever I thought the necessary information was available in standard references, I have hurried on; but I have indicated what these references are.

This book was first printed in 1952 in a preliminary edition. I taught from it at the University of Missouri, the University of Utah, and the University of Southern California. Teachers at about a hundred other institutions used it; a few of them have written helpful observations. Dr. Mardel Ogilvie, of Queens College, the author of *Speech in the Elementary School,* wrote me a well-thought-out letter of valuable suggestions. Many of my students expressed their reactions vividly. They advised me to shorten the title from *Teaching Speech in the High School* to *Teaching Speech,* pointing out that many of the pages were as applicable to college instruction as to high school teaching. They advised me to beef up certain chapters, particularly those in the middle of the book. They contributed hints, sources for materials, kinds of assignments, and other useful ideas from their own specialties and backgrounds.

Once I wrote in an article: "We fret over the beginners because they make foolish mistakes, or because they have not had enough hours in this or that. Sometimes they are too strict, sometimes too bookish, sometimes overly inclined to give tests; but their virtues of enthusiasm, fresh point of view, freedom from family responsibilities, and willingness to expend their time and energy highly commend them. Exceptions quickly leap to mind, but as a group the beginning teachers supply most of the energy and vivacity that brighten the school day, and it may be that they also supply their full share of the day's inspiration."

I address this book to the beginner everywhere, and to those of vaster experience who still have a beginner's curiosity about teaching procedures, and a beginner's affection for the teaching profession.

LOREN REID

note to the fourth edition

The foreword was written in the summer of 1951, and appeared with little alteration in the first three editions of *Teaching Speech*. I let it stand much as it has previously appeared. I do not see how I can better express my concern with the problem of the beginning teacher, especially if I can include in this category the experienced teacher who seeks new ideas and approaches.

Many of the teaching problems that were discussed in the other versions persist, and new ones have arisen. I suspect the current edition shows, in subtle ways, the effect upon classroom teaching of such trends as these: (1) the growing complexity of the discipline, with increasing attention to empirical procedures; (2) the competition for the students' attention and interest of speech versus other disciplines; (3) a heartening emphasis upon the humanities and the social studies, following a period when the principal thrust was upon the sciences; (4) the greater sophistication, the enhanced freedom of spirit, and the generally superior preparation of students at all levels; (5) the use of a varied and imaginative lot of teaching aids and assists; (6) the impact of federal support, both as it increases and as it decreases; (7) rising enrollments, particularly at colleges, including community colleges, and universities.

In any revision the author retains features that have proved useful and adds material in response to readers' suggestions. A new teacher seldom has sufficient examples, so I have retained specific illustrations from former editions and have added new ones. Collectively they suggest areas into which the teacher can venture to find examples of his own. I have substantially increased the amount of reference material. The lists of texts are reasonably full though not complete. Often a teacher has the name of an author or a title in mind, so the lists will help him secure the exact information he needs. In the appendix are addresses of publishers, manufacturers, and regional and national associations.

Invariably the reader will have to adapt the book to his own situation. It is not practical to say, "The paragraph that follows applies to colleges but not to high school or junior high." Nor can one say, "This assignment will work better in a suburban high school than in an inner city school." The teacher's art is fragile and what is excellent for one is poor for another.

Once again I wish to express my appreciation to my departmental colleagues at the University of Missouri, Columbia, for their advice and assistance.

Off the campus I have addressed inquiries to perhaps three or four hundred people: directors of state activity associations, state superintendents of education, speech supervisors, directors of the first course at the college level, high school and college specialists in specific areas, officials of regional and national associations, and publishers. They have responded with a cordiality that makes me feel doubly grateful.

Knowing well that I am likely to make startling and unforgivable omissions, I express my thanks to the following for allowing me to make use of certain materials:

William Work, executive secretary, Speech Association of America; Thomas D. Houchin, executive secretary, Speech Association of the Eastern States; Kenneth E. Andersen, executive secretary, Central States Speech Association; Dwight L. Freshley, editor, *Southern Speech Journal*; Robert Vogelsang, executive secretary, Western Speech Association, for permission to print excerpts from the publications of their associations and for other kinds of information.

Logan Wilson, president, American Council on Education; Becky Bogard, economic assistant, American Association of University Professors; Glen Robinson, director, research division, National Education Association, for permission to print excerpts from journals and publications of their associations and for statistical and other types of data.

Charley A. Leistner, director of the Committee on Discussion and Debate Materials, National University Extension Association, for information about debate and discussion topics and Committee policies.

William H. Inglis, administrator, American Educational Theatre Association, Martin L. Jones, editor, *Bulletin of the American Association of University Professors,* for permission to print excerpts from their journals and publications.

Ronald L. Smith, executive secretary, International Communication Association and Paul D. Brandes, Kim Giffin, and Kendall Bradley, for permission to print excerpts from the *Journal of Communication.* Gifford Blyton, president, American Forensic Association, for permission to print excerpts from the *Journal of the American Forensic Association* and other materials.

Floyd R. Merritt, director, Ohio State High School Speech League; Lavinia McNeely, supervisor, English and Language Arts, Louisiana State Department of Education; H. David Fry, assistant executive secretary, Illinois High School Association; Herman H. Brockhaus, Wisconsin High School Forensic Association; Gladys Dieruf, librarian, University Extension, University of Wisconsin; Fred B. McDonald, director, elementary and secondary education, New Mexico Department of Education; Hugh Seabury, Iowa High School Forensic League, Herman F. Benthul, assistant superintendent, curriculum development, Dallas Independent School District, for permission to print excerpts from materials published by their offices and for other information.

Wilbur E. Gilman, Queens College, for historical data about speech associations.

Ralph G. Nichols, University of Minnesota, St. Paul, for information about research in listening.

John Christopher Reid, University of Missouri, Columbia, for assistance in interpreting computer and other statistical premises and data.

Holt, Rinehart and Winston, Inc., for permission to print excerpts from Halbert E. Gulley, *Discussion, Conference, and Group Process,* 2d ed., 1968.

Little, Brown and Co. for permission to print an excerpt from Robert Beloof, *The Performing Voice in Literature,* 1966.

Addison-Wesley Publishing Co., for permission to print an excerpt from Dwight Allen and Kevin Ryan, *Microteaching,* 1969.

E. P. Dutton and Co., for permission to print *The Spires of Oxford* by Winifred M. Letts. Copyright 1917 by E. P. Dutton and Co. Renewal 1945 by Winifred M. Letts.

Random House, for permission to print an excerpt from Gilbert Highet, *The Art of Teaching,* 1950; and from Kahlil Gibran, *The Prophet,* 1953, both published by Alfred A. Knopf, Inc.

The Amidon Press, for permission to print an excerpt from E. J. Amidon and N. A. Flanders, *The Role of the Teacher in the Classroom,* 1963.

University of Chicago Press, for permission to print an excerpt from Wayne C. Booth, *The Rhetoric of Fiction,* 1951.

The editors of *Look,* for permission to print an excerpt from the issue of June 29, 1965.

Appleton-Century-Crofts, for permission to print an excerpt from Henry L. Ewbank and J. Jeffery Auer, *Discussion and Debate,* 2d ed., 1951.

Fearon Publishers, for permission to print an excerpt from Robert F. Mager, *Preparing Instructional Objectives,* 1962.

Jean J. Madden, director, Alumni Activities, and James R. Spieler, manager, Annual Gifts Progressive Development Fund, University of Missouri, Columbia, for statistics on alumni giving.

Elmer Ellis, University of Missouri, for permission to quote from *Toward Better Teaching.* Robert S. Daniel for permission to use the *Teacher Evaluation Questionnaire* developed at the University of Missouri, Columbia, and for suggestions about evaluation.

Fred McKinney, University of Missouri, Columbia, for suggestions about counselling and related psychological applications.

Many editors and publishers reminded me that the material I wished to quote was freely available under the "fair use" agreement, but I nevertheless appreciate the courtesies extended.

Mardel Ogilvie, Herbert Lehman College of the City of New York, and Margaret L. Wood, Northern Illinois University, have given invaluable help with chapters of the manuscript, for which I am most grateful. Other readers unknown to me, selected by the publisher, have directed attention to all manner of points, substantive and rhetorical, that guided the final shaping of the manuscript.

Other professional assistance is acknowledged at appropriate places in the text.

My wife, Gus, out of her hundreds of hours of supervising university teachers of freshman English, has provided specific ideas which I have shamelessly filched. Some of these come under the heading of method, others under philosophy.

My relationship with McGraw-Hill has extended over many years. Clarence T. Simon, late consulting editor of its Speech Series, cheered me by his enthusiasm for the notion that McGraw-Hill might bring out this revision. Frederic W. Hills, Publisher, Social Science, Humanities, and Foreign Languages, provided the mix of encouragement and general directive that were invaluable in getting the project under way. Robert A. Fry, Speech Editor, took over the manuscript in its early stages and has been on the battle line since, with all kinds of editorial and other professional advice and counsel.

The reader will not go far wrong if he concludes that many good points of the book come because of persistent prodding from people listed above and from others, and that its spectacular faults result because the author at times failed to listen and heed.

LOREN REID

Teaching Speech

Part One
preview

So, Mr. M'Choakumchild began in his best manner. He and some one hundred and forty other schoolmasters, had lately been turned at the same time, in the same factory, on the same principles, like so many pianoforte legs. . . . He knew all about the Water Sheds of all the world . . . all the histories of all the peoples . . . all the productions, manners, and customs of all the countries, and all their boundaries and bearings on the two-and-thirty points of the compass. Ah, rather overdone, M'Choakumchild. If he had only learnt a little less, how infinitely better he might have taught more!

He went to work . . . not unlike Morgiana in the Forty Thieves: looking into all the vessels ranged before him, one after another, to see what they contained. Say, good M'Choakumchild. When from thy boiling store, thou shalt fill each jar brim full by-and-by, dost thou think that thou wilt always kill outright the robber Fancy lurking within—or sometimes only maim and distort him!

Charles Dickens in *Hard Times*

1

preview of a profession

And you, America,
Cast you the real reckoning for your present?
The lights and shadows of your future, good or
*   evil?*
To girlhood, boyhood look, the teacher and the
*   school.*

Walt Whitman

Let us hope that this moment finds you in a pensive mood, strongly committed to the teaching profession, and willing to gain insight into possibilities that may lie ahead. Education is currently described as a rapidly growing field, full of promise. The purpose of these pages is to describe trends that are powering present-day inquiries into teaching and learning.

Admittedly all that can be done here is to sketch the situation briefly. As former Harvard president James Bryant Conant, author of *The American High School Today,* told an audience of high school principals: "Writing about American education is almost as breathtaking as writing about international politics. Before a book is in print, parts of it are already out of date."[1] The statistics here and elsewhere will, however, serve to record the present scene, and even after the figures themselves are no longer applicable, the picture of trends will continue to be helpful.

---

[1] *Time,* January 29, 1965, p. 56.

Students: In the Mass

We are in the midst of a social phenomenon: more people are attending school today than ever before. As a general estimate, one out of every three persons in the total population goes to school. A broad figure is seventy million: fifty-two million in elementary and secondary schools, eight to nine million in higher education, nine to ten million in adult classes. The totals are huge; we are, after all, a population that is ninety-eight percent literate.[2]

Indications are that enrollments will steadily increase. Since World War I the changes have been staggering. Of the sixty students in my high school graduating class, only three received any kind of college education, though half a dozen good institutions were within seventy-five miles of us. If all the college students of my generation could have been assembled, they would have found ample seating room in a dozen of the great university stadiums in the Mississippi Valley. We numbered considerably less than a million.

Now the picture has vastly changed.

After World War II, enrollments began to increase steadily. (The war had interrupted educational plans as well as breaking homes, dislocating families, delaying marriages.) In the latter years of the war, educational authorities began to contemplate the problem of educating GI's. No one, however, anticipated the extent of the rush back to school when the war was over. I recall conducting an informal survey among the hundred or so air force cadets I was teaching at Syracuse University. The great bulk of them declared that they did not intend to complete their education when the war was over. "We will be too old," they said; "we will be too far behind ever to catch up." But the war ended sooner than anyone anticipated. Moreover, they changed their minds; financial support was available for tuition, books, supplies, and other necessaries, and they flocked back to the campuses. Many who had never previously considered this step undertook a college education. Some had not even been graduated from high school, but were admitted to college on the basis of tests or other evidence.[3]

At the same time thousands of new homes were started. The total number of marriages per year did not increase greatly—1.5 million before the war, 1.6 million afterwards—but the new couples were eager to have families. The great American baby boom got under way. From 1935 to 1945 the number of annual

---

[2]To learn exact figures for any one year, consult these convenient sources: *Statesman's Yearbook, World Almanac, Britannica Book of the Year,* or releases issued periodically by the United States Office of Education.

[3]Reports from abroad indicate that many Americans in service do not intend to return to the campus. Like other veterans, however, they may change their minds when they return to civilian life, review their career plans, and reassess the educational requirements for those careers.

births had slowly increased from 2,155,000 to 2,735,000. In 1946, however, it leaped to 3,288,000. Never before had as many as three million babies been born in one year in the continental United States. Year by year the number climbed steadily until in 1961 it touched a high point of 4,317,000. Slowly it began to decline; in 1964 the number was 4,070,000. By 1968 the baby crop was down to 3,335,000, and further declines were predicted. White and black families alike are affected.[4]

The babies born in the mid-forties supplied the base for college attendance in the mid-sixties. Youngsters born during the peak year of 1961 will be storming the gates of college in 1977 and 1978. Business and industrial leaders are studying birth figures with tremendous personal and financial interest. These youngsters will have to be fed, clothed, housed, supplied with sports cars, and color TVs. The prospective teacher can also view this never-ending parade with relish. As long as babies are born ignorant and uninformed, teachers will be in demand. Not only are more children being born, but they are staying in school longer. Of one thousand fifth graders who toddled off to school in 1946, 553 made it all the way through high school. Such a survival figure would have seemed astronomical to my fifth-grade teacher. Hardly a fourth of her fifth graders saw their names on a commencement diploma. She would have been even more astounded by the record of the fifth graders of 1959; 721 of every 1000 graduated.[5] Thus the holding power of the schools is steadily increasing. Personal, social, and economic factors are on the side of students' getting as much education as possible.

A survey by the editors of *Look* revealed the deep-seated attitudes of people about education. Of the teenagers interviewed, 65 percent listed college as a principal objective; 41 percent expressed regrets about the inadequacy of their education thus far. Given their lives to live over, 43 percent of the adults would have got more education. Given their choice of occupation, they chose teaching over every possibility except business. As for their children, they preferred teaching to every profession save medicine.[6] In any survey of this sort a good deal of wishful thinking creeps in—many who would *like* to have a diploma or a degree would not have sustained the interest to *work* for it; even so the statistics are remarkable.

A statistic of particular interest to Americans: the United States sends 40 percent of its young people to colleges and universities. By contrast, Great Britain and France send about 10 percent. The rioting students of London and Paris in 1968 would have been delighted to settle for what Americans enjoy and take for granted.

---

[4] Basic data from U.S. Census Bureau; U.S. Department of Health, Education, and Welfare; *World Almanac*. Decline among whites has fallen from 117.7 babies born to women aged 15-44 (1957) to 77 (1968); among nonwhites the decline has been from 163 to 115.
[5] The American Council on Education, *A Fact Book on Higher Education*, 1968, p. 8048.
[6] *Look*, June 29, 1965, p. 21.

For the future, these figures are projected:

1. Elementary school enrollment is expected to level: 36 million in 1965, 36 million in 1975.

2. High school enrollment will continue to follow an established rate of increase: from 12.9 million in 1965 to 16.6 million in 1975.

3. College and universities will move from 5.5 million in 1965 to 9.1 million in 1975.

All sorts of interesting lesser statistics are buried in the larger figures. Community colleges will continue to expand in this ten-year period: from 840,000 to 1,685,000. Graduate schools will need to accommodate more than double their enrollment: 582,000 to 1,140,000.[7]

Reviewing statistics like these, a young person accepting his first teaching appointment can feel reasonably certain that the demand for teachers will be strong and continuing. Although there will be plateaus and reversals, the Carnegie Commission on Higher Education has proposed that by the year 2000, no American be deprived of the chance to go to college by barriers of race, geography, income, age, or quality of early schooling.

Teachers: Too Few, Too Many

One fact emerges: increasing numbers of teachers are available to instruct the increasing numbers of students. In some fields the supply is ample; in others, the market belongs to the seller. One summer there appear to be too many Ph.D's in physics; another sees too many in English or theater. Black colleges complain of a brain drain; their good teachers, they say, are being lured away. Rapidly rising enrollment in colleges of education and graduate schools has created surpluses in certain disciplines and in certain regions. These surpluses will affect poorly trained teachers more than others. And of course these statements have to be reinterpreted each school year and in each part of the country.

Every prospective teacher should review the situation for himself. Different regions have different rates of growth and development. The teacher placement official of your own college or university is a good place to start an investigation.

Further information can be secured from the placement services of learned societies such as the Speech Communication Association, the American Educational Theatre Association, or the American Speech and Hearing Association (see Appendix E for addresses). These and other associations maintain facilities at their annual conventions for appointing officers to meet with prospective can-

[7]The American Council on Education, *A Fact Book on Higher Education,* 1968, p. 8005.

didates. Although the demand for elementary school teachers has slackened in most parts of the nation, the demand for high school and college teachers should at least be moderate. The well-educated teacher with one or more graduate degrees will be in an especially favorable position in the decade ahead.

Salaries: Up, but not Enough

Each of the previous editions of this text has included typical salary schedules from public school systems; the current exhibits are in Chapter 19. Applicants for elementary or high school positions may write superintendents of schools in which they are interested and secure copies of the salary schedule. In general these observations are true:

1. Schools pay teachers on the same basis regardless of whether the teaching assignment is in the elementary grades, junior high, or senior high.

2. Schools have a graded series of salary increments, based upon length of service.

3. A few schools have merit increases in addition to the automatic increments.

4. A few schools pay the teacher a modest additional sum for extra duties such as directing plays, directing debate, supervising school publications, supervising student organizatons, or serving as school clinician.

5. Other factors being equal, a teacher with a master's degree will receive substantially more per year than a teacher with comparable length of service holding a bachelor's degree. The economic return from higher degrees is obvious; the personal satisfaction of having an additional year's preparation is especially noteworthy. Intermediate steps between bachelor's and master's degrees are frequently found on public school schedules, so that the teacher receives additional compensation for a semester's graduate study, or for a couple of summer sessions, beyond the bachelor's degree.

College and university salaries have gradually increased. In 1956 the average faculty salary would buy about 12 percent more goods and services than it would in 1940. Since then the average annual *real* increase (taking into consideration factors of inflation) has ranged from 2 percent (1968) to 5 percent (1965), or about 4 percent a year on the average.[8] The best source of information about faculty salaries continues to be the summer issues of the *AAUP Bulletin,* and should be consulted by those who wish the latest estimates.

Whether salaries continue to increase at these or other rates, level off, or

---

[8] These figures are in terms of the 1939 dollar which equals 100; the 1968 dollar equals 250.4. The source of these calculations is *AAUP Bulletin,* Summer 1969, pp. 192 f.

decrease, depends on the state of the national economy and the importance of education to it. A key figure to watch is the Gross National Product (GNP), a figure that can be put, roundly, at a trillion dollars. Education needs a larger share of the GNP than it has received if students are to be taught adequately in the numbers required. Following are indications of this larger share:

1. *Tuition Fees.* Nearly every year the colleges and universities of the country announce a further increase in fees. Years ago Harvard Economist Seymour E. Harris, in a report to the Central Association of College and University Business Officers, called tuition increases the biggest untapped source of additional income. He correctly observed that college and university expenses were increasing more rapidly than tuition advances and, at that time, urged that the tuition bill be quadrupled.[9] Administrators have repeatedly reminded alumni that tuition fees do not cover educational costs.

The president of Brown University, when announcing a tuition increase, added that Brown students were paying $800 per year less than the actual total cost of their education, and that much of this $800 was being taken out of the hides of their professors. The president of Grinnell College reported that the college was then spending $810 more than the student paid the college—again an automatic subsidy for each student. Substantial tuition increases are regularly announced each spring and summer across the nation as college administrations and governing boards study anew the constantly rising costs of instruction. In 1969-70 tuition at major public colleges and universities jumped 16.5 percent; the median went from $369 for resident students in 1968-69 to $430 in 1969-70.

Annual tuition increases of even 4 or 5 percent mount rapidly. At land-grant schools tuition for out-of-state students is being raised more rapidly than for in-state students. This kind of move is made only in response to strong local pressures. It overlooks the fact that college graduates often do not take up permanent residence in their home states, and, if the tuition differential becomes too large, will tend to make colleges and universities more provincial.

2. *Alumni contributions.* Do students, after graduating, repay these costs? Alumni of the 1,344 institutions reporting to the American Alumni Council and the Council for Financial Aid to Education contributed $400,300,000 during 1969-70. The average annual alumni gift in 1969-70 was $53.73, an increase over previous years. Other categories of gifts to colleges and universities totalled nearly $1.3 billion. It is apparent from these figures that alumni support is increasing substantially, even despite campus unrest. Nevertheless, colleges are not recovering their costs from alumni.[10]

[9]*Time,* May 25, 1959, p. 70.
[10]The American Alumni Council and the Council for Financial Aid to Education, *Voluntary Support of Education,* 1969-1970.

3. *Corporation and foundation support.* In this decade business is expected to make contributions in excess of half a billion dollars a year. More than one billion dollars comes annually to colleges and universities from all sources of voluntary support.[11]

4. *Federal support.* Grants and scholarships from the National Defense Education Act have had great impact on the financing of educational expenses of both individuals and institutions. The Elementary and Secondary Education Act of 1965 provided more than one billion dollars for the first year of operation, most of it for Title I, aimed at the educational needs of culturally deprived children. Other titles provided library books and textbooks, special equipment, funds for special cultural, educational, and scientific programs, funds for research in educational techniques, support for state education agencies. The amount of federal or state support any given year depends upon current problems, about which the teacher can keep himself informed through national associations.

5. *More of the student's educational dollar should go for educational necessities.* This statement represents a hope, not a fact. Critics of the educational scene deplore the expense entailed in excessive use of automobiles on the campus and unusual social events, which may involve costly entertainment, dating, or clothing expenses.

As times change, the American public distributes its income differently among items like food, housing, clothing, taxes, medical costs, travel, insurance, education, recreation. As education becomes more and more important to the average family, parents will not only adjust the size of their family, but arrange their budget to provide the necessary schooling for the children. The trends noted briefly above suggest an increasing share of the GNP for education.

Speech and the School

Figures are slow reading, but the statistics presented in this chapter describe conditions under which teaching will be done. A teacher can expect:

1. *More students to teach.* The student population is rising, even faster than the teacher population. The increase in enrollment will be counteracted only in part, at the college level, by stiffer entrance requirements and less patience with academic delinquents.

2. *Greater use of teaching devices* that can be accommodated to large numbers of students. Closed circuit TV instruction and portable videotape recorders are in wide use in more than four hundred institutions of higher learning. Following in

[11]Council for Financial Aid to Education, Inc., "The Key Reporter," *After Ten Years,* 1963. In 1969 the Council reported $1.8 billion.

the wake of this development is a greater interchange among institutions of visual materials in the field of speech. Other possibilities are short, supplementary programmed materials in book or film form, and more intensive application of computerized tutor-teaching and test scoring. Learning laboratories are becoming an established facility; talking typewriters are attracting attention.

3. *Reexamination of ways to use the teacher more effectively.* Assistant or apprentice teachers should assist with record keeping, paper grading, quizzing, and other important duties. Even in the elementary schools the journals are beginning to report classes of seventy-five and more pupils under the charge of a trained teacher and one or two assistants. The lecture-laboratory method of teaching public speaking at the college level, described in Chapter 4, illustrates a procedure designed to meet budget limitations and at the same time to expose larger numbers of students to senior lecturers.

4. *Reexamination of the curriculum.* Faculties may shorten the school year, with or without adopting the trimester plan. Some institutions are beginning the fall semester early in September, so that final examinations will be completed before the Christmas holidays; this move generally results in a slightly shortened semester. Reading periods or self-study periods are being substituted for formal classes. Institutions may offer short courses, without requiring registration or grades, which continue only as long as students are interested. One survey showed four hundred colleges following a plan that halts formal instruction during January. The students use the month for a variety of pursuits, following individual preferences, both on and off the campus, often for college credit.

5. *Attention to the superior student.* This problem, always a major one in a system of mass education, will continue to be studied as the necessity for leadership in humanities, social studies, and the sciences becomes keener. Honors programs, studies, and colleges will be established. Bright students in secondary schools will have opportunities to accelerate their programs in various ways.

6. *Attention to the disadvantaged student.* The image of the student as white and middle class is changing. Students of widely varying ethnological backgrounds are part of the campus population today. Special programs or adaptations of regular programs will have to be instituted to compensate for inadequate educational backgrounds.

7. *The student will need to be responsible* for more of his own education. Despite the best intentions of every one, he may find fewer remedial, elementary, or review courses available. If he fails to make his grades, he may find his probation requirements stiffer.

8. *The student will become increasingly involved in policy making.* This long-established feature of educational decision making has received new emphasis because of campus events of the late sixties. To a certain extent, students have long been consulted about standards of conduct, the school calendar, student

publications, and other activities. In other less formal ways they have long been able to make their preferences known in both curricular and noncurricular matters. They quickly perceive for example, poor teaching or poor course content. Now they are being given more opportunities to express their opinions in committees that have responsibility to make recommendations and take action.

9. *The secondary school will become more and more of a college preparatory institution.* More than half of the high school graduates now attend college. Accordingly, secondary school teachers will need to provide more college preparatory courses. Remedial courses in speech, along with those in English and mathematics, are disappearing from the college curriculum. This move naturally follows the improvement of instruction in elementary and high schools.

10. *More new colleges and universities are being established.* In the quarter century since 1945, more than three hundred new branches of established universities and new universities have been created. By 1985, writes New York University's Allan Cartter, every existing school will have to double its size and one thousand new ones will need to be created to accommodate everyone wanting a higher education.

11. *The number and size of community colleges is increasing.* The number of community colleges approaches eight hundred, more than one quarter of them built in the last decade. Enrollment nearly quadrupled in the decade 1960-70. As the needs of community college students emerge, each discipline will have to prepare special material for the improvement of instruction. Students' interests and motivations, their feelings about themselves, their educational and sociological backgrounds, their interest in vocational and industrial careers as well as in the professions, will add a new concern to the problem of teaching communicative principles and skills in all fields.

Preview of Your First Class

So much for this brief "Preview of a Profession." Now you should reflect upon the role you are preparing yourself to play. With little effort you can imagine your first teaching assignment. You will report for duty to the chairman of your department or to the principal of the school, wondering if he still remembers the individual, i.e., you, he hired last spring. You will also wonder whether he is looking forward to meeting you with eagerness and anticipation, or whether he will open the interview by saying, "We've faced a little emergency; we've had to cancel your contract . . ." The chances are that he will be glad to see you, that he has put you on that inspired document, the payroll, and that, marvel of marvels, he will be able to hand you a mimeographed roster with your name on it, show you your mail box, and hand you a key to your office.

You will not quite be a teacher, however, until you attend your first staff meeting. Here new teachers will be introduced, and speeches about the history, the tradition, the prestige of the department or the school will be given. There will be talk about grades, and records, and special rules, to which you will give closer attention than you ever did to your professors. No doubt you will also be advised not to gossip about your colleagues or date your students. Your new chief will talk from a long list of notes, compiled over the years from the lessons of experience. No matter how long the list is, however, it will not be long enough, for *you* are sure to do something which no list could have anticipated.

After the meeting breaks up, you will have a day or two to your own devices—schools always call teachers together sooner than necessary—which you will use to unpack, to get acquainted with your new colleagues, to check over your books, notes, and school equipment.

Eventually the first day of school arrives. Walk to school that morning deliberately, because although you may teach a thousand classes, or thirty thousand, there is only one first class. You may arrive at the building early and watch the students come and go. If you are a high school teacher, you will go to your room before any of the students arrive. Life is safer that way. If you are a college teacher, you may make an entrance as the final bell rings. This will be your first class. Take a deep breath, and plunge ahead.

Most of this book is designed to help you get ready for that first class and those that follow it. Methods classes are sometimes described as valiant efforts on the part of the professor to teach the student to swim on dry land. If this book is to avoid that criticism, it will need to summon a keen imagination so you can see the water. If you are now teaching you will be able to test the ideas of the book at once. If your first teaching assignment still lies in the future, you will need to imagine yourself putting some of the ideas of the book into practice.

An old rule that guides sailors during a storm is: "One hand for the ship, one hand for yourself." If when the ship is tossed you do not help steer the vessel, it will be lost; and if you do not hold on yourself, you will be lost. As you study the problems of your own teaching, you will also need to study problems affecting the entire profession. Those who are capable of growing and changing with the needs of this dynamic society will experience the full excitement of the future. And now go ahead and meet that first class.

Assignments

1. Report as assigned on one of the following topics:
    a. The birthrate as related to increasing enrollments.
    b. Relationships among high school enrollments, high school graduates, college enrollments.

c. A study of the projected elementary school enrollment: public schools versus private schools, girls versus boys, your state versus national figures.
d. A study of the increasing secondary school enrollment; public schools versus private schools, girls versus boys, your state versus national figures.
e. A study of the increasing enrollment in higher education; public schools versus private schools, girls versus boys, your state versus national figures.
f. Shortages or surpluses in the teaching profession.
g. Comparative study of secondary school and higher education enrollments, United States versus Great Britain; United States versus France; United States versus USSR. As a starting point, consult the latest encyclopedia yearbook.
h. Suggested educational reforms and possible effects on number and quality of students.

Questions for Classroom Discussion

1. What difficulties do you foresee arising out of (a) increasing tuition, (b) increasing federal aid, (c) increasing taxes?

2. What steps should be taken to make sure that worthy students are able to stay in school?

3. More than one-third of the persons of college age go to college. Do you see any indications that this ratio may increase?

4. What are possible sources of new teachers? married women? retired officers? retired corporation workers? (On this last point, a letter from Belle G. McGuire, staff assistant of the American Association of University Professors, noted that General Electric compiled a list of 136 of its employees, past fifty, who felt that they were competent to teach *college English*; 70 percent of this number *had Ph.D.s in English.*)

References

American Council on Education. *A Fact Book on Higher Education.* Washington, 1968. Charts covering many aspects of enrollment, population increase, federal expenditures, corporation growth, and the like. The Council also publishes pamphlets on specific topics: *The Federal Investment in Higher Education* (1967), *Federal Programs for Higher Education: Needed Next Steps* (1969). Other sources are unpublished data from the Office of Education; Bureau of Census reports; *Statesman's Yearbook.*

National Education Association. Public School Salaries Series: Research Reports. Washington, 1968. A series of bulletins covering many aspects of salary.

National Education Association. *Estimates of School Statistics, 1968-9; Research Report 1968-R16.* Washington, 1968. One of many authoritative statistical studies by NEA.

Statistical Abstract of the United States. Issued annually.

World Almanac. Issued annually.

Note. To keep abreast of the changing picture in education, see current issues of *School and Society; U.S. News and World Report; Higher Education and National Affairs,* published weekly by the American Council on Education; the quarterly issues of the *Bulletin of the American Association of University Professors. Spectra,* published by the Speech Communication Association, often supplies leads to information of particular value to its readers. Consult also citations in current issues of the *Education Index.*

The United States Government issues pamphlets covering all aspects of education. Write for Price List 31, *Education,* issued periodically (available without charge from the Superintendent of Documents, U.S. Government Printing Office, Washington, D.C. 20202). Your university library is a subscriber to the *Monthly Catalog* of U.S. Government publications. The Office of Education issues a list of its publications each year. This list may be secured from the Superintendent of Documents, or from the Publications Distribution Unit, Office of Education, Washington, D.C. 20202.

Students will be particularly interested in the educational situation existing in their own states. For statistics, write the state department of education or the secretary of your state teachers association.

(At the end of Chapter 18 is a list of extremely valuable, frequently consulted references. Scan this list so that you will know what kind of reference material is available to you.)

speech: its nature, its aims

[The educated man] *is at home in any society, he has common ground with every class; he knows when to speak and when to be silent; he is able to converse, he is able to listen; he can ask a question pertinently, and gain a lesson seasonably.*

John Henry, Cardinal Newman

Seven years of silent inquiry are needful for a man to learn the truth, but fourteen in order to learn how to make it known to his fellowmen.

Plato

In the long history of American higher education no educational movement has been more striking than the emergence and development of the discipline comprehended by the terms speech, drama and the theatre, rhetoric and public speaking, discussion and debate, oral interpretation, voice and speech science, speech pathology and audiology, radio-TV-film, communication.

For the time being I shall use the single word *speech* to embrace these interrelated studies. I realize that speech was not brought forward to be used in this all-inclusive sense until the discipline was well established. I am also aware that after being put on trial for a few years the term was not considered inclusive enough to serve this widely expanding discipline. Many departments prefer the title "speech *and* dramatic art," or "speech *and* theater." On many campuses drama, speech pathology-audiology, radio-TV-film, exist as separate departments, often in different divisions. Nevertheless, I use *speech* in this text as a serviceable approximation. I use it as some one else might use *English* to embrace linguistics, grammar, composition, and literature—even *American* literature.

I use speech, further, because in this treatment I am concerned with origins rather than specialization, and it is at the beginning that the unified nature of the discipline seems clearest. The term speech, moreover, is brief. People who have become accustomed to thinking of themselves as speech teachers, teaching speech courses, participating in speech contests, will continue using the word in this context. Alongside them are people who prefer to think of themselves as speech communication teachers, teaching speech communication courses. As the two terms coexist, however, it will be appropriate for this book to refer to speech communication as well as speech to remind the reader of the increasing emphasis on communication.

Regardless of preferences about terminology, we are in substantial agreement about the importance of the concept of communication as we go about the business of teaching public speaking, reading aloud, acting, phonetics, speech correction and pathology, listening and audiology, discussion and debate, scenery and costuming. Communication-oriented terms appear in courses taught, and in textbooks used, by professors in speech departments. All of us are concerned about getting a message across, whether we are lighting a stage, studying a dialect, establishing a mood, or spinning an argument. All of us are concerned about the listener—whether he is hearing, or overhearing; watching or gazing; soaking us up or letting us bounce off; agreeing or disagreeing; in the room with us or at the end of an electronic impulse, on the earth or on the moon; sharing an instant with us, or picking up our message hours, days, or weeks later, in the medium we used or in another. Or perhaps the message begins and ends with the same person, a kind of communicating or communing with oneself. And we are concerned about what the listener does with this message, whether or not he reacts to us, at the moment or later, as we hoped or whether through him our message or a part of it gets around to other people, or is allowed to fade away.

Origin of Speech

A brief note is in order here regarding the term speech. Before World War I, John P. Ryan, then chairman of the Department of Speech, Public Speaking, Reading, and Dramatic Art at Grinnell College, sought a single term to cover all aspects of this growing field. He did not like oratory, expression, speech arts, elocution, or even rhetoric. He discussed these possibilities in the *Quarterly Journal of Speech Education,* January 1918. Public Speaking was his preference for the title of a course rather than as the name for a field or department: "It hinders rather than helps toward a right recognition of the department in the curriculum." The best title, he continued, "is Department of Speech. The word *Speech* is old, short, simple, stable, well-known, accurate, common, learned, definite, extensive, and academically acceptable for it connotes the art and denotes the science, or just as well it denotes the art and connotes the science. . . . Now is the time for teachers of speech to reorganize and to rename their department."

Ryan was not alone in this push for a change of title. *The Quarterly Journal of Speech Education* had previously been called *The Quarterly Journal of Public Speaking.* Clarence E. Lyon, then at the University of South Dakota—the first of a long line of great speech teachers to come out of that state—made a survey of thirty-six departments and found twenty-three separate departments of public speaking. His study, regional in nature, identified only institutions in the Mississippi Valley. Maud May Babcock of the University of Utah located additional departments of public speaking all over the country: Amherst, Vanderbilt, West Virginia, Oregon, to pick only four examples from her extensive list. These surveys were made in 1915 and are reported in the April *Journal* of that year. There seemed no great rush after the 1918 Ryan article to change the name. Advertisements in the *Quarterly Journal of Speech Education* for 1918 included those for The Department of Public Speaking of the University of Wisconsin and the School of Oratory at Kansas Wesleyan. An ad also appeared for the Northwestern University School of Oratory and Physical Education (Ralph B. Dennis, Director). By 1921 it still called itself a School of Oratory, although before the year was out it was advertising its School of Speech.

What was wrong with the terms *oratory, elocution, expression,* etc., that Ryan and his contemporaries displaced? For reasons not fully explored, communication terms easily become pejorated. People who study and practice oratory, elocution, or expression are easily led into excesses that color the term and make it undesirable, just as the people who populated salons turned the word into saloons and finally brought about the banishment of the word from genteel society. If such terms as speech, journalism, mass media, even communication, are in their turn supplanted, it will be because their superfluities have been emphasized at the expense of their essence.

The year 1921 was a turning point for speech; after that year it became firmly entrenched on campuses as a field of study. Up to that time eleven masters' degrees had been awarded but not a single doctorate. In 1922 the first Ph.D. was awarded by the University of Wisconsin to Sarah Stinchfield whose dissertation was titled: "The Formulation and Standardization of a Series of Graded Speech Tests." Then came a notable acceleration of masters' degrees: twelve in 1923 to forty-eight in 1927. By 1934 the total number of graduate degrees conferred by fifteen institutions reached almost one thousand, including forty-three doctorates. All of this was done in a mere dozen years—1922-1934. By 1941, 3,893 degrees had been awarded, of which 241 were doctorates. By 1971 the total exceeded thirty-five thousand, with more than four thousand doctorates. Easily within the memory of emeritus professors, the discipline has gone from one graduate degree to more than thirty-five thousand. These degrees come from more than one hundred and fifty campuses, each degree program being established only after study by faculty and administration committees usually composed of senior professors from the humanities, the social studies, the sciences.[1]

The Meaning of Speech

To repeat, any explanation of speech must emphasize the concept of communication. Speech is basically a form of communication between speaker and listener. Ordinarily the medium used is that of the spoken word, with its tones and inflections, but since utterance is accompanied by facial expression, bodily posture, and gesture, speech properly and naturally includes these visible elements as well as the audible features. Communication can be carried on by words alone, as over the radio, or in the dark; communication can also be effected by gestures and signs alone, as in pantomime.

The serious student will, however, find his investigations carrying him far beyond this elementary description. Underlying every single term in the foregoing description is a wealth of chemical and physical detail that we are beginning to understand, plus a touch of human genius that may forever be hidden from us. *Speaker* comprises an organism that creates and produces symbols: this process embraces a facility with nerves and muscles, a combination of chemistry, electricity, and awesome magic, which produce the combination of sounds, tones, noises, grimaces, and posturings that make up a message. These do not die inside the organism, but are transmitted through the air, sometimes through an electronic circuit (microphones, receivers) or both. This transmission process subjects the message to varying degrees of deterioration, depending on distance, competing stimuli, efficiency of the electronic system. *Listener* comprises another organism—or a hundred or million other organisms—equipped with reception apparatus that picks up the visible and audible symbols constituting the message, again with deterioration. (The listener may find it difficult to

---

[1] These statistics come from the indispensable reports collected and interpreted by Franklin H. Knower. I know of no discipline that has for such a long period of years kept such accurate records of its graduate production.
See also Robert C. Jeffery, "Analysis of Speech Association of America Membership on the Eve of 'Phase Two,' *Quarterly Journal of Speech,* October 1962. With other information, it gives the thirty institutions awarding the largest numbers of bachelors', masters', and doctoral degrees.

hear, or suffer some distraction, or be disposed or not to receive symbols eagerly.) Finally, *listener* makes an interpretation of the symbol: he understands or does not understand; he reacts as *speaker* had hoped, or in some other way; he *feeds back* to *speaker* messages that may affect what *speaker* does next.

Communication thus enters into speaking, reading, acting, the improvement of articulation or voice. A speaker may wish his listeners to understand why lightning strikes, so they will discount the many superstitions about it. A nervously pacing actor, looking frequently at a big clock up center stage, wants his listeners to develop a feeling of suspense. A reader tells about Tom Sawyer whitewashing the fence, wrapping into the narrative certain emotions and attitudes. The speech clinician spends hours with his pupils on voice or articulation exercises—not that the speech sound or vocal tone is an end of itself, but that the mastery of these details makes the pupil more effective as a communicator.

The Domain of Speech

The domain of the discipline is the act or process of communication. No institution, system, or process can exist without it. Take as an example the scientist working in his laboratory. This task would appear to be a lonely and isolated one. First, however, the scientist must ask: Has this problem been solved already? Are others working on it? Second, he needs to communicate with others: to gain financial support, to seek technical assistance. Third, when the experiment is finished, he needs to tell two groups of people about it: other scientists, to whom he will talk in a technical language, and laymen, to whom he will talk in everyday idiom. Actually, the lonely scientist is becoming more and more scarce. The big problems call for teams of scientists. If one of the team cannot communicate effectively, he is not only less of a communicator but less of a scientist.

When the teacher of speech talks about communication, however, he means more than a crude, barren, minimal operation. Holding steadily in mind the communicator, the message, the medium, the receiver, he wants the communicator's thought or attitude to stimulate the receiver with maximum effectiveness. The teacher of oral interpretation guides students in a careful study of a poem, or an essay, or a speech. This study should lead to a penetrating inquiry into author, setting, circumstances, and other relevant factors. Mind, voice, and body must then be set to work, in a disciplined manner, at the task of putting word meanings into visible and audible symbols. If what is done is sincere, honest, and intelligent, the listener will have a fuller appreciation of the work than he would have had otherwise. The teacher of acting performs much the same task, using different conventions and a different medium. The speech clinician may appear at times to be working entirely with the vocal problems of the communicator, but he, too, is well aware of voice and articulation as parts of the total communicative act. Enough has already been said about rhetoric and public speaking to show again the interactions of speaker, message, and listeners to understand, to change or modify a belief, or to take action.

Speech is based on principles that are teachable and usable. Its practitioners are aware that there are exceptions to these principles, and so it is not a science, per se, though certain aspects of it, such as phonetics, pathology, and audiology, have solid scientific underpinnings. It is not merely a technique, a knack, a skill. None of these words says enough; principle, method, system, rationale are more accurate. As they master the principles, students improve, and their improvement is noticeable both to themselves and to their classmates. Although there are backward glances at native talent and genius—the claim that speakers are born and not made—there is a positive insistence that nearly everyone can improve. This belief finds strong support in the study of the careers of eminent speakers—those who might be thought to have had the greatest natural gifts. Clay, Webster, Calhoun, Bryan, Roosevelt, and others gained public speaking experience in the classroom or the debating society. Each served an arduous apprenticeship. Webster, for example, was so seized with stagefright at Exeter Academy that he could not speak at all. From this tender beginning he rose to the heights.

The discipline of communication has close ties with nearly every other discipline. Graduate students regularly find their assignments carrying them to the classics, linguistics, physics, psychology, education, language, mathematics, chemistry, physiology, and law. They customarily seek out supporting courses in other disciplines. One writing a dissertation, for example, on a nineteenth-century controversy would find it advisable to take courses in history, literature, political science. If he had an experimental problem, he would pursue psychometric and statistical studies. If his field was speech pathology, he would study anatomy, neurology, psychology, physiology, and related fields, just as the family doctor would consult with orthodontists, pediatricians, orthopedic surgeons, clinical psychologists, and others. The graduate student in drama draws upon other arts, and from history, psychology, literature, and sociology.

As the Committee on the Nature of the Field of Speech has put it, speech, like other contemporary academic disciplines, has expanded into specialized study. The report of the Committee continues:

> Today the specialist in speech may find his interests akin to those of the linguist who analyzes the structure of spoken language, the psychologist who studies verbal behavior, the sociologist who relates social structure to symbolic interaction, the anthropologist who studies the structure of speech and language as reflecting the structure of culture, the philosopher who investigates the problem of meaning in everyday language, and so on.[2]

[2]Donald K. Smith, Andrew T. Weaver, and Karl R. Wallace, in *Speech Teacher*, November 1963, pp. 351-355.

Gilbert Highet in *Art of Teaching* says:

> Communication . . . is one of the basic activities of the human race; it is . . . an art without which genius is dumb, power brutal and aimless, mankind a planet load of squabbling tribes. . . . Teaching is only one of the many occupations that depend upon it, and depend upon it absolutely.[3]

Statements that set forth the qualifications of an educated person, or that define the place of a discipline in the curriculum, include the requirement that one be able to express himself orally. The nature of our discipline as described in the foregoing pages suggests its relevance to society, its concern with intelligent inquiry on the part of both teacher and student, and its usefulness to the individual as he goes about his business of making a living.

Historical Origin of Communication

Communication is, therefore, the concept that brings unity to the many aspects of the discipline. Actor, reader, clinician, broadcaster do not live worlds apart from one another. Though they operate in widely different situations, they start with similar basic principles.

Historically these disciplines developed from a common origin. Originally the name of the discipline was rhetoric. Early statements in the field of rhetorical theory were informal, but eventually systematic treatises appeared. Many of these latter contained observations about the management of the voice, so in a way they foreshadowed current speech correction and pathology. Some of them also offered comments about drama and the theater, but this area independently brought forth treatises in *poetics*. The discussion that follows, however, is limited in the main to the development of the rhetorical aspects of the field of speech.

Rhetoric has been defined as the rationale of discourse. The discourse may be entertaining, expository, persuasive. It may be spoken or written, though for the most part these pages will deal with spoken discourse.

So far as there are records, the discipline goes back five thousand years. Egyptian papyri roughly dated 2900 B.C. contain bits and pieces of rhetorical advice.[4] The *Precepts* identified with Kagemni and Ptah-Hotep clearly show that the Egyptians were concerned about principles of speech. "If you carry a message from one noble to another, be exact in the repetition . . . give his message even as he hath said it." This statement foreshadows the current interest in listening. "If you are in the council chamber, follow the procedures." This

---

[3] New York: Alfred A. Knopf, 1950, p. 97. Used by permission.
[4] *See:* Giles Wilkeson Gray, "The Precepts of Kagemni and Ptah-Hotep," *Quarterly Journal of Speech,* December 1946, pp. 446-454.

statement foreshadows parliamentary orderliness. "Avoid speaking of that of which you know nothing . . . . If you know what you are talking about, speak with authority, and avoid false modesty." This statement is good advice in all times and places.

The Greeks and Romans systematized rhetoric, as they did politics and many other studies. It has been wisely observed that if a modern thinker starts down a long, dusty road of reflection, he will not have gone far before he meets an ancient philosopher trudging back. Corax in 466 B.C. was the first to make clear that rhetoric involved principles—that it was not merely a knack or skill or gift sent from heaven—and that these principles were teachable and learnable. He demonstrated further that rhetoric had a structure, an organization, an architecture, a design—and that a message set in a frame would be clearer and more persuasive than one lacking pattern or contour. The human race never learned a wiser or more enduring lesson. From his slender quiver Corax drew another powerful bolt: since human problems are wrapped in contingencies, alternatives, and choices, rhetoric must involve itself with that which is likely and believable as well as with that which is certain and provable.

Corax's rhetoric was a vast improvement over the timid Egyptian cautions and admonitions. Contemporaries can be proud to practice the same intellectual discipline that Corax and his pupils helped to develop. But mightier rhetoricians were still to come. Plato, like Corax, saw the virtues of form. The message should have a head, a body, and a tail, like a living creature. But Plato saw more. As he looked around him, he observed the varying mood and temper of listeners—the nature of the human soul, as he called it—and noted that the message must be adapted to the different kinds of soul: the calm, the angry, and so on. Plato criticized much of rhetoric, but he also gave the discipline powerful support. According to Plato, without rhetoric, even one who knows the truth is unable to persuade. The truth itself is valueless—but the combination of truth and rhetoric forms a lever that can move the earth.

Aristotle drew upon the substantial body of rhetorical theory developed by Plato and dozens of others. Moreover, he heard effective oratory in the courts and in the public places. Following his natural bent, he constructed a system of criticism that was the first model of communication theory. Following are five of the leading Aristotelian ideas:

1. A listener can be persuaded in any or all of three ways: through the character of the speaker, through the logic of the argument, through his own feelings and emotions. Any other way of persuading a listener, such as with the help of a shotgun, would have to be called nonrhetorical. Even so, rioter and demonstrators blend symbols of force (the raised clenched fist, the shotgun, the pavement cobblestone) with the more conventional symbols so intimately that rhetoricians may decide to glance at these symbols as well.

2. The character of the speaker is of paramount importance. This statement has grown in significance through the years. The increasingly complex nature of knowledge forces us to depend upon one another more than ever. When you find yourself talking to your students about source credibility you are not so far from Athens as you might imagine.

3. A speech has four parts. The simplest strategy would be to state your case and then prove it—these would seem to be the only essential moves. But you are advised to open with an introduction and finish with a summarizing, interpreting, or action-seeking conclusion. Awareness of and information about the listener cannot be overlooked in making decisions about the speech plan.

This notion has proved extremely helpful over the years. Think again of the pupil in the classroom, reporting on a school project. He is so full of his subject that he forgets his classmates are still empty. So he plunges into the middle of his exposition. Places, events, and people, are named but not identified. The listeners are as puzzled as playgoers who arrive late. Somewhere in his education this pupil overlooked the Greeks. Better remind him to start at the beginning (Plato); listeners being what they are he should open with a listener-oriented introduction (Aristotle). The instruction in organization that you received, and that you will impart to your own students, may be more subtle and sophisticated than the four parts notion, but you will meet many in your classes who would do well to master this solid, basic architecture before they start building gables, turrets, windows, and cornices.

4. The end and object of the speech is the audience—the listener—the judge. Aristotle elaborates on and systematizes Plato's notions about the audience. Listeners can be viewed according to their age, wealth, position, mood, and temper. From this theory, contemporary teachers of speech fan out richly in many directions: mood, tone, bias, information, competence, predilection, image, role, value systems.

5. Language is a matter for careful attention. First of all, it must be clear. Second, it must have interest; it must be vivid, colorful, striking, and forceful; it should use metaphor, inversion, parallel structure. (We can easily perceive from this advice, the lengths to which the communicator must go to stimulate the receiver.) Each of these qualities must be appropriate to listener and setting. English and speech teachers, playwrights and sermonizers, presidents and copywriters, all spend countless hours on this ancient formula.

Aristotle applied the same kind of intellectual vigor to the basic questions about drama and the theater. In his *Poetics* he talked about plot, character, diction, thought, melody, and staging. He discussed the requirements for a tragic hero, the formula for developing a plot, the catharsis to be wrought in the spectator. He even commented on the history of the art: the increase in the number of actors from one to two and three, the reduction of the amount of choral chanting, the introduction of painted scenery, the discarding of grotesque early diction. He saw the close relationship between rhetoric and poetic (for example, the speaker could learn about delivery by observing the actor, and the playwright could enhance his play through the application of principles of rhetoric). The two arts, however, were beginning to develop their own rationales.

The history of rhetoric need not be discussed lengthily, other than to call a few illustrious names. Marcus Tullius Cicero—the "sweet Tully" of succeeding centuries—acquired the unique distinction of being the only celebrated orator to set down a systematic treatise on the theory of oratory. Quintilian, well known to historians of education as well as to teachers of speech, evolved a theory of teaching the young speaker that covered his entire career. He started by suggesting the selection of a proper nurse (she should not have a faulty dialect) and concluded with advice about the proper time to retire (well before being completely done in). He also offered advice about speech outlines, the delivery of short speeches, the use of words, standards of pronunciation, the expert study of selections that are to be read aloud.

The Greek and Roman rhetoricians and their successors also began the study of speech pathology. Classical writers and those who followed distinguished differences in loudness and quality. They observed weak voices and thin, hoarse and rasping voices. They wrote advice about the speed of utterance. They noticed that breathiness obscured resonance and carrying power. They were aware of mannerisms such as excessive heaving and panting. They noted that a few pupils hoisted phlegm from their lungs and sprayed their listeners. They commented on vocalized pauses like *uh, uh, uh.* They advised against visual intrusions such as excessive movements of the tongue or lips. They did not, however, set down much in the way of therapy: singing, proper diet, and exercise appeared to them to be generally efficacious.

Much of what the early rhetoricians said can also be applied to the improvement of language. Cicero's contributions to style are well known. High school students can today venture only a little way into Latin before they confront Cicero. He shook Latin style, loosened it up, replaced its formal correctness with colloquial vigor, and introduced all sorts of stylistic adornments.

In the Middle Ages the spokesmen for the Catholic Church needed to develop and defend their doctrines against both schism and heresy. This defense called for close reasoning, a need that sent priests like Saint Augustine back to logic and rhetoric. Eighteenth-century England, busy with the development of a parliamentary system, concerned with the need for communication in the law court, the pulpit, and the university, provided a fruitful climate for intense rhetorical output. The nineteenth century was particularly busy with matters of language and style. On the list of distinguished theorists are English, Scottish, Irish, and American names—one from this last group being John Quincy Adams, scholar, diplomat, president, congressman, and lecturer on rhetoric at Harvard.

The steadily mounting interest in science of the twentieth century stimulated a system of communication that combined clarity and persuasiveness. In turn, rhetorical principles themselves have been supported or modified by experimental investigation. Researchers in speech and also in sociology, psychology, and social psychology have launched inquiries concerning the credibility of the source, the organization of the message, and the behavior of the receiver. The line of thought, however, is continuous; old questions are cast in new language and approached through new techniques.[5]

Philosophy: Aims, Purposes

Whenever a teacher discusses the aims of speech education, he becomes in some measure a philosopher. Before he has uttered half a dozen paragraphs he will have reflected one or more schools of thought and will have identified himself in all sorts of ways. Accordingly, therefore, you should take a shrewd look at your own philosophy to discover how deeply you have become involved and where to go from there.

If you do not search your philosophy to see how it may be applied to speech education, you will be unable to participate intelligently in important discussions that go on in inquiring circles. Out of a clear blue sky someone may ask you, "Just what do you mean by *speech* (or *speech communication*)?" This question may not be easy to answer impromptu. In summer school you may be defending a thesis, and a committee member may impale you on this thorn: "What is the purpose of your research?" The answer calls for orientation: if you have not previously prepared a place to which you can retreat, you are in difficulty. Or you are in the office of an administrator seeking funds, when he suddenly inquires, "Why should we put more money into drama?" Once again you are in a situation that calls for philosophical thinking. I recall an interview in which a candidate's brilliant explanation of the values of intercollegiate debate deeply impressed the committee of professors of science, history, and language. And actually the candidate considered communication theory, not debate, his major field of competence.

The Aims of Speech Education

Questions such as these are usually asked by people in superior positions who have the right to an answer. At least they have the right to be curious. Whenever a teacher discusses his field with knowledgeable persons, he needs to be well-grounded in its broader implications. No doubt in college you preferred acting in

[5] Much of the foregoing discussion is adapted from Loren Reid, "The Discipline of Speech," *Speech Teacher,* January 1967.

a play to studying theater history. Practice teaching packed more thrills per minute than philosophy of education. As a student you could afford these preferences and prejudices. As a member of the teaching profession—and it is amazing how quickly a beginning teacher finds himself at full status—you will need all the breadth and depth of vision that you can command.

How can a beginning teacher reach the point where he can say with assurance, "My philosophy of teaching is thusandso?" What is wrapped up in philosophy?

Basically, the philosophical attitude is reflective, thoughtful, examining, meditating, encompassing. Among the topics it is reflective about are experience, meaning, truth, purpose, relevance, value. Philosophy is concerned with the meaning of life, the significance of the world in which man lives, the concept of standards and values. The method of philosophical reflection involves careful definition, avoidance of inconsistencies, comparison of differing views, and conclusions or viewpoints that hold up under critical examination.

As a field of study, philosophy includes metaphysics, wherein reality, appearance, the nature of the self, and the nature of matter and mind are considered; epistemology, which seeks to learn what makes knowledge valid; logic, which is concerned with principles of valid reasoning; ethics, which inquires into conduct; and aesthetics, which considers the nature of beauty. At times philosophy resembles religion; at other times it seems closely related to psychology; at all times strongly allied to science. You have no doubt begun to see that some of your notions about speech have a philosophical cast. Whenever you ponder the place of communication in society, or in the educational system, you are necessarily philosophical in your method of inquiry. Inquiry becomes especially necessary whenever society in general and the educational system in particular are disturbed, harassed, or under fire.

Let us imagine that your philosophical development is still at a humble, curbstone level and that someone has asked you to state your philosophy of teaching. Suppose you reply, "Well, I believe that every assignment should be so flexible that students with a wide variety of talents and interests can profit from it." As philosophy, this simple thought is in the same category as the statement of the service station operator who declared, "My philosophy is to give service. Anybody can sell gas."

If we examine your statement and that of the service station operator more closely, we can say that each is a small part of a larger system of thought. The service station man evidently subscribes to the current notion that the purpose of his business is to serve the driver. Early in their business careers, he and others who serve the public learn that they cannot afford the luxury of neglecting the customer. Competition is much too keen. Your statement is also a part of a larger system of thought. It grows, perhaps unconsciously, out of your ideas about equal educational opportunity for all. Probably most American educators would applaud, not challenge, your democratic point of view.

I have a friend, however, who teaches history at Oxford. He too believes in democracy, but he has a different concept of education. He has no interest in teaching everybody. When he interviews a prospective student he tries to make sure that the young man already has a serious interest in history, and moreover is ready to specialize in some special aspect or period. If during the interview the student gives the impression that he is not well prepared, this Oxford professor discourages him at once. Oxford is apparently not interested in "a wide variety of talents and interests"; Oxford is interested only in the best. As you see, it is not necessary to go back to ancient Sparta in search of a different philosophy of education. Oxford is close enough.

Does this point of view seem far-fetched? Suppose you find yourself teaching in a university of ten thousand people. Ten years go by, and enrollment increases to twenty thousand. Still the students roll in, and you find your classes larger and larger. Many of your students have grave educational deficiencies. What becomes of your philosophy then? Will you still search out a "wide variety of talents and interests"? Will you then construct a new philosophy—college education is for the leaders, the students of high potential, or will you accommodate your instruction to different kinds of Americans?

Actually my Oxford friend and my American colleagues are both examining their attitudes on this point. Oxford (and other British) faculties are asking: "Are we teaching too few students? Can we admit large numbers of poorly prepared students?"

Philosophy quickly leaves the curbstone level and leaps into highly organized and systematic ways of thinking. You will gradually need to do the same. Most of your ideas about conduct, religion, art, science, and the like, have already been profoundly influenced by minds of the past. The ideas of great thinkers first spread to other great minds, and gradually seep down to the masses. Without realizing it you may hold a mixture of ideas from old pagans like Plato, religious systems like Christianity or Judaism, scientists like Darwin, philosophers like Dewey or Nietzsche, psychoanalysts like Freud. Perhaps you have already begun to think of yourself as an Aristotelian, a pragmatist, an idealist. You may even be far enough along to call yourself a socialized-Rousseauian, a neo-Deweyite, or a meta-Augustinian; you should however, use phrases like these with care, or you will intrigue only those who like to take what is already simple and befuddle it with what is obtuse.

Speech Viewed Philosophically

The necessity of having a sound viewpoint may be illustrated by an example. Some years ago the Contest Committee of the Commission on Secondary Schools made a report to the national speech association about speech contests and recommended that interscholastic speech contests should be discontinued. Certain harmful aspects of speech contests had come to the attention of school administrators and the recommendation of the Contest Committee was a drastic one. To have adopted it would have meant the elimination of interscholastic high school debating, speaking, and interpretation contests. A committee from the Speech Association of America, however, worked with the North Central's Contest Committee to restate sound educational goals under which speech contests could be conducted; and the Commission itself adopted the report of the combined committee.

You should read the results of the deliberations of these two committees.[6] Part of the report, suggesting its philosophical foundation, follows:

> Communication makes possible group living; and speech, as the chief means of communication, is the universal instrument of social cooperation and coordination. From the most ordinary convention to the most complex political discussion, speech is used more often and more widely than any other means of communication. The world of today is for most persons a speaking and listening world. . . .
>
> In a free society, the welfare of all the citizens depends ultimately upon public opinion. If they do not have the ability to form wise judgments on the basis of information and arguments presented to them, then the wise and the unwise will suffer together the consequences of their mutual failure to present and to comprehend sound courses of action. . . .
>
> If we are not to be deluded by the fraud that government by decree is safer than government by discussion and debate, then all our people must be made increasingly able to participate effectively in public affairs—in the union, in the church, in the corporation, in the legislative assembly, and in the Congress. A citizenry able to differentiate between sound and fallacious reasoning, to distinguish between acceptable and shoddy evidence, to tell an honest speaker from a verbal swindler—this is the minimum essential for the survival of a free and responsible society in a chaotic world.

Speech Communication and the Needs of Students

Sometimes a teacher is asked to tell a group of parents or faculty how speech communication fits into the curriculum. The General Committee of the Cooperative Study of Secondary Standards listed the following needs of students:

1. To learn to live with other human beings.

2. To achieve and maintain mental and physical health.

3. To learn to live in their natural and scientific environment.

4. To receive sound guidance.

5. To learn logical thinking and clear expression.

6. To prepare for work, for further education, or for both.

[6]*Quarterly Journal of Speech,* October 1951, pp. 347-358.

7. To learn to use leisure time.

8. To learn to live aesthetically.

Speech communication is involved in all eight of these needs. Training in informal speaking, in discussion, in oral interpretation, and in the arts of the theater can make invaluable contributions to the growth of students.

Another useful list is the "Ten Imperative Needs of Youth," proposed by the Educational Policies Commission. They are:

1. The development of marketable skills.

2. The development and maintenance of physical fitness.

3. Understanding the rights and duties of citizens in a democracy.

4. Understanding the significance of a family.

5. Knowing how to produce and use intelligently both goods and services.

6. Understanding the methods of science.

7. Appreciating beauty in literature, art, music, and nature.

8. The ability to use leisure time well.

9. Respect for others.

10. Ability to think rationally, express thoughts clearly, and to read and listen with understanding.

Statements of educational goals appear frequently, changing little over the years. Agreement seems to have been reached on principles such as these:

1. Students need to be educated for employment, for civic leadership, for participation in democratic activities.

2. Students need to be given the kind of academic training that will prepare them to understand and appreciate their fellow men, and to join in the common enterprise of improving the society in which all must live.

3. Students need to learn methods of investigation and research, so that fields of knowledge will continue to be deepened and widened.

4. Students need to be given a basis to enhance their intellectual and aesthetic resources, to rid themselves of biases and provincialisms, to enrich themselves culturally.

Teachers of all disciplines, as they read such statements as these, will be able to see how they and their colleagues can make contributions to the general good. The need for effective communication looms large in every paragraph. Robert Frost's famous informal definition of a college education, "hanging around till you've caught on," can be translated, from our point of view, as meaning listening enough and discussing enough till you've caught on.[7]

You will find it helpful to discuss these and other basic aims to show students how speech communication fits into the educational program. Often students become so occupied with daily assignments that they do not clearly see where they are headed. You can do them a service by explaining what education is about and by describing the role played by the discipline you teach.

General Aims

Every teacher should develop for himself a statement of aims and purposes. To do so is to achieve more than a textbook requirement. All teachers should know the purposes of their subject in order to present their work to administrators and laymen and, even more to the point, to give their teaching proper emphasis and direction. The aims outlined below may be helpful in formulating your own statement of goals.

1. *Improve voice, articulation, and other fundamental processes.* The term fundamentals is widely used, often with different meanings. To some it means simply "first steps" or "basic principles"; a book entitled *Fundamentals of Teaching* would presumably discuss the elements of teaching. Etymologically the word is related to foundation; it means groundwork or underlying principles. From that meaning an easy step leads to such synonyms as basic, essential, elemental, important, primary.

To others fundamentals suggests the foregoing but also a further meaning. The fundamental processes of speech or the fundamentals of speech include elements common to all forms of communication. Voice and articulation are fundamental in this second sense; whether an individual communicates by speaking, reading, interpreting, or acting, he uses voice and he articulates sounds. Language is another fundamental. In all forms of communication, words or an equivalent are employed: sometimes one's own words, sometimes those of another. Visible symbols, such as posture, gesture, and various kinds of action, are needed. *Fundamentals* also includes another important aspect: listening.

To bring each student to minimum standards in the fundamental processes is a responsibility of the teacher of speech communication at all levels of instruction. Each student should be able to speak words with reasonable distinctness. His voice should be adequately flexible and pleasant. He should be able to use language accurately. Posture, poise, and movement should be motivated. During the course the teacher will be concerned with a variety of activities and assignments, but he should be on the alert for opportunities to improve his students in these fundamental aspects.

[7]Quoted by Martha Wright in *American Association of University Professors Bulletin*, December 1966, p. 433.

Because work on fundamentals is less exciting than work on speeches or debates or plays, teachers are likely to hurry over the necessary routines. The answer is to find ways of making basic materials interesting; the suggestions in subsequent chapters may be helpful. Another part of the answer is, when working on debates or plays, to insist upon the use of good voice, articulation, bodily action, and the like, along with rebuttal practice or principles of characterization.

2. *Improve personality.* I approach a discussion of personality with some forewarning. I have never advocated, and do not now advocate, detailed studies or inventories of personality problems, except by those teachers who are properly trained and have valid reasons. Yet anyone can see that effective communication of content is inextricably bound up with qualities of personality. Teachers must do what they conveniently can to enhance the credibility of their charges. "Men are proved by their speeches," said Demosthenes, "whether they are wise or foolish." "If you would create something," said Goethe, "you must be something." "What you are," said Emerson, "speaks so loud I cannot hear what you say." A great teacher of public speaking put it this way: "The speaker's character may almost be called the most effective means of persuasion he possesses." Clearly I am not thinking about the improvement of personality per se, but as it is related to communication. Caution is indicated; the teacher's competence is presumably limited to problems in communicating.

What problems of personality come to the attention of the teacher who is seeking to help a student improve communication?

One thinks first of those who lack self-confidence, self-assurance, poise. Anxieties and tensions of various sorts hinder thinking and speaking. With some students the teacher meets this problem immediately, head-on, and must turn his attention to it before he can proceed with further instruction.

Intellectual integrity is an asset needed by those who wish to communicate effectively. How can a student make a speech if, consciously or unconsciously, something about him says, "This is exaggerated"? The "something" may stem from superficial habits of preparation; or from language that overstates the evidence. Here the teacher, by showing the student that words are sharp-edged tools, may be able to teach the student to think more precisely and thus to express himself more believably. The interpreter or the actor wants his listeners to weep for Hecuba, but as the performer himself does not understand why this weeping should be done, the listener views the appeal with detachment. Certainly you can neither act nor read without having paid your debt to the intellectual demands of what you are reading. Again, the teacher is able to stretch and sharpen the intellectual perceptions that lead to integrity of performance.

Good judgment is a priceless quality, one most associated with adulthoood. Good judgment comes to reside in an individual when he has successfully made hundreds of decisions. We may concern ourselves with making good decisions that are related to the process of communicating; what to say, what not to say; what to put in, what to leave out; how to appraise this bit of evidence and that; how to interpret this meaning or the other one; which values or attitudes were meaningful, which were not. Imagine a teacher who was a specialist in bad judgment; who urged interpreters to search out strange and unwarranted meanings, or speakers to enunciate exaggerated and unbelievable facts. Certainly in such an environment the other principles of good communication would be hatcheted before they got under way.

Imagination is another quality useful for communication. Where would the drama be without imagination? What could be done with problems of stage design, stage lighting, characterization, line reading, if imagination were absent? In how many hundreds of ways can imagination give wings to good sense? For good judgment may be a plodding fellow without its widewinged companion. Many times a day a good teacher will get the student to do something with imagination that a hundred times before the student has done only routinely and mechanically. George Campbell in his *Philosophy of Rhetoric* suggested, two centuries ago, that an idea presented with liveliness or vivacity would be more persuasive than one lacking these qualities.

Teachers of other disciplines may interest themselves in the student's personality; the teacher of speech communication cannot escape it. He comes face to face with listlessness, timidity, belligerence, dependence, insecurity, all in ways that hinder communication. He does not need to preach or moralize; his opportunities are immediately at hand, ready to be exploited in an unpretentious way.

3. *Teach the principles underlying the various forms of effective communication.* Parliamentary procedure develops leadership by teaching a mastery of motions and the principles of voting and presiding. Public speaking says much about gathering, selecting, adapting, arranging, organizing, and presenting material, all aspects of learning to think clearly. Interpretation has special ways of looking at the intellectual and emotional content of a selection. The theater arts employ a variety of exercises calling for the use of creative faculties.

If the teacher is to achieve this aim of the course he must have specific training in many different kinds of communication. Most teachers would include in the list the following: conversation, interviewing, speechmaking, debating, discussion, reading aloud, pantomime, acting, radio and TV speaking. Some teachers would add one or more of the following: parliamentary procedure, choral reading, phonetic transcription, history of the theater, puppetry, vocabulary building. One teacher will argue that the principles of communication can be taught through a single activity, such as choral reading; whether the problem is one of poor articulation or excessive timidity, choral reading will improve it. Another teacher will make the same claims for debating; another for acting. A more realistic evaluation would appear to be that debating is superior for certain intellectual values, choral reading or acting for some of the imaginative qualities, and that a general course that planned to do the best job of teaching communicative skills would employ a variety of activities. The Joint Project on the Individual and the School stated: "Well-taught subject matter is the school's chief instrument for stimulation."[8]

4. *Prepare students for participation in a democratic society.* This purpose is so valid that it needs little more than a mention. We are citizens first, teachers and students second. The present tensions of war, or for that matter of everyday living, hit teachers and students alike and are likely to last for years to come.

Students are better prepared for citizenship in this republic if they are competent in public speaking, discussion, and debate, both as participants and as listeners. The classroom provides opportunity for talking about topics concerned with democracy: our attitude toward minority groups, the importance of intelligent voting, the improvement of economic and social conditions, the understanding of the American tradition, the methods of that form of communication known as propaganda, the value of clear thinking and clear speaking, the ability to recognize the Big Lie. Democracy exists at every school level: a problem of student government, or management of the school cafeteria, or good sportsmanship at football games, or consideration for others, can improve a student's understanding of democracy as well as his speaking skill. The teacher should point out the implications of these topics, so that students will see speech as one of the ways of participating more fully in the democratic process. Interpretation and dramatics, as well as speechmaking, can enliven the democratic idea: their vivid presentation of situations and attitudes can make democratic living more meaningful.

5. *Improve ability to think and to listen.* The average student listens with only a fraction of his potential; the figure has, in fact, been set at 25 percent. No one has ever set down a figure for thinking effectiveness or speaking effectiveness, but, given a good teaching and learning situation, the average student in a year-long course should double his competence. In every activity that the class undertakes the teacher should try to wring from it every opportunity to improve both thinking and listening.

Specific Aims

In developing aims for individual courses in public speaking, debating, dramatics, interpretation, fundamentals, and the like, the teacher will impose certain specific aims on the general aims suggested above.

The total procedure goes like this: first the teacher formulates a statement about the kind of society for which he is preparing his students. In that statement, the concept of democracy will loom large. Second, he reviews the

[3]Quoted by Wanda B. Mitchell, "Planning the Course," in *Speech Teacher,* November 1969, p. 262.

general aims of his course: the responsibility he has toward the fundamentals of voice, articulation, language, and action; the qualities of personality and character he thinks he can develop. And finally he asks himself, what principles of effective communication can I exemplify in this course? That question leads him to formulate specific aims.

If, for example, he is thinking of a beginning public speaking course, he will set down such questions as: How can I teach students to choose topics, gather material, organize their ideas, and the like? What shall I teach about studying and analyzing audiences? Shall I try to develop greater competence in speaking through the use of models or classroom examples, or both? If he is thinking of the specific aims of a class in oral interpretation, he will raise such questions as these with himself: How can I teach students to study materials for oral presentation? What literary forms shall I especially try to get them to recognize? What techniques are useful for conveying different thoughts and emotions? In general the specific aims of courses deal with principles of communication, both on the transmitting and the receiving ends.

As the teacher moves from general, overall purposes to daily segments of instruction, he is likely to phrase his objectives in behavioral terms. Behavioral language comes easier to a speech teacher than, perhaps, to those of other disciplines, since many assignments call for speaking, writing, inquiring, reacting, listening, formulating, demonstrating, and other observable actions. He is not likely, however, to deal exclusively in behavioral objectives as he also seeks to bring about appreciation and insight. I recall instances of sudden insights, a relationship, a principle that never before had been so fully grasped. I can recall the teacher, the room, the situation, the mental excitement. Likely I made no outward sign and the teacher may or may not have realized what he had done. Readers who recall the popularity of behavioristic psychology between World Wars I and II and, after a few years, the reaction against its built-in limitations, will embrace neobehaviorism with poise, even as they approve its insistence upon clearly stated, observable, outcomes of classroom instruction.

With respect both to general aims and specific objectives, keep your students informed about what you are doing and why you are doing it. The student does not have your perspective on affairs, and easily bogs down in the day by day routine. Accordingly, if you can bring some vision into his life, you do him a service. If you show him how the assignments in your class support the aims of the course and at the same time fit into his own plans for a career, you make his study and preparation more meaningful.

Every teacher will have to present this material in his own fashion: some do it solemnly, and some with a light touch. All ways are better than leaving the student in the dark. The second week of the course, after teacher and students become acquainted, is a good time to talk about course aims, purposes, and philosophy. Your discussion will make the student feel more sure that the course is well motivated, and that even though you are proceeding small bit by small bit, you know what you want the class to achieve. The middle of the term is another good time to review what has happened, and what is still to be achieved. Best of all, in a different way, is the last day of the course; at this point the students can join in the discussion, look with you into the future, and predict how the skills and appreciations they have developed will fit into their future careers.

Assignments

1. Select one of the following courses and report, from your own reading and experience, what it contributed to you. Cite evidence for claims made.
    a. Fundamentals of speech
    b. Public speaking
    c. Discussion
    d. Debate
    e. Speech pathology
    f. Phonetics
    g. Oral interpretation
    h. Acting
    i. Play direction or production
    j. Stagecraft
    k. Radio, TV, film

2. Select one of the above courses and report, from your own reading and experience, its contribution to better citizenship. Cite evidence for claims made.

3. Compare and contrast the educational philosophy current in the United States with that current in Great Britain or some other country with which you are familiar.

4. Prepare a critique of the aims of speech as given in the chapter. Compare and contrast with statements given in other textbooks or in courses of study (your library may have a collection).

5. Choose one of the aims given in the chapter. Develop this aim in behavioral language: what behaviors would be observable if the aim were successfully carried out?

Questions for Classroom Discussion

1. Compare and contrast *speech, communication,* and *speech communication* as terms describing the discipline. Comment on this definition of *speech*: "Speech is ongoing multisymbolic behavior in social situations carried on to achieve communication. We define communication as a social achievement in symbolic behavior" (Baird and Knower, *Essentials of General Speech,* 3d ed., p. 6). Comment on this description of the area of speech in speech communication: "Spoken symbolic interaction is the central focus of study in the speech-communication area" (Kibler and Barker, eds. *Conceptual Frontiers in Speech-Communication,* p. 18).

2. Comment on the organization of present-day departments. Note especially departmental structure regarding theater, speech pathology, radio-TV-film.

On your campus are these areas part of the department of speech? Are they organized in separate departments or divisions? What is the practice on other campuses? (Consult college and university catalogs or advertisements in professional journals.)

3. What is the domain of your specialty within the discipline? How would you describe the community of scholars that practices this specialty? What methods of inquiry (research) are used?

4. Review the requirements for a bachelor's or master's degree on your campus. Are they too broad? too specialized?

5. Select a specialty within the discipline and discuss whether it contributes to national defense or national welfare. In other words, can you justify the use of federal funds to support it?

6. What speech courses, if any, should be required of prospective teachers of other subjects? Public speaking? interpretation? discussion? a special course?

References

Anderson, Martin P. "A Mid-Century Survey of Books on Communication." *Journal of Communication* December 1964. Lists the ten most significant books in the field of communication during the decade 1950-59.

Berlo, David K. *The Process of Communication.* New York: Holt, Rinehart, & Winston, 1960.

Black, John W., and Moore, Wilbur E. *Speech: Code, Meaning and Communication.* New York: McGraw-Hill, 1955.

Borden, George A.; Gregg, Richard R.; and Grove, Theodore G. *Speech Behavior and Human Interaction.* Englewood Cliffs: Prentice-Hall, 1969.

Braden, Waldo W. "Teachers of Speech as Communicators." *Speech Teacher* March 1966.

Brigance, William Norwood. "Demagogues, 'Good' People, and Teachers of Speech." *Speech Teacher* September 1952.

Bryant, Donald C. "Rhetoric: Its Function and Scope." *Quarterly Journal of Speech* December 1953.

Contest Committee of the Speech Association of America. "A Program of Speech Education." *Quarterly Journal of Speech* October 1951.

Dance, Frank E.X., ed. *Human Communication Theory: Original Essays.* New York: Holt, Rinehart & Winston, 1967. Contributions of anthropology, neurophysiology, psychololinguistics, speech, and other disciplines.

"Democratic Practices in Secondary School Administration." *Bulletin of the National Association of Secondary-School Principals* October 1951. See especially the article "Why Beginning Teachers Fail," and the articles on the imperative needs of youth and the major objectives of secondary education.

Dickens, Milton, "Laws of Experimental Research." *Western Speech* Autumn 1960.

Eisenson, Jon; Auer, J. Jeffery; and Irwin, John V. *The Psychology of Communication.* New York: Appleton-Century-Crofts, 1963.

Erickson, Keith V. *Dimensions of Oral Communication in Instruction: Readings in Speech Education.* Dubuque: William C. Brown, 1970.

Haberman, Frederick W. "Toward the Ideal Teacher of Speech." *Speech Teacher* January 1961.

Highet, Gilbert. *The Art of Teaching.* New York: Alfred A. Knopf, 1950.

Jeffrey, Robert C. "Analysis of Speech Association of America Membership on the Eve of 'Phase Two.' " *Quarterly Journal of Speech* October 1962.

Kibler, Robert J., and Barker, Larry L. *Conceptual Frontiers in Speech-Communication.* New York: Speech Association of America, 1969.

Klotsche, J. Martin. "The Importance of Communication in Today's World." *Speech Teacher* November 1962.

Lang, William C. "Public Address as a Force in History." *Quarterly Journal of Speech* February 1951.

McLaughlin, Ted J. "The Responsibility of Speech Departments in Time of Revolt." *Speech Teacher* January 1967.

Miller, Gerald R. "On Defining Communication: Another Stab." *Journal of Communication* June 1966.

Nilsen, Thomas R. "Free Speech, Persuasion, and the Democratic Process." *Quarterly Journal of Speech* October 1958.

Rahskopf, Horace G. "Speech at Mid Century." *Quarterly Journal of Speech* April 1951. See also the brief commentary at the end of the article entitled "The Goals of Speech Education" by J. P. Ryan, *Quarterly Journal of Speech Education* January, 1918.

Reid, Loren. "The Discipline of Speech." *Speech Teacher* January 1967.

Schmidt, Ralph N. "A Philosophy to Guide Us in Teaching Public Speaking." *Speech Teacher* January 1956. Relates public speaking to Aristotelianism, Platonism, pragmatism, and other philosophical schools.

Schramm, Wilbur, ed. *Mass Communications.* 2d ed. Urbana: University of Illinois Press, 1969. *The Science of Human Communication.* New York: Basic Books, 1963.

Sereno, Kenneth K., and Mortensen, C. David. *Foundations of Communication Theory.* New York: Harper & Row, 1970.

Smith, Donald K.; Weaver, Andrew T.; and Wallace, Karl R. "The Field of Speech: Its Purposes and Scope in Education." *Speech Teacher* November 1963. An official document of the Speech Communication Association, it has been reprinted in leaflet form and can be ordered in quantity from the national office.

Smith, Raymond G. *Speech Communication: Theory and Models.* New York: Harper & Row, 1969.

Thompson, Wayne N. *Quantitative Research in Public Address and Communication.* New York: Random House, 1967. Chapter 6, "The Teaching of Public Speaking," reviews studies pertinent to teaching method.

Wallace, Karl R. "Goals, Concepts, and the Teacher of Speech." *Speech Teacher* March 1968.

————. "The Substance of Rhetoric: Good Reasons." *Quarterly Journal of Speech* October 1963.

Walter, Otis M. "On the Teaching of Speech as a Force in Western Culture." *Speech Teacher* January 1962.

Weaver, John C. "In the Power of the Tongue." *Central States Speech Journal* August 1966. In this keynote address at the annual CSSA conference, a university president and former dean affirms the importance of speech as a discipline.

Weirich, Dorothy Q. "Participating in Community Affairs." *Speech Teacher* November 1969. Imaginative suggestions that help relate school to community.

Yeomans, G. Allan. "Speech Education: A Terrible Responsibility." *Vital Speeches* March 15, 1964. Includes excerpts from correspondence with prominent Americans about the value of speech education.

History of Speech Education

Students and teachers seeking to acquire historical depth about the teaching of speech in this country should consult:

Wallace, Karl R., ed. *History of Speech Education in America: Background Studies.* New York: Appleton-Century-Crofts, 1954. Twenty-eight chapters dealing with all aspects of speech education: early rhetorical theory, elocutionary training, the literary society, intercollegiate debating, phonetics, teaching the deaf, outstanding teachers, speech organizations, educational dramatics, high school dramatics, professional theater schools.

Gray, Giles Wilkeson. "A Bibliography of Studies in the History of Speech Education from 1925." *Speech Teacher* January 1956.

Part Two
the classroom

"If ye had a boy wud ye sind him to colledge?" asked Mr. Hennessy. *"Well,"* said Mr. Dooley, *"at th' age whin a boy is fit to be in colledge I wudden't have him around th' house."*

Finley Peter Dunne

3

planning a
high school course

Sir, while you are considering which of two things you should teach your child first, another boy has learnt them both.

Samuel Johnson

Since readers of this book have likely had twenty or thirty hours of professional education, they have already been exposed to basic principles of planning course outlines and units of instruction. We begin with statements of purpose—we would be foolish to plan assignments until we knew where we were headed—and in formulating our purposes we move through two layers of objectives: general statements that say something about basic philosophy, and specific statements about what we want students to achieve from each instructional segment. We plan assignments that advance toward these objectives, reviewing the resources at our command, including books, films, and related materials, and pondering different styles of classroom activities: lecture, discussion, demonstration, student performance. We become curious to know how well we are doing our job, and here we rely upon quizzes and tests to supplement daily observations of student behavior. Finally, after the grades are in and the students have moved on, we review strong and weak points. We may conclude, to switch to a golfing image, that we did well with the woods and the putter but not so well with the irons. We then review and revise the course outline. Surely every certificated teacher, or undergraduate student headed for a certificate, has gone or will go over this ground in length and depth.

41

A word about objectives. As suggested in the preceding chapter, students of psychology and education in the post-World War I period were influenced by behaviorism, a school of thought led by John B. Watson and others, that stressed that human beings were best studied by observing what they actually did. In part this was a revolt against the introspectionism then in vogue. Watson's contributions did not lead to a complete picture of human learning. He and his followers made excessive claims about the importance of the observable part of human behavior and dealt too cautiously with thought, introspection, idea, imagination, and similar notions that could not be easily observed. Research and investigation continued, and in the fifties and sixties neo-behaviorism emerged, though the adjective became behavioral instead of behavioristic. Adherents of this school do not disclaim the importance of inner, mental activity, but place emphasis on what can be noted and measured.

Hence those who are most involved in research about learning advise teachers to state objectives, at least in part, in behavioral language. Thus while it is proper to say, as was said in the preceding chapter, that students of speech should become better members of a democratic society, you and I should at some point be specific about this aim, and ask ourselves what observable things we can ask students to *do* in a classroom that suggest they are actually on the way toward becoming better citizens. Otherwise, how can we appraise the value of instruction? How can we tell whether we taught what we set out to teach?

In his book *Preparing Instructional Objectives,* Robert F. Mager poses the problem in this way:[1]

Words open to many interpretations	Words open to fewer interpretations
to know	to write
to understand	to recite
to *really* understand	to identify
to appreciate	to differentiate
to *fully* appreciate	to solve
to grasp the significance of	to construct
to enjoy	to list
to have faith in	to compare
	to contrast

[1] This inexpensive paperback manual is well worth reading in full. It is published by Fearon Publishers, Inc. (address in Appendix D). *See also* the books edited by Benjamin S. Bloom, David R. Krathwohl, and others, *Taxonomy of Educational Objectives* (listed in the References at the end of this chapter).

The *Course Guide in the Theatre Arts at the Secondary School Level*[2] is an excellent example combining general with behavioral statements of objectives. To illustrate, under the heading of "Teacher Emphasis," the *Guide* has these suggestions:

> Emphasize the important role of aesthetics in the student's daily life.
> Encourage a broad exposure to all the fine arts.

Immediately following is another heading, "Behavioral Evidences of Student Awareness and Response," with such statements as these:

> If the objectives of this section are realized, each student will demonstrate, to a degree, behavioral evidences similar to the following:
> Will begin to respond to the theatrical situation by (a) expressing opinions that relate his own experiences to the work at hand (this can be demonstrated by comments as "That's true" or "That's the way it happens" or "That isn't the way you do that"); (b) showing involvement in the scene being performed as indicated by changes in facial and physical expression.
> Will begin to develop an attitude of discrimination toward an art experience by (a) recognizing and using terms other than superlatives in the discussion of theatrical work; (b) recognizing differences among television, film, and theater; (c) making positive statements, such as "Let's do this as a scene" or "I would like to act this out" or "Let's do that again."[3]

Actually teachers of speech have always operated in the midst of considerable observable student behavior whether or not they use the language of the behavioralists. Behavior is our natural environment, our protective coloration. We have always been where the action is, whether in the front of the room, the back, or in between. Our students discuss, debate, read aloud, act, participate in all sorts of exercises and demonstrations. Even so this new emphasis will help sharpen our perceptions.

What now follows are specific suggestions about what activities can go into a high school speech course. Other suggestions may be found in the following chapter, "The College First Course," and in the specialized chapters on public speaking, oral interpretation, etc. From these and still other sources the teacher can construct his own course of study, in the light of his own objectives and his own ways of appraising the result of his instruction. The discussion of the

Published 1968 by the American Educational Theatre Association (address in Appendix E).
Ibid., p. 9. These brief excerpts do not do justice to the *Course Guide*. Students and teachers are advised to study it not only for its suggestions about the theater, including readers theater and chamber theater, but also because its approach will be helpful in formulating one's own objectives in other segments of the course.

year-long high school course that follows is based upon the assumption that the course meets five days a week for approximately forty-five minute periods, with twenty-four or fewer students. (1) It plans a series of major units. (2) It indicates the total amount of time that may be spent on each unit. (3) It incorporates suggestions for daily assignments or activities. These suggestions may be amplified by reading pertinent chapters later in the book. (4) It stresses a point of view for each unit, mentioning significant achievements to be attained. No attempt is made to be consistent in the style from unit to unit; less is said, for example, about clinical speech and play directing, since books in those fields traditionally illustrate the teacher's viewpoint.

Orientation (1 week)

Part of the first day of school will be taken up with routine announcements and registration details. You may, however, find time to introduce yourself, announce the text, describe the wide variety of activities that a speech class embraces, and talk about the importance of communication not only in the home and the school, in social situations, and in business and industry, but also as it is related to good citizenship. Your purpose should be (a) to set the tone and (b) to describe the content of the course, so that before the bell rings the students will have a good idea of what will happen during the semester.

The traditional way of opening, after the foregoing preliminaries, is to ask each student to talk about himself: he should give his name and tell about his interests, hobbies, and experiences. You may demonstrate to students what you want done by introducing yourself to them: tell them your name, spelling it if necessary; describe your interests, hobbies, and experiences; mention briefly your educational background. The students may then talk in turn, at first each one standing by his seat, though later in the period you may vary the procedure by asking each one to come to the front of the room.

If this activity becomes so mechanical that students merely recite their names plus two or three sentences of biographical material, the teacher needs to ask questions. Here is a point at which students of limited environmental or educational experience will need sympathetic prompting. The reports of field workers in the inner city, for example, clearly state that young people in this category are likely to reply in monosyllables or short phrases. While supervising student teachers in small high schools I have often observed a similar situation: an assignment that the student teacher and I had thought would occupy a class for a full period, was completed in fifteen minutes. Hence the student should be encouraged to amplify the response that he has wrapped and bundled into a short phrase. One technique is to get a thread of discussion started through all the talks. If you are able to start something about favorite games or hobbies, you may, through questions, get a student to add to, or compare and contrast, his experience with that of others who preceded him. On another level you may get students to say something about their politics, or their favorite public figures, in addition to autobiographical material. Many students take politics seriously, and are proud to be Democrats or Republicans; in such a situation the teacher can make good-humored comments about each new addition to the Democratic or the Republican column. A variation is to ask students to indicate whether they are liberal or conservative, radical or reactionary. These terms mean more than traditional political labels, and are intriguing enough to provoke various kinds of observations. Sometimes the student body is engaged in a lively issue that may be discussed as a part of these first speeches; for example, after the introduction proper, each student may speak in behalf of his candidate for the next president of the class, or on whether the school should organize a cafeteria or engage in competitive football.

The assignment has the virtue of having been used by hundreds of teachers at all levels from the elementary school to the adult education class. It requires ingenuity on the part of the teacher, but if the discussion becomes spirited, with a free play of good humor, fears and anxieties are quieted and the class bell rings almost too soon. The students leave feeling that the class is going to be all right, and the teacher has learned something about guiding and stimulating discussion: how to take a pupil who expected to be able to say only a few words, encourage him with questions, and thus lead him into making a talk of respectable length.

Variations on this traditional procedure have been devised, especially by teachers who feel that the student will be more at ease talking about someone other than himself. You may divide the class in twos, let each twosome chat a few minutes, and then ask each member of the couple to introduce the other. If members of the class are not well known to one another, you may ask students who have not yet spoken to review the names of those who have. After four speakers have introduced themselves, for example, ask another student to identify the four by name. After eight speakers have spoken, ask still another to identify all eight. By the end of the hour everybody should know everybody's name. This device is frequently used in adult classes of business men, where memory of names and faces is stressed. It ought to be useful in a class where the students come from different neighborhoods.

A good followup for this first speaking experience is to invite each student to make a narrative talk of three to five minutes in length. "Your talk tomorrow will be the same kind as the one you just completed: tell us about your most embarrassing experience, or your most exciting adventure." Since everyone has been sorely embarrassed, or scared half to death, he should have little trouble in finding a topic. A variation, suggested by teachers who think this topic too egocentric: report an interview with someone else who has an interesting job or hobby. Your criticism of and suggestions for this first round of speeches may emphasize the principles of interest (use of specific example, vivid language, dialogue, humor, suspense) and should be as encouraging and commendatory as the situation warrants: this speech is, after all, the first one.

The first part of the course is the proper place to talk about communication theory. In this connection a statement prepared by William D. Buys, Charles V. Carlson, Hite Compton, and Allan D. Frank, under the auspices of the Secondary School Speech Interest Group, appearing in the November 1968 issue of *Speech Teacher* under the title "Speech Communication in the High School Curriculum," should be consulted.

After offering a rationale for a communication theory approach (considering the Darwinian, Freudian, and economic revolutions which focussed attention upon individual human beings behaving in ways that reflect cognitive and affective processes), Carlson, et.al., offer a variety of questions for discussion and proposals for activities. They consider both interpersonal and intrapersonal communication and have compiled a selected bibliography covering the whole range of their study. Here are two brief samples from their work. Under the heading of intrapersonal communication they ask such questions as: Am I afraid to meet new people? Can I start a conversation? Am I able to enter a conversation which others have begun? . . . How do I learn? Am I able to predict what will result from my thinking? Am I able to recognize facts? Am I able to distinguish fact from opinion? Do I enjoy the process that is termed intellectual? Under the heading of interpersonal communication they suggest such activities as: For each speaking assignment, develop a parallel listening assignment . . . such as . . . have listeners write out the speaker's central idea and intent . . . have listeners list what they consider to be the important information presented by the speaker . . . compare these lists with the speaker's perception of important information.

A byproduct of this exercise and the few that follow is to perfect your knowledge of the needs and abilities of the particular class. From your practice teaching and other experience, you have collected general notions but each day will bring specific insights and impressions and you will find yourself mentally rearranging the curriculum furniture in order to teach each group most effectively.

Voice and Articulation (1 week)

Since the improvement of voice and articulation is one of the *fundamentals* of communication described in the previous chapter, you should start your discussion of these concepts early in the course.

Prepare mimeographed sheets of sentences such as those illustrated in Appendix A, and bring to class your supply of criticism sheets (Appendix B) Although the first round of speeches may yield adequate knowledge about the needs and abilities of your students, for a complete check even an experienced teacher needs the help of designed test sentences. As the student reads Sentence 1 of the testing sentences, "Paul looked up at the ripest plum on the tree," listen for the *p* sounds to see if they are clearly articulated. Most students have no difficulty with *p*'s, or, for that matter with any of the sounds in the first six sentences (occasionally a youngster will say "tlass" instead of *class*, or "bid man" instead of *big man*). In Sentence 7 *some* and *missing* may be heard as "thum" and "mithing" or as "shum" and "mishing." In similar fashion proceed through the entire list. This method of making a survey is of value to the teacher whose ear may not be trained adequately to enable him to catch all the defective sounds in a more complex performance. The form also includes a classification of voice problems, so that a notation may be entered about any voice difficulty that is observed. The rating scale of 1 to 5 gives a chance to make an overall, subjective impression ranging all the way from very poor to very good. Later the survey sheets can be studied, the defects being classified and grouped for purposes of later instruction.

On the following day you may show each student his score card. Give him also a copy of the test sentences, and read them one by one to illustrate the various kinds of speech habits that occur. Invite the students to compare their differing methods of pronunciation, pointing out that we approach these problems in the spirit of inquiry and analysis. You may demonstrate dialectal differences, if you have had training in phonetics: some individuals pronounce *Paul* like *pole*; in *carry* some use the vowel of *bad*, some that of *bed*. Often *fighting* comes out as "fightin.' " You may also demonstrate sound substitutions, omissions, insertions, and additions. "Thum" and "shum" certainly do not sound like *some*. "Witer" and "woad" in Sentence 20 are not acceptable for *writer* and *road*. You may illuminate your discussion by relating experiences of your own with students who have had speech difficulties. Your choice of experiences needs as always to be related to the backgrounds of your own students. If you have students of differing national or racial backgrounds you may want to bring out differences between home talk and school talk, assigning to each dialect its own sphere of usefulness. Invite each student to read the test sentences again to see if he can, with care, improve in distinctness. From time to time you may find it necessary to demonstrate mechanics of sound production: *l* is made with the tip of the tongue, not the lips, and so on.

You should, after this systematic presentation, strive for ingenious ways of introducing exercise material, to keep the unit from becoming monotonous. Competition may enter: ask five students to read a short group of sentences, the class indicating which one is most clear. Or let the performers stand out in the hall in front of a microphone, while the class listens through the loud speaker placed in the room. Later the best speakers in each group of five can compete against one another, and the less successful ones compete for a consolation prize. Telegrams may be dictated over the loud speaker to the class; the omission of familiar connectives makes clearer articulation necessary. "FAY INJURED MEET PAN AMERICAN FLIGHT SEVENTY MONDAY BRING NURSE" contains interesting possibilities for error, the most obvious being "seventeen" for *seventy* and "hearse" for *nurse*. Tongue twisters also afford a few moments' diversion.

Members of the class may contribute examples of misunderstandings that arose because of faulty articulation. One girl thought she heard a boy ask her over the telephone, "Are you going to the dance Saturday," and answered, "No." The boy then said, "Well, I'm sorry," and soon thereafter hung up. Later she learned that the boy had actually said, "Would you like to go to the dance Saturday," and so he was quite surprised when she said simply, "No." His "Well, I'm sorry" sounded rude but in reality was courteous under the circumstances.

Instruction in voice is equally important. You may talk about good breathing and proper resonance. Class exercises in breathing, relaxation and resonance can be found in Chapter 6. You may find it interesting to have the class memorize a short selection, such as the speech of Marullus in Act 1 of *Julius Caesar*, which requires variety of voice, ranging all the way from pleading and beseeching to scorn and anger.[4] The famous nose scene in *Cyrano de Bergerac* is another often-used vocal stunt.

The class should also be shown how the voice can be used to communicate ideas. A single word like "Yes," or "No," or "George" can be spoken to suggest a variety of meanings. Simple exercises such as the following demonstrate how effectively the voice can express different shades of meaning.

Question: "Will you loan me fifty cents to go to the show?"
Response: "Yes." (Of course.)
          "Yes." (I will, but I'm not too enthusiastic about it.)
          "Yes." (I'm not sure I have fifty cents.)
          "Yes." (I'm afraid I'll never see it again.)
          "No." (Positively, flatly, no.)

Such exercises as these anticipate the units in interpretation and drama later on in the course.

Stand six students on one side of the room, and one opposite. The one walks over to the six and says aloud, "Who's in charge here?" One at a time each member of the group steps forward and says, "I'm in charge." Let the class decide who was the most convincing. Did the one who spoke loudly and aggressively seem to be the most in charge? Or was it the one who spoke quietly and confidently? Or paraphrase King Lear and his daughters. King Lear asks each in turn:

Which of you shall we say doth love us most?
. . . What says our . . . daughter?

Each girl, in a sentence or two, tries to convince him that she does. Let the class discuss who would make the best heiress.

[4] For additional materials, see Chapter 6, "Improving Voice Articulation, Other Elements of Language."

Conduct imaginary tryouts for a play. Each aspirant is to read the same short selection—four or five lines. Who read it the most convincingly? To what extent do voice and articulation help make reading convincing?

Keep instruction in voice and articulation as practical as possible, using most of the time for actual drill and practice. The physiology and anatomy you learned in college was primarily for your background, and need not be relayed here. Try to give each pupil help with his essential problem. If you can start him on the road to improvement this week, you can build on this beginning throughout the course.

Some teachers strongly recommend that four to six weeks, or even longer, be spent on this unit instead of only one week. That decision needs to be made by each teacher. The teacher in Hawaii, working with students whose language habits reflect strong Oriental influences, faces a different problem from that existing in a mainland suburban school. In other parts of the nation the background is Spanish, Chicano, Negro, Indian, Eskimo. Moreover, these ethnological differences may be compounded by environmental conditions. In integrated schools, the teacher may be faced with one set of needs from white students, another set from black students. In each situation the teacher should find sensible projects that will improve the communicative abilities of each boy and girl in both his home and school environment. References at the end of Chapter 6 may suggest a lead. If the problem needs more classroom time than usual, the teacher will need to expand instruction here and drop some of the units that follow. Certainly this segment of the course offers rich opportunity for full and rich development. Voice alone may be treated under the heading of pitch, loudness, quality, and duration, with interesting assignments worked out under each heading. If you decide to spend only the minimum time suggested here, you may continue the instruction indirectly throughout the remaining units. If a student has spent his life perfecting bad habits of articulation and voice, he will not make phenomenal improvement in a few days.

You may show how personality is reflected in voice and articulation. Most people feel that they can analyze character by listening to the individual's voice; a calm, relaxed, responsible person would not be likely to talk in a shrill, hurried way; a forceful executive type of individual would not speak with hesitant, mumbling articulation. One observer of the contemporary scene commented that some people say "Hello" in the tone of voice they would use for "Drop dead." Encouraging a shy person to speak up, to assert himself, to take his full share in conversation and discussion, may be the first step toward shaping him into a bolder and more forthright communicator.

Informal Speaking (4 weeks)

Whether the unit described below belongs in senior high or junior high depends upon the school and the students. Quite likely it belongs in both places, the instruction and the nature of the assignments being adapted to the level. In the same class the teacher may find students who come from homes that practice all the social amenities, and from homes that have none. The same statement may be true of college classes. Students who feel more at home in group activities than in solo activities may additionally profit from such informal speaking assignments as accompany instruction in social introductions, conversation, and interviews.

Begin with an analysis of the proprieties underlying social introductions, as many conversations open with an introduction of the principals to each other. Find out from the group what problems people have in making introductions. Do they find themselves forgetting to make the necessary introductions? Do they know how to put every person at ease? Does their inexperience lead them to forget the names of people they know well? Are they as at home among adults as among people of their own age? Do they feel the verbal formulas they use are too mechanical? After friends are properly introduced, do they know how to continue the conversation so as to include the new arrivals? Many other problems should be revealed by the discussion.

The rules governing social introductions are important, and the teacher will need to know them; two matters are paramount. One is the opportunity to advance the instruction in voice and articulation: many introductions are garbled because some name was improvidently mumbled. More significant is the opportunity to continue the development of the student's personality. In business and social circles a mark of poise is the ability to make new friends. Advancement seems to go to the young man or woman who can not only handle an assignment proficiently but who can also meet the public. The teacher can detect the individual who is at a loss for words, and can suggest specific things to do to help fill the great, silent voids. In all likelihood these individuals have not received much help in such matters at home, so that classroom exercises may represent first-time experiences for them.

Most textbooks suggest specific exercises. Usually the teacher needs to prepare a set of realistic situations: two girls are talking together, and a boy comes up who knows one of the girls but not the other; the girl who knows him greets him, and presents him to her companion. A girl greets her date at the door and presents him to her parents. A boy takes his date to the drug store, and runs into two of his friends, whom he presents to her. Your mother visits you at school, and you present your teachers to her. While you are attending the football game with your father, you meet one of your teachers, and introduce the two men. All of these situations and many more like them are enacted by students in front of the class. For variety you may intersperse such tomfooleries as "While you are walking down the street with your grandmother you meet an old friend, the president of Mrs. Brockton's School for Girls; introduce the two"; but these are strictly for comic relief.

After a day spent discussing the principles of social introductions, and two or three days spent in dramatizing specific situations and in reporting on outside experiences with social introductions, the unit logically moves into conversation. (After you meet a person, you need to be able to enter into conversation with him.) Your next activity, therefore, can well be a discussion of principles of conversation. What are common faults? Let your students develop the discussion with you: write on the board, for example, the various points as they are made. Another interesting classroom discussion is to answer the question: "If high school students want to become good conversationalists, what topics should they try to inform themselves upon?" Put on the board the topics suggested.

For classroom exercises, some teachers divide the class into small groups and assign each a topic to discuss. Suppose your discussion reveals that big league baseball is a topic of conversation that everyone should be informed upon. Select four or five eager fans, and ask them to demonstrate a conversation about baseball. Do the same for other topics, assigning each member of the class to one group. If your students are more sophisticated, choose a more challenging topic: higher education, foreign policy.

You may also put on the board a list of conversational situations that seem difficult. Is it difficult to extend condolence to a friend that has lost a near relative? Is it difficult to tender, and receive, congratulations? Is it difficult to talk to the date's parents? Is it difficult to use the telephone? Is it awkward to open a conversation with a new student? Divide the class into committees, assigning each committee to one of these problems. Each committee gathers all useful information, and reports. Or if this seems too structured, several conversations may be carried on in different parts of the room, and some other arrangement be devised to share conclusions. Discuss specific formulas that may be used. For condolences, one class suggested: "We are all so sorry to hear about the bad news at your house." To a date's father, another class evolved: "You would certainly have been very proud of Jennifer, Mr. Jones, if you had heard her speech in class today." Specific help of this sort aid each young person to figure out phrases that are useful for *him*.

Improvisation and *sociodrama* are words frequently heard; you can combine them in assignments to improve conversation. The purpose of sociodrama is to act out, spontaneously, a dramatic situation. Corporations use sociodrama to train executives: the aspirant is put in an imagined situation, for example, a labor squabble, in which one of his fellow trainees represents an unhappy worker, another his foreman, and he himself is the plant superintendent. On the spot he listens to both sides and evolves a solution. You can pose a difficult conversational problem and assign students to talk it out, improvising as they go along. To arouse interest, read conversations from your favorite fiction: the spy successfully outmaneuvers his captors, the diplomat negotiates an understanding with his opposite number.

Students seem to need guidance in learning how to make the kind of small talk that bridges the interval between the meeting of a new friend and the discovery of solid, mutual interests. Apparently they do not appreciate the importance of small talk; they must think that newly introduced persons immediately hit upon topics of moment. Casual inquiries such as "Where is your home, Miss Blank" or "Who are you with, Mr. Roger" or "Is this your first visit to Chicago, Dr. Quack" or "So you're from Gary; did you know a Ruth Allen in the lumber business there" are courteous inquiries of mature and poised individuals who have learned that interesting conversations start with humble beginnings. What are the equivalents among teenagers?

Some persons upon being introduced immediately start discussing an incident of the day simply as a way of breaking the ice. A good rule to follow when initiating conversation is that of "one more question." Just at the point when one feels that a new acquaintanceship is about to die an undeserved death, ask "one more question" to give it a fresh start. Two people meet casually in the street, and both may say "hello" and pass on; but if one should stop to ask "one more question," an interesting conversation may develop. At a party or game one meets many people, often merely to exchange greetings; but if one asks "one more question," a friendship may begin.

Many faults of conversation grow out of problems intimately related to speech. Here is a student who answers all efforts to be friendly with "yes" and "no." "Have you lived very long in Topeka," says the new acquaintance, mentioning a topic upon which our student should be able to discourse for hours; but our student says not "Yes, my father bought the Brown hardware ten years ago and we have been here since," not "Yes, my parents came here from Chicago last year," but simply "Yes." Years later he will start to work in the Brown hardware, and the customer, about to buy an expensive power mower, will say, "Is this a pretty good buy?" "Yes" may be all the student is able to say unless he profits by his speech course. Love affairs, happy marriages, opportunities for promotion, various forms of recognition, may all be starved by monosyllables. Of course, the evils of the opposite extreme need to be noted: people can talk too much as well as too little.

Often boys and girls (and for that matter, adult men and women) do not succeed in saying exactly what they mean. For this reason their attitudes are sometimes misunderstood, and they may be thought to be less friendly and cordial than they really are. The words "yes" and "no" do not convey so much information as students think. If a friend asks you to do him a special favor, and you respond with a mild "yes," he will think you are not very eager to help him. If you are really pleased, the mild "yes" has not fully expressed your attitude; perhaps you should have said, instead, "yes, I certainly will," or "yes, I'll be delighted to," or "sure will, no trouble at all," or "I'll do it right away." I have heard high school boys and girls turn down dates to parties with a flat colorless "no," when probably they were genuinely disappointed. I have also overheard something like this: "I'm so sorry I can't go, I've already made a date; I wish I had known you were thinking of asking me." About five years of growing up and learning to live with people lie between the two refusals. If students can be taught to hold on to the conversational thread until they succeed in finding the words they seek, adopting an attitude of friendliness and candor, they will not only avoid embarrassing situations, but will find their relationships with others much more pleasant.

Attention should also be given to telephone conversation. Everyone should know how to answer both a business and a residential phone; how to hold the mouthpiece so that words will be clear; how to speak naturally. Circulars may be secured from the telephone company; these also stress the importance of not talking too long, and the golden rule of consideration for others on your party line. You may also want to offer advice about the advisability of posting near the phone a list of emergency numbers (and follow up on this advice). This is ordinary horse sense of the kind parents often think teachers do not have.

Your study of conversation leads naturally into the problem of interviews. You may begin by discussing the types of interviews: applying for a position, making a sale, securing information from an authority or expert. You may continue by eliciting from the class ideas about good principles to follow in each of these types, and, conversely, the common faults.

Before you make assignments of exercises illustrating, for example, the interview used in applying for a position, find out what experience members of the class have had themselves. Have the girls applied for positions as camp counselors or salesgirls? If so, have some of them demonstrate good interviews. Let one girl take the role of playground director, and let others interview her for the position, one at a time. The class may discuss the strong and weak points of each application. The boys have no doubt had experience in applying for various summer and part-time positions: grocery stores, camps, construction engineers, post offices, newspapers, and the like. Let them demonstrate interviews of the types they are familiar with. Find out, also, what experience members of the class have had in selling. Let them demonstrate good and bad selling techniques. Discuss principles of interviewing for information; ask each student to interview some older person on a topic with which the elder is familiar, and report to the class the results of his interview. This interview may take the form of a vocational inquiry: if a student wants to enter a trade, a business, or a profession, let him interview a practitioner about the advantages and disadvantages and the type of preparation needed.

The interview presents priceless opportunities for the development of the ability to communicate on a practical level. Many job seekers are unable to make a good case for themselves; they minimize their training and experience to the point where the prospective employer loses all interest. In boom times when anybody can get a job, the ability to conduct an interview is less important; but when jobs become scarce and a good position is at stake, the successful applicant will need to be able to give a fair accounting of his talents. Interviews are also conducted for the purpose of gaining information.

The teacher should prepare an ample list of situations covering social intro-ductions, conversation, and interviewing. Much of the time may actually be spent in enacting these situations, but opportunity should be provided for discussion of the principles involved.

In developing this or any other unit of instruction the teacher needs to be guided by the age, maturity, and sophistication of the students in the class. If your students come from upper-income families, they may need less of this sort of instruction. If they come from low-income groups, they need help with situations realistic to them. Some teachers, in fact, would place a unit such as this in the elementary grades or junior high. Much, however, depends upon the mood created by the assignment and by the choice of situations and illus-trations. Nor should a teacher be misled by apparent sophistication. I have known high-caliber university students who did poorly in interviews because they fumbled the casual questions of the interviewer about their educational ambitions, their social or political opinions. Almost without exception the high school texts in wide use have substantial chapters about conversation and interviewing that you will find stimulating to draw upon for assignments and discussions.

Parliamentary Procedure (2 weeks)

As instruction in parliamentary procedure has been generally dropped from the college first course, this outline suggests that two weeks of instruction may profitably be included in the high school course. Students in large high schools have an immediate need for it in connection with their many clubs. Students in small high schools may find it important especially in communities where the 4-H, FFA, or similar programs are prominent.

In a two-week unit, the teacher can cover fairly well the subsidiary motions and a dozen others. He can develop an understanding of what is meant by precedence; a general knowledge of how to make, discuss, amend, and vote upon motions; a familiarity with standard references.

As many teachers who have never studied parliamentary law will read these paragraphs, this is a good place to say that a teacher must continually be a learner, and some matters he learns best by trying to teach them. In this connection a teacher in English methods one day propounded an intriguing theory for the beginning teacher. The field of English literature is so broad (she argued) that the beginner should pick for complete coverage only authors familiar to him. If his knowledge of Wordsworth and Shelley is only sketchy whereas his appreciation of Tennyson and Browning is richer, let him pay his respects to the former but dwell longer on the latter. Later in summer school (the argument continued) he can fill in the gaps by taking the proper courses.

The argument is a neat one and fits in well with the busy schedule of the high school teacher who has the problem of working up new courses the first year out of college. An important shortcoming of the argument, however, needs to be pointed out. The student should not have to suffer too much for the inadequate background of the teacher; the gaps might be too broad. The field of speech is also broad, and whereas the teacher can easily skip debating, in which he may have had little practice, and amplify choral reading, in which he has had much, he should be willing to plunge into a new field and explore it with his students. Obviously he may not feel like doing much plunging the first year. Yet one may have a career of fifty years as a teacher, and it would be a tragedy to dodge an idea a whole lifetime.

Taking such a plunge proved for me a profitable although at the time embarrassing experience. One high school had had a long tradition of parliamentary law: my predecessor had taught it many years. Yet in seven years of college and university study I had not received ten minutes' instruction in the subject. A persistent axiom says that a good way to learn something is to try to teach it to others. I would either have to teach parliamentary procedure, or omit it. I decided to teach it. I started by discussing the duties of the presiding officer and ways of making, seconding, and voting upon main motions. This material is certainly the simplest in the parliamentary law books. Each day that followed I limited the practice and discussion to two motions; this was about all I could trust myself to master, but actually I kept abreast of student ability to assimilate. Next year the teaching of parliamentary procedure was much easier.

If you have never taught parliamentary procedure, secure a copy of *Robert's Rules of Order Newly Revised*[5] and two or three of the newer manuals and proceed. Teach one or two motions a day—starting with the conventions of the main motion, proceeding to the subsidiary motions one by one, and ending with a few of the privileged, incidental, and renewal motions.

The unit on parliamentary procedure makes a substantial contribution to that aim of the course which states that speech communication is vital to training in living in a democratic society. The basic rule is our deeply rooted concept that every man should have his say, with the final decision by the majority. Times arise, however, when the majority moves too slowly to suit the minority, even when the minority assembles, parades, and petitions; then the minority may be driven to tearing up pavements, building barricades, breaking heads. The shouting, too, becomes violent, and the quiet assumption of one man, one vote is scorned and jeered. But when the tumult has quieted, the mob realizes that its leaders have no program, and turns its back on them. Then the strategy changes: the new, but by no means novel, strategy is to work inside the structure, not outside it. The majority has become more sensitive and more responsible, and objectionable features are altered.

Moreover, the unit on parliamentary procedure helps develop presiding skills. Though a good chairman needs to be forceful, he needs also to be fair and

[5] Scott, Foresman, 1970. The first major revision since 1915.

tactful. These assets of leadership are respected by all. At times the chairman is wiser to overlook a minor rule in order to avoid harassing the group by mere mechanics, provided he is assured that wishes of members are being respected.

Listening (1 week)

Throughout any course, high school or college, the teacher will give attention to the problem of listening. If the assignment calls for speeches, members of the class will need to listen attentively if they are to criticize intelligently such factors as use of evidence or plan of organization and adaptation; if it calls for oral readings, listeners may be invited to appraise the reader's appreciation of thought and emotion; if it calls for acting, the listeners will have opportunity to express their reactions to the characterization.

The vital importance of good listening is not new or novel. Epictetus once wrote, "There is an art of hearing as well as of speaking. . . . To make a statue needs skill; to view a statue aright needs skill also. . . . One who proposes to hear philosophers speak needs a considerable training in hearing. Is that not so? Then tell me, on what subject are you able to hear me?"

Investigators have uncovered much specific information about the art or skill of listening itself. Research also shows that the ability to listen and remember varies widely from individual to individual, and that the difference in listening is not solely related to intelligence. When at the University of Minnesota a comparison was made of the one hundred best and worst listeners of a freshman class, some ten differences were spotted distinguishing the best listeners from the worst. Among them:

1. *Poor listeners usually declare the subject uninteresting* after the first few sentences. Having made this decision, they conclude it is not worthwhile to listen. A good listener is more patient, more judicious, and will continue to listen because he realizes that what is being said might turn out to be useful to him.

2. *Poor listeners are overly critical of the speaker's delivery or appearance.* Receiving an unfavorable impression of the speaker, they decide not to listen carefully. This finding helps explain the tendency of beginning students of speech to be overly critical of mannerisms. Since this is the way many people are, speakers (and teachers) should give a thought to their dress and general appearance so as to make this first impression a favorable one.

3. *Poor listeners listen only for facts.* The good listener listens for facts, but also tries to get the underlying principle or generalization involved. The poor listener is likely to miss the application of the example or illustration—to the good listener, this may be the illuminating part of the speaker's contribution.

4. *The poor listener tries to outline all his notes.* Or he places his dependence entirely on a single note-taking system. The good listener has various systems of

taking notes. If the speaker's material is well organized, he takes the ideas down in outline form. He does not waste time, however, trying to outline the unoutlineable; for such a speech he employs a different system of note taking.

5. *The poor listener usually avoids difficult listening.* His background of listening experiences includes more of the simple situations than of the complex ones. On TV, for example, he would spend relatively more of his time listening and viewing westerns, and less with "Meet the Press."

These and other characteristics of good versus bad listeners can profitably be called to the attention of students.

Ralph G. Nichols, an authority on listening with wide teaching experience, believes that four listening abilities need to be taught. One is to overcome distraction, to learn to listen regardless of noises, dialect, or poor articulation. Another is to learn to detect the organization of a message: the central ideas and supporting statements, the lists or enumerations, the chronological or other sequences. A third relates to attitude: to keep an objective frame of mind, to avoid anger or other upsetting emotions. The fourth is to appraise a message: to judge its evidence, its logic, its inferences.[6]

The following will be helpful in developing your own unit in listening:[7]

Listening

I. General aim:
    A. To develop a willingness on the part of the student to assume the responsibilities and seize the opportunities that efficient listening affords.

II. Specific aims:
    A. To build a proper attitude toward listening.
    B. To aid in general language development by seeking the best listening opportunities.
    C. To broaden the student's encounter with and acceptance of ideas.
    D. To establish values in listening as a tool for dealing with propaganda.
    E. To enable the student to carry away at least the major points of an oral communication.
    F. To teach the student listening with a purpose.
    G. To enable the student to give form to his listening experience.

---

[6] I am indebted to the researches of Dr. Nichols for the foregoing. *See: Are You Listening,* written by Nichols and Leonard A. Stevens, published in 1957 by McGraw-Hill Book Co., Inc., and the January 1958 selection of the Executive Book Club. *See also* their article, "Listening to People," in *Harvard Business Review,* September-October 1957, pp. 85-92; and these Nichols's articles: "This Business of Listening," *American Trade Association Executives Journal,* January 1956; "Do We Know How to Listen," *Speech Teacher,* March 1961.

[7] Adapted from *Speech and Drama: Tentative Guide for High School Teachers,* pp. 24-27. Issued in 1961 by the New Mexico State Board of Education.

III. Content and procedure:
   A. Listening for a purpose.
      1. Consider the purposes or general ends of speaking in terms of the listener.
      2. Determine if the listener has more, or fewer, or different purposes from the speaker.
   B. Analyze the process of attention as it relates to listening.
   C. Discuss the hearing mechanism as the key part of the enabling process of listening.
   D. Explain why people so often say, "You don't get what I mean."
   E. Review propaganda devices as preparation for listening.
   F. Listening as well as reading, writing, and speaking depend on structure.
      1. Review patterns of composition such as time and space.
      2. Anticipate devices speakers may use in giving unity to their speeches as themes, motives, slogans, various forms of repetition.
      3. Associate major points with each other.
      4. At the end of the speech reexamine your purpose and review again the ideas that you want to take away with you.
      5. Try out the ideas on someone else who listened to the speech. Compare notes on the major points.
   G. Discuss the function of internal verbalization and how it may interfere with listening.
IV. Suggested activities:
   A. Have the students stop all activity and during five minutes of classroom quiet write down all the different sounds they can identify.
   B. Discuss the sound spectrum and how it brings us information.
   C. Have a student read a very short story and at the conclusion ask each student to write an abstract of the story. Read these aloud and notice the variability of recall.
   D. Have each student make a one-sentence statement. Analyze what it means and what it could mean. See if some student can quote the sentence verbatim, if it is moderately long. Attempt to paraphrase the statement. Determine if the oral style could be improved.
   E. Allow class members to state in their own words what their favorite pieces of literature mean to them. Use the literature selected as listening exercises.
   F. Listen to effective radio and TV commentators. Discuss the degree of effectiveness that these men have achieved in composing speeches for the listener or listener-viewer.

Suggestions for Teaching Listening

The Dallas Independent School District has developed an especially useful guide for providing work lists of aids, guides, and outcomes: *Language Arts for Secondary Schools: Curriculum Guide* (Dallas, 1967, pp. 72-73, 79). The following suggestions relate to listening:

Ask students to appraise themselves as listeners.

Give specific suggestions about things to listen for: how a pause amplifies humor, how a speaker developed an idea by illustrations, how facial expression heightens mood or meaning.

Show how a listener can become discriminating in his listening through his choice of radio and TV programs, movies.

Expected Outcomes: Listening, Observing

Improves as an intelligent listener, a careful observer, and a logical thinker.

Recognizes the power of effective speech in a democracy.

Realizes the essential part effective speech plays in personality development.

Practices keen observation in relation to accepted usage.

Demonstrates ability to benefit by constructive criticism.

Check List for the Student Listener

Do I give the communicator my full attention, listening from his first words, putting aside everything else and concentrating on him? From his point of view, do I seem to be bright-eyed and attentive, or do I emit distress signals?

Do I listen sympathetically and courteously? Do I avoid distractions? If I disagree, do I nevertheless hear him out and await a proper time to reply? Do react to humor, suspense?

Do I distinguish between evidence and opinion? between persuasion and propaganda?

Do I note whether the communicator is overstating or understating? overplaying or underplaying?

Am I aware of digressions?

Can I follow his reasoning, staying with him to the end? If his reasoning is faulty, am I aware of the flaws?

Do I make a mental note of ways to praise him? or of suggestions that will help him improve? or of questions that will give us additional clarification or information?

Can I relate the performance to the assignment—i.e., is he practising good theoretical principles? Can I relate it to my own experience?

Can I compare or contrast the performance with an earlier performance of the same individual?

Have I aided the performer by attentive listening?

Can I summarize the main points in a speech? state the theme of a reading or play? call the characters by name?

Can I see why the speaker uses certain materials, cherishes certain values, creates certain attitudes?

Do I steadily increase my ability to appraise evidence and form judgments about ideas?

Have I learned any new words? or anything new about the use of language?

Would one or more of the following words describe my listening: *creative, distinguished, mature, retentive, judicious, sympathetic, courteous, passive, neutral, prejudiced, disinterested, distracting, annoying?*

Speechmaking (5 weeks)

Some teachers feel that too much stress has been placed on speaking in the high school course, and that some of the time given to speaking should instead be devoted to small group discussion. Part of the argument is that in later years the student will find himself involved more frequently in discussion than in speech-making. On the other hand, the relatively fewer speeches (meaning reports, presentations, demonstrations, and the like to audiences of modest size as well as longer, more formal types) that one does make have unusual importance in forwarding his career as citizen or as business or professional man. Moreover, speechmaking is a competence that requires the help of a person like you, and the encouragement that can come from a classroom audience.

A provocative way to open the public speaking unit is to adapt the classic illustration appearing in Professor James A. Winans's *Speech-Making.*[8] Yesterday (your story goes) I went to (name of theater) to see (name of film currently showing). I walked away from the theater, and as I stood at the corner of (well-known intersection), I happened to notice an old Buick coming down the street on my side. A woman was driving it. As she drew near me, she seemed to lose control of the car; it careened wildly from side to side, and smashed into a truck. As I stood there (name a student in your class) happened to walk by, and he saw me and asked what had happened. I began to explain the accident, and as I talked (name and name) came along and joined our group. I went into greater detail, and added my views about the licensing of drivers. Meanwhile (name, name, and name) joined our group, and pretty soon our whole public speaking class was there, along with many others. Someone yelled at me, I believe it was (name), to stand on the box that happened to be on the sidewalk, and so I did, continuing with my comments.

No doubt by this time the class has become alerted by your discussion, and

[8]p. 11.

everyone is pleased to be included in your obviously fictitious incident. At this point you review the incident, observing that it started with a conversation between you and (name) and ended by your climbing up on the box and talking to a group of fifty people. The class will agree that your performance at the end could certainly be called public speaking. You then raise the question, "At what moment did I stop conversing and begin making a speech?"

A student may hurriedly observe that the speech began when you stepped up on the box: you then parry the remark with another question, "Could I have made a speech without the box? Is a platform necessary for public speaking?" That position seems to be indefensible so another student may observe that you were speaking, not conversing, when your group reached a certain size. Did nineteen people make the incident a speech whereas eighteen made it only conversation? Is fifteen the deciding number? or twelve? If you had twenty people grouped in chairs and sofas in a large living room, would it be possible for members to carry on conversation, or would they make a series of speeches? Someone may comment that the speech began when you finished your narrative and started to give your opinions about licensing drivers. Is a speech, then, limited only to certain kinds of topics?

The discussion affords an opportunity to bring out the superficial resemblances between speech and conversation, and to review the elements that the two have in common. From there you may point out the profound differences between the two, since after all a speech is not a conversation. So far as your class is concerned, however, the conversational approach of the speaker to his audience is entirely teachable; if his speaking sounds like good, lively, natural talking, he is building on a good foundation.

Teachers who have a strong interest in group process as well as in speech making can slant this illustration in that direction.

Students may have erroneous notions that should be quieted early. A questionnaire similar to the following is useful:

If you had to give a speech before a class, which one of the following items would be most important?

To use good grammar
To speak fluently
To have a beautiful voice
To have good choice of words
To stand properly and use good gestures
To pronounce words correctly
To have the class listen attentively

Of 846 high school students, 254, or 30 percent, checked the item which most teachers would consider the most important: "To have the class listen attentively." Two-hundred and twenty-two, or 26.2 percent, checked "to speak fluently"; 170, or 20 percent, "to pronounce words correctly"; 104, or 12.2 percent, "to use good grammar"; 62, or 7.3 percent, "to stand properly and use good gestures." Only two students checked "to have a beautiful voice." A student who thought the end of speechmaking was to "have a beautiful voice" would make different preparation from one who thought it was "to use good grammar"; both might wonder why the class did not always "listen attentively."

The field of public speaking is so extensive that you will need to make careful selection of what to present. Conventionally, speechmaking is viewed under these headings, roughly listed in the order in which the speech is prepared and delivered:

1. Choosing a subject on which to speak, one that can be related to a specific audience, limiting it to a scope that can be handled in the time allotted.

2. Collecting material, including personal experiences, ideas gained from interviewing, and ideas from books and periodicals.

3. Organizing ideas into a form suitable for presentation.

4. Putting the ideas into effective language. Again, each step is taken with a specific audience in mind.

5. Rehearsing.

6. Presenting the speech to the audience.

Beginning the Speech

Preliminary instruction should be given in order to acquaint the students with the usual courtesies of speechmaking. Advice similar to the following appears in many textbooks:

1. Walk purposely but deliberately to the center of the room. When you reach the center, stop, smile a little, look over the audience. Avoid any appearance of being rushed or flustered; good speakers take their time getting under way.

2. Begin your speech deliberately, in order to forestall the common tendency to stumble over the opening words. This practice requires the speaker to have his opening sentences well in mind.

You can demonstrate this procedure by making a short talk of a minute or two. A good method of impressing the idea upon the class is to ask each member to give a "one-sentence speech." This exercise involves coming to the front of the room, pausing, looking over the audience, and then speaking one sentence of what might be a longer speech, such as: "Mr. Smith, fellow students: Reading he headline in this morning's *Tribune* about the draft makes me feel that some of us boys will not be around here much longer." Or: "Mr. Smith and fellow sufferers: This morning as I came to class I said to myself, 'What a fine school this would be if we didn't have to have teachers.' "

The exercise usually produces both serious and amusing ventures, as illustrated, and gives painless instruction in the important matter of getting a speech under way. The "one-sentence speech" can be used on other occasions, as a way of having the class review quickly a principle that the teacher has explained.

Speeches of one or two minutes in length are as a rule more desirable at the beginning of the course than are longer speeches of ten minutes. If short speeches are given, everyone gets a chance to perform, and the hour moves rapidly. Longer speeches may require three or four periods for a single assignment; these speeches should be saved for later in the year, after everyone has had a certain amount of instruction.

Most beginning speakers need training in organizing ideas more than in any other aspect of speaking. For this reason, and the further reason that organization is easily teachable, the speechmaking unit should include it. Basic principles are reviewed in Chapter 7.

After the principles of organization are understood, the class may be requested to give a short speech on any subject, the speech itself to have each of the major parts of the well-organized speech. Criticism may be directed towards matters of organization: did the speech have an introduction with a central idea, specifically stated? Did it have a body? Did it have a conclusion? For the following hour the assignment may be repeated, with the further requirement that the central idea be (1) clearly stated, and (2) immediately restated in other words. For example: "There are three different steps in the process of giving blood to the blood bank. I want to explain each of these three steps so that you will know what will be expected of you if you volunteer to be a blood-bank donor." Since a clearly conceived central idea is the essence of a well organized speech, this second assignment focusses the thinking of the student on this principle.

On the next round of short speeches the student may be asked to give attention to the introduction. In order to intrigue his imagination into seeing new possibilities of introducing speeches, the teacher may read selections of striking introductions from famous speeches. Another round may be given to emphasizing the conclusion. The use of examples and illustrative material, the appropriate selection of visual aids, and the improvement of gesture and bodily activity are matters for further instruction. Note especially the contributions of the new rhetoric: elements in the situation that govern speech preparation and delivery; analysis of listeners—their needs and wants, their attitude towards speaker and subject.

Chapter 7 on "Improving Thinking" and Chapter 8 on "Improving Delivery" contain pertinent suggestions.

Additional Assignments

The following assignments may be worked into the schedule as seems desirable

The class meets at a dinner, in a restaurant, the school cafeteria, or a home After the dinner the students give a program of speeches on some humorous theme.

The class gives a series of "Believe It or Not Speeches," each speaker describing the most unusual situation he has encountered.

A series of speeches is presented as a part of a radio program. Use any public address system, putting the microphone in an adjoining room. By all means have an announcer to supply appropriate introductions, station breaks, and commercials. Or use screens, with a picture frame aperture, and call it TV.

On a tape recorder record a program of speeches, or a group conversation. Your comments on the recorded speeches, will be helpful; remember to be charitable and encouraging as listening to one's own recording may be a dismal experience.

The search for suitable topics for speeches is challenging. Assigned topics often do not work out well. As a change, however, a program of talks about Lincoln or Washington might brighten a long February hour—or a program about heroes of other ethnic groups: Blacks, Indians, Chicanos, Orientals, Puerto Ricans.

Take advantage of local situations. Remember the New York City English teacher who asked her class to write on "What I Know About Narcotics." To another teacher basketball scandals suggested classroom speeches on "Is Athletics Overemphasized?" A third provided an assignment on student restlessness—not only in the United States but in England, France, Italy, and Japan. The obvious difficulty with assigning a single topic to a class is that a few members will not know anything about narcotics, nor care whether athletics is overemphasized. For these students, suggest alternate possibilities.

Organize a speaker's bureau. The better speakers in your class should prepare a twenty or thirty minute speech, on a topic about which he has an unusual fund of information. Perhaps one of your students has lived in Alaska, another is an expert at swimming, a third has a hobby of guns or quilts, a fourth has taken part in a demonstration. Prepare a folder about your speakers and their topics and send the information to the program chairmen of local organizations.[9]

Utilizing a familiar radio-TV format, plan a series of speeches on a "You Are There" theme. These can be rhetorical (Churchill's 1946 Iron Curtain Speech, Kennedy's inaugural, King's 1963 "I Have a Dream"), or non-rhetorical (landing on the moon). If you have a portable videotape recorder you can make the assignment highly realistic.

[9]*See:* Jack B. Simpson, "A Speakers' Bureau for High Schools," *Speech Teacher,* November 1952.

Train speakers to take part in Community Chest, Red Cross, March of Dimes, Cancer, Heart and similar campaigns. Each speaker can appear before a luncheon club, church circle, social club, or other organization. On a national Boy Scout Sunday, one teacher had every student in her class speaking briefly in a church.

Trade programs with another teacher whose class meets the same hour as yours. The other class need not be a speech class; interesting programs can be supplied by English, history, manual training, home economics, or Latin classes. Your team of speakers visits the other class, and its speakers or demonstrators come to yours.

On the day before Christmas vacation, when students are too restless to follow their regular schedule, plan a mock trial, complete with crime, defendant, judge, attorneys, jury, and, of course, a bailiff and sheriff.

You may borrow interesting assignments from those used by college teachers (see Chapter 4, "The College First Course").

Group Discussion and Debating (4 weeks)

Discussion takes many forms. A classroom recitation is a type of discussion, the teacher acting as group leader. Questions are asked and points of view presented, all focussed upon the problem before the group. A formal speech may be followed by a discussion, the audience participating by asking questions, or by making short talks either supporting or opposing the speaker's position. A panel discussion is one in which a group, termed a panel, explores an assigned topic. A symposium resembles a panel except that it is more carefully prepared: each individual presents his topic as a short talk. Afterwards opinions may be exchanged informally.

The broad field of discussion is so rich with possibilities for the high school class that you should read two or three of the texts in the field. First of all you should impress upon the class that the purpose of an organized discussion is not just to "argue" in the commonly accepted sense of the term, but (usually) to solve a problem. Next you should bring out the idea that the members of a discussion group are not "for" and "against"; they are relatively open-minded. The problem may have several solutions, and the group may need to explore the merits and demerits of each before reaching an agreement. You will discuss the responsibilities and duties of the chairman, one of whose jobs is to keep the participants from wandering from the main line of thought. See Chapter 9, "Group Discussion," for additional suggestions about both principle and practice.

Debating

Debating as a classroom activity is looked forward to with anticipation. English and history classes, as well as speech classes, often schedule debates on topics that have grown out of classroom arguments. The two teams select the best evidence available supporting their contentions, and listeners vote either as to which team did the more effective debating, or as to which side of the question they now believe. Many great American and British orators took part in debating clubs or societies during their school days. Debating, properly conducted, is unexcelled as a means of improving the ability to speak well. No other speaking activity can approach it. It is an intelligent solution to the problem of holding the interest of the superior student.

The topic for the first round of classroom debates should be relatively simple. A school that had a playing field but no stadium suggested the topic, "Should our school district build a stadium?" The debaters on both sides secured their arguments from their teachers, their parents, and their neighbors. One student interviewed a contractor, who provided an estimate of the costs; another interviewed an insurance agent, who talked about liability; another talked to a coach of a school that had a stadium; others interviewed football players and other students. The result was an intelligent picture of the problem of financing a stadium. The debaters aroused interest in the question, and were later invited to present their debate at the school assembly. Another team of four interested itself in the matter of high school fraternities and sororities. Not much was known about these semi-illegal groups, but the debaters unearthed material both for and against them. The perennial concern with athletic contests, narcotics, military training, poverty, hunger, labor unions, student government, and segregation, suggests other possibilities. For later rounds of debates the class may undertake the national high school question, explained in Chapter 15.

Second Semester: Reading, Acting

The foregoing outlined assignments have been designed to suggest the content of the first semester of a one-year elective high school course. This first semester began with the problem of studying student needs in voice, articulation, and speechmaking, proceeding to informal speaking situations and thence to formal situations in speaking, discussing, and debating. The assignments now to be suggested are taken from the fields of interpretation and drama. The emphasis upon fundamentals should be continued, but the applications should deal with the problem of expressing the words of others as written in essays, short stories, poems, and plays.

How to Study a Selection (2 weeks)

A good way to approach the teaching of the unit on interpretation is to begin with the study of a short selection. Take one of your own favorite poems, informal essays, or speeches, and provide each student with a copy. Read it aloud, or let students read parts of it in turn. Ask questions to bring out the meaning. See if you can get the students to appreciate the various good qualities of the selection. I have seen young teachers develop exciting class hours with the ngersoll selection (see pp. 230-231), and with "The Highwayman," "When I Was)ne and Twenty," and others. Your high school text includes other possibilities.

In these two weeks bring out various principles of good reading: some of hem inductively, growing out of class discussion; others didactively, growing)ut of your lecture or demonstration. See the discussion in Chapter 10, "Interpretation."

Reading Various Types of Prose (4 weeks)

)iscuss with your class various types of prose, arranging them, from the point of riew of reading difficulty, from the simple to the complex. You may develop a ıst of items similar to the following.

. *The written speech.* Examples can be found which are simple and conversational in nature. Others, however, show careful composition, like Ingersoll's "At the Tomb of Napoleon."

!. *The informal essay.* Consult almost any book of college composition for xamples.

!. *The formal essay.* Bacon's, Emerson's, Burke's, are examples.

+. *The short story.* This literary form not only has exposition, but also contains iescription and narration. Dialogue may be introduced, which presents a special iroblem.

You may not be able to have every student read an example of every type. You may elect to choose a few types and have all students work on these. Again, ee Chapter 10.

Reading Poetry (4 weeks)

\t this time you may introduce any of the special problems of reading poetry iot previously discussed—principles growing out of meter, rhythm, figurative anguage, mood, and the like.

From a list of the different types of poetry, select for your group the types hat seem most promising.

A part of this time may be spent in choral reading (see pp. 233-235).

Special Project in Reading (4 weeks)(optional)

\ contest, special program, or individual repertoires may be developed here. \ssembly programs or programs for special groups may grow out of such irojects as these.

History of the Theater (1 week)

After so much vigorous performance, the class may begin the unit on dramatic
with a discussion of the history of the theater and some of the conventions and
traditions of the stage. The Greek origin of the drama; the miracle and mystery
plays, morality plays and the early comedies; the Elizabethan theater of Jonson
Marlowe, and Shakespeare; the eighteenth-century theater of Garrick, Sheridan
Goldsmith, and Siddons; the nineteenth-century theater of Wilde, Pinero, Jones
Fitch, Gillette, Ibsen, Gorki, Belasco, Stanislavski, and others; and the contemporary theater all represent an intensely fascinating story. You may use pictures
slides, and stage models to highlight your narrative. Students may give reports
draw floor plans, or make actual models as their contribution. If you are a
home in dramatic literature, you may profitably read samples of the various
styles so as to make some of the playwrights come to life. Although teachers
may omit altogether any consideration of theater history, its materials are so
entertaining and inspiring that the topic certainly deserves the modest week se
aside in the present syllabus.

Elements of Acting (2 weeks)

On beginning the unit on acting, an exciting narrative to read to the class is
Lesson One in Boleslavski's little book, *Acting: The First Six Lessons*.[10] Lesson
One describes a situation in which a high school girl, fresh from high school
dramatic triumphs, interviews the Great Director in order to further her career
on the stage. The girl, sympathetically characterized by Boleslavski as The
Creature, attempts to give The Director a sample of her artistic abilities, and
does not do very well. Yet she seems to have a genuine impulse, so The Director
takes pity on The Creature, and gives her further lessons in acting. The subsequent lessons may be too involved for a high school class, but the first lesson
presents a situation with genuine charm.

Dozens of simple experiments may be conducted to show the class how
posture or position alone can tell a story—without words or movement. Have
two boys face each other, both glaring. Then have one lower his eyes; immediately a different story is told. Have two girls face each other, both glaring; then
have one turn her back, both continuing to look stern and serious. This story is
different from the one told by the two boys. Ask another student to go to the
door and listen, intently, without movement; from her posture the class may be
able to tell whether she hears her sweetheart, a burglar, or a mouse. Boleslavski's

[10] *Theatre Arts,* 1933.

rst lesson, incidentally, shows that The Creature was asked to reveal her acting bility by showing how she would listen to the faint scratching of a mouse.

After this experiment, progress to pantomime: the telling of a story without ords, but with movement. Almost any high school speech text or college text a acting contains suggestions: a spectator at a tennis game; a baseball pitcher; a udy hall teacher; a man reading a newspaper, and dozing off; a woman nswering a telephone; a girl awaiting an important date; a patient at the entist's office. Give the class many suggestions; let the students act some of em impromptu; demonstrate the importance of making every movement ecific. Pantomime shows the importance of detailed movement in building lot and developing character. Discuss Red Skelton or Marcel Marceau.

If the teacher can also impress the members of the class with basic customs d traditions of the stage, his discipline problems will be greatly minimized and e will achieve much better results with his group. The class always experiences a rilling moment when two or three young actors, unaided by makeup, costume, r much in the way of props, succeed in creating an illusion by the magic of eir line-reading and characterization.

Characterization; Short Scenes (3 weeks)

he problem in teaching dramatics, as in public speaking, is to plan the daily ogram so that as many students can receive individual help as possible. ne-character scenes are helpful for this reason; if the scenes are not too long, ch member of the class will have an opportunity to contribute. Individual riations in stage business and action can be worked out.

The teacher should have simple properties and a few pieces of furniture as inimum equipment. Modern school buildings often contain a speech or drama om provided with a small stage; lacking formal equipment, the teacher can ake use of folding screens, tables, benches, stools, a telephone, a buzzer to mulate a doorbell or a ringing telephone, and an arsenal of assorted weapons. ith this much prompting, the imagination of the listeners will supply the rest.

At least two methods are useful for handling longer selections. One is to take one-act play and cut it into appropriate short scenes. A cast is then selected for ch scene. The various casts present their scenes in turn, thus forwarding the ity of the plot, though the part of each character is taken by a succession of dividuals. Teachers usually try to find plays containing three or four major aracters so that each person will have action and lines while he is on the stage.

Another possibility, if the play has a small number of characters, is to assign e same role to several people. In the Quintero play, *A Sunny Morning,* the incipal characters are an aged man and woman, Gonzalo and Laura. As the ot develops Gonzalo discovers that Laura is his boyhood sweetheart, but does t let her know that he recognizes her. Laura has meanwhile discovered that

Gonzalo is her faithless fiancé of years ago, but she too does not reveal that she recognizes him. Both parts offer intriguing opportunities for line reading and characterization. If the girls in the class prepare the part of Laura, and the boys Gonzalo, various boy and girl combinations can be tried out during the class hour. Perhaps outstanding couples will materialize, each giving its own twist to the characterization. *A Minuet* by Louis Parker is another familar one-act play in which most of the action is carried on by a man and a woman; in this play the time is the French revolution, the principal characters are two royalists, and the scene is a jail.

Plays with more than two characters present new dramatic problems. Those that are best by far for classroom use are, again, those in which the roles are about equally prominent. The first act of *The Romancers* by Rostand presents an unexpected variation of the Romeo and Juliet theme. In this play the father of the hero and heroine pretend to be bitterly opposed to the match, but in reality strongly favor it, and evolve underhanded maneuvers to insure that the young couple actually falls in love. The parts are simple, and the opportunities for broad characterization are many. An even better exercise is the Pyramus and Thisbe interlude in *A Midsummer Night's Dream,* with such notorious characters as Pyramus and Thisbe, the lovers; Bottom the Weaver; a character who plays the part of the Wall; and another who portrays the Lion. This robust comedy provides rugged entertainment, and has the practical advantage that copies of the play are readily accessible.

The teacher-director may exercise great imagination in developing these units. In "Pyramus and Thisbe" he may conduct tryouts for the whole class, ending up with four or five people assigned to each principal role: five Lions, five Walls, and so on. As he works out the ludicrous business with one cast, the others quickly see the possibilities in the comedy. Eventually he may come out with four or five complete casts.

If for no other reason than the fun, two or three days may be spent on stage makeup. A modest assortment of paints, liners, and powders can produce unusual results. If you are not a makeup artist your first demonstrations may not be very convincing, but the important problem is to suggest the possibilities and let the members of the class experiment upon each other. Students who have unusually artistic abilities will achieve striking results almost from the first. One of the by-products of this activity is to train students to become better observers of people: to study facial expressions is alone an engrossing human experience.

In planning the unit read also Chapter 14, "Directing a Play."

Radio and Television Broadcasting

The teacher will need to make a decision about instruction in radio and television. If his own experience has been limited, he may want to begin by occasional assignments, as parts of other units, set in a broadcasting framework. With a public address speaker in the classroom, for example, and a microphone outside of it, he has a setting for a newscast, an interview, or a play.

If he is prepared to spend more class time on broadcasting, he has a wide variety of topics from which to select:

History of broadcasting	Production problems
Broadcasting as a social force	Technical glossary
Broadcasting as a political force	Voice, articulation, pronunciation
Equipment	Critical listening

Kinds of programs: news, sports, interviews, dramas, documentaries, quiz shows, special events, commercials, readings of poetry or prose.

For sample units, including statements of objectives, consult high school texts and syllabi (e.g., Little Rock, Nebraska, Missouri). The Michigan Speech Association curriculum guide series has a booklet, "Radio and Television in the Secondary School." Other references are given at the end of this chapter and at the end of Chapter 4.

The Louisiana *Guide,* which suggests six weeks for the broadcasting unit, has the following objectives for the student:

I. Understanding
   A. To realize the importance of broadcasting to life in a democratic society.
   B. To recognize that the nature of broadcasting necessitates split second action.
   C. To learn the importance of developing critical standards whether one is a participant in a show or a listener.
II. Skills
   A. To gain confidence when speaking before a microphone.
   B. To learn to handle a script noiselessly.
   C. To master the time requirements.
   D. To learn techniques for different types of speaking and writing.
   E. To learn the importance of working cooperatively to produce an acceptable product.
   F. To learn terminology and to communicate through hand signals.
II. Attitudes
   A. To develop an appreciation of good broadcasts.
   B. To listen to programs more intelligently.
   C. To increase literary appreciation.
   D. To appreciate the vocational aspects of broadcasting.[11]

[1] Adapted from *Guide for the Teaching of Speech in Louisiana High Schools,* p. 103. Older readers will recall the presidential magic of Franklin D. Roosevelt in his first inaugural, his fireside chats, and his Monday-noon message to Congress following Pearl Harbor Sunday.

Starting with the 1960 Kennedy-Nixon debates, each national campaign ha
increasingly stressed the importance of broadcasting. The presidential image
demonstrably formed and shaped through his television appearances. At times c
crisis, whether local, state, or national, the public depends upon broadcasts fo
explanation and guidance. In the event of a widespread power blackout, th
transistor radio can save the day. At the high school level it would seem tha
appreciations and attitudes of the highest significance can result from the uni
on broadcasting.

High School Texts

Standards to be followed in choosing a text have frequently been discussed an
need not be reviewed here. The text should have an acceptable philosophy: i
should have the ring of authority, written by teachers who understand th
special needs of high school students. It should serve the purposes of the specifi
course for which it is to be adopted: a course with a variety of speech activitie
calls for a different text than one which stresses public speaking, for example, o
dramatics.

On two criteria of selecting a text the teacher can be critical. One is language
Scan the pages and inspect the vocabulary: if the pages are dotted with difficul
words, many of your students will not be able to understand what they ar
reading. Study the style: even if the words are simple enough, the sentences may
be cumbersome or dull. Inspect the examples: see if they are timely and realistic
Note particularly the level of style; avoid texts that are too simplistic if you
class is sophisticated.

Another criterion is that of typographical appearance: size and style of type
selection of illustrations, use of white space in headings and margins, and
clearness and readability of the page. Modern high school texts have undergone a
radical change in the last few years. They use a variety of type arrangements and
headings, with illustrations, sketches, maps, cartoons, graphs, and diagrams. The
pages have a striking, dramatic appearance. Old style texts used solid pages of
type, gingerly varied by a few timid side-headings, with few illustrations. Again
choose a speech text that not only meets the usual standards, but looks as
challenging as a language, English, or social studies book.

Speech texts are designed for about three different kinds of classes. *On Stage
Everyone* by Barnes and Sutcliffe or *The Stage and the School* by Ommanney
are planned for semester or year courses in dramatics. They are concerned with
acting, theater history, characterization, projection, rehearsing, production. *Ease
in Speech* by Painter is designed for a semester or year class in speechmaking. It
emphasizes planning the speech, organizing ideas, adapting to audience. and the
special problems of informing, convincing, impressing, and entertaining. *From
Thought to Speech* by Hanks and Andersen is a high school text on speaking
focussing on the motivating process to show students how to reach, hold, and
move a group.

Other texts have different approaches. The teacher interested in selecting a book for a course that embraces a variety of activities has several texts to select from. *The New American Speech* 3d ed., by Hedde and Brigance; *Speaking and Listening* by Weaver, Borchers, and Smith; *Speech: A High School Course* rev. ed., by Sarett, Foster, and McBurney; *Speech in Action* by Robinson and Lee; *Modern Speech* by Irwin and Rosenberger; *Speak Up* by Adams and Pollock; are some that have had a wide following among high school teachers. The Hedde-Brigance book has these sections: everyday speech, fundamentals, public speaking, special discussion, interpretation, and dramatics. The Weaver-Borchers book covers a wide range of activities, giving primary attention to fundamental processes and to many types of informal speaking. It is also useful for various kinds of integrated courses. The Sarett-Foster-McBurney book has sections on first principles, speech composition, public speech; and a section on interpretation, choric speech, dramatics, and radio, television. The Robinson-Lee book has sections on formal and informal speaking, interpretation, play production, radio, and television. The Irwin-Rosenberger book has sections on informal speaking, speech preparation and delivery, discussion and debate, interpretation and broadcasting. The Adams-Pollock book has such basic sections as everyday speech, more formal speech, and interpretive speech. This summary is however, only a brief guide to the amount of attention paid by each text to the different speech units. Some have a single chapter, for example, on dramatics; some have several chapters. Review these and others before making your selection. See the list of high school texts at the end of this chapter. And remember that revisions of these, and entirely new titles, will continue to appear at the rate of at least one new volume a year.

Before adopting a text you may find it helpful to make a tabulation of the topics discussed by the books under consideration. The list may include conversation, interviewing, discussion, debating, parliamentary procedure, preparing a speech, delivering the speech, using the voice, articulation, pronunciation, reading aloud, story-telling, choral reading, declaiming, theater history, acting, directing, producing, playwriting, puppetry, radio and TV speaking. Of special importance will be those topics you plan to teach in your own course. Your tabulation will give you a quantitative view of each text.

A guide to new books are review sections of such publications as the *Speech Teacher,* the *Quarterly Journal of Speech,* the *Educational Theatre Journal.* Whenever a new book appears the editors of these journals assign it for review to a competent person, who writes an analysis of its strong and weak points or at least a comment about what is in the book.

Making a Lesson Plan

A teacher should make a plan for every class, setting forth purposes to be accomplished, procedure to be followed, and the assignment for next time. The plan may refer to the general purposes of the unit, the specific aims for the day and may mention ways of appraising the achievements of the students. For som class periods the plan may be brief, perhaps only a mental outline; for others will be detailed.

The lesson plan below is purposely constructed in detail. An experience teacher with a strong background in this particular field would need a week time to exhaust the possibilities of the ideas suggested. By example an question, he could spark a lively discussion of the importance of language an specific instance. A beginner would cover the plan more rapidly; he might nee all this material to see him safely through a single class period.

A Unit in Speechmaking (October)

General purposes of the unit: To improve the student in such fundament processes as voice, articulation, language, and bodily action. To teach improve ways of choosing a topic, gathering material, organizing ideas, adapting t audiences, and delivering the speech. To improve the student's ability to thin and listen. To show how both as speaker and listener he may become a bett member of a democratic society.

Plan for a Single Class Hour

Specific purpose: To have the student demonstrate his knowledge of the usefu ness of each of a specified number of standard reference works.

Procedure: The students should bring to class copies of *World Almana Webster's Dictionary of Synonyms,* Stevenson's *Home Book of Quotation Roget's Thesaurus,* and a dictionary, such as *Webster's Seventh New Collegia* or *The American Heritage Dictionary of the American Language.* Illustrate th use of these works with examples such as the following:

World Almanac: Since this is baseball season, show how this book could b used for material for a speech about the world series. Read the figures showir how the total gate receipts and other income is divided among the players, th leagues, and the commissioner. A player on the world championship team (fe example) receives in excess of $15,000, whereas one of the runner-up tea might receive $10,000, or more. Read other statistics, such as batting and hittir records. Show how figures may be used in speeches.

Show how much more convincing it is to say "Babe Ruth's lifetime home ru record of 714, or his record of knocking 60 home runs in 1927, has never bee equalled in a season of 154 games," than simply to say, "Babe Ruth knock more home runs in one year than anyone ever has, and more home runs in h lifetime than anyone ever has." Better still, use exact figures and then interpr them, using comparison, contrast, or other methods.

Show other uses of the almanac: for example, any student interesting in goi

) college can learn the size and other select facts about any institution of higher
:arning in the country; developments of the space age, or zip code numbers, can
lso be researched in the almanac.

Webster's Dictionary of Synonyms: Show how the book distinguishes among
ie meanings of such words as the following:

uy, purchase
hange, alter, vary, modify
opy, imitate, mimic, ape, mock
iithful, loyal, true, steadfast
;norant, illiterate, uneducated
ft, raise, rear, elevate, hoist, heave, boost
ffense, sin, vice, scandal
ition, allowance, dole, pittance
:rious, solemn, sober, earnest
:nd, attend, mind, watch

Roget's Thesaurus: Show how this book may be used to teach one to employ
greater variety of interesting words.

Instead of *wonderful,* say: wondrous, surprising, unexpected, astonishing,
mazing, admirable, fascinating, astounding, startling, dazzling, striking, electri-
ying, stunning, stupefying, petrifying, confounding, bewildering, flabbergasting,
taggering, breath-taking, unheard of, incredible, unimaginable, overwhelming.

Instead of a *plan,* you may have: a scheme, design, project, proposal,
roposition, suggestion, resolution, motion, system, organization, germ, forecast,
rogram, bill of fare, base of operations, platform, plank, policy, contrivance,
tratagem, alternative, master stroke, stroke of policy, bright thought or idea,
ounterplot.

Instead of *news,* you may have: information, report, story, yarn, copy, filler,
itelligence, tidings, word, advice, message, communication, bulletin, rumor,
earsay, cry, buzz, town talk, topic of the day.

Instead of *telling,* you may: disclose, discover, lift up the veil, break the seal,
iy open, lay bare, bring to light, make evident, divulge, reveal, let into the
:cret, breathe, utter, blab, preach, let the cat out of the bag, tell tales, come out
rith, whisper about, make public, break the news.

Not so well known as Roget but even better is J.L. Rodale's *The Synonym
'inder* (Rodale Books, Emmaus, Pa. 18049).

Stevenson's *Home Book of Quotations:* Recall speeches of half a dozen
iembers of the class, and show how they might have used quotations from
tevenson or other sources to make their speeches more distinctive. Raise the
uestion of whether quotations should be memorized or read. (Better known
ian Stevenson, because widely distributed by the Book-of-the-Month Club, is
artlett's *Familiar Quotations.*)

Dictionary: Ask the class which of the following information can be found i a good dictionary:

1. Spelling of a word
2. Pronunciation
3. History of the word, or etymology
4. Whether or not the word is hyphenated
5. Occasionally, a picture illustrating the word
6. Proper names, like *Sioux* or *Thespian*
7. Dates of birth and death of famous men and women
8. Pronunciation of names of famous men and women
9. Pronunciation of well-known places
10. Definitions of technical or scientific terms
11. This city and its population

Many dictionaries will contain all of the foregoing information, plus man technical and scientific words. Your home town may even be listed unless i population is less than 5,000.

Assignment for next time: Go to the library and find answers to the followir questions:

1. For what is Walter Reed noted? Walter Johnson? Walter Cronkite?

2. What are the dates of King Charles I of England? Charles de Gaulle? Wh: United States Presidents have been born in the twentieth century?

3. In what year was the Battle of Waterloo fought? In what year was the Bay Pigs?

4. Give the distance for the world ski jump, the world record broad jump, t world record discus throw, the world record mile run.

5. Name the world heavyweight boxing champions (or principal contender after Muhammad Ali vacated the title in 1967.

Assessing the outcome: Note whether the student has demonstrated r searched facts, interesting use of language, applicable quotations, and oth details.

Team Teaching

It is beyond the scope of this text to offer specific suggestions about adaptir units of instruction to nonconventional or experimental curriculum design

ach teacher needs to be alert to opportunities and adapt methods of instruction
 ways that seem promising and feasible.

Team teaching, for example, has been utilized in a variety of situations.
eachers of literature, composition, and speech can work out programs of
udies in which each teacher offers his specialty. Richard W. Clark describes a
roject in which a social studies teacher and a speech teacher combined an
dvanced speech course with a course in contemporary world and domestic
roblems. The fifty seniors in the class were divided into two political parties,
ho put on party conventions and conducted a campaign. After the election, the
oup formed a bicameral national legislature. The author also suggests com-
ning world history and the general speech course, and comments also on an all
peech course, conducted by a team composed of a public speaking specialist, a
ice science specialist, and a drama-oral interpretation specialist.[12]

A considerable advantage of team teaching is the opportunity to see one or
ore of your colleagues in action. You may find qualities of good teaching that
ou want to emulate. By the same token your colleagues may borrow ideas from
ou.

Along with team teaching comes a variety of unit or modular scheduling
ocedures. Instructional units may be arranged so as to occupy shorter or
nger periods of time than customary. So we have option periods, and mini-
urses. Just as these standard time zones are being broken down, so also are
any physical restrictions. School buildings are being constructed all over the
ountry with fewer inner walls and with more moveable partitions. Power-
erated sliding doors make it possible to make big rooms out of small rooms, or
ce versa. In a large room different kinds of instructional activity may be going
 at once. Students receive a greater number of stimuli, participate in a wider
riety of activities, and have greater freedom from supervision. In a loose sense
e situation recalls the pioneer one-room school, the teacher offering instruc-
on in an assortment of subjects, sometimes teaching a single grade, sometimes
vo or more at the same time, the bright students helping the slower ones, and
ose in one grade overhearing what goes on in another. Now the teacher has
finitely more help, but frontier flexibility, adaptability, and resourcefulness
as a small but sympathetic echo in the modern school.

Team teaching also suggests team learning. Role playing comes to mind;
stead of talking about a principle, act it out for a change. Instead of one
udent giving a report on, for example, slum clearance, let two or three do it
ne such team utilized taped interviews with residents, color slides, etc.).

At the university level, drama, oral interpretation, and public address appear
 a general course in humanities, alongside English literature, foreign literature

Richard W. Clark, "The Speech Teacher as a Member of a Teaching Team," *Southern Speech Journal,* Summer 1966, pp. 184-189, citing Wanda B. Mitchell, "Why Try Team Teaching," *Bulletin of the National Association of Secondary School Principals,* January 1962, pp. 247 ff.

in translation, art, music, philosophy. Each segment of the course is conducted by a specialist from the appropriate discipline. Survey courses within the department, comprising phonetics, voice science, rhetoric and public address, oral interpretation, drama and the theater, speech education, and radio-TV are often similarly managed by a team of specialists.

Those who have experimented with team teaching urge the importance of making careful study of content and outcomes. Consideration also needs to be given to the existing teaching loads of those who undertake the new assignment. Quite possibly team teaching projects tend to be short-lived, the exception being those in which the course is carefully thought through, and for which the teachers concerned are able to keep up their enthusiasm and that of the students.

Microteaching

Microteaching is a plan used in both student teaching and for the improvement of teachers in service that is characterized by four features: (1) the size of the group being instructed consists of only four or five students; (2) the lesson lasts only a few minutes, not an entire class hour; (3) the teacher attempts to demonstrate a specific principle of effective teaching; (4) a supervisor is present who, with or without the aid of a tape or videotape playback, reviews with the teacher the effect of the instruction.

The instructional skills best developed in the microteaching situation are those that can be readily demonstrated and observed. Among them are (1) stimulus variation—adding variety to the teaching style through movement, gesture, different kinds of dialogue with students; (2) set induction, preparing a class for the instruction; (3) closure, the use of transition, summary, or review so that the students will have a feeling of achievement; (4) reinforcement skills, learning various ways to reward student participation; (5) asking different kinds of questions; (6) using specific illustrations and examples.[13]

This procedure is mentioned here since a 1968 survey indicates that microteaching is used in 53 percent of all teacher-education programs. If the reader has not been exposed to it during his undergraduate days, he may find it used as part of a teacher-improvement program later on.

Other Resources

The teacher should exploit whatever special resources the school possesses. In front of me is a clipping about a junior high school amply equipped with com-

---

[13]*See:* Dwight Allen and Kevin Ryan, *Microteaching.* The summary above comes from Chapter 1. The book is clearly written, specific, and of value to teachers at all levels.

ters. The computer sets a problem; the student attempts the problem; if he
misses it, the computer supplies a hint; if he gets it right, the screen lights up
with blue letters saying "Stupendous!" "You're marvelous!" and the like. Students were seen to blush under such praise, even though they knew a teacher
had programmed those comments. One girl punched an error, instantly realized
her mistake, and covered the screen as if to fend off the wrong answer until she
could supply the right one. Language laboratories also come up with materials to
hasten the development of linguistic skills.

Many of the newer instructional techniques focus on visual and auditory
equipment that is widely available. Tape recorders, including those with car-
tridges and cassettes, are at hand in every community. Classrooms may be
equipped with opaque projectors so that a teacher can put an outline on the
screen, or a selected bit of review or demonstration material, or a picture, and
use it as a focus for discussion. Portable videotape projectors are relatively
inexpensive and simple to use, though not entirely foolproof. These make
possible playbacks of all kinds of student performance. Programmed instruction
devices and materials are available: phonetics, parliamentary procedure, aspects
of speech composition. Although the procedures of reserving and transporting
equipment may be considerable, the teacher who clambers over these barricades
can add something new to the class hour (picture yourself climbing two flights
of stairs carrying a playback, a long roll of charts, or an armful of anatomical
models).

A Final Word

The foregoing material is not cast specifically in the form of lesson plans. In
preparing these, suit your preference as to arrangement and content. You will
need to consider not only the what but the how, day by day and week by week.
What is expected of the student by way of homework? What will be the nature
of the recitation? What is to be the assignment for the next meeting? How will
this day's work contribute to desired outcomes?

Two ideas may be presented by way of final admonition. Keep your philosophy of aims and purposes in the foreground; through them you unify the
course. If you agree that it is important to strengthen the personal resources of
the individual and help him become a better individual and citizen, let those
goals motivate your reading. If you want to improve his ability to communicate,
keep that thought also in mind. Finally, after you construct a syllabus, do not
become enslaved by it. Do not be too concerned if you cannot achieve all you
had planned. A syllabus represents a grand strategy for the course; tactical
procedures have to be altered to suit the progress of the class. The overriding
advantage of a syllabus is that it can be constructed in leisure; after a school year
gets under way, event follows event with such rapidity that a teacher finds it
difficult to regain the same sort of perspective.

Assignments

1. A practical assignment is to prepare a syllabus for one or more units o course. Preliminary study and locating of materials will help the prospect teacher do a better job when he begins his actual teaching.

2. Collect sample courses of study from state departments of education. See 1 list given below.

3. Do the same for requirements for certifying teachers of speech. Write two three state departments of education, asking for a leaflet setting forth 1 requirements for a teacher of speech. Arrange the class collection into exhibit which all can study.

4. Teachers using this book as a textbook in a speech education course m assign such projects as the following:

   Investigate opportunities for graduate study in speech, dramatic art, spee pathology, etc. Collect bulletins from representative schools offering t doctorate or the master's degree (see Appendix C). Find out what fellowsh or scholarships may be available in your own institution, or in nearby schoc Look ahead to Chapter 19 for further suggestions.

   During the early part of the course, you should begin collecting certe materials that will require correspondence, so that when you need t materials they will be at hand.

   Make a list of high schools in which you might like to teach. Write t superintendent of that high school a letter in which you indicate that yo class is reviewing salaries, and ask him for the schedule now in effect in I school system. Most school boards have these prepared on mimeograph sheets. My students have found it helpful to give serious attention to t financial side of teaching, and the schedules your class collects will supp ment the material to be found in Chapter 19.

   Make a collection of materials necessary for a director of debating, or director of dramatics. Secure copies of debate handbooks and other aic Write for copies of play catalogs from two or three of the leading publishe (See Appendix D.) These materials will contribute to a realistic discussion these extracurricular activities.

Questions for Classroom Discussion

1. In these days when the entire curriculum is under scrutiny, how can yc justify speech education? Do you see in the high school course opportuniti for intellectual stimulation or cultural growth?

2. More specifically, how would you compare the mental activity involved algebra with that involved in preparing a speech? how does training scientific method compare with constructing a debate brief? how would yc compare the study of literature in an English class with the study of literatu for oral presentation? or for presentation on the stage?

3. In what ways does training in speech help a student become a better busine

or professional man? or a better citizen? a better student in other courses? Conversely, how does a strong background in science, social studies, and the humanities help a student in the speech class?

. Would you like the curriculum better if it were all science? all social studies? all foreign languages? *all speech?*

. Discuss: "The real frill in education is the *poor* teacher of any subject. The real asset is the *good* teacher of any subject."

. How can each of the customary units taught in the high school be upgraded intellectually and culturally? What will be the result if these units are weakened intellectually, imaginatively, and creatively?

. Comment on Quintilian's thought that the educational process is a series of "arranged victories."

References

Courses of Study

Most state departments of education and a good many city school systems have published courses of study, prepared by committees of classroom teachers. A list of titles appears below. Consult also the collection in your college or university library.

The following list is incomplete and subject to change. It includes titles from a survey of all state departments plus a limited selection of city schools. Courses of study in language arts not listed below may have sections on speech and drama. A few states are not included because their courses of study are in process of preparation or revision and tentative titles or publication dates could not be supplied.

A nominal charge is often made to nonresidents of the city or state for which the course of study is designed.

Basic Speech Curriculum Guide for the Junior High School Level (1966). Division of Instructional Services, State Department of Education, Lincoln, Nebr. 68501

Oral Reading: A Bulletin for Language Arts Teachers (1969). Public Schools, Tulsa, Okla. 74801

Guide for the Teaching of Speech in Louisiana High Schools (1966). State Department of Public Education, Baton Rouge, La. 70804

Guide for the Teaching of Speech, Secondary Level (1969), Public Schools, Little Rock, Ark. 77201

Language: A Curriculum Guide for Special Education (1966). Department of Public Instruction, Madison, Wis. 53702

Oral Language Development (1968). Alaska Department of Education. Juneau, Alaska 99801

Teaching of Speech in High School (1967). Office of Commissioner of Education, Austin, Tex. 78701

Guide for Speech, Dramatics, Radio and Television (1959). State Department of Education, Jefferson City, Mo. 65101

Oral Communications in Kentucky Schools (1968). State Department of Educa
tion, Frankfort, Ky. 40601

Communication in the Secondary School (1960); *Speaking and Listening*
(1970). State Department of Public Instruction, Springfield, Ill. 62700

Speech and Theatre in the Secondary School (1970). State Department of
Education, Tallahassee, Fla. 32300

The Speech Arts (1967). State Department of Public Instruction, Dover, De
19901

Secondary Speech Guide (1970). State Department of Education, Honolulu
Hawaii 96800

Teacher's Guide to High School Speech (1966). English Curriculum Center
Indiana University (Distributed by Speech Communication Association).

Language Arts for Secondary Schools: Curriculum Guide (1967). Independer
School District, Dallas, Tex. 75204

Curriculum Guides, published by the Michigan Speech Association, distribute
by National Textbook Corporation (address in Appendix D). Among th
titles are: *Dramatic Arts in the Secondary School, Basic Speech in the Senio
High School, Discussion and Argumentation-Debate in the Secondary Schoo
Speech in the Junior High School, Speech Activities in the Elementar
School, Radio and Television in the Secondary School, Oral Interpretation i
the Secondary School.*

Speech and Drama: Aids and Suggestions for Teachers (1961). New Mexic
State Board of Education, Santa Fe, N. Mex. 87501

A Course Guide in the Theatre Arts at the Secondary School Level (1968
Published by the American Educational Theatre Association.

Language Arts (primary, intermediate, upper grades—three separate bulletin
(1962). State Department of Public Instruction, Phoenix, Ariz.

(Write the National Educational Association, Department of Supervision an
Curriculum Development (address in Appendix E), for their current list o
curriculum yearbooks, if you are interested in a broad study of curriculun
problems.)

Speech and Other Subjects

Elementary School

Davidson, Donald. "Grammar and Rhetoric: The Teacher's Problem." *Quarter*
Journal of Speech December 1953.

Granfield, Geraldine. "The Integration of Speech with English in the Hig
School Curriculum." *Speech Teacher* March 1953.

Kosh, Zelda Horner. "Helping Children Develop Effective Oral Commun
cation." *Speech Teacher* March 1957.

Oberle, Marcella; English, Robert H.; Piquette, Julia C.; Irwin, Ruth Becke
Abernethy, Rose L.; Ogilvie, Mardel; and Searles, Myrtle; Hunter, Mary Alic
Simmerman, Amy Jean; Kupferer, Albert F.; Nurk, Maude. "A Symposium
Speech for Elementary Schools." *Speech Teacher* November 1960.

ilvie, Mardel. "Creative Speech Experiences in the Elementary Schools." *Speech Teacher* January 1958.

—"Oral Communication in Elementary School Living." *Speech Teacher* January 1957.

ilvie, Mardel; Pruis, John J.; and Hahn, Elise. "Bibliography of Speech in the Elementary School." *Speech Teacher* November 1953.

rsteck, Bennett J. "Speech at the Core of the Core Curriculum." *Speech Teacher* November 1953.

nith, Dora V. "A Curriculum in the Language Arts for Life Today." *English Journal* February 1951.

ymposium on Teaching Speech." *Western Speech* Summer 1957. Introduction, Waldo W. Phelps. "Speech in the Primary Grades," Helen S. Grayum. "Speech in the Sixth Grade," Betty Dobkin. "Speech and English in the Junior High School," Jerry Craycroft. "Speech in the History Class," L. Day Hanks.

ells, Charlotte G. "Speech in the Full School Program." *Elementary English* April 1951.

General Interest

Secondary School

len, Dwight W., and Ryan, Kevin A. *Microteaching.* Reading, Mass.: Addison-Wesley Publishing, 1969.

hbaugh, Kraid I. "Teaching the Art of Conversation." *Speech Teacher* March 1957.

han, David F. "A Technique for Teaching Audience Awareness and Audience Response to High School Students." *Speech Teacher* January 1964.

om, Benjamin S., ed. *Taxonomy of Educational Objectives, Handbook 1 (Cognitive Domain).* Krathwohl, David R. et al., *Handbook II (Affective Domain).* New York: David McKay, 1956, 1964.

ys, William E.; Carlson, Charles V.; Compton, Hite; and Frank, Allan D. "Speech Communication in the High School Curriculum." *Speech Teacher* November 1968.

rr, Marjory W. "The High School Speech Course." *Western Speech* Summer 1968.

rtright, Henrietta H.; Niles, Doris S.; and Weirich, Dorothy Q. "Criteria to Evaluate Speech I in the Senior High School." *Speech Teacher* September 1968.

ickson, Marceline:; Stevens, Walter W.; Hoogestraat, Wayne E.; Watkins, Lloyd I.; and Graham, John. "Improving Speech Programs: Needs, Trends, Methods— Part I." *Speech Teacher* January 1963.

hring, Mary Louise. "The High School Oration: Fundamentals." *Speech Teacher* March 1953.

bson, James W., and Kibler, Robert J. "Creative Thinking in the Speech Classroom: A Bibliography of Related Research." *Speech Teacher* January 1965.

84   Teaching Speech

Gibson, James W. "Creativity in the Speech Classroom." *Central States Speech Journal* May 1964.

Glaser, Robert, ed. *Training Research and Education.* New York: John Wiley 1965.

Hettinger, Esther. "Speech in the High School." *Western Speech* Fall 1957.

Klausmeier, Herbert J., and Goodwin, William. *Learning and Human Abilities* 2d ed., New York: Harper & Row, 1966.

Konigsberg, Evelyn. "Making Drill Functional." *Speech Teacher* March 1952.

Konigsberg, Evelyn; Cortright, Rupert L.; Nelson, Oliver W.; and Robinson, Kar F. "Principles and Standards for the Certification of Teachers of Speech in Secondary Schools." *Speech Teacher* November 1963. See also "Speech Education in the Public Schools." *Speech Teacher* January 1967.

McNess, Wilma. "An Orientation Course in Creative Skills for First Year Junior High School Students." *Speech Teacher* November 1952. An imaginative, yet practical, outline of assignments and activities for junior high students.

Mager, Robert F. *Preparing Instructional Objectives.* Palo Alto: Fearon Publishers, 1962.

Meyer, John L., and Williams, Frederick. "Teaching Listening at the Secondary Level: Some Evaluations." *Speech Teacher* November 1965.

Mitchell, Wanda B.; Kenner, Freda; Metcalf, Marguerite Pearce; Collins, Betty May; and Weirich, Dorothy Q. "Advice for the Beginning Teacher of Speech: A Symposium." *Speech Teacher* November 1969. See their excellent articles: "Planning the Course," "Motivating Students," "Discipline," "The Use of Audiovisual Aids," "Participating in Community Affairs."

Nelson, Oliver W. "Speech in the Secondary School." *Western Speech* Fall 1957.

Nichols, Ralph G. "Material for Courses in Communication." *Quarterly Journal of Speech* December 1952.

O'Brien, Joseph F. "Henry M. Robert as a Presiding Officer." *Quarterly Journal of Speech* April 1956. Background reading about the old general whose work on parliamentary procedure "has outsold *Tarzan of the Apes, Mrs. Wiggs of the Cabbage Patch,* and *Little Lord Fauntleroy.*"

Phelps, Waldo W. "Organization of the High School Speech Program." *Southern Speech Journal* Spring 1955.

———."The Panel-Forum as a First Assignment in the Secondary School Speech Fundamentals Class." *Speech Teacher* September 1952. Specific help with a specific assignment.

"Radio and Television in the Secondary School." *Bulletin of the National Association of Secondary School Principals* October 1966.

Rickey, James T. "Secondary School Speech Texts: An Evaluation." *Central States Journal* February 1964.

Roberts, Mary M.; Kuhr, Manuel Irwin; Schmidt, Robert; Kline, H. Charles; Holley, Donald L.; White, Harvey; and Verderber, Rudolph F. "Improving Speech Programs: Needs, Trends, Methods, Part II." *Speech Teacher* March 1963.

Seabury, Hugh F. "Objectives and Scope of the Fundamentals Course in Speech in the High School." *Speech Teacher* March 1954. Unit headings: 1. Oral interpretation of prose; 2. Explanatory speeches with visual aids; 3. Phonetics, diacritical marks, spelling, pronunciation, and articulation; 4. Informatory and explanatory speeches on speech content; 5. Oral interpretation of poetry; 6. Discussion; 7. Parliamentary procedure; 8. Radio plays; 9. Individual and group pantomimes; 10. One-act play unit; 11. Extemporaneous speeches on topics from *Time, Newsweek,* and *American Observer;* 12. Argumentative speeches.

Secondary School Interest Group. "Fundamentals of Speech: A Basic Course for High Schools." *Speech Teacher* March 1959. Content and scope of the basic high school course.

Timmons, Jan, and Giffin, Kim. "Requirements for Teachers of Speech in the Secondary Schools of the United States." *Speech Teacher* March 1964.

Wheater, Stanley B. " Team Teaching in a Course in Speaking and Writing." *Speech Teacher* September 1966.

Wilson, Lewellyn L., and Newcombe, P. Judson. "Speech Education in Canadian Higher Education." *Speech Teacher* November 1968,

Winans, James A. *Speech-Making.* New York: Appleton-Century, 1938.

Interpretation, Drama

See: references at the end of chapters 10 and 14.

High School Texts

Adams, Harlan M., and Pollock, Thomas C. *Speak Up.* rev. ed. New York: Macmillan, 1964.

Allen, R.R.; Anderson, Sharol; and Hough, Jere. *Speech in American Society.* Columbus: Charles E. Merrill, 1968.

Barnes, Grace, and Sutcliffe, M. J. *On Stage, Everyone.* rev. ed. New York: Macmillan, 1961.

Braden, Waldo W. *Public Speaking: The Essentials.* New York: Harper & Row, 1966.

Brandes, Paul D., and Smith, William S. *Building Better Speech.* New York: Noble and Noble, 1964.

Dolson, A. F., and Peck, Alberta. *The Art of Speaking.* 2d rev. ed. Boston: Ginn, 1966.

Griffith, Francis; Nelson, Catherine; and Stasheff, Edward. *Your Speech.* rev. ed. New York: Harcourt, Brace & World, 1960.

Hanks, Day, and Andersen, Martin P. *From Thought to Speech.* Boston: D.C. Heath, 1969.

Hedde, Wilhelmina; Brigance, W. Norwood; and Powell, Victor M. *The New American Speech.* 3d ed. Chicago: J. G. Lippincott, 1968.

Irwin, John V., and Rosenberger, Marjorie. *Modern Speech.* New York: Holt Rinehart & Winston, 1961.

Lamers, William M. et al., *The Speech Arts.* Chicago: Lyons & Carnahan, 1966.

Markert, Edward E. *Fort's Speech for All.* Boston: Allyn & Bacon, 1966.

Masten, Charles, and Pflaum, George R. R. *Speech for You.* Evanston, Ill.: Row Peterson, 1961.

Motter, Charlotte Kay. *High School Drama.* Englewood Cliffs: Prentice-Hall 1970.

Nelson, Theodore F., and Atkinson, W. Kirtley. *Speech and Your Personality* Chicago: Benj. H. Sanborn, 1955.

Nelson, Oliver W., and LaRusso, Dominic A. *Oral Communication in the Secondary School Classroom.* Englewood Cliffs: Prentice-Hall, 1970.

Ommanney, Katherine A. *The Stage and the School.* 3d ed. New York McGraw-Hill, 1960.

Painter, Margaret. *Ease in Speech.* 4th ed. Boston: D. C. Heath, 1962.

Reid, Loren. *Speaking Well.* Columbia: Artcraft Press, 1962.

Robinson, Karl F., and Lee, Charlotte. *Speech in Action.* Chicago: Scott Foresman, 1965.

Sarett, Lew; Foster, W. T.; and McBurney, James H. *Speech: A High Schoo Course.* Boston: Houghton Mifflin, 1956.

Summers, H. B.; Whan, F. L.; and Rousse, Thomas A. *How to Debate: A Textbook for Beginners.* 3d rev. ed. New York: H. W. Wilson, 1951.

Weaver, Andrew T.; Borchers, Gladys L.; and Smith, Donald K. *Speaking and Listening.* Englewood Cliffs: Prentice-Hall, 1956.

See also: the references at the end of Chapter 14, "Directing a Play," and Chapter 15, "Directing Debate."

Parliamentary Procedure

Auer, J. Jeffery. *Essentials of Parliamentary Procedure.* 3d ed. New York Appleton-Century-Crofts, 1959.

Bosmajian, Haig. *Readings in Parliamentary Procedure.* New York: Harper & Row, 1968.

Carmack, Paul A. "Evolution in Parliamentary Procedure." *Speech Teacher* January 1962.

Davidson, Henry A. *A Handbook of Parliamentary Procedure.* New York Ronald, 1955.

Gray, Giles Wilkeson. "Point of Emphasis in Teaching Parliamentary Procedure. *Speech Teacher* January 1964.

Gray, John W., and Rea, Richard G. *Parliamentary Procedure: A Programmed Introduction.* Chicago: Scott, Foresman, 1963.

Hellman, Hugo. *Parliamentary Procedure.* New York: Macmillan, 1966.

O'Brien, Joseph F. *Parliamentary Law for the Layman: Procedure and Strategy for Meetings.* New York: Harper & Brothers, 1952.

Rea, Richard G., and Gray, John W. "Teaching Parliamentary Procedure Through Programed Instruction." *Speech Teacher* January 1964.

Robert, H.M. *Rules of Order.* newly revised. Chicago: Scott, Foresman, 1970.

Sturgis, Alice. *Standard Code of Parliamentary Procedure.* 2d ed. New York: McGraw Hill, 1966.

Wiksell, Wesley. *How to Conduct Meetings.* New York: Harper & Row, 1966.

Teaching of Speech; Speech for Teachers; Readings

Balcer, Charles L., and Seabury, Hugh F. *Teaching Speech in Today's Secondary Schools.* New York: Holt, Rinehart & Winston, 1965.

Barrett, Harold. *Practical Methods in Speech.* New York: Henry Holt, 1959.

Braden, Waldo, et al., *Speech Methods and Resources: A Textbook for the Teacher of Speech.* New York: Harper & Row, 1961.

Ecroyd, Donald H. *Speech for Teachers.* 2d ed. Englewood Cliffs: Prentice-Hall, 1969.

Erickson, Keith. ed. *Dimensions of Oral Communication Instruction: Readings in Speech Education.* Dubuque: Wm. C. Brown, 1970.

Fessenden, Seth A.; Johnson, Roy Ivan; Larson, P. Merville; and Good, Kaye M. *Speech for the Creative Teacher.* Dubuque: Wm. C. Brown, 1968.

Friederich, Willard J., and Wilcox, Ruth A. *Teaching Speech in High Schools.* New York: Macmillan, 1953.

Huckleberry, Alan W., and Strother, Edward S. *Speech Education for the Elementary Teacher.* Boston: Allyn & Bacon, 1966.

Mulgrave, Dorothy I. *Speech for the Classroom Teacher.* 3d ed. Englewood Cliffs: Prentice-Hall, 1955.

Nelson, Oliver W., and LaRusso, Dominic A. *Oral Communication in the Secondary School Classroom.* Englewood Cliffs: Prentice-Hall, 1970.

Niles, Doris. "Notebooks for Neophytes." *Speech Teacher* March 1959. Interesting ideas about motivating students.

Ogilvie, Mardel. *Speech in the Elementary School.* New York: McGraw-Hill, 1954.

———. *Teaching Speech in the High School: Principles and Practice.* New York: Appleton-Century-Crofts, 1961.

Phillips, Gerald M.; Dunham, Robert; Butt, David; and Brubaker, Robert. *Development of Oral Communication in the Classroom.* New York: Bobbs-Merrill, 1969.

Pronovost, W.L. *Speaking and Listening in the Elementary School.* New York: David McKay, 1959.

Rasmussen, Carrie. *Speech Methods in the Elementary School.* New York: The Ronald Press, 1950.

Reid, Loren. "How to Improve Classroom Lectures." *Bulletin of the American Association of University Professors* Autumn 1948.

———."On First Teaching Speech." *Speech Teacher* January 1952.

Robinson, Karl F., and Becker, Albert B. *Effective Speech for the Teacher.* New York: McGraw-Hill, 1969.

Robinson, Karl F., and Kerikas, E. J. *Teaching Speech: Methods and Materials.* New York: David McKay, 1963.

Sorrenson, Fred S. *Speech for the Teacher.* New York: The Ronald Press, 1952.

Van Riper, Charles, and Butler, Katherine. *Speech in the Elementary Classroom.* New York: Harper & Brothers, 1955.

Weaver, Andrew; Borchers, Gladys; and Smith, Donald L. *The Teaching of Speech.* Englewood Cliffs: Prentice-Hall, 1952.

References about the art and the career of teaching appear at the end of Chapter 19.

the college first course

*The ablest teachers can teach little things
best, if they will.*

Quintilian

Whatever the field, its "First Course" presents a challenge to the teaching profession. It reaches as many students in a given institution as all other courses in the department added together. Its syllabus is subject to continual modification.

As a part of the preparation of this chapter in the former edition of this work, I collected syllabi from more than a hundred colleges and universities, and drew conclusions that seemed warranted by a study of these outlines. I later collected sixty additional course outlines from thirty-nine different institutions, and still later another thirty-six from twenty-five institutions. The discussion that follows includes items from the first survey, but is guided in large measure by those supplied for the later collections.

Trends

As in other disciplines, substantial changes have been made during the last decade in the organization and content of the first course.[1]

It will be fitting for the reader to add, silently, after such statements as this, "judging by the institutions surveyed." After all, more than one thousand departments are offering some kind of first course. The author's sample, however, included distinguished and progressive departments, both large and small. The faculties were educated in graduate departments of speech throughout the United States.

Different kinds of student participation.   Less time is spent in making sho
(5-10 minute) speeches; more time is given to group discussion: of an assigne
speech, of a collateral reading in communication theory, of a film viewed c
record heard. Instances of communication breakdown may be presented as
case study, followed by discussion of individual reports, or enacted as a
exercise in role playing. Short speeches are usually not omitted altogether, bu
are reduced in number. Much less time is spent in voice and articulatio
exercises. Parliamentary procedure is rarely taught as a unit of the first cours
though problems of presiding and of participating in discussion are considere
   It is difficult to state the extent to which these kinds of changes are takir
place; on the basis of the sample inspected, 20 or 30 percent are makir
significant use of these different kinds of assignments. Titles of the courses giv
only a partial clue. Of nine popular titles, three include the word commun
cation: "Fundamentals of Speech Communication," "Principles of Or
Communication," "Oral Communication." Six other titles are: "Fundamenta
of Speech," "Principles of Speech," "Elements of Speech," "Public Speaking
"Fundamentals of Public Speaking," "Essentials of Public Speaking." Prophec
is hazardous; probably those first courses that put a major emphasis on spee
making will continue in the majority, but the fundamentals teacher should b
trained in group process as well as in speechmaking.

Greater use of supplementary materials.   Whether the student spends most c
his time in speechmaking or in other kinds of participation, he is steadily bei
exposed to increasing amounts of collateral reading. At one time supplementa
assignments were given in other speech texts, which were placed on libra
reserve, or to collections of speeches: anthologies of "classified speech models
such annual volumes as *Representative American Speeches* or *Vital Speeches c
the Day.* These kinds of resources are still widely used, but added are anthologi
of materials on controversial issues. Books by professors within the discipline c
communication theory and speaking behavior are popular. The offerings b
scholars in related fields also appear on reading lists: Suzanne K. Langer, Wende
Johnson, S. I. Hayakawa, Wilbur Schramm, B. F. Skinner, Roger Brown, Ca
Rogers, Kurt Lewin, Erich Fromm, Marshall McLuhan, Paul Watzlawich, Edw
T. Hall.

Increase in the amount of written work.   Instructors have long require
outlines and lists of references as evidence of the preparation of major speeche
along with midsemester and final written examinations. Written analyses c
speeches heard or read are also honored by long tradition. In addition son
instructors require students to keep notebooks or communication diaries, or t
submit reports on other kinds of communication experiences or situations.
readily observable corollary is that a greater part of the final grade is based upc
the student's written work. Many people used to say, "Base two-thirds of th
final grade on speaking performance, one-third on written work"; the trer

seems to be to increase the value of the written work to 40 percent, and two syllabi put 50 percent.

Change in methods of instruction.   Many departments use the plan, described in early editions of this work as the University of Missouri lecture-laboratory method, of having individual sections meet jointly for lectures, individually for recitations. A multisection three-hour course of twenty sections can thus call three hundred or more students together once a week for lectures (and group written examinations) and still allow each of the twenty sections to meet twice a week with its own instructor for discussion and speechmaking. The lecture hour can be spent viewing a film, listening to recordings, listening to select students demonstrate an assignment, listening to a live or TV lecture. Uniform examinations can be administered during the lecture hour, avoiding the necessity of each section instructor constructing his own examination. Various instructors can participate as a team in giving the lectures. Course content can thus be more controlled, grading standards for the tests can be agreed upon, still leaving the responsibility for assigning a final grade to the individual instructor. Two advantages accrue: (a) lectures should attain a higher standard; (b) saving in instructional costs allows each section to be smaller (at Missouri, about twenty). A demurrer to the lecture-laboratory plan is entered by Ralph R. Leutnegger. He reports that the Michigan State University staff favored the use of lectures, but the students polled on the question, whether mass lectures by different instructors helped them learn better than if they had met solely with a laboratory instructor one more hour per week, divided evenly for and against. If the lectures were to be continued, students voted two to one in favor of many instructors rather than one expert for the entire term. (Students are often put in the position of being asked to vote whether they like a given plan, without having had the actual experience of the substitute plan.) After a two-year trial, however, the staff, which had tried various plans, decided to abandon the lecture system.[2]

Many departments are concerned that students often spend too much time listening and too little in actual speaking. As Thomas R. King puts it in the Florida State University syllabus: "We claim to be primarily concerned with the teaching of the encoding of oral verbal behavior, but in a class of twenty-five each student spends only 1/25 of the time on an assignment encoding, and 24/25ths decoding." At Florida State each student attends only two-thirds of the class sessions; he spends the remaining one-third of his time viewing video-tape lectures, working through programmed learning materials,[3] listening to

---

[2] "A New Approach to the Teaching of Voice and Diction," *Southern Speech Journal*, Fall 1963, pp. 62-67.

[3] One investigation reports that the amount of learning through programmed instruction is greater than through the videotaped lecture. Philip R. Amato, whose study with public speaking lectures support this finding, at least in part, urges that further experimentation in this area be given high priority. ("A Comparative Study of Programmed Instruction

sample speeches illustrating the next assignment from the dial-access equipment at the Media Center, and similar activities. Net gains seem to be that section enrollments can be increased and at the same time each student can give more speeches. The class is admittedly experimental, says the syllabus, and the results should be judiciously appraised.

On many campuses sharp limitations on available classroom space will hold most classes strictly to the conventional pattern. An instructor could do a variety of things during the hour if he had an empty classroom next door, and even more if he has a central recording, viewing, and listening facility. Note also that the activities described in paragraph 1 above are designed to work the student more vigorously during the class hour (as King would put it, keep him from wasting his time).

Peer group instruction—calling upon students for certain instructional tasks, such as helping to appraise and grade speeches—has been given some trial. Given the proper kind of general supervision, report Gordon Wiseman and Larry Barker, students seem to assign the same kinds of grades as instructors. They also comment on class attitudes and motivations, and classroom attendance.[4]

Current Features

Although course outlines show a certain uniformity of practices and assignments, they also reflect individual features as demanded by the needs and abilities of specific departments.

Common Features

Performances should be of moderate length. Only a few institutions found a place for speeches or readings longer than ten minutes. Four to ten minutes was the customary length. Short talks or critiques of two or three minutes are often used.

About six major performances, plus numerous shorter appearances, constitute the average number for one semester.

Some evidence exists that the speeches are getting a little longer, and the

---

and Videotaped Lectures as Part of a Course in Public Speaking," *Speech Monographs,* November 1964, pp. 461-466). Regional and national speech conventions frequently have sessions devoted to programmed and videotape instruction.

[4]"An Appraisal of Peer Group Instruction," *Central States Speech Journal,* May 1966, pp. 125-130.

See: Gordon R. Owen, "The Beginning Course: Don't Renovate—Innovate," *Speech Teacher,* January 1970, pp. 74-75. Speech classes of thirty-five students are divided into five laboratory groups, each meeting in its own room, administered by peer groups. "Instructors float from group to group, guiding, suggesting, leading oral evaluation, and completing written evaluations on as many speakers as possible."

number is being reduced, so that on the whole fewer class hours are being spent on performance. This trend is a result of the growing desire to have more class time spent in discussions of principles.

A reasonable degree of uniformity is sought among the various sections of multisection courses. The syllabus is, in most instances, a calendar or schedule of lectures, teacher-led discussions, and student participations. Usually the program is spelled out week by week. The new teacher, therefore, should prepare himself to teach the syllabus as written by the departmental staff. A department with twenty different sections of Speech 101 does not want to stand responsible for twenty different versions of the course, some of which might overlap and duplicate other courses in the department. The instructor who joins this department should at the outset bend his best efforts toward teaching Speech 101 as planned, not his own original Speech 101½, nor the first course of the institution he just left. After he has gained experience with Speech 101, he will know better what changes to present to its staff. Exceptions may arise, and to cover this eventuality one syllabus states: "We do not ask that all classes be identical, but we do hope that the same basic areas will be covered." Other departments provide for experimental sections where proposed new departures can be tested. The advantages of carefully discussing a new proposal with chairman and colleagues, in advance, are too numerous to catalog.

A strong plea is made for originality. Various documents explain plagiarism. "Close adherence to the content and arrangement of a single article, or speech, as occurs in condensation or digest, will be considered plagiarism," writes one staff. "All speeches are to be ORIGINAL," writes another, with emphasis. "If quotations are used, they should be acknowledged. If larger sources are used for general inspiration or form, such sources SHOULD BE CREDITED." Still another says: "Speeches should reflect *personal* thought, opinion, or experience; although complete originality cannot be demanded, speeches must be an expression of the student's own thinking and not merely an oral report of a written article or a previously heard speech. You are expected to create the speech you deliver."[5]

This statement also is clear and cogent: "A hearer demands of the speaker that he shall have done his own thinking. . . . Beware of the one-article speech, in which facts, tone, style, and point of view are all supplied to him ready made. . . . What is necessary?. . . an *intimate aquaintance* with the facts. . . the applying of his own *judgment* to his materials. . .applying *imagination* to his materials."

Historical note: A paragraph like this would have sounded ridiculous in 1899. A pronounced shift away from memorized selections to speeches on topics chosen by the student himself was engineered by James A. Winans, at Cornell University, about 1900. His most distinguished student of those early years, John P. Ryan, carried this idea to Grinnell College and developed and extended it.

Still another syllabus notes that although the student will often have to depend on the work of others for information and ideas, he should acknowledge these sources and give them the stamp of his own mind by reflecting on them by applying his imagination to them, and by achieving a new synthesis with them. "A summary of other people's works not bearing these marks of originality will not receive credit." Another syllabus observes that "point of view and structure of the speeches must be entirely one's own, except where specific indebtedness is acknowledged."

The ethical distortion obvious in plagiarism leads one syllabus to comment on another ethical problem: gross distortion of information, or blatant exploitation of such emotions as fear and prejudice. It recommends that these matters be called to the attention of speaker and class so that they can be discussed.

A true extempore style is generally insisted upon. "Neither impromptu (unplanned) nor memorized speeches are acceptable," says one syllabus. "All speeches are to be delivered without notes," comments another. "Notes will NOT be used on the platform except for quotations and statistics," observes a third. "The plan of the speech should be ALIVE in your mind." Another syllabus allows a single note card, containing about a score of words, during the first half of the course, but during the second half the student should be prepared to speak without notes.

By far the greater number of syllabi are silent on the matter of notes, though the extempore point of view is everywhere implied. If a syllabus wants a written speech to be read aloud, it specifically assigns it. And it is worth observing that the manuscript speech is coming into the curriculum, even at the first-course level, in a few institutions. This concession to current political and professional practice is accompanied by instruction about how to prepare and present manuscript speech.

The institutions surveyed use thirty different texts and fourteen different books of readings. A few use a selection of references instead of a text; a few do not mention the text used. The wide variety of textbooks is a commentary on the prodigious output in the field since 1960. Contrast the situation with the one that existed before World War II: Charles H. Woolbert's *The Fundamentals of Speech* was adopted by more than seven hundred colleges and universities. Woolbert's and three or four other texts completely dominated the field. A limited number of texts still enjoy wide sales, not wholly unexpected, considering the current size of college and university enrollments.[7]

[6]Maxine M. Trauernicht, "Woolbert as a Teacher," *Speech Teacher,* September 1960, p. 201.
[7]*See:* James W. Gibson, Charles R. Gruner, William D. Brooks, and Charles R. Petrie, Jr., "The First Course in Speech: A Survey of U.S. Colleges and Universities," *Speech Teacher,* January 1970.

The search continues for ways to upgrade the content of speeches. The use of a book of readings is one method, as is the required reading of current newspapers and magazines. Says one syllabus: "Select a general problem from which you may develop individual subtopics for the various speaking assignments." Another uses the "Common Materials" plan as a means of arousing interest in worthwhile topics. The class is given a list of topics for investigation, from which each student chooses one, and then participates in speechmaking and discussion on his topic. The trend toward improved speech content has been noted in previous editions of this book.

Since departments are using books of selections to supplement speech textbooks, I should like to review some of the advantages and disadvantages. Our colleagues in English departments regularly supplement texts in composition with books of readings, and have done so for decades.

The problem is to stimulate the thinking of students. The difficulty with a speech based entirely on personal experience is that many listeners can quietly reflect that the speaker's experience may be only a little more or a little less than their own. The speaker does not have to extend himself to meet problems of gathering and selecting speech materials.

To avoid so much of the commonplace, the instructor asks the class to read a speech or article on a controversial or provocative subject, and make a speech based on it. This type of assignment has some advantages but also runs into some difficulties. If the article deals with, for example, flying saucers or extrasensory perception, the teacher may find that a substantial percentage of the speeches coming from that assignment are merely parrotings or paraphrases of the ideas in the reading. The average student's speech does not show much personal reaction or reflection nor much adaptation to the audience. He would have been better off to have stuck to a topic related to his personal experience; here at least is a chance for animation and enthusiasm. Hence the teacher, in assigning a reading, needs to warn: "Don't summarize the article; react to it. Bring in your own reflections. Make the material *yours*. Show how it affects or is vital to your immediate listeners." Some books of readings contain provocative queries after each selection.

Giving the assignment this direction, the instructor will have good luck with some students and not with others. If a student has previously read material about flying saucers, he can at least compare what he knows with the article in the book of readings. But he may not yet have seen a flying saucer, read about one, nor be particularly interested in one. With a selection on ESP he might do better; he may have noted the strange coincidences of life and may have pondered that more than chance operates in human destiny. Another student may not care anything about either flying saucers or ESP.

The instructor has still another possibility if the book has a *series* of speeches or articles about flying saucers or some other field of inquiry. The student may then compare and contrast. Various observers report having seen these objects; the Air Force solemnly avers that it can account for all but 6 percent in natural, scientific ways. As the student reads the series, he meets contrasting points of view. Some articles conclude that flying saucers exist, others that they do not.

A whole class that has read materials on the same topic can participate in a lively discussion. To be sure, the discussion may bear on flying saucers or ESP rather than on principles of speaking, but the instructor can keep it from getting entirely out of hand by inquiring into logic, the rules of evidence, the *tone* of the individual articles. Does Source A seem scientific, detached, competent? Does the missing 6 percent unchecked or unverifiable flying saucers bear any significance? Is 94 percent certainty sufficient? Does it matter whether the source is a professor of astrophysics at Harvard or a Welsh preacher? When a student reads widely and then makes a speech about what he reads, he is brought face to face with problems both of point of view as well as with selection and arrangement. For flying saucers substitute juvenile delinquency, student unrest, narcotics, ecosystems, propaganda, communism.

Still another possibility, used by a few departments, is to choose a book of selections that consists of articles about outstanding speeches, speakers, or rhetorical theory. Here the student can bring a certain amount of personal experience as a speaker or as a listener to speeches. Maybe he has heard Muskie, Kennedy, Johnson, Nixon, Humphrey, Agnew, King. His speech need not be entirely paraphrase.

If there were a foolproof way of improving speech content, departmental course outlines would show more uniformity than they do. What we all seek to develop is the ability to combine personal experience and reflection *with* the ideas of others (properly acknowledged), hoping that the outcome is so original and so creative that the instructor can say: *Nobody but Joe X could have given that speech. No audience would have enjoyed or appreciated the speech any more than the group he actually faced as he delivered it.*

Assignments Common to most Courses

1. *A speech of introduction.* In this short first talk, the student introduces himself and talks about his general background, interests, or vocational aims. This assignment was discussed in the preceding chapter. Some course outlines call this an *icebreaker* speech. One syllabus adds: "Bring your textbook to class. This is a tactful way of saying don't miss that first class, and don't leave the text at home."

Variations are reported. Divide the class in pairs at the first meeting; each student interviews his partner in preparation for a two- to three-minute speech of introduction to be given at the next meeting of the class. At that meeting, after each speech, the audience asks questions of the person introduced. Another syllabus suggests that in a speech of self-introduction the student should discuss

n aspect of his personality—preferably a strong belief or opinion—which
cquaints listeners with him as a person. A question and answer period follows
he speech.

The assignment not only gives each student an opportunity to try himself out
s a communicator, but gives the entire class information about the potential of
he group: its special traits, qualities, interests.

. A narrative or personal experience speech. This speaking assignment logically
follows the speech of introduction; it seems to say to the student, "You
ntroduced yourself to us in your first talk; now, in another talk, tell us more
bout yourself."

The narrative speech is in one way easy, in another way difficult. It is easy in
hat it keeps the student comfortably grounded in materials with which he is
familiar. It is difficult to keep these materials from falling into the dull and
commonplace. Precede this assignment with a discussion of the requirements of
good narrative speaking: locale, characters, selection of details, and especially
he importance of complication (conflict) and climax.

One syllabus suggests the use of a narrative speech dealing with an incident
hat made a profound impression upon the speaker: one that changed his life,
brought him to his senses, altered his point of view, brought him face to face
with an entirely different way of living, shattered a false idol, turned him from a
scoffer into a believer, resulted in a strong or meaningful insight.

3. *A one-point speech.* This assignment introduces the student further to the
principle of organizing. He is invited to choose his own topic and develop it
through one reason or one example. One course outline asked for "one point
with support," followed by another talk having "one point with two supports,
documented." Comments another outline: "An idea, stated just once, is rarely
comprehended by an audience. . . . The present exercise calls upon you to take a
single idea and find supports for it that will enable both you and the audience to
dwell upon it, and thus readily to grasp it."

One syllabus comments that the one-point speech looks deceptively simple
but can prove difficult for those not used to bringing their ideas to a sharp focus.
t offers meaty suggestions:

a. The theater of the absurd exposes the contradiction between our idea of
how the world ought to be and our experience of the way it actually is.

b. The influential leaders of the Negro revolt are "black nationalists."

c. The stock market is painfully sensitive to political decisions in
Washington.

d. Most women college graduates still see themselves chiefly as potential
wives and mothers.

e. Student activism is directly related to the academic quality of the college
or university.

f. The one thing new, popular novels (or plays or movies) have in common is
—————————— .

4. *An expository speech.* Teachers are finding that today's well-prepared students are responding to expository assignments of a more sophisticated sort. For example:

Exposition of a definition. From one list: Buddhism, capitalism, dialectic, esthetics, functionalism, impressionism, jazz, Judaism, logical positivism, truth, zen. From another: aristocracy, empathy and sympathy, inflation, justice, persuasion, rationalization. From a third: manifest destiny, counterpoint, field linguistics, cubism, gross national product. From a fourth: friendship, love, black power, soul, sovereignty, nationalism. From a fifth: status symbol, inelastic demand, planned obsolescence, cultural lag, charismatic leader, marginal utility.

Exposition of an opinion. Make the opinion clear, says one course outline. Make the audience understand it; you do not need to convert your listeners. Show wherein you agree with others who hold this opinion. Show the reasoning and evidence that led you to this point of view. Example: revisionist theories of young American historians.

Exposition of a problem. School dropouts, for example; juvenile delinquency, drug addiction, racial tension. Comments one syllabus, helpfully guiding the student to subtopics: show that the problem chosen for discussion is dangerous, degrading, injurious; show it prevents the operation or growth toward an ideal; show that it is fundamental in that it causes other problems; show that it is recognized by experts, or by large numbers of people.

Exposition of values. Values and value-judgments have long been significant in rhetorical theory. The central value of any age; values of patriotism, courage; values that led to great moments in history, such as the Renaissance or the romantic movement; such values as those of Socrates, Moses, Lincoln; the values, misplaced or otherwise, of today.

Exposition of a cause. Explain the causes of, for example, price changes, inflation, crime, farm surplus, a disease, good grades, genius, the deterioration of the environment.

5. *An expository speech using visual aids.* This assignment is designed to perfect the expository talent and at the same time to get the student to handle objects, move around, and generally develop bodily freedom. This assignment will be more effective if the student is made fully aware of the wide variety of visual aids available—maps, graphs, and charts are just a starter. Related to this assignment is one in which the student is asked to explain a process or skill in which he uses gesture and bodily action.

One department requires each student to design a pictorial model of communication, develop and defend it.

6. *A speech to persuade.* Sometimes called a speech to *convince* or *to change belief.* Says one syllabus: "Alter the belief of the listeners on such topics as

ompulsory class attendance, lengthening the electrical engineering curriculum, dopting the policy of four-year eligibility in intercollegiate athletics."

One assignment shows Toulmin's influence: "Establish a claim through estimony, statistics, and specific instances. Affirm a persuasive proposition hrough the use of *massive documentation* [italics added]. Illustrative claims: .. 'Inequalities exist (do not exist) in the present draft system,' 'Marijuana is (is ot) harmful of itself,' 'The Peace Corps is (is not) a success.' "

. *A speech to persuade.* Sometimes called an *action* speech or a speech to ctuate. Here the speaker is invited to choose a topic of a sort that listeners can eact to by specific behavior. He is to urge a realistic and specific course of ction: as one syllabus says, "enroll in a particular professional society, subcribe to a specific periodical, etc." He is urged to demonstrate good reasoning, se of evidence, clear organization, valid motive appeals and interest factors.

One syllabus, recalling the principle of *selective exposure* that leads listeners o prefer the speaker whose views agree with theirs, reminds students that most ersuasive speaking can be designed simply to *reinforce* views currently held. In hese instances the speaker should not be content to reinforce the listener's ttitude, but should get him to do something about it. Everybody knows the alue of exercise, the syllabus continues; perhaps the student speaker can ersuade the listener to utilize the free swim and gym hours. It continues:

1. Be well informed: read this book; watch this TV documentary; subscribe to this journal; attend this lecture.
2. Utilize the cultural opportunities of the campus: visit the museum; catch the Berlin Philharmonic concert; take in the exhibition at Memorial Hall.
3. Protect yourself: lock your apartment when you leave; fasten seat belts; on the campus after dark, walk only with another person.
4. Give time and energy to others: sign up for the tutorial program; buy UNICEF note and holiday cards; give blood.
5. Work for international understanding: go to the foreign student teas; sign up for Comparative Political Systems.

Other Speaking Assignments

ollowing is a variety of assignments developed by one or more courses:

he workout speech.   The student plans his speech, as usual, but is interupted by students or teacher and is asked questions about his organization, his election of evidence, etc. Or the teacher may interrupt to offer a comment bout delivery.

he inquiry speech.   Says one course outline: "Maturity . . . is the willingness o suspend judgment . . . life teaches us that snap judgments may be wrong . . .

sound opinions must be based on study." In this speech the student makes an inquiry into some current problem: for example, regulations governing student driven cars. Student drivers are often, at first, vexed and annoyed by the rules one syllabus explains; impartial inquiry gives all concerned a better appreciation of the complexity of the problem. Inquiry into the problem of civil rights often turns up various solutions. Other examples: What, actually, is the effect of cigarette smoking? What is the best time for military service?

The impromptu speech.   This assignment is probably used more frequently than appears in the survey of outlines. A variation introduced into one course: "Impromptu speeches of evaluation: sixty to ninety seconds, immediately following the round of extempore speeches."

The speech contest.   In some departments the semester speech is a traditional activity, having special attraction for the superior student.

The panel or symposium speech.   This assignment is set up in a variety of ways. In one department the instructor brings a list of topics to class: Should we have a national lottery? How can the United Nations succeed? How can we prevent depression (inflation)? etc. Students are invited to add to the list. Eventually the class is divided into groups of three to five according to preference of subjects and each group is given a date on which to present its panel or symposium discussion. A variation is to use the buzz session approach: select the one topic of greatest interest to the class, divide the class into four or five groups, station each group in a different part of the room, let each group select a chairman (he should try to get the group to follow the "processes of thinking" pattern, say one syllabus), and discuss the topic for twenty or thirty minutes. In the closing minutes of the hour a representative of each group reports the conclusions of his group.

A forum or question period may follow the more formal series of speeches.

Note also that the topics considered may include those related to the social relevance of speech: The Ethics of Persuasion, The Impact of Radio and Television, Freedom of Speech in Contemporary American Society, The Role of Propaganda in Contemporary American Society.

The sales speech.   A practical variation of the speech to actuate. Says one syllabus: "You must sell an article to the highest bidder. This is a cash sale. Sympathy bidding or planted bidders are against the rules. You may sell a service, article of clothing, book, etc." Says another: "Sell your reading lamp. Sell a copy of *Roget's Thesaurus*. Most of us are tough customers." This type of speech is also likely to appear in courses in public speaking for business and professional men.

Assignments on listening. These can take a variety of forms: listening for application of principles of speaking, appraising evidence, discriminating between fact and opinion, testing authorities, identifying linguistic or propagandistic devices, critiquing classroom speakers or outside speakers, both on content and on application of principles of speaking. One syllabus suggests these items: statistics, analogies, circumstantial data, opinions, inductions, deductions classification, consequence, disjunction), propaganda devices (name calling, glittering generalities, testimonials, card stacking).

Many course outlines set up an assignment in which the student is asked to listen to a campus or community speaker and report on his effectiveness. Often he is provided with a set of questions or guidelines so he will know what to listen for. One department also provides its students with a complete sample report. In general the student is asked to appraise both content and delivery of the speaker.

Ethics of speechmaking. Classical theory and modern application of the ethical and moral responsibilities of the speaker. Usually presented in lecture and discussion form.

Speech of praise or of appraisal. May be based on a famous novelist, playwright, poet, scientist, inventor, statesman, minister, speaker; on an "unforgettable character" in your neighborhood; on your father, mother, or other relative.

Reading aloud. Many course outlines included an assignment in reading aloud. Often the assignment was in fact a combination reading-and-speaking exercise. For example: "Select a significant poet. Present a six-minute program of his poetry. Your personal comments about the poet will be an important part of the assignment, and will be included in the time limit." Or: "Select a piece of narrative prose that can be read in x minutes or less. Precede it with relevant comments about author, selection, locale, or characters. In reading it, try to achieve a direct, communicative, story-telling attitude." Still another syllabus asks students to select a passage from an essay, a biography, a work of fiction or travel. "Attention to voice and articulation is begun here," it comments.

Discussion of a case involving a communication breakdown. One syllabus features this type of assignment. The instructor distributes a handout describing an incident in which a worker was dismissed for ignoring a company rule— "willful insubordination." The case is read and discussed. These alternatives appear: the worker should be reinstated; the company's act was right; some compromise should be worked out. Each student is asked to render his decision, citing reasons. The class is divided into three groups based upon their decision, and given the rest of the hour to draw up the best possible case for their opinion. In the subsequent meeting, each group is allowed to present its reasons. At a third meeting the instructor announces his decision.

Variants: (a) "A team project. In teams of three, reproduce by role playing communication breakdown that at least one of the group has experienced. On person may narrate." (b) "Role playing: new truck role play, one group with foreman, another group with no foreman. Dorm counselor and/or laborator assistant role play: effects of status on communication."

Log.   Keep a log, preferably a looseleaf notebook, in which you enter analysi of class discussions, individual speeches, or case studies, analyses of commun cation situations or incidents from your residence unit, family groups, studen committees. Following is a sample log entry, an analysis of a classroom di cussion:

> I observed a very interesting pattern in the first day of our small grou meetings. The members were Jane, Wanda, Bobbi, Susan, Cindy, Robert, an myself. The pattern was one of dominance of the group by Bobbi. She wa very outspoken about declaring the mimeographed material to be ridiculou and everyone was very quick to agree. After dismissal of the discussio question, Bobbi talked to Myrna about campus politics; Susan joined in little later, then Cindy, Robert, and Jane listened. Neither Robert nor Jan said more than four or five sentences in the opening discussion. I did n listen, being uninterested.
>
> I think that the pattern that our group followed was due both to perso ality traits and to the effect of early interactions in the group. Bobbi strike me as being an open, aggressive person who is not awfully perceptive. (Th last point I inferred from the fact that she thought and said that our who group participated in the discussion of mimeo sheets and campus politics For this reason she tended to talk the most (since I believe that speech is form of aggression) at the beginning of the discussion. Robert and Jane, wh seem to be timid persons, did not speak at the beginning of the discussio perhaps because they were intimidated or talked down by Bobbi. It interesting that these patterns remained throughout the class period, probabl demonstrating that initial patterns of interpersonal relations in a group ten to be perpetuated by the group.
>
> In addition, I think that my own withdrawal from the day's activity an my indifference to the course is my own method of aggression. I resent bein dominated.

Feedback.   One syllabus stresses the importance of feedback in discussion c speeches and the analysis of classroom activities. The quality of a student feedback is a factor to be considered in the grading, it suggests. Anothe assignment: "Rectangle demonstration or variant thereof, demonstrating relativ advantages and disadvantages of presence or absence of feedback. Suggeste topic: 'Should public speaking be abolished?' "

Advice to the teacher.   (a) "Develop *principles*, not how-to formulas. (b) "Beware of talking about oral interpretation, or extemporaneous discours

tc. as though they were being taught as isolated short courses. Keep all
nchored to the basic theoretical framework." (c) "The increasing sophistication
f our freshmen suggests that we do not need to spend so much time on 'getting
cquainted' or 'conquering stage fright' types of assignments." (Most syllabi use
hese assignments but in a more vigorous fashion than a decade ago.)

peech of disagreement.   "Attack the main idea, or an important supporting
lea, in a speech delivered by another member of the class during the previous
ound (or, perhaps, earlier in the semester). State clearly and correctly the idea
eing attacked."

ublic relations speech.   The student should speak in behalf of some industry
rganization, or institution, and show that it has high ideals of public service and
worthy of public support.

tudent's level of information.   One syllabus provides an "Identification
est" of fifty names to be given the first week of the semester in order to
ncourage students to read widely. The list includes authors, sports figures,
tatesmen of various countries, artists, musicians.

urrent controversy.   The first course has traditionally encouraged the dis-
ussion of controversial ideas. In their search for topics, students invariably
light upon matters close at hand. Here are two pressing lines of thought:

1. Improved dialogue between teachers and students. Whatever else has
appened because of worldwide dissent, the faculty has become more sensitive
 student thinking than before; not particularly to militants, who generally have
o constructive program, but to those who can not only raise the questions but
ave workable suggestions about the answers.

2. Ethnological studies. Contributions of the black community, the Latin-
merican community, the Indian community, and of other ethnological groups
 our culture have often been ignored. Not only in the first course but in
dvanced courses the teacher will need to incorporate appropriate materials.
extbooks, anthologies, critical articles are rapidly increasing in number. To
eep abreast, attend conferences and conventions; read current issues of learned
urnals. A list of suggestions of specific things to do appears in Ronald K.
urke's forum article in the April 1969 *Quarterly Journal of Speech*. Read it and
lso the reply by Jeré Veilleux. Robert L. Scott and Wayne Brockriede, *The
hetoric of Black Power*, Harper, 1969, contains selected essays and also a
ibliography.

Surveys

urveys enable the teacher to update his instruction.

A survey by Norman T. London of the first course in one hundred and five southern colleges showed that these topics were included: extemporaneous speaking (more than 90 percent), followed by diction, voice, listening, discussion, impromptu speaking, interpretation (less than 50 percent).[8]

A survey by Paul L. Dressel and Frances H. DeLisle of 322 institutions of higher learning reported that 51 percent had some form of requirement in speech. A demonstration of proficiency only was required by only 8.1 percent; 21.7 percent required a one-term course; 0.6 percent required more than one term but less than one full year; 0.6 percent required a two- or three-course, one-year sequence; 2.2 percent required two years or more; 10.6 percent included speech in a distribution option; and 7.1 percent required speech as part of an integrated course.

Among the trends in speech requirements measured by the study were the following: (1) the number of institutions requiring a one-term course has remained virtually the same over the ten-year period studied; (2) speech as an option in the distribution requirements increased over the ten-year period by four percentage points; and (3) speech as a part of an integrated course declined by five percentage points.

For comparison purposes, the study revealed that, over a period of ten years, the following changes took place: (1) the percentage of schools requiring one year of English Composition declined from 60 percent to 48 percent; (2) the number of schools requiring one year of literature courses declined from 4 percent to 37 percent; and (3) the number of institutions requiring two years of a foreign language in college or its equivalent advanced from 58 percent to 67 percent.[9]

A survey of 564 colleges and universities (including community colleges) by James W. Gibson, Charles R. Gruner, William D. Brooks, and Charles R. Petrie Jr., previously cited, provides information about the administration of the first course (enrollment, class size, problems of staffing) and also about course objectives and content.

Course objectives and percentages responding (schools checked more than one objective) are reported as follows:

1. Development of effective oral communication   3.

2. Development of effective delivery   2

3. Gain knowledge of communication theory and practice   2

4. Develop and improve organizational skills   2

5. Develop listening ability   1

---

[8] Norman T. London, "Professional Attitudes Towards a First Course in Speech and Its Requirement in Southern Colleges," *Southern Speech Journal,* Winter 1962, pp. 142-147
[9] Paul L. Dressel and Frances H. DeLisle, *Undergraduate Curriculum Trends,* American Council on Education. Cited in *Spectra,* April 1969, p. 15.

6. Develop critical abilities and standards   15

7. Improve pronunciation and use of voice   14

8. Gain self-confidence and self-insight   14

9. Learn audience analysis skills   12

0. Improve research abilities   11

he eleven items that followed each ranked 9 percent or lower, including use of ⸱idence, participation in a group, and, at the bottom, knowledge of parlia-ᵉntary law.

These data are subject to interesting interpretations. Speechmaking (a single ⸱eaker talking to an audience) ranks higher than group participation. Effective ⸱livery (including use of voice) ranks higher than might have been expected. ⸱lf-confidence and self-insight are given more attention than might have been ⸱pposed, considering the prevailing belief that students are more poised than in ⸱e days of the early studies about speech anxieties. Logical aspects of com-ᵘnication are emphasized over emotional and motivational aspects. Communi-⸱tion theory and listening are more prominent than two decades ago.

Course objectives should be viewed alongside the list of units taught, also ⸱ported in the survey. Of twenty-three items reported, the highest priorities are ⸱ven to informative speaking, persuasive speaking, delivery, supporting material, ⸱tlining, reasoning, audience analysis, and topic selection—in that order—again ⸱owing the emphasis upon public speaking as the backbone of the first course. ⸱scussion, for example, is eleventh on the list and communication theory ⸱urteenth.

One other statistic reported is that more than 50 percent of the respondents ⸱ satisfied with their courses as now taught (which can also be interpreted as ⸱aning that nearly 50 percent are not satisfied with their courses as now ⸱ght).

These surveys and the discussion in this chapter present a description of the ⸱te of the first course at the beginning of a new decade.

Assignments

Secure a copy of a syllabus for a first course, and revise it in the direction of what you consider to be good current practice.

Compare and contrast a selection of current textbooks and report on the essential likenesses and differences.

Secure a copy of a syllabus for a first course in some other discipline, preferably the humanities and social studies, and report on features that have significance for good syllabus construction.

Prepare a statement of goals or outcomes for the first course, to guide you in determining content and procedures for the course.

5. Plan in detail a segment of a first course, with reference, if feasible, to course you might yourself teach.

6. From the point of view of your specialty within the discipline, appraise th importance of that specialty in the first course.

Note. Think of these assignments as realistic, on-the-job projects. Make full us of available sources of material.

7. Report on the section, "Some Wild Card Exercises for Your Browsir Pleasure," in Elwood Murray, Gerald M. Phillips, and J. David Trub (exercises by Alton Barbour), *Speech: Science-Art,* Indianapolis, 1969, pp. 25 ff. ("A group of us sat down the other day and came up with a list (speeches we would like to hear. . . ." "Can you list some 'laws of scienc which are no longer true? What sciences exist now that didn't exist ten yea ago? What does this say about our 'knowledge' of the world we live in?")

8. Increasing attention is being paid to the use of games as instructional device Read William I. Gorden, "Academic Games in the Speech Curriculum *Central States Speech Journal* Winter 1969, and comment on implications f(your teaching specialty.

Questions for Classroom Discussion

1. In the usual first course, is too much time spent on speechmaking, n(enough on discussion of theory?

2. Is the proportion of time usually spent on reading aloud in the first cour too little, too much, about right?

3. Is it preferable for students to have the responsibility of choosing subjects f(their own speeches, or should they base their topics on books of selection

4. Suggest ways of managing written work in the first course: use of outline references, listening reports, logs, or journals.

5. Do you approve of the apparent trend toward basing more and more of t grade on the written features of the first course?

6. Considering that parliamentary procedure has practically dropped out of t first course, what place should now be assigned to it? Should it be taught discussion courses? In a special course of one or two semester hours? Shou it become a standard part of the high school speech course? Are the minimum essentials of parliamentary procedure that are essential for go(citizenship?

References

Of General Interest

Amato, Philip P. "Programmed Instruction and Speech: Part 1: History, Prin ples, and Theories." *Today's Speech* September 1965.

Baird, A. Craig; Gehring, Mary Louise; Kerr, Harry P.; Bosmajian, Haig A.; a White, Eugene E. "Symposium on Using Speech Models." *Speech Teach* January 1967.

lankenship, Jane. "On the Teaching of Style." *Speech Teacher* March 1964.

oase, Paul H. "Speech in the Liberal Arts College." *Central States Speech Journal* November 1964.

oase, Paul H., and Glancy, Donald R. "And Gladly Will They Learn, and Gladly Teach." *Speech Teacher* November 1966.

raden, Waldo W. "Putting Rigor into the Teaching of Speech." *Today's Speech* September 1963.

roadrick, King; McIntyre, Charles J.; and Moren, Richard. "TV Teacher's Report." *Speech Teacher* March 1962.

yers, Burton H. "Speech and the Principles of Learning." *Speech Teacher* March 1963.

hesler, Mark, and Fox, Robert. *Role-Playing Methods in the Classroom.* Chicago: Science Research Associates, 1966.

levenger, Theodore Jr. "A Rhetorical Jigsaw Puzzle: A Device for Teaching Certain Aspects of Speech Composition." *Speech Teacher* March 1963.

edmon, Donald N., and Rayborn, David W. "Closed Circuit Television and the 'Required' First Course in Speech." *Speech Teacher* November 1965.

edmon, Donald N., and Frandsen, Kenneth D., "A 'Required' First Course in Speech: A Survey," *Speech Teacher* January 1964.

ast, James R., and Starkey, Eleanor. "The First Speech Course: Rhetoric and Public Address." *Speech Teacher* January 1966.

croyd, Donald H. "New Directions in Teaching Voice and Articulation." *Speech Teacher* September 1967.

isher, B. Aubrey. "The Persuasive Campaign: A Pedagogy for the Contemporary First Course in Speech Communication." *Central States Speech Journal* Winter 1969.

ibson, James W.; Gruner, Charles R.; Brooks, William D.; and Petrie, Charles R., Jr. "The First Course in Speech: A Survey of U.S. Colleges and Universities." *Speech Teacher*, January 1970.

iorden, William I. "Academic Games in the Speech Curriculum." *Central States Speech Journal* Winter 1969.

aakenson, Robert. "Training for an Industrial Speakers' Bureau." *Today's Speech* February 1965.

ance, Kenneth G. "The Character of the Beginning Course: Skills and/or Content." *Speech Teacher* September 1961.

ance, Kenneth G.; Devito, Joseph A.; Baker, Elson E.; and Ragsdale, J. Donald; "Symposium: Evaluation in the Public Speaking Course." *Speech Teacher* March 1967.

ildebrandt, Herbert W., and Sattler, William M. "The Use of Common Materials in the Basic College Speech Course." *Speech Teacher* January 1963.

ildebrandt, Herbert W.; Brandes, Paul D.; Tedford, Thomas L.; McNally, J. R.; Graham, John; Hopkins, Jon; and White, Hollis L. "Symposium on Using Common Materials." *Speech Teacher* November 1967.

ohnson, Martha, and Richardson, Don. "Listening Training in the Fundamentals of Speech Class." *Speech Teacher* November 1968.

Leutenegger, Ralph R. "A New Approach to the Teaching of Voice and Diction." *Southern Speech Journal* Fall 1963.

London, Norman T. "Professional Attitudes Toward a First Course in Speech and Its Requirement in Southern Colleges." *Southern Speech Journal* Winter 1962.

_____. "Professional Attitudes Toward a First Course in Speech and Its Requirement in American Colleges." *Speech Teacher* January 1964.

McClerren, Beryl R. "Creative Teaching." *Speech Teacher* September 1966.

McCroskey, James C. "Toulmin and the Basic Course." *Speech Teacher* March 1965.

Owen, Gordon R. "The Beginning Course: Don't Renovate—Innovate." *Speech Teacher* January 1970.

Tolch, Charles John. "Methods of Programming Teaching Machines for Speech." *Speech Teacher* September 1962.

Wiseman, Gordon, and Barker, Larry. "An Appraisal of Peer Group Instruction." *Central States Speech Journal* May 1966.

Textbooks

The following is a selection of texts available for classroom use. Collectively they cover a wide variety of approaches: public speaking, voice and articulation, adult or other specialized classes. Some are academic and technical, some are otherwise.

When ordering copies, specify the latest edition; some titles are known to be in process of revision as this list is being prepared. For appraisals, read the reviews in *Quarterly Journal of Speech* and other scholarly publications. For announcement of new titles, see recent issues of these journals. Consult also the "Check List of Books" appearing in the *Directory of the Speech Communication Association.*

Abernathy, Elton. *Fundamentals of Speech Communication.* 3d ed. Dubuque: William C. Brown, 1970.

_____. *The Advocate: A Manual of Persuasion.* New York: David McKay, 1964.

Andersch, Elizabeth G., and Staats, Lorin C. *Communication for Everyday Use.* 3d ed. New York: Holt, Rinehart & Winston, 1969.

Andersen, Martin P.; Lewis, Wesley; and Murray, James. *The Speaker and His Audience: Dynamic Public Speaking.* New York: Harper & Row, 1966.

Auer, J. Jeffery. *Brigance's Speech Communication.* 3d ed. New York: Appleton-Century-Crofts, 1967.

Baird, A. Craig; Knower, Franklin H.; and Becker, Samuel. *General Speech Communication,* 4th ed. New York: McGraw-Hill, 1971.

Baker, Virgil L., and Eubanks, Ralph T. *Speech in Personal and Public Affairs.* New York: David McKay, 1965.

Blankenship, Jane. *Public Speaking: A Rhetorical Perspective.* Englewood Cliffs: Prentice-Hall, 1966.

Braden, Waldo W. *Public Speaking, The Essentials.* New York: Harper & Row, 1966.

rigance, William Norwood. *Speech: Its Techniques and Disciplines in a Free Society.* 2d ed. New York, Appleton-Century-Crofts, 1961.

ronstein, Arthur J., and Jacoby, Beatrice F. *Your Speech and Voice.* New York: Random House, 1966.

rown, Charles T., and Van Riper, Charles, *Speech and Man.* Englewood Cliffs: Prentice-Hall, 1966.

rown Speech Communication Series. A series of 128-page paperbacks covering speaking, interpretation, discussion, basic skills; additional titles in preparation. Dubuque: William C. Brown, 1967 and later.

ryant, Donald C., and Wallace, Karl R. *Fundamentals of Public Speaking.* 4th ed. New York: Appleton-Century-Crofts, 1969.

———. *Oral Communication.* 3d ed. New York: Appleton-Century-Crofts, 1955.

uehler, E.C., and Linkugel, Wil A. *Speech Communication: A First Course.* New York: Harper & Row, 1969.

ass, Carl B. *A Manner of Speaking.* New York: G. P. Putnam's Sons, 1961.

randell, Judson S.; Phillips, Gerald M.; and Wigley, Joseph A. *Speech: A Course in Fundamentals.* Chicago: Scott, Foresman, 1964.

rocker, Lionel, and Hildebrandt, Herbert W. *Public Speaking for College Students.* 4th ed. New York: American Book, 1965.

romwell, Harvey, and Monroe, Alan H. *Working For More Effective Speech.* Chicago: Scott, Foresman, 1964.

ance, Frank E. X. *The Citizen Speaks.* Belmont, Calif.: Wadsworth, 1962.

ickens, Milton. *Speech: Dynamic Communication.* 2d ed. New York: Harcourt, Brace & World, 1963.

ietrich, John E., and Brooks, Keith. *Practical Speaking for the Technical Man.* Englewood Cliffs: Prentice-Hall, 1958.

croyd, Donald H.; Halfond, Murray M.; and Towne, Carol C. *Voice and Articulation.* Chicago: Scott, Foresman, 1966.

hrensberger, Ray, and Pagel, Elaine. *Notebook for Public Speaking.* 2d ed. Englewood Cliffs: Prentice-Hall, 1956.

isenson, Jon, and Boase, Paul H. *Basic Speech.* 2d ed. New York: Macmillan, 1964.

llingsworth, Huber W., and Clevenger, Theodore Jr. *Speech and Social Action: A Strategy of Oral Communication.* Englewood Cliffs: Prentice-Hall, 1967.

rway, Ella A. *Listening: A Programmed Approach.* New York: McGraw-Hill, 1969.

isher, Hilda B. *Improving Voice and Articulation.* Boston: Houghton Mifflin, 1966.

ilman, Wilbur E.; Aly, Bower; and White, Hollis L. *An Introduction to Speaking.* 2d ed. New York: Macmillan, 1968.

rasham, John A., and Gooder, Glenn G. *Improving Your Speech.* New York: Harcourt, Brace & World, 1960.

Gray, Giles Wilkeson, and Braden, Waldo W. *Public Speaking: Principles and Practice.* 2d ed. New York: Harper & Row, 1963.

Hellman, Hugo E., and Staudacher, Joseph M. *Fundamentals of Speech: A Group Speaking Approach.* New York: Random House, 1969.

Hance, Kenneth G.; Ralph, David C.; and Wiksell, Milton J.; *Principles of Speaking.* 2d ed., Belmont, Calif.: Wadsworth, 1969.

Holm, James N. *Productive Speaking for Business and the Professions.* Boston Allyn & Bacon, 1967.

Jensen, J. Vernon. *Perspectives on Oral Communication.* Boston: Holbrook 1970.

Juleus, Nels G. *Perspectives on Public Speaking.* New York: American Book 1966.

Kelley, Win. *The Art of Public Address.* Dubuque: William C. Brown, 1965.

Larson, Orvin. *When It's Your Turn to Speak.* New York: Harper & Row, 1962

Lewis, Thomas R., and Nichols, Ralph G. *Speaking and Listening.* Dubuque William C. Brown, 1965.

Linkugel, Wil, and Berg, David M. *A Time to Speak.* Belmont, Calif.: Wadsworth 1970.

Lomas, Charles W., and Richardson, Ralph. *Speech: Idea and Delivery.* 2d ed Boston: Houghton Mifflin, 1963.

Martin, Howard H., and Anderson, Kenneth E. *Speech Communication.* Boston Allyn & Bacon, 1968.

Mayer, Lyle V. *Fundamentals of Voice and Diction.* 3d ed. Dubuque: William C Brown, 1968.

McBurney, J. H., and Wrage, Ernest J. *Guide to Good Speech.* 3d ed. Englewoo Cliffs: Prentice-Hall, 1965.

McCall, Roy C., and Cohen, Herman. *Fundamentals of Speech,* 2d ed. New York: Macmillan, 1963.

Mills, Glen E., and Bauer, Otto F. *Guidebook for Student Speakers.* New York Ronald Press, 1966.

Minnick, Wayne C. *The Art of Persuasion.* 2d ed. Boston: Houghton Mifflin 1968.

Murray, Elwood; Phillips, Gerald M.; and Truby, J. David. *Speech: Science-Ar* Indianapolis: Bobbs-Merrill, 1969.

Monroe, Alan H., and Ehninger, Douglas. *Principles and Types of Speech.* 6t ed. 1967. Also *Principles of Speech Communication.* 6th ed. Glenview, Ill. Scott, Foresman, 1969.

Mudd, Charles S., and Sillars, Malcolm D. *Speech: Content and Communication* rev. ed. Scranton: Chandler, 1969.

Nadeau, Ray E., *A Basic Rhetoric of Speech-Communication.* Reading: Addson-Wesley, 1969.

Olbricht, Thomas H. *Informative Speaking.* Glenview, Ill.: Scott, Foresman 1968.

iver, Robert T. and Cortwright, Rupert L. *Effective Speech.* 5th ed. New York: Holt, Rinehart & Winston, 1970.

iver, Robert T.; Zelko, Harold P.; and Holtzman, Paul D. *Communicative Speaking and Listening.* 4th ed. New York: Holt, Rinehart & Winston, 1968.

hillips, David C. *Oral Communication in Business.* New York: McGraw-Hill, 1955.

hillips, David C., and Lamb, Jack Hall. *Speech as Communication.* Boston: Allyn & Bacon, 1966.

ahskopf, Horace G. *Basic Speech Improvement.* New York: Harper & Row, 1965.

edding, W. Charles, and Sanborn, George A. *Business and Industrial Communication: A Source Book.* New York: Harper & Row, 1964.

eid, Loren. *First Principles of Public Speaking.* 2d ed. Columbia, Mo.: Artcraft Press, 1962.

____. *Speaking Well.* Columbia, Mo.: Artcraft Press, 1962.

ogge, Edward, and Ching, James C. *Advanced Public Speaking.* New York: Holt, Rinehart & Winston, 1966.

oss, Raymond S. *Speech Communication: Fundamentals and Practice.* 2d ed. Englewood Cliffs: Prentice-Hall, 1970.

t. Onge, Keith R. *Creative Speech.* Belmont, Calif.: Wadsworth, 1964.

amovar, Larry A., and Mills, Jack. *Oral Communication: Message and Response.* Dubuque: William C. Brown, 1968.

andford, William Phillips, and Yeager, Willard Hayes. *Principles of Effective Speaking.* 6th ed. New York: Ronald Press, 1963.

arett, Lew; Sarett, Alma Johnson; and Foster, William T. *Basic Principles of Speech.* 4th ed. Boston: Houghton Mifflin, 1966.

cheidel, Thomas M. *Persuasive Speaking.* Glenview, Ill.: Scott, Foresman, 1967.

hrope, Wayne Austin. *Speaking and Listening: A Contemporary Approach.* New York: Harcourt, Brace & World, 1970.

mith, Donald K. *Man Speaking: A Rhetoric of Public Speech.* New York: Dodd, Mead, 1969.

oper, Paul L. *Basic Public Speaking.* 3d ed. New York: Oxford University Press, 1963.

trother, Edward S., and Huckleberry, Alan W. *The Effective Speaker.* Boston: Houghton Mifflin, 1968.

hompson, Wayne N. *Fundamentals of Communication: An Integrated Approach.* New York: McGraw-Hill, 1957.

erderber, Rudolph F. *The Challenge of Effective Speaking.* Belmont, Calif.: Wadsworth, 1970.

alter, Otis M., and Scott, Robert L. *Thinking and Speaking.* New York: Macmillan, 1968.

eaver, Carl H. *Speaking in Public.* New York: American Book, 1966.

Weaver, Carl H., and Strausbaugh, Warren L. *Fundamentals of Speech Commur cation.* New York: American Book, 1964.

Wilson, John F., and Arnold, Carroll·C. *Public Speaking as a Liberal Art.* 2d e Boston: Allyn & Bacon, 1968.

Zimmerman, Gordon G., and Duns, Donald F. *A Guidebook to Public Speakin Philosophy and Practice.* Boston, Allyn & Bacon, 1964.

Collections of Speeches, Source Books, Supplementary Materials

Aly, Bower, and Aly, Lucile. *American Short Speeches.* New York: Macmill 1968.

Arnold, Carroll C.; Ehninger, Douglas; and Gerber, John. *The Speake Resource Book.* 2d ed. Chicago: Scott, Foresman, 1966.

Baird, A. Craig. *American Public Addresses: 1740-1952.* New York: McGra Hill, 1956.

Berquist, Goodwin F., Jr. *Speeches for Illustration and Example.* Chicago: Sco Foresman, 1965.

Black, Edwin, and Kerr, Harry P. *American Issues: A Sourcebook for Spee Topics.* New York: Harcourt, Brace & World, 1961.

Borden, George; Gregg, Richard; and Grove, Theodore. *Speech Behavior a Human Interaction.* Englewood Cliffs: Prentice-Hall, 1969.

Bosmajian, Haig A. *Readings in Speech.* New York: Harper & Row, 1965.

——. *The Principles and Practice of Freedom of Speech.* Boston: Hought Mifflin, 1970.

Braden, Waldo W., ed. *Speech Methods and Resources.* New York: Harper Row, 1961.

Brandt, Carl G., and Shafter, Edward M. Jr. *Selected American Speeches Basic Issues.* Boston: Houghton Mifflin, 1960.

Carlile, Clark S. *Project Text for Public Speaking.* rev. ed. New York: Harpe Row, 1962.

Crocker, Lionel. *Rhetorical Analysis of Speeches.* Boston: Allyn & Bacon, 19

Gibson, James. *A Reader in Speech Communication.* New York: McGraw ᴴ 1971.

Hildebrandt, Herbert W. *Issues of Our Time.* New York: Macmillan, 1963.

Laser, Marvin; Cathcart, Robert S.; and Marcus, Fred H., eds. *Ideas and Issu Readings for Analysis and Evaluation.* New York: Ronald Press, 1963.

Linkugel, Wil A.; Allen, R.R.; and Johannesen, Richard L. *Contempor American Speeches.* 2d ed. Belmont, Calif.: Wadsworth, 1969.

Lomas, Charles E. *The Agitator in American Society.* Englewood Cliffs: Pr tice-Hall, 1968.

Reid, Ronald F. *An Introduction to the Field of Speech.* Chicago: Sc Foresman, 1965.

Schwartz, Joseph, and Rycenga, John A. *The Province of Rhetoric.* New York: Ronald Press, 1965.

Scott, Robert L. *The Speaker's Reader.* Glenview, Ill.: Scott, Foresman, 1970.

Steinberg, Charles S., ed. *Mass Media and Communication,* vol.1 of *Studies in Public Communication.* New York: Hastings House, 1965.

Stewart, Charles J., and Kendall, J. Bruce. *On Speech and Speakers: An Anthology of Writings and Models.* New York: Holt, Rinehart & Winston, 1968.

Thonssen, Lester, ed. *Representative American Speeches.* New York: H. W. Wilson, annual.

Thonssen, Lester, and Finkel, William L. *Ideas that Matter: A Sourcebook for Speakers.* New York: Ronald Press, 1961.

Wrage, Ernest J., and Baskerville, Barnet. *American Forum: Speeches on Historic Issues, 1788-1900.* Seattle: University of Washington Press, 1969.

_____. *Contemporary Forum: American Speeches on Twentieth-Century Issues.* Seattle: University of Washington Press, 1962.

Radio, Television

Abbot, Waldo, and Rider, Richard L. *Handbook of Broadcasting: The Fundamentals of Radio and Television.* 4th ed. New York: McGraw-Hill, 1957.

Chester, Giraud; Garrison, Garnet R.; and Willis, Edgar E. *Television and Radio.* 3d ed. New York: Appleton-Century-Crofts, 1963.

Griffith, Barton L., and MacLennan, Donald W., eds. *Improvement of Teaching by Television.* Columbia: University of Missouri Press, 1964.

Hilliard, Robert L., ed. *Understanding Television: An Introduction to Broadcasting.* New York: Hastings House, 1964.

Lawton, Sherman P. *Introduction to Modern Broadcasting: A Manual for Students.* New York: Harper & Row, 1964.

Starlin, Glenn. *Speech Communication Via Radio and TV.* Dubuque: William C. Brown Co., 1969.

(*Note.* The Television Information Office, 745 Fifth Ave., New York, N.Y. 0022, issues a monthly leaflet on Television Highlights.)

the alleviation
of speech tension

It was with awe as well as eagerness that I braced myself for the supreme ordeal. . . . I need not recount the pains I had taken to prepare, nor the efforts I had made to hide the work of preparation.

Sir Winston Churchill

I have sometimes had a wish to speak, but . . . dreaded exposing myself, . . . and remained in my seat, safe, but inglorious.

Edward Gibbon

ʼhen students reflect on the contributions of the speech course, they are likely ᴑ report a considerable gain in the ability to think, to create, to deal with ideas ᴉd attitudes. They are also likely to note specific details growing out of their ᴉastery of the art of communication. Somewhere along the line they will ᴋobably comment on their own gain in poise and self-confidence. Though ᴉudents are more assured and forthright than those of a generation ago, they are ᴉlled upon to face situations of increasing variety and complexity and many ᴉfferent kinds of confrontations; the speech class can provide experiences that ᴉll help those who feel ill at ease to overcome their difficulties.

The phenomenon that used to be referred to as *stage fright* is now described ᴉ some of the research literature, newer texts, and course syllabi in different ᴉrms: *speech tension* or *speech anxiety*. This terminology has a freshness to

115

commend it as well as greater accuracy. Teachers also find themselves using the word *reticence*. Little reason exists for abandoning the term *stage fright* altogether; it is strongly rooted in lay usage and is generally familiar to students. Many teachers feel that by using the newer terms, at least occasionally, they may be able to put the discussion on a more objective plane.

Teachers have many approaches to the problem of helping students to manage the tensions that grow out of communicating to groups of listeners. One approach is to discuss the problem at length: explain what it is like, how it affects different people, what degree of severity is exhibited, to what extent self-assurance can be gained by experience. This explanation may be nontechnical in nature, using the language of the layman, or it may be wrapped in terms familiar to those who study the psychology of emotion. Personality tests, schedules, or inventories may be administered. Another approach is not to treat speech anxiety systematically at all; the teacher may answer questions that anyone cares to raise, or give an occasional word of counsel, but not go beyond that point.

Whether or not the instructor gives specific instruction about managing tension and anxiety, he needs to plan his syllabus with the problem in mind: he will begin with simple performances, moving only slowly to the more difficult types; his criticisms and suggestions will be encouraging; he will undoubtedly avoid talking too much about transient mannerisms. He may give the class opportunity to discuss the overall problem with him.

The following suggestions should help to either plan an informal lecture or as background material to guide a class discussion.

Common Experience

Many people experience tensions arising out of communication situations. Floyd I. Greenleaf surveyed 384 students at the University of Iowa and found that 6 percent reported themselves as severely bothered by stage fright, 45 percent as moderate, and 33 percent as mild. Only 16 percent reported no stage fright. A questionnaire administered to 789 students at the same institution revealed the following list of symptoms: dryness of throat or mouth, forgetting, excessive hesitation, inability to finish, tension in the abdominal region or stomach upset, weak voice or inability to produce voice, stuttering or stammering, speech rate too fast or slow, tremors of knees and hands, excessive perspiration, accelerated heart rate, difficulty in breathing, inability to look at audience, feeling that audience is disapproving.[1]

Some of these symptoms have been measured experimentally. In a fundamentals course at Redlands University, investigators arranged a situation in

[1] "An Exploratory Study of Stage Fright," *Quarterly Journal of Speech,* October 1952, pp. 326-330.

which a hundred students, fifty men and fifty women, each gave a three- to five-minute extemporaneous talk. At the conclusion of his talk each student, instead of returning to his seat in the classroom, was asked to step into the adjoining anteroom before rejoining the class. In the anteroom his pulse rate and blood pressure were taken by a registered nurse. The pulse and blood pressure rates were measurably affected even by the making of this fairly routine speech in more than 90 percent of the speakers; obviously good and poor speakers alike were affected. In a related experiment, these measurements were taken before the speech and even greater pulse fluctuation was observed.[2]

A few hours after they had talked to their speech sections, four hundred and twenty men and women enrolled in a beginning public speaking course were asked to select statements that best described their experience in talking before the class. The figures represent the percentage of the total group that selected the statement:

I am in a state of nervous tension before getting up to speak. (70%)

It is difficult for me to search my mind calmly for the right word to express my thoughts. (57%)

Fear of forgetting causes me to jumble my speech at times. (40%)

My voice sounds strange to me when I address a group. (37%)

Only 6 percent of the group reported that speaking in public was "a pleasurable experience unaccompanied by any doubts or fears."[3] Kim Giffin and Kendall Bradley, who have carried on considerable research into speech anxiety at the University of Kansas, report that more than a fourth of the students they surveyed were more than "just bothered" by lack of skill or experience in speaking.[4]

Stage fright is not limited to stages and platforms, but is found on athletic fields, in operating rooms, and a hundred other places where human beings have listeners and onlookers. It is a universal human experience. The anxiety that an individual suffers before a performance, and perhaps while he is going through it, has a counterpart in most fields of endeavor. Football players, amateurs and professionals alike, are tense before an important game. Professional musicians are nervous before a concert, even when playing a program they have presented many times before. Surgeons become apprehensive before a critical operation. People who want to borrow money, or apply for a job, or sell a short story, have

Milton Dickens and William R. Parker, "Physiological, Introspective, and Rating-Scale Techniques for the Measurement of Stage Fright," *Speech Monographs,* November 1951, pp. 251-259.

Howard Gilkinson, "Social Fears as Reported by Students in College Speech Classes," *Speech Monographs,* 1942, pp. 141-160.

Kim Giffin and Kendall Bradley, "Group Counseling for Speech Anxiety: An Approach and a Rationale," *Journal of Communication,* March 1969, pp. 22-29.

described themselves as walking around the block repeatedly before they finally generated enough courage to enter the building. The common element seems to be either the lack of experience in the particular situation, or the presence of an audience or its equivalent; sometimes both elements appear.

Many eloquent speakers had to struggle through depths of fear and anxiety before they mastered the art of public address. The disastrous maiden speeches of Sheridan and Disraeli are known to students of British oratory. History will record that Britain's greatest orator during the first half of the twentieth century was Winston Churchill—who, as a young member of Parliament, meticulously prepared several possible lines of thought, so fearful was he that he might have to debate something which he had not previously studied. To him the preparation of a speech was "a vulture in the sky." Mark Twain once said that if he were going to be hanged he would know he could make a good showing, but he was not always so confident that he could make a successful speech.

The problem also arises with actors and actresses on stage and TV, with radio performers, and others. Theater history is filled with instances of performers who virtually had to be dragged on stage the opening night, so frightening was the prospect of facing the audience out front. Radio and TV performers also have their share of nervousness. The quiet and still of the soundproofed radio studio shatters the aplomb of the average person. The engineers working at their control boards do not seem so comforting as the faces of a live audience; and the microphone itself seems a forbidding instrument. Many radio performers solve the problem by inviting a studio audience to supply the needed person-to-person contact. A TV studio presents its own psychedelic atmosphere. The dazzling lights overhead, the cameras stealthily gliding about yet always keeping the great glass eye toward the front, the distractions caused by members of the crew waving signs and pointing at this and that, the added responsibility that comes when the performance is taped, all give the performer a unique tension.

A survey of university professors who had occasional public lecturing experience in addition to their regular teaching, revealed only two persons who did not report some early speech tension. Bryan, describing his fear during the Cross of Gold speech, later said that only the knowledge that he had a good conclusion kept him going. Governor Leslie R. Shaw, a notable stump speaker at the turn of the century, and a member of Theodore Roosevelt's cabinet, said: "If a man doesn't get nervous, he is going to make a poor speech." Henry Ward Beecher was one of the eloquent pulpit orators of the last century. For forty years he drew nearly three thousand people each Sunday morning and each Sunday evening to hear him preach at Plymouth Church in New York City. Yet on occasion, he testified, as he entered the church and walked toward the pulpit, he prayed that the Lord would strike him down so that he would not have to preach. Exceptions appear, especially among those who are constantly called upon to speak in public. In his abstract of the Knisely dissertation, Milton Dickens had these observations to make about the sixty prominent contemporary public speakers investigated:

. The average experienced and successful speaker had stage fright in at least a part
»f his speaking activity, but the reactions were mild and occurred infrequently.

:. The only factor which seemed to coincide consistently and positively with
he decrease of stage fright among these speakers was that of frequent and
egular speaking experiences.[5]

Undoubtedly, even a hardened lecturer who can face a run-of-the-mill,
opular audience week after week without a tremor, would find anxieties
eappearing if he had to make an unusually important speech before a critical
udience.

It will therefore be helpful, after the first round of speeches, to inquire which
peakers had speech tension, what kind, and to what extent. Probably the great
najority will report in the affirmative, even those who seemed self-confident. If,
owever, you asked each student to write on a slip of paper the names of his
lassmates he thought were scared, the list will be short. Often a student who
eports feeling a good deal of anxiety is surprised to learn that most of his
lassmates observed little or no tension. Caleb W. Prall used sixty-one speech
eachers and graduate students to check observable degrees of anxiety; he
oncluded that judges underestimated student fears more frequently than they
verestimated them. Paul D. Holtzman, using three groups of nonexpert judges,
lso found that the observations of the judges did not agree with the reports
nade by the speakers themselves. These studies show that speech tension does
ot show nearly so much as students usually think.[6]

A certain amount of anxiety is probably essential to the best speaking
erformances. Speech tension may not be necessary for a good classroom
·cture, since that, for the teacher, may be a routine performance. It may not be
ecessary for a good popular lecture, since that for many experienced lecturers is
lso fairly routine. But once in a while a teacher or a popular lecturer gets
orked up; he has a message of uncommon import; and if on these special
ccasions the speaker delivers not merely a good but a brilliant speech, his
peaking was probably accompanied by a little tension. Experimental evidence is
eing reported that does not entirely support this point of view, but it neverthe-
·ss persists as a belief among teachers of speech. The problem therefore
ecomes not to eliminate the tension, but to control it.

Related to Experience. Students in a beginning public speaking course,
·hether in high school or college, show wide variations in the amount of
revious speaking experience they have had. Interviews with hundreds of
tudents at the University of Missouri who had done poorly in a simple test
volving the making of a short talk show that almost invariably they had had

Speech Monographs, June 1951, pp. 124-155.
·rom unpublished doctoral dissertations, University of Southern California. Quoted by
    Edward R. Robinson, "What Can the Speech Teacher Do About Students' Stagefright?"
    Speech Teacher, January 1959, pp. 9-10.

little speechmaking activity. They had not participated in assembly programs, debates, or plays; they seldom if ever gave oral reports in class; they had usually not been officers of organizations; they had not been members of groups that offered opportunities for speaking. Accordingly, the making of a talk even on a simple subject was a somewhat new and strange experience.

Three Forms of Speech Tension

Speech tension takes three forms. One may be described as *audience tension:* the speaker is keyed up, but his voice is under control and his fluency is unimpaired. An advanced form is *audience fear:* the speaker is so nervous that his voice or his train of thought falters, or both. A third form is *audience panic:* the speaker cannot face the group at all, or if he begins his speech, he breaks down and quits before he has gone very far.

Audience Tension

A student may therefore ask himself the question, "What form of tension do I have?" (Some students may feel they have all three!) Although there is physiological similarity in bodily chemistry as one goes from excitement to fear and back to excitement again, much practical difference exists between audience *tension* and audience *panic.* The difference in speaking experience may be a score or a hundred speeches. Audience tension may have these symptoms: nervousness, excitement, an increase in the pulse rate, a feeling of constriction in the throat or chest or stomach, trembling of the hands or knees. After the speaker gets under way he feels much less apprehensive; in fact he may feel quite in command of the situation. It may then be said of him as Gorgias said of Socrates: "Socrates, you have an unusual attack of fluency."

Audience Fear

The second form, properly described as audience *fear,* is something of a different sort. Here the individual undergoes one or more symptoms that actually make his speaking deteriorate. His voice may become squeaky, his words may sound muffled, his flow of ideas may falter. The list of sensations is a familiar one. Often there is a pounding of the heart, a thumping as ominous as if the speaker had run several blocks to make his speaking engagement, taking the platform before he had a chance to recover his wind. Knees wobble and hands become shaky and moist, or hot and dry. Inhalation and exhalation are accomplished with difficulty. The tongue becomes parched and the mouth dry, so that the speaker needs to drink quantities of water, without ever quite being able to get his speech mechanism properly cooled and lubricated. The feeling in the stomach is miserable: Irvin S. Cobb must have had what we call audience fear in mind when he described how a man feels "when he has a speech turning around in his system and is wondering whether it is going to come sloshing out, rich in proteins and butterfats, or just clabber inside of him and produce nothing but a thin whey."

The speaker who suffers from audience fear is a man abandoned by the gods. The expectations of the ordeal are terrible enough, but the actual performance is worse. He wants to stop, but he has to go on, and reveal his suffering in the presence of witnesses. He may stumble over his first sentence; he may mispronounce words; he may lose control of his voice; he may make a foolish statement like "Mr. Chairman" when he means "Madame Chairman," or commit a spoonerism like the mayor who introduced the President: "Ladies and gentleman, the President of the United States, the Honorable Hoobert Heever." A fortunate wretch may eventually get control of himself, and finish without further difficulty. Or he may have to fight the demons throughout his entire address.

Audience Panic

Audience *panic* is an entirely different order of experience. This person may not even be able to read to an audience from a manuscript, or stand up and tell his name and address, or say a few words about a profession which he has followed for years. Even if he is cajoled to the front of the room and catapulted by bogus flattery into beginning a speech, he may break down before a few sentences are finished and be compelled to retire. This severe type of reaction is becoming increasingly rare, at least in college classrooms.

Speech Tension Can Be Alleviated

Various studies show that speech tension can be modified, lessened, and generally made manageable through the experience of a speech course.

Stanley F. Paulson administered the Gilkinson Personal Report on Confidence as a Speaker to 271 students enrolled in a speech course at the University of Minnesota. After ten weeks of speech training they again filled out this report. Bell Adjustment inventory scales were also utilized. Moreover, another group of fifty-six students filled out the Gilkinson form before and after giving a speech to a section other than their own. Among the conclusions were: (1) Both men and women showed significant increases in confidence during the ten-week course; (2) the improved confidence tended to remain even though they spoke to an audience composed of strangers.[7]

Edward R. Robinson, in a useful article, cites a number of experimental

"Changes in Confidence During a Period of Speech Training," *Speech Monographs,* November 1951, pp. 260-265.

studies. The Leyden study cited reported that "the experimental group receiving speech training showed significant improvement in . . . social behavior." The Hayworth investigation of 850 students showed that, even with differing methods of instruction, anxiety was alleviated, and that for that purpose many short speeches were better than fewer long speeches. The Garrett study concluded that "students should have training and experience in the classroom." Robinson also cited studies by Moore, Rose, Edwards, Eckert, Keyes, and others, and concluded: "Almost without exception studies which have tested specific methods for the development of confidence have shown that repeated performances will increase confidence."[8] A small class participating in an experiment at Northern Illinois State College reported extreme nervousness during the first speaking performance and practically no fright in the final speech.[9] Using a novel test administered before and after a speech course, Paul D. Brandes concluded that the beginning course reduced the anxiety of students toward situations where fear of speaking was involved.[10]

Ways of Managing Speech Tension

If students are successfully to be taught to manage their apprehensions and anxieties, by far the first requisite is that the teacher develop an atmosphere in his classroom that is cordial and relaxing. People do not think or speak well when they are under too much tension. An ingredient of classroom strain is the feeling that the ever-watchful teacher, seeing all and hearing all with his eagle eye and his lynx ear, will confront the student with a classified list of faults as soon as the performance is finished. By his very attempt to offer constructive criticism, the teacher may defeat a part of his own purpose.

The delicate aspects of the art of criticism will be saved for a later chapter. So far as stage fright is concerned, this principle is worth stating right here: students accept criticism better after they have developed confidence than they do while they are still feeling uncertain and insecure. Undoubtedly, therefore, comments based on the beginner's first speeches, or readings, should be generous and reassuring. Pick out the individual's strong points, and, by commending them get them firmly established as speech habits. Some of his faults will correct themselves as he becomes less nervous, or as he watches others, or as he profits

---

[8]*Speech Teacher,* January 1959, pp. 10-11. *See also:* the review article by Theodore Clevenger, Jr., "A Synthesis of Experimental Research in Stage Fright," *Quarterly Journal of Speech,* April 1959, pp. 134-145. Clevenger concludes that the stage fright an individual feels, the stage fright an observer sees, and the physiological disruptions that can be recorded by a meter, are three variables that are fairly independent.

[9]Louis Lerea, "The Verbal Behavior of Speech Fright," *Speech Monographs,* August 1956, p. 233.

[10]Paul D. Brandes, "A Semantic Reaction to the Measurement of Stage Fright," *Journal of Communication,* June 1967, pp. 142-146.

y your lectures or demonstrations. After he has conquered some of his first xperiences, you can begin to make your criticism more specific.

Charles R. Gruner reported the number and percentage of New York students /ho checked factors in the speech course that caused reduction in their own ensions and anxieties. Items most checked were:

Factor	Number checking	Percent checking
Practice	101	89.4
Enlarged understanding of speech	75	66.4
Attitude of instructor	62	54.9
Attitude of classmates	62	54.9
Better understanding of self	53	46.9
Understanding nature and causes of speech fright	52	46.0
Increased liking for speech	39	34.5
Feeling of having done well as a speaker	32	28.3

le commented particularly on the attitude of the instructor and the attitude of lassmates, and thought that the high response to "understanding nature and auses of stage fright" was the result of discussions by the teachers on this opic.[11]

The Gruner study, an earlier study by Ernest Henrikson that he cites, and the iiffin and Bradley study referred to earlier in the chapter, all stress "attitude f classmates" as an important factor in lessening speech anxiety. Giffin and radley particularly refer to the importance of the listener as a variable in the peech-anxiety complex, not only as a member of an audience, but as an idividual with whom the speaker has an interpersonal relationship. They wrote:

> One's view of oneself as a communicator necessarily requires feedback from other people. If the feedback is negative and indicates to a person that his social self is inadequate, he will fear and tend to avoid communication situations.

s a part of his teaching procedure, therefore, the instructor should encourage avorable comment from members of the class about one another. Assurances rom one's peers that his general speaking behavior is moving in the direction of oise and self-confidence help build the speaker's self-image. In addition to what

Charles R. Gruner, "A Further Note on Stage Fright," *Speech Teacher,* September 1964, p. 223.

the teacher can do in class to stimulate peer approval, he may find some ways outside of class. If he hears John praise Jack, and Jack is not within earshot, he may say to John, "Tell Jack that, won't you, he'll be pleased that you valued his speech." Sometimes when I seem to have a difficult problem with a student, I take another student into my confidence, and ask him to contribute a private word of encouragement. All of us have to work through as many channels as we can. The researches and surveys already cited indicate that some students are reached one way, some another.

Speech tension can be reduced in other ways. For example:

1. *Use humor.* Beginning speakers usually take themselves too solemnly. Lincoln, Ingersoll, Wilson, Roosevelt, Churchill, Kennedy, and most other great speakers and teachers had an unfailing sense of humor. Tension and anxiety cannot exist in the presence of laughter. A speaker need not tell a funny story; a turn of phrase, an illumination of a situation, are all sufficient to break the ice.

2. *Relax.* Most people feel that trying to relax physically helps immeasurably. Before you face the audience, take some bending and stretching exercises. Draw a few deep breaths; yawn a few times; move about. These activities should add to your physical, and therefore to your mental, well-being.

3. *Have a message.* Speakers must talk on subjects they are personally concerned about. They must be alive, enthusiastic, mentally on fire. When the speaker is over his depth, when he is paraphrasing an article instead of probing his own study and reflection, when his imagination breaks down before the task of intriguing his hearers in the facts to be presented, when his intellectual resources are shallow, then the setting for stage fright is 100 percent complete. Facts are not dull; facts are dynamic, exciting, persuasive. The dullness lies in the inferior selection, interpretation, application, or presentation.

This point is important to keep in mind. Often when a student breaks down in a speech, an important part of the trouble is that he is trying to talk on an unfamiliar topic. He might talk very stumblingly and hesitatingly about national defense, but be notably fluent about the generation gap.

4. *Don't take the situation too seriously.* Advice like this needs to be dispensed cautiously, of course, as one should always try to do his best in every situation. The simple fact remains, however, that student performances are not a do-or-die matter. The world will not cave in if the speaker stumbles over a word, or even if he runs howling from the classroom. The other students are primarily too worried over their forthcoming performances to be too critical of the person who happens to be, at the moment, in front. The student who sets too high a standard for himself is compounding his own misery.

5. *Organization.* The human listener has limitations. The speaker should boil his ideas down to four or five main points; two or three are even better. Let these main points represent the quintessence of the case. Disregard the rest; save them

or another day—or better, use them if the audience asks questions. Sam Jones, a popular platform humorist, used to say, "My speeches are like a train. First I roll out the locomotive; then I attach as many cars as the occasion requires; and when the end of my time approaches, I hook on the caboose." For a beginner, two or three boxcars are plenty; and he should be sure to have a caboose handy, or he won't know how to stop.

. Use visual aids. If a speaker can provide himself with something to handle or demonstrate, he will usually feel more comfortable. Use a map, to which you can relate the main points of your talk; or a series of charts, on which the principal ideas or key words are displayed; or the actual object itself, which you can explain part by part.

. Conviction. A speaker must have the courage of his convictions. For illustrations, read John F. Kennedy's *Profiles in Courage.* Even if his purpose is merely to explain, and not at all to induce belief, he needs the self-assurance of knowing what he is talking about. Students should avoid discussing topics that they know little about or that they do not fully believe in. They should have the powerful conviction ascribed to the Southern orator: "I will debate secession, suh, with man or devil, suh, at any time or in any place; and what I lack as a speakuh, suh, will be more than made up by the subject."

. Rehearsal. It is easy to forget to remind students that rehearsal is a good preventive for anxiety. Tell the student that after he has planned his speech he should take himself to his room and say the speech aloud. He may discover that he has planned ten minutes, whereas the time limit is supposed to be five; he can therefore eliminate part of his speech and thus make his task easier. Moreover, he will become accustomed to hearing himself talk, which will take some of the strangeness away from the actual speaking situation itself. Many, many experienced speakers give time to rehearsal. Recall the story of Gladstone, who was overheard walking in his garden one evening, saying, "I had not intended to address the House tonight, but the remarks of the honorable gentleman . . ."

It is silly to be reticent about rehearsing a speech. Try the talk out on a roommate, a date, or a spouse. Practicing a speech is in the tradition of rehearsing a play, a concert, or other public performance. Go behind stage just before the curtains go up, and you will see actors and actresses going over lines or practicing business. Visit a radio or TV station, and you will see the announcers reading their scripts or cue cards aloud just before they go on the air. Great piano players practice the afternoon before a concert. Football and basketball players toss the ball around right up to game time. Only a beginning speaker would make the mistake of giving his listeners a first-time-through speech. You will, of course, need to tell the student that the purpose of rehearsal is not to memorize words, but a sequence of ideas and examples.

. Seek experience. The good speakers are experienced speakers. A speaker may have to make a certain number of speeches against his inclination in order to prepare himself for the speeches that are important. Edward Everett advised the

young man who asked the secret of oratory: "Whenever anyone is foolish enough to ask you to speak, you should be foolish enough to accept." A sure way to help students control stage fright is to give them repeated experience in speaking.

10. *Giving a speech can be exciting.* Perhaps we talk too much about speech *worries* and too little about speech *rewards.* A good speech can be an exciting experience. The ability to hold an audience in your hand, even if only for moments, as you tell a story that has suspense, pursue a cogent argument clearly and vividly, lead by reasoned steps to an irrefutable conclusion, win the respect of your adversaries for your viewpoint, is well worth the time and worry of preparation.

11. *Be alert to the student's progress.* In dealing with speech tension, the teacher should not forget what he has learned about reinforcement. A good observer will note even slight progress and be alert to praise any degree of improvement. Sometimes a student will ask, "Did you notice whether my organization (or choice of strategies, or range of materials, etc.) was better? I've been trying to improve it." Such a question as this helps to see what the student's immediate goals are. If the student does not initiate such a dialogue, the teacher can ("Is there some question you want to ask us about your speech?"). Obviously any specific kind of improvement that you or the other students can observe and praise, helps to deal with the general problem of anxiety.

12. *Avoid adding to the problem.* Regrettably, speech tension is sometimes abetted by the teacher himself. Perhaps he has had so little experience with actual speechmaking that he cannot truly fathom the inner turmoil of the student. Perhaps he is overly critical, and in a way that inhibits rather than stimulates. This kind of obstacle is frequently reported in the literature. It should not be exaggerated, however. The actual situation is undoubtedly something like this: most teachers are successful with most students; some teachers can reach a larger majority of their students than others can; no teacher can wholly reach out to every student.

13. *Be sensitive to the student's self-concept.* Students sometimes present difficulties that are not easily resolved with the usual resources of the classroom. Their self-concept, shaped over the years by family, neighborhood, and previous school experiences, may be subjected to further influences in your classroom. A black student in a class of white students, or vice versa, may have not only the usual difficulties of any beginning speaker but others growing out of his special relationship to the class. It is not necessary to detail these: economic differences, attitudes, social dialect, the simple fact that he is a minority of one. Far less complex, no doubt, is a lone girl in a class of boys, an adult in his forties in a class of eighteen-year-olds, an exchange student from a foreign country. In situations like these a teacher must redouble his efforts to capture the student's point of view. A personal conference may be indicated.

I prize the experience of having taught on different campuses. At Hawaii many students were of Oriental background. Teaching overseas for the University of Maryland brought all sorts of situations because of the mix of students found on an American military base: military and civilian, private and colonel, male and female, races and nationalities, military specialties. In one class was a sole commuter from a base fifty miles distant; twice a week he drove that distance in order to meet the speech requirement and thus earn his diploma. He was a commissioned officer in his late twenties; his work was commendable, ranking him in the top fourth of the class. After the last meeting of the term he lingered for a chat, saying that one of the gratifying aspects of the class had been that the other students had accepted him. I was surprised. "Why shouldn't you have been accepted? You are an American, like the others, serving the country overseas; you are the same age as many of the others, and have had a comparable military experience." "Yes," he explained, "but I am the stranger; I came from a different base." If this relatively slight difference bugged one bright student, think what the feelings might be when differences are vastly greater.

One student suffered genuine audience panic; he was unable to speak before the class at all. A German who had joined the American forces in order to become a citizen more readily, he had spent a long time in a concentration camp and had endured its brutality. His English was understandable but just barely. Nothing I could say could get him to his feet. I enlisted the help of his classmates who knew him out of class, but they could not convince him that other students were sympathetic and understanding. I could not even persuade him to continue in the course as a nonparticipant. His first thought was to drop out of school altogether, but we managed to persuade him to transfer to another course where there was little likelihood that he would need to make an oral presentation. Later my student accomplices and I decided that all we could claim was that we had done him no harm; our resources were too slender. Maybe we softened him up so that a day might still come when he would be more amenable to some other speech teacher.[1 2]

4. *Take a speech course.* The evidence is impressive that the practice one gains in a speech course helps the student to overcome a large share of his difficulties. Many students insist that this improvement is an important contribution of the course.

Approaches that Do Not Help

Certain approaches, used principally by laymen, are of little real help and may actually be harmful.

[2]H. Bedford Furr reports a preliminary study in which a course in business speaking contributed to improvement of the self-concept in (probably) personal, social, and moral-ethical realms ("Influences of a Course in Speech Communication on Certain Aspects of the Self-Concept of College Freshmen," *Speech Teacher,* January 1970, pp. 26-31). *See also:* Ernest G. Bormann and George L. Shapiro, "Perceived Confidence as a Function of Self-Image," *Central States Speech Journal,* Autumn 1962, pp. 253-256.

"Pick out a friendly person in the audience and talk to him." This advice frequently appears in print, but is not good doctrine. Every member of an audience likes to feel that the speech is addressed to him; this attitude is reenforced if he can catch the speaker's eye now and then. To speak to a single person is fine for that person, but not helpful to others present.

The advice is especially ridiculous when applied to a group conversation or conference. An individual who addressed his remarks only to one person would lose communication with the rest of those present.

"Look just over the heads of your listeners." The idea behind this fraudulent counsel is that if the speaker can avoid looking directly at any one person, he will be less embarrassed. Those who offer this advice apparently feel that listeners will *think* the speaker is looking directly at them; any teacher can demonstrate in half a minute that this supposition is fallacious.

The best place for the speaker to look is into the eyes of his listeners. Instead of being embarrassed by them, he is likely to receive friendly encouragement: a thoughtful countenance, a generous smile, a nod of agreement, are part of the feedback that is heartening to the speaker.

"Say repeatedly to yourself, 'I'm a better man than they are, I'm a better man than they are.'" Again, this puts the speaker into the wrong mental attitude. What he should be saying repeatedly to himself, as he begins a speech, are the opening words of his talk: once he gets them safely launched, his problem of anxiety begins to recede.

You may find it entertaining to relate these theories in order to put your own more thoughtful approach in better perspective.

The Teacher's Own Experience

The foregoing comments may be helpful in counseling students. As years go on, you will become better able to advise beginning speakers. You will yourself need to gain two sorts of experience: first, that which comes from repeated conversation with beginning and experienced speakers, to learn their ways of managing their nervousness; and second, and more important, the experience that comes from the speaking you yourself do. One who frequently goes through the actual business of addressing an audience can best appreciate the beginner's problem.

As a counteroffensive against the beginner's fear, you should remind him again that communication, whether speaking or acting, before a microphone or not, is a stimulating human activity. The approval of an audience is rewarding. To have an audience absorbed in what you are saying is an outcome for which your preliminary apprehension is a modest price to pay.

Assignments

1. Extend your reading about speech tension in the newest available references. Consult recent issues of *Speech Teacher, Speech Monographs, Journal of*

Communication, or other sources listed in *Education Index, Psychological Index.*

Questions for Classroom Discussion

. Discuss your own experiences with speech tension as speaker, reader, actor, announcer. Compare these incidents with similar experiences in other fields: athletics, journalism, business, social situations. Enumerate devices that have helped you, mentioning particularly counsel or suggestion received in the classroom.

. What amount of time should be spent discussing speech tension in the classroom? Will full and complete discussion of symptoms and manifestations of speech tension overemphasize the problem, or help students to understand and thereby overcome it?

. Tell the class about examples of extreme speaking behavior that have come to your attention.

References

peech tension has been given systematic study by teachers of speech. Much experimental investigation is currently being conducted. The following references will be helpful to those who want to make a thoughtful study of the problem. Many textbooks on public speaking also contain helpful advice (see the list accompanying Chapter 4).

ormann, Ernest G., and Shapiro, George L. "Perceived Confidence as a Function of Self-Image." *Central States Speech Journal.* Autumn 1962.

randes, Paul D. "A Semantic Reaction to the Measurement of Stage Fright." *Journal of Communication* June 1967.

levenger, Theodore Jr. "A Synthesis of Experimental Research in Stage Fright." *Quarterly Journal of Speech* April 1959.

levenger, Theodore Jr., and Phifer, Gregg. "What Do Beginning College Speech Texts Say About Stage Fright?" *Speech Teacher* January 1959.

ickens, Milton; Gibson, Francis; and Prall, Caleb. "An Experimental Study of the Overt Manifestations of Stage Fright." *Speech Monographs* March 1950.

ickens, Milton, and Parker, William R. "An Experimental Study of Certain Physiological, Introspective and Rating-Scale Techniques for the Measurement of Stage Fright." *Speech Monographs* November 1951.

urr, H. Bedford. "Influence of a Course in Speech-Communication on Certain Aspects of the Self-Concept of College Freshmen." *Speech Teacher* January 1970.

iffin, Kim, and Bradley, Kendall. "Group Counselling for Speech Anxiety: An Approach and a Rationale." *Journal of Communication* March 1969.

reenleaf, Floyd I. "An Exploratory Study of Stage Fright." *Quarterly Journal of Speech* October 1952.

runer, Charles R. "A Further Note on Stage Fright." *Speech Teacher* September 1964.

Henrikson, Ernest H. "Some Effects on Stage Fright of a Course in Speech." *Quarterly Journal of Speech* December 1943.

Low, Gordon M., and Sheets, Boyd V. "The Relation of Psychometric Factors to Stage Fright." *Speech Monographs* November 1951.

McKinney, Fred. *Psychology of Personal Adjustment.* 3d ed. New York: John Wiley & Sons, 1960. Chap. 14, "Emotional Stability"; Chap. 15, "Self Confidence."

Paulson, Stanley F. "Changes in Confidence During a Period of Speech Training." *Speech Monographs* November 1951.

Robinson, Edward R. "What Can the Speech Teacher Do About Students' Stage Fright." *Speech Teacher* January 1959.

improving voice, articulation, and other elements of language

Though the full articulation of words is necessary, to count and number, as it were, every letter, is disagreeable.

Quintilian

he teacher needs to offer instruction in a cluster of elements relating to language: voice, articulation, pronunciation, syntax, word usage. The capabilities f his students will range all the way from severe handicap to elegant talent, rom the grossly inarticulate to the eloquent.

At the outset the teacher needs to make decisions about the spectrum of ifficulties that he will attempt to manage, in and out of class. These decisions epend on his own resources and on those provided by the institution. He may fer certain kinds of problems directly to the speech clinician, if there is one; ith these problems his own instruction will be in support of the clinician's commendations. If there is no clinician, he will have to do what he can on his wn. Systematic instruction in grammar falls in the domain of the English class, ough the speech teacher will lend a hand as occasion presents itself. He is not xpected to deal in depth with syntax or vocabulary though here again he can ffer useful generalizations.

With each passing year, the speech communication class contains a wider riety of student needs and aptitudes. College teachers are told that entering

students, judging by tests of aptitude and achievement, are increasingly bette
prepared. At the same time colleges are admitting students with good potenti
whose backgrounds, because of home, family, and neighborhood condition
have not exposed them to the same quality of education. High school an
elementary school teachers similarly face this problem. Disadvantaged student
may be put in an especially exposed position because the dialect that they fin
entirely serviceable at home is not nearly so communicative at school. Socic
linguist Roger Shuy observes that to the teacher "their speech may seer
careless, inconsistent, or awkward. But in fact, the children are being ver
careful, consistent, and graceful within the dialect they know."[1] Hence th
teacher should know a little about the reason for variations in dialect; he shoul
also be able to recognize these variations. This chapter offers basic suggestion
and points to additional reading.

The Speech Clinician

We start with the speech clinician. Like practitioners in other parts of th
discipline of speech communication, his tradition is ancient and honorable, goin
back at least as far as the Greeks. In the course of their investigation into th
principles of effective communication, classical rhetoricians had proceeded but
little way before they discovered the individual with difficulties of voice an
articulation. They observed voices that were weak, thin, harsh, and in other way
not only unpleasant but unserviceable. They noticed differences in dialec
Gorgias of Sicily, for example, charmed the Athenians because of the foreign a
of his articulation. Other problems of articulation like the feeble *rho* or th
garbled *lambda,* they found less charming. They also puzzled over difficulties c
inhalation and exhalation: too much or too little breath, wheezy intake of ai
droplets of saliva sprinkled over near bystanders, and other sorts of nois
components that interfered with clarity of communication. Their notions c
therapy were vague and indefinite: diet and exercise were freely prescribec
They also had various sorts of aphasias and other organic disorders, but posse
sors of such ailments were tossed over the nearest cliff. Better methods are no
available, both to the classroom teacher and to the speech pathologist.

Over the last two decades the increase in the number of professionally traine
speech clinicians attached to public school systems has been tremendous. In th
fifties, the national conventions of the American Speech and Hearing Associ
tion attracted a few hundred teachers and clinicians; in the seventies attendanc
reached a few thousand. If you find yourself teaching in a school with a sta

[1] Quoted by Barbara Sundene Wood and Julia Curry in "Everyday Talk and School Talk c
the City Black Child," *Speech Teacher,* November 1969, p. 283.

linician, you should refer students with speech difficulties to the office for
diagnosis and treatment. If your school does not have such a person—and the
demand outweighs the supply—you will need to use your own resources. In this
situation, the suggestions of this chapter may be helpful. Many should be useful
to teachers of subjects other than speech.

Teachers who have not studied clinical methods often do not know how
specific the clinical approach is. Not having been trained to listen to details of
sound and voice, they can only judge the total effect. A clinician will make a
mental list of defective sounds, if any, whereas someone else can at best make
only general such observations as "indistinctness," "words swallowed," "mush in
the mouth."

The speech survey procedures in Appendixes A and B should be of help even
to those without much clinical training. By listening to sentences and focussing
attention on specific sounds, the teacher may observe those that are defective,
provided also standards of normal articulation are well fixed in mind.

The classroom teacher needs a practical viewpoint for managing a speech
defect. His own training and the ever-present problem of class load, time, and
energy determine the kind and amount of clinical help that he can give. Another
consideration is the student himself: his interest, talent, and future vocation. A
serious defect for a student with professional ambitions may be trivial for one
who would never use speech in an artistic way.

Procedure for Managing Problems of Articulation

In managing problems of articulation, the teacher may proceed as follows:

Ask the student to repeat. This simplistic method is the ancient approach of
family and friends. It reminds the student that he has misgauged the size of the
group or the acoustics of the room. A more impressive way is for the teacher to
say, "Did everybody hear that?" And when hands appear, "They didn't get it
over there," thus giving the student an idea of the distance over which to project
his voice. Or if the student said, "I read a book by mmfmmph," the teacher can
say, "You read a book by whom?" thus giving him credit for part of his
utterance but not for the uncommunicated fragment. Some general observations
may also be pertinent: more energy is required to recite in class than to converse
with a single individual, a proper name or technical term introduced for the first
time needs to be spoken with extra care, a communicator should not let his
voice weaken nor his precision of articulation fail at the all-important end of the
sentence.

Demonstrate the student's problem to him. If the simplistic method does not
work, and it may not succeed the first time, the teacher will need to give the
student further insight. The student must *hear* what he is doing improperly. A

tape recorder is invaluable in these situations: through the playback the studer
can hear his own voice. If, for example, he repeatedly mumbles the closir
words of sentences, the tape will demonstrate the fact. Or he may be vocalizir
pauses excessively. If a recorder is not conveniently at hand, the teacher ma
need to demonstrate the problem. Often the applicable principles can better b
brought out inductively, by class discussion, than by the teacher's categoric;
statement.

If the problem involves one or more sound substitutions, the procedure
more detailed:

Demonstrate an acceptable way of making the sound. Have the student watc
and listen as you make, for example, an *"l."* When the sound seems to b
mastered in isolation, try it in syllables—*lee, lah, lo,* etc.—and then in simpl
words: *late, line, let,* etc. Test not only the initial but the medial and fin;
positions: a student who says "way" for *lay* may be able to pronounce the *l* i
feel without difficulty. From words proceed to phrases or sentences.

If a student speaks a word unacceptably, like "fwight" for *flight,* you ma
interrupt him, pronounce the word correctly three or four times, and ask him t
repeat it; with that stimulus, he may be able to go on without difficulty. Or yo
may need to go back to a simpler stimulus, like *lie* or *light,* which are similar t
but easier to say than *flight.* Again, utilize a tape recorder.

Let the student *see* how the sound is made. So far you have used primarily a
auditory stimulus: you may also use a visual stimulus by letting the student se
you make the sound. The *l,* for instance, is made with the tip of the tongue hel
against the gum ridge, the tongue relaxed so that the sound comes out over th
sides. The student who says "fwight" for *flight* is using his lips, thus producing
w, instead of an *l.*

Use other senses. On occasion you may use a tactual or kinesthetic stimulu
A student who says "berry" for *very* is using both lips instead of touching h
upper teeth to his lower lip. You may need to tuck his lip under his teeth with
tongue blade or other instrument in order to help train him to curl the li
unaided.

Speech pathologists advise that the student make as many different kinds o
responses as feasible instead of letting the teacher do the work for him. Let th
teacher speak *flight-fwight,* the student responding whether the two are alike o
different; the teacher then continues with *fwight-fwight, flight-flight,* and othe
variations. Focus his attention on your lip and tongue action (you can grossl
exaggerate visual features and still produce the sound) and let him indica
whether the pairs are alike or different. Let him utter paired sounds and als
indicate whether they are alike or different.

Use repetition. After a student has learned to make the sound correctly, h
should be encouraged to repeat it a few times so as to fix it in mind. Th

ocedure is ordinary good sense. Sometimes ask him to say it both the new way
d the old way in order to emphasize the new skill. Time is required in order to
ake the new habit automatic. The student easily relapses into old habits. If,
wever, he can produce acceptable sounds at will, he has made a good
ginning.

Speech pathologists have devised numerous games and other approaches to
proving speech. These play methods are useful in teaching younger children. If
u find yourself becoming interested in this area, you should plan to take a
urse. Many universities offer a course for the classroom teacher in methods of
eech correction.

Sounds that Prove Troublesome

ggestions for dealing with some of the most troublesome sounds are given
low.

Consonants

s-z

Test sentences: Some of the ball bats are missing.
The zeal of the player was amazing.

Even at best *s* and *z* are noisy, characterized by friction. Three types of defect
common: the whistling *s* or *z,* like that employed by older persons with
ntures; the substitution of *th* for *s* or *z,* as in "thum" for *some* or "amathing"
amazing; and the lateral *s* or *z, bats* and *zeal* sounding like "batsh" or
heal." The *th* for *s* substitution can often be corrected by a moderate amount
drill, but the other faults are more difficult to improve and will require many
actice sessions. Students with certain foreign language backgrounds may un-
ice the *z,* i.e. substitute *s* for *z.*

th[θ, ð]

Test sentences: Both of the thin men were affected by ether.
Either breathe in this way or give up swimming.

English is one of the few languages in which *th* sounds occur. Speakers of
ench, Spanish, Russian, and Oriental languages are likely to say "dees" or
es" for *this* and "deze" or "zeze" for *these.* The correct position of the
gue is easy to demonstrate: the tip should touch lightly the lower edges of
upper front teeth. A fairly acceptable classroom pronunciation can be
ured in short order, but if the sound is prevalent in the community the
dent will continue to use the dialect of his contemporaries and elders.

f-v

Test sentences: Frank was laughing at the giraffe.
Vera and the other wives are leaving.

The *f* and *v* sounds can usually be articulated without difficulty, except among younger pupils, who may substitute *p* or *b* for *f* and *v*. *Vera* thus becomes "bera" and *leaving* becomes "leabing." If you study your own speech mechanism and note how in producing the sounds your upper teeth touch your lower lip, you may be able to help the student acquire the correct sounds by instructing him to imitate you.

k-g

Test sentences: The class brought a sack of candy to the circus.
The big man is lagging behind the man with the gun.

Three pairs of consonants, *p-b, t-d,* and *k-g* are known as stop or plosive consonants. Of the six, two are likely to cause difficulty for younger students. The childhood tendency to say "tat" for *cat* and "dod" for *dog* may persist into the higher grades. Sometimes a student who has no difficulty whatever with *cat* or *corner* may say "tlass" for *class.* One who substitutes *t* for *k* or *d* for *g* trying to make the tip of his tongue do what the back of the tongue normally does.

A fairly common difficulty with this group of sounds is the tendency to explode or aspirate them too lightly, so that the speech lacks distinctness. Or to put the matter another way, if the articulation seems lazy and careless, these sounds may be among those at fault. There is a difference between *mine* and *mind,* between *boy* and *Boyd,* between *miss* and *mists,* between "Babtist" and *Baptist,* between "twenny" and *twenty.* The sounds should not be over-stressed but they should be articulated clearly enough to make words distinct.

zh [ʒ]

Test sentence: He had a vision of a new garage painted azure.

The *zh* sound does not occur frequently; most of the instances in which it does occur are in words of French origin. Although the second *g* in *garage* is often pronounced with the *g* of *gem,* preference exists for the *zh* sound. *Rouge, azure, beige,* and many *-sion* words like *vision* call for the *zh* sound.

l

Test sentence: Leo heard the bell tolling in the loft.

The l sound is a lateral consonant, so called because with the tip of the tongue held against the upper gum ridge, the sound waves are emitted over the sides of the tongue. The most common substitution is of *w,* so that *Leo* would sound like "weo" and *loft* like "woft." Oriental students may substitute *r* for *l.*

r

Test sentence: The writer drove over the road himself.

The *r* is one of the last to be mastered by the child learning to talk; some childhood difficulties may still persist into the high school and college years.

ove, for example, may sound like "dwove." A famous member of Roosevelt's ɔinet liked to discuss "wecipwocal twade agweements." If the student substi-
:es a lip sound, he will produce "twy" and "kwy" for *try* and *cry.* Students of
·eign language background usually substitute a different variety of *r* for the
glish *r.* It is not easy for one with an *r* from one language background to
ster the *r of another.*

m, n, ng [ŋ]

Test sentences: The man attempted to move his right arm.
No one knew what happened in the ninth inning.
Ring out the old, the chorus sang.

These three nasal consonants do not usually cause difficulty among students,
hough organic obstructions, like enlarged adenoid tissue, may block the nasal
ssageway and cause *man* to sound like *bad, inning* like "iddig." Faulty habit
y product the same effect. Vowel sounds, especially those preceding or
lowing nasal consonants, may themselves be nasalized. Improvement of a
sal voice therefore usually begins by making good vowel sounds even when
re are nasal consonants in the word. [n] may be substituted for [ŋ], as in
ɪnin' " for *inning.* [ŋg] may be substituted for [ŋ], as in "ring gout" for *ring*
t.

w, wh [ʍ, hw]

Test sentences: Will fixes the wagons in the winter.
The white foxes howl when he whistles.

Some students, principally in the East, do not distinguish between the
ɔnunciation of *where* and *wear, what* and *watt, whale* and *wail,* and similar
ɪrs of words. Students of foreign extraction sometimes substitute *v* for *w* or
, so that *will, wolves, when, whistles* sound like "vill," "volves," "ven,"
stles." The difference in the saying of *v* and *w* or *wh* is easily demonstrated: *v*
abiodental, or made with lip and teeth, whereas *w* and *wh* are bilabial, made
th both lips.

Diphthongs

ai, ou, oi [aɪ, aʊ, ɔɪ]

Test sentences: I said fix the tire, not the fire.
No houses are built in the downtown district.
After much toil the men brought in the oil well.

A diphthong is a blend of vowel sounds: compare *ah* and *I, Don* and *down, all*
1 *oil.* When a student weakens the second element of the diphthong or
ɔstitutes a vowel for it, *tire* might sound like *tar, fire* like *far, down* like *Don,*
ʋ like *tall, oil* like *all.* Sometimes the diphthongs in words like *down town* are
ɪwled almost into a triphthong: "daeown taeown." Other variations, difficult

to represent with key words, also are heard in New England, parts of the Midd
West, parts of the Southwest, and other areas.

Vowels

i as in hit
e as in met
a as in man

Test sentences: He did not intend to hit the little boy.
In September Ned received a pen and pencil set.
He received a bad gash in the back.

Students of foreign extraction sometimes have difficulty with words like *di*
and *hit,* speaking them like "deed" and "heet." In parts of the Middle West a
Southwest *pen* and *pencil* sound like "pin" and "pincil," and *September* t
comes "Septimber." In certain metropolitan areas *bad* and *gash* may sound li
"bed" and "gesh."

Attention should be given generally to developing skillful enunciation of t
vowels. Most of the music of the voice lies in the vowels; accordingly, they ne
to be sustained in order to secure vocal resonance, but the process should not
overdone or the result will be artificial.

Voice Improvement

Teachers who want to give their students substantial training in voice improv
ment will need to plan as follows: discuss in class the basic requirements for t
production of good vocal tone; demonstrate helpful exercises; spend a fe
minutes periodically in class on a setting-up program; work out a simple for
whereby each student can keep a home record of his practice. If these conditio
are fulfilled, most students will be able to demonstrate notable improvement
voice in a semester's time.

You should not find it necessary to make a technical excursion with yo
students into the field of voice science. You will of course need to familiari
the class with such terms as *quality, pitch, loudness, duration,* so that they w
be able to interpret the voices around them. Since tone is produced on t
exhaled breath stream, a good supply of breath, steadily under control,
essential; since tone is initiated by the vibrating of the vocal cords (vo
folds), a good vocal cord impulse, free from unnecessary strain or tension, is
requisite; and since the final tone is the result of modification by t
resonating cavities, attention needs to be paid to the throat, mouth, and na
resonators.

You may be able to borrow from the physics laboratory a few pieces
apparatus in order to illustrate these principles. Tuning forks of different siz

th resonators, are helpful; the forks demonstrate pitch, and when a vibrating
·k is placed on top of a resonator, the increase in loudness helps to make an
portant point. If one of your students has a trombone or trumpet, have him
·duce various tones with the mouthpiece attached and unattached: the dif-
ences in quality will be striking. Turning the tone control knob of an ordinary
lio shows what happens when various frequencies are modified: the tone can
 made more or less boomy, as highs or lows are intensified or attenuated. The
st part of the demonstration, however, is that which can be made with the
'ferent voices in your classroom. Take a sound like "ah," and have each person
istrate the differences in quality, pitch, loudness, and duration.
Most students can improve if they give attention to the importance of
·aking with the best voice possible. One may easily fall into the habit of
·aking not quite loudly enough, or of lowering the pitch on the last words of
·tences, or of letting his voice get too high-pitched on the last words of
·tences, or of letting his voice get too high-pitched when he talks louder. Some
·too much air escape as they speak, making the voice breathy. Although the
·vice to slow down is too frequently given, many students would get better
cal results if they did speak more slowly. Other students talk in a monotone,
·king their ideas less commanding.

Voice and Personality

·e relation between voice and personality is an overriding consideration. The
·ice responds quickly to physical and emotional states: it is hardly conceivable
·t a forceful voice can come from one who is exhausted, frightened, or
·ef-stricken. Accordingly, one who is constitutionally tired, fearful, repressed,
 amused would reflect his prevailing mood in his voice. Do we not recognize,
 at least think we recognize, the voice of the girl who is afraid of her own
·dow, the neighbor who is a chronic complainer, the society matron who is
·d and haughty, the executive who is overly brisk and efficient? A student
·o has a weak voice therefore needs a little emotional underpinning as well as a
·v pages from the anatomy and physiology of sound production.
That is precisely why training in speaking, reading, and acting is so helpful in
·ice improvement: it helps generate the proper attitude for effective communi-
·tion with an audience, and thus bears directly upon the mechanics of voice.
·vertheless, the frontal attack on voice problems has its place, and is the
·mary consideration of this chapter.

Breathing and Relaxation

·ercises dealing with breathing and relaxation are fundamental to most kinds
·voice improvement.

Many texts are available which discuss in detail helpful breathing exercis
These few will help students to understand the principles involved:

1. Observe the differences between inhalation for normal breathing and inha
tion for speaking. The speaker inhales quickly, usually through the mouth. Nc
also the differences in exhalation when breathing normally and when speakii
The speaker exhales slowly, speaking on the outgoing breath stream.

2. Inhale, then sound the vowels *a, e, i, o, u,* on the outgoing breath strea
Control the breath at all times, so that the *u* sounds as clear as the *a.* Work
what the singer calls the legato style: smooth, even, sustained vowels. Vary t
exercise by uttering the vowels at the normal speaking rate. Continue to spe
each vowel in good voice, especially avoiding the common fault of lowering t
pitch too much on the last sounds uttered. (The teacher with training
phonetics will recall that the *a* as in *mate,* the *i* as in *line,* and the *o* as in hoi
are technically diphthongs.)

3. Do the same, counting from 1 to 10 instead of using the vowels.

4. Inhale, then exhale, making the sound *s-s-s.* See who in the class can susta
this sound the longest. Repeat, using other fricatives, like *z, f, v, th, sh, zh.*

5. Pronounce the following vowel sounds: *ee* (as in *meet*), *i* (as in *hit*), *e* (as
bet), *a* (as in *bat*), *a* (as in *palm*), *a* (as in *awe*), *o* (as in *home*), *oo* (as in *boo*
oo (as in *mood*). In making these sounds the front of the tongue and the jaw
progressively lowered from *meet* to *bat,* and the back of the tongue and the j
progressively raised from *palm* to *mood.* Beginning with *palm* and continui
through *mood,* the lips are progressively more rounded. Sound the entire ser
of vowels, trying especially to make a full tone.

Exercise material of this sort needs to be prepared in abundance. Gra
Fairbank's *Voice and Articulation Drillbook* is useful. *Communication Skil
Voice and Pronunciation* by Mardel Ogilvie and Norma S. Rees has live
sprightly, authoritative instruction and exercises. See these and other referen
at the end of this chapter.

Many other breathing exercises may be located in appropriate texts. In sor
instances the standard breathing exercises, unaccompanied by speech, may
recommended. If the student keeps a daily record of how many seconds he c
speak on the outgoing breath, he can discover whether he is increasing vi
capacity.

Relaxation exercises also find a place in voice improvement programs. It
difficult to relax directly and consciously the small muscles of the throat a
larynx involved in resonance, so the usual procedure is to approach the proble
indirectly by learning to relax the larger muscle groups of nearby regio
Achieving a general physical or emotional relaxation is also helpful. The object
not to relax every muscle, since some must be contracted in order to produ

und, change pitch, etc., but to relax opposing or interfering muscles, primarily
open and enlarge resonating areas.

Have each member of the class put his books to one side or on the floor, sit
pright in his chair, let his head fall forward, and allow his arms to hang loosely
his sides. Eyes should be closed, mouth slightly open. Complete silence should
evail for the duration of this exercise. The teacher should savor and relish this
oment, as wholly quiet intervals do not often occur in school.

Free the neck muscles of tension, so that the slightest push would toss the
ad from side to side. Let the arms hang lazily at the sides. Raise the feet and
gs and let them fall heavily to the floor. Try to clear the mind of troubles.

Turn the head first to one side, then to the other. Rotate the head slowly,
st to the left, then to the right. Move the head as far backward as it will go,
en forward. Lift your head up toward the ceiling, so as to stretch the neck.
est, then repeat.

With the head facing forward, open the mouth as wide as possible. With the
outh open, try to move the lower jaw in a circle: down, side, up, side. With the
w relaxed, say *yah, yah, yah; yaw, yaw, yaw.* Relax the throat by yawning.

An interesting demonstration is to have selected members of the class read a
w lines; then let the whole class practice breathing and relaxation exercises;
en have the same students read again. Usually improvement is noticeable: the
ercises tend to lower pitch and improve resonance.

Teachers may not want to take sufficient class time to go through the entire
gimen every day. A few repetitions may be desirable, if students can be
couraged to continue on their own. Work in new exercises every day, to avoid
onotony. This might be one of the long-remembered units of the course.
udents should also be reminded that breathing and relaxation have a beneficial
ysical value. For some kinds of nervous disorders, relaxation is specifically
cessary. People who have to work under heavy tension often keep themselves
ysically and mentally fit by a short period of rest and relaxation after the
onday meal.

Four Attributes of Voice

ou need also to turn your attention to the four attributes of voice: pitch,
udness, duration, quality. As pitch and loudness are the most readily identi-
d, start with them.

tch.   Improvement of vocal pitch involves two factors. One is that of getting
e voice in the right pitch range, or key; another is that of avoiding a
onotone.

The pitch of the voice is largely fixed by physical factors. Sopranos can n be transformed into altos, nor baritones into tenors. Fortunately the norm range of the human voice is about three octaves, so that if an individual voi can be placed within that range, it can be developed into something reasonab serviceable so far as pitch is concerned.

You need not assume, however, that the particular pitch range each student using is necessarily the best one for him. He may have allowed his voice become too high or too low. After demonstrating what pitch is, have ea student read two or three sentences at different levels. Select the one that see the easiest for him and that offers the best possibility for future improvemen If a piano is available, you may demonstrate the upper and lower limits of t pitch range that each student is using. Using a fairly open vowel like "ah" "oh," let each student utter it at as low a tone as he can serviceably produ then go up the scale by half tones until he reaches his upper limit. He may a work with slides, i.e., taking "ah" and speaking it on one pitch, then sliding upward or downward to a neighboring halftone, fulltone, tone-and-a-half, even more. An inflection of a full octave is not uncommon. Practice the inflections with words like *yes, no,* or phrases like *come here, go back, oh, r* and the like. From almost any dramatic selection you may choose two or th sentences containing emotional dialogue. Use these as drill materials in order bring out differences in pitch.

Most students find this sort of exercise helpful. Quite likely no one has ev shown them the capacities of their own voices for expressing ideas. A stude who has been monotonous in his conversation may get a deeper insight into t possibilities of his voice. The degreee of friendliness with which one says *hel* for example, is largely a matter of pitch. You will find students who ha devoted years to the giving of wrong impressions about themselves because th voices were lacking in the warmth, enthusiasm, and responsiveness that conventionally communicated by (largely) pitch inflections.

Modification of pitch should be under the supervision of a teacher; a stude may get into difficulty if he attempts too much self-improvement. Boys and gi sometimes try to lower their voices too much, thereby robbing themselves resonance and carrying power. One student developed a pitch much too low f her because she tried to sing alto in the choir instead of tenor. The direc needed another alto, and this student obligingly tried to remodel her voice. any of your students has any ambition to improve, he should do so while y can guide him.

Loudness.   Proper exercise will help almost anyone increase loudness a carrying power. Exercises similar to the following are used:

[2]*See:* J. Richard Franks, "Determining Habitual Pitch by Means of Increased Read Rate," *Western Speech,* Fall 1967, pp. 281-287. Reviews the methods of Fairbanks, V Riper, and others to determine optimum pitch. Suggests the use of rapid oral reading the point of using a monotone, and then assuming that monotone to be the speake habitual pitch.

Take the class into a large room. Give each student a passage to read (a) in a hisper, (b) in a loud voice that will reach the back of the auditorium, and (c) in voice that will reach the middle row. Have a third of the class in the front ws, a third in the middle section, and a third in the back of the room. Each observer should report on each performer. Some students may find that their voices do not carry as far as they expected; in other words, they are unable to dge their vocal power. After each student has had a chance to review the ports on his voice, let him try again, helping him judge his loudness by propriate signals from the auditorium.

A variation is to read a word, like *mortar,* while the listeners indicate whether ey heard *order, mortar, border,* or *water;* then another word, like *shut,* while s listeners check *shook, shout, shut, shot;* and so on.

Count from one the highest number you can reach in one breath, beginning th a whisper and increasing in loudness. Begin at the number reached and unt backward, gradually diminishing in loudness.

uration; Rate.   When we speak of the duration of a tone, we refer to the agth of time it is prolonged. We can say "o-o-o-oh," as when surprised, or aply "oh," as when disappointed. Duration is akin to rate; the longer individu- sounds are prolonged, the fewer words per minute, or the slower the rate. ot all sounds can be prolonged; it is hard to hold on to [p]). Long pauses tween words also slow down the number of words per minute.

Students naturally and normally take different amounts of time in making unds. Expressed in rate of words per minute, students may speak all the way om ninety to two hundred. No objection should be made to rapid speech, ovided the speaker is communicative. If the student speaks so rapidly that teners cannot always understand him, he needs to give attention to duration.

The best exercise is the simplest one of letting each student read a short ection or make a short talk. Discuss with him the matter of distinctness and e use of pause. You may very properly have much to say on the subject of using, as beginning speakers are invariably too hurried. The experienced eaker knows the value of emphasizing an idea by a moment of silence.

Variation in rate is as important as variation in pitch. When a speaker is king at his normal rate, and then suddenly slows down to clinch an important a, his audience feels the contrast in voice as a way of emphasizing the idea. ace a student learns to make effective use of duration and rate, he is not isfied again to speak like a metronome.

ality.   Improvement of voice quality is one of the challenging problems nfronting the teacher. Quality is the characteristic that distinguishes one voice om another when factors of pitch, loudness, and duration are similar. It is the sic tone of the voice. Appropriate descriptive words are *pleasing, mellow, ll-rounded, resonant, rich, full, melodious,* and the like. Less desirable voice ality is described by *metallic, muffled, breathy, nasal, denasal, hoarse, thin.*

The quality of a voice is the result of a complex blend of a basic soun the fundamental, and a series of overtones of progressively higher pitch. If tl fundamental tone vibrates at the rate of 128 cycles per second, the average pit of a male voice, the first overtone would vibrate at 256, the second at 384, tl third at 512, and so on by multiples of 128. As this blend of tones pass through throat, mouth, and nasal cavities, some overtones are amplified a' some are diminished. The improvement of voice quality is thus related to t' size, shape, and general condition of these cavities. To put the matter anoth way, voice quality is improved by adjusting, usually enlarging, the throat a' mouth cavities, and by regulating the amount of sound that goes into the nas cavity. The foregoing explanation is simplified; the problem is complex a' worthy of review by the teacher.

Relaxation exercises, especially of the throat and jaw, are helpful in impro ing quality. A study of the operation of the soft palate in opening and closi the gateway to the nasal passages is also valuable. Good vowel sounds contair degree of nasal resonance; lacking this resonance, they are somewhat dull, b' with too much they take on the thin, unpleasant sound of nasality. Since t' student cannot entirely trust his own ear in judging his voice, he needs to rely ' your ear and your artistic sense. Reading exercises in which the student som times tries to be harsh, sometimes shrill, sometimes as melodious and bell-like his sound production as possible, help him to explore the capacities of his voi'

Generally speaking, the improvement of voice quality calls for extensi amounts of artistic endeavor. Consider the relatively few opportunities that tl average boy or girl gets to improve vocally. He converses, recites, interview yells at athletic contests. None of these calls for much from the voice other th' enthusiasm and energy. Do many of your students take part in plays, read stori or the Bible aloud, take singing lessons, or sing in choirs? Are they called up' to interpret a poem orally, considered an exacting test of the capability of tl voice? If you can interest your students in taking part in extracurricul activities that call for the use of the voice, especially those where they recei some guidance or direction, you will forward their progress. Humming, singin reading aloud, even taking a spirited part in conversation, all have their place.

You may also discuss the care and hygiene of the voice. Excessive shouting not considered good; and the practice of continuing to yell even when hoarse especially harmful. Students sometimes show up in colleges with harsh voic that they date back to their cheering-squad days. Many conditions of sore thro also call for voice rest. Excessive use of tobacco or alcohol is harmful to go' vocal tone.

Standards

The question often arises about the proper standard or level of dialect suitab for educated Americans.

For decades linguistic geographers have mapped dialects, community by community and region by region, recording pronunciations and expressions common to a given area. Ten major regional areas have been defined: eastern New England, New York City, Middle Atlantic, Southern, western Pennsylvania, Southern Mountain, central Midland, Northwest, Southwest, North Central.[3] In brief, the dialect one chooses for himself should have a regional acceptability; the southern speaker will use the variety of southern speech that is acceptable to that region. Within that region he may use two or three different variants: a formal style in the pursuit of his own business or profession; more colloquial styles for informal use. All of these statements must be interpreted with good sense and judgment. One is more informal talking to a single customer than presenting an award at a company banquet. One is more formal talking to some customers than others. An individual has a message to get across, and does not want individual peculiarities of his own dialect to make it less clear or less convincing.

With respect to primitive languages, anthropologists argue that such a language is suited to its culture and meets the needs of those who speak it.[4] By analogy a dialect not in wide or general use can also be said to be suited to its culture and to meet the needs of those who prefer it. They can be happy with it and think it meddlesome of one to seek to alter it. These statements and judgments are all proper in a given context. Teachers, however, whether they teach speech, history, science, or golf, seek to increase the potential of each of their students. We operate in a society in which the individual is not class-bound, occupation-bound, or region-bound. He does not have to work at his father's trade nor live in his father's house. An individual may well find himself on a different social, economic, or cultural level from that of his parents. The dialect that seemed to meet his teenage needs may not entirely meet his adult needs. In the classroom a student needs to learn to see what his teacher sees, hear what his teacher hears, perceive what his teacher perceives. No one claims that the process is simple or easy, whether it involves acquiring a new dialect or new concepts of other sorts. Sometimes educational tasks are mastered although the student drags his feet all the way, fever raging and wounds bleeding. Many students will eventually outdistance their teacher, discovering relationships he never dreamed of, and thus society is able not only to hold its own but improve itself.

In some classes the problem of dialect will seem unimportant; the students already have habits of articulation, pronunciation, and syntax that seem appropriate to their vocational aspirations, so the teacher's problem will be one of modest proportions. In other classes the problem may be so severe that the teacher will want to devote a good part of the course to it. If he finds himself in Peace Corps, inner city, or similar teaching situation, he will need to meet the

---

For a detailed discussion *see:* C. K. Thomas, *An Introduction to the Phonetics of American English*, 2d ed.

See: Dell Hymes, "The Anthropology of Communication," in Frank E.X. Dance (ed.), *Human Communication Theory*, pp. 4-5.

problem in terms of student needs and aspirations. He may need informatio about the linguistic system employed by children of various racial and nation origins—the reasons underlying their sound substitutions and alterations. He ma need to pay attention to nonverbal features: sounds and tones (paralinguistics gestures, facial expressions, body stances and distances (proxemics). Observa tions of field workers show that lower-class children respond in short answers c monosyllables; they need to be reassured more frequently than others abou what the field worker really wants to know; they are more likely to use the fir or second person than the more generalized and abstract third person; the responses are generally more reticent, more passive; they need more encourag ment to participate. The implications for classroom instruction are obvious.[5]

In various ways the teacher can establish the point that each dialect has i virtues. In some situations "Her went to town" does the job better than "Sl went to town." A pronunciation deemed faulty in one situation may b elegantly designed for another. The usual approach is to urge students whos home dialect differs from school dialect to acquire another way of communic ting. The eagerness with which pupils will acquire another way depends in larg measure upon the image that they can see of themselves operating in a large economic, political, or social community. As a single example, note the increa ing number of black entertainers, athletes, office holders and office seekers, ar militants who can, on TV, demonstrate a flawless variety of one of the standa regional dialects (and who presumably, in other situations, could speak equal flawlessly a social class dialect).

Walter Loban writes:

Regional accent rarely causes serious educational or social problems. Or can speak standard English with a Texas, New England, Gulf Coast, or Gre Plains flavor, and be entirely acceptable to voters, clients, or customers. Wh does cause difficulty is social class dialect: pidgin, Cajun, Appalachian, Ozar various Negro dialects, and other variations spoken by poorly educated culturally different Americans.

He comments that these dialects differ enough from standard structure ar usage to cause problems in communication as well as in social and person relationships. To deal with such problems in school requires sound knowledg human values, and great delicacy, for human dignity and the self-image of th pupil are at stake. Because here we have, he continues, a fluid, open societ where individual worth counts for so much, yet language "still operates

---

[5]Frederick Williams and Rita C. Naremore, "On the Functional Analysis of Social Cla Differences in Modes of Speech," *Speech Monographs,* June 1969, pp. 77-102. See tl article itself for further discussion, specific examples, and additional references.

eserve social class distinctions and remains one of the major barriers to ossing social lines."[6]

Teachers should appreciate the positive advantages of social class dialect and t merely give lip service to it. In visiting various places in Hawaii, accompanied students, I was at times extricated from minor embarrassments, or given ompter service, when my student escort made a vigorous application of pidgin the situation. The problem also comes up in connection with students from reign countries who are presumably highly articulate in their own language. y experience in teaching students from Taiwan, for example, or Latin America, s to discover that often these students wanted only to learn enough about glish to get by, since they planned to return to their native countries and ere expected to speak little English. In this way they resemble students who efer their social class dialect and do not expect to pursue a career involving a ed for any other dialect.

Pronunciation

onunciation refers to the uttering of sounds in a traditional or conventional nner. A mispronunciation is not necessarily a speech defect; it usually dicates that the word was not learned correctly. *Scintillate* with the first llable as "skin" is a mispronunciation. But one who says "kewpon" instead of oopon" for *coupon* is only exercising personal preference.

The traditional approach to the improvement of pronunciation is to compile ist of frequently mispronounced words and drill the class on them. No doubt is plan involves a vast amount of waste effort, as there is little profit in rning to pronounce *marital, flaccid, acclimate,* and *conversant* if the student es not use any of the words in his speaking vocabulary. Assuming that the list words for class drill is well selected, the graver danger exists that the teacher y impose old-fashioned standards of pronunciation. The pronunciations you rned in your high school days of words like *apparatus, government, bouquet, rilegious, oleomargarine, presentation, program, educate,* and *secretary* may old-fashioned today.

Every teacher should develop an interest in the pronunciation of words. He ould routinely call the attention of every student to any word not pronounced ceptably. Pronunciation suggests all sorts of social and intellectual implications

Teaching Children Who Speak Social Class Dialects," *Elementary English,* May 1968, pp. 592-618.

A change from one dialect to another sometimes has undesirable consequences; the individual may become uncertain about his native dialect and overly conscious or overly pedantic in the use of the new dialect. *See:* Malcolm Lieblich, "Be Proud of Your Brooklyn Accent," *Today's Speech,* May 1969, pp. 53-54.

to the average listener. Any one who uses *alias, facade, protégé,* and *marital* suggests that he is a person of some intellect; but if he pronounces the second syllable of *alias* as *lye,* if the *c* of *facade* is pronounced like *k,* if *protégé* is in two syllables instead of three, and if *marital* comes out like *martial,* listeners just as immediately realize that the speaker is not so well educated in these matters as they at first assumed. Rightly or wrongly, we tend to assume that if a person mispronounces a word, he does not know much about the idea represented by that word. One who has spent years in musical circles will utter words like *concerto, pianissimo, fugue, aria,* and *ensemble* with accuracy and precision; conversely, one who fumbles with these words will be assumed not to know much about music.

Even if a teacher is not a trained clinician, he can insist upon sufficient accuracy of articulation to make meaning clear. It is difficult to imagine one saying *"speech* department" so hurriedly that the listener hears *"police* department," but muddled articulation, or careless listening, or both, will produce this amazing result. The customer did not understand the salesman at the auto supply store who spoke of *bouncing* the front wheels; what the salesman was trying to say was *balancing.* A visiting speaker giving a formal address in a notoriously old auditorium happened to say, "I am pleased to be here in famous old Dickens Hall," and was astonished when a roar of laughter greeted his words; what had happened was that his somewhat Southern pronunciation of *hall* sounded to northern ears like *hole.* Technical terms, proper names, and unusual words need to be uttered with care if the listener is to understand clearly. And if the speaker mumbles excessively, if he drops his volume at the ends of sentences, if he omits sounds or syllables, if he starts to pronounce a long word but loses interest in it half way through and lets the ending trail away, the hearers have to guess from the context what the obliterated words were. There is, therefore, a practical need for distinctness that all teachers should insist upon.

Pronunciation is made doubly difficult because English is not a phonetic language; that is, the spelling of English words does not always give an accurate clue to the pronunciation of these words. *Cough, through, though, enough,* and *hiccough* do not rhyme with one another. *Read* can be pronounced two ways, and *need, kneed,* and *knead* are pronounced identically. The *or* of *tailor* is pronounced *er,* and silent letters abound in *psychology, phthisis, gnat, wreck* and *sleigh.* Words like *one, busy,* and *women* do not make much sense phonetically. Few people pronounce accurately the twelve months of the year. *July* loses a vowel, *August* a *t.* So many other inconsistencies can be demonstrated that we should be much more charitable toward one another than we are.

In your teaching, seize the opportunity now and then to talk about pronunciation. Do not be any more dogmatic or prescriptive than you can avoid; when you hear variant pronunciations of *closet, with, orange, farm, horse, your thing, quay, idea,* and the like, find out from your students who uses what. The American language is growing and changing. You will be in a strong position you argue that there are regional and cultural variations in dialect, that each region and culture has its own levels of acceptable pronunciation, and that people who speak one standard regional dialect acceptably do not need to learn another.

Speakers of Foreign Language Background

Years ago while visiting in Boston I stopped at a subway ticket office to inquire when the next car left for Harvard. The elderly lady at the window took a quick glance at her assistant before she replied: "The next cah leaves for Hahvahd at half past fouh" [kaː], |haːvəd], |haːf paːst fovə]. As I turned to leave I overheard her say, "Talks funny, don't he?" Long afterwards I found myself in the little English town of Whitby, in northeast Yorkshire, on the North Sea, inspecting such tourist sights as the romantic remains of the Abbey and the statue of one of Whitby's distinguished citizens, Captain Cook. For souvenirs, I stopped at a little stand and asked for "three postcards, please." The clerk stared at me and said, "Are you from Australia?" "No," I replied, "from Missouri." "Ah," she continued, "I knew you were a stranger as soon as I heard your foreign accent." Back in the United States, I found myself in a Chicago hotel; I boarded an elevator and heard the dark-haired, dark-eyed girl call the floors: "one, two, t'ree"; that, to me, was foreign accent.

A *foreign language* is a language not yours, and a *foreign accent* is a way of speaking that is strange to you. Each language has a certain number of sounds constituting its sound system, and the sound system of one language differs in many details from that of another. An American learning French or German has difficulty with the *r* sounds of those languages together with a host of other difficulties, and as long as these persist, he will forever speak those tongues with a foreign accent. The reason is that he has to learn to utter a different kind of *r* as well as some other sounds new to him. On the other hand, a French, Spanish, or Oriental speaker will likely pronounce *fish* as "feesh"; a German speaker would do well enough with *fish,* but, along with the French and Oriental speakers, would have difficulty with any *th* combination. French, Spanish, and Italian speakers have difficulty with the vowel in *fish* as it does not exist in their languages. Frenchmen who cheered Woodrow Wilson as his car drove along the boulevards cried "Weelson! Weelson!" (Germans would have had no trouble with the vowel, but would have tripped on the initial consonant: "Vilson! Vilson!") When Eisenhower appeared, they called out: "Eek! Eek!" and their greeting to a later president was "Neexon!" Almost no "foreign" speaker can say "okay" or "Coca-Cola" as an American does. Oriental speakers often substitute *r* for *l,* or *l* for *r.* My Tokyo guide continually referred to me as his "crient," spoke of his "Engrish ranguage ressons," and once called attention to the "five o'crock lush our."

When learning a second language, or when trying to help one of a non-English background improve his English pronunciation, one needs this information about the other language:

1. What sounds are pronounced identically both in English and the foreign language?
2. What sounds are found in English, but not in the other language?
3. What sounds are found in the other language, but not in English?
4. What sounds in the two languages are basically similar but still have slight differences?

Speakers of other languages may have to learn one or more of the following English sounds: the vowel in *hit,* the vowel in *put,* the vowel in *bird,* the *th* in *thin* and *this,* the *ch* in *chat,* the *j* in *judge,* etc. (the list is not complete). A teacher working with a student of foreign-language background will need to prepare such a list for his own student, and add to it other sounds from the student's language which require some important modification. He then needs to give instruction in these sounds: in isolation, in words and syllables, in phrases, in simple conversation. Each language also has its own tune, or melody, or pattern of inflections; a British speaker, for example, will say "Did you go?" with a different inflection from that used by an American. The drill materials embodying phrases and simple conversation will need to consider melody therefore as well as articulation.

Serious Speech Handicaps

What advice can be given to the teacher who has in his class one who has serious breaks in fluency (usually called *stuttering*), severe foreign accent, cerebral palsy, or cleft palate? If the institution has the services of a speech clinician, the student can be referred to the clinic for special help. Only a trained person can make the proper study of such cases, as causes and symptoms vary from individual to individual. If you also have an opportunity to confer with the pathologist, you may receive valuable suggestions. Otherwise you should manage the student with thoughtfulness and consideration. Let the student contribute what he can to the class discussion, without the feeling of too much hurry or pressure. Moreover, study the problem in books listed in the references at the end of this chapter.

Final Word

The teaching of this unit presupposes a certain minimum of training on the part of the teacher in the fields represented. The material is exact and not easily self-taught. The teacher himself needs ear-training before he can fairly judge others; otherwise he may make decisions of doubtful value. If his training has not included course work or the equivalent in voice and diction, phonetics, speech correction, and speech therapy, he should handle this unit carefully and study the problem as he goes along.

Assignments

1. Review textbooks in voice and articulation and report on exercise and drill materials useful for (a) individual (b) classroom use. Refer to titles listed at the end of Chapter 4.
2. Report on speech correction programs currently in effect in various states. Consult recent issues of the *Journal of Speech and Hearing Disorders* for relevant articles.
3. Construct a unit on voice and articulation improvement for a course or segment of a course that you might presumably teach.

Questions for Classroom Discussion

1. Can you account for the apparent levelling off of interest in improving voice and articulation as a part of the college first course?
2. What are minimum standards for voice and articulation in public performance? in private communication?
3. Does the upsurge of concern for racial groups bespeak a modification of standards of acceptable regional speech?
4. What standards of pronunciation prevail in your community? Have you felt that your usual, normal dialect is acceptable in other parts of the country? Should a student develop two dialects, one for school, one for home?
5. How can students be motivated to embark upon a long-range program of voice and articulation improvement?
6. How can foreign students, who plan after their education in this country is completed to return to their home country, be motivated to develop the best possible American speech?

References

kin, Johnnye. *And So We Speak: Voice and Articulation.* Englewood Cliffs: Prentice-Hall, 1958.

llen, Harold B., ed. *Teaching English as a Second Language: A Book of Readings.* New York: McGraw-Hill, 1965.

ernstein, Basil. "Elaborated and Restricted Codes: Their Social Origin and Some Consequences," in Alfred Smith, ed. *Communication and Culture.* New York: Holt, Rinehart & Winston, 1966.

152   Teaching Speech

Black, Martha. *Speech Correction in the Schools.* Englewood Cliffs: Prentice Hall, 1964.

Bronstein, Arthur J., and Jacoby, Beatrice F. *Your Speech and Voice.* New York: Random House, 1967.

Byrne, Margaret C. *The Child Speaks: A Speech Improvement Program for Kindergarten and First Grade.* New York: Harper & Row, 1965.

Carrell, James. *Disorders of Articulation.* Englewood Cliffs: Prentice-Hall, 1967.

Carrell, James, and Tiffany, William R. *Phonetics: Theory and Application to Speech Improvement.* New York: McGraw-Hill, 1960.

Crocker, Lionel, "Teaching Public Speaking to Upward Bound Students," *Western Speech* Summer 1970.

Darley, Frederic L. *Diagnosis and Appraisal of Communication Disorders.* Englewood Cliffs: Prentice-Hall, 1964.

Ecroyd, Donald H.; Halfond, Murray M.; and Towne, Carol C. *Voice and Articulation, a Handbook.* Glenview: Scott, Foresman, 1966. Also: *Voice and Articulation: Programed Instruction; Voice and Articulation: Recorded Exercises* (7 discs).

Egland, George O. *Speech and Language Problems: A Guide for the Classroom Teacher.* Englewood Cliffs: Prentice-Hall, 1970.

Eisenson, Jon. *The Improvement of Voice and Diction.* 2d ed. New York: Macmillan, 1965.

Eisenson, Jon, and Ogilvie, Mardel. *Speech Correction in the Schools.* 2d ed. New York: Macmillan, 1963.

Ervin, Jean Conyers; Grundman, Mary Ellen; Peabody, Elizabeth A.; and Sterns Gladys M. *An Automated Program in Speech Therapy.* Washington: Institute of Modern Languages, 1966. Tapes also available for articulation exercises.

Fairbanks, Grant. *Voice and Articulation Drillbook.* 2d ed. New York: Harper & Row, 1960.

Finocchiaro, Mary. *Teaching English as a Second Language: In Elementary and Secondary Schools.* rev. ed. New York: Harper & Row, 1968.

Fisher, Hilda B. *Improving Voice and Articulation.* Boston: Houghton Mifflin 1966. (Tape to accompany book.)

Gordon, Morton J., and Wong, Helene H. *Manual for Speech Improvement.* Englewood Cliffs: Prentice-Hall, 1961.

Grasham, John A., and Gooder, Glenn G. *Improving Your Speech.* New York Harcourt, Brace & World, 1960.

Hahn, Elise; Lomas, Charles W.; Hargis, Donald E.; and Vandraegen, Daniel *Basic Voice Training for Speech.* 2d ed. New York: McGraw-Hill, 1957.

Hanley, Theodore D., and Thurman, Wayne L. *Developing Vocal Skills.* 2d ed New York: Holt, Rinehart & Winston, 1970.

Hejna, Robert F. *Speech Disorders and Nondirective Therapy.* New York Ronald Press, 1960.

Hymes, Dell. "The Anthropology of Communication" in *Human Communication Theory: Original Essays,* edited by Frank E. X. Dance. New York: Holt Rinehart & Winston, 1967.

Johnson, Kenneth. "Improving the Language Skills of the Culturally Disadvantaged." In *Teaching Disadvantaged Pupils*. Chicago: Science Research Associates, 1967.

Johnson, Wendell; Brown, Spencer F.; Curtis, James F.; Edney, Clarence W.; and Keaster, Jacqueline. *Speech Handicapped School Children*. 3d ed. New York: Harper & Row, 1967.

Jones, Merritt B., and Pettas, Mary. *Speech Improvement: A Practical Program*. Belmont, Calif.: Wadsworth, 1969.

King, Robert G., and DiMichael, Eleanor M. *Improving Articulation and Voice*. New York: Macmillan, 1966.

Loban, Walter. *The Language of Elementary School Children*. Champaign: National Council of Teachers of English, 1963.

——. "Teaching Children Who Speak Social Class Dialects." *Elementary English* May 1968.

Luper, Harold L., and Mulder, Robert L. *Stuttering: Therapy for Children*. Englewood Cliffs: Prentice-Hall, 1964.

Mayer, Lyle V. *Fundamentals of Voice and Diction*. 3d ed. Dubuque: William C. Brown, 1968.

Nash, Rosa Lee. "Teaching Speech Improvement to the Disadvantaged." *Speech Teacher* January 1967.

Ogilvie, Mardel, and Reis, Norma S. *Communication Skills: Voice and Pronunciation*. New York: McGraw-Hill, 1969.

Robinson, Frank B. *Introduction to Stuttering*. Englewood Cliffs: Prentice-Hall, 1964.

Thomas, C.K. *An Introduction to the Phonetics of American English*. 2d ed. New York: Ronald Press, 1958.

Van Riper, Charles. *Speech Correction: Principles and Methods*. 4th ed. Englewood Cliffs: Prentice-Hall, 1963.

——. "The Speech Therapist Speaks to the Communications Staff." *Speech Teacher* November 1958.

Van Riper, Charles and Butler, Katharine. *Speech in the Elementary Classroom*. New York: Harper & Row, 1955.

Van Riper, Charles. "The Speech Therapist Speaks to the Communications Staff." *Speech Teacher* November 1958.

Van Riper, Charles, and Irwin, John V. *Voice and Articulation*. Englewood Cliffs: Prentice-Hall, 1958.

Wells, Charlotte G. *Cleft Palate and Its Associated Speech Disorders*. New York: McGraw-Hill, 1971.

Wood, Barbara Sundene, and Curry, Julia. "Everyday Talk and School Talk of the Black Child." *Speech Teacher* November 1969. See the article itself for discussion and for additional references.

7

speechmaking: improving thinking

There is no way to make a good speech without having something to say.

James A. Winans

Thought is the fibre . . . of eloquence.

Woodrow Wilson

The point at which teachers of most disciplines join hands is in the effort to teach students to think. Such mental competencies as observing, analyzing, defining, classifying, interpreting, and relating are needed in all fields.

What kinds of thinking fall within the domain of our discipline? Mathematics, for instance, works with numbers and quantities, and their patterns and relationships. A mathematician's thinking might be improved by teaching him to discover new systems of numbers or quantities, or new patterns and relationships, which would enable him to solve problems that had previously been difficult or impossible. When, however, he discussed his discovery and tried to make it clear or persuasive, he would call upon, not principles of mathematics, but tools of communication.

The historian works with incidents, events, movements. He reads correspondence, journals, newspapers, official documents, records, and other testimony; he compares, contrasts, reflects, seeks motives. The historian is not content to record a list of incidents but seeks larger meanings. When he lectures and clarifies or interprets his thinking, he becomes part practitioner of the discipline of history, part practitioner of speech communication. Assuming the mathemati cian's thought and the historian's thought were worthy of consideration by others, it would be a grave social loss if both these scholars were naive or inep about principles of communication.

As soon as a mathematician or historian prepares his ideas for oral communi cation to others, he is likely to think as a practitioner of speech communication He may select, order, arrange, rearrange, amplify, expand, illustrate, work ove. the wording and phrasing, establish his credibility, reveal value judgments display his enthusiasm and conviction, remove or assuage doubts, relate to the interest and concerns of his listeners: these can all be seen to be major topic: in speech textbooks. By common consent, if he seeks to put his message ir writing, as a poem, play, story, or essay, he calls upon principles found in the domain of the teacher of English.

Hence when the teacher seeks to improve the thinking of his students, as it is to be displayed in their speeches, he addresses himself to such problems as the foregoing. He thinks of the communication model, source-channel-receiver, plu feedback, and tries to buttress the student's ideas at all points by using principles of communication. Selecting and arranging, putting into language, establishing the student's authority to speak on the topic, stimulating the attention of the listeners, all come within his purview. Since the language we are talking about is spoken language, he thinks of the student's voice and how it can express the student's enthusiasm and conviction. Since the spoken language is conveyed by a human body, he addresses himself to problems of gesture and action. Voice and action are, or should be, ways of communicating thought.

Since the teacher is first of all an informed citizen, he may have advice to offer about the *ideas* that student speakers bring to him and to the class from other disciplines. The student's mathematics may be at fault, or his history, and quite possibly the teacher or other students will do something about the quality of the speaker's thinking in his own discipline. These kinds of suggestions are, of course, happy byproducts of the classroom. The teacher has a basic and primary responsibility to see that the principles of his own discipline are made to operate effectively.

As has often been observed, principles of speech communication sometimes have more room to operate given a subject matter that is problematical, debat able, or complex. A statement like *John's roses won a ribbon at the state fair* offers only limited possibility for language refinement and audience adaptation. But our students are going to need to wrestle with mightier problems: war and peace, the nation's defense, commerce, taxation (to start with an older list), social and political liberties, religious freedom, personal morality (to continue with newer additions). They will need to exert wise leadership on these issues and they should address themselves to these matters while in school. The disci plines vested in these issues cannot solve them with their own discipline bound techniques; the body politic has to be consulted; this means narration, exposition, persuasion. All sorts of analyses, interpretations, confrontations, refutations, planes of emphasis, must be made before final policy decisions can be taken.

The problem of improving thinking is two-fold: to work within the discipline, and, so far as the teacher's breadth of information will permit, outside it. The latter is considered first.

We can begin to eliminate topics that are too trite or too simple for the student. Early in every teacher's career comes the day when he has heard one speech too many on "The Benefits of Athletics" (although Douglas MacArthur once made a magnificent speech to a West Point audience on the contributions of football), or "Our Trip to the West Coast" (yet nearly every issue of the *Saturday Review* contains a sophisticated travel article). At once the teacher ponders the problem of persuading students either to break out into loftier themes or to deal more satisfyingly with the simpler notions. Hazards lie in either direction. If he momentarily envies teachers of language, science, and social studies whose students give oral reports on their meaty outside readings and investigations he will learn from them that they often find themselves listening to dull, lifeless paraphrase that shows little personal reaction to, and minimum learning about, the topics being reported on. As has been observed, a high percentage of classroom reports pass from the reporter to the listener without going through the mind of either.

Hence the central problem: continually to extend the range and significance of subjects that students are able to discuss meaningfully and interestingly. (Confidential note to the reader: where your author writes "speech" or "report" you can freely substitute "conversation," "interview," or "group discussion"— perhaps even "theme," "book report," or "term paper.")

Ever since C.L. Shannon and Norbert Wiener published studies describing their mathematical theory of communication, scholars have given increasing attention to the amount of *information* in any given message. Information is something the listener did not previously know, or knew only imperfectly, and therefore something that hits him with a certain amount of surprise, excitement, or wonder. "Something the listener does not know" must be appraised in terms of the specific listeners out front; certainly they will not exhibit much delight, surprise, excitement, or wonder at hearing things they know very well.

Choosing a Topic

Where does a speech begin? It may begin with an audience, as when a program chairman says, "We want you to address the Rotary Club." It may begin with an occasion: "We want you to be the speaker at our annual awards banquet." It may begin with both: "Talk to the city council at its public hearing on Friday." The speech may have other beginnings, but the first task of the speaker is to choose a topic; and teaching him how to manage that situation is one of your critical teaching problems when you attempt to raise the standard of speech content. Similarly, the starting point for any other kind of oral performance, such as a report, is to stimulate the student to *search out a good topic*. The student must either exploit more significant subject matter, or present the usual fields in a more striking way.

How can you help students choose better subjects? One good answer can be given: sit down with each student individually and, in conference, explore the possibilities that confront him. You cannot give him topics, but you can discover his qualifications, and accordingly help him uncover interests that he may have passed over. You can learn about his talents, his hopes and ambitions, the range of his intellect, sympathy, compassion. His best subjects must be related to his own experience; he cannot talk very well about some other person's experience. In your conference you may be able to move the discussion through *general* subject to *specific* topic and perhaps even to concrete *supporting materials*.

In the speech class, as in other classes, exposing and uncovering the interests and experiences of students is not easy. A topic may be so familiar to a student that he is unable to realize its novelty. Imagine a girl, lithe as a willow wand, graceful as a bird. Her first talk on "The Newest Miracle Drugs" does not carry much conviction; conference reveals that she worked it up from a magazine article. She is a dancer, and her next talk on ballet, with its absorbing insights into this demanding art, is a high point in the class hour. Perhaps she urges us, teacher and students alike, to read Agnes de Mille's absorbing, brilliantly written book, *Dance to the Piper*.

In the field of history, a classic instance of student nearsightedness is the incident of a young woman who might have given a routine report on a nineteenth-century political figure. Inquiry by the professor revealed that she was a distant relative of an Iowa senator, whose descendants still had the senator's letters and manuscripts, so at the professor's prompting she turned to that topic with brilliant results.

All these examples are unusual, yet many a student must have gone to work on a second-best or third-best topic because of failure to explore all of the facets involved in making a choice.

If you are not able to have a conference with every student, you must do the next best thing; show the class the kind of questions you would ask if you did have a personal interview. Encourage students to dig into their own experiences. Give them examples of successful speeches you have heard from other high school or college students. A farm boy talks about mule-breeding; a former worker in nightclubs tells how the public is fleeced; a girl who worked in a reducing emporium tells how people are taught to take off weight; a boy who won a state chopping contest shows how to handle an ax; a sergeant back from Pacific regions tells how his patrol discovered an enemy cache; a boy of Apache descent discusses the economic plight of the Indian; an alumnus tells what was wrong with the job corps; a former NASA employee analyzes problems of space exploration; a Peace Corps volunteer explains the political situation in Nepal; a lifeguard demonstrates artificial respiration; a lepidopterist talks about collecting beetles; a boy who had not seen his father for ten years describes their reunion; an armored-truck driver's helper narrates the monotony of handling cash; a graduating senior pleads for loyalty to the alma mater; a baby-sitter reports hitherto unrevealed statistics; a girl presents evidence to show that women drivers are more reliable than men drivers; and so it goes.

A List of Suggested Subjects

This fine list of topics still will not help the student who cannot handle an ax or mount a beetle. One teacher kept a notebook on his desk in which he had written several hundred possible titles, adapted from textbooks in public speaking, his own experience as a teacher, and a dozen other sources. Typical entries in this notebook were the following, designed to reach the student who feels he has never done anything worth talking about:

1. The class has learned that you recently read a book. We extend you an invitation to speak to us about this book, telling us why we should (or should not) read it.

2. We understand you are well versed in lunar geology and geography. We invite you to interpret for us your revisionist theories about the origin of the moon.

3. Each member of the class is attempting to decide which particular profession or craft he should follow as a life career. We understand you have already reached a decision and should like to know the motives that influenced you.

4. Members of the class have been thinking about their schedule of courses and comparing the value of various classes. We have learned that you especially enjoyed a course in (blank) and are eager to know why you advise us to enroll.

5. It has been rumored that you have been dissatisfied with this institution. We invite you to air your views and tell us how you think the school should be run.

6. We understand that you recently attended a certain play. Will you appear at the next meeting and tell us why we should (or should not) attend this performance?

7. The class has learned that you have definite opinions upon the subject of segregation (or socialism, church attendance, the next election, the international situation, ecological imbalances). We invite you to discuss these opinions and tell us why you believe as you do.

8. Members of the class have been discussing instructors they have had during their academic career. We have learned that you have a favorite. We urge you to tell us the qualities of personality and methods of procedure that made this teacher effective.

9. We have been led to believe that you have made a special study of the influence of the military-industrial complex in the United States. We would be interested in hearing your analysis.

10. Certain instructors are holding examinations in their courses next week. From your experience with examinations, have you discovered new evidence as to their value?

From any standard textbook on public speaking you may read to your class other lists of subjects. Turn the pages of a dozen textbooks until you locate good lists of topics; take them to your class, and use them as examples of what other students have talked about.[1] You may, however, spend a whole class hour talking about subjects for speeches and offering many examples, but still not reach some student. At the end of the hour he is as puzzled as ever. Nothing in his experience seems related to speechmaking. Accordingly he falls back upon the method made traditional by thousands of beginning speakers: he reads a magazine article and decides to speak about it. To make the situation as bad as possible, let us suppose he ventures to talk about "Deep Sea Diving."

Is the situation irretrievable? You would need a large sheet of paper to list the errors wrapped up in this single decision of his. Has the speaker ever seen a deep sea diver? No. Has he previously read about deep sea diving? No. Did the article awaken a former, though slight, interest in deep sea diving? No. Has the class shown interest in the topic? No. Yet on occasion a student, using skill in selection, arrangement, and adaptation, can make a magazine article interesting, though the practice of using one single source is, as a general rule, discouraged. Deep sea diving as a subject contains novelty. Oceanography and ocean exploration are matters of public interest and concern. The student may avoid plagiarism by giving credit to the magazine, and if he familiarizes himself with the ideas, but uses his own language, he may be able to recapture for his listeners the excitement of the original article. He may not, either; but he certainly would have been no better off discussing the benefits of athletics.

The illustration leads into another problem of choosing a topic. Sooner or later students find their fund of personal experiences and interests exhausted and then have to go afield for new materials. When a student does find himself talked out, when his own experiences no longer seem to contain anything amazing, he especially needs to consult the library. He may look in public speaking textbooks, or he may pick up a volume of the *Readers' Guide to Periodical Literature:* the list of titles given there may enlighten him. Warn him again, however, of the danger of making his speech merely a summary of a single magazine article.

---

[1] *See:* Raymond S. Moss and Margaret Davis Barto, "Choosing Controversial Speech Subjects," *Speech Teacher,* March 1956.

Speeches on Current Topics

ne should probably not plan a speech without first asking himself the question, Is anything special or significant currently happening about which I am quali-ed to speak?"

Events in the news constitute an urgent source of topics. A student who can xplain the significance of what is going on in the Near East or in Africa, or why 1ere is an epidemic of plane crashes, or why the faculty is justified in lowering 1trance requirements, commands attention from those who want to be better 1formed. If a student by virtue of his own training or background cannot be 1fficiently authoritative, he can enhance his position by explaining that he 1ade a special point of gaining the information by reading or interview, or both. uch topics as "Alaska's North Shore," "The San Andreas Fault," "The Current tatus of NATO," "The Case Against Wearing Furs," "The Middle East Crisis," The Fight Against Inflation" illustrate the kind of subjects that frequently reak into the news.

A student making a thorough search for a topic may also ask himself, with :spect to the day on which he is scheduled to speak, "What day is today?" laybe it is the anniversary of Beethoven or Iwo Jima, the invention of the eamboat, the adoption of the Constitution or of the fifteenth amendment. nnouncing that "today is the anniversary of —" may give you a reason for 1lking on the subject.

Topics for Reviews or Reports

he student assigned to give a review or report on a book or subject for 1vestigation also has a problem of choosing a topic. First of all, he must decide *hich* book, or *which* field of investigation, guided by the suggestions the :acher has provided. The teacher should urge the student to consider several ossibilities before making a final choice. Just as the speaker may be unwise to repare the first topic that comes to mind, so also should the student planning a :view or report consider various possibilities. "Of all these books or topics," he 1ould ask himself, "which am I most genuinely interested in?" "And of these ossibilities," he should immediately continue, "which can I interest the class 1?" This second question is the one likely to go unanswered.

Once the book or the subject is selected, important limiting and narrowing eeds to take place. If a student is to report on David Kahn's mammoth but 1teresting book, *The Code Breakers,* he must plan at the outset to cover only a art of the book. He can limit his discussion to the breaking of German and 1panese codes by American cryptanalysts, leading to victory at Midway and elsewhere; or the solution of the Linear B code of ancient Crete; or the problem of sending messages to other beings in outer space, or solving those that might be sent to us. If a student is to report the result of a field trip on voting preference he should probably not attempt to detail each interview, though he may narrate one or two unusual experiences for color and interest, but he should give the major part of the time to the really important part of his study—the interpretation of his findings.

Gathering Materials

Once a student gets past the stage of reporting personal experiences, he needs to augment his fund of information with research materials. Even a personal experience speech may be bolstered with additional data, but other kinds of talks are certain to be improved by research. One reason for insisting upon the thorough preparation of speeches is that the preparation itself—the reading and sifting of evidence—tends to persuade the speaker as to the proper side to take of the policy to recommend.[2]

A painless way to gather materials is to interview experts. One student became interested in cancer when a relative was stricken with it, and decided later to make a talk on the subject; but realizing that her information was limited, she decided to interview the chief of the nearby cancer hospital. He gave her facts and examples, and even supplied her with large charts for use in her talk.

The most frequently consulted sources, however, are books and periodicals. Every student should be made aware of the inexhaustible possibilities of the library. A student who leaves your course with a full appreciation of the range of information to be found in books is already on the road to wisdom. He should learn to turn to the library almost instinctively; he may never amount to much as a speaker until he does.

Consider the boy who gave a fair report on deep sea diving. Suppose he comes from an inland area and has never even seen the sea, much less a diver—what of it? Through the library he can become something of an authority on the subject. He can learn about the kinds of apparatus used, and the limitations of each kind. He can become acquainted with outstanding personalities. He can read about exploring sunken treasure ships, and raising submarines. He can learn of the hazards of failure in the air supply, accidents to hose and lines, fights with sharks, and the deadly peril of the bends.

The real problem with the talk on deep sea diving was that the speaker had read only a single article. Once he reads two good articles, he is in a different

[2]Stanley E. Jones, "Attitude Changes of Public Speakers During Investigative and Expressive Stages of Advocacy," *Speech Monographs,* June 1966, pp. 137-146.

)sition with respect to the speech. He can now compare, contrast, select. These ental operations are the essence of speech preparation. Reading the second ticle made a better speaker of him; reading other articles may make him still :tter. A teacher feels he makes his greatest progress when he arouses students › *think;* when he gets them to read widely, compare ideas, and react to what .ey read. No one is interested in glib paraphrase or restatement; what is needed alert, critical, original thinking.

The best way to teach students how to use the library is to take them there ﾑd show them or have the librarian show them the location of important books. :re is the *Readers' Guide,* here is the *New York Times Index,* here is the *ﾑucation Index,* here are encyclopedias general and special, here are atlases and manacs, here are yearbooks and dictionaries. If a trip is impractical, a solution to bring a few standard reference works to class. Either way, it is worthwhile › spend time acquainting students with the common references; many people :ver fully appreciate a dictionary and an encyclopedia until they have seen ﾑem through a teacher's eyes.

To test the value of the instruction, organize a treasure hunt based on ference works. Give each member of the class a mimeographed sheet on which ›pear twenty questions. What was Willie Mays's home run record in 1970? How d was President Kennedy when he was elected? The answers to these and other ﾑestions can be found in the library. Such an exercise would appear to send ost of the students on a second tour of the library; if this additional tour is ﾑnducted during the class hour, each person will have an incentive to do the hole job himself.

Like other good ideas, this assignment needs to be followed up during the :ar. If the content of a speech seems thin, ask the student where he could have ﾑne to find better material. Keep the memory of those old friends, the card talog and the periodical indexes, green in his mind. One cannot do a good job ՝ thinking unless he has something to think about.

You may encourage students to use the reference room of the library by quiring speeches on topics that require investigation. This assignment intro- ﾑces the study of note-taking. The note card has never proved popular with ﾑdents; it is a ritual of scholars. College students are required in freshman ﾑglish to submit a term paper accompanied by a convincing stack of note cards; ﾑt many write the term paper first, the note cards afterwards. Later, when term ﾑpers are due in other courses, they may take their notes in bulk fashion on eets of loose-leaf paper. Perhaps you should be willing to settle for any way of cording notes, provided that the source is written down along with the notes. speaker may be asked to give the origin of a statistic by chapter and verse; the ﾑds are against such questioning but teachers should go to great length to tablish habits of accuracy.

A teacher may help students improve content by setting the class to work at a ecial project. As described in an earlier chapter, students may undertake to find out as much as possible about local history, a foreign country in the news, historical event or period, a persistent problem such as crime or housing, a outstanding book or play. This type of assignment simplifies the matter of choosing a topic and gives the student practice in selecting and organizing h material, and in learning to think about what he reads.

Teaching Organization

You may also improve the content of student speeches or reports by teachir basic principles of organization. This again is one of the ways in which a goc mind thinks: through a plan, an outline, a design, a system, a strategy. Organiz tion has already been touched on in Chapter 3, but it needs to be emphasize here. Organization is the oldest rhetorical principle. Corax, Plato, Aristotl Cicero, Quintilian, and a hundred others, have written suggestions for arrangir the idea of a speech.

Once the student has selected his general subject, and has gathered materia about it, he finds that he has accumulated more than he can use. This is as should be. He must then decide what to leave out: and the decision of what t omit is as important as what to include. The success of the speech, in fact, ma depend on what is left out. Counsel students, therefore, not to attempt to tell a they know. Narrow the general subject down to a specific topic: and tha specific topic becomes the basis of the *central idea* of the speech. This principl is also important in giving reports on research topics. Beginning teachers wi recall from graduate seminars and undergraduate classes that many reports ar not so interesting as they should be. One fault is that the reporter includes to much; he tells the class even more than the professor really wants to know. A investigator should read widely, not for the purpose of *reporting* every detai but for the purpose of being able to *interpret* a somewhat *limited* part of h study.

Beginners with little training in speaking should take this as an article of fait Don't talk about "Water Pollution," but ask yourself "What is the most interes ing aspect of this topic?" The answer might be "Pollution in Lake Erie" (c some place closer to home). Limit the topic specifically, pour on the vivid detai and you have a fair chance of holding interest. "Water Pollution" however, foredoomed to failure unless you are allotted much more time than is customar in classrooms. It would have been vague, and generalized. Other examples can b multiplied from your own experience. Nearly always the best classroom speeche or reports are those made on a *sharply limited* subject, with enough *speci details* and *examples* to make the ideas clear.

After formulating the *central idea,* proceed next to list the supporting poin or reasons. If the central idea is "Abraham Lincoln had three outstanding trai of personality," the supporting statements might be:

I. His resourcefulness helped him make the most out of his meager facilities.

I. His humor brightened many a dark moment.

I. His generosity helped his enemies forget their bitterness.

Iere you have three distinct, nonoverlapping, categories. Support each statement with an appealing example, and you have the basis of an impressive ve-minute speech. You may know enough about Lincoln to talk for an hour, ut you have very kindly agreed with yourself to limit your speech to Lincoln as personality, and leave out Lincoln as a president or Lincoln as a speaker.

You may hand out to students a list of suggested outlines, following the arying patterns of *definition, time order, space order, series of reasons,* etc. For xample:

Definition

entral idea:[3] How can *burglary* be defined?

upporting statements:[4]

I. Burglary involves breaking and entering a dwelling.

I. Burglary involves the intention to commit a felony.

I. Burglary takes place in the nighttime.

Solving a Problem

entral idea: How can we encourage an intellectual atmosphere on this campus?

upporting statements:

I. We need orientation courses in social studies, humanities, and science.

I. We need more discussion groups for student participation.

I. We need more high-quality lectures and concerts.

Space Order

entral idea: Here is my blueprint for an ideal classroom building.

upporting statements:

I. The basement should contain special facilities for recreation.

I. Classrooms should be located on the first and second floors.

I. Open-shelf reading rooms should be located on the third floor.

he *central idea,* properly stated with respect to the situation, listeners, etc., is usually a part of the *introduction* of the speech. The usual design or strategy is to open with comments relating the subject to audience interests, followed by a statement of the central idea of this specific speech.

he *supporting statements,* when amplified, become the body of the speech. Note again that the student initially has a substantial list of supporting statements, but limits them to the number that he can manage in the time allowed. In deciding which statements to include and which to leave out, he will consider his listeners: what will be new to *them,* interesting to *them,* useful or stimulating to *them.*

Series of Reasons

Central idea: [My state] should lower the voting age to 18.

Supporting statements:
   I. Eighteen-year-olds now shoulder a wide variety of responsibilities.
  II. Eighteen-year-olds today are well educated.
 III. Eighteen-year-olds are self-supporting.

I have often invited students to hand in brief outlines, illustrating differen kinds of development, and in their contributions is this sample:

Time Order

Central idea: The landing on the moon was a series of planned ventures involvin manned spacecraft.

Supporting statements:
   I. Apollo 7 demonstrated the ability to locate another spacecraft in orbit.
  II. Apollo 8 made a successful round trip journey from the earth to the moor
 III. Apollo 10 approached the moon's surface with the LEM, a specially de signed landing vehicle.
  IV. Apollo 11 and Apollo 12 put men on the lunar surface.

After these steps have been refined, the speaker needs next to think about conclusion. (Many book reports, field investigations, scholarly presentations, an the like simply *run down,* with no final summary or interpretation.)

The simplest type of conclusion is the *summary* or *recapitulation.* Perhap every talk should have a final review, if only a cursory one. It leaves the listene with loose ends tied up and with a final picture of the whole talk. Th conclusion can usually be improved however, if, after the summary, the speake follows with an *appeal,* a *plea,* an *interpretation.* "This is what I have said," th speaker concludes, as he summarizes, "and this is what I think we should d about it," or, "and this is what I think it means." The speaker may conclud with an *application* to a specific situation; or a *quotation;* or some combination A good conclusion adds to the impact of a speech. Many times a sermon tha seems quite ordinary for the first fifteen minutes has been raised to sublim heights by what was said in the last five. The speaker should work to a clima: that has been thought through in advance. In making these decisions the studen has his listeners well in the foreground of his thinking.

Ordinarily the speaker does not prepare his *introduction* until after *body* an *conclusion* have been worked out. Not until then does he really know what h wants to introduce. To help students plan better beginnings and endings to thei speeches, bring to class a collection of public speaking textbooks and speec anthologies, and read samples of what good speakers have done.

As a brief review of possibilities of introductions, consider these:

riking statement: "In ten years it will be impossible to get from here to
ィicago by train." Or: "Last week a teacher at the Grant School happened to
y something to her second-grade class about Adolf Hitler. 'Who's Hitler?' asked
e children."

ιestion: "Did you know that every college and university student received, at
e opening of the school year, a scholarship worth $800—and this in addition to
   other grants, awards, and scholarships that were distributed?" (This speaker
ιde the point that since members of the faculty were paid inadequate salaries,
e cost to each student was $800 less.)

ιotation: "There is an old saying attributed by a New Bedford mate on a
ιaler, to his ill-humored captain, 'All I want of you is a little see-vility, and
ιt of the commonest, gol-darndest kind.' I have been thinking about the
palling lack of courtesy between the younger generation and its elders, and I
ιuld like to make a plea today for a little old-fashioned, New England
ι-vility. . . ."

rsonal reference: "I cannot tell you how pleased I am that Professor Magoo
ι s given us this opportunity to report on . . ."

ιstration: "The other day my father received an insurance notice from the
ιover Insurance Company. 'Dear Mr. Haggis,' it said. 'We want to congratulate
ι u on the fact that your son has turned 16 and has received his driver's license.
ιis note is to inform you that your insurance premium has been increased to
ι 52.38 . . .'"

The method of teaching organization, then, is to talk about each of the parts:
roduction (including the central idea), body, conclusion. Some teachers re-
ire an outline with every talk; others require outlines only until the process
ι ms clear.
You may find the problem of teaching organization clarified by explaining
ι *nsitions.* A transition summarizes the point just made and introduces the
ιnt to follow; it may also relate both points to the central idea. For example:

As I have just explained, one of the principal advantages of spraying fruit
trees is to control insects and disease. Another important advantage is to
increase the amount and improve the color of the fruit.

ιis transition indicates that the central idea has to do with advantages of
ιaying; the first two points are now entirely clear. Or:

As you see, you can reduce by exercising, but it is a slow process. There is
a better way; to undertake a scientific diet.

In these two short sentences the speaker has reviewed his first point an introduced his second. He has also reminded his listeners of his central ide how to reduce. Furthermore he has suggested that, important as the fir point is, the second point is of greater significance. Winston Churchill transitions were as clear and brief as an interstate highway sign. After digression about the Royal Air Force, for example, he said, simply: "I retur to the Army."

Transitions are a form of *repetition* or *restatement.* The content of a speech more easily remembered by an audience when the speaker repeats the mai divisions. Three or four repetitions in a speech of length may not be too many The human mind may be impressed by an idea, but may quickly forget. If lat in the speech the speaker repeats the idea, the listener has a certain satisfactio in recognition. Beginning speakers are hesitant to use repetition, and eve experienced speakers may not use repetition as much as they should. Advertisir companies have learned that the repetition of a slogan increases sales; otherwi they would come out with a new slogan every week.

Using Examples

The importance of specific examples needs to be reemphasized. Two wor heighten the audience's estimate of a speaker: the phrase *for example. Fc example* puts the speaker on common ground with his audience; *for examp* gets him down to cases. A speech needs certain generalities, but it becom necessary to show by examples how these principles can be worked out.

A series of speeches was once made on these topics: "Socialized Medicine "The Humane Society," "New Developments in Lubricating Oil," "The Coinsu ance Clause," "A Program of Job Instruction," "Patronize Your Local Dealer For some reason there was a complete lack of examples in every speech. Ever talk was generalized and therefore less interesting. "Socialized Medicine" migl have had an example showing either the operation of the present or of tt proposed system. "The Humane Society" might have related an incident shov ing what happens when a pet is picked up by the dog catcher. "New Develo ments in Lubricating Oil" might have had an example describing the improve performance possible with new detergent oil. "The Coinsurance Clause" bad needed illustrations. "A Program of Job Instruction" might have contrasted tt bungled beginning of a new worker who did not understand his new job with tt efficient output of one who had been properly instructed. "Patronize Yot Local Dealer" presented the advantages of having someone at hand to service purchase when new parts or adjustments are needed; specific examples wou have been entertaining. You can help your students improve by commendii their use of examples and, when a speech has none, by suggesting possibilitie

Improving Language

teaching students to improve their choice of words we also improve the ntent of speeches. Enlarging vocabulary is a fascinating activity for students, ce their interest has been aroused. As good an approach as any is the idental comment: "Charles in his speech said that students should not be *sured;* that's a good, useful, everyday word that we ought to add to our aking vocabulary. Most of us would have said *blamed* or *scolded.*" If in every y's comment about speeches you include a mention of striking words or rases, you may encourage students to use better language. You do not need to ch for *supercilious, vituperation, dalliance, querulous;* you may issue praise *gladden, princely, bewildered. Although, since, moreover, accordingly,* bring ief as connectives from the constant *and, but, for. Wonderful* and *interesting* overworked; so is *thing.* If your class becomes absorbed in the meaning of rds, introduce it to *Roget's Thesaurus* and *Webster's Dictionary of Synonyms.* ow your students how the *Thesaurus* reminds them of words they may rlook.

Webster's and other dictionaries of synonyms discriminate among meanings. e discussion in *Webster's* of *beautiful* and nine synonyms (*lovely, pretty,* nely, good looking,* etc.) takes two full columns of fine type, and is worth iewing. *Beautiful,* it is made clear, has the richest significance of all: it xcites the keenest pleasure, the imagined perfection associated with one's nception of an ideal." A speaker or reader who fully appreciated the deeper aning of *beautiful* would utter it with much more feeling than would one who ught it meant no more than *good looking.*

The use of numbers and figures is worth discussing. *Many, hundreds, thou-* ds, millions* can readily be improved upon. Not "Far too many of our ssmates were in traffic accidents last year," but "I know of at least six boys three girls who were in traffic accidents last year." Not "People live a good l longer nowadays," but "Twenty years has been added to the life span since rld War I." Not "The public debt has mounted to billions of dollars," but ie public debt is now two-hundred and seventy-five billion dollars." Some- es the speaker will want to say, emphatically, "The budget for this town is enty-three thousand, one hundred and fifteen dollars and thirty two cents," sometimes it will be sufficient to say "more than seventy-three thousand lars"; either is better than "a lot of money." Sometimes he will want to make gure vivid by comparison or contrast; these devices are illustrated in most lic speaking textbooks. You can improve content of speeches (and discus- is) by insisting upon a realistic treatment of statistics.

By the same argument, specific words everywhere are better than generalized statements. *Sycamore* is better than *tree, mud cat* is better than *fish.* A speak should use specific verbs as well as specific nouns: *ambled, tottered, wavered, a* more vivid and picturesque than *came* or *went.* Call attention to the examples they crop up, and now and then offer pointed advice to the laggards.

Everybody knows that the *character* of an individual is revealed to h listeners largely by his use of words. If he indulges excessively in *absolute positively,* and other loose modifiers, if he declares that something *alwa happens* instead of the more accurate *sometimes happens* or *frequently happe* or *has been known to happen,* or *happens in 30 percent of the cases studied,* he makes loose assertions about races, religions, nationalities, or professio certain listeners are likely to discount his accuracy. Before long they w conclude that if he is careless with facts they know about, he may be inexact facts that they do not know about; and so what might have been a report speech of promise ends up in an atmosphere of doubt and uncertainty. / teachers can contribute to a student's maturity by interesting him in fairness a accuracy of statement.

Ability to Define, Analyze, Classify

So far as exposition and argument are concerned, the teacher has a cent interest in the ability of the student to do critical thinking. The principles th one needs to develop are discussed in detail in nearly any textbook on speaki but can be briefly stated here. Are necessary terms clearly defined? Once definition is established is it maintained throughout? Are areas of discussi properly bounded, grouped, limited, so that a sharp focus can be made? Are t partitions or classifications logical? Are causal relations demonstrably valid? arguments from analogy are used, are the points of comparison acceptable? the method is inductive, are there sufficient instances? Are the instances rep sentative? Are there negative instances? Are the claims warranted?[5]

These and related topics are basic to critical thinking. The student may n yet be aware of the importance of *definition.* You may need to be the first demonstrate to him that *classification* demands a high order of mental alertne Make a collection, from textbooks or from other reading, of arguments th contain major fallacies and expose the class to a selected few as a way of getti a discussion started.

---

[5] *See:* Allan D. Frank, "Teaching High School Speech to Improve Critical-Thinking Ability *Speech Teacher,* November 1969. Outlines an experimental class that emphasiz instruction in testing evidence, logical inference, validity of statements. Speech demonstration, speech to analyze emotional thinking, definitions of abstract term inductive speech, deductive speech, casual analysis speech, and similar assignments.

Improvement of the Quality of Thinking Is Foremost

ou will be well repaid for giving special attention to ways of improving the 1ality of the student's thinking. To summarize, the task is twofold. You can ork on better selection of ideas, better arrangement, more accurate use of evi- ence and language. You need also to exercise a generally superintending influ- ce over the materials he brings from other disciplines. In his article, "Teaching ritical Thinking," Robert G. Gunderson observes: "Inadequate information is 1 important cause of both poor speaking and poor writing. . . . We should not 1ly urge the student to search for new facts, but we should show him how to scover and use those he already has."[6]

Assignments

ake a survey of a number of public speaking textbooks to learn how they cover the following topics:

1. Speech topics

2. Speech materials

3. Organization

4. Adaptation to audience

an a discussion suitable for a speech class on the following topics:

1. Suggestions for speeches

2. Kinds of materials suitable for speeches

3. How to organize a speech

4. Examples of unusual introductions

5. Examples of unusual conclusions

6. Examples of transitions and summaries

7. Examples of examples

8. Rhetorical strategies

peech Teacher, March 1961, pp. 100-104.

Questions for Classroom Discussion

1. A Gallup poll listed the following ten domestic topics as being those that the
American people were most concerned about:

a.	Improving public education	45%
b.	Reducing amount of crime	41%
c.	Conquering "killer" diseases	37%
d.	Reducing unemployment	35%
e.	Helping people in poor areas	32%
f.	Reducing discrimination	29%
g.	Improving housing	21%
h.	Improving highway safety	18%
i.	Reducing air pollution	17%
j.	Beautifying America	3%

   The percentages indicate the frequency of responses. Review these topics a
   possibilities for classroom speeches or discussions. Note which ones have
   special appeal for your classroom listeners.

   Here is another short list of topics, each with a certain urgency: overhaul o
   foreign aid, political integration of Europe, smoking and health, expansio
   of the Peace Corps and job corps, financial problems of hospitals growin
   out of medicare, population explosion, college or high school dropout
   peaceful exploration of outer space, automation and thinking machine
   Britain and the Common Market, war in Asia, policy in Cuba and Lati
   America, TV in courtrooms, labor unions, accomplishing integration by law
   problems in space exploration, the political future of current preside
   tial hopefuls (select one), management of news, any controversial suprem
   court decision.

2. How does the organization of a *speech* differ from that of a *theme?*

3. Do good contemporary speakers exemplify principles of good organization

4. How can the content of speeches be improved: choice of topics, selection o
   content, accuracy and felicity of language?

5. Should topics be assigned? Is it a useful exercise to have a class read
   provocative, controversial article and then have everyone make a speec
   about it?

6. What is the place of speeches on simple topics, those based largely o
   personal experience or observation?

7. Comment on: "The enemies of all liberty flourish and grow strong in th
   dark of the enforced silence."

8. Do the traditional principles of public speaking (i.e., freedom of speakin
   flourish in an atmosphere of close supervision—i.e., in some corporation
   businesses, military situations?

9. How significant is public speaking as a social force? as a professional asset? a
   an aid to good government? Does public speaking aid an individual as

citizen, as a member of a business or profession, as a member of social or religious groups?

0. How important is the character of the speaker in public speaking? How do such factors as integrity and honesty influence the effectiveness of academic exercises like book reports, historical or scientific investigations?

1. How honest are the rhetorical procedures of selection, emphasis, amplification, identification with the group, praise of the listener, etc.? Should we (or can we) fight our way (according to Plato and Aristotle) with the bare facts alone?

2. Do we need to defend the use of appeals in speaking? Do we need to defend the arts of delivery? Is there a difference between a good and an effective speaker?

3. How can the classroom teacher use principles of speaking to improve his lecturing? What opportunities can he find for improving himself as a speaker?

References

Im, Richard S. "Buzz Sessions About Books." *The English Journal* January 1951. Describes procedures used to stimulate classroom discussion about books.

owell, Laura. "The Process-Inquiry Speech." *Speech Teacher* September 1952. Spells it out, like one teacher talking to another.

onham, Wallace B. "Why Experiment? The Case System in College Teaching of Social Science." *Journal of General Education* January 1949. Those interested in the case system of teaching (i.e., by problem, solution, and discussion), will find this treatise readable.

owling, Fred. "Teaching Impromptu Speaking." *Speech Teacher* September 1957.

ynn, Lawrence J. "The Aristotelian Basis for the Ethics of Speaking." *Speech Teacher* September 1957.

ank, Allen D. "Teaching High School Speech to Improve Critical Thinking Ability." *Speech Teacher* November 1969.

underson, Robert G. "Teaching Critical Thinking." *Speech Teacher* March 1961.

enderlider, Clair R. and White, Eugene E. "A New Emphasis in Teaching Public Speaking." *Speech Teacher* November 1952.

uger, Arthur N. "The Ethics of Persuasion: A Re-Examination." *Speech Teacher* November 1967.

cNess, Wilma. "An Orientation Course in Creative Skills for First Year Junior High School Students." *Speech Teacher* November 1952.

Murphy, Richard. "The Speech as Literary Genre." *Quarterly Journal of Speec* April 1958.

Sawyer, Thomas M., Jr. "In Defense of Explanatory Speeches." *Speech Teach* September 1957.

Simpson, Jack B. "A Speakers' Bureau for High Schools." *Speech Teach* November 1952.

Wallace, Karl R. "An Ethical Basis of Communication." *Speech Teacher* Janua 1955.

Walter, Otis M. "Creativity: A Neglected Factor in Public Speaking." *Speec Teacher* September 1954.

Note: For a list of high school texts, see the references at the end of Chapter For a list of college texts on public speaking and fundamentals, see th references at the end of Chapter 4.

8

speechmaking:
improving delivery

The height of art is to conceal art.

Quintilian

One of the first arguments to arise in the theory of public speaking was whether content or delivery is more important. Like many controversies, this one dates back to the Greeks. Aristotle thought a speaker should be able to make his way by the logic of his discourse; he should know the underlying facts and the inescapable probabilities. Delivery, he admonished, was not an elevated subject of inquiry but needed to be considered for practical reasons. Demosthenes, his contemporary, declared that delivery was all-important. The three rules of good speaking, he is reputed to have stated, were first, action; second, action; third, action.

The Greeks passed the argument to the Romans intact, no solution having been agreed upon. Cicero, the only speaker of note who ever wrote systematically about the theory of speaking, observed that delivery was the sole and supreme agent of eloquence. Quintilian, whose ideas about speech training won him a place in general education, was reserved in his praise of delivery, but devoted many pages to voice, enunciation, and gesture.

Most students of public speaking since Quintilian have followed his lead. Significant content and effective delivery are both inescapably necessary. The graphic arts play an increasingly important role in communication. Television gives us opportunity not only to hear the speaker's words but to formulate opinions about his sincerity. Newspaper reports of TV speeches often refer to the speaker's appearance or gestures.

Paul Heinberg's suggestion about the relative importance of content an delivery in determining the general effectiveness of speeches has raised puzzlir questions. College teachers listened to tape recordings of two kinds of stude speeches: self-introductions and persuasive talks. Their conclusion: delivery w; almost twice as important as content in determining the general effectiveness self-introductions, and almost three times as influential as content in the pe suasive situation. Heinberg speculates that the lesser impact of content m; reflect adversely upon the attitudes of society today, and that greater emphas should be given to analytic listening in speech courses.[1] Sorting out the imm diate question from those of longer range, the reader can note that as always tł teacher must give attention to all aspects of speech preparation and presentatio and that he cannot neglect the improvement of the speaker's delivery.

Some teachers put little stress on delivery, other than to commend tł student for posture, conversational voice, and eye contact. Other teachers g beyond this minimum, working not only for alert posture but for a variety (bodily attitudes and highly varied flexibility of voice. This chapter will discu methods whereby these goals may be achieved.

What Kind of Presentation?

The presentation of a speech is closely related to the method of preparation us by the speaker:

A speaker may write a speech and memorize it. This method was made famo by the great orators of a century and a half ago. After completing his researc the speaker wrote out his speech, committed it to memory, and delivered it the audience. This method is not used much today, for two reasons: first, tł problem of forgetting the speech is ever-present, and second, the speaker wł uses this method finds it almost impossible to conceal the fact that he is utterir memorized words. In every beginning class a few students are likely to try either because they misunderstand the nature of modern speaking or becau they are too fearful to trust themselves to think on their feet.

A speaker may write a speech and read it. Many speakers use this method b few use it well. Most people who read a speech make a mechanical process out it. When listeners see a speaker pull a manuscript out of his pocket, the conclude they are in for a bad time, and they usually are.

A beginner will do better with the manuscript speech if, while writing it ou he is careful to use the language of speaking rather than the language of writin

---

[1] "Relationship of Content and Delivery to General Effectiveness," *Speech Monograph* June 1963, pp. 105-107.

As the language of speaking has shorter and more striking sentences, is more vivid and colorful, and especially is more direct, this kind of language set down on paper results in a speech that is easier to read aloud. If, further, the beginner will do a few simple things to break the monotony of reading, he has an even better chance to improve his presentation. For example, he should look at his listeners as much as possible; he should look up from his paper and paraphrase a sentence or a paragraph now and then; he should interpolate comments that do not appear on the page. These devices tend to break the monotony of presentation.

When Churchill prepared a speech that was to be read aloud, he walked up and down his study, thinking over his ideas, and dictating them to his secretary. This process guaranteed that the words would sound like talk. Roosevelt also used the method of dictating speeches. Truman, Eisenhower, Stevenson, and Kennedy read their speech manuscripts over ahead of time to make sure they would sound right.

Undoubtedly beginners should not be allowed to read speeches. They need to acquire a direct method of speaking, and to accomplish this goal, they cannot use manuscripts. A speaker who has extreme stage fright might use a manuscript, though some teachers would object even to this concession, but he should be weaned away from his written text at an early date.

speaker may prepare an outline and speak from notes. Most training in public speaking today comes under this category. Many experienced speakers are likely to take a few notes with them to the platform. Many experienced teachers will permit students to use a few notes while speaking. The beginning speaker should use them, however, simply to help him bridge the transitions; he should not give the appearance that he is leaning heavily on them. The teacher should, moreover, be alert to make sure that students are placing less and less dependence on notes as the semester progresses. It is saddening to visit a class that has been in progress for most of a semester, and see student after student take a sheaf of notes to the platform and obviously act as if the success of the speech hinged on the use of the notes. It is even more saddening to see students search out their notes just when they are making an emphatic point. If, however, the listeners see a speaker glance at his notes, catch the idea, and then speak for a few minutes before he takes another glance, they are not likely to be distracted.

Those who are beginning their teaching of public speaking should develop in their students a true extempore style. Make sure that their voice and manner shows that they are thinking on their feet. A student who has overdone the memorization part of his preparation will sound too hurried and a little mechanical. A student who has too many notes in front of him unconsciously drops into a reading tone instead of a conversational tone. You should be patient with the student who needs notes, in order to give him confidence, but you need to prod him into using fewer and fewer props. Left to his own devices he is not likely to make an effort to use fewer notes, so you will need to stiffen you requirements gradually.

An excellent book is *Speech Practices: A Resource Book for the Student of Public Speaking.*[2] It provides reproductions of actual notes used by speakers and shows convincingly that in modern good practice experienced speakers use a minimum of notes, and those principally as a guide to the sequence of ideas. *Speech: Idea and Delivery* has a facsimile of a portion of a manuscript by Adlai Stevenson; the complete typescript contains seven hundred corrections and revisions.[3] Students of public address who have inspected Truman manuscripts at Independence, Roosevelt manuscripts at Hyde Park, or Wilson manuscripts at the Library of Congress, have viewed typescripts with handwritten inter lineations, many added at the last moment.

A speaker may speak without advance preparation. The ability to speak impromptu is a great asset to an individual. Many students take courses in speech primarily to achieve this ability. It is an especially invaluable asset in conference, law court, or legislative assembly, as these situations call for immediate responses. In planning a speech course, most teachers allow time for impromptu speaking.

The importance of this activity can hardly be overestimated. Properly handled it shows the student that he *can* be reasonably fluent on his feet. It helps bridge the last gap between faulty memorization or poor use of notes, and direct, animated, audience-reaching, delivery.

A Method of Preparation

What general advice can a teacher give for preparing a speech? Most teachers think it is advisable to write the speech out, not with the idea of committing it to memory, but to gain practice in putting the thoughts together. After the speech is written, the beginner may prepare a brief outline, on a card, using key words or phrases. Holding this in his hand, or placing it on a table, he should practice the speech aloud, to hear the ideas flow, and to see how much time is consumed. This rehearsal should be done in as lively and direct a manner as feasible. After he has practiced the speech two or three times, the speaker will find himself becoming more fluent; he will even find himself using some of the same language at each rehearsal, and at other moments improving the phrasing. He will never get the language fixed rigidly—in fact, he should not attempt this—but he will become confident of the progression of ideas. When he has finished this rehearsal, he will have a good idea of what the speech will sound like.

---

[2] By Waldo W. Braden and Mary Louise Gehring.
[3] By Charles W. Lomas and Ralph Richardson.

While he is practicing, the speaker should give attention to eye contact. He should visualize various persons sitting around the room, and, as he speaks, he should look at each one of them. He should, moreover, imagine that he is talking directly to them in a lively, earnest manner. He should give thought to his posture, to make sure that his body suggests an alert person.

Minimum Essentials

The minimum essentials of eye contact, conversational voice, and posture themselves represent a degree of achievement. Good posture indicates a measure of poise; or to put the argument the other way, a speaker who has learned to stand comfortably before an audience has increased his own feeling of self-confidence. The ideal of good posture is that the speaker should suggest readiness without stiffness. Hands appear more natural at the sides than in coat pockets, or clasped behind the back, or gripping notes. Teachers help a student to feel better about his problem by advising him to clench his fists slightly: this effects a compromise between what seems natural to him and what is acceptable to the audience. The beginner often wants an all-purpose position that will be suitable for an entire speech. No one position is good enough for this, but hands-at-sides is certainly better than arms-folded, hands-behind-back, hands-in-pockets, hands-grasping-lectern.

Just as there is no all-purpose posture, so there is no all-purpose voice. A conversation-like voice is usually nominated for this spot, and fills it fairly well, especially since it leads the beginner away from monotones and sing-songs. In fact the conversational voice may be suitable for all of the customary situations, if it is sufficiently lively and energetic. With a few classes a teacher can discuss vocal variations that are not particularly conversational but, used sparingly, are strikingly effective. Actually, however, though I use the word *conversational,* I do so primarily for lack of a better word. The textbooks that speak of conversational quality in delivery usually append the notion that the method being advocated is conversation *plus;* lively and animated speaking, not quiet, subdued muttering; a tone of voice that is not patterned but has the normal variety of inflections heavily underscored with earnestness and moral conviction. To be entirely candid, I have admired passages from Roosevelt, King, Churchill, Kennedy, Stevenson, Dirksen, and Johnson that are cadenced and emotional, and I find myself forgetting what Professor James A. Winans put into his books and taught his students on the Missouri campus, and inwardly applauding the highly charged cadences of a speaker who is stirred and moved. By the same token I would approve of some of this in student speaking though I dislike as much as anyone the use of chants or sing-songs that drift through a whole speech in disregard of changes of meaning.

Teachers strive to instill good eye contact at the outset. Every speaker should look directly at his audience; more than that, he should look at every person, if the group is small, or at least at every section of the room, if the group is large. If he is carrying on a conversation with five people, he tries to look into the eye of each in turn; this ideal so far as possible should be achieved before an audience. Good speakers make every listener feel, "He is talking directly to me."

No good way has been discovered of avoiding this responsibility. Looking just over the heads of listeners fools nobody; the speaker who practices this deception seems to be talking with unfocussed eyes. Gazing at the ceiling, out of the window, or aimlessly around the room makes listeners feel uncomfortable. Staring at the floor makes the speaker seem inept and inexperienced. From the first, therefore, teachers advise students to look at the audience.

Dealing with Mannerisms

All sorts of mannerisms will show up in the early speaking experiences of the class. A boy will repeatedly tug at his ear or nose; a girl will keep glancing down at her notes; perhaps several will look only at one part of the audience or will ignore it altogether. You need not be in a hurry to point out these mannerisms or comment on them. Most of them are self-correcting; they result from lack of experience in speaking, and as the student gains experience, they will disappear. To call attention to self-correcting oddities makes the student unnecessarily aware of them. Even those that are deeply rooted will be supplanted by useful movements as the student learns more about bodily activity. Instead of saying "don't twirl your ring," "don't twist your handkerchief," give positive suggestions as to what can be done with the hands: utilize a few simple gestures, or a visual aid.

Vocal mannerisms like "er" and "uh" are hard to eliminate indirectly; the student utters these unconsciously, and has to be made pointedly aware of them. A suggestion here is to make a list of all who vocalize the pause, and set aside part of a period to work on this entire group, one at a time.

A study by Gerald R. Miller and Murray A. Hewgill suggests that the speaker of normal fluency is more believable, more credible, than the speaker who vocalizes pauses or who repeats initial syllables of words. The fluent speaker appeared more *competent* than the nonfluent speaker to the approximately 160 students in Michigan State University speech classes that participated in the experiment.[4] The objection to *uh's* and *er's* by listeners is thus seen to be based on more than aesthetic considerations.

Students themselves will likely put more emphasis on mannerisms than you

---

[4] "The Effect of Variations in Nonfluency on Audience Ratings of Source Credibility," *Quarterly Journal of Speech,* February 1964, pp. 36-44.

o. When talking about their speeches to one another they will comment on individual peculiarities that you seem to have overlooked. Lay audiences seem also to be aware of speakers' idiosyncracies. This is what happens: when the speaker becomes dull or involved, listeners lose interest in what he is saying, and accordingly give more attention to his way of speaking. On the other hand, if he is unusually inspiring or entertaining, either they ignore his mannerisms or they conclude simply that they are an acceptable part of his way of speaking. Such distinguished speakers as Kennedy and Churchill had a basketful of individual mannerisms, but these seem unimportant alongside their statesmanship and their eloquence.

The researches of Ralph G. Nichols[5] and others suggest that this preoccupation of students with the mannerisms of speakers is deeply rooted. An experiment was conducted at the University of Minnesota to test the retention ability of a large group of students. One finding was that poor listeners tended to judge the worth of a lecturer by the quality of his delivery. If he overused his notes, if he had a poor voice, if his speech were indistinct, if he had mannerisms, they tended to conclude that the content of his lecture was not good.

Teachers should therefore realize that in every listening group will be people overly sensitive even to lesser faults of delivery. Accordingly, although today we are individually convinced that the *message* is more important than the *manner* of its presentation, we must deal with listeners as they are and we must therefore bring speakers up at least to minimum standards of delivery.

The Time to Criticize Delivery

An important distinction exists between the method of improving content and of improving delivery. You may evaluate a student's speech content at your leisure—after his speech is finished, at the end of the class hour, or after school that day—provided your notes are complete enough to refresh your memory. But problems of delivery should be attended to at once. If a student does not talk loudly enough, interrupt him, or signal him then and there, so that he may immediately make the necessary adjustment. If a student does not look at his audience, stop him and show him what is implied by good eye contact. If he does not emphasize his words enough vocally, interrupt him and question him about the meaning he is trying to convey.

If his gestures are feeble or inept, show him what to do. An alternative is to allow him to finish and then take him back over selected passages. The teacher is an active person when working on problems of delivery, conducting demonstrations as well as making comments.

See: Ralph G. Nichols and Leonard A. Stevens, *Are You Listening.*

Improving the Speaking Voice

So far as the voice is concerned, the making of a good speech requires energy
Secure records of Roosevelt, Churchill, Truman, Kennedy, Nixon, and other
and play them to your class; let the students hear for themselves the physica
power that is being poured into the words. Many other characteristics of th
speaking voice can be pointed out: the use of pitch and loudness to emphasiz
words; the employment of various kinds of pauses; and occasionally eve
changes in quality. Of the speakers named, the contrasts are perhaps mor
notable in Churchill, who at times, as has been noted, put unusual depths c
feeling into his utterance. A part of this effect is the result of the way he uses h
voice.

All men in public life who have done considerable speaking or campaignin
have learned to use their voices in a striking and forcible way. Business an
industrial executives at large conventions, labor leaders at union conclave:
distinguished ministers in their pulpits, all speak with energy and feeling. Th
quiet conversational tone of a teacher talking to a small class or of a docto
talking to his patient fades away in the presence of the robust delivery of activ
speakers. A little of this force and drive ought to seep into classroom speaking. I
a student chooses a topic about which he has real concern, like military trainin
student government, war and peace, city politics, or university regulations, h
should be able to command a voice that carries conviction.

You can develop this more realistic type of speaking in your classroom if yo
give your students encouragement and instruction in this direction. Forcefu
speaking may not come easily to students; a beginner may speak "We must get a
the bottom of this scandal and never rest until the causes are brought to light" i
much the same tones that he would use in saying "We begin by washing th
dog's head and ears and proceed gently until we finish the tail." In the firs
sentence words like *bottom, scandal, never rest,* and *brought to light* sugges
strong feeling that should be expressed by suitable vocal inflections. In th
second sentence, the voice can be as gentle as the washing; most audiences wil
not care whether the washer gets as far as the tail or not.

As a teacher, you may use several techniques to help beginning speaker
improve the flexibility of their voices. As most beginners fill their speeches wit
generalized statements, you should encourage them to use illustrations, ex
amples, personal experiences. As these materials contain colorful language, th
speaker is likely to use a more interesting voice. You may carry this suggestion
step further by pointing out the value of employing dialogue: instead of "H
asked me what I was doing there," say "He grabbed me by the arm and said
'Where do you think *you're* going, Buster?' " Or this line, in different vein: "W

peatedly asked ourselves the question, 'How are we going to win?' " The
otation gives opportunity to suggest mood or feeling as well as the bare idea
elf. You may take such statements as "The team is in a bad situation," and
ow how to emphasize *bad* to bring out the full meaning (and of course there
e a full score of better words than *bad—desperate, regrettable, deplorable,
taclysmic* and *disastrous,* all of which invite a little vocal treatment). At the
ne of Dunkirk, Churchill declared: "What has happened in France and Belgium
a *colossal military disaster.* " You may also encourage the student to make his
lk more direct by using *you* and *we,* and by referring to previous speakers:
ou've all seen the headlines in the *Times";* "As Mary just pointed out in her
lk. . ."

Fundamentally each student must develop his own vocal style. Some speakers
veal innate force and conviction using only moderate vocal energy, whereas
hers use a loud voice that persuades no one. Neither speaker may be so
fective as he should be, but for different reasons. These speakers require your
ntinued study. If you can help them with their basic problems, you will
deniably be making a lasting contribution to their experience.

An observation I made after spending hours in the strangers' gallery of the
ouse of Commons and listening to Hyde Park speakers and Englishmen in
tion elsewhere, is that the English speaker uses more pauses than his American
unterpart. The pause is the natural child of the act of thinking on one's feet,
owing the speaker reflectively groping for a word or for the next rung on his
ental ladder. The use of the pause also comes with age and experience, to
mericans as well as Englishmen, and the seasoned speaker has learned that the
oment of silence after an important idea allows the listener a moment to
gitate. Invariably beginning speakers operate without pauses. They have too
uch stuff for the time allowed and they know it, and scamper along accord-
gly. They also know it is more comfortable sitting with the classroom audience
an standing before it, so they hurry along to exchange the worry of standing
r the peace of sitting. Other reasons will also suggest themselves. The
structor may then, quite profitably, comment on the use of the pause, with
monstrations. The lesson, however, is not easily learned.

Teaching Gesture and Action

e teaching of specific gestures (palm up, clenched fist, etc.) has passed the
ak of its popularity, as has the teaching of certain conventions of platform
ovement (advancing, retreating, transitional steps, etc.). Teachers were not
fficiently rewarded by their successes and were dogged by their failures—the
dents who never seemed to be able to endow their newly acquired movements
th naturalness and motivation.

As the speaker is man seen as well as man heard, the teacher cannot igno: the problem of gesture altogether. A minimum achievement is to help th student free himself of mannerisms that distract listeners and thus interfere wit communication. Much of this improvement, as pointed out elsewhere, occu without direction from the teacher because the student steadily feels more . home in the speaking situation. A further achievement is to encourage th student to work for visual variety as well as for vocal variety. Question hi about his convictions: does he mean what he says? do his ideas have signif cance? relevance? are they vital? do they touch us? must we act on them? now How do speakers use facial expression? gesture? You and some of your studen can demonstrate gesture and action, and with the class evolve principles. Ho much further you go than this depends upon your experience and the interes and inclinations of the students.

Improving Action through Visual Aids

Teaching students to use visual aids is a way of improving their skill i exposition; it has the additional benefit of getting them to use more bodil action, and thus enlivens their delivery. The following series of assignments ma be used for short talks.[6]

1. Give a talk using a blackboard sketch, drawing, or map. Suggestions: "Place to Visit in Green County," "What Makes Lightning Strike," "The Nations o Africa," "How to Read a Contour Map," "The New Federal Budget," "How t Lay out a Subdivision," "Causes of Traffic Accidents," "New Proposals fo Foreign Aid," "The ABM System," "Pollution in This Area." What is sought i not a show and tell performance but the exposition of a subject for which visual aid is not only a convenience but a necessity.

2. Give a talk using an actual object for demonstration. Suggestions: "Kinds o Resonators," "How to Make Artificial Lures," "How to String a Racket," "Car Tricks for Dull Dates," "Common Types of Barometers," "A Demonstration o Fencing," "My Father's Sword Collection."

3. Give a talk using your body to demonstrate a skill. Suggestions: "How t Model a Dress," "How to Jump the Low Hurdles," "How to Tap Dance," "Basi Strokes in Tennis," "How to Play Center." Variation: make a speech in whicl you ask a classmate to assist you with the demonstration: "A New Type o Artificial Respiration," "Basic Holds in Wrestling," "A New Dance Step," "Th Art of Self Defense."

[6]Adapted from Loren Reid, "On First Teaching Speech," *Speech Teacher,* January 1952 pp. 4-5.

Instruction in the effective use of visual aids should by all means be a part of the beginning course. As the foregoing list of assignments suggests, students may make use of maps, graphs, charts, mock-ups, and the actual objects themselves. They may use moving pictures, slides, filmstrips, and recordings. They may use mimeographed or typed handouts. They may use their own bodies (not strictly speaking a visual *aid*). They may borrow a classmate for demonstration purposes.

Homemade graphs, charts, maps, and the like are useful devices. In certain ways they are more effective than those made by professionals—at least the homemade variety suggests that the speaker himself has labored with crayon and chalk in the interest of his listeners. You can profitably invite an artist to visit your classes to demonstrate simple lettering and sketching. Or, as a starter, secure fifty to one hundred sheets of newsprint from the local newspaper office, a few boxes of crayolas, and let your class practice making visual aids.

You will need to make suggestions about the effective use of these devices. The visual aid should be large enough to be easily seen. Lettering on charts or graphs should be instantly intelligible. Judicious use of color is attention-holding. Sometimes large pictures may be cut out of magazines and pasted on the charts as a way of illuminating a point. Each visual aid should be kept out of sight until the time comes to use it; some speakers mount their charts on the wall, but fasten a sheet of blank paper in front of them until the proper moment comes. Each speaker should carry his own supply of thumb tacks, scotch tape, pointers, extension cords, and similar devices. Rotary clubs, church pulpits, and other places where people make speeches almost never provide these materials. Mechanical gadgets as recording machines and projectors should be tested beforehand.

Principles and Kinds of Gesture

Several principles of good gesture have been formulated. One is *variety*—do not weaken a good gesture by too much repetition. Another is *purposiveness*—use a gesture with a genuine desire to emphasize the idea. Another is *wholeness*—use the whole body, not simply the hand and forearm. Another is *timing*—let the gesture accompany or precede the forceful idea, not follow it.

In explaining gestures, teachers are not interested in giving instruction about a standardized set of forms, but are primarily concerned with demonstrating the conventions, which each individual may vary. Some speakers gesture closer to the body than others, although any gesture should avoid hugging the body too closely. When gesturing, speakers should look at the audience, not at the gesture. Teachers sometimes attempt to encourage gesture without any preliminary explanation about the conventional forms, but often this plan does not work so well.

President Kennedy's speaking mannerisms brought him a good deal of mild ridicule during his campaign and in the early days of his administration. Newspapers called two of his favorite, awkward gestures the *chop* and the *swoop*. With expert advice and practice he steadily improved in the essence of good delivery if not in the refinements, so that reporters could write this description at the time of the Cuban missile speech:

> That youthful looking man appeared in complete command; he was engaged in a sober discussion of subjects that mean life and death to the nation and to the world. . . .
>
> His staccato, unemphatic delivery, the quiet smile sometimes dimly but gently lighting up his features—all this contributed to inspire a sense of confidence and respect.[7]

Aside from this impressive speech, in effect a solemnly delivered state paper, Kennedy's delivery was most effective when he was extemporizing: during campaigns, for example, or in the opening moments of a speech when he was establishing common ground with his listeners, before he turned to the manuscript before him.

So many speakers are content simply to stand quietly behind the lectern and follow notes and manuscripts that students may get the idea that bodily action is not essential. Once, however, your students have an opportunity to witness a first-rate speaker who exemplifies not only good content, but vivid and expressive bodily action as well, they will not be satisfied to speak any other way. The use of bodily action is one more method by which communication with an audience may be made effective.

Assignments

1. Consult a number of contemporary textbooks of public speaking and compare and contrast their treatments of delivery.

2. Work out units in radio or television speaking, with special reference to means of improving delivery.

3. Compare and contrast the advice given concerning delivery in classical works like those of Aristotle, Cicero, and Quintilian, with that suggested by contemporary textbooks.

4. Compare and contrast the advice given concerning delivery in nineteenth-century works on rhetoric and elocution with that suggested by contemporary textbooks.

[7] *The Reporter*, January 3, 1963, p. 12. For a detailed description of Kennedy's delivery, *see:* James G. Powell, "Reactions to John F. Kennedy's Delivery Skills During the 1960 Campaign," *Western Speech*, 1968, and included in J. Jeffery Auer (ed.), *The Rhetoric of Our Times*, pp. 313-322.

Questions for Classroom Discussion

1. Comment: "Content is like the right hand, delivery is like the left."
2. Is sufficient attention being paid today to the improvement of delivery?
3. Consider prominent speakers who members of the class have recently heard. Would your critiques of these speakers include mostly comments on content, or comments on delivery?

References

Auer, J. Jeffrey, ed. *The Rhetoric of Our Times.* New York: Appleton-Century-Crofts, 1969.

Braden, Waldo W., and Gehring, Mary Louise. *Speech Practices: A Resource Book for the Student of Public Speaking.* New York: Harper & Bros., 1958.

Brooks, William D., and Strong, Judith W. "An Investigation of Improvement in Bodily Action as a Result of the Basic Course in Speech." *Southern Speech Journal* Fall 1969.

Dowling, Fred. "Teaching Impromptu Speaking." *Speech Teacher* September 1957.

Kruger, Arthur N. "The Extempore Speaking Contest." *Speech Teacher* September 1956.

Lomas, Charles W., and Richardson, Ralph. *Speech: Idea and Delivery.* 2d ed. Boston: Houghton Mifflin, 1963.

Nichols, Ralph G., and Stevens, Leonard A. *Are You Listening.* New York: McGraw-Hill, 1957.

Reid, Loren. "On the Reading of Convention Papers." *School and Society* January 10, 1948.

Schmidt, Ralph N. "Speaking a Written Speech." *Today's Speech* February 1963.

See: the list at the end of Chapter 4 for contemporary textbooks dealing with public speaking and fundamentals.

group discussion

The hour is late, and the agenda is long.

John F. Kennedy

An activity utilized by teachers of all subjects and at all levels of instruction is classroom discussion. Discussion has, moreover, attained a commanding prominence in business, professional, industrial, and governmental circles. Research in group process is going forward at an impressive rate.

Purposes

Discussion has two principal purposes. One is to disseminate information, to compare points of view, to offer advice. A group participating in discussion for this purpose is ordinarily not trying to invent, to legislate, or to petition. It may be inquiring into the features of British universities, ways of improving instruction, the management of the news, the desirability of student representation on school committees, the appeal of *War and Peace.* Everyone will have opportunity to present his point of view, to defend his ideas against opinions of others, to lend his support to those with whom he agrees, to correct errors of fact and sometimes to be corrected, to gain new insights. The discussion is intellectually satisfying if, out of the differences and disagreements, a consensus is reached (a) on those matters on which the group substantially agrees and (b) on those points at which the group agrees to disagree.

A second purpose of discussion is to solve a problem: the group plans to issue a recommendation, petition, directive, or order, and will take a vote or poll to crystallize the sentiments of those present.

The purpose of discussion ordinarily flows from the nature of the group. A steering committee usually discusses problems with the idea of taking action or at least of making a recommendation for action. A class, however, discusses a problem chiefly to learn more about it. Yet situations differ. One class, for example, investigated the desirability of substituting a pass-fail grading system for that of the conventional letter grades. Members read articles in journals and through correspondence, learned how the system was working in other institutions. Deciding that the problem was too significant to keep confined to the classroom, the group approached the student organization with information and recommendations. Using this ammunition, the student government took the problem to the faculty and administration, the result being that a modified pass-fail system was inaugurated.

The Discussion Process

Discussion is often contrasted with debate. The participants in debate have made up their minds in advance as to which side of the proposed question they wish to defend. A debate therefore consists of arguments for a proposal confronted by arguments against a proposal. There is not likely to be much exploration of the middle ground, nor much change in any speaker's opinion.

Participants in discussion usually have not made up their minds in advance. The chairman states the question and those present act as a group to feel it out. Toward the end of a discussion, however, different points of view emerge as participants begin to disagree about various aspects of a problem. Even so, compromises may be proposed as the middle ground is explored, and since the discussion process is informal, participants may find themselves modifying their views as the problem becomes better understood. Individuals who are highly argumentative may not become first-class discussion participants until they learn to join with the group in analyzing objectively all angles of the question.

The discussion process is often described in language that originated with John Dewey. Discussion begins with (1) a felt difficulty, which is then (2) defined and analyzed; next (3) comes a listing and consideration of practical solutions, (4) a choice of the most feasible solution, often followed by (5) a consideration of how to put it into effect.

A three-phase way of looking at the discussion process has been devised by Robert F. Bales and Fred L. Strodtbeck. During the first phase discussants spend most of their time either asking for or giving orientation, information, and confirmation. In the second phase the preponderance of the communications ask for or give opinion, analysis, appraisal and judgment, feeling or wish. In the final

hase the communications ask for or give suggestion, direction, possible modes
f action. As Halbert E. Gulley observes, this method of analysis has points of
semblance to the Dewey plan. He correctly notes that the discussion leader
oes not need to follow any scheme rigidly but can take advantage of useful
ontributions whenever they are made. Still, the leader should have *some* plan,
ven though he may need to alter it. As Gulley illustrates:

> If a busy man boarded an airliner in Chicago to fly to St. Louis and the
> plane landed in Indianapolis, then in Denver, and then in Little Rock, he
> would naturally ask what had gone wrong. If the stewardess explained that
> this particular pilot did not like to plan his flight in advance but preferred to
> fly happily from airport to airport as he happened to pick up a radio signal,
> the busy man would be justifiably furious. Yet people spend more time in
> discussions than in airliners and they often suffer such a fate, travelling with
> discussion leaders who neglect to plan a route in advance.[1]

Sometimes discussion proceeds in an orderly arrangement from analysis to
ossible solutions to best solution. Sometimes the creative process refuses to be
nanneled into a set groove, but instead expresses itself in irregular, unsum-
oned, and unannounced hunches and flashes of insight. Many kinds or variants
f the discussion process have been developed.

Types of Discussion

onventional types of discussion and newer variants are listed and briefly
escribed in the paragraphs that follow.

Group Discussion with a Leader

this type of discussion, the leader makes an opening statement explaining the
uestion or problem: "Are teachers' strikes justified?" or "Should the electoral
ollege be modified?" He opens the discussion and then urges the group to
articipate, following as closely as seems necessary the usual problem-solution
utline. To this end he makes the necessary transitions as he leads the group
om one phase of the discussion to another, and closes with a summary of what
as been decided or agreed upon.

Discussion, Conference, and Group Process, pp. 208, 211-213. He cites the Bales-
Strodtbeck study from Cartright and Zander, *Group Dynamics: Research and Theory*,
pp. 624-638. He notes also the spiral model of Thomas M. Scheidel and Laura Crowell,
"Idea Development in Small Discussion Groups," *Quarterly Journal of Speech*, April
1964, pp. 144-145. The thought of these authors is that a group does not always
progress in linear fashion from problem to solution, but moves outward in its elaborating
and agreeing-disagreeing, yet onward in that it makes progress toward a decision.

Panel

A panel is a conversation in front of an audience. It is characterized by an informal interchange of opinion as contrasted with the series of short speeches that compose a *symposium* (see below). Three members, plus a chairman or moderator, is a good number for a classroom panel; this small size means that everyone will have a chance to participate, and still allow time for discussion by the class before the bell rings.

The most serious problem of this century is undoubtedly the population explosion. Years ago Ortega y Gasset in *The Revolt of the Masses* identified it as a problem of the modern age, pointing out that up to 1800 Europe had not succeeded in attaining a population greater than 180 millions, then in less than a century and a quarter it leapt to 460 millions.

A panel discussion on this vital topic could be planned with students representing the points of view of engineering, agronomy, and sociology, plus a presiding officer. Three panel members, at the most four, plus a chairman, is a workable number.

The chairman could open by commenting on the importance of the subject: the two billion people living in underdeveloped, underfed countries; the estimated rate of growth of the populations of Asia, Africa, and South America. He could also view the serious aspects of the population explosion in highly developed countries. The Mississippi Valley, for example, is one of the most fertile regions on the globe. In fifty years its population is expected to triple.

The chairman's introduction should lead into, yet not steal from, the first topic: "What is the present situation?" The panel speakers could talk about protein shortages and widespread malnutrition, world tension, crowding, poor utilization of manpower. Each member of the panel would presumably have something cogent to offer from the field he had researched. Agronomy suggests talk about depleted soils, engineering about floods, sociology about congested areas.

The second phase of the discussion should answer the question, "What can we do to meet the problem?" Here the panel conversants could offer possible solutions: family planning, building of roads and dams, building of fertilizer plants, improvement of storage and distribution.

The third part of the discussion naturally follows: "What appears to be the best solution to the problem?" Here the panelists might talk about plans that have already been put into effect, or partially into effect, or that have been tried in one part of the world but not another. Flood control, irrigation systems, loans to individuals and to nations, improvement of sanitation, opportunities for useful and productive work, distribution of better varieties of rice and other food grains, and principally the dissemination of birth control information, are topics that would likely pass in review. One feature of the solution would probably be the establishment of priorities: all of the foregoing solutions have merit but need to be implemented in a practical sequence. The chairman might urge the panelists to formulate a resolution, or a series of resolutions, that represents the consensus.

The composition of the panel depends largely upon the interests of available students. Conspicuously absent from the illustrated panel is material from economics and political science. Doubly conspicuous is the absence of the problem of communication; much needs to be explored about persuasion, exposition, exhortation, in small group discussion and through mass media.

Thousands of Americans have visited Brazil and other Latin-American countries, Hong Kong, Singapore, and other Chinese and Malaysian areas, Vietnam and neighboring regions, Nepal and Pakistan, Calcutta, Benares and other Indian cities, the Arab countries of the Middle East, and have been appalled by the sight of hundreds and thousands of children growing up in depressed environments, and by the sight of hundreds and thousands of adults, doing almost no work at all, or working with primitive tools. Most have gone as tourists but many as experts and consultants. Literature on conditions in American cities is multiplying. Materials on the topics are, accordingly, plentiful.

A few minutes should be saved for class participation after the panel contributions. A problem is that the usual class period is hardly long enough. A discussion often starts out slowly and haltingly, sometimes not becoming lively until ten minutes before the end of the hour; then the participants and class members alike become enthusiastic and interested, and the bell rings amid a flurry of excitement. A college seminar of two hours can use the panel type of discussion effectively. If, however, time is limited, keep the panel to three members plus moderator, as suggested.

Whatever the panel, the choice of topic for discussion should be a joint venture of teacher and students. List on the board the promising suggestions and choose the best ones by vote. In a class of twenty-four, six panels may be elected. After the panels have been heard, let the class elect the best chairman and panel, and conduct a final discussion, inviting in another class for a guest audience. The idea of a discussion contest is not new: some teachers regularly conduct them, picking the best discussants at each round and sending them into successive rounds until the best of all has been chosen.

Symposium

The symposium is more formal in structure than the panel. It begins with a statement from the moderator about the problem or question, then follows with a series of short speeches. After the speeches, the discussion becomes informal as the members of the symposium question one another. After this interlude, the listeners may ask questions.

As a typical project assume that teacher and class have selected "What Should Be Done to Promote Greater Safety on the Highway?" The chairman in a brief talk describes the gravity of the present situation: the number killed approaches sixty thousand, says the National Safety Council; more people have been killed on the nation's highways in this century than have been killed in all American wars. Speaker A talks about what is now being done: education, highway patrol, student traffic policy. Speaker B talks about highways: good and bad types of highway design and construction, the importance of a highway engineer to a safety program. Speaker C talks about drivers: bad driving habits, driver's license laws, men versus women drivers, drivers under twenty-five versus older drivers. Speaker D takes as his topic alcohol and gasoline, indicating why the two should never be mixed. He describes England's spectacularly successful breatholyzer law, and notes the increasing strictness of state laws against driving while drunk. The chairman invites questions and comments from the audience. At the end he summarizes the important points made during the discussion.

Other Types of Discussion

A *forum* period is the time allotted to the audience for questioning the leader, lecturer, panel, or symposium speakers. This practice gives rise to such self-explanatory terms as *panel-forum, symposium-forum, debate-forum, lecture-forum* when a panel, symposium, debate, or lecture, respectively, is followed by a question period.

Round table, staff conference, committee meeting, meeting of governing board or *board of directors, colloquy, bargaining session, training session, workshop, public hearing* are more or less specialized forms of discussion that do not call for special treatment here. With the exception of the last-named, the *public hearing,* the discussions are usually carried on by closed groups, with no audience present. These groups explore questions or problems, the chairman following a discussion outline or a more formal agenda. Preassigned speeches may be made, as by a budget officer or supply officer at a staff conference, or by the representative of an organization, institution, or individual at a public hearing or bargaining session; but these formal interludes are likely to be followed by highly informal discussion. The *round table* is so called because the participants sit around a large table, in a fashion that suggests each is on an equal footing with everyone else; the discussion that follows is likely to be exploratory or informative rather than policy-making. A *colloquy* resembles a panel except that the term *colloquy* suggests the presence of highly qualified experts (although the distinction is not hard and fast; panel experts may be as authoritative as colloquy experts). Meetings of *committees, governing boards, boards of directors,* may or may not be open to the public, and may or may not hear expert opinion or testimony. Usually they work from an agenda, and are expected to bring in reports, recommendations, fact-finding studies, and even resolutions or decisions.

A *buzz session* is an informal committee meeting. This device is often used with large classes or audiences. After a speech or panel of speeches, listeners are divided into small groups. This division may be prearranged; each individual when he enters the room may be given a buzz session assignment, or the moderator may announce, after the preliminary speeches, "Look under your chair, and you will find your assignment to a buzz session, and the name of your chairman." The individual groups then go to different parts of the room, or to different rooms, elect a recorder or secretary, and discuss the material that has been presented to them. At the expiration of the assigned time limit, the groups reconvene, and their chairmen, or recorders, report summaries of the various discussions.

Discussion Variants

Discussion is often stimulated by devices other than the formal problem-solution approach.

Role-playing (psychodrama, sociodrama) is a device that may be used to initiate a discussion. Instead of a formal statement by a moderator or chairman, a small group may enact an improvised play showing customer complaints, good and bad on-the-job instruction, and the like. A worker may be assigned to play the part of the boss, a foreman may be asked to assume the role of a green beginner.[2]

The case method. Instead of beginning with a question, "Shall N——, caught stealing a watch from another student's locker, be expelled?" the case method begins with a narrative of the circumstances under which the watch was stolen. Details can be supplied about the accused student, conditions in the locker room, the types of offenses for which the punishment is expulsion. The group decides what action to recommend.

Classroom-tested cases may be found in a number of textbooks. Most of them come from areas such as student discipline, employer-employee relationships, crime and criminals.[3]

Values of Discussion

Values of discussion include:

The group will nearly always foresee more difficulties, explore more facets, visualize more outcomes, and produce better solutions than can a single individual.

---

ee: Peter E. Kane, "Role Playing for Educational Use," *Speech Teacher*, November 1964, pp. 320-323.

For sample cases and a discussion of the method, *see:* Irving J. Lee, *Customs and Crises in Communication.* Lee observed the case method in operation in almost a hundred class hours at the Harvard University Graduate School of Business. Cases may also be found in Norman R. F. Maier, *Problem-Solving Discussions and Conferences*; John D. Glover and Ralph M. Hower, *The Administrator: Cases on Human Relations in Business. See* also William M. Sattler and N. Edd Miller, *Discussion and Conference*, chapter 18, Appendix D; Gulley, pp. 351-363.

Discussion improves group spirit. People like to be consulted. They like to be i on prospective developments. They cherish a feeling of being a member of th group.

Discussion helps remove misunderstanding. Points of friction between facult and students, between labor and management, and between other groups even between nations—can often be resolved through discussion.

The agreed solution is more likely to work. Some bugs will have been remove by the process of discussion itself. The individuals participating, moreover, wi exert extra effort to make the solution work. Those involved in spac ventures, for example, from technicians to mission control workers t astronauts, became confident that each mission would be successful becau the problems had been fully confronted and discussed.

In a study involving 132 high school students, Waldo Phelps and Miltc Dobkin contrasted conventional methods of teaching high school civics and a experimental approach including an extended series of problem-solving pan forums, preceded by brief instruction in discussion theory. The investigato concluded that the teacher may use a third of the course time in panel di cussions without sacrificing mastery of basic content, thus giving the superic students special opportunity for intellectual leadership.[4]

Examples

So that the teacher will be better able to stimulate the interest of students i discussion, the following illustrations are suggested:

The Constitutional Convention. In 1787 delegates from the colonies met i Philadelphia. A variety of antagonisms was represented: large states against sma states, Northern states against Southern, free states against slave states, Nev York against almost everybody.

It is difficult to imagine the host of topics on which the delegates ha conflicting interests. It helps to remember that those present represente sovereign states. Few thought of themselves as being Americans; the delegat identified themselves as Virginians, New Yorkers, Pennsylvanians. They ha different kinds of money and were properly suspicious of another's currenc They had had boundary disputes and trade disputes.

Just as they came from different backgrounds, so also they had differir opinions about what to do. Some wanted to amend the old Articles of Confede ation; others wanted to draw up a new instrument. Some wanted a federatio

[4] *See:* "The Influence of Problem-Solving Panel Forums on Learning High School Civics *Speech Teacher*, March 1957, pp. 126-138.

ɔme a confederation. Other disagreements came to light as the meetings dragged
ɔn.

Days came when delegates were discouraged, but somehow they managed to
ʞeep in session and work out adjustments for their differences. Fortunately
ɪere was a strong desire to produce a new document that all the colonies could
ɔccept. Moreover, there was relatively less disagreement on such matters as
ɪacing the common defense and the regulation of commerce in the hands of the
ɪntral government. Wise and influential men were present who had had a long
ɪssociation with the processes of discussion. George Washington was a fine
ɪresiding officer, partly because of his prestige, and partly because of his vast
ɪxperience with groups. Another persuasive individual was Benjamin Franklin.
ɪnce when the going got rough he told an entertaining story; on another
ɔccasion he offered a prayer; at the conclusion of the deliberations he appealed
ɔ everybody to sign the document, whether or not he personally agreed with
ɪery line of it, simply because it was the best the group had been able to work
ɪut.

This chapter will offer advice a few pages further on about the importance of
ɪe *agenda*. The Constitutional Convention also had an agenda; part of it is
ɪnown to history as the Virginia Plan. At one stage of the discussion, part way
ɪrough this agenda, the convention deadlocked, because no one could formu-
ɪte a method of resolving the conflicts between large states and small. Now if a
ɪroup begins its deliberation by adopting an agenda, it makes at least a tacit
ɪromise to itself to consider all of it. When in the Convention deadlock occurred,
ɪe presiding officer decided to drop that item and proceed to the next on the
ɪst. Later the group returned to the troublesome point, and reached an agree-
ɪent.

The Convention could easily have failed to achieve its primary mission; that it
ɪd not speaks much for the ability of those present to develop ideas through
ɪiscussion.[5]

ɪvention of the Airplane. The use of continual discussion by Orville and
*ɪilbur Wright in their invention of the airplane will be noted at once by any
ɪacher of speech who reads the standard biographies of these resourceful and
ɪnaginative men.

Wilbur and Orville Wright manufactured, sold, and serviced bicycles in

---

ɪrom Loren Reid, "The Engineering of Ideas," *University of Missouri Bulletin,* December 8,
1958, pp. 15-21. Most of the examples in this section of the chapter are adapted from the
address printed in this bulletin. The speech may also be found in W. Norwood Brigance,
Speech: Its Techniques and Disciplines in a Free Society, pp. 545-550. For a discussion
of the adopting of the Constitution, *see:* Carl Van Doren, *The Great Rehearsal;* Lindsey
S. Perkins, "The Convention of 1787: A Study in Successful Discussion," *Western
Speech,* October 1954. Perkins concludes that the convention prospered, among other
things, because of: (1) the ability of the delegates to attack problems with imagination
and integrity; (2) rules of order permitting full discussion; (3) constructive reasoning in
resolving and preventing conflicts.

Dayton, Ohio. Before 1900 they became interested in the possibilities o constructing a flying machine, and began, like every good scientist, by reading a the articles they could find on the subject. More material was available than on would realize. Many people, both in this country and in Europe, were intereste in gliding and flying.

The Wright brothers spent more than three years building and testing differ ent kinds of gliders. Whereas other pilots had tried to control the glider b shifting their bodies and swinging their legs during flight, the Wrights undertoo to develop a system of levers that would change the angles of the surfaces o wings, rudder, or elevator. They found the problem tremendously complex, an they endured many dispiriting hours. Early in their experimenting, howeve they had developed the habit of discussing problems together. They found th practice helped them think more clearly about what they were trying to do.

At one point in their gliding experiments, for example, they observed tha occasionally one wing would start to drag and dip, so that the plane, instead o responding to the usual methods of control, would dive to the ground wing firs This phenomenon, which today is called the tailspin, was puzzling to th Wrights. They called it "well-digging" and could not figure out the cause. The realized that well-digging had something to do with the tail, because the earlie tailless gliders did not exhibit this phenomenon. One evening Orville, th younger brother, sat down to give the problem concentrated thought. Eventuall he arrived at what he decided was the solution, and hunted up Wilbur to explai his theory. Orville had decided that the tail vane, originally a rigidly fixe surface, needed to be hinged. Wilbur agreed, and pointed out a relationship i the angle of the tail surfaces to that of the leading edges of the wing surface Through this discussion they evolved a method of controlling tail and win surfaces with a single cable. This idea, the result of experiment, observation, an discussion, has been called one of the greatest inventions in the long history o air transport.

On another occasion the Wrights were concerned with propellers. No on could tell them how to make a propeller; no information was available about th proper length, width, or pitch. They looked into the subject of marine prope lers, but found that no one had evolved a theory of propeller thrust; that who problem had simply been treated as a matter of trial and error. The Wrights ha many discussions about propeller theory and propeller design. At one poir Wilbur had one idea, Orville an entirely different idea. After long conferenc they were as far apart as ever—except that Wilbur had gone over to Orville position, and Orville had accepted Wilbur's argument. They continued the experimenting, and their discussion, and formulated a workable theory. Aviatio experts today credit the Wrights with having developed a propeller that was 6 percent efficient—the best that had been designed up to that time.

In the year 1903 on December 17 they assembled their machine on the beac at Kitty Hawk, North Carolina, at ten thirty in the morning. They were s

nfident of success that they told the photographer where to stand so he could
t a picture of the machine in the air. It was Orville's turn to be at the controls;
ments after starting the engine he was rolling down the track they had built
r a runway. That first flight lasted only twelve seconds, but it established the
:t that a heavier-than-air machine could be built and flown.[6] The habit of
.cussion established by the two inventors had sharpened their thinking and
ided their steps through the long months of study and experiment.

Other Problems and Issues

ery human effort has a *rhetorical* ingredient. The building of such great
dges as Brooklyn, Eads, and Golden Gate, the construction of the Erie Canal,
juired exposition and persuasion. Most of this took place in discussion
uations: dialogs, conferences, hearings. In 1969 the centennial of the building
the first transcontinental railroad was observed. The rhetorical aspects of this
pendous 1869 event have still not been fully explored. One city builds a giant
morial arch; another decides to issue an invitation to the Olympic committee;
hird plans a world exposition. The teacher of discussion will find instances of
: important talk that must take place between the time that a citizen gets an
a and his fellows implement it.

Examples of the discussion and decision-making process in government are
ion. In October 1962, President Kennedy was advised that Soviet missiles had
en discovered in Cuba. Immediately he summoned his advisers and explored
: situation from every angle. All possible options and choices were reviewed.
one time the group seemed to favor massive military intervention. Further
cussion revealed disadvantages in that move, and finally the decision was
de to quarantine shipments of offensive missiles by sea. The President went
the air to inform the country about the steps that were being taken. Later he
id tribute to the discussion process: he was convinced that if he had had to
:e action without full consideration of the crisis, he would not have been able
act as effectively as he did.

In 1964, President Johnson personally intervened in a railroad labor dispute
t was almost five years old. The Illinois Central had already shut down and a
tional strike was scheduled to get under way in a few hours. Representatives
the railroads had agreed to the President's request for further discussion, but
: unions had refused. The President persuaded them to meet again, appealing
inly on the basis of the hardship that a national strike would cause. They
eed to postpone the strike fifteen days. Bargaining teams and mediators then

niversity of Missouri Bulletin, pp. 16-18. Based on standard biographies about the Wright
Brothers, and also on material supplied by the Smithsonian Institution (where the Kitty
Hawk plane is on permanent exhibit). See: Wolfgang Langewische, "What the Wright
Brothers Really Invented," Harper's Magazine, June 1950, pp. 102-105.

went to work in earnest. After thirteen days and nights, with only two da⟨ remaining, agreement was reached.

Because the issues were quietly solved, the whole incident has been general forgotten. If, however, the nation had been plunged into a bitter railroad strik⟨ the consequences would have sharply affected the entire population.

In 1969, Neil Armstrong, Buzz Aldrin, and Mike Collins achieved an i⟨ pressive landing on the lunar surface. Many fields of study contributed to tl⟨ achievement, but from our point of view it must also be considered a rhetori⟨ triumph. Details will steadily emerge but certain high points were evident once. Eight years of effort on the part of three-hundred thousand peop⟨ powered by twenty-four billion dollars, could not have put two men on t⟨ moon without tens of thousands of hours of *conversation, discussion, persu⟨ sion, exhortation.*

Starting with Vanguard, weighing twenty pounds, we soon found ourselv⟨ making plans to launch larger and heavier craft, using the 1.5-million pou⟨ thrust of the Saturn booster. Then what to do? After still more discussion, ⟨ decided not merely to launch a space station, or to buzz a man around t⟨ moon, but to step on the moon itself. In 1961 President Kennedy, in ⟨ memorable speech, so advised Congress. Appropriations had to be foug⟨ through committees and through Congress; the space agencies themselves had ⟨ discuss all manner of problems. In all, it was reported that ten thousa⟨ different questions had to be answered that year by scientists and technicia⟨ before the dream of a lunar landing could even be made to look like a realizab⟨ possibility. At one time space headquarters was fully committed to a pl⟨ (earth-orbit rendezvous) of assembling a craft in global orbit, and from th⟨ point detaching the lunar-landing module to proceed to lunar orbit and then to lunar descent—then all the way back to rendezvous with the mother-craft ⟨ global orbit. One knowledgable scientist, through persuasion, was able to g⟨ higher headquarters to abandon this plan in favor of one in which the space cra⟨ would proceed to lunar orbit, and then the landing module would descend to tl⟨ lunar surface and return. Certainly this was a significant job of exposition ar⟨ persuasion. Dropped along the way was the notion of shooting a vehicle fro⟨ Cape Kennedy directly to Tranquillity Base in one single, awesome blast.

Discussion also preceded the decision to televise the actual stepping ⟨ Armstrong and Aldrin on the surface of the moon and their subsequent activi⟨ of scooping rock samples, planting the American flag, and deploying scientif⟨ instruments. In this discussion was a conflict of basic values. The argumen⟨ against televising the scene came under the heading of added risk and decreas⟨ safety: more weight to carry, hence more fuel. Better stick to the main job: g⟨ there, take a few snapshots, collect rock samples, and then get the m⟨ back. And as matters turned out, the fuel supply came within seconds of bei⟨ exhausted. The arguments for televising stated that the scientific mission cou⟨ be accomplished, safely, but that there would be an added plus: apart from tl⟨ scientific value of the continual photography of the locale came the conside⟨

tion of the stimulus to the human spirit, all around the world, of being able to
articipate in this stirring event. How fortunate for mankind that this latter view
revailed.

Full credit is due to the material and technical resources that made the
anding possible, with its potential of planetary exploration later on. In listing
he talents of our people, however, we must once more include our genius for
reative talk. In this environment we assimilate foreign-born intellects as well as
hose nurtured at home. It is an easy step from the discussions at Philadelphia
nd at state conventions that resulted in the adoption of the Constitution to the
iscussions in hundreds of committee rooms and laboratories that resulted in
chievements in outer space.

Techniques of Presiding

he presiding officer sometimes is the president of the organization with a
pecific responsibility to work out a solution to a problem; at other times he is
mply a discussion leader.

In either instance, he should be able to get along with others; to preside with
ict and fairness; to keep in the background and draw out others present; to
xpress himself clearly when he opens a discussion, guides it, and summarizes it;
⊃ guide the group through the various aspects of analyzing the problem,
athering solutions, and working out the most feasible solution.

The suggestions below apply in the main to the more conventional discussion
tuations. Procedures like role-playing, brainstorming, and presentation of cases
all for modifications.

Advance Arrangements

Vhatever the nature of the discussion, certain plans need to be made in advance.
hese questions are suggested:

ow is the question to be worded? It should not be too broad, or too narrow.
 should have good focus. Often the question form is used: "Should students
nish college before doing military service?" or "How can we increase interest in
ne ecumenical movement?"

ho is to participate? Unless the membership of the group is fixed, the
residing officer needs to invite the participants. Different points of view should
e represented: in a discussion of "The Tensions of City Living," the discussants
acluded a corporation executive, the president of a labor union, a judge, and an
ditor. Each saw the problem differently, and the group as a whole was able to
over a variety of aspects. Moreover the participants were well-informed and
rticulate. If you were a social studies teacher planning a class discussion of the
orthcoming city election, you would certainly want students representing both
Reform" and "Liberal" tickets who were not only interested in city politics
ut who were also able to express themselves well.

What kind of discussion plan should be worked out? For a policy making
group like a student council, advising the administration about the calendar, the
agenda could look like this:

Agenda for a Conference

I. Minutes of last meeting.
II. Consideration of next year's calendar.
A. Report of committee on examinations.
B. Report of committee on review week.
C. Report of committee on calendars of other institutions.
D. Report of committee on student questionnaire.

For a public meeting, the discussion plan may include such questions as, "What
is the nature of the problem?" "What are possible solutions?" and "What is the
best solution?"

Is a rehearsal or preliminary discussion necessary? Usually a discussion is improved if the participants meet in advance and agree upon a discussion outline
and the points of view that each is to express. Even in formal committee sessions
it is helpful to mail an agenda to the participants before the meeting, or to
notify key people ahead of time to be prepared to discuss certain aspects. The
hope is to avoid irrelevant wandering and still not hinder spontaneity.

What publicity should be given the discussion? If the public is to be invited
possible news channels should be explored.

What visual aids are to be employed? Here the leader should ask himself what
will be necessary in the way of graphs, charts, slides, films, exhibits.

What other arrangements need to be made? Here the check list consists of items
concerned with reserving the room, notifying or reminding the participants
procuring and preparing ash trays, scratch pads, copies of the agenda or outline
name cards, and the like. At a Press Congress of the World each delegate was
provided with an agenda, a loose-leaf notebook to record notes, an ash tray,
microphone so that his remarks could be heard throughout the hall, a name card
an identifying badge. Pages were on duty to carry messages, and hostesses with
pots of hot coffee circulated among delegates at strategic intervals. These are
elaborate arrangements indeed; but delete the microphones, pages, and hot
coffee, and what remains is simply standard equipment for any conference
Some of these details like an agenda, pad of paper and pencil, used even in
classroom discussion, would clothe it with importance.

Procedures During the Meeting

The presiding officer should note the following suggestions:

1. *Make the preliminary remarks brief.* The presiding officer should introduce
the participants; state the topic; open the discussion with a brief comment. After
the comment, he may then introduce the first speaker, or ask a question. He

ɔening remarks can become too lengthy. He should take care of essentials, but
, quickly as possible should get the discussion under way.

Insert brief summaries. He should guide the progress of the discussion by
:casional brief summaries that tie the discussion into the agenda or program
ıtline.

Ask questions. Consider the forms that a question may take:
a. *Indirect* question (aimed at no one in particular). "How prevalent is
dishonesty in examinations?" or "What are some of the procedures used by
cheaters?"
b. *Direct* question (aimed at a specific individual). "Dean Jackson, how many
cases of academic dishonesty have come before your office this year?"
c. *Relay* question. Someone asks a question of the chairman, but he relays it
to the group: Member: "Mr. Chairman, how extensive is the problem of
cheating?" Chairman: "You've heard the question, 'How extensive is the
problem of cheating.' Dean Jackson, can you answer that?"
d. *Reverse* question. Someone asks a question of the chairman, but he
reverses it to the questioner himself: Dean Jackson: "Mr. Chairman, how
extensive is the problem of cheating?" Chairman: "Well, to start with, Dean
Jackson, how many cases has your office turned up this year?"

Classroom teachers who would like to improve their own techniques of
ıding discussion sometimes realize, to their surprise, that they do not make
fficient use of questioning; or that their questions invariably follow the same
ttern; or that they can use reverse or relay types to keep the discussion
ntered in the group.
Questions are invaluable in meeting situations that arise during discussion.
ıis list of suggestions by Henry L. Ewbank and J. Jeffery Auer is indispensable:[7]

. *To call attention to a point not yet considered:* "Has anyone thought about
is phase of the problem?"

. *To question the strength of an argument:* "What reasons do we have for
lieving this argument?"

. *To get back to causes:* "Why do you suppose Doakes takes this position?"

. *To question the source of information or argument:* "Who gathered these
tistics that you spoke of?" "Who is Mr. Gish whose opinion has been
ɔted?" "Do you know that as a fact, or is it your opinion?"

. *To suggest that the discussion is wandering from the point:* "Can someone
ı me what bearing this has on our problem?" "Your point is an interesting
e, but can't we get back to our subject?"

ᵣead the complete list of questions in *Discussion and Debate*, pp. 287-288. Quoted here
by permission of Appleton-Century-Crofts.

6. *To suggest that no new information is being added:* "Can anyone ad anything to the information already given on this point?"

7. *To call attention to the difficulty or complexity of the problem:* "Aren't w beginning to understand why our legislators haven't solved this problem?"

8. *To register steps of agreement (or disagreement):* "Am I correct in assumin that we all agree (or disagree) on this point?"

9. *To bring the generalizing speaker down to earth:* "Can you give us a specifi example on that point?" "Your general idea is good, but I wonder if we can make it more concrete. Does anyone know of a case . . .?"

10. *To handle the impatient, cure-all member:* "But would your plan work in a cases? Who has an idea on that?" "Hadn't we better reserve judgment until w all know more about this problem?"

11. *To suggest that personalities be avoided:* "I wonder what bearing this has o the question before us?"

12. *To suggest that some are talking too much:* "Are there those who haven spoken who have ideas they would like to present?"

13. *To suggest the value of compromise:* "Do you suppose the best course c action lies somewhere between these two poins of view?"

14. *To suggest that the group may be prejudiced:* "Is our personal interest i this question causing us to overlook the interests of other groups?"

15. *To draw the timid but informed member into the discussion:* "Spelvin, her lived for quite a while in China. Suppose we ask him whether he ever saw . . .?"

Beneath these helpful and specific statements lie basic realities familiar t these authors that must not be dropped from view. The statements themselv are the outer workings of an inner set of assumptions about the functions of participant. They are ways of drawing out the information, the inferences, th value judgments that an individual may possess. They suggest mutual respect an affection rather than antagonism or distrust. They bespeak relevancy rather tha irrelevancy. Presumably the decisions of the group will react to the good c mankind, not the opposite.

In this connection, the teacher may want to observe that at times a group ha to submerge its selfish preferences in order to serve a higher ethic. Edmun Burke once told Bristol voters that he served their long-term rather than the short-term interests in Parliament, and, beyond that, national rather than loc good. The men of Bristol forced him to withdraw from that particular conte but he found a wide and universal base for his talents. From your own studen you may be able to draw twentieth-century parallels. What about corporatio executives that find themselves accused of price-fixing conspiracies? They mu have offered advice in discussion groups, and were seduced by short-term, selfis mpensation rather than the desire to serve their fellow-men. In your teaching discussion, as in other segments of your course, you should be well supplied t only with practical recipes and suggestions, but also with a broad concept, undergirding philosophy, and a high ethic.

Dean C. Barnlund's observations show that the following represent the incipal functions of the group leader and the number of times this function is observed:[8]

Summarizing or asking for summary 51
Directing group to new or former issues 44
Ascertaining group opinion 38
Resolving differences 33
Insuring recording of decisions 29
Stimulating further exploration of ideas 27
Checking time limits 23
Noting digressions from agenda 22
Clarifying agreements or disagreements 22
Restating problem or reorienting 19
Suggesting agenda or method of proceeding 16
Providing clarification of problem 13
Securing selection of leader or secretary 11
Noting need for further information 11

Experienced presiding officers raise this question: Can a discussion have *too* ich guiding? On this point the chairman must ever exercise judgment. Out of iat appears to be wandering, digressing, or reminiscing may develop the idea at best solves the problem. A discussion may be slowed down simply to give eryone his say; but what is lost in minutes may be gained in morale. Experienced chairmen combine careful guidance with flexible management so as to hieve the greatest amount of stimulation and creativity. Not the smallest talent a sense of humor, or at least a sense of proportion, to help the group get over e bumpy spots.

The teacher is advised to invite the class to supply examples of different kinds leadership. At one end of the scale is the individual who supplies no dership at all. He is helpless, inept, bungling. He wastes time in trivialities. mbers of the group have to remind him about actions and procedures. At the her end of the scale is the autocrat who has to do everything his own way. He minates the scene, is intolerant of the ideas of others, keeps discussion at a nimum. Between these extremes are many desirable patterns of leadership,

ean C. Barnlund, "Experiments in Leadership Training for Decision-Making Discussion Groups," *Speech Monographs*, March 1955, p. 6. For a helpful scorecard for rating group leaders, see the Barnlund-Haiman Leader Rating Scale, *Speech Monographs*, March 1955, p. 10.

depending upon the personality of the individual.[9] Good leaders develop th
own style of handling the situations that appear on Barnlund's list just above.

Ernest G. Bormann has studied the behavior of small groups for many yea
His conclusions about qualities of leadership will repay careful reading. T
desire to be a leader is strong in nearly everybody; out of eighty discussi
participants interviewed in one survey, only two indicated a dislike of lead
ship.[10]

Techniques of Participation

It follows that members of the group as well as their chairman have duties a
responsibilities. These can be brought out by class discussion. Something like t
following may emerge:

Keep the agenda or discussion outline in mind. A member of the group will th
be able to make his contributions at those times when they will be m
pertinent.

Understand the nature and purpose of discussion. A member will thus be able
enter into the problem-solving (or information-disseminating) spirit of the grou

Avoid excessive talkativeness. Sometimes the most useful member of the d
cussion group is the one who has the most to say. Almost any discussion lea
of practice, however, knows the type of discussant who requires too many wo
to express his ideas, and who is too aggressive and dominating.

Avoid excessive silence. A participant cannot offer information which he d
not have. In almost any discussion, moreover, are certain aspects about whi
some participants know nothing at all. On the other hand, just as it is easy to f
into the habit of saying too much, it is also easy to fall into the habit of sayi
little or nothing. And then, "sometimes the quiet fellow has already said all
knows."

Good discussers avoid the extremes just described. They are active menta
throughout the discussion. They supply information; they ask questions; th
challenge or stimulate differing points of view; they help keep the discussion
the main track. Avoiding personalities, they stick to the central problem. Th
are ready to praise a point well made and to help the chairman draw o

[9]*See:* Richard R. Wischmeier, "Group-Centered and Leader-Centered Leadership: An Exp
imental Study," *Speech Monographs,* March 1955. "Full moderation [keeping discussi
focused, making suggestions regarding analysis of problem, clarifying discussion] v
more favorable than partial [moderation] to progress towards consensus," William
Utterback, "The Influence of Style of Moderation on the Outcomes of Discussio
Quarterly Journal of Speech, April 1958.
[10]*Discussion and Group Methods: Theory and Practice.* Chapter 10.

meone who may be hesitant. Their own contributions sparkle with specific :ts and pointed examples.

To help a student gain insight into his own habits of discussion, let him study s list:

. Do I let other people do the talking?
. Do I feel inhibited when I am expected to contribute?
. Do I talk to the point?
. Do I have trouble keeping conversations going?
. Do I let fear of saying the wrong thing stop me from saying what I mean?
. Is it easy for me to persuade others to accept my views?
. Do I often know what I want to say, but not how to say it?
. Do I give a favorable impression of myself when I talk?
. Do I have difficulty putting complex ideas into words?
Do I find myself thinking of what I am going to say instead of listening to other person?
Am I overcritical of what other people say?[11]

Basic Principles

ong with forms and types, the teacher should introduce students to basic nciples describing behavior in groups. Interpersonal relationships and group namics are being intensively researched. The theory that is being formulated readily be applied to experiences that students themselves have observed. u can generate classroom assignments that give students insight into the ways t they and their peers operate in groups.

ver is the influence one member has over other members of the group because his position or past reputation. In the first instance he may have a higher title n other members, i.e., president, colonel, dean; he may have had greater erience; he may enjoy prestige because of his literary, artistic, political, letic, or social standing. In the second instance he may have acquired a utation for being well-informed, possessing tried judgment, or evolving novel itions; he may be well-liked. A participant in a discussion may thus be sified as high power, average power, or low power.[12]

e is the pattern of behavior exhibited by a participant. The teacher may want present this concept from discussion literature and invite students to suggest ous types: information-seeker, harmonizer, procedure-follower, summarizer,

dapted from questionnaires appearing in Laura Crowell, Alan Katcher, and S. Frank Miyamoto, "Self-Concepts of Communication Skill and Performance in Small Group Discussions," *Speech Monographs*, March 1955, pp. 23-24.
ulley, pp. 280-285; Sattler and Miller, pp. 287-291.

coordinator, aggressor, recognition-seeker, special interest pleader. Behind the
labels is the kind of content found in discussions: supplying information, aski
helpful questions, lending encouragement and support, recalling related decisio
or procedures, getting the discussion back on the track, appealing for harmoi
evolving a compromise—and the opposites.[13]

The teacher may lead into this concept by asking students to consider t
various roles they themselves play. Any given person may be an expert or
layman, a leader or follower, an enthusiast or a passivist. In some situations I
advice and counsel are more prized than others. Leadership follows informatic
skills, experience, thoughtfulness, communicativeness; it shuns ignorance, inco:
petence, inexperience, boorishness, inarticulateness.

Conformance is the pressure put by the group on the individual to meet
acceptable standard of behavior. In discussion situations this can be interpret
as a pressure to accept the reasoning of the group instead of questioning
Excessive conformity is likely to reduce the amount of group creativity
resourcefulness. No one likes to be in a minority of one, yet often a minori
opinion, well stated, can influence the outcome.[14]

Communication networks are patterns through which talk flows. A group
people sitting around a table, each freely talking to every other person, illi
trates a network with all channels open. This kind of network exists ideally ir
class which is not too large and in which everyone is free to contribute. It mig
also exist in a student council or a drama club. It would be highly constricted
a shop where the foreman gave orders to each worker, the workers having lit
or no opportunity to influence shop procedure.

As people like to be consulted, to recieve and to give information, they w
be most productive in communication situations where channels are ope
Research has been conducted with a variety of kinds of communication n
works, in some of which the flow of talk has been, experimentally, restricte
You may find it stimulating to read in this area and report some of the
experiments to your students.

Appraising Discussion

After a discussion has ended, you should appraise it: was it good, bad,
indifferent? Were the solutions or decisions wise? Who participated most or le
effectively?

Various objective plans of appraising discussion have been developed; i

[13]Gulley, pp. 161-162; Sattler and Miller, pp. 331-332; Bormann, chapter 9.
[14]A number of interesting experiments are collected in Sattler and Miller, pp. 129-133. S
Bormann, pp. 268-269, 310-313.

hough they have only a limited usefulness, they serve to enliven the critique. ?or instance:

. Keep a running tally of the number of times each one participates. Your table nay look like this:

Cargill — 23
Gebhard — 18
Hessmann — 16
McDonald — 9
Sullivan — 0

'his tally provides a rough index of the amount of activity, but says nothing bout quality.

.. A variation is to keep a tally with a *plus* for each helpful contribution, a *zero* or a neutral contribution, a *minus* for digressing, sidetracking, blocking, or an •verly aggressive contribution:

Crews — 0++000000
Sampson — ++++
Burke — 00 − 0 − 00 − 0
Page — 0000+0
Voltman — 0+0

'his tally suggests that Crews made two useful contributions early in the liscussion, but continued his comments after he had finished his constructive •bservations; Sampson spoke less frequently but made valuable contributions; 3urke hindered more than he helped; and so on.[15]

.. Make a chart showing the positions of the discussers around the table, ndicating each participant with an X. After the preliminary remarks of the •residing officer, draw a line from his X to the one who speaks next; next a line rom that X to the X representing the next speaker; and so on. You can tell from he chart whether much of the discussion centered around the presiding officer a closely guided discussion) or whether there are other clusters of lines (a •osely guided discussion). You can also observe who is relatively active and who s relatively passive.

.. Combine one or more of the foregoing techniques with oral critiques by the eacher or by a panel of critics. Invite comment on soundness of reasoning, use •f evidence, worth or ingenuity of the solutions, interest of the discussion, •pecific contributions of individuals, and so on.

[5] For still other methods of appraisal, *see:* William E. Utterback, "Evaluation of Performance in the Discussion Course at Ohio State University," *Speech Teacher*, September 1958, pp. 209-215, and any recent textbook on group process.

5. A variation is to draw a grid, listing participants along the left-hand column. At the top of other vertical columns are comments describing various kinds o contributions: "Offered information," "Clarified issue," "Encouraged others," "Digressed," and the like. Tally marks are placed in appropriate columns. The chart makes possible not only a quantitative but something of a qualitative statement about the discussion.

Before adjournment the leader may call upon previously appointed student to comment on the discussion *as a discussion*. Was there enough information? A what points did the discussion lag? Was it too permissive or too controlled? Did useful contributions go by unremarked? Did anyone who seemed to want to contribute fail to be recognized? Was the agenda covered? Were participant overly critical or the opposite? In general what weaknesses and strengths were revealed?

The Teacher's Use of Discussion

From the foregoing discussion of purposes, types, examples, and procedures, the teacher may gather suggestions for varying the recitation period. A class which regularly employs the lecture system for example, may add variety to the daily fare by introducing an all-student panel on some aspect of the subject. Teacher of English, social studies, foreign language, fine and applied art, physical education, mathematics, science, and other subjects can discover topics in their field that can be adapted to discussion.

Attention should also be directed to the recitation, since here, too, teaching skills can be developed. A few common faults can be profitably mentioned:

The continual talker. This teacher does not use discussion at all. The teacher who supplies the answers along with the questions robs the class hour o stimulating thinking. This point does not apply to large university classes; here the problem is met in part by supplementing the lecture with discussion sections. Sometimes, however, even in the discussion session the leader does too much talking. Learning should be an active process, with the student exploring the question along with the teacher wherever possible.

The fill-in-the-blanks exercise. As discussion this rests on the same level as the foregoing procedure. "Kennedy's opponent in the 1960 campaign was—doe anybody happen to remember? ... That's right—Nixon! And who ran against Nixon in 1968—does anybody recall? ... Yes, sir, Humphrey."

The pas de deux. This ballet term is a specialty dance for two performers, and may be used to describe the extended duet between the teacher and a student during which others in the class sit in patient expectation.

he same old few. Closely related to the foregoing, this situation arises when the *t*eacher asks an indirect question and hands appear in the air. This forest of *w*aving palms creates the impression that everybody in the class has read the *le*sson. Instead of continually calling on the same few, chop down one of the *p*alms that is not waving.

he easy mark. "Let's get the teacher off the subject . . ."

he fast draw. This teacher asks a question but supplies the answer before the *c*lass has opportunity to reflect. After asking a question it is helpful to pause. *M*ake it a long pause, if necessary; a few students will realize that the teacher is *g*oing to stay with the question until a *student* answers it.

Undoubtedly those who read these paragraphs will see that the foregoing are *su*bstitutes for discussion. They suggest that the teacher should instead prepare *a*n agenda for the lesson, a discussion outline, with a mixture of information-*se*eking questions and questions that seek appraisals, comparisons, reflections, *ge*neralizations. If the discussion is profitable the student will see the topic in a *n*ew light. He may feel that he has helped to form or shape or create the concept *p*resented during the hour. "To be learning something," wrote Aristotle in the *P*oetics, "is the greatest of pleasures, not only to the philosopher but also the *r*est of mankind, however small their capacity for it."

Parliamentary Procedure

*Y*our teaching of group discussion may or may not be preceded by a segment on *p*arliamentary procedure (see Chapter 3). If such a segment is included, the *su*ggestion of this text is not to teach it merely as a complex of rules and *r*egulations. Here are two lines of thought:

1. Our debt to the British parliament. Now in the eighth century of its *e*xistence, Parliament developed its procedures out of trial and error:

a. The presiding officer should be clothed with sufficient authority and prestige to enable him to enforce his decisions. He should enjoy long tenure in office. The notion that an assembly should have a different presiding officer everyday seemed eminently fair on the face of it, but proved unworkable. The ability to preside requires a certain talent plus a body of specialized information; experience ripens one and augments the other.

b. The business before the house should be put in the form of a main motion or resolution. Talk should be directed towards this resolution; other discussion is irrelevant and out of order. Parliamentary debate took a great stride forward once the assembly developed the concept of a main motion.

c. Opportunity for participation should be available to every member. Whatever limitations are set should apply to all. The House of Commons, for example, has a rule that no member shall speak a second time (except to clarify a statement, answer a question, etc.) until others have spoken. The presiding officer operates with scrupulous fairness in recognizing members who wish to speak.

d. Every member should have one vote. Schemes to give privileged people, such as university graduates, more than one vote had short duration. Admittedly a vote reflects an individual judgment, and some individuals are wiser, more impartial, and more experienced than others; the overriding assumption, however, is that these differences cancel out. Moreover, nearly all parliamentary decisions are on problems of policy, not of fact, and the best wisdom of the group needs to be ascertained.

e. A majority vote determines the outcome. Originally, Parliament followed the plan of requiring a unanimous vote before any decision could be taken. Again, this seemed eminently fair and reasonable. But the impossibility of securing unanimity on controversial questions quickly became evident. The alternative was to canvass the votes on each side of the question and abide by the wish of the majority. Disappointment is great when a side loses by a single vote, but this possibility must be accepted once the general principle is agreed upon. In the event of a deadlock, the speaker is given the responsibility of breaking the tie.

These procedures were incorporated into United States Senate rules when Thomas Jefferson, then Vice President and its presiding officer, formulated his manual of procedure. Jefferson did not follow all of the rules of Parliament. He did not like its cumbersome method of voting nor certain ceremonial practices, but he did accept the heart and core of its body of principles. In the main they have also found their way into *Robert's Rules of Order* and other manuals.

2. *The relation of parliamentary procedure to representative government.* Concepts such as the right of every person to speak his piece and to vote are the essence of representative government. The better an electorate is informed, and the more effectively its divergent points of view can be expressed, the wiser its decisions. We are not a country where differences are followed by revolutions. Ours is a legitimate government, nearing the end of its second century of existence, firmly rooted in the consent of the governed and dedicated to life, liberty, and the pursuit of happiness. All sorts of minority groups have their say but ultimately they stand or fall because of a decision arrived at in a parliamentary manner.

At times groups emerge that deny the basic parliamentary assumption. They seek to overturn the current system but can only substitute negatives for it. They are mighty on the strong questions but weak on the quiet answers. The leaders are particularly baffled when the followers ask, "What do we do next?" The followers then see that whereas before they had *something,* now they are being offered *nothing.* Whereupon the old leaders are discarded and the shift is made to new leaders who seek to enhance the *something* but by working within the parliamentary framework.

A Final Word

The field of discussion opens broad possibilities for motivation. Business management is, for example, a popular study on most campuses. Principles of management are so widely applicable that one who understands them can find an important niche in any business or industry: merchandising, electronics, petroleum, airlines, drugs. From our point of view, management is in large part a matter of small groups: committees, boards, teams, dealing with personnel, sales, research, finance, public relations. On the campus the student learns method, theory; on the job he learns corporate details involved with steel, fabrics, insurance, utilities, or whatever. An alumnus who works for a telephone corporation declared: "To learn what I needed to know about the telephone business was relatively easy; learning to work with people proved to be the real test."

Take a Sunday classified advertising section to class and read the ads seeking junior or senior executives, top management or middle management; let students see for themselves where group-process fits in. If this approach seems too materialistic, shift the emphasis to government, medicine, the ministry, education, Peace Corps. Each of these suggests a decision making system, the focus being placed on committees, boards, teams: people consulting, exploring, persuading, inquiring. Actually you will find yourself talking not only about discussion, but also about interviewing, conversation, speechmaking, even interpretation and drama—the works.

Discussion methods are becoming increasingly prominent in the speechmaking course at both high school and university levels. Lines of approach suggested in this chapter may be pursued in the sources cited and in others that follow below.

Assignments

1. Prepare an oral report (the teacher will assign time limits) on one of the types of discussion described in the chapter. Read as widely as you can about it in discussion textbooks and in other sources. Consider how it is used in education, in business, in government. Suggest subjects or topics for high school or college classes.

2. Work out a teaching unit in discussion for a high school or college fundamentals course. Be especially specific as to your assignments, classroom procedures, illustrative material, suggested topics.

3. Divide the class into groups of four or five. Each group is to take a class period and put on a demonstration of a specific type of discussion.

4. The class will select a timely question; choose a moderator; divide into buzz

sessions of four or five each; choose a chairman and recorder for each buzz session. On a stated day the moderator will present a preliminary discussion of the question selection. After this presentation, the buzz sessions will retire to different parts of the room and discuss the question for twenty to thirty minutes. At the end of that time, the group will reconvene and the moderator will call on the recorders for reports.

Questions for Classroom Discussion

1. What is discussion? a way of solving a problem? a procedure for determining "truth"? a method of training leaders? a device for building morale? a second-rate substitute for a trained executive? a way of assembling and mobilizing facts? a way of pooling ignorance? a form of persuasion?

2. What are the kinds of discussion: round table, symposium, panel, group, staff conference, buzz session, brainstorming session, teacher-led classroom discussion, demonstration discussion, role-playing, others? What new methods or techniques have appeared in the last few years?

3. Should a discussion yield recommendations, facts, solutions, definitions, random comments? Is the end-product of discussion tangible, intangible, or both?

4. What are the faults and flaws of discussion: too time-consuming, too random, too wasteful, inefficient, unproductive?

5. What are the materials of discussion: facts, opinions, arguments, reasons, comments humorous and otherwise, orders, directives?

6. In what kind of political, social, economic, and intellectual atmosphere does discussion thrive?

7. Give instances of history-making discussions; discussions in business, legislative, or educational circles that produced notable results.

8. What is the function of the chairman: planner and visualizer, provoker of contributions, stimulator, check-rein, summarizer, referee, evaluator?

9. What is the function of the participant? What if he talks too much? talks too little? talks beside the point? irritates others? overstates or understates?

10. What is the function of the agenda? When should it be followed, when modified or abandoned?

11. How is a discussion appraised: purpose, number of contributions, kind of contributions, intellectual or emotional ferment generated, validity of solutions, decisions or judgments reached?

References

Of General Interest

Baird, A. Craig. *Argumentation, Discussion, and Debate*. New York: McGraw-Hill, 1950.

Bales, Robert F. *Interaction Process Analysis: A Method for the Study of Small Groups*. Cambridge: Addison-Wesley, 1950.

Barnlund, Dean C., and Haiman, Franklyn S. *The Dynamics of Discussion*. Boston: Houghton Mifflin, 1960.

Barnlund, Dean C. *Interpersonal Communication: Survey and Studies*. Boston: Houghton Mifflin, 1968.

Bormann, Ernest G. *Discussion and Group Methods: Theory and Practice*. New York: Harper & Row, 1969.

Braden, Waldo W., and Brandenburg, Earnest. *Oral Decision-Making: Principles of Discussion and Debate*. New York: Harper & Brothers, 1955.

Brigance, W. Norwood. *Speech: Its Techniques and Disciplines in a Free Society*. 2d ed. New York: Appleton-Century-Crofts, 1961.

Cartwright, Dorwin, and Zander, Alvin, eds. *Group Dynamics: Research and Theory*, 3d ed. New York: Harper & Row, 1968.

Cathcart, Robert S., and Samovar, Larry A. *Small Group Communication: A Reader*. Dubuque: William C. Brown, 1968.

Collins, Barry E., and Guetzkow, Harold. *A Social Psychology of Group Processes for Decision-Making*. New York: John Wiley & Sons, 1964.

Cortright, Rupert L., and Hinds, George L. *Creative Discussion*. New York: Macmillan, 1959.

Crowell, Laura. *Discussion: Method of Democracy*. Chicago: Scott, Foresman, 1963.

Ehninger, Douglas, and Brockriede, Wayne. *Decision by Debate*. New York: Dodd, Mead, 1963.

Ewbank, Henry L., and Auer, J. Jeffery. *Discussion and Debate*. 2d ed. New York: Appleton-Century-Crofts, 1951.

Glover, John D., and Hower, Ralph M. *The Administrator: Cases on Human Relations in Business*. 4th ed. Homewood, Ill.: Richard D. Irwin, 1963.

Gulley, Halbert E. *Discussion, Conference, and the Group Process*. 2d ed. New York: Holt, Rinehart & Winston, 1968.

Hare, A. Paul. *Handbook of Small Group Research*. New York: Free Press, 1962.

Hare, A. Paul; Borgotta, E. F.; and Bales, Robert F. *Small Groups: Studies in Social Interaction*. Part III, rev. ed. New York: Alfred A. Knopf, 1966.

Harnack, R. Victor, and Fest, Thorrel B. *Group Discussion: Theory and Technique*. New York: Appleton-Century-Crofts, 1964.

Lee, Irving J. *Customs and Crises in Communication*. New York: Harper & Bros., 1954.

Maier, Norman R. F. *Problem-Solving Discussions and Conferences: Leadership Methods and Skills*. New York: McGraw-Hill, 1963.

Potter, David, and Andersen, Martin P. *Discussion: A Guide to Effective Practice*. Belmont, Calif.: Wadsworth, 1963.

Sattler, William M., and Miller, N. Edd. *Discussion and Conference*. 2d ed. Englewood Cliffs: Prentice-Hall, 1968.

Utterback, William E. *Group Thinking and Conference Leadership*. rev. ed. New York: Holt, Rinehart & Winston, 1964.

Van Doren, Carl. *The Great Rehearsal.* New York: Viking Press, 1948.

Wagner, Russell H., and Arnold, Carroll C. *Handbook of Group Discussion.* 2c ed. Boston: Houghton Mifflin, 1965.

Special Studies

Becker, Samuel L.; Murray, James N., Jr.; and Bechtoldt, Harold P. *Teaching by the Discussion Method.* A special publication issued by the University of Iowa, 1958, reporting an experiment with television discussion, small group discussion, and the lecture method.

Brown, Charles T., and Pruis, John J. "Encouraging Participation in Classroom Discussion." *Speech Teacher* November 1958.

Crowell, Laura; Katcher, Allen; and Miyamoto, S. Frank. "Self-Concepts of Communication Skill and Performance in Small Group Discussions." *Speech Monographs* March 1955. Note the questionnaire items for exploring one's self as communicator.

Discussion contests: Cathcart, Robert S. "The Case for Discussion Contests." *Speech Teacher* November 1957; Shepherd, David W. "Some Observations on High School Discussion." *Speech Teacher* September 1955; Shepherd, David W., and Seal, Forrest L. "The Discussion Contest: Requiescat in Pace." *Speech Teacher* January 1957.

Forbes, Allen E. "Discussion Today." *Western Speech* Spring 1959.

Gray, Giles Wilkeson. "Points of Emphasis in Teaching Parliamentary Procedure." *Speech Teacher* January 1964.

Harshbarger, H. Clay, and Becker, Samuel L. "Teaching by Discussion or Television." *Quarterly Journal of Speech* December 1956.

Kane, Peter E. "Role Playing for Educational Use." *Speech Teacher* November 1964.

Mills, Glen E.; Windes, Russel R., Jr.; Robinson, James L.; Christophersen, Merrill G.; Freeley, Austin J.; Giffin, Kim; Lashbrook, Brad; Anderson, Kenneth E.; and Polisky, Jerome B. "A Symposium on Debate and Discussion." *Speech Teacher* March 1960.

Phelps, Waldo; Hanks, L. Day; and Neef, Harold. "The Influence of Speech Activities on Learning United States History." *Speech Teacher* March 1959. Reports a controlled experiment with 133 students. Fifty-five reported "speech activities stimulated greater interest and effort"; eighteen reported "speech activities discouraged interest and effort." Every teacher of social studies should read this and the preceding reference for the discussion of problems pro and con.

Watkins, Lloyd I. "Some Problems and Solutions in Teaching Group Discussion." *Speech Teacher* September 1961.

Wischmeier, Richard R. "Group-Centered and Leader-Centered Leadership: An Experimental Study." *Speech Monographs* March 1955. Appraises the two types of leadership under such categories as "Which group got off to a better start?" "Which group reached a more satisfactory solution?" and others.

See also: references at the end of Chapter 15.

10

---

interpretation

I can read Browning so Browning himself can understand it.

Mark Twain

Reading remains to be considered. Only practice can teach how a boy may know when to take breath, where to divide a verse, where the sense is concluded, where it begins, . . .what is to be pronounced with greater slowness or rapidity, with greater animation or gentleness than other passages. . . . So that he may be able to do all this successfully, let him understand what he reads.

Quintilian

f speaking is the oldest form of human communication, reciting story and verse nust be the second. Oral interpretation has a long and distinguished tradition to vhich each century has contributed modifications. Especially in recent years the neory of reading aloud has received penetrating study. Old strictures have been ltered or laid aside. The reader's communication of meaning, feeling, attitude, one, continues with increasing sophistication as man's social, humanistic, and cientific horizons are expanded. The modern teacher-critic offers more by way f imagination and insight, less by way of rule. More sympathetic to modes and tyles that expose the richness of structure and content, he does not lay so heavy hand on departures from tradition and formalism. New types of group reading re evolving, and evolutions of these new forms. Hence at those points in the year's schedule when instruction in interpretation comes to the foreground, the classroom teacher needs to be as knowledgeable as possible.

Good oral reading is necessary in a wide variety of communicative situations. For example:

1. The extempore speaker who wishes to support his reasoning by reading a precise statistic, a quotation from an authority, or other type of evidence. Unless the read-aloud bit is as effective as the rest of the speech, the attention of listeners sags when the reading starts.

2. The speaker who wishes to read his entire speech from a manuscript. Most speakers read poorly. Even experienced speech readers have been known to throw prepared speech texts away and substitute extemporaneous remarks; occasions arise, however, when the manuscript is necessary and must be read effectively.

3. The discussant or debater who, because of the nature of this form of communication, must incorporate quoted materials into his presentation.

4. The student who enjoys acting and would like to appear in amateur or even professional performances must manage his lines well if he is to perfect his characterization.

5. The classroom teacher who wishes to read a passage aloud, instead of paraphrasing it, because of the special elegance or clarity of its wording.

6. Various situations in which information must be presented verbatim, such as the reading of rules and regulations, directions, orders, directives, or steps in a process.[1]

Note that some of the foregoing are utilitarian, some artistic, some both.

In addition to its significance in these kinds of communication, oral interpretation especially commands our admiration as an art to be practiced in its own right. Inflections, intonations, changes in rate and loudness, intervals of silence carry meaning just as do the words themselves. Facial expression, movement, action, bearing, and gesture are also a part of the complex of understanding, attitude, feeling, that are to be expressed by the reader and received by the listener. Robert Beloof makes a convincing case for the oral presentation of literature. Thinking not only of the critical study of a piece, but also of voice and body, he writes:

If the reader has learned wrongly the vocal and bodily experience, the poem is beyond him. If he reads with a singsong rhythm or some other ironbound vocal pattern, this limitation will not merely impair his reading

[1] *See:* Ordean G. Ness, "The Value of Oral Interpretation to the Student in General Speech," *Speech Teacher,* September 1956.

aloud; it will impair his silent reading, for surely the evidence points out that one needs to know the proper vocal patterns even to read silently—providing that one is reaching for the profound rather than the superficial level.

Most students can manage the basic, biologically oriented tones, Beloof continues, "hate, greed, love, pain, those tones whose lingual signals they would adequately have developed in their own bodies by imitation of the normal bodily, vocal, and verbal signals of their everyday environment." What escapes them are tones "arising out of a more complex, more sophisticated level of verbal signals than they were likely to have encountered during their openly imitative period: tones of irony, ambiguity, and other complicated balances of attitude." These they must achieve not only through "a purely book-bound, purely intellectual effort"—which is admittedly valuable—but by making them read aloud, and listen to good reading by others."[2]

Experience in reading aloud is being introduced into first courses at both college and high school levels. Not only teachers of speech and English, but teachers of other subjects should read to their students from time to time. This advice assumes that the teacher can read with sprightliness, enthusiasm, and projection. Every field has vivid materials that can be enhanced by oral presentation. Hopefully the teachers of these subjects have been exposed during their college days to good principles of oral interpretation. Most students can recall teachers whose reading was a high point in the day, and can report that these classes would otherwise have been much less rich.

Basic Point of View

This chapter is not written for the specialist teacher but for the new teacher planning a unit in interpretation, either at the high school level or as a part of the college fundamentals course. Teachers of other subjects, however, who read this discussion and who pursue their inquiry further, will glean helpful suggestions in reading aloud more effectively.

As the teacher begins to plan his course segment, he can profitably reflect along these lines:

1. Instruction in oral interpretation should include both theory and practice. Interpretation is developing a significant corpus of principle that makes it not only an integral part of the field of speech but also gives it a significant role in liberal education. To have the segment of the course dealing with interpretation consist entirely of performance would be poor pedagogy. Yet the student should not be exposed solely to theory, either; he needs opportunity to improve his own competence.

Robert Beloof, *The Performing Voice in Literature*, pp. 7-8.

2. Depending on the type of course and the needs of students, the teacher wi
likely make a selection from the following:

a. *Types of literature.* Beginning with relatively straightforward forms an
moving to the more complex, the teacher can choose from different types o
literature in this order: (i) the speech, (ii) the informal essay, (iii) the narr;
tive, (iv) drama, (v) poetry. Without attempting to teach a literature cours·
the teacher should explain the problems that each type presents to the reade·

b. *Principles of interpretation.* Instead of making the main headings of th·
unit different types of literature, he can instead take up in turn those basi
principles that can be applied to any type. Among these are: (i) use of th·
voice: pitch, loudness, duration, quality; (ii) facial expression, bodily actio·
posture; (iii) articulation; (iv) analyzing content, a concern of highest impo
tance; (v) tone; (vi) language, rhythm, meter; (vii) techniques of presentatio·

c. *Activities or projects.* Especially when the teacher elects to give onl·
limited time to interpretation, as in a general course, he may want to choose
specific project and spend all of the available class time on it. Some of th·
first-course syllabi reviewed in Chapter 4 assigned part of a play, a poem fro·
a favorite author, or a narrative selection. The instruction focusses on th·
single assignment. The high school teacher planning a year course similar t
the one described in Chapter 3 might allot six to eight weeks to interpr·
tation, and cover a limited range of projects: for example, an informal essa·
(which poses no problem of characterization), a narrative selection (perha·
one in which the story is told entirely in the first person, with little or n
dialogue); a poem (preferably a relatively simple lyric or narrative). When th·
assignments are pointed toward an assembly program or a festival or tourn;
ment, the teacher reviews previous instruction as needed to fit the specif·
project.

Types of Literature

Each type of literature presents its own challenge to the oral reader. The teache·
should consult the references at the end of this chapter in order to gain a fir·
grasp of essential requirements.

The speech. It has been well said that the reading of speeches is an acquire·
taste. A speech is so particularly adapted to a specific audience at a specific tim·
that it is likely to contain allusions that an uninformed reader will miss. To cate·
the mood and tone of the situation is also a prime requisite. Once the spirit c
the speech is grasped and the meaning well understood, the reader will need t
present it with the deliberateness that is characteristic of public address. Th·
delivery of good speakers suggests also energy, vitality, and concern.

The essay. The informal essay rambles merrily along, delightfully and casually

The tone may be ironic, whimsical, reminiscent, wistful, full of awe or wonder. The formal essay is closely packed, with longer, more complex sentences and paragraphs, subtle bindings and harnessings, placing a greater burden on the memory span of both reader and listener.

The universal problem in reading these kinds of materials is to make the performance sound more like lively *talk* than like rote *reading.* If the reader can make the sentences sound like animated talk, he has made a good beginning. The cadence of inexperienced oral readers invariably has a pattern, a singsong, that flattens and levels the pitch and loudness variations that normally characterize directness and spontaneity. Vocal inflection is just as likely as not to come at the wrong places, showing that the reader has not fully studied the material. Hence, at times the teacher will need to interrupt the student and ask questions that compel more accurate thinking. Clues can be found in adverbs and adjectives, in striking choices of verbs, in variations from usual word order, in repetition and parallelism. In one of the most famous sentences of this century, "Never in the field of human conflict was so much owed by so many to so few," these observations can be made: *never,* at the beginning of the sentence, out of usual word order; *field of human conflict,* with much more distinctiveness than, for example, "in the course of history"; the parallelism of *so much, so many,* and *so few,* the first two phrases contrasting with the third.[3]

The narrative. Here the reader must suggest the character telling the story, whether it is Huck Finn or Holden Caulfield. If the narrative opens into a dialogue, the reader will need to portray the characters. He must employ subtle changes of voice, or bodily posture and tension, or both, to suggest each character. Meaning, attitude, tone, emotion call for more variety than, for example, the formal essay. The student will need to locate essential details that identify *time and place,* establish *point of view,* lead to the *complication,* work towards the *climax.* Other basic issues are suggested in Wayne C. Booth's indispensable *The Rhetoric of Fiction.* Where he writes *author,* the student may to an extent substitute *interpreter:*

> How can an author make sure that his most important dramatic moments will be heightened rather than obscured by their surroundings? . . . How can he prevent a sentimental reading of this character or a hostile reading of that one? How can he insure that when this character lies, the reader will not be taken in—or, when desired, that he will be? Answers to these and numerous similar questions . . . can provide a beginning in the effort to understand the rhetoric of fiction. . . .
> The novel comes into existence as something communicable, and the

Other famous phrases: *iron curtain, black power, Ask not what your country can do for you, ask what you can do for your country.* Also (though not from a speech): *That's one small step for a man, one giant leap for mankind.*

means of communication are not shameful intrusions unless they are mad
with shameful ineptitude.[4]

The drama. This type of literature requires the reader to tell the story throug
the lines of the participants, without the benefit of narrative or expositor
paragraphs. As with the narrative, vocal inflections, subtle changes of stance c
muscle tension, restrained gesture, and facial expression are utilized to sugges
the flow of dialogue from one character to another and to the listener.

Principles of Interpretation

Certain principles of interpretation have already been suggested in connectio
with the foregoing discussion of literary types.

The essence of oral interpretation, as of public speaking, acting, or any othe
form of communication, lies not in the written word itself but in the word a
uttered. Interpretation requires the utmost of the reader's ability to analyz
content and to express that content through voice and body.

The teacher may illustrate this basic point for students in a score of ways, bu
an example that deserves to be better known than it is comes from the career c
the brilliant Sara Siddons. For many years she was the supreme lady of th
theater—the Sarah Bernhardt of the eighteenth-century London stage. Her inte
pretation of numerous distinguished roles, particularly of Lady Macbeth, was t
the sophisticated audiences of her day moving and stirring.

Up to 1785 London playgoers had become accustomed to certain tradition;
renditions of scenes from Macbeth. During the sleepwalking scene, for exampl
Lady Macbeth had invariably carried the candle even while she was trying t
wash blood off her hands. As the young Mrs. Siddons studied the script (it w;
her habit to read, ponder, underscore key words and phrases, experiment wit
various interpretations), she became convinced that Lady Macbeth should con
on stage, put down the candle, and then proceed with the scene and tl
subsequent hand washing. To her mind the digital dexterity of the old tradition
of hand washing while candle holding at the same time, was not dramaticall
sound. So expert a dramatist as Richard Brinsley Sheridan, hearing that st
proposed to make this violent alteration of traditional method, pleaded with he
even at the last minute, not to set down the candle. Her dramatic instinc
convinced her, however, that she should proceed as she had planned; she di
and the scene was powerful. She made other changes; instead of reading tl
answer to Macbeth's statement, "If we should fail?" as "We fail?" (how ir
probable!) she changed the interpretation to "We fail" (if we fail, we fail, an
that's that). Her facial expression, both as she listened to Macbeth's lines and i

---

[4]Wayne C. Booth, *The Rhetoric of Fiction,* pp. 64, 397.

he read her own, augmented the impressiveness of the scene. London playgoers noted the changes at once and were excited by them. She settled for good the question of what to do with the candle and other traditional practices. She found a meaning in Shakespeare's words that had been lost on others. Her vocal and bodily interpretations were likely too rich for our blood but were eminently satisfying to those who saw and heard her.[5]

The teacher will want to read widely into ways of analyzing material for oral interpretation. A point of view is stated by Don Geiger: "If a piece of literature is representation of experience, we probably best *understand* it when we have experienced it, and work in oral interpretation holds out the possibility for something of this meaningful experience."[6] Hence a student not only reads about a selection and the selection itself, but adds a dimension to his preparation when he begins to read the selection aloud. In his analysis he asks questions growing out of the situation: who is speaking and to whom? when and where does the action take place? Still further (writes Geiger): What is the content of the speaker's (narrator's) utterance? why does he utter it? what does it mean?[7]

Whatever is revealed by a study of the selection must be expressed through the physical resources of the interpreter. Frances L. McCurdy reminds the interpreter that he may be called upon to express, for example, not merely satire, but a particular kind of satire; not merely irony, but a special kind of irony. Moreover: "The oral interpreter must not only be aware of the tone of the writer; he must determine the tone of the narrator whom the writer chooses as his fictional voice." She writes:

> The oral interpreter who speaks for a narrator addressing a fictional listener must be alert to the responses of that imagined listener. For example, the passionate woman in Browning's "The Laboratory" watches the reactions of the maker of potions to her demand for a suitable potion. She speaks in a particular place of fumes and vapors surrounded by vials of bright-colored potions. . . . To be sure the interpreter does not adopt an Italian accent or sniff the fumes, but he must be able to feel the body tensions of the jealous woman, to see the old chemist stooping over his bench, to hear the soft hissing of the vapors in the laboratory, to be aware of the power that the old man now holds and to calculate the use he may make of this power.[8]

Good literature is written painstakingly. Authors tell about writing a few pages of prose a day, or a few lines of verse. Often they work from an outline

Yvonne Ffrench, *Mrs. Siddons: Tragic Actress*, pp. 109-117.

The Sound, Sense, and Performance of Literature, p. 4.

The Dramatic Impulse in Modern Poetics, p. 21.

"Oral Interpretation as an Approach to Literature," in Thomas L. Fernandez (ed.), *Oral Interpretation and the Teaching of English*, pp. 10-11, 13. Wilma Grimes and Alethea Mattingly, *Interpretation: Writer-Reader-Audience*, pp. 32-33, also suggest questions to ask in connection with "The Laboratory."

prepared in advance and changed or modified as they proceed. Words, phrase
incidents, are selected with deliberate intent. An author may mull over half
dozen words before making his final choice. To use the one word that express
the exact thought is invariably the principal determiner: at times the poet wi
even accept an inexact rhyme, or an essay writer will vary his scheme or patter
rather than settle upon a menial word that trifles with his meaning. Recall Mar
Twain's dictum here: the difference between the right word and the almost-rigl
word is as great as the difference between lightning and the lightning-bug. Eve
Lincoln chided Douglas with the distinction between a horse chestnut and
chestnut horse.

When you can get the student to realize the sweat, the anguish, the incessar
trial and toil, the pondering, the tearing up and starting over, the repeated draf
that go into the choice of words and incidents, of plans and designs, he will n
rest until he has exposed for himself the reasons behind the choices.

The incident of John Keats and his good friend Leigh Hunt is wort
recounting. Keats and Hunt were sitting in the same room, Keats writing an
Hunt reading. At one point Keats looked up and said, "What do you think
this? 'A beautiful thing is an unending joy.' " "Good," said Hunt, "but not qui
perfect."

Here was criticism blended with encouragement—in all the world is there
better formula for creative teaching?—and Keats restudied the line. Pretty soo
he spoke up: "How is this? 'A thing of beauty is an unending joy.' " "That
better," responded Hunt, "but still not quite it." Keats studied his paper furthe
and spoke again: "What do you think of this? 'A thing of beauty is a jo
forever.' " "That," said Hunt, "will live as long as the English language
spoken."

Would your student prefer that Keats had written, "A *lovely thing* is a jo
forever?" And in the Keats context, is not *thing,* usually a word to throw awa
and replace, for once in its long existence invested with glory and majesty
Would he like *bit* or *object* better? Would he improve on Keats if he wrote, "
beautiful thing is a joy forever?"

For the Gettysburg ceremony Lincoln wrote, "This nation shall have a ne
birth of freedom." At the last minute he changed it: "This nation, under Go
shall have a new birth of freedom." Thus was he impressed by the battlefiel
itself, as he saw where thousands of brave men, some living and son
dead, had recently fought. The ceremonial speech of its era was the Kenned
inaugural. The young president worked over draft after draft; one change h
made was in the opening sentence: he altered "We celebrate today not as
victory of party but the sacrament of democracy" to the simpler, more el
quent contrast: "We observe today not a victory of party but a celebration
freedom." Busy, discouraging, war-filled years have flown by since that speec
was composed and delivered; if you were to read it aloud today you woul
wonder at this passage:

Let every nation know, whether it wishes us well or ill, that we shall pay any price, bear any burden, meet any hardship, support any friend, oppose any foe to assure the survival and the success of liberty.

s Kennedy promising too much, offering too much, venturing too much? Is it tter to spend our primary energies closer to home? Does a nation alternate its riods of confidence with periods of despair, so that given another turn of the eel, the sentiment of this passage will be reaffirmed? The phrases are there, e rhetorical pattern bright and clear; if the setting now looks different to us, ould the reader speak these words with some admixture of historic irony? It is t always easy to understand meaning. A reader would feel ridiculous to read a ection with impressive solemnity when closer study showed him that the thor wrote with ironical intent. In *Hamlet* are the lines:

What a piece of work is a man! how noble in reason! how infinite in faculty! in form and moving how express and admirable! in action how like an angel! in apprehension how like a god!

ese lines could be read to show wonder, awe, admiration; but, thrown into a ferent situation, as they were in *Hair,* the reader subtly indicated that he was couraged about humankind and depressed as he witnessed the gulf between n's promise and his actual comportment.

You may have insightful discussions trying to unveil the architecture of the em, or of the story or play. A thought planted at the beginning may be peated or exploited later. If the first statement of the thought is read just ht, the listener will grasp and appreciate its repetition or development. alysis may uncover a logical or emotional progression, a climax or anticlimax. e reader's interpretation will enhance the listener's perception of the design. oreover, the analysis of structure yields valuable clues about the larger meaning the piece. The listener may fancy he is listening to a casual statement or a ies of isolated events, when all at once, through the reader's artistry, the aningful whole emerges (as in *The Playboy of the Western World*). Again, nbolism has been a fruitful technique of writers and critics, and the reader o misses the symbol is certain to come up with a story about a sea captain rching out a giant whale instead of the other story several layers deeper.

Interpretation also requires extraordinary sensitivity of facial expression. dily activity is considerably restrained. If the reader is presenting Mark ain's fabulous piloting adventures in *Life on the Mississippi*, he will direct the aight narrative part generally forward towards the listeners. As other char- ers enter the story, he will by a glance place them slightly toward one side or other as the plot requires. For example, he might direct the lines of Horace by ("By the shadow of death, but he is a lightning pilot!") slightly towards left. Listeners will thus associate these changes of direction, along with

appropriate changes of facial expression and vocal modification, with Twa
himself, the apprentice and narrator, and with Bixby, the veteran. As t
steamer moves steadily towards the perilous Hat Island crossing, the reader w
show the mounting tension both by subtle changes of voice and by increasi
muscle alertness. As Bixby, the reader will never literally reach out and grab
imaginary steering wheel to yank and twist the craft through the shall
crossing, but with heightened yet disciplined bodily tension he will convey
the listener what is actually happening.[9]

Charlotte I. Lee, in a chapter filled with practical suggestions on techniqu
points out that the interpreter of a telephone conversation does not need to p
one clenched hand to the ear to suggest a telephone, especially since the oth
hand is holding a book, but he can insert the word "Operator" before giving t
number, and complete the illusion of using a telephone by the manner
speaking. Nor, she continues, does Juliet need to pick up an imaginary pois
vial and hold it high for the audience to see before quaffing its contents; rath
the interpreter can visualize for the audience a vial in the palm of the hand
even lying on the reading stand. In one example the overt gesture is dispens
with altogether and in the other it is reduced in scale.[10]

I always found it helpful to discuss situations such as these with studem
repeatedly soliciting "other ways" of handling business and action. Some of t
suggestions were less than inspired, but the good sense of the class invariab
asserted itself and the improvisations are helpful in making the central poi
memorable.

The average human voice is readily capable of expressing fear, calm, ang
disgust, alarm, and the like, in real-life situations. Interpretation, however, mak
a twofold challenge to the student. First, he must learn to express the
emotions when the stimulus is a printed page, not an actual event. Any o
trapped in a burning building can scream for help with fervor and convictic
but a passage from literature may also call for an anguished cry and the read
cannot burn down a building just to get the proper mood. Second, as alrea
suggested, he may need to call upon a wider variety of vocal expression than
normally uses. This statement is not to urge him to be overly sensational but
observe that he may have latent vocal resources he has not drawn on. So
students, for example, are unresponsive even in situations calling for m

[9]*See:* Wallace A. Bacon, *The Art of Interpretation,* pp. 80-84; Charlotte I. Lee, *O*
Interpretation, pp. 311-333. Jeré S. Veilleux, *Oral Interpretation: The Recreation*
Literature, gives a chapter to specific questions (using the eyes, handling excerp
planning a program, a dozen others) that a student might ask in connection wi
improving his own ability to read aloud (pp. 108 ff.). Geiger, *The Sound, Sense, a*
Performance of Literature, has in Chapter 9 specific insights about expressing attitud
actions. Louise M. Scrivner, *A Guide to Oral Interpretation,* has many teachal
suggestions both about analysis and about the improvement of student techniques.
[10]Lee, pp. 319-321.

:pression of pleasure or excitement. Interpretation requires the student to pry
s eyes loose from the page, to come out from behind the book, to unbolt his
nds from the lectern—in short to project and communicate so that listeners
it front can share the experience.

Humor, excitement, wistfulness, sorrow, suspense, anger, envy, are only a few
' the tones that the reader may wish to suggest. Consider these passages:

> I am loath to close. We are not enemies, but friends. We must
> not be enemies. . . . The mystic chords of memory, stretching
> from every battlefield and patriot grave to every living heart and
> hearthstone all over this broad land, will yet swell the chorus of
> the Union when again touched, as surely they will be, by the
> better angels of our nature.
>
> Abraham Lincoln, *First Inaugural Address.*

> A sense of duty pursues us ever. It is omnipresent, like the
> Deity. If we take to ourselves the wings of the morning, and
> dwell in the uttermost parts of the sea, duty performed or duty
> violated is still with us, for our happiness or our misery.
>
> Daniel Webster, *The White Murder Case.*

> There was once a prince, and he wanted a princess, but then she
> must be a real princess. He traveled right around the world to
> find one, but there was always something wrong.
>
> Hans Christian Andersen, *The Real Princess.*

> Colts grew horses, beards turned gray,
> Deacon and deaconess dropped away,
> Children and grand-children—where were they?
> But there stood the stout old one-hoss-shay
> As fresh as on Lisbon-earthquake day!
>
> Oliver Wendell Holmes, *The Deacon's Masterpiece.*

> Rustum gazed, and gazed, and stood
> Speechless; and then he uttered one sharp cry:
> "O boy—thy father"—and his voice choked there.
>
> Matthew Arnold, *Sohrab and Rustum.*

> **Christina.** Speaking of insults, though, what explanation can
> *you* offer *me* for your rudeness to me as a guest in your house?
> **Mrs. Phelps.** I have not been rude to you.
> **Christina.** You have been appallingly rude. . . .
>
> Sidney Howard, *The Silver Cord.*

Each of these excerpts strikes its own emotional note. The Lincoln select
is an appeal to patriotism: for the Union, not merely for a section. The Webs
selection is solemn; the Andersen selection is wistful; the Holmes selectio
mock serious; the Arnold selection is anguished; the Howard selection is ang
Study and analysis are necessary to reveal the proper mood and tone. T
following come into review:

The use of imagery. Figurative language is imaginative, not exact, and acco
ingly serves to suggest moods or states of mind. Note "the mystic chords
memory," "better angels of our nature," "wings of the morning."

Repetition. Repeating a word or phrase may give the selection an emotio
impact: "princess," "duty."

Rhyme. Rhyme itself has an emotional effect. Perhaps the age of the one h
shay is suggested by the unchanging rhyme of the five lines quoted: *gray, aw
they, shay, day.*

Meter. The internal rhythm of lines adds to the emotional effect. The successi
of stressed and unstressed syllables, arranged in patterns which themselves ha
slight variations, is appreciated consciously or unconsciously by the listener. T
break in the meter of the Arnold selection probably heightens the anguish of t
father's discovery: " 'O boy—thy father!'—and his voice choked there."

Other poetic devices. The use of musical or unmusical sounds and of alliterati
also heightens emotion. "Soft is the strain when Zephyr gently blows" v
Pope's way of writing a line full of *s* and *z* sounds to suggest a breeze; he a
wrote

When Ajax strives some rock's vast weight to throw
The line, too, labors, and the words move slow

to show that a series of short words, chosen with a special ear, suggest t
strained lifting of a heavy weight.

Specific words. Often a subtle reason need not be sought to explain an em
tional effect; a simple word, accurately used, may have powerful resul
"Rude," repeated in the Howard excerpt, is a blunt word. "Appallingly rude'
stronger than "fearfully rude," "terribly rude," "awfully rude," "shockin
rude," "frightfully rude." "Appalling" implies overwhelming, frightening, alm
beyond human power to alter. In the Arnold selection several words contribu
to the effect of anguish. "Gaze" says more than "stare," considerably more th
"gape" (which has an entirely different connotation) or "peer." The repetiti
"gazed, and gazed" adds something further. "Speechless," "sharp cry," a
"choked" also intensify the deep emotion.

These and other selections may form the basis for a class discussion fferences between poetry and prose. You will probably want to avoid subtle stinctions, if you recall your own puzzlement over rhetoric versus poetic, but ou will find it profitable to comment upon the more obvious characteristics of oetry. As they affect the reader, the following are noteworthy:

he problem of suggesting the rhythm, without being carried away by it. If the ythm is followed literally, the effect is mechanical and patterned. There is no tistry in "It was MANY and MANY a YEAR ago," when accented syllables are reremphasized. Rhythm must be subordinated to meaning: an instance occurs hen meaning runs from one line into a following line. In

I call

That piece a wonder, now . . .

e major pause comes after *now,* not after *call.*

he frequent inversion of word order appearing in poetry. "We galloped all ree" is to be read as if that order were perfectly plausible, clearly meaning "All ree of us galloped."

he poetic use of imagery. Does "Drink to me only with thine eyes" mean more an "Show in your eyes how much you love me?" If so, the reader's task is to ll by his interpretation how much more it does mean, and if he can succeed, he n make the song, familiar as it is, take on richer connotations. What does the oet mean when he says "[I] trouble deaf heaven with my bootless cries" or The Wordly Hope men set their Hearts upon Turns Ashes—or it prospers . . ." The stag at eve had drunk his fill." Good poetic imagery shows that the poet as chosen his words carefully for their emotional weight, a quality that should : reflected in the reading.

The foregoing are only elemental differences between prose and poetry. obert G. Ingersoll in his speech "At His Brother's Grave" used poetic qualities this carefully prepared address: "For whether in mid sea or among the eakers of the farther shore, a wreck must mark at last the end of each and all." inston Churchill's speeches also contain rhythm, imagery, and inversion of ord order, as when he said: "It is not given to us to peer into the mysteries of e future. Still I avow my hope and faith, sure and inviolate, that in the days to me the British and American people will for their own safety and for the good all walk together in majesty, in justice, and in peace."

In discussing the rhythm of poetry, talk about the different varieties. The ythm of "That's my last Duchess painted on the wall" is not the same as "I rang to the stirrup," and both differ from "Hail to thee, blithe spirit." You ay bring in *iambic, anapestic, trochaic,* and *dactylic,* and similar technical rms.

Exercises for Class Study

You may want each member of the class to study and read the same selectio
The excerpt from Robert G. Ingersoll's most famous lecture illustrates ma
qualities of prose style:

> Do not tell me that you have got to be rich in order to be happy. We ha
> a false standard of these things in the United States. We think that a m
> must be great, that he must be famous, that he must be wealthy. That is al
> mistake. It is not necessary to be rich, to be great, to be famous, to
> powerful, in order to be happy. The happy man is the free man. Happiness
> the legal tender of the soul. Joy is wealth. Liberty is joy.
>
> No, it is not necessary to be great to be happy. It is not necessary to
> rich to be generous. It is not necessary to be powerful to be just. When t
> world is free, this question will be settled. A new creed will be written.
> that creed, there will be but one word, "Liberty." Oh, Liberty, float n
> forever in the far horizon, remain not forever in the dream of the enthusia
> dwell not forever in the song of the poet, but come and make thy hor
> among the children of men.
>
> I know not what thoughts, what discoveries, what inventions may le
> from the brain of the world; I know not what garments of glory may
> woven by the years to come; I cannot dream of the victories to be won up
> the field of thought. But I do know, that coming from the infinite sea of t
> future there shall never touch this bank and shoal of time, a richer gift, a ra
> blessing, than liberty.
>
> A little while ago I stood by the grave of the old Napoleon. It is
> magnificent tomb of gilt and gold, fit almost for a dead deity. I gazed up
> the sarcophagus of rare Egyptian marble in which rest at last the ashes of th
> restless man. I leaned upon the balustrade and thought of the career of t
> greatest soldier of the modern world.
>
> I saw him walking upon the banks of the Seine contemplating suicide
> saw him quelling the mobs in the streets of Paris. I saw him walking at t
> head of the army in Italy. I saw him crossing the bridge of Lodi with t
> tricolor in his hand. I saw him in Egypt in the shadow of the Pyramids. I s
> him conquer the Alps and mingle the eagles of France with the eagles of t
> crags.
>
> I saw him in Russia, where the infantry of the snow and the cavalry of t
> wild blasts scattered his legions like winter's withered leaves. I saw him
> Leipsic in defeat and disaster, driven by a million bayonets, clutched like
> wild beast, banished to Elba. I saw him escape and take an empire by t
> force of his genius. I saw him upon the frightful field of Waterloo, whe
> Chance and Fate combined to wreck the fortunes of their former king, an
> saw him a prisoner on the rock of St. Helena, with his arms calmly fold
> behind his back, gazing steadfastly out upon the sad and solemn sea.

And I thought of all the widows and orphans he had made, of all the tears
t had been shed for his glory; of the only woman who had ever loved him
n from his heart by the ruthless hand of ambition. And I said, I would rather
·e been a poor French peasant and worn wooden shoes; I would rather have
·d with the vines growing over the doors and the grapes growing purple in the
·; yes, I would rather have been that poor peasant and gone down to the
·gueless silence of the dustless sleep, than to have been that impersonation of
·ce and murder known as Napoleon the Great.

"At the Tomb of Napoleon," from *The Liberty of Man, Woman, and Child*

In your discussion of Ingersoll, you may mention a few facts about his career;
·ny thought him the greatest orator of the nineteenth century. His lecture on
· *Liberty of Man, Woman, and Child* was delivered in 1877, when he was
·y-four years old. He gave it in Chicago before five thousand people; he held
·audience entranced for three hours; when he finished and left the platform,
·people cheered until he returned; when he asked them if he could talk
·ther half-hour, many shouted, "Yes—all night"; so he continued until mid-
·ht. His central theme was that men and women should free themselves from
·gious persecution; that woman should be assigned a place of equality with
·n; that love, rather than fame or power, should be the guiding spirit of human
·duct.
You may call attention to the fact that some sentences are long, some short;
·uch contrasts as "rest at last the ashes of that restless man"; to parallelism, as
·series of "I saw's"; to metaphor, such as "mingle the eagles of France with
·eagles of the crags"; to alliteration, like "dreamless dust"; to the use of visual
·gery; to the use of adjectives. Students will miss much unless you point out
·se features and label them.
You may follow this assignment with one in which you ask each student to
·ite a short speech, and analyze it in the way that the class analyzed the
·ersoll speech. When the student reads his speech to the class, you may
·ıment that speakers often read their speeches from a manuscript (though it is
·ifficult way of making a speech interesting), and demonstrate that a speech
·ın read is more effective if the speaker reads with full knowledge of content,
·h energy and vivacity, with conversational flexibility of voice, and with the
·s on the listeners as much as possible.
Other assignments may deal with other types of prose. The informal essay
· the short story are interesting to younger students. A good procedure is to
·gn a short essay, perhaps one in the text, so each one will have a chance to
·d it aloud and participate in the general discussion of content and meaning.
·the next assignment each student may then select a different essay, and read
·o the class. The teacher may visit the school library, dig out twenty or thirty
·rt, interesting essays, and review each briefly for the class, saying just enough
·intrigue a prospective reader. Students who have meager library facilities at

home will welcome this help, whereas those who want to go further afield m
do so.

After the experience with the prose essay, the class may turn to a short stoɪ
The story contains the problems of the informal essay plus the additional one
dialogue, which calls for characterization. Probably the teacher should beg
with the study of a short story from the text or book of selections, for
discussion of general principles; later each student may select a story of his ov
to cut to an assigned length and read to the class.

Selections of poetry abound in every textbook. Consider the following:

The Spires of Oxford

I saw the spires of Oxford
    As I was passing by,
The gray spires of Oxford
    Against a pearl-gray sky.
My heart was with the Oxford men
    Who went abroad to die.

The years go fast in Oxford,
    The golden years and gay,
The hoary Colleges look down
    On careless boys at play.
But when the bugles sounded war
    They put their games away.

They left the peaceful river,
    The cricket-field, the quad,
The shaven lawns of Oxford
    To seek a bloody sod—
They gave their merry youth away
    For country and for God.

God rest you, happy gentlemen;
    Who laid your good lives down,
Who took the khaki and the gun
    Instead of cap and gown.
God bring you to a fairer place
    Than even Oxford town.[11]

Every generation has to cope with war, and every generation develops its ow
attitude towards the nation's struggle. In the nineteenth century, although me
fully realized the horrors of war, speakers and journalists could and did dram
tize its opportunities for service and sacrifice. Many a young man, working in

[11]Winifred M. Letts, *The Spires of Oxford and Other Poems.* Copyright 1917 by
P. Dutton & Company. Renewal, 1945, by Winifred M. Letts. Reprinted by permissiᴇ
of the publisher.

ore or on a farm, with little chance of avoiding the daily monotony, found
mself swept up into combat, and discovered within himself a quality of
ourage, or leadership, or capacity for suffering and hardship that he did not
now he had. World War I, with which the poem deals, still possessed some of
at excitement; liberty and freedom needed to be fought for, and the enemy
as clearly identified. The men of Oxford left their rowing, their cricket, their
ormitory fun, their bowling, and many of them, for country and for God, gave
eir merry life away. The reader may interpret from a base of these and other
eas that he gathers were in the mind of "I," the woman who wrote the poem.
    younger generation of students that sees war differently, may attempt an
terpretation not out of 1917 but out of threescore years later. On some details
I will have to agree: the skyline of Oxford is marked with gray spires (recall the
ollegiate Gothic buildings of your own campus), the sky is nearly always
earl-gray, the buildings are ancient (though modern structures are beginning to
opear), the Thames still flows nearby, the grass is perpetually green and lush, as
refully manicured as a golf-green, Oxford is indeed a fair place (avoid the
dustrial areas), and war still turns boys into men (the British use *gentlemen*
ore than we do).
    Narrative poems involving humor, suspense, or conflict, like Noyes's "The
ighwayman," Cowper's "John Gilpin's Ride," Browning's "The Laboratory" or
How They Brought the Good News," or Kipling's "Tomlinson," are good to
ustrate principles of reading; later you may proceed to such poems as the
onnets of Shakespeare, Browning, or Wordsworth, Keats' "Ode on a Grecian
rn," or I Corinthians XIII. Because the oral reading approach to poetry is so
olid, you may succeed in quickening a student's appreciation in a way he has
ot before experienced.

Choral Reading

ou may want to try with your class some variety of choral reading.

nison reading is reading in concert, everyone speaking the same words at the
me instant. It is suitable for short reflective poems, but, unless skillfully
one, lacks the interest of other varieties of choral performance.

ntiphonal reading divides the choir into two parts, one part asking questions,
r stating problems, and the other part answering the questions or resolving
e problems.

efrain reading carries the narrative through the use of a solo performer or a
uo, the chorus supplying a refrain which is repeated at intervals.

mpersonative choral reading combines acting or pantomime with reading. Two
r more readers may present short scenes in pantomime, or as readers acting
ut their lines, the chorus coming in to supply connecting narrative or refrain.

As clear articulation and good line reading are necessary for choral readi[n]
the teacher should undertake this activity towards the end of the unit, althou[gh]
teachers sometimes use it as an interest-arousing device and begin with cho[ral]
activity. The first procedure in organizing the class into a choir is to divide t[he]
males into light and dark voices, and the females into light and dark voices; t[his]
plan makes it possible to work for various tonal effects. The teacher then nee[ds]
to provide copies of poems with which to work, studying them with the class [to]
assign certain lines as solo parts, others as group parts; some for light voic[es,]
some for dark, some for the whole chorus. For example:

Does the road wind up-hill all the way?	Li[ght]
Yes, to the very end.	D[ark]
Will the day's journey take the whole long day?	Li[ght]
From morn to night, my friend.	D[ark]

Christina Rossetti, *Up-Hill*

Gay go up, and gay go down,	
To ring the bells of London town. . . .	
Kettles and pans	*Light* (
Say the bells at St. Ann's.	*Light* (
You owe me ten shillings,	*Dark* (
Say the bells at St. Helen's.	*Light* (
When will you pay me?	*1st S*(
Say the bells at Old Bailey.	*Li*[ght]
When I grow rich,	*2nd S*(
Say the bells at Fleetditch.	*Li*[ght]
When will that be?	*3rd S*(
Say the bells at Stepney.	*Li*[ght]
I am sure I don't know	*4th S*(
Says the great bell at Bow.	*D*(
When I am old	*5th S*(
Say the bells at St. Paul's.	*D*(
Here comes a candle to light you to bed,	
And here comes a chopper to chop off your head.	

Anonymous

Actually, choral reading is no longer taught by most teachers, many of wh[om]
were led to believe that it could be successfully managed with little or no eff[ort]
or study. Demonstrations at teachers conventions and conferences had sti[mu]
lated such interest that teachers must have said to themselves, "This is ea[sy,]
colorful, and reaches many students at once—I can do this." The expec[ted]
results did not follow. The simplicity proved to be deceptive. It was like [the]
magic vegetable knife which in the hands of the state fair pitchman tur[ns]
radishes into flowers and carrots into graceful spirals but at home transform[s]

erything into a pile of chips. Only a relatively few teachers had the talent and
e persistence to make a verse-choir performance hold the attention of a large
dience. Wallace A. Bacon describes with real enchantment a choral interpre-
tion of Euripides' *Hercules Furens* at the beautiful theater at Epidaurus.
While the voices differed in quality and pitch," he wrote, "they were as one in
tacking and sustaining words and phrases. The effect was electric. The listener
lt at once the strange position of the chorus in the play: actor and yet not
tor; part of the action and yet not part of the action; human being and yet not
human being but a force. This was orchestration in the fullest sense."[12]

Choral reading will regain its popularity—not through the efforts of teachers
ho think it is easy but through those who appreciate its subtleties. Teachers
n find it highly useful as a classroom exercise—it does involve the whole group,
d it does provide a sheltering situation where the more reticent student can
mpt the fates with his efforts. As a group, students can try differing interpre-
tions and the teacher can illustrate principles of reading aloud.

Readers Theater

current favorite among teachers who like group interpretation activities is
aders theater. Such professionals as Charles Laughton, Agnes Moorehead, and
dith Anderson got it off to a good start in the early fifties with productions of
n Juan in Hell[13] and *John Brown's Body,* which for some years played to
rge audiences on campuses and elsewhere all over the country. *Brecht on
echt* and *Under Milk Wood* were other early productions. Readers theater is
e presentation, from a script, of plays or other material cast in dramatic form.
general it follows the traditions of oral interpretation—reading from a manu-
ript—but it may include scenes in which the readers leave their manuscript and
t their roles, following conventions of the theater.

Teachers of speech or English have often studied plays by assigning different
rts to different students sitting in the classroom. Imagine the students taking
eir chairs and books to the front of the room and projecting the scene to the
ass; they read not to each other but to the group. This maneuver has added
terest to the recitation, though the presentation has come but a small way

P. 307. Karl F. Robinson and Charlotte Lee, *Speech in Action,* illustrate choral reading
with selections from "The Negro Speaks of Rivers" by Langston Hughes; "The Ballad of
the Oysterman" by Oliver Wendell Holmes; "Jazz Fantasia" by Carl Sandburg; "The
Disagreeable Man" by W. S. Gilbert; "Waiting for the Birdie" by Ogden Nash; "Stage
Directions" by William Rose Benét; "The Lovely Shall be Choosers" by Robert Frost
(pp. 364-370). Shelley's "Ozymandias" is a classroom favorite; *see* Chester C. Long,
"The Poem's Text as a Technique of Performance in Public Group Readings of Poetry,"
Western Speech, Winter 1967, pp. 16-29.
Laughton and Moorehead with Charles Boyer and Sir Cedric Hardwicke called themselves
the "First Drama Quartet."

toward the sophistication of readers theater. Instead of letting the students sit
chairs, provide them with stools, and reading stands on which to place the
books; this technique gives them greater freedom in coming and going and
handling their scripts. Assume further that they do not read to the class unt
after they have given the material such careful study that they are fully aware
what the play is about and are not riveted to the written pages in front of ther
Opportunity for dramatic impact is at once enhanced.

Readers theater has evolved its own conventions through experienc
Questions as these are given varied answers: How shall the script be managec
Where does the individual look when he is reading? May a reader interpret mo
the production to two hours and a half. (The playwright himself, fond of h
own brainchild, reportedly liked a still earlier version that never got on t
stage—rumor was that it was a full five hour show.)

The answers to these somewhat technical questions grew out of reade
theater's own developing theory. Lighting effects may be devised to show whic
readers are on stage, just as the scene is shifted from one area to another in tl
conventional theater through the use of spots. If lights are not used, readers m
still all remain on stage, exits and entrances being shown by the play's contex
Or readers may come and go. Although generally the performers read their lin
out towards the listeners, they may, in a particularly vital bit, forsake the
books and act the scene out. Music or dancing may be introduced; occasional
hand props or costumes of an unpretentious sort are used. Spirited discussio
are heard at conventions about whether this or that bit of technique is appr
priate to readers theater, but the simple fact is, happily, that directors are st
highly experimental. For the most part reading conventions prevail, with the ar
of acting, public speaking, and dancing secondary, the principal determinan
being taste, judgment, and imagination. Keith Brooks offers this definitio
"Readers theater is the combining of expert readers and minimal staging wi
great literature in a manner that is theatrically stimulating."[14]

Teachers have adapted the principal features of readers theater to the hi
school class and the college first course. Possibilities abound also for public
semipublic performances, as at assembly programs. Nor is this activity bei
restricted to speech classes. English teachers are adapting readers theater to tl
oral presentation of the literature being studied. Science or social studi
teachers add variety to their classes by letting students read dramatized versio
of incidents drawn from the history of science or from political and soci
history. Out of the simplicity and unpretentiousness of the class exercise c
come enjoyment and fuller appreciation of the material.

Margaret A. Nielsen notes particularly the usefulness of readers theater as
classroom exercise. A class may be divided into working panels, she observe
each working on the assignment. The shy student gains support from the fa

[14] "Readers Theatre: Some Questions and Answers," *Dramatics*, December 1962, p. 14

hat scripts may be used and from participation in a group rather than in a solo event. At the same time the advanced student receives full challenge in interpretation of character and in line reading. She also comments on the possibility of using readers theater productions as programs for literature classes and as assembly and community programs.[15]

More and more college and university students are acquiring personal experience as participants in and as spectators at finished readers theater programs. As a form of interpretation, the appeal of readers theater is unmistakeable. Favorite titles include *The Thurber Carnival, The Tempest, Uncle Vanya, The Caucasian Chalk Circle, Abraham Lincoln in Illinois, Animal Farm, Saint Joan, Spoon River Anthology, Canterbury Tales, King Lear, Fall of the City,* the poetry of Yevtushenko and Lindsay.[16] Classroom exercises, necessarily less ambitious, can capture the essential effectiveness of group reading from a script. As a starter, the teacher may read *Readers Theatre Handbook* by Leslie Irene Coger and Melvin R. White. Their exposition of principles, with descriptions and pictures showing how some twoscore productions were actually staged ("Part Two: This Is the Way it Was Done"), and their selection of sample scripts, are helpful to stimulate the teacher's own interest and imagination. Dr. Coger has also written a helpful description of a readers theater production of *Up the Down Staircase.*[17] Aside from the development of the thread of the story out of a wide variety of incidents, the production incorporated many side effects. A school bell marked transitions; voices were heard over an intercom; the songs that Paul composed for the teachers were sung by the teachers for whom he had composed them; and at the end a siren, after the grim jump from the window.

Some teachers may want to venture into a relatively newer form properly called "chamber theater." Originated and named by Robert S. Breen of Northwestern University's School of Speech, it is a way of presenting nondramatic fiction.[18]

The Explanatory Introduction

On many reading occasions the student may preface his performance simply by announcing the title and author. Many teachers, however, like to combine speaking and reading by asking him to open with a brief explanation about the selection, supplying details about its author, telling why he chose it, or identifying locale or characters.

See: "Readers Theatre," in *A Course Guide in the Theatre Arts at the Secondary School Level,* American Educational Theatre Association, 1968, pp. 103-106.
See: Newsletter issued by the Interpretation Division Group of the Speech Communication Association.
"Let it Be a Challenge! A Readers Theatre Production of *Up the Down Staircase," Dramatics,* February 1969.
See: A Course Guide in the Theatre Arts at the Secondary School Level, pp. 107-110.

Whether or not he prepares an introduction, the student will quickly find th
he is necessarily under severe time limits. There may be fifteen or thirty studen
in the class to be heard in a restricted number of days. He may have fifteen (
twenty minutes or half that time. He will likely have to make sharp cuts in tl
material. The first rule is that almost anything can be cut—the *Readers Dige*
made a fortune from this formula; the second is that the cut version c;
sometimes be better for reading aloud than the whole selection. Practice
cutting is good training, as it requires the student to discriminate between less
and greater, principal and subordinate, essential and surplus. Instead of readi
all opening paragraphs, he may substitute for them a swift paraphrase.

Cutting may be a positive blessing for beginners. Just as experienced acto
can make a lengthy, talky play interesting to an audience, less experienced acto
that cannot hold the attention of listeners for three hours would do better to c
the production to two hours and a half. (The playwright himself, fond of I
own brain-child, reportedly liked a still earlier version that never got on tl
stage—rumor was that it was a full five hour show.)

Recitals: Programs

Teachers who wish to develop individuals professionally may extend the sugge
tions given in this chapter into a public program by talented students. On son
campuses the individual recital is a well-established tradition. A forty- or fift
minute program can be constructed from scenes from a long play, or it may I
based on selections from a single writer: poems of Carl Sandburg, or dramat
monologues from Shakespeare or Browning. It may develop a theme, like tl
seasons, travel, love, "Conrad and the Sea." One program, entitled "The Stuff
Owl," described itself as "an anthology of bad verse—containing some of tl
most hilariously awful poems written since the eighteenth century." The floo
gates were opened wide, the bars let down, the rule book torn asunder, tl
stuffiness emptied out of the room, and listeners were treated to an hour of fu

The speech department of Jamaica (N.Y.) High School made a selection
poems by major black poets for reading aloud. Here are their choices: *From t*
Dark Tower, Countee Cullen; *Dreams, My People, Dream Variation, Mother*
Son, Langston Hughes; *Sympathy,* Paul Laurence Dunbar; *My Mother,* Clau
McKay; *My City,* James Weldon Johnson; *I Heard a Young Man Saying,* Ju
Fields; *In Honor of David Anderson Brooks, My Father* (Pulitzer award), I
Real Cool, Gwendolyn Brooks; *Sonnet to April,* Alice Dunbar-Nelson; *Progre*
Unlimited, J.M. (from a collection of poems by ghetto children, *The Me Nobo*
Knows, ed. Stephen M. Joseph).[19]

[19]The selection committee: Rose Kirchman, Ruth Barlas, Judith Watts, Jean Fulson, Lin
Sadur. My thanks to Dr. Mardel Ogilvie for calling my attention to this collection.

A theme such as the eerie world of the illiterate could be used as a guide for
ecting excerpts from William Stryon's *The Confessions of Nat Turner*. Nat
nself, who has mastered the labels on jars and barrels, attempts to read a
ok, but finds none of his familiar words: sugar, ginger, capsicum, cloves; Little
ɔrning carries up from the cellar a keg marked "molasses" instead of the keg of
il" he had been sent to get, because he did not know what the label said; Hark
empts to escape to freedom, his principal guide being intermittent glimpses of
ᴇ North Star; he wanders night and day, this way and that, unable to read the
rnpike signs; what he thinks might be Richmond, Baltimore, and Washington
ᴇ only Jerusalem, Drewrysville, and Smithfield, and so he is picked up after
ıg, aimless wandering, only a few miles from home.

The contributions of interpretation to the student are well worth keeping
fore him. He learns more about words, their logical meanings and emotional
pacts. His knowledge of literature should be enhanced, as he and other
ᴅdents work with a wide variety of selections. His imagination specifically and
ᴊ emotional sensitivity generally should be heightened. If his primary interest is
speaking, what he learns about reading will serve him in good stead. If it is in
ting, he will have made a start on one of the basic problems of the actor. And
may learn from his experience that interpretation itself may prove to be his
ımary interest. I prize my good fortune at being able to study under and to
serve gifted teachers of interpretation, and although I have elected mainly to
ınder in the field of public address, I have often observed that at times
tinguished public speaking seems much like poetry, and that, lodged in the
ıl of a public speaker, are qualities also belonging to the interpreter, the
ɔphet, the minstrel, and the mime.

Assignments

Work out a unit for the teaching of interpretation, covering an appropriate
length of time (four to eight weeks). Compare it with the suggested unit
presented in Chapter 3. Include the necessary materials: exercises, examples,
etc.

Work out a unit for the teaching of choral reading, covering an appropriate
length of time (three to six weeks). Include necessary exercises, examples.

Compile lists of selections for each of the following literary forms. The
teacher may suggest how many to list under each category. The titles should
represent materials suitable for high school students.
  a. Lyric poems
  b. Narrative poems
  c. Dramatic monologues
  d. Speeches
  e. Informal essays
  f. Formal essays
  g. Short Stories

h. Plays
i. Humorous declamations
j. Dramatic declamations
k. Original orations

Questions for Classroom Discussion

1. Differentiate among interpretation, impersonation, and acting. (An old que tion, impossible to settle to everybody's satisfaction, but needs to be pere nially reviewed.)
2. To what extent is interpretation basic to public speaking? to drama? to su professions as teaching, ministry, the law?
3. What standards should be applied in choosing materials for interpretatio How can the appreciation of students for good literature be stimulated?
4. At what levels should interpretation be taught? What differences do you s in method of teaching at these levels?
5. In the interpretative art, what part is creativity and what is recreativity?
6. To what extent should imitation be used as a teaching device? Consid (a) the imitation of the teacher; (b) the imitation of recordings or oth models.
7. Describe the extent to which lighting, staging, costuming, props, soul effects, "acting techniques," are being used in readers theater productions. specific; use examples that you have observed. Conclude with a set guidelines.
8. Study the form "Achievement in Reading Aloud," in the next chapt Prepare a revision that will incorporate your own objectives.

References

Texts and Books of General Interest

Aggert, Otis J., and Bowen, Elbert R. *Communicative Reading.* 2d ed. N York: Macmillan, 1963.

Armstrong, Chloe, and Brandes, Paul D. *The Oral Interpretation of Literatu* New York: McGraw-Hill, 1963.

Bacon, Wallace A. *The Art of Interpretation.* New York: Holt, Rinehart Winston, 1966.

Bahn, Eugene, and Bahn, Margaret. *A History of Oral Interpretation.* Minn polis: Burgess, 1970.

Bamman, Henry; Dawson, Mildred; and Whitehead, Robert. *Oral Interpretati of Children's Literature.* Dubuque: William C. Brown, 1964.

Beloof, Robert. *The Performing Voice in Literature.* Boston: Little, Brow 1966.

ooth, Wayne C. *The Rhetoric of Fiction.* Chicago: University of Chicago Press, 1951.

rooks, Keith; Bahn, Eugene; and Okey, L. La Mont. *The Communicative Act of Oral Interpretation.* Boston: Allyn & Bacon, 1967.

———. *Literature for Listening: An Oral Interpreter's Anthology.* Boston: Allyn & Bacon, 1968.

ampbell, Paul. *The Speaking and the Speakers of Literature.* Belmont, Calif.: Dickenson Publishing. 1967.

iardi, John. *How Does a Poem Mean.* Boston: Houghton Mifflin, 1959. The discussion of various selected poems is helpful to the teacher interested in heightening his own competence in analyzing poetry.

oger, Leslie Irene, and White, Melvin R. *Studies in Readers Theatre.* Brooklyn: S & F Press, 1963.

ernandez, Thomas L., ed. *Oral Interpretation and the Teaching of English.* Champaign: National Council of Teachers of English, 1969.

french, Yvonne. *Mrs. Siddons: Tragic Actress.* London: Derek Verschoyle, 1954.

rye, Northrup. *The Well-Tempered Critic.* Bloomington: Indiana University Press, 1963.

ahagan, Winifred, et al., eds. *A Course Guide in the Theatre Arts at the Secondary School Level.* Washington, D.C.: American Educational Theatre Association, 1968.

eeting, Baxter M. *Interpretation for Our Time.* Dubuque: William C. Brown, 1966.

eiger, Don. *The Sound, Sense, and Performance of Literature.* Chicago: Scott, Foresman, 1963.

———. *The Dramatic Impulse in Modern Poetics.* Baton Rouge: Louisiana University Press, 1967.

rimes, Wilma H., and Mattingly, Alethea Smith. *Interpretation: Writer-Reader-Audience.* Belmont, Calif.: Wadsworth, 1961.

astings, Henry C. *Spoken Poetry on Records and Tapes: An Index of Currently Available Recordings.* Chicago: American Library Association, 1957. Lists 581 records and tapes and references to 136 anthologies.

aughton, Charles. *Tell Me a Story.* New York: McGraw-Hill, 1957. An anthology of the favorite selections of a distinguished reader and actor.

ee, Charlotte I. *Oral Interpretation.* 3d ed. Boston: Houghton Mifflin, 1965.

ichards, I.A. *Practical Criticism.* New York: Harcourt, Brace, 1929. Also available in paperback. The heart of this book is a series of thirteen poems, followed by chapters on principles of criticism.

obb, Mary Margaret. *Oral Interpretation of Literature in American Colleges and Universities.* rev. ed. New York: Johnson Reprints, 1968.

obinson, Karl F., and Lee, Charlotte. *Speech in Action.* Glenview, Ill.: Scott, Foresman, 1965.

Scrivner, Louise M. *A Guide to Oral Interpretation.* New York: Odyssey Press 1968.

Thompson, David W., and Fredricks, Virginia. *Oral Interpretation of Fiction.* 2 ed. Minneapolis: Burgess, 1967.

Veilleux, Jeré. *Oral Interpretation: The Re-creation of Literature.* New York Harper & Row, 1967.

Walters, Donald N. *The Reader: An Introduction to Oral Interpretation.* New York: Odyssey Press, 1966.

Woolbert, Charles H., and Nelson, Severina H. *The Art of Interpretative Speech Principles and Practice.* 5th ed. New York: Appleton-Century-Crofts, 1968

Articles

Bacon, Wallace A. "The Act of Literature and the Act of Interpretation," i Thomas L. Fernandez, ed. *Oral Interpretation and the Teaching of English* Champaign: National Council of Teachers of English, 1969.

Bowen, Elbert R. "The General Education Approach to Interpretative Reading. *Central States Speech Journal* Autumn 1958.

———. "Promoting Dynamic Interpretative Reading." *Speech Teacher* Marc 1958.

Brooks, Keith. "Readers Theatre: Some Questions and Answers." *Dramatic* December 1962.

Brooks, Keith, and Bielenberg, John E. "Readers Theatre as Defined by Nev York Critics." *Southern Speech Journal* Summer 1964.

Coger, Leslie Irene. "Interpreters Theatre: Theatre of the Mind." *Quarterly Journal of Speech* April 1963.

———. "Theatre for Oral Interpreters." *Speech Teacher* November 1963.

Dennis, Ralph B. "One Imperative Plus." *Quarterly Journal of Speech Education* June 1922. A classic.

Geiger, Don. "Emotion in Poetry: The Oral Interpreter's Special Respon sibility." *Southern Speech Journal* Fall 1955.

———. "Oral Interpretation and the Teaching of Literature." *Speech Teacher* September 1962.

Grimes, Wilma H. "Oral Interpretation and Criticism: A Bibliography." *Western Speech* Spring 1958.

Hargis, Donald E. "Interpretation as Oral Communication." *Central State Speech Journal* Spring 1960. Selected bibliography on contemporary theory

Kershner, A. G. Jr.; Thompson, David W.; Gilbert, Edna; Lee, Charlotte I Mouat, Lawrence H.; Nelson, Severina E.; Smith, Joseph F.; Murphy Richard. "Teaching Interpretation: Students Recall Methods of Earl Leaders." *Speech Teacher* November 1962.

Krider, Ruby. "A High School Course in Oral Interpretation." *Southern Speech Journal* Spring 1957.

lacArthur, David E. "Readers Theatre: Variations on a Theme." *Speech Teacher* January 1964.

lcCoard, William B. "An Interpretation of the Times: A Report of the Oral Interpretation of W. H. Auden's *Age of Anxiety.*" *Quarterly Journal of Speech* December 1949. How a Pulitzer prize-winning poem was studied for oral presentation.

lcCurdy, Frances Lea. "Oral Interpretation as an Approach to Literature." Thomas L. Fernandez, ed. *Oral Interpretation and the Teaching of English.* Champaign: National Council of Teachers of English, 1969.

——. "Reading Symbols of Poetry." *Speech Teacher* January 1966.

larcoux, J. Paul. "Current Trends in Literary Analysis for Oral Interpretation: An Overview." *Speech Teacher* November 1966.

larlor, Clark S., ed. "Readers Theatre Bibliography: 1960-64." *Central States Speech Journal* February 1966. Lists about 250 titles for readers theater: plays, poems, prose, together with a selection of books and articles on theory and practice. Prepared by a committee of the Interpretation Interest Group. For the years covered, it is an indispensable survey by competent teachers.

lattingly, Alethea S. "The Listener and the Interpreter's Style." *Western Speech Journal* Summer 1964.

loorehead, Agnes. "Staging 'Don Juan in Hell.' " *Western Speech* May 1954.

ahskopf, Horace G. "The Curry Tradition." *Speech Teacher* November 1968.

eclam, Herta. "Choric-Speaking in Greek Tragedies Performed by Students." *Speech Teacher* November 1962.

obb, Mary Margaret. "Growing a Taste for Poetry." *Speech Teacher* November 1963.

eilleux, Jeré. "The Interpreter: His Role, Language, and Audience." *Speech Teacher* March 1967.

he SCA Interpretation Division.   Valuable teaching materials are compiled from time to time by members of this division, and are distributed free, or at nominal cost, at the annual conventions of the Speech Communication Association. All members are eligible to enroll in this division and be placed on its mailing list, to receive the *Newsletter* and other publications and materials. Officers are listed in each issue of the *SCA Directory.*

11

---

testing, grading, examining

*I was gratified to be able to answer promptly,
and I did. I said I didn't know.*

Mark Twain

If we could measure the ability of a student both at the beginning and end of a term, we could determine how much he had learned. If we could make exact measurements at intervals during the course, we could tell how well he is progressing: whether he is learning more or less rapidly than others, and, what is more important, which are his relatively strong and weak points. Standardized tests would tell a teacher whether his students were better or worse than students in other institutions or than his own students of a former year.

At present, however, no paper-and-pencil test exists that will measure the effectiveness of a speaker, a reader, or an actor. We need to rely upon the judgment of the observer. On matters of ratings, teachers will disagree just as drama critics or book reviewers will disagree; yet despite differences of individual opinion, a consensus usually emerges that says A gave the best speech in class today, or Bs report was the best we have had all semester, or C did not do so well today as usual, or D has made the greatest progress to date.

Many teachers have devised criticism forms to assist them in arriving at a well-balanced judgment regarding the various elements of the act of speaking, reading, or acting. A simple one for judging the oral reading of a selection appears on the following page. You may add still other items that you wish to call attention to in your critique. Such a form will help you to keep each of these features in mind as you listen to the reading. You may devise different forms for different kinds of performance, ranging from informal speaking to debating and acting.

Achievement in Reading Aloud

NAME OF STUDENT . . . .

SELECTION . . . .

Item	*Comment*
Understanding and projecting the thought	
Understanding and projecting mood, tone	
Bodily activity, facial expression	
Voice control	
General effectiveness	
Other comments	

This form is not a *measuring* instrument. It may not even include *all* the features of a successful performance. It says nothing about whether one item is more important than another. To *measure* achievement in reading aloud, you would need a form in which you assign numerical values to each item, as follows:

Understanding and projecting the thought	1	2	3	4	5
Understanding and projecting mood, tone	1	2	3	4	5
Bodily activity, facial expression	1	2	3	4	5
Voice control	1	2	3	4	5
General effectiveness	1	2	3	4	5

Total: —— points

The numbers are interpreted as follows: 5, superior; 4, excellent; 3, adequate; 2, fair; 1, poor.

After filling out thousands of criticism forms and rating scales in speaking, reading, debating, and dramatics, I have come to the conclusion that their chief value is to assist the teacher in learning to arrive at a balanced judgment. At first it is easy to overemphasize some elements of the total performance and under-emphasize others. As the teacher becomes more sophisticated, he will do about equally well whether he fills out a prepared form or writes comments on a blank sheet of paper. The criticism form has this usefulness to the student: if he becomes aware of a certain difficulty, he likes to know whether he is improving with respect to it, and the form helps him compare similar features of two recitations.

The achievement scale has the additional feature of the numerical score, making possible a sort of comparison on total performance, so that individuals can be ranked and graded. The more consistent the rater is, the better the score card is as an instrument of ranking and grading. If, however, the rater is inconsistent, comparisons are, to that extent, meaningless. The same criticism, of course, applies to any kind of grading, ranking, or scoring. It is intriguing, occasionally, to score a round of speeches or readings on a scale; students find the procedure interesting, or at least novel, and the scale calls attention vividly to outstanding weaknesses as well as to principal strengths. Scales are also useful in grading contests, festivals, or tournaments. Note especially the space marked *comment;* observations here will help the student in a specific way that the fistful of numbers will not.

Observations about Grades

The score cards just described measure the student's talent in a specific type of performance. Often this score needs to be translated into a grade. Teachers are unwilling, however, to base a student's entire grade on his *talent;* this procedure, they believe, gives too much advantage to the student with previous experience. They like also to consider *improvement.* Grading therefore becomes a complex process.

The grade is an appraisal of a student's work. Moreover, it tells how he rates in comparison with other students. The grade of B indicates that the student's achievement was above average, perhaps even notably above average. After a teacher has listened to a dozen speeches, and has assigned each one a grade, he should take a look at the list of grades in order to make sure that they reflect a true comparison: to see that the best students have actually received the highest grades, the poorest students the lowest grades, and the others in between. Students scrutinize a teacher's grades sharply on this score: a student may be disappointed in his grade of B, but more willing to accept it if he finds that poorer students received C, and only those who were obviously outstanding received A.

Other observations may be made about daily grades. You should be as consistent as possible: an A in October should mean about the same as an A in May. If, therefore, a student receives Cs in the fall, Bs in the winter, and As in the spring, he is making improvement. You should try to make each grade as judicial an evaluation as possible, and avoid the temptation to raise grades just to give a student encouragement. Other students may want a little of this encouragement, and the whole business leads to interesting complications. By the same reasoning, you should avoid rebuking students by giving them low grades; give them what they earn. Use other ways of encouraging or reprimanding.

Avoid making deductions from grades for petty or crotchety reasons. These always seem silly when aired in the presence of adults. Keep a record of your grades. Visualize students looking over your shoulder; that will put you in the proper frame of mind for imagining their conversation when they walk down the hall asking one another, "What did he give you?" A student does not seem to question his daily marks; apparently he feels that if one of your marks is low, he can, by working harder, raise it next time. This judgment will be confirmed if he sees others being graded according to the same standard of performance. A student will discuss his final grade and have much to say about the way in which his grades were averaged or weighted, but it does not often occur to him to question the daily marks themselves at the time he is pondering his final grade.

If as you go from assignment to assignment you keep the foregoing aspects in mind, your problem of compiling quarter or six weeks' grades may not be so difficult. About ten days before these grades are to be handed out, study your class rolls and *make an estimated grade for each student.* Give attention to those students about whom you have a close decision to make, so that during the following days you can get new evidence. Compare grades to see if you have each one in the right relative order. If you take these precautions, your grades should turn out all right.

Computing Final Grades

The problem of computing final grades is more complex. How shall you appraise written work as compared with oral work? Should you give more weight to later grades than to earlier ones? How can you recognize improvement in computing the final mark? What percentage does the final examination count towards the final grade? What deduction should be made for absences? All of these questions have to be answered in arriving at a final decision.

Give two or three times as much weight to oral work as to written work. Written tests and examinations do not need to play the major part, as you can learn from oral performances much of what the student knows and can do. *But note:* the nationwide trend is toward giving increasing weight to written work.

Students are being given a more rigorous foundation in *theory* and *principle* than a decade ago. The weight you assign should represent the amount of emphasis *you* are putting on written work and oral performance in *your* course.

Give more weight to later grades than to earlier ones. You are more interested in what your students can do in May than in what they could do when they entered the course. In following this plan, you are giving consideration to improvement as well as to ability.

Do not put too much weight on final examination grades. Your final course grade should represent the caliber of work the student has done during the term, not merely what he did on the final examination. A student's final examination may be higher or lower than usual; he may have put on a burst of speed at the end, or he may have been ill or under tension. Use the final examination primarily as a means of deciding doubtful cases. If a student has fluctuated between B and C, and you are dubious which mark he has earned, leave the decision to the final test. As a rule of thumb, count the final examination about two or three times as much as a weekly grade.

The principal reason for giving the final examination greater weight occurs in classes that are so large the student does not have opportunity to recite. In speech communication classes, however, you may call upon each student two or three times a week.

Make deductions only for excessive, unexplained absences. Life gets complicated and students have to miss school. Illness also occurs. Perhaps the work can be made up; here again teachers should be charitable. A student may return to school after a severe illness and, in a weakened condition, will have to face not only current work but makeup assignments. Save your rancor for the truants; you can overlook a few absences by conscientious students.

Consider typical grading problems as they arise at the time of compiling final grades. For purposes of simplification, assume that six letter grades are typical of the work of the whole term; and that the seventh grade represents the final oral or written examination. Assume also that the final examination grade counts twice as much as any other grade, a modest weighting.

Some of your students will be easy to grade, as follows:

	1	2	3	4	5	6	Final Exam
G.H.A.	A	A	A	A	B	A	A
C.J.B.	C	C	B	C	D	C	C
J.A.C.	B	C	B	B	B	C	B

G.H.A. is entitled to a final grade of A; he has only one B on his record. C.J.B. has earned a C; his B and D average C and his other grades are C throughout. J.A.C. has a clear B. Undoubtedly during the course these students, as they saw their daily grades, ranked themselves as A, C, and B respectively.

	1	2	3	4	5	6	Final Exam
F.W.D.	C	C	C	B	B	B	B
G.J.E.	C	C	C	C	B	B	B
K.V.F.	C	B	C	B	C	B	B
F.C.G.	C	C	B	C	C	B	A

These students show varying patterns of improvement. F.W.D. and G.J.E. seem reasonably entitled to a B. The latter has more Cs than Bs, but his Bs were made late in the course, and one of them is the final examination grade. K.V.F. and F.C.G. have been more erratic in their record, but their grades average B—and with some credit for improvement would likely appear in the B column.

Often you run into such complex problems as these:

	1	2	3	4	5	6	Final Exam
J.K.I.	A	A	B	C	C	C	C
M.V.J.	B	B	B	B	C	C	C
K.R.K.	B	A	C	B	C	D	C

These illustrate progressively weaker preparation and failure to improve. A grade of C would appear to be fair enough for the latter two, and perhaps even for J.K.I. On the basis of ability, J.K.I. has shown a little more than F.C.G., who was rated B; but F.C.G. shows some improvement throughout the course, whereas J.K.I., after his first three grades, never rose above the C level.

How can you reassure yourself that the set of grades which you are in process of preparing is equitable? One is to ask yourself whether the students who received As are demonstrably better than those who received lower marks. Study all of those who received the same mark, and see if they are a relatively homogeneous group so far as ability and attainment are concerned. See if a margin of difference exists between your lowest A and your highest B, between your lowest B and your highest C. Give thought to the failing grades you have recorded; be sure that you have clear and demonstrable reasons that will make sense to grownups. Imagine two of your students comparing grades—review their records for the term and see if your final grades are plausible. Go over your grades with the greatest care; be sure you copy them accurately; then stick to them.

Another way to arrive at a final grade is to go through an elimination process. For a given student, you may see at once that he has not earned an A or an F. You now have the choices B, C, D. You rule out D, because his work is average or better, not below average. You now have B and C. Hence your task boils down to the problem of appraising the quality of his work to determine whether he has attained B or C. (Note the latter part of the sentence: it does not read, "whether you give him B or C." The focus is on what he has *achieved*, not what the teacher is going to *give* him.) Nearly every calculation that you can make comes eventually to a choice between two letters. At the outside, you are likely to misappraise his work only by a single letter. You are almost never likely to be *two* letter grades off.

Go over your grade records with care; check and crosscheck to be sure of the arithmetic; avoid clerical errors in reporting student grades. Once your grades are turned in, stick to them—only arithmetical or clerical errors should be subject to change.

"Handbooks" for students specifically advise the student to put pressure on the teacher to get him to change grades. These "manuals" urge the student to portray the calamity that will befall him if the grade goes in as is. He will be inducted into military service, have to leave school, etc. Older teachers will not be overawed, say the books, but younger teachers will have guilt feelings and will succumb. My scouts inform me that "change-of-grade slips," which once were used sparingly, are now being used in increasing and distressing numbers.

Invariably the reasons given for requesting a change of grade have nothing to do with academic achievement. The student may have a personal problem; he appeals to you to "take this into consideration" and adjust his grade accordingly. He may be facing military service, and will have to terminate his enrollment because his average has fallen too low. Such a crisis is indeed, serious. Or it may be his desire to be initiated into a fraternity or to play football. Now, because of the grade received in your course, he will be unable to be initiated or to play football. And that predicament is far from inconsequential to him: it looms as a major disappointment.

Often in presenting his case the student will make it clear that *your* grade is the one that is causing all the difficulty. If your grade can be altered, the difficulty will be cleared up. But his academic record consists of *many* grades, independently arrived at by *many* teachers. How can one single grade be more decisive than another? A few questions, or inquiry at the principal's or dean's office, usually reveals that *many other grades* are also low. The student has come to you because he feels he has an opportunity to have your grade altered. If he is unsuccessful in his conversation with you, he will review his situation and select the next most likely prospect, unless you succeed in convincing him that this whole procedure is academically improper. It has been well observed that grades should measure a student's accomplishments, not his needs.

A new teacher especially, but an experienced teacher as well, should discuss this type of problem with administrators and colleagues. Such a discussion will ground him solidly in school policy. Grades should not be changed for non-academic reasons. To do so is to be manifestly unfair to other students. Moreover it does the profession of teaching and learning a disservice.

Some things you *can* do for students. If a student misses work for valid reasons, you can give him opportunities to make it up. You can defer a deadline on an assignment. You can help him locate a tutor. You may refer him to testing or counseling services. If he brings his problem to you *during the course,* you can extend to him these kinds of assistance.

Illness is often the number one problem. The school can provide ways for a student to make up work missed during short-term illness, though actually it is not set up to handle long, complicated illnesses. Certainly when a situation gets to the point where an individual is more of a *patient* than he is a *student*, he can not complete a full load of work. He may have to drop some or all of his courses.

Another problem arises when a student neglects one course in order to work on others. Maybe he is struggling with botany, and robs speech and history of their share of his study-time in order to survive botany. So far as you are concerned, he has become more of a *nonstudent* than a *student.* He may survive botany, but may be a casualty in speech and history. After the grades are in, he may ask the speech and history teachers for special consideration so that he can avoid probation, make a fraternity, enter graduate or professional school. Or the nonstudent role that he is adopting in your course may spring from financial difficulties (he has to spend more time in outside work) or family problems (father died, or parents are getting a divorce). When the final grades are reported he realizes that his school work has suffered. His recourse again is to ask for "special consideration." Actually and undeniably his difficulty is heartrending. You will find yourself reflecting, "Why is this student having to face so depressing a problem—the dimensions of which would stagger even an older person?" You can talk to him as a friend, as a counselor—you may see solutions that had not occurred to him—but as a teacher, you cannot change a grade.

Quite purposively I have not dealt with a basic question, that grades should be abolished altogether. Reforms may be just around the corner. For any number of reasons, however, institutions now find it desirable to report the quality of intellectual achievement of each student. Society has provided an education for the youth, and society wants to know how well he has done. The device of grades seems to meet the needs of society. The grading system has, of course, been made subject to continual review. On many campuses students are being allowed to take certain kinds of courses on a Pass-Fail (Satisfactory Unsatisfactory) basis. In the past this plan, or some variety of it, has been repeatedly tried and abandoned. When I was a student at the University of Chicago, the graduate division was employing a P-F system. In order, however, to label the truly distinguished student, the grade of H was introduced. Hence P-F became H-P-F. Teachers then began to use other designations: H—, P+, P—. The mixture seemed much the same as before. Before long Chicago went back to conventional letters. The educational climate may change, however, to the point that P-F becomes increasingly popular. That will do away with all decisions except the most painful of all: the distinction between P and F. So, the grading philosophy you evolve for A-B-C-D-F will still apply to P-F.

Giving Examinations

References cited at the end of this chapter give information about the preparation of examination questions. The choice of the teacher is between the essay and the objective type of question.

Essay questions are open to certain objections. One is that subjective factors enter into grading. Consistent ways of marking style, language, spelling, syntax, organization of details, and selection of examples are difficult to contrive. Another is that essay examinations test only those facts that the student can recall; they cannot measure facts that the student may be aware of, but unable to reproduce. Still another is that they offer opportunities for writing around the question instead of directly answering it.[1]

Objective questions are also open to criticism. Those of the true-false type especially encourage guessing. They may stress unimportant details. Statements may be ambiguous: a multiple-choice question may have two or three equally good answers.

Teachers everywhere have given the problem thought, and have devised various solutions. If essay and objective examinations are alternated throughout the term, students for whom one type seems unduly difficult are not overly handicapped. When the essay type is used the teacher should make the questions specific enough to discourage discursive replies. In grading he should read the answers to question 1, scoring them on a comparative basis, before proceeding to question 2. Some teachers like to circulate, or put on an opaque projector, model answers to essay questions.[2] When objective examinations are used, the teacher should observe the usual cautions. He should favor multiple-choice, with four or five items under each question, over true-false. He should be sure that the longest statement is not necessarily the correct answer. He should avoid giveaway words like *always* and *never*. He should not use statements that suggest an answer to some other question. His correct statements should be well distributed among answers A, B, C, D, and E, making sure that C contains the lesser percentage of right answers as that item is most frequently chosen by guessers. He should avoid patterns of answers as a student might hit upon the hidden scheme. His questions should test important implications as well as minor details.

In his article "The Measurement of Speech," Jack Douglas quotes suggestions by C.T. Simon for making grades on essay questions more reliable: (1) Before grading essay questions, write out answers to serve as a standard. (2) Grade one question at a time through a set of papers. (3) Reverse the order of the papers in grading the next question in order to compensate for alterations in the standard. (4) Fold back the cover page of the examination books in order not to know whose paper is being graded. See the complete article in the *Speech Teacher*, November 1958.

See: "John P. Ryan's Art of Teaching," *Speech Teacher*, November 1959, p. 293.

If the examination, whether essay or objective, is to achieve its educational purpose, the teacher should, well in advance, discuss it with the class. Everybody should be clear on what ground is to be covered, and what is to be considered relevant. Lists of review questions can be provided, or chapters to be included can be agreed upon. This procedure gives the student specific tasks to accomplish during his reviewing period. When the teacher says, "You may omit this and this and this, but review thus and thus and thus," the student can launch his review with more confidence.

In preparing questions, the teacher should bear in mind that any item so difficult that no one can answer it is worthless as a discriminating item. Likewise, any item so simple that everyone can answer it is also worthless. Once having promised to quiz the class over a certain number of chapters, you should include questions from each chapter. A student hates to spend time reviewing material and then not have a chance to reveal his information. Teachers occasionally meet this problem by including the following question:

"Write down a question for which you reviewed that did not appear on the test; then answer that question."

As suggested above, the principal objection to true-false or multiple-choice questions is that students quickly turn up ambiguities that never crossed the teacher's mind. You may meet this objection by instructing your students: "If you feel any item is ambiguous, proceed as follows: Write down an answer; put an asterisk in front of the answer, and, on the back of the sheet, write a short explanatory statement." This opportunity sets his mind at ease; you may read his responses and be guided accordingly. Often the student puts down the right answer, indicating that he read the question as you intended; occasionally he points out a genuine ambiguity, and his statement gives you a chance to credit his answer. Of course with large classes you may need to deny the student this happy comforter. If you are using machine-scored tests, you will not be able to confront the computer with these thorny alternatives; it would either turn itself off or recycle itself and start anew at the beginning.

Since a teacher spends many hours preparing sets of multiple-choice or true-false questions, he naturally wants to use them for more than one semester, especially since his item analysis suggests modifications. Dangers exist, however, in reusing sets of questions. He probably does not teach exactly the same things each semester, and students are quick to detect old items that did not come up for discussion in the current term. A more serious reason for not reusing old tests is that copies of the questions get into circulation. Residence halls are diligent about keeping their files of questions up-to-date, as the competition for grades is keen among them. Half a dozen students who have taken the same two-hundred item objective test, can, by putting their heads together after the test, reconstruct a substantial portion of it. Once this summary gets into the files, one who has read it before the exam has an advantage over one who has not. If a teacher prepares a fresh set of questions for each examination, if he ıssures himself that no unauthorized person can see the questions before examination time, and if he takes ordinary precautions against cheating, he is warranting to his students that the examination is being administered under truly competitive conditions.

With large classes, the essay examination has fewer defenders. Part of its obsolescence is deserved: if the teacher must reply on others to read the papers, answers are not graded with uniform rigor. To compensate for this built-in inequality, the teacher instructs students to make answers specific, or at least to include certain reasons or concepts ("What are the component elements of *power* and which is most important?" . . . "Analyze three specific principles of audience adaptation."). In other words, the essay question itself is becoming more objective.

At the same time the objective examination is enrolling more supporters. Computer scoring of prepared answer sheets, increasingly used at all levels of instruction, puts at the disposal of the teacher an enormous amount of data about student performances on his test. The answer sheets are scored, more accurately than human beings can score them (if the computer errs, it is likely to make a gross mistake that is detectable). The accompanying printout analyzes each question; tells the teacher what percentage of the class selected the correct answer; tells how many students attained each score, thus giving the range and the distribution; records the mean, the median, the standard deviation. The student can look at the printout and learn his own score, his rank in the class, and his percentile ranking.

The teacher who analyzes the results of his objective tests, whether he does it with pencil and paper or has a computer do it for him, can discover useful things about his method of instruction. Suppose 95 percent of the class correctly answers Question 1. If this item reflects a concept that you especially wanted students to master, you may conclude that you presented it about as well as one could. If 23 percent of the students correctly answer Question 2, and this item also reflects a concept that you especially hoped students would learn, you can review your instruction on this point. Clearly you need to do something more by way of exposition, demonstration, repetition and review, questioning. With respect to certain difficult items, you might conclude that these represented lesser points that might be comfortable to know but not essential. With respect to another difficult item, you might conclude that you had not given the student reason to believe that he would be quizzed on that type of material. Hence you remind yourself to do a better job of discussing with your students what to expect.

Certainly everyone has had experience with bizarre examinations. I recall a French class in which we spent the semester translating from French into English, but on the final we were given passages in English and told to translate them into French. I recall a Greek literature class in which we came to the final examination primed to discuss *Works and Days,* the *Iliad,* and the *Odyssey* in copious detail—authorship, plot, characters, language and composition—but the instructor entered the room and wrote the following on the board:

1. Hesiod.
2. Homer.

and then departed. I have tried to tell myself that this was a high-level challenging, stimulating, creative set of questions, but I do not sound very convincing to myself.

The Problem of Cheating

Conducting examinations brings the teacher face to face with the problem of cheating. Cheating seems to be less prevalent in high school than in college, but it is prevalent enough.

Since cheating is a natural consequence of grading, the teacher should understand the nature of grades. The chapter has already pointed out the importance of grading by a consistent standard, so that a student will not be penalized by erratic peculiarities of individual teachers. Apart from these considerations, grades are an accepted measure of value, like money. Money is a means to an end, not an end in itself, and a modest supply helps to enrich the journey through life. As an end in itself, however, money can narrow and demean life. Grades are also a means to an end, and happy consequences attend a good GPA: awards, scholarships, interviews. Made a grim and unyielding goal however, the pursuit of grades can bind and circumscribe the educational experience.

Teachers have faced the difficult problem of appraising student achievement and progress, and of assigning grades, with honor and conscience. No widespread charge has ever been made that members of the teaching profession can be dishonorably influenced in their awarding of marks. Teachers have taken their responsibility quietly and earnestly, without the self-consciousness of oaths, pledges, or creeds, and as a profession have upheld a good standard of judgment.

Cheating results when teachers are careless and students are weak-principled. If the teacher does not safeguard his examinations, the wrong eyes may see them. If he asks the same questions repeatedly, pupils may show up at the test forewarned. If he does not use alternate sets of questions, pupils with long rubber necks and sharp young eyes may select a few points from their neighbors. If he uses the same set of questions for different sections of the same course, pupils may exchange helpful information between periods. If he does not proctor the test systematically, written aids may quietly appear. If he writes the questions on the board, pupils may confer about answers while his back is turned. If he dictates true-false statements, pupils may signal answers to one another.

College students know all these devices; only when they become teachers does wisdom desert them. Undergraduates are sophisticated about cheating, and can speak with authority on both the causes and the cures. Once an undergraduate receives his diploma and becomes a teacher, he seems to become naive and has to learn afresh.

The pernicious feature of cheating is that the student cheats not only himself but his classmates. He cannot advance himself into a higher bracket without running the risk that he will push someone else into a lower bracket. Meanwhile students in the class who observe the cheating feel bound by a strange honor not to report the cheater, even though they themselves directly suffer by his action. That is because many students feel that cheating is merely a game played between student and teacher, instead of a vicious method by which one student takes advantage of others.

The morale of a class can be seriously lowered by muddle-headed administration of a test: students of integrity will suffer anguish when others use dishonest means to gain an advantage. Cheating on examinations is far more deplorable than cheating at games or sports, because whereas the results of athletic contests are for most persons only of secondary importance, grades earned become a permanent part of the record, and may, at least for a few years, affect employment, college entrance, or military status. Other competitions may be immediately affected, as, for example, class honors or scholarships.

For these reasons, and for the more important reason that the classroom should set a high standard of morals, the teacher should do everything possible to protect the integrity of the examination. A part of this task is to make students realize that cheating is not a prank but a serious offense. Students should not be allowed to traffic in matters that affect adversely the careers of others.

Importance of the Grading System

Over the years one hears strange stories about grading practices. On the opening day of a class a teacher said to the students, "I am going to give each student in this class an A; so from now on we can enjoy the course, without worrying about marks." The repercussions were tremendous. What the teacher did was simply to abolish the grading system. On a number of occasions beginning teachers have embarrassed themselves by erratic grading. One teacher had a genius for giving the wrong grades to the wrong people. When her first grades were distributed, it was made evident to the students, the other teachers, and the principal, that she had given As to mediocre students and Cs to those of superior talent. Morale in her class hit rock bottom; no good reason remained for taking her assignments seriously. Parents called the principal's office. Agonizing conferences were necessary before she was able to redeem herself. Apparently she started her teaching career with no clear idea of standards; she kept haphazard and incomplete records, and was slow to become acquainted with her students.

Every teacher consciously or unconsciously develops into a strict, average, or

easy marker. Everyone knows how students interpret grades: a B from Miss Y
they say, is as good as an A from anyone else, because "Miss Y almost never
gives As"; whereas an A from Mr. Z is not worth much, because "anybody can
get an A from Mr. Z." The problem goes deeper than students realize. Both Miss
Y and Mr. Z are doing them a grave injustice, because Miss Y and Mr. Z are
following eccentric schemes of grading, not the one used by the institution for
certification to colleges or graduate schools, prospective employers, and pos-
terity in general. Miss Y's scheme of grading contains only the letters B, C, D,
and F, for all practical purposes; whereas Mr. Z's scheme seems limited to A, B,
and C. The strong advice of this book is to avoid the example of either Y or Z,
but instead to follow the traditional system of the institution.

You can compare your grading habits with those of other teachers by
consulting your colleagues. Whether you teach in a high school or college, you
will quickly learn that the administration is concerned about the grading standards of teachers. From time to time the registrar or admissions officer will be
asked to compile all sorts of statistics about grades: the percentages of As, Bs,
Cs, Ds, and Fs earned by all freshmen, or all students in English, or all engineers;
institutions with computer systems can easily supply any sort of tabulation
desired. From these statistics the administration can determine which divisions,
which departments, or which individuals, are strict or easy graders. Eventually
this comes to a study of *your* grade percentages. The principal of a high school
or the chairman of a department will receive a tabulation like this; one of the
names below will be yours:

Sample Report on Teachers' Grades

	PERCENTAGE OF				
	A	B	C	D	F
Mr. Able	0	5	47	36	12
Miss Baker	3	7	60	21	9
Mr. Charley	7	20	50	17	6
Mr. Dog	9	23	52	8	8
Mr. Easy	12	22	49	12	5
Miss Fox	20	26	48	4	2
Mr. George	27	24	39	6	4
Mr. How	41	41	16	2	0

You can easily see what reputation the school or department would get if
every instructor graded like Able and Baker; or, for that matter, like George and
How. And assuming that the list represented a group of instructors teaching a
beginning class in fundamentals, you can easily see what reputation the course
would get if all instructors graded like Able and Baker, or like George and How.
A teacher needs to make the careful discriminations necessary to use five letters

rades with wisdom, sense, and fairness. This is easier said than done, but if this oal is to be attained at all the teacher must establish fair and reasonable tandards and apply them with some consistency.

When a teacher is judicious in his grading, when he keeps students informed bout their progress, when he looks with charity upon the shortcomings of oung people yet upholds his ideals for them, when he keeps personalities out of ie little black book, when he can make friends yet avoid favoritism, he can do s well as can be expected with traditional grading systems. Grades have a aradoxical importance; the teacher should compile them accurately, yet not mphasize them. The greater significance is to be placed on a teacher's sugges-ons, comments, and criticisms, not upon his grades. I have known many utstandingly good teachers, and of them students say, "I enjoy my class so uch and I am getting such a great deal from it that I don't care very much what ade I get." To be sure they do care, but for a while at least the teacher has entered their attention on something more lasting.

Assignments

Construct multiple-choice or matching questions for such units as may be suggested by the teacher.

Report on methods of constructing and grading objective or essay tests.

Report on typical rating scales as described in contemporary books about public speaking, debating, interpretation, drama, and speech pathology.

Questions for Classroom Discussion

What are some of the ways in which students use their high school and college transcripts?

Would it be desirable to have the grades of all high schools comparable? What advantages do you see? What disadvantages?

What advantages or disadvantages are there if the *speech* grades ran notably higher or notably lower than the grades of other classes?

In a staff of teachers all teaching the same course—freshman English, required physical education, fundamentals of speech—what disadvantage do you see to the course if one teacher gives notably higher (or notably lower) grades than his colleagues?

References

ostrom, Robert N. "The Problem of Grading." *Speech Teacher* November 1968.

ouglas, Jack. "The Measurement of Speech in the Classroom." *Speech Teacher*

November 1958. Sensible discussion of the problem of testing and measuring Useful list of references.

Goyer, Robert S. "The Construction of the 'Objective' Examination in Speech." *Southern Speech Journal* Fall 1962.

Gruner, Charles R. "Behavioral Objectives for the Grading of Classroom Speeches." *Speech Teacher* September 1968.

Holtzman, Paul D.; Oliver, Robert T.; Sawyer, Thomas M. Jr.; Wiksell, Wesley Hildebrandt, Herbert W.; and Stevens, Walter W. "A Symposium on Evalua tion, Criticism, and Grading." *Speech Teacher* January 1960.

White, Eugene E. "A Rationale for Grades." *Speech Teacher* November 1967.

Sample Questions

The following questions have been selected from examinations supplied b the directors of various fundamentals courses. Four types are represented true-false, matching, multiple choice (by far the most frequently used in th examinations studied), essay.

Devise criteria by which a question can be measured. Is the judgment or info mation sought "significant," "necessary to know," "unimportant"? Does i appear to discriminate between good and poor students? Does it illustrate sound principle of test construction? or does it illustrate a common fault c test construction? Can it be answered by a person who has not had th course? Does it seem to be an important item? Other criteria will occur t you.

True-False

1. Discussion is a competitive venture.
2. Oral interpretation requires that both the intellectual and emotional conten of literature be conveyed to the audience.
3. A conglomerate of people waiting on a corner for a bus have a common goa though not common roles.
4. Style may be defined as everything that has to do with expression, choice o words, syntax, delivery.
5. The authors of the text state that there is no need nor can there be a genuin outline in discussion.
6. Questions of fact make better discussion questions than do questions o policy.
7. The size of a person's vocal folds has little bearing upon the pitch of person's voice.
8. It is generally agreed that 175-200 words per minute constitute a satisfactor rate for public speaking.

Matching

(i)

1. The factor most necessary in order to develop confidence for speaking.
2. The theory that language perceptions are culturally determined.
3. The tendency to adjust conflicting perceptions.
4. The speaker's awareness of the responses of his audience.
5. Opinions or evidence which are accepted by both the speaker and his audience.
6. Defined by Aristotle as the discovery of the available means of persuasion in any given case.
7. The support, evidence, validation, and reasoning used by a speaker to develop his ideas.
8. A form of supporting material in which the opinion of an expert is employed.
9. A method of idea development employing a question which requires only a mental response from the listener.
10. The persuasive impact of the speaker's character, personality, and background.
11. Argument which takes the form of an extended comparison.
12. Portion of the trachea wherein vocal sound originates.
13. The speaker's choice of language.
14. Mode of speech delivery in which the speaker has made prior preparation, but has not memorized nor does he employ a manuscript.
15. A schematic format illustrating all of the important elements of the communication process.

A. Sapir-Whorf hypothesis
B. cultural determinism
C. careful preparation
D. extemporaneous
E. personal evidence
F. analogy
G. communication model
H. proof
I. rhetorical question
J. audience participation
K. larynx
L. pharynx
M. style
N. common ground
O. speaker adjustment
P. common materials
Q. testimony
R. persuasive speaking
S. feedback
T. cognitive dissonance
U. vocabulary development
V. rhetoric
W. audience cognition
X. ethos
Y. suasion
Z. an outline

(ii)

The following statements are based on Lincoln's speeches. Each statement on the left may be associated with one speech listed on the right.

1. This speech was given in Bloomington. It praised the newly organized Republican party. The reporters were so excited they threw away their pencils.

2. At the conclusion of this closely reasoned speech, the 1500 present stood and cheered like wild Indians.

A. First speech, campaigning for state legislature.
B. Lost speech.
C. House Divided speech.
D. Cooper Union speech.
E. Gettysburg Address.

3. Lincoln gave many short speeches: farewells, speeches to regiments, platform speeches, etc. This one he said would be short and sweet, "like the old lady's dance."

4. In this speech he talked about the 39 founding fathers, finally accounting for 23 who believed (as Lincoln did) that the Federal Government could regulate slavery in the territories.

5. Webster once began a speech by saying, "When the mariner has been tossed for many days" he takes his first opportunity to locate his true latitude. Lincoln began this speech with the same idea in simpler language: "If we could first know where we are . . . we could better judge what to do, and how to do it."

6. The preparation of this speech preyed on his mind in Washington, on the train, in his hotel room the night before.

Multiple Choice

1. "Just consider the source" suggests a speaker who is indulging in (a) a false analogy; (b) the *post hoc* error; (c) an *ad hominem* attack; (d) an appeal to authority.

2. The standards peculiar to informative speaking are (a) intelligence, character, good will; (b) accuracy, completeness, unity; (c) ethos, pathos, logos; (d) data, warrant, claim; (e) inquiry, reinforcement, persuasion.

3. Which of the following critical comments indicates a constructive attitude on the part of the critic? (a) "your speech was poorly organized"; (b) "your arguments were not sound"; (c) "you didn't look at the audience"; (d) "you should have covered less material and gone into more depth"; (e) "your grammar was incorrect."

4. To Mr. Wellfed, the word "grandma" recalls cherry pie, roast turkey, potatoes, and gravy. To Jack Knife, member of the Black Dragon teenage gang, the word "grandma" reminds him of a fat old lady who keeps children while their parents work. To the grandson of Grandma Moses, the word "grandma" recalls beautiful paintings. Which of the following describes the type of meaning involved: (a) denotative; (b) structural; (c) connotative; (d) multiple.

5. Note the following: "Jones will do good work at X university. He did good work at Y university and X and Y universities are comparable in ways that affect grades. Also, both have similar scholastic standards. Hence we may expect Jones to do good work at X university." This speaker developed his

point with (a) description; (b) deduction; (c) specific instances; (d) analogy; (e) none of the above.

6. When the speaker begins his argument by observing "as you all know, the town bridge collapsed yesterday," he is using (a) first order data; (b) second order data; (c) third order data; (d) fourth order data.

7. Howard C. Wilkinson's speech, "How Separate Should Government and God Be?" is especially noteworthy for its (a) use of ethical proofs; (b) extended conclusion; (c) use of historical examples; (d) use of narrative.

8. Good articulation is characterized by (a) appropriate force; (b) controlled rate; (c) flexibility in frequency; (d) clear, distinct, sound formation; (e) pacing utterance to meaning.

9. If you wanted to describe your future spouse to your parents so that they would have a favorable impression (without leaving out any negative points), you would, following the advice of McCroskey (a) quickly describe all negative characteristics first, then emphasize positive characteristics; (b) describe all positive characteristics first, then the negative ones; (c) alternate negative with positive characteristics; (d) not worry about your order of presenting positive and negative characteristics.

10. Recognizing the influence of selective exposure, attention, and recall, if you were a political candidate, you should spend your TV money on (a) one-minute spot advertisements; (b) quarter-hour weekly broadcasts at the same time each week; (c) half-hour addresses to the nation; (d) hour-long specials.

11. Communication models are useful to students of speech for all of the following reasons except (a) they increase our understanding of the process of rhetorical communication; (b) they facilitate the organization of communications research; (c) they direct our attention to the problem of noise which may enable us to reduce such interference in communication; (d) they are prescriptive in that they explain how to improve one's speaking ability.

12. Usually in preparing a speech the first thing a speaker should do is to (a) read voraciously; (b) interview his professors; (c) think himself empty; (d) converse with his friends; (e) start writing.

13. Style in speaking is that part of the art which emerges from (a) the speaker's image; (b) choices and combinations in languages, their grammatical construction, and their psychological impact; (c) the care with which the speaker prepares his person and his platform surroundings; (d) the customs of the time in which he speaks; (e) the relative beauty of a given speech.

4. A listener comments, "It wasn't at all clear what you were saying. Why didn't you structure your speech differently?" The "noise" here is probably (a) in the encoding process; (b) in the audience analysis; (c) in the receiver; (d) in the source's thinking.

5. As a member of the Speakers Bureau, you are asked to give your speech, "Dorm Living" at a freshman orientation. In adapting your speech to the audience, select the factor about which you need the *least* information (a) socio-economic level; (b) sex; (c) age; (d) knowledge of the audience; (e) expectations of the audience.

Essay

(i)

You have been appointed to the position of Director of Communications a Texas Instruments, Inc. It is your conviction that a basic public speaking cours for junior executives of the company would improve communications bot within the company and with the company's customers. However, you mu convince the company's board of vice presidents that your proposal has meri Although three or four of them sympathize with you, three or four are oppose and the rest are undecided. "We don't need any classical orators," says one. "L them join Toastmasters," says a second. "Public speaking is a natural talen either you've got it or you haven't," comments a third. Thus, your work is cu out for you. The effectiveness of your presentation will determine whether yo get your course.

A. Outline the speech you would present.
B. Call attention to special features of the speech you have designed t appeal to your particular audience. Regard your audience as a grou of intelligent, hard-headed business men.

(ii)

Define *eight* of the following terms. Where appropriate, also illustrate th concept and discuss its significance: (a) latitude of acceptance; (b) motive; (cognitive dissonance; (d) value; (e) motivated sequence; (f) audience; (g) identif cation; (h) source credibility; (i) suggestion; (j) reference groups; (k) congruit principle; (l) argument.

(Note: The short-answer or identification type of question is a usef compromise between the essay and the objective question. Instructors wh generally give essay questions often include identification items as a way putting at least part of the test on an objective basis.)

Choose *three* of the following problems and write fairly complete essays o them.

A. To what extent do you think Aristotle's theory of persuasion is mad obsolete by the ideas of Kelman, Festinger, and Kenneth Burke? Detail th ways in which it has or has not been made obsolete.
B. Much is said and written about the importance of persuasion in th decision-making of the society and the growth of the person who studies i If you had to challenge such statements, what would you argue are the limit tions and dangers of persuasion?
C. Outline in some detail your ideas about the nature and functions propaganda. Include a definition of propaganda, assumptions about effecti strategy and tactics, and factors you think determine the success or failure a propaganda campaign.
D. Discuss the methods and contributions of experimental studies in persuasio Refer to research studies.
E. Evaluate the ethics of the view which says, "truth is what sells," "truth what you want to believe," and "truth is that which is not legally false

(Note. In your critique of the foregoing five statements, ask yourself: (1) nder what circumstances should students be given, or not be given, choice or >tional questions ("answer 3 out of 5")? The standard objection is that udents are not writing the same exam, thus, in a competitive situation, making •mparisons more difficult. (2) What suggestions would you give students, •fore the exam, as to what to review? Looking at (C), do you find the second ntence helpful to give the student an idea of what the instructor will be oking for in the answer? Looking at (D) would you say, days before the exam, ⁄ou will be required to comment on research studies by author and approx- 1ate title," or "You will be given a list of research studies, from which you will ake selections and on which you will comment?")

12

the art of criticism

*Criticism, carried to the height worthy of it,
is a majestic office, perhaps an art, perhaps even
a church.*

Walt Whitman

*I have derived continued benefit from criti-
cism at all periods of my life, and I do not
remember any time when I was ever short of it.*

Sir Winston Churchill

Every one likes a little compliment.

Abraham Lincoln

he word *criticism* carries with it the idea of rebuke, correction, or faultfinding.
riticism, however, is favorable as well as adverse: it comes from a Greek word
leaning to *discuss, judge,* or *discern.* The ancient meaning should be restored to
1e classroom: let the moments devoted to criticism be regarded as periods of
iscussion, judgment, discernment.

Some day when in pensive mood you should reflect upon the art of criticism.
egin by looking backward over high school and college days, dwelling on the
istances when criticism played a part in shaping your education. Recall a
:acher, wiser than most, who took the trouble to give you thoughtful appraisal
f your resources. You may also recall bits and pieces of advice that helped you
) think more clearly about yourself.

You are now the official critic; students look to you for help in achieving

their goals. A teacher's responsibilities are important, but that of offeri
criticism is especially grave. What you say may have far-reaching effect.

Basis of Good Criticism

Good criticism must grow out of a liking for the student or at least out of a
honest interest in his growth. Of Northwestern's Lew Sarett it has been writter

> One of his strongest claims to greatness . . . was his deep interest in th
> individual: his problems and potentialities. He had an almost uncanny abilit
> to put his finger on the driving force of a person's life, to dignify that force a
> he guided the student to a pride in his own talents and possibilities, and t
> crystallize the youth's determination to make his life contribute to the goc
> of the world community.[1]

This short paragraph suggests the point of view from which criticism begin
Illinois's (Iowa's) Charles Henry Woolbert had the same trait:

> [He] was loved, honored, and respected by all of the students who can
> into contact with him. . . .
> He was interested in and interesting to, not only speech students, bu
> athletes, politicians, scholars, and ne'er-do-wells. He was friend and adviser t
> all. . . . He found the minutes and the energy with which to greet eac
> student who came to him. He met them all with that keen interest an
> freshness which is usually reserved for the first few in the morning.[2]

And further:

> To watch a teacher who was honestly interested in stimulating students t
> "think" their way through a speech situation was exhilarating. We knew tha
> *something* worthwhile would happen during each hour spent with him.[3]

Grinnell's John P. Ryan's influence is epitomized as follows:

> Many who knew him first as teacher, later looked to him as adviser, an
> still later as a loyal personal friend. His students sought his help in selecting
> career and in getting established in their own professions. . . . They sent the
> sons and daughters to Grinnell, with earnest, parental advice to take h

---

[1] Emily Kimball Lilly, "Great Teachers of Speech: I. The Young Lew Sarett," *Spee
Teacher, January 1955.
[2] Andrew Thomas Weaver, "Charles Henry Woolbert," *Quarterly Journal of Speech,* Febr
ary 1930.
[3] Severina E. Nelson, "Great Teachers of Speech: II. Charles Henry Woolbert," *Spee
Teacher, March 1955.

famous course in public speaking. His counsel, his continued support, and above all the warmth of his friendship will always live in their memories.[4]

One of Ryan's students, Iowa's Harry G. Barnes, has been memorialized in ıese words:

> Harry Barnes was a fine classroom performer. He was alive and stimulating. He enjoyed large classes wherever he taught. . . . But . . . he was at his best in helping a student unravel a problem. He was unbelievably wise. Students left his office with their heads a little higher and their self-esteem a little stronger. In this land there must be a thousand men and women who will say that this was so. This great talent he carried with him to the end of his days.[5]

The quality of personal appreciation of the good labors of students is built ɛeply into the careers of scores of famous teachers of speech. This list of ibutes could continue for many pages, but would be incomplete without these ›w words about Wabash's William Norwood Brigance:

> Briggie was esteemed by his students as a great teacher. His classes were challenging. The instances that documented his exposition became motivating influences that pulled each student to levels of excellence he had not before achieved. . . . His life was devoted to bringing out the best in others.[6]

If, therefore, a teacher is to manage students, he must have a warm concern ›out them. Kahlil Gibran put it in these well-known phrases:

> No man can reveal to you aught but that which already lies half asleep in the dawning of your knowledge.
> The teacher who walks in the shadow of the temple, among his followers, gives not of his wisdom but rather of his faith and lovingness.
> If he is indeed wise he does not bid you enter the house of his wisdom, but rather leads you to the threshold of your mind.[7]

Important ingredients of criticism would therefore appear to be: a lively ıterest in the student; a feeling for his possibilities of development; and a ·alization that although this growth must come slowly, even erratically, persis- nt effort on the part of the student and steadfast concern on the part of the ·acher will make it come surely.

)uarterly Journal of Speech, April 1951.
'Shop Talk," Quarterly Journal of Speech, December 1955.
ohn W. Black, Central States Speech Journal, Spring 1960, p. 22.
·he Prophet, New York: Alfred A. Knopf, 1935, pp. 64-65. The Prophet is so famous that to quote it seems trite, yet it is continually being rediscovered with astonishment by people expressing, wonderingly, why-haven't-I-been-told-about-this-before.

What Criticism Is and Is Not

When a teacher criticizes acting, he weighs and appraises it: he shows where th
characterization was honest and convincing, where it fell short of those qualitie
In arriving at his judgment he may discuss voice, articulation, action, faci
expression, understanding of the meaning or feeling, and a dozen other catege
ries. When he criticizes reading, he similarly proposes a judgment about th
effectiveness of the performance: he may talk about voice and body, unde
standing and interpretation of thought, emotion, and attitude. A criticism of
speech, or a conversation, or a report or demonstration is likewise an appraisa
Criticism usually proceeds through analysis: the total performance is broken int
various elements, which in turn are evaluated; but the result is a synthesis,
judgment about the performance as a whole. The teacher-critic suggests a way c
improvement so that the student will know what to do better next time.

One of the advantages of using score cards is that they remind the teacher c
the importance of viewing the whole performance instead of being overly critic:
of a single aspect of it. Consider, for example, speechmaking, described b
classical rhetoricians as being an art made up of five arts.

Art number 1 is the art of creating or discovering good and sensible ideas. Tt
speaker accumulates evidence, argument, example and illustration, testimon
from authority. From this storehouse he evolves comparisons, relationship
solutions.

Art number 2 is the art of selecting and organizing. Mastery of this art guides tt
student as to what to leave out of his speech and what to put in; and in wha
order to arrange what is selected.

Art number 3 is the art of using language. Certain words are more forceful, vivi
persuasive, and accurate than others. "Iron curtain" was retained in the mine
whereas "great wall" would have passed unnoticed. Relevant, pertinent fac
call for clear, incisive language.

Art number 4 is the art of memory. A student needs to have ideas at the tip o
his tongue, so he can draw upon them *when* he needs them. He may also b
called upon to answer questions, to develop his ideas at greater length, t
defend his evidence or reasoning.

Art number 5 is delivery. The use of voice and body helps the student immeasu
ably in making words effective.

Imagine a speaker *weak in ideas*. His information would be inaccurate, h
judgment unfounded, his counsel superficial. His influence could not be lastir
among thoughtful people.

Imagine a speaker *weak in selecting and organizing*. His speeches would be rmless blobs, difficult for him to present, difficult for listeners to remember. Imagine a speaker *weak in the use of words*. His ideas would seem vague and olorless; his utterance would consist of trite sayings. The two great arts of iving ideas and of clothing them in well-chosen words are almost inseparable. s soon as you take any crude, raw idea and begin to shape and form it, even st to make it clear and understandable, you are calling upon the principles of sing language.

Imagine a speaker of *weak memory*. He would have to write his speeches and ad them. He would hardly dare take his eyes off the page. He would be elpless in a question and answer period.

Imagine a speaker of *poor delivery*. He might be so inaudible that you could ear him only with great difficulty. He might mumble so much that you would iss the meaning. He might lull you into inattention by a chant or singsong esentation.[8]

Now imagine a teacher who attended only to the visual and audible features, le matters that comprise *delivery*, and overlooked a salient weakness in *ideas*, *ganization, language,* or *memory.* A similar list of things-to-look-for could be olved for reading aloud, or interpretation, or other kinds of communication, ch item in this list being essential to good criticism.

This two thousand-year-old concept is still giving good mileage, although we so ask ourselves searching questions about the speaker's values, attitudes, role, lf-concept; the listener's information, attitudes, biases; the extent to which eaker identifies with listener; the speaker's image, credibility, ego-involvement.

Some teachers are such fine critics that the period spent in criticism is fully as osorbing as the time spent listening to performances. As the teacher reviews rious student contributions, his observations are so penetrating, so helpful, and illuminating that the class receives new inspiration. At times, however, a acher goes through the motions of criticizing, but never actually analyzes and dges. The result may be description or explanation, but not criticism. The four amples below illustrate types of comments that sound like criticism, but tually are not. The examples apply to speech making, but may be applied to her forms of communication.

The student may present an analysis of the famous "New Truck" case, inging out ideas of his own, as well as adding material he has dug up in his ading. After he has finished, the teacher may review the speech, mentioning ch principal reason and paraphrasing the supporting material. These comments ay be attractive, but what the teacher has done in fact is to give a short speech oout the case where the student gave a longer one. *Summary is not criticism.*

The student may make a speech on an essay he has read, "Every Man His

\dapted from Loren Reid, *Speaking Well,* pp. 5-6.

Own Historian," and after he has finished, the teacher may take the floor an
give additional ideas of his own about this famous Becker essay. He may n
even refer to the student's reflections at all. The result is that the student ga
one speech about historical study, whereas the teacher gave a different one. Tl
student's train of thought stirred up in the teacher an associated train of idea
Free association is not criticism.

3. The student may make a speech on "The Ethnic Studies Program Reviewed
and after he has left the floor, the teacher may step forward and describe tl
effort with such adjectives as wonderful and interesting. As a result the stude
is aglow, and for a moment may believe that he has received penetratii
criticism. Merely to call a speech wonderful, however, is not to give a fir
criticism of it. One teacher calls a speech *interesting* whenever he can think
nothing else to say. *Abstract generalized approval* may contain 98 perce
sawdust and only 2 percent criticism. A teacher who can say only *wonderful*
marvelous when he hears an above average speech will lose the respect of h
class. By the same reasoning, *abstract expressions of disapproval* like *terrible* ar
awful are remote from useful criticism. Benjamin Franklin was right when I
wrote, "Blame-all and praise-all are two blockheads."

4. The student may make a speech on "The Development of Hybrid Corn," ar
after he has completed his remarks the teacher may offer a detailed commenta
on mannerisms. He may describe how frequently the student cleared his throa
how he held his notes close to his body, how he fingered the buckle of his be
Overattention to one aspect of speechmaking is only a part of criticism. Tl
critic needs to study both content and delivery if he is to arrive at a val
judgment.

The foregoing examples are by no means rare. An untrained critic may spe
half the period talking about performances he has just heard. He may couch h
praise and blame in empty words. If he is listening to reading or acti
performances, his possibilities of using bogus criticism are just as numerous. I
may talk pleasantly about the choice of selection, ranging widely elsewhere
literature. He has rich opportunity for using meaningless expressions of approv
and disapproval. He may talk brilliantly on trivial details. When the bell rings, I
may not have offered much helpful suggestion.

Adapt Criticism to the Student

If the teacher wants to improve his worth as a critic, he must keep sever
principles in mind. One is that it is more important to study the person bei
criticized than it is his performance. Human beings are sensitive to commen
made about them. A word of praise may be remembered forever, especially if
is vivid or unusual. A word of disapproval may carry a good deal of sting where

You will find that some students are more teachable in this respect than others. Suppose you make an observation such as the following:

Next time you speak . . .

These words themselves state the problem obliquely, putting the whole matter in the future, without being too blunt about the speech just heard . . .

. . . pick out two or three main points that do not overlap, and discuss them one at a time. By making sure that your principal points do not duplicate one another, your speech will be better organized and will move ahead more rapidly.

One student, listening to this comment, will nod thoughtfully and later will execute your suggestion. Another will argue it out with you:

But my speech today didn't have any overlapping. My first point was on soandso, whereas my second point was on suchandsuch . . .

The teacher should not care whether he wins this particular argument or not. A good tactic is to withdraw from that aspect of the controversy, and discuss a part of the speech where ideas were better organized, using it as a standard that the other parts of the speech could approach. Assure the class that no teacher is interested in showing a student up, or proving him wrong, or poking fun at a shortcoming; a teacher is interested in tomorrow, and next week, and twenty years later, and only for that purpose does he offer suggestions for improvement.

One way or another the teacher has to learn who can be taught and who can only be argued with. Students in the latter group must gain insight into the emotional attitude that blocks their progress. The teacher may develop this insight with a discussion of study habits and mental attitudes that encourage self-improvement. Sometimes, however, students are so impervious to criticism of their weaknesses that the only approach is a personal interview, where problems may be frankly discussed without the presence of an audience.

Make Criticism Meaningful

No one formula will reach all people, but as universal a rule as any is to begin criticism by discussing the good points of the performance. The advantages of positive reinforcement have been demonstrated with rats and men alike. Mention as many favorable features as you honestly can. Candid approval opens the recipient's mind, and allows him to shed some of his tension. If you then mention possibilities for future improvement, he is mentally disposed to follow you. End your comment, however, on a note of praise; repeat again the outstanding good item in the performance.

Beginning teachers ask, "What if you can find nothing to praise?" Experienced teachers also have to ask that question. We must remember that speaking and reading aloud are difficult and complex acts. If nothing else avails, describe the pupil's improvement. *Improvement* is a word of magic.

The language of criticism is of the utmost importance. Contrast these two statements:

> Your speech today, Susan, was really wonderful. It was really outstanding. It was really interesting from first to last.

These are heady and exciting words, delightful to hear, even though lacking in specific content. Yet this statement is better:

> Susan, last night I thought a long time about the speeches you have made in this class. I remembered how much we liked your talk on "How Wide is The Communication Gap" and we voted your next speech on "Dropouts and Hangouts" the best heard that day. Your talk today was just as good. A reason is that you work variety into your speeches: you combine example, quotations from authority, humor, and today you used a little dialogue, all woven together to make your central idea stand out. Everything you said seemed selected with this particular group of listeners in mind.

You have paid Susan two stimulating compliments, one by showing a sustained interest, and the other by showing that you have listened attentively enough to be able to pick out and label a quality of speechmaking that she should consciously seize upon and strive to perfect.

Make your criticism, therefore, full of meaning. Take notes so that you can recall concretely what you want to criticize. The *exact statement of a student's own words* is helpful; your quotation will enable the other members of the class to follow your comments. Discuss the *performance*, not the *person*, but show your interest in the person, and be specific about the remedy. Finally: nothing that has been said rules out the necessity of being blunt and forthright when the situation demands it. Wayne N. Thompson rightly observes that critiques cannot always be both informative and complimentary.[9]

Students learn at their maximum rate when, after making a speech, giving a reading, acting a part, writing a test, they are quickly made aware of the results. *Delayed* reinforcement—the criticism delayed until next week, the term paper handed back a month late—has reduced value. One of the advantages of programmed instruction is that if the student makes an error on card 5, he learns about it on card 6; if he gives the correct response on card 11, he sees a hearty "very good" on card 12.

---

[9]*Quantitative Research in Public Address and Communication*, p. 151.

The nature of the speech communication class—much student talk and participation, little teacher lecture; frequent short performances instead of infrequent long performances; frequent student-teacher interaction; classes of moderate size, tending to reduce the gap between teacher and student; group assignments, so that students tend to rehearse or study together, outside of class hours, guaranteeing that learning goes on between classes; festivals and tournaments, offering additional, outside, motivations—is designed to encourage learning on an observable (behavioral) basis. In fact if you wanted to set up a situation that would facilitate maximum learning, you would end with something very much like a speech communication class.

Keep Minor Details in Proportion

After you have mentally analyzed a performance and are ready to make suggestions for improvement, you should ask yourself one further question: suppose this student changed this performance as I have suggested—would it truly be better? Assume that you are about to tell him to hold his hands at his side instead of holding them behind his back: would that improve the speech? Only to a minor degree. Suppose he is acting a part and you have told him to turn more to the audience: will that improve his acting? Not in any important way. Perhaps you have told him to slow down, or speed up, or talk louder—you may or may not have made an important contribution. What, then, should you have said? These things, no doubt, but also something more vital: a suggestion about analyzing the audience, limiting the subject, using more vivid material, if a speech; perhaps a better way to interpret the character, to ferret out the meaning, to suggest the emotion, if a play. The trivialities need to be kept in proportion.

Avoid calling attention to minor faults that will correct themselves automatically. Beginning performers will reveal various kinds of mannerisms sheerly from nervousness. Why catalog and describe them? As soon as students gain experience they will relax, nervousness will largely disappear, and superficial movements vanish. They will be more likely to improve if you ignore these self-correcting faults. If bad habits persist, you need to take a hand; even so, remember the Greek epitaph: "The visits of many physicians have killed me." You cannot continually pull students up by the roots to see if they are still growing.

The strong tendency of beginning teachers to talk about trivialities and nonessentials has a counterpart in the teaching of English. If you read a theme and limit your corrections to matters of punctuation, spelling, split infinitives, pronoun references, and agreement, you will improve the student's paper about 10 percent. If the student's paper has vivacity, energy, imagination, originality, it knows the really priceless ingredients. If it lacks those virtues, try to discover why, and begin criticism from there. No one objects to a teacher's marking the grammar provided he only starts there and works up to something significant.

One final suggestion to the critic: at times ask yourself, what did the student omit, leave out, fail entirely to do? If he makes three speeches and has no humor in them, or uses no specific examples, call this lack to his attention. You have thereby done him a much greater service than to teach him to hold his hands at his side. If he acts three different roles and interprets each the same way, review for him the study and research through which a characterization is built. When you are at a loss to find an approach to the problem of helping a student develop, ask yourself what he is overlooking or omitting.

Stress Praiseworthy Features

One method of conducting a critiquing session is to open by saying, "Did any one notice anything unusually good about any of the speeches (or other kinds of performance) this hour?" A student may respond by commenting favorably upon the organization of A's speech, which gives the teacher opportunity to review the special features of good organization that the speech displayed: transitions, summaries, elements of coordination and subordination, and the like. The next question may be, "Any other interesting features of A's speech?" proceeding to a further discussion of the talk. As these compliments should give A a solid basis of reassurance, you may decide to go to the next speech without any adverse criticism whatever; or you may think it wise to mention casually something like "A, you seemed to look nearly all of the time at these five students over here; next time try to look at everybody in the room." You would, however, probably elect to overlook anything that came under the heading of a trifling symptom of nervousness that would correct itself.

After the discussion of A's talk is completed, you may continue by asking, "Did you notice anything unusually good about some other speech?" and thus proceed to a second discussion. Eventually you will have talked about every performance; not necessarily in chronological order, but in an easy and convenient way as various points occurred to the class.

Good teachers point out that what weakens a speech is not the presence of *faults* but the absence of *virtues*. This principle can be illustrated scores of times from the experiences of eminent speakers. Edmund Burke became a powerful figure because of the strength of his ideas; his delivery was sometimes indifferent. Sir Winston Churchill's language commends itself to us along with his courage and fortitude; his was not a top flight voice, though he used it remarkably well.. William Jennings Bryan had a magical way with audiences, though his influence was not lasting. Henry Clay could get more people to listen to him and fewer to vote for him, the saying goes, than anybody. Eisenhower in his press conferences had a rambling sentence structure, but nevertheless a commanding and reassuring presence. Abraham Lincoln was called a baboon but managed to be genuinely eloquent.

What teachers most need to develop in the beginner is confidence and self-assurance, tempered with as much judgment and good sense as can be expected.

The secret of speaking effectiveness is locked in *content*. A teacher should ever urge students to seek out facts, to use examples, to express thoughts in fair and exact language. If a student's talk is filled with loose generalities, his voice and action are also likely to be unimpressive. Encourage him, therefore, to use illustrative material; he can thus be expository at some moments, narrative at others, and this variety of content will, or should, introduce variety into the presentation. Be alert also to the quality of the thinking that is going on, the validity of the evidence and other forms of support, the basic sincerity and conviction of the individual.

Where this discussion has mentioned *speeches* and *speechmaking,* the reader may mentally substitute, at times, plays, skits, characterizations, oral interpretations, reports, or other types of performances. Once again theory urges the teacher to amplify and magnify and solidify the virtues of the presentation as a surer way of gaining improvement than, negatively, to nibble away at faults. Both types of criticism have a place, but the emphasis on the student's good qualities is what is important. And to repeat, a basic source of effectiveness in these activities lies in content; when one interprets the words of another, as in an oral reading or a play, he must understand the content in its intellectual and its emotional aspects.

Suppose the critic teacher uses the other approach, and elaborates on trifling faults: "this is poor, that is unsatisfactory, the other is inadequate." The student will lose heart, just as the teacher would himself if a supervisor were sitting at the back of the classroom ever ready to call him to task. Moreover, even if the student learns to minimize his little mannerisms, he has arrived at best at only a neutral position. Buried inside every student is a second teacher, a self-teacher, and this is the person you want to reach; through your encouragement you can get the student interested in teaching himself, and thus you loosen a force that will guide and direct him years after he has left your class.

Interviewers making a public opinion poll participated in an experiment in which half of the interviewees were praised for their answers to the questions, half were not. The results indicated that praise reduced the number of "don't know" responses, increased the originality and number of answers, and yet did not make the interviewees insincere or dishonest in their responses.[10]

Class Participation in Criticism

Teachers like to have members of the class participate in the criticism of a performance. The procedure encourages more careful listening, through which

---

[10] Joan B. Field, "The Effect of Praise in a Public Opinion Poll," *Public Opinion Quarterly,* Spring 1955, pp. 85-90.

the student can gain suggestions for his own improvement. The strong approval of a classmate is, moreover, a fine tonic.

The first exercises in class criticism need guidance. Teachers should themselves take the lead in the critique until the students gain a better idea of what to listen and look for. Members of the class can then be led to the proper critical attitude by, at first, being invited to comment on the desirable features of the performance, as suggested above. Questioning by the teacher of student critics will help teach them to be more specific. If a classmate said that A had a convincing characterization in his role in the play, the teacher can follow up by asking what made the role convincing, searching out details about movement, voice, facial expression, understanding the lines, etc. Interesting discussions develop which give members of the class a feeling that basic principles are indeed being studied.

Questions about the aim or purpose of the student—"What did he seek to accomplish? What was his central theme? What mood or tone did he establish?" —are of the first order of importance.

Methods of Criticism

The methods of criticizing are important to review. You may offer your comments after each performance. This may not be the best procedure, and it is the most time consuming. It requires the greatest alertness on your part; as soon as the student finishes, you need to take the floor. It cuts the class hour into shreds.

You may wait until the series of performances is finished, then discuss all of them in one session of ten or fifteen minutes. This procedure allows you to make comparisons and contrasts, to pick out one or two important critical points and relate each effort to it. For example, if after listening to six speeches you decide that most of them had a weak ending, you could center your discussion on the art of concluding, going through the series of speeches, and picking out the good and the mediocre conclusions.

You may criticize after each second performance, or each third performance, thus breaking the class hour into two or three divisions. This method has advantages. For one, you do not focus quite so sharply on any one student, since you can mention points in which each of them excelled, or one or two matters in which all of them could improve. For another, you can save a little classroom time.

You may, after a series of performances, invite students to make short talks of appraisal. Name your student critics in advance, so they may take proper notes. Or appoint one student to comment on articulation and pronunciation, one on quality of supporting data, one on general effectiveness, and so on through the list of items. Or follow each performance with a student criticism

Still another method is to take copious readable notes on each performance, and at the end of the class give each student his card of notes. That method is economical of time, and gives the student ideas in writing that he may study at leisure.

You may also ask each student to write a comment about each other student. Assuming the assignment for the day is a two-minute reading, give each student a slip of paper for each of his classmates. After the class, collect the comments and distribute them. Each one will take with him a number of slips of paper, bearing comments about his reading. A good variation of this procedure is to collect the slips yourself, and prepare an exhibit for the next day's class. Across the top of a bulletin board, write headings for columns: Critic A, Critic B, Critic C, and so on. Along the side write the names of the performers. Thumb tack the slips in the proper squares, so that all of Critic A's comments will appear in his vertical column. Let the class study the bulletin board, and determine which critics are the best. You will notice striking facts: you will see that Critic G observes nothing but delivery, his comments being on voice or action; whereas Critic R notices only pronunciation or grammar. The exhibit reveals the listening habits of students. You may repeat the exercise later on, and see if the students have begun to look and listen for a greater variety of factors.

You may use a check list or score card; see the examples in Chapter 11. In using these, however, give thought to the sections headed "Comments" or "Remarks." You may use a tape recorder or moving picture or TV camera.

A final method of criticism is to call each student in for a conference. This is the college method, and may be too time-consuming for high school. Some students, however, can be reached only through interview, so if you have slow-learning individuals, invite them to confer with you.

We do not improve in a straightforward line. We move ahead, fall back, thrust further ahead, this time a little more than before; slip and fall back but perhaps not so miserably as formerly; mark time for so long that we think we have done as well as we can ever do, then find ourselves beating our old mark; then comes a humbling setback; then forward again. We have good days and bad days. But if we keep steadily at it, we may surprise ourselves by our achievement. You should point these facts out to students; biography is rich in illustration.

Encouraging Self-Criticism

Frederick W. Haberman has written an absorbing description of teacher-critics at work:

Back-stage at the Wisconsin Union Theatre I once observed a young student come to one of the technical theatre assistants, who was a graduate student, and ask for help in the building of the upper half of a Dutch door.

The student was not very skillful with the tools of his extra-curricular trade. With the hammer he bruised the wood; with the saw he beveled its edges. The teaching assistant could witness this mutilation no longer; besides, he decided, this guy was hopeless. Taking saw and hammer in hand, he said, "Watch me." He created a fine Dutch door in jig time. He was happy and proud when all was finished; but the student was neither.

In contrast, on another occasion, I observed a teaching assistant who was asked by a student how to build something that would look like a big boulder on the stage. The assistant agreed to help. He explained when necessary, offered a guiding hand when really needed, but stood by most of the time and watched even when the boy made silly mistakes. But the boulder was made. Two people were proud and happy. The student had created a boulder; the teaching assistant had helped to create in another human being a skill and an appreciation of something. Both the door and the boulder that were created in that shop will be thrown away; but there is in one boy a modicum of skill and understanding and appreciation that may last a lifetime.

I shall not say that one teaching assistant was better than the other or that one will be more valuable to civilization than the other. For the one is a performing artist and the other is a teaching artist. We need both.[11]

The art of criticism is usually thought of as a one-way plan of communication, the teacher taking the initiative and furnishing the ideas. Quite likely the best criticism does not proceed this way at all. Instead of saying to a student, "You did soandso," or "You never seem to do soandso," your better approach may be to ask, "What do you think of your performance? Where do you think you could have improved? What were you trying to achieve?" and in that way start the wheels of improvement turning within the student. Or you may ask the student an open-ended question: "Is there anything you would like to ask me to comment particularly on?" Often we talk too much, and do not listen enough. We are too free with advice and not sufficiently patient to help the student seize the initiative.

As a step in this direction, you may take a few minutes someday to talk about the importance of being willing to ask questions.[12] The reluctance to participate is awesome. Point out once again that the class is composed of beginners; that no one is supposed to know it all; and that if any principle is not made clear, those who are confused should ask questions. Encourage them to ask questions to verify their own knowledge; sometimes a student thinks he has

[11] "Toward the Ideal Teacher of Speech," *Speech Teacher,* January 1961, p. 5. The article also appears in Keith Erickson (ed.), *Dimensions of Oral Communication Instruction. Readings in Speech Education,* pp. 233-244.
[12] This suggestion has also been made elsewhere in this book. Every teacher must get his students to participate. They must develop confidence in their own ideas, and gain practice in expressing them. They must open up the channels of reception: to learn to listen, to give and take, to share.

aught an idea, and if he would ask a confirming question, he could reassure
.imself. Remind them that if one person is confused, others may be also, and a
;uestion will thus benefit many. Tell them that a part of the fun of teaching is in
answering their questions: and not alone of teaching—almost any kind of expert
.kes to talk about his specialty. The modern classroom welcomes questions, is
.rateful for questions, gives special attention to questions. Perhaps if you can
;sue a call for questions two or three times during the course, you can open for
.ll present this broad avenue of information.

Once you have encouraged students to ask questions, you have greatly
.orwarded the art of criticism. You have broken down a bit of the formality of
.he classroom. You have brought teacher and student closer together. You have
hrown out the desk and chairs and have brought in the log.

Nothing in this chapter should be taken to mean that criticism is a simplistic
.rt that can be practised brilliantly by all. Teachers' comments and students'
omments about one another may range all the way from helpful and insightful
.o damaging. Each teacher will have to study each student performance and
letermine the best way to improve it, or to help the student improve himself.
Ay observations of teacher-critics have been on the optimistic side: the chances
.or a fair amount of success at the outset are favorable and for improvement
ven more so.[13]

Assignments

. Visit a class in speechmaking, interpretation, or acting, and take notes on
performances. Afterwards, compare your observations with those of other
students.

. Listen to a TV or radio speech, round table, dramatic performance, newscast,
or other program. The teacher or class may agree in advance which program
to observe. Afterwards, compare your criticisms with others of the class.

. Ask several members of the methods class or the teaching staff to visit a class,
contest, or festival where performances can be judged. Afterwards, the judges
should compare their rankings or grades and give reasons for their decisions.

Questions for Classroom Discussion

. To what extent should students participate in criticism sessions? Do students
value the praise of their classmates?

. What is the best *time* for criticism: after each performance? after each two or
three performances? at the end of the class?

[3]For a review of methods of the art of criticism and of some of the difficulties inherent
herein, see the articles and the introductory section in Erickson, Chapter 3, pp. 246 ff.

3. Is it possible that whereas most teachers should be kindly in their critique others might be effective by being blunt and outspoken? If a teacher is blu₁ and outspoken, what offsetting qualities of personality should he have ¡ order to avoid demoralizing the student?

4. Are written comments preferable to oral? of equal value to oral? worthles

5. What use should be made of formal check lists or score cards? Should they ₤ used exclusively, as a supplement to other forms of criticism, or not at all?

References

Auer, J. Jeffery, ed. *Antislavery and Disunion, 1858-1861.* New York: Harp₁ & Row, 1963.

Baird, A. Craig, and Thonssen, Lester. "Methodblogy in the Criticism of Publ Address." *Quarterly Journal of Speech* April 1947.

Brigance, William Norwood, ed. *A History and Criticism of American Publ. Address.* 2 vols. New York: McGraw-Hill, 1943.

Bryant, Donald C., ed., *The Rhetorical Idiom.* Ithaca: Cornell University Pres₁ 1958.

Dedmon, Donald N. "Criticizing Student Speeches: Philosophy and Principles. *Central States Speech Journal* Februrary 1967. Reviews pedagogically soun₁ principles of criticism.

Erickson, Keith, ed. *Dimensions of Oral Communication Instruction: Reading in Speech Education.* Dubuque: William C. Brown, 1970. See the articles b₁ Gerald M. Phillips, Donald N. Dedmon, Paul D. Holtzman, Eugene E. Whit₁ Jack Douglas, William I. Gordon, and the author's introduction to th₁ section.

Howes, Raymond F., ed. *Historical Studies of Rhetoric and Rhetoricians.* Ithac₁ Cornell University Press, 1961.

Montgomery, K. E. "How to Criticize Student Speeches." *Speech Teach₁* September 1957. Suggests specific questions to ask, particularly with refe₁ ence to organization and support of main ideas.

Reid, Loren. *Speaking Well.* Columbia: Artcraft Press, 1962.

——, ed. *American Public Address: Studies in Honor of Albert Craig Bair₁* Columbia: University of Missouri Press, 1961. Contains essays of interest t₁ the teacher-critic.

Richardson, Ralph. "Adlai E. Stevenson, Hollywood Bowl, October 9, 1954. *Western Speech* May 1955. A clear and vivid report of a contemporar₁ address. Includes a reproduction of the Stevenson manuscript showing th₁ speaker's underscoring and interlineations and, in a parallel column, the actual speech as recorded on tape, with the speaker's interpolations and audience cheers.

Thompson, Wayne N. *Quantitative Research in Public Address and Communication*. New York: Random House, 1967.

Thonssen, Lester; Baird, A. Craig; and Braden, Waldo W. *Speech Criticism*. 2d ed. New York: Ronald Press, 1970.

morale:
yours and the students'

Let the horse worry. His head is bigger.

Old Hungarian Proverb

When I was a child, I besought Thee with no little earnestness that I might not be flogged at school, but Thou didst not hear me.

St. Augustine

.uch of the art of teaching is the art of working with students. Thousands of
asses are taught by people moderately well prepared as to subject matter but
arful of their ability to maintain a good class atmosphere. Any teacher, high
hool or college, wants the morale of his students to be as high as possible. He
so wants to keep his own morale at a livable level.

This chapter is written with the problem in mind broadly and generally. The
acher may be young or old, someone with a recent bachelor's degree, or
meone who left a degree behind years ago to pursue a career in the armed
rces or to rear a family. The subject may be physical education or industrial
ts, French or physics; if most of the examples come from speech, it is because
ost though not all of the readers of this book are teachers of speech, and that I
aw largely, as I must, from my own observation and reflection.

Most of this discussion about morale is based on the internal conditions of
e school: intramural situations, those within the walls. But events of these
cades have dealt savage blows to the morale of both students and instructors.

The high mortality rate among presidents and deans has been obvious; les apparent is the slow erosion taking place in the classroom. So far as externa situations are concerned, those institutions have fared best which had already made some adaptation to changing times, and which have carried on ample dialogue with their friends and supporters. So far as internal situations are concerned, speech shares with certain other disciplines the advantage of working with relatively limited numbers of students in each class. The teacher gets to know each student by name, and the discussions of current issues and o problems of communication gives all present an opportunity to make their view known. Even so, teachers and students operate under stresses that differ from decade to decade, and each one should contribute something to the genera morale.

At workshops and conferences the questions I am asked most frequently have to do not so much with course content but with morale, with the genera conduct of a class. In these situations the problem that surfaces most frequently concerns *motivation*. Arouse a student's interest and you can do no wrong; fai to catch his interest and you can do no right.

Most of the answers you will have to dig out of yourself. How do you motivate yourself to do (a) the things you like to do, (b) the things you need to do, (c) the things you should do? On your list of preferences how do you rank teaching a class, writing a research paper, grading examinations, canvassing for school or community project, making a speech, setting up a part or a readin program? Is there anything in your own experience that you can share with student? Have any values, rewards, or satisfactions accrued that might appeal to others?

Students may be reminded of the ways in which speech can serve them i their own vocational choices. In this connection, the learned societies serving ou discipline have prepared pamphlets and other materials that can be secure from the national offices. I conducted my own survey by writing the personne departments of fifty of America's largest corporations, asking in what ways student who had majored in speech (I had in mind college graduates) could be useful to their organizations. Some responses follow:

Chase Manhattan Bank of New York: "I would say your graduates with speec experience and training would have their best chances in our Personnel Depart ment. We employ a great many people for interviewing, counseling, and trair ing. . . . We have noticed in recent years an imperative need for improved verba communications on the part of the officers of the Bank. . . . Banking is becom ing increasingly aware that its officers must be able to meet and inform the public in a sundry variety of speaking situations."

Xerox: "Success in marketing is largely dependent upon a person's ability to communicate. . . . The present nature of our products does not require a highl

pecialized vocational background so that a person with a good liberal arts
ducation is highly acceptable."

nternational Shoe Company: "Thorough training in courses related to speech
ould be good training . . . in departments such as public relations or sales, and
so to enter the business as management trainees."

nternational Harvester Company: "Individuals who have training in public
peaking would be best qualified to serve in the sales department or possibly
ublic relations."

eneral Electric: "We think of sales trainees for the field sales force; positions in
mployee and community relations; recruiting and engineering programs, union
elations, employment practices, safety training, employee publications. . . . [In
dvertising and sales] a creative sense, with the ability to present advertising
ctivities and programs verbally, is very important."

And so on, throughout the list. A phrase that continually appeared was
management trainee," suggesting that individuals with good speech traits would
ave a head start toward a career in higher management. And what are the
equisites for success in this area? "Ability to make correct and timely deci-
ons" comes first: any relation between this trait and what the speech teacher
as to say about gathering and appraising facts, evidence, opinions, and adapting
ese to the prospective listener? "Ability to work with higher management"
nd "ability to motivate subordinates" are also desirable managerial talents.[1]

You can also show the relation between good speaking and good citizenship. I
ways feel a sense of professional pride, as if I had been the individual's teacher
yself, when I hear a treasurer's report clearly and interestingly given, a
ell-stated argument in a hearing before a city council, a good presentation at a
ospital or library board. Nor need interpretation and drama be overlooked:
ccasional public and semipublic performances are a part of most social, civic,
d commercial organizations, and even modest talents can bring satisfaction
d appreciation.

The Institution and the Staff

hen you are considering a teaching position, you should look carefully at the
stitution, the administration, and the faculty. Of primary importance is the
stitution. What kind of image does it have in the community, or, for that

ee: *The Research and Development Engineer as Manager: An Analysis of the Management Development Needs of Engineers at the NASA Manned Spacecraft Center,* Houston: Manned Spacecraft Center, October 1968, p. 23. I am grateful to Charles R. Row
for calling this study to my attention.

matter, in the country? What kind of reputation does the department enjoy
You would not find it easy to reverse a direction that was headed toward goal
different from those you set for yourself.

Good classroom morale begins with the institution as a whole. If teachers an
administrators lack mutual regard, their poor morale infects the students. If th
attitude of teachers toward one another is poor, the individual teacher has
difficult time making his way. If the relation between teachers and students
poor, faculty and administration have a joint problem. Once you have selecte
the institution, and have given it the seal of your approval, support it. Stan
with your colleagues in the task of enforcing the regulations, protecting instit
tional property, maintaining standards, and the like. Carry your share of th
load; since your job of managing students will be easier in a well-run institutio
than in a poorly ordered one, let your actions contribute to the welfare of th
whole.

The influence of the administration makes itself felt in various ways o
college campuses and in high schools. If you are looking over several college
choose one, other things being equal, where members of the faculty enjo
independence and freedom from a multitude of oppressive regulations. If yo
are approaching high schools in search of a post, select one where good disciplin
is the order of the day, and where superintendent and principal are sure t
support the teacher in the management of difficult cases. Among the distinctiv
intangible influences of an institution is the quality of its academic instruction
If students, teachers, and administrators alike put the major emphasis upo
study and learning, problems of classroom discipline should be minimal.

Everyone carries a share of the morale burden. No one can indulge in th
luxury of idle gossip about colleagues. It is no part of your responsibility t
undermine the work of other members of the staff. You can rest assured that i
you criticize the history teacher, before the sun goes down the history teache
will hear about your comment, likely in an exaggerated form. Many teachers lik
to talk shop with their spouses, but in the same breath, in the tactful way tha
they know best, they must make sure that what is said over the breakfast table i
not repeated over the back fence. Teachers need to follow the ethical practice
firmly established by physicians, lawyers, priests, and others, that certain kind
of confidences, professional opinions, and judgments are not to be proclaimed
If you indulge in loose gossip, you will find that your own position in the schoo
will be less highly respected, and you will notice less help from others with you
own problems of maintaining morale.

Institutional Routines

A first job of a new teacher is to acquaint himself with procedures. He needs t
know the basic organization of the institution, the way in which its courses an
activities are scheduled. He must learn how to deal with absences and othe
irregularities. He needs information upon half a hundred details about thi

ecific school. A reason why opening meetings of the year are important is that
ey are the agency to orient the new teacher. The topics discussed may seem
moved from classroom teaching, but they are nonetheless central to the whole
oblem.

The average American high school carries on such a variety of services that
e new teacher feels the demands of absence reports, attendance records,
ank-day deposit books, special assemblies, and a host of assorted campaigns and
ives conspire to defeat his professional aims. Bel Kaufman's *Up The Down
aircase* illustrates these procedures to the fullest. The American college also
as its host of activities in the form of committee meetings, registration assign-
ents, announcements, reports, and the like. Most of these activities come about
cause the modern school is no longer thought of simply as an institution for
e socially fortunate and intellectually gifted; it serves students having a wide
nge of needs and talents. Every teacher is expected to cooperate in all aspects
f the program, and to give attention to the forms, reports, and requests for
formation that come to his box. If the department chairman or principal needs
formation about absences, and asks his staff of fifteen teachers to provide it
r him, he will not be able to compile his results until the fifteenth teacher has
sponded. As tolerant as an administrator needs to be of the busy schedules of
s teachers, he cannot help becoming impatient if the same two or three
achers are always negligent about their records. To put it another way: some
embers of his staff will file their reports promptly and accurately; some are
isurely, but still competent; a few seem always rushed, harried and inaccurate.
hese few invariably bring the needed information a little late; they rush into
e office puffing and panting, hair blowing or coattails flying. Luckily they are
ot firemen; though bells would ring, whistles blow, and lights flash, they would
ever quite get off their own pads and the fire truck would make many a trip
ithout them. About all they could do would be to keep their own bunks nice
d tidy.

I would like to write that order, system, method, and a halfway decent
unctuality are only minor assets. I can recall a few highly gifted professors
hose lectures were stimulating and entirely satisfying even though we knew
at any record they kept on us was random and capricious. I can also recall a
w orderly and systematic souls whose teaching was dull and uninspiring. But
e bulk of the argument is on the other side, favoring the person who can
aster system and method and harness it to the service of his greater talents.
ost of the better teachers fall in this category. Moreover, I think of the
eticulous laboratory records of Edison, the fine grasp of detail of wartime
inister Churchill, the careful planning of Pitt or Nelson. In your lawyer's files
e notes on every matter you have consulted him about. Your physician asks
ou two score routine questions in order not to overlook one significant detail;
e orders several laboratory tests though he is certain the results will be
egative, rather than have you pay the penalty of an unsupported judgment. Out
f record and detail come a statesman's or general's strategy, a lawyer's counsel,

a physician's diagnosis. In the pursuit of his career, a teacher must jot his ow
notes, file his own data, keep his own records. Some of these must be set dow
on official or semiofficial forms, and it is on the careful recording and punctu
reporting of these data that the administrator on one side and the student on th
other set great expectation.

Yet a good institutional person is more than simply a prompt filer of report
He sees the problems of the whole school, and its place in the community. H
puts in a good word whenever he can. He may now and then come up with
good idea for the benefit of the school: a plan for a cafeteria, a speci
conference, a recreational project for the staff. He is certainly going to sper
hours on committees. Although in certain business and corporate circles th
concept of the organization man is overworked, the point of this brief observ
tion is simply to call attention to the fact that a teacher has solemn responsibi
ties not only to his students but also to his colleagues. These solemn respons
bilities may include disapproval of certain procedures, or enthusiasm for th
establishment of different routines but in all fairness criticism and reform shou
first follow the inside track, in private confrontation with the people immediat
ly concerned.

The Dilemma of Discipline

A teacher will not really enjoy teaching until he can understand studen
Teachers have two goals: one, to learn as much as they can about the various a
pects of their subject; two, to acquire what practice they can in working wi
people.

Those who have taught for years notice a dilemma in the problem of disc
pline. Qualities prized in life include ingenuity, audacity, daring, and adve
turousness. The genius of the American people rests on these qualities. On t
other hand, qualities prized in the classroom include obedience, adherence to th
rules, and respect for the authority of the teacher. Teachers are justly puzzled
know how they may reconcile these opposites.

Parents, too, fall astraddle the same dilemma. A father who narrates wi
pride his own escapades as a student is pleased to learn his son is leading
well-ordered life at school. Parents should probably take alarm at a grade ca
describing their son or daughter as "neat, obedient, dependable, easy to wo
with." Perhaps they should save their allowance increases for cards readi
"audacious, imaginative, daring, and venturesome." Presumably, however, the
feel that a child who is neat, obedient, and easy to work with as a child w
miraculously acquire boldness and originality when he grows up.

Perhaps the way out of the dilemma is to note that there is a time to b
methodical, honest, trustworthy, cheerful, and obedient, and also a time to rai
questions. There is time to enforce the rules stoutly and a time to bend them
favor of a teacher or student bearing an original or creative notion. Much soci

etterment, improvement of working conditions, increased wages, and tolerance
f other races and faiths have come about because certain groups were no longer
ocile. Although Americans are capable of bold action, they are also well-
isciplined when the need arises. We pay our taxes, line up for ration cards, and
ı general do what the man says at least as long as he makes good sense. Lord
rougham once said: "An educated people is easy to lead but hard to drive; easy
ɔ govern but impossible to enslave."

Dealing with Minor Infractions

irst of all, the teacher needs perspective in dealing with the minor infractions of
ıe classroom. One who has some understanding of the perennial problems of
ıe school, the Asian mysteries of growing up, and the mores of parents and
ıxpayers will put in its proper place the incident of a student writing notes or
tters in class. He can take notice of the restlessness and energy of his charges
ıd at the same time maintain order. He notes the difference between the
rst-timer and the repeater. He can distinguish between the case-hardened
ffender whose standards have become distorted or vicious and the run-of-the-
ıill student whose motives are fundamentally honest.

Because going to school is hard work, students often attempt to ease their
ırden and make their lives bearable by trying to dodge an assignment or skip
ass altogether. If a student can evade a report, invent an excuse, get outside
ɔlp on an assignment, foul the class bells, or take advantage of a substitute, he
ill probably seize the opportunity to do so. These attitudes are a part of the
merican tradition, an aspect of the battle between young people and their
ders. Such performances contribute to the maturing of a new teacher on about
ıe following schedule: at first he is trusting, sympathetic, naive; then after
ıving been outsmarted and sold down the river a few times, he becomes
ıspicious and even a little cynical; finally he recovers some perspective, as he
es his pranksters mature and begin to amount to something, and handles his
ɔblems with greater wisdom. Obviously I am not here including the restless,
responsible minority seeking to disrupt the institution altogether. Many of
ıem, actually, are nonstudents.

A teacher of speech communication has a special problem in the matter of
assroom management. A lively class is more responsive, more creative, and
akes greater progress than one that is timid. Fears and anxieties about per-
ɔrming in front of others are more easily dealt with in an atmosphere of freedom
ıd relaxation. A dull, stolid class is uninspiring enough for a social studies or
nguage teacher, but it is doubly difficult for the teaching of speech. A lively
ass, however, easily becomes a little too lively, and the teacher may fool him-
lf into thinking that he is managing the class whereas the class is in actuality
:having as it pleases. Alertness and responsiveness are the qualities sought, not
ɔnfusion and distraction.

Personality Clashes

At times almost insoluble personality clashes arise between teacher and student
The teacher has lost patience with the student and the student has lost confi
dence in the teacher. The best approach is a frank discussion with the student
entirely objective, and without attempt to exaggerate—if anything, describe th
picture in favor of the student. Review what he has done that seemed out o
line, and the different measures you have already taken in an attempt to mee
the situation. Give him an opportunity at this point to set the record straight
usually you can well afford to accept any arguments he offers. Your purpos
after all is not to win an argument but to settle a larger situation. Then move th
discussion into the broadest possible field so as to leave behind the immediat
causes of friction. Inquire, candidly: "Do you like your studies? Do you like th
students pretty well or not? Are you fond of the teachers, or do you think thei
stuff is dull?" Or: "What do you do outside of class? Do you have hard work t
do? Would you describe yourself as a nice sort of a person, kind, generous
thoughtful, and well-intentioned, or do you think you are on the ornery side
hard to get along with?"

No one can begin to suggest all the possibilities; some of the foregoin
approaches may even be exactly the opposite of the proper procedure, but the
have the common purpose of attempting to get the student to stand up for hi
school, or for the other students, or for his fundamental seriousness of purpose
Make him defend these things, for a change, instead of trying to undermin
them. Chances are you will make more progress through a discussion of this sor
than by the most eloquent argument on the topic, "Why You Should Pa
Attention in Class." Or go at him in this way: "The semester has just begun, an
since you don't want to continue in my class, let's talk to your adviser and see i
we can find you something in social studies." Or: "Since Mr. Jones also has
speech class, suppose I go to him and tell him you and I are having a lot o
trouble, and offer to trade you to him in return for someone who can't get alon
with him."

Teachers have observed that classes differ greatly: one may have thre
sections of beginning Spanish or of sophomore English, and quickly note tha
the three are not only different from one another, but also that they stand apar
from anything in past experience. You may have the good fortune to start you
career with four or five good classes, and reach the end of your first semeste
assured that the difficulties of teaching are greatly overrated; then next semeste
you may find yourself teaching classes with which you can make little headway
Two or three obstreperous individuals may be the root of your trouble; or th
whole class may be listless and indifferent.

Conference is Helpful. Whenever a teacher runs into a difficult problem c
working with students his best tactic may be to have a conference with eac

ndividual involved. You may announce the conference as one to go over the work of the semester or to hand back papers or outlines, but you can easily lead the discussion into the problem gnawing at you. Although in these conferences you may easily dominate the situation, underscoring the law and the gospel and declaring that in the future you will tolerate no more such nonsense, you may find it wiser to let the student do most of the talking, limiting your efforts to questions that will draw him out further, or encourage him to put his difficulties into words. The latter procedure is more rewarding. Young people do not have numbers of close companions, and a good listener is a pearl of great price. You may even get the student to suggest a remedy for his own misbehavior. This approach proceeds upon the assumption that most real reform will have to come from within; reforms handed down from above have a short life. The Rogers nondirective approach has much to commend it. The secret weapon that has any chance of closing the generation gap is the art of listening. The gap, incidentally, has to be closed from both ends.

Out of such conferences a teacher gains information about the attitudes of students. He learns, for example, that classroom noise always sounds louder to the teacher than to the students: the saddest wails come from pupils who are scolded when they weren't making "ANY noise AT ALL." He learns that students are more alert than they appear to be: "I don't see why you think I'm not interested, Miss J.—this is one of my FAVORITE courses." He learns that pupils are making more progress than he suspected: "My grades don't show it, but I'm learning a LOT." And he learns that the student who was the most restless, the most inattentive, and the most distracting to others, was apparently unaware that he was doing the slightest thing out of line. No irony is intended in the foregoing comments: they simply reflect the tenor of conferences reported by teachers.

Students often present situations about which the teacher feels incompetent to advise. Perhaps the problem is one which every individual has to decide for himself, like whether to borrow money to stay in school or to work outside while in school at some sacrifice of grades. It may be a knotty personal or family problem. Even in these situations, however, the teacher can help the student clarify the issue, and is often able to suggest an angle that the student had overlooked. After all, the teacher is at least from four to eight years older than his students and can view life's catastrophes from that much perspective. He knows far better than they the resources of the institution and the community: counseling, clinical, financial, medical, legal.

Other Approaches.   When serious infractions occur you should realize that the influence of the institution is tremendous. The principal or the dean may want to call in the parents for a discussion or he may need to separate the student from the school altogether. Threats are not advisable unless you are prepared to carry them out. A university teacher once said, "If you don't like this lecture, you can get up and walk out," and the class of three hundred students did so.

Often it is better to say, "If there is any further disturbance, I'll——" and the
shake your head grimly as if the punishment were too horrible to contemplate
If you avoid committing yourself specifically, you may act as you please whe
the storm breaks.

Classroom confusion may be the result of a general school discipline that
too lax. Perhaps the faculty should discuss the matter and take steps in concer
Or maybe the activities selected for classroom participation are too elemental c
too difficult. Don't spend time in needless worry. If you cannot handle
discipline situation yourself, seek advice. You do not have to be a lone agen
older and more experienced friends are willing to advise you. Teachers naturall
hate to disturb a superior with classroom difficulties, yet he may be the one wit
the requisite power and authority to solve the problem. He has resources at h
command that you do not have.

Maintain a Professional Attitude

A teacher is a counselor, a guide, a friend, an older scholar; he is not
ringmaster, a warden, a baby-sitter, a slave driver. He may be a parent but he
not the student's parent. (He may be able to exert more influence, in som
directions, than the student's parent.) The following suggestions contribute t
more effective teaching:

Plan a good opening day. Explain what the course is about; establish its plac
in the curriculum and in society; describe the kinds of activities and assignment
refer to your testing and grading procedures. In short, conduct such a discussio
that when the bell rings students will have a clear notion of why it is a good ide
for them to be in the class, how it will contribute to them as individuals, an
what your standards and expectations are. The tone in which this material
delivered is important; some of your own interest and enthusiasm ought to shin
through.

Some of my colleagues are convinced that this is one of the most importan
hours of the term—to give a preview of what is ahead, to tell what the course
all about. From a good discussion students may receive encouragement, reassur
ance; they may see some possibilities that had not occurred to them, or, in
moment of reflection, readjust some of their misconceptions.

Show your interest in your subject. Through the centuries there have alway
been people interested in scholarship for its own sake: much of what has bee
preserved from the past comes to us because of the enthusiasm of ancien
philosophers and their disciples, monks in monasteries, university professors, an
teachers everywhere. In teaching it is not enough to be passively interested; on
should show his interest, manifest it, radiate it. One should express what h
chosen career means to him. This quality of zeal is of the highest importanc

tudents appreciate and respect the enthusiasm of a teacher for his subject. As
ne student put it, "If the teacher is full of enthusiasm, some of it is just bound
ɔ rub off on us."

ɔterest students in the art of teaching and learning. Consider the opposite—
ɪe teacher whose lackluster manner clearly says, "Well, students, here we are
gain—we have to face another hour of this terrible old [supply a subject from
our own student days]." If you employ visual aids, point out their usefulness
ɔ learning devices. If you like objective tests, explain their advantages and tell
ow they are constructed. If in preparing a lecture or a lesson plan you have
ɪtilized some unusual or intriguing methods, point them out. Give students an
ccasional glimpse of the world from your end of the classroom.

Your interest will give students insight into the art of teaching and increase
ɪeir respect for the profession. If you have suggestions about ways of studying
ɪd learning, pass them along. Engage the class in a discussion of "How I Prepare
 Speech," or of "The Best Way to Write an Examination." Your charges will
ɔend years following the career of student; your advice may prove significant to
ɪem.

'ake assignments specific. In adult life, people like to know clearly what is
ɕpected of them. We operate most efficiently when our instructions are
ɕplicit. We want to know when we are to use our judgment and when we are to
•llow established procedure.

Students also like to know exactly what is expected of them. When assign-
ents are vague, students complain in aggrieved fashion that they do not
ɪderstand what the teacher wants, and they therefore make minimum prepara-
ɔn. Only the conscientious students will come back for further instruction.
ccordingly, a good teacher will try to make the assignment clear and interest-
g. Since everyone needs to make his contribution to the master problem of
aching pupils how to study, he should explain each assignment so that each
ɪtener will know not only what it is but also how to prepare it.

Ordinarily an assignment should be given at the end of the class hour, so that
ɪudents will leave the room with the next project in mind. Presumably students
•me to the class with the current day's work foremost in their thoughts, so that
e teacher finds it easy to take up at once what they have just prepared. He
ay, therefore, have to break into an interesting discussion five or ten minutes
•fore the bell rings in order to present the assignment for the next hour.

The cardinal rule in making an assignment is to give specific examples of the
oject you have in mind. Suppose your class is made up of seniors, and you
•nceive the idea of speeches on vocational opportunities. Your thought is to
k each student to interview a citizen now active in a desirable business or
ofession, and discuss with him the opportunities in that vocation. In making
e assignment, you may invite the class to suggest vocations and people to be
ɪterviewed. Before the assignment is completed, every student should have

decided whom he is to interview, what kinds of questions he may ask, when h
report is due, and how many minutes he is allotted for his talk.

It is only fair to say that in spite of his best intentions a teacher sometim
becomes absorbed in his teaching and the bell rings without his having made a
assignment: in his distraction he can only mumble a few words about "read t
next ten pages," and promise himself to do better the next time.

On college campuses especially, instructors prepare a list of assignments f
the whole term. Weekly assignments, examinations, term papers, are fully s
forth. The student can then plan his evening and weekend study accordingl
The assignment sheet relieves the instructor of the necessity of commenting c
each class project, though he should refer to its salient features occasionally wi
such exhortation as may be needed.

Talk to students as if they were responsible and capable individuals. Gi
them your trust and confidence. Avoid any inclination to patronize them. It
entirely possible to maintain this attitude toward the class as a whole, and y
deal realistically with the fact that a few individuals may from time to time de
your optimism. Avoid the silky "we" and "our" when "you" and "your" a
meant, as in "When we hand in our assignments tomorrow, we must rememb
to write our names in the upper left-hand corner." If you disapprove of smokin
proclaim the rule as a matter of sanitation, fire regulation, or personal prefe
ence, without moralizing. A teacher needs to build the character of his student
but smoking is a poor basis on which to construct a lecture about the good lif

Don't be overawed. There are more than twenty thousand teachers of spee
communication in the country, and by and large they are getting along all righ
Speaking, discussing, debating, radio and TV speaking, managing speech diso
ders, reading aloud, and directing, staging, and acting in plays all have a go
deal of inherent solidity and substance about them to command the interest c
students. Discipline may not turn out to be so grave a problem as you imagin

Keep cool under pressure. Every day brings its vexations, as well as its successe
sometimes, it seems, difficulties pile up out of all proportion, whereas meda
and kind words fail to appear. If an emergency arises that tests your temper, ar
you handle the situation calmly, you are in a better position afterwards than
you had lost your patience. This advice is not written entirely to outlaw plai
healthy anger. Yet hasty scolding is often unjustified and unwarranted. Inatte
tion or improper behavior sometimes arises from perfectly understandab
causes. A teacher should investigate before jumping to conclusions. One teach
reprimanded a young man who three days in a row failed to turn in h
assignment. The student had nothing to offer in his own defense, and the teach
reproved him sharply. Later the teacher learned that this student had to wo
nights, in order to augment his family's income. Naturally she was embarrasse
to realize that she had not given him a fair hearing. A girl developed the habit c
dropping off to sleep in class, even when the discussion seemed fairly lively. Sl

eemed reasonably ashamed and penitent about the matter when the teacher scolded her, but was not able to correct the situation. Later she began to realize that her health was failing, and examination revealed a severe infection. She spent some days in the hospital before she was discharged. When she returned to school she was attentive, and the teacher realized that he had been unreasonably severe.

An incident that happened in a university class throws light on the problem. A tardy student stopped after the hour to explain why he had been late for class. His wife had fallen and had hit her head against the sharp corner of a kitchen table; the student had taken her to the hospital, and thus had been delayed. This explanation was acceptable, and when the student repeated it, the professor reassured him cordially that the matter was entirely all right. The professor thought everything was settled, but half an hour later the student was back, bringing with him a pale-looking, drawn-faced girl with a mountain of gauze round her head. "I just wanted you to see," the student explained, "that my wife was really hurt, like I said." The student must have had experiences with suspicious teachers that made him feel his unsupported word could not be accepted.

Unquestionably situations arise when a spirited reprimand clears the air, and makes possible a better atmosphere in the classroom. The technique, however, loses its efficacy if it is repeated too often. Incessant scolding, nagging, and prodding should be replaced by more effective approaches.

Act with firmness if a bad situation arises. A student may become so perennial a discipline problem that the teacher may dread that particular class. If methods of quiet persuasion fail to work, take firmer steps. You have a responsibility to the rest of the class and to yourself not to let a worrisome situation continue.

At times a speech teacher can unravel a personality problem where other teachers are helpless. The nature of speech courses gives individuals a chance to express themselves and to work cooperatively with others; these opportunities may interest the pupil where some of the more traditional courses cannot. On the other hand students may show up in school who should not be there; years of mismanagement cannot always be corrected by the limited means the classroom teacher has at hand.

Be fair. Your decisions, your judgments, and even your grades pass in review before many students. If you favor certain individuals or certain groups, your practice will soon be advertised throughout the school. Avoid dating your own students. If a teacher, however, keeps his social interests from prejudicing his classroom responsibilities, he can feel free in many ways to enjoy the companionship of students in their games, sports, class and school activities, and social functions.

Learn what you can do best. A teacher should put his best foot forward, but at first he needs to learn what his best foot is. One who reads competently has a sure way of holding the interest of a class; some teachers can read speeche poems, plays, scholarly reports, current events in science or foreign policy intriguingly that the students listen with great intentness. Other teachers have gift of criticism and analysis; students sit entranced listening to a review of the skills as speakers or actors or in presenting a demonstration in science or ma class. Some teachers can take a four-line poem and spend an hour bringing o its deeper meanings. Others are good lecturers; still others skilled questione One teacher of national reputation has a special ability to get students interest in word definitions. Another talks absorbingly about pronunciation. Anoth ranges widely in literature and drama. Some teachers are good lecturers, b poor discussion leaders: they talk interestingly, but find it difficult to draw t class out. Some teachers cannot act well, but are skillful in utilizing somewh crude demonstrations to suggest new possibilities to the student actor. In h early teaching days the beginner will do well to exploit the methods that see most successful to him, but should try to improve gradually other teaching skil

Seek interrelationships among disciplines. Knowledge is not compartmentaliz even though curricular organization makes it appear so. Much of what you tea can be related to other fields of instruction. Bring these connections out, a help the student to discover them for himself. Tie your classroom discussions the current scene. How would your students answer the question: "Do y think about the class at any time other than when you are in class or prepari an assignment?" To get an affirmative answer to that question you need to bre through to where the students live.

New plays, movies, and books, recent speeches, current events, select campus happenings can often be mentioned in connection with a lecture discussion. You do not need to labor the point or beat it to death; simply let support, briefly, the assignment of the day.

Case Studies of Individual Differences

Much of the problem of heightening student morale involves trying to unde stand each one as a person. It is difficult to predict, for the beginning teacher, of the different types that he is likely to meet. The following descripti comments reflect varieties of situations that arise.

The Problem of Capacity

The first phenomenon about students to come to the attention of a teacher the vast difference in their intelligence. The IQ of students may range all the wa from 80 to 200.

I had an introduction of sorts to Joe Consull. The superintendent had calle me into his office early in the fall to describe him. "We think very well of Jo

e is popular, loyal to the school, and has many talents. He can do passably in
l his subjects except English and one other. English is a real problem for him. If
ou can help him there, we can work out his other class. If a little extra effort
ill make it possible for him to graduate, it will be a great thing for him."

I resolved to make every explanation in that English class as clear as I knew
ow. I can hear myself saying, "Our language is made up of different kinds of
ords, called parts of speech. All of the words that are names of something we
ll nouns. *Car* is a noun—it is the name of a thing." And so on. Then came
entification and recognition. What is the noun in the phrase, *fast horse?* Then
Joe: identify the noun in *the yellow wagon.*

"Yellow," says Joe, after some reflection.
"Why do you say yellow?"
"It's the noun."
"What's a noun?"
"It's the name of something, like you said."
"Is yellow the name of something?"
"Yellow is the name of yellow. It's the name of a color."

That moment taught me how difficult it is to be clear. A thousand times since
en I have seen the whole problem of teaching come to a sharp focus in a
oblem at once simple and profound. The room grows quiet, and students
onder what the teacher will do next. Perhaps he should retrieve his dignity, and
rriedly explain that yellow now and then bobs up as a noun, but is ordinarily
adjective. Perhaps the new grammar will give him a retreat. Or maybe his
gnity will stand a moment's anguish while he continues: "Joe, you got ahead
me there—you're in tomorrow's lesson. Would you mind if I gave you another
ample that is similar in one way, but different in another? Identify the noun
the phrase, *old woman*."

"Woman."
"Why didn't you say *old?*"
"Because *old* is not the name of anything."
"And *woman* is?"
"Yes."
"*Woman* is the name of what?"
"Well, it's the name of a kind of human being."
"Now let's go back to *yellow wagon.* Does it look any different to you now?"
"Yes it does." One might say, if he likes the sound of rich descriptive
ssages, that an electric thrill went through the class.
"What is the noun?"
"There are two nouns, *yellow* and *wagon*."

Progress comes in small packets: it is the great secret of the art of teachin
As the years passed I met Joe a hundred times, in high school, in college,
graduate school. A slow burner, a literal-minded person, he never quite sees th
difference between a vowel and a consonant, between a speech and an oratio
between *impromptu* and *extempore*. Who does? "When you use the wor
prevalent in this multiple-choice test," he will ask, "do you mean 'in a majorit
or simply 'frequently'?" "Why do we need," he will inquire on another occasio
"one symbol for [ʌ] and another for [ə]?"

Teachers learn much from the Joes—they remind us that minds do not run
the same groove. They command us to make it clear, keep it simple, drive
home, glue it down. They compel us to rethink concepts that more glib min
readily accept.

My introduction to Ed Minster was different. "I hear you have Ed Minster
your public speaking class," said my colleague who taught science. He spok
Ed's name much as he might say Lord of the Manor.

I can see Ed now, sitting in the front row, chunky, of average height, wearir
glasses, a little awkward. He quickly demonstrated a vocabulary and a fund c
information above average. Knowing something about Edmund Burke (IQ 150
Charles James Fox (IQ 145), William Pitt (IQ 180), and Thomas Babingtc
Macaulay (IQ 190) must have prepared me for my first brush with Ed Minste
One day I came to class with slips of paper with topics for impromptu speeche
We had a talk on something like "What I Would Do If I Were President," an
then I handed Ed a slip reading "My Favorite Motion Picture Actress."

Ed took it and read it. "I am willing to talk about 'My Favorite Motic
Picture Actress' if you wish, but I wonder if you will give me a topic that is
little more difficult."

The class was quiet, as if this were a test moment awaited all these days. "A
right," I said, "let me have your slip." I wrote a few words on it, and put
under a book on my desk. "I am going to call on the other members of th
class," I said, "and then we'll have your talk on the topic I just wrote down.
anyone else wants a special topic he may have one, but my suggestion is that fc
this first speech we keep to the list of topics as prepared." We heard the roun
of speeches, then we came back to Ed. If he were going to do somethin
superior, I at least wanted the other talks out of the way, so the students wh
followed would not be embarrassed by the comparison.

"Do you know anything about Benedict Arnold?" I asked, handing him th
slip on which I had written that name.

"Of course," he said, not boastfully, not arrogantly—everyone knows ol
Benedict Arnold.

"All right, talk for two minutes about him."

I remember something of what he said. Benedict Arnold was a traitor to h
country. In reality, however, whether or not a man is a traitor depends upon th
point of view. If the Revolution had been unsuccessful, George Washingto

might have been regarded as a traitor. Benedict Arnold admittedly nurtured a hostile intent toward the young United States, but for a moment let us see what can be said in his favor. It was a talk showing originality of thinking.

Days later when I again handed out topics for impromptu speaking, he asked for a special theme. "You gave me a historical subject last time," he said, "give me a different kind this time." I replied, "Well, talk about heat." "All right," he replied, "shall I talk about the commercial applications of heat?" "No," I answered, "that's too easy: talk about the basic, elemental nature of heat." So he did: the concept of heat is not easy to grasp: even a block of ice contains heat, as contrasted with something as cold as zero, and especially when you think of the formidable depths of absolute zero, 460 degrees lower still.

After class we talked about his speech. "You've had your fun," I said, "and I've had mine. In reality there are few simple topics, just simple ways of handling them. Actually, a highly perceptive talk can be made on 'My Favorite Motion Picture Actress.'"

I believe he left the class that spring a more understanding sort of person. Since Ed, I have known many brilliant and talented young men, though perhaps no one with a more dazzling mind than he possessed. On my intellectual scale Joe and Ed represent two different extremes of capacity. The critics who write the articles about how little history or geography students know, or how poorly they do in science, or how wretchedly they write, must have stepped into a classroom only yesterday. College and high school teachers have known this patent fact for generations. Teachers also can report that other students know vast quantities of history, geography, and science, and can speak and write with surprising movement and clarity. You will have to learn this, too, and once you have, some of your newness as a teacher will have been forever erased, and you will face a class with a great sureness and presence.

The Problem of Interest

To say that students have different degrees of intelligence tells only part of the story. Teaching is further complicated by the fact that some have more interest or motivation or a better attitude than others. The cases of Edie Sanders and Natalie Clarkson illustrate two aspects of this problem.

In a sophisticated school where the girls were nicely groomed, wore nail polish, rouge, and lipstick, Edie knew nothing of the art of personal adornment or decoration. Her hair was carelessly arranged, her face and arms not always clean. She wore shabby shoes and an ill-pressed dress. She had little interest in life. She was not sullen or bitter; she was listless. She was one of the community's disadvantaged.

Where do you start to unravel a personality that other teachers have abandoned as hopeless? Do you show unusual interest, overwhelm the person with displays of praise and enthusiasm?

If the important rule of teaching is that changes of attitude have to com from within, perhaps the best approach is one that is simple and honest. Take a assignment in reading aloud and imagine the criticisms that may be made. No "Edie, that was unusually good, that was outstanding, you really stole th show," but "Edie, you made a nice start; if you like, you may look out ove your book directly into the eyes of your listeners: watch me now—when I glanc downward the class can see only my eyelids, but when I look out they can se my eyes, and my face therefore becomes more expressive." The point is to trea Edie like everyone else in the class. She is not the recipient of special attentio she is instead the beneficiary of a greater gift—equality in a group where she ha long considered herself an inferior.

I wish I had kept a record of the days that followed. As it is, I recall only th dramatic features of Edie's development. One day she tried rouge and lipstick although since she had not used soap and water, the effect was startling. Soa and water were never in the vanguard of civilization anyway; they came la to Edie, as to the human race. Later came a day when she did her first classroo performance with a little verve. Still later she was on an assembly program an was applauded by students and visitors. Gradually but surely she became a accepted member of the school community.

Matalie, timid and reserved, was brought to school by her mother. Mr Clarkson patiently hunted up Matalie's instructors, telling each that her daughte was shy, but bespeaking our patience and assuring us that Matalie's interest ar eagerness would repay our efforts. Her words were sparkling jewels of unde statement. Of many alert, attentive students in that school, Matalie was out standing: a petite, dark-haired, dark-eyed sophomore, who quickly commande the admiration of her classmates in the class in dramatics.

She used to sit on the edge of her chair, watching everything that went o She never took her eyes off the teacher, listening as though she were hearin words that would never again be spoken in her lifetime. With the same intentne she would watch the performance of the dullest classmate.

Is a part of the normally slow progress of students simply a lack of willingne to concentrate on the matter at hand? Would all students learn more rapidly they gave their hearts and minds to the teacher's instruction? Matalie had th tremendous gift of being teachable.

Every teacher can call to mind examples of student alertness. In a letter fro a teacher who had eight weeks of experience behind her was this notation: " kept five boys after school today. I stepped out of the room for a moment, an when I returned they were gaily tossing a chair back and forth." The studen had an abundance of energy, and this was a good way to expend it. The lette recalls George, a six-footer who never seemed comfortable in a chair. He seeme to be always restless, always in motion, always wanting to be somewhere else.

A student's account in the teacher's bank of patience can eventually b overdrawn; George was generally in arrears. Finally he transferred to anoth ollege. I supposed he had learned nothing whatever. Yet one vacation he came to tell how much he owed to his training in speech. At the other campus he had applied for a scholarship, and one day found himself in the anteroom of the dean's office. Through the thin walls, he could hear the other candidates, one at a time, state their needs; as he listened he realized that most of them were rambling and hesitant. Their faltering recalled to him the advantage of speaking to the point, so he organized his ideas, presented them lucidly, and won the scholarship. I decided he had learned something when I was not looking.

High school students are more responsive, volatile, and explosive than their college counterparts. These characteristics sometimes encourage, sometimes discourage, the teacher. If the morale of the class is good, his announcement of a new project may be received with considerable enthusiasm. If morale is mediocre, new assignments may be greeted with frowns and groans. The climate, however, changes like New England weather. I have heard practice teachers report such experiences as this: "I told the class that we were going to study pantomimes, and they grumbled like children. After a day or so, however, they became excited about pantomimes." A high school student is fairly uninhibited about exclaiming either "This is fun!" or "Why do we have to do this?"

By the time he has spent a year or two in college, the student has lost much curiosity and enthusiasm. Something has disappeared in the educational process. Where the beginner is likely to be fooled is in thinking that students who appear unresponsive and indifferent are also uninterested. Some appear listless and inattentive, but in reality they are probably just exhibiting their priorities. A student should be careful about what he wants out of his college career because he is almost sure to get it.

In moments of pessimism the teacher sometimes wonders what happens to the enthusiasm of freshmen on their way to becoming seniors. How marvellous everything is those first weeks—rushing, the prospect of classes, the team, the band, even the president of the institution. Comes the senior year, candles do not twinkle so brightly at the founders' day banquet, teachers are a mix of indifferent to fair, team and band are better on nearly every other campus, the president is less glamorous. If enthusiasm is there, it is harder to spot. Practice teaching sessions bring it out again, however, and so also do graduate and professional schools.

In between the freshman year and the graduate school, the college teacher must keep up his own morale and be unflagging in his own preparation. From time to time, students have varied preoccupations and distractions: curricular and extracurricular competition, finances, problems at home. But let us not make the art of teaching too difficult. Let us paraphrase Lincoln: "You can please all of the students part of the time and part of the students all of the time, but you cannot please all of the students all of the time." Those odds ought to be good enough for anybody. Lincoln also said to a critic who disapproved of his speech: "There are some fleas a dog can't reach."

The Problem of Application

Students also differ in their application and industry. Application is related to interest; we give our time to matters that engage our fancy. It is also related to energy. Mark Twain once wrote, "If I were a pagan, I would erect a statue to energy, and fall down and worship it." An abundant supply of energy is a gift both to teachers and students. Some people have three or four good hours a day; others move from one constructive task to another for six, eight, twelve, or more. The supply of energy varies as an individual moves through high school and college. Often, late-sleeping college sophomores develop into jet-propelled seniors.

Each class, therefore, contains people with varying habits of application. Your A students are without exception those who prepare their assignments carefully everyday of the week. They step to the head of the class early in the school term, and never relinquish their position. You will also have in your class some Bs-who-want-to-be-As. They cannot maintain the fast pace set by the As, but they do pretty well, and they comfort themselves by saying that when examinations roll around, they will turn on the power. But everybody is a good student at examination time; your A student also turns on the power, and your B-who-wants-to-be-A is still, by comparison, a want-to-be. Your C group includes people who are medium week after week, and also a few who sometimes attain B or A, but who also drop to D or F. Thus again, faulty or irregular habits of application make themselves felt.

The teacher's interest is focussed; he knows where he is going. The student's interest is diffused; any given class is only a part of his day, and he may not be quite sure how all the parts fit together.

Put the Emphasis on the Individual

So much for capacity, interest, and application: three characteristics of students everywhere. "The actual teaching in a school," once wrote William Lyon Phelps, Yale's great professor of English, "is the least of the teacher's difficulties. The central problem is that of understanding the students."

You will need to plan your lesson for your first class with the thought that you will be teaching students with wide differences in capacity, interest, and application. As you gain experience you will learn to vary this plan during the class meeting itself, in order to make your instruction more suitable. Methods of making these adaptations will be discussed in later chapters. After a few weeks you will surprise yourself by the ease with which you can adapt to student differences. Among other devices, you will provide yourself with a supply of instances and examples, or classroom activities, to keep your recitation afloat. You will need to make your assignments and explanations clear, to reach those of low capacity; you will need to introduce variety, to stimulate interest; you must give thought to different sorts of motivations, to gain your share of the student's expendable energy.

Improving Morale through Good Teaching

Matters of discipline and other classroom problems tend to disappear in the presence of effective teaching. Most of this book is concerned with the improvement of instruction; the paragraphs below primarily serve to summarize.

The art of teaching may be looked at from four different points of view, recalling the conventional four ends of speaking. A teacher makes use of (1) informing, (2) persuading, (3) impressing, and (4) entertaining. Here again I have in mind teachers of all subjects.

The Art of Informing.   Fundamentally, the job of the teacher is to explain, to simplify, to elucidate, to draw out, to illuminate, to analyze: in short, to make clear. What are ways in which theories and principles may be made clear? The following are suggested:

Use a preview or overview of what is to be taught. Orient the student generally before teaching him specifically. Give him a bird's eye glimpse of what is to be covered. Everybody knows about *feedback*; the preview is *feedforward*.

Use transitions and summaries. A transition helps the student to connect one part with another; a summary provides a recapitulation or review.

Use repetition. Repeat three, four, or five times, in different connections, the ideas you especially want to fix in the student's mind. What may be fairly clear on Friday may be forgotten Monday; recall the ideas by reviewing and restatement.

As you explain a point to a class, the natural flickering of attention may cause a student's mind to wander; your repetition or restatement of the point helps put him back on the track. The forecast of what is going to occur, followed at the end of the hour by summary and freshened the next hour by review, improves teaching. Some teachers achieve a reputation by repeating a phrase year after year. In one institution the lecture of a history teacher on "Charlemagne cut the age of confusion in two" became a classic; students might forget the details of Charlemagne's career, but they remembered that Charlemagne put a period of orderly rule between two confused eras. In another institution a psychology teacher repeated, "Never worry at night." Do your worrying in the daytime, he insisted, while the mind was alert enough to solve problems; "never worry at night" when the mind is fatigued and cannot think clearly. Most teachers do not strive for dramatic repetitions like the foregoing but at least employ the principle as a part of the daily work.

Ask and invite questions. Unless a student can put an idea in words, he has not mastered it. Encourage students to ask questions; many a student seems never to open his mouth except to put something in it. Learning should be active, not passive; questions and discussion bring students into the picture. Use a variety of questions: some elicit routine facts, others stimulate interest and curiosity.

You might find it helpful at the outset to assure students that you welcome their questions. When questions begin to appear, then give them special attention; and repeat your invitation to ask questions until everybody gets the idea. Students in graduate seminars are sometimes as silent as the grave when the professor first calls for discussion, but repeated interest on his part in their queries and comments leads them to become more responsive.

Use blackboard drawings, charts, models, maps, diagrams. A single visual aid may be worth many words.

A university teacher of vocal anatomy demonstrated this versatility exceptionally well. Once his task was to explain how the muscles of chest and abdomen function during breathing. In the course of three lectures he did the following: (1) He drew diagrams of the structures on the blackboard, using colored chalk. (2) He displayed large charts, showing schematically the positions of muscles before and after inhalation. (3) He personally demonstrated forcible inhalation and exhalation, showing on his own body the location and operation of muscle groups. (4) He asked students to come before the class to demonstrate the same principle. (5) He used a balloon-like device to demonstrate the operation of the diaphragm. (6) He passed around photographs of pictures in textbooks and similar sources. (7) He used specially prepared dissections made by medical students. In all of these presentations and demonstrations he constantly used questioning, summary, review, and repetition, all bound together with illustrations and amusing examples to make his points vivid. He might also have used (8) slides and (9) moving pictures, though he did not happen to do so.

Teachers may use pictures of speakers and actors, models of sets and theaters, tape and phonograph recordings, anatomical and phonetic charts and devices, maps, charts of parliamentary rules, graphs showing progress of members of the class, collections of facial types for makeup projects, and scores of other devices. You will find in Appendix D a list of manufacturers and distributors of visual and auditory aids to teaching.

Use films and filmstrips. Teachers of all subjects are giving added attention to the use of films and filmstrips. Committees from the Speech Communication Association, the American Educational Theatre Association, and other groups are compiling lists of available films in these areas. Eventually in all fields there will evolve recommended lists of films based upon the judgment of scores of teachers and students.

Criticisms of educational films are numerous. Some are not designed for high schools and colleges; it is disappointing to schedule a film and find it was planned for the fifth grade. Others are dated by the costumes of the actors. In some instances sound is poor, photography inadequate, or the acting stilted. Students are sophisticated moviegoers and are not deceived by an inferior product. Many releases, however, are exceptionally fine.

Three types of subject matter may be considered. Films on historical persons or events may throw light on speechmaking: good films are available on Webster, Wilson, Churchill, Kennedy, even Hitler. Films on specific speech topics may explain a principle: as for example, those on stage fright, conference, voice, gesture, parliamentary procedure. Films on teenage topics may serve as a stimulus for the development of discussion skills: as for example, those on problems of dating or personal morals.

Use a variety of teaching methods. The possibilities of using different kinds of materials are suggested above; the variety of teaching methods is equally rich. Divide the class hour into two or three parts: allow time for discussion, time for performance, time for making the next assignment. This procedure helps to keep students from becoming restless. Talk about organization, then let each student make a skeleton speech of half a minute's duration illustrating the principal divisions of the talk. Talk about problems confronting society, the schools, the nation, getting students to discuss the problems of the educated citizen. Other possibilities will be suggested throughout this book. Teachers of natural and social sciences, foreign language, the fine and applied arts, should apply the principle of *variety* in their planning. If the teacher usually talks all the time, or conducts the same sort of question-and-answer dialogue all the time, he should search out other possibilities.

The Art of Persuading.   Important as information and informing are, they do not constitute the whole of life. People do not become better speakers or better teachers simply by offering more information. You can fill the trough only so full of fodder and no fuller. Hence some discussion on persuading, impressing, entertaining.

Every teacher learns, for example, that after giving students a substantial amount of information, a straight-from-the-shoulder persuasive appeal to apply this knowledge can be effective. Such a plea can set up an immediate goal that students can understand and reassures them that the teacher is interested in their progress. A swimming teacher wanted the members of his class to swim twenty laps of the pool. When the last week of the class rolled around, no one had as yet been able to swim farther than half that distance. The teacher, a former high school debater, gathered his class around him on the edge of the pool, and made an eloquent appeal to the swimmers: he told them that the achievement was within their grasp, he reminded them of the thrill of being at home in the water instead of trying to fight it, and he reviewed for them the importance of relaxed stroking and rhythmical breathing. As he talked he became enthusiastic and excited about the importance of what he was saying. When he finished, the boys dived into the pool and swam the twenty laps without too much difficulty. Through good exposition, he taught his charges to swim ten laps; with the additional aid of persuasion, he got them to double their performance.

The example is not isolated. Athletic teams invariably do better the second half of the contest after having been exposed to the exposition (explaining mistakes, pointing out weaknesses) and the persuasion of the coaches. The fascinating biography of Notre Dame's Knute Rockne illustrates that his success was fully as due to persuasion as to exposition. Sales managers get their salesmen together for conventions largely to exhort them to increase their efforts. Directors of debating and of dramatics get more out of their students after a persuasive appeal. Teachers of all subjects find it helpful to use persuasion as well as exposition.

When you find an occasion to deliver a good pep-talk, take the long view; put your talk in a broad setting. Remind your students of the reasons why every young person should seek as much education as possible, bringing in social, vocational, and cultural aspects. Look with them into the future, when each will take his position in the world to earn a living and rear a family. Mention that although some of their older acquaintances may be self-educated, no substitute is nearly so efficient as the school, where a student may command the services of many highly trained people to teach him the things he needs to know. Students lose sight of the great goal because of the burden of daily tasks. Awaken some pride in their own institution, and what it has contributed over the years to the community and to the country. Give attention to the values of your subject, reviewing what they mean to the many aspects of a student's life, now and in the future. A thoughtful discussion along these lines will give each listener an opportunity to review his own ambitions.

Interest. The personality of the teacher is an important factor in his ability to persuade. As just stated, if he has affection for his subject, his persuasion will carry the mark of integrity. He should also show his interest in his students by being aware of the things they participate in: the social, athletic, religious, and avocational events of the school and community. Praising a student is one way of showing an interest in him. Whether you praise a student face-to-face, or praise him to a classmate or to another teacher, seems to make little difference: in a school the word quickly gets around, and the indirect way may in the long run be as effective. Criticizing a student is another way of showing an interest in him, if he is convinced of your competence, honesty, and good will.

Candor. Enthusiasm is the art of pardonable exaggeration: when a student says, "The best city in the country is Oklahoma City, Oklahoma, my home town," or when a teacher says, "Speech is the most important subject in the curriculum," or when the cobbler says, "There's nothing like leather," we are willing to overlook the exaggeration and personal bias out of respect for the speaker's strong preference. The counterpart of enthusiasm is candor: the impact of frankness as a persuasive attribute is disarming, and therefore often compelling. "Why did you act like that," says the annoyed principal to the teacher, and when the teacher says, with conviction, "I don't know—I guess I'm just stupid," the principal finds himself mellowed, and with little to say. We say admiringly, of a physician, "If he can't cure you, he admits it," and of a teacher, "If he doesn't know, he isn't afraid to say so." Aristotle put it wisely: we are less likely to punish the servant who freely confesses his mistakes.

Candor reveals itself in more important ways than in willingness to admit a fault. If certain outside reading is difficult and dry in spots, say so; don't describe it as being fascinating. "This assignment is not so easy to read as I should like, and for a while I debated whether to substitute instead a popular article. The popular article, however, had so many extravagant ideas in it that I decided not to assign it, even though it is entertaining. I am however going to put both of them on reserve in the library so that if you find the first one too difficult for you, you may turn to the second."

Special devices. Successful teachers use a variety of persuasive devices that may be mentioned in passing; many of them at least enliven a moment in the class hour. One professor at times gives an abnormally long assignment; when the students grumble, he discusses with them what should be the proper length of an assignment, and eventually compromises by reducing the task to the figure he originally had in mind. He feels the discussion is valuable, and the class feels it won a moral victory. Another uses a form of negative suggestion; he asserts his fears that a project is too ambitious, whereupon the class, in the mood of a boy taking a dare, mobilizes its energies and spiritedly undertakes the task. Another makes exaggerated or provocative statements in class, or takes an unpopular position, as ways of stimulating discussion. No doubt these devices are successful because the class finds them diverting and entertaining, and because professor and students alike realize that no one is really being fooled.

Contests of various kinds, both formal and informal, are excellent means of persuasion. Present an award; its nature or value is immaterial. One day while shopping for a prize, I visited a theatrical supply house and bought a supply of rabbits' feet of the kind used in makeup. These trophies proved captivating. On other occasions I have presented copies of *Roget's Thesaurus*; and on still others ordinary pencils. After a round of classroom speeches, it is interesting to take a class vote, each member writing the name of the speaker who made the best talk and the speaker who has shown the greatest improvement. This twofold award recognizes those who plug along as well as those who have special talent. Every institution has ways of recognizing outstanding merit. The individual who makes the best effort gets the scholarship, the game ball, the prize, the election to the hall of fame.

In memory of a distinguished teacher, the alumni of one school provided a tablet with a series of bronze plates. Each year all seniors who had taken part in speech activities were invited to submit their records: debates, plays, assembly programs, speech contests. On the basis of these records the committee named the outstanding girl and boy of the year and engraved their names on the bronze plates. Teachers thought the memorial encouraged students to seek a well-rounded training in all of the various aspects of the curricular and extracurricular program. Scholarships and awards are substantial ways of rewarding the superior student.

So many institutions have a special club for promising and talented students that no further mention need be made of this method of sustaining interest.

These persuasive or motivating devices have a place in planning the course. They are not a substitute for clear, straightforward teaching, but add excitement to it. Competition is a part of American life. Teachers recognize the dangers of too much competition, but an occasional contest, with recognition for as many of the competitors as possible, encourages participants to put forth an extra effort.

The Art of Impressing.   Teachers may attain some of their goals by *impressing* as well as by *explaining* or *persuading*. The term *impressing* is used in its technical sense: it does not mean to "make a good impression" on the students but simply to impress them with the breadth and the depth of the subject matter. One reason why John Erskine was a great teacher of English literature, writes Clifton Fadiman, was this capacity for impressing: "Erskine not only loved his subject but reverenced it. . . . He challenged us to understand what we were reading . . . . He called upon us for a kind of mental exercise that is ordinarily devoted to mastering 'hard' subjects."

If students are to respect literature, mathematics, or science, they must be impressed with the wisdom of these subjects. Speech, for example, is not simply the mechanism for uttering sounds. Its role as an agency of communication makes it a vital essential in business, industry, science, religion, statecraft; vital, because nothing can flourish without it. Students are not likely to see beyond the scope of the simple activities of the classroom unless the teacher takes occasion to explain the larger implications. How would the course of events be changed if the American people, for a few months, could have direct communication with the Russian people, in order to interpret and explain in simple terms the true state of world affairs? Or looking at the problem of the individual, what difference will the ability to speak well make in his personal, social, civic, and professional life? Occasionally we hear about seniors majoring in the humanities, or social studies, who apply for Woodrow Wilson, Danforth, Rhodes, or other important scholarships. After preliminary eliminations based largely on grades, survivors are summoned by regional committees for personal interviews. As the candidates' competence in their major fields has already been established, they are likely to be questioned about other interests. A physics major from Iowa may be interviewed by a philosophy professor from Illinois; seeking a common basis for conversation, the professor might ask the candidate his views about racial tension, or, more simply, what's new on the Iowa campus. One bright English major was asked to name her favorite magazines, and through a combination of limited interests and nervousness could respond only with *Better Homes and Gardens*. She had feeble answers to other questions of a general nature and her stock with the regional interviewers fell to zero. Straight A students in various fields realize that because of large undergraduate classes, they have had little chance to participate in lively discussion. Often they see the scholarship awards go to students who are more poised and responsive. The college public speaking class, with its requirement that students make speeches on significant topics based on personal reflection and on reading books, newspapers, and magazines, still offers an opportunity to improve one's communicative talent, whether to an audience of fifteen classmates or to a single Woodrow Wilson regional examiner.

Take a copy of the *Wall Street Journal, New York Times*, or other large paper to class (this suggestion has been given previously), and in the want ad section, note the inquiries for "sales managers," "junior executives," "special representatives," and similar positions where the ability to speak well would be an obvious asset. Tell about the success of former students in attaining rewards or recognitions. Here is one student who secured an important position in a large bank, in competition with a score of others. Here is another who successfully completed a campaign for prosecuting attorney. Here is a third who made an important presentation before a legislative committee. If an alumnus visits school, invite him to tell your class how his speech training has been helpful.

A discussion on the moral obligations of a speaker may also serve to impress students with the dignity of the subject. Quacks and freaks in this country do not last very long: wildeyed politicians achieve a momentary success with their schemes, but their influence is brief. Demagogues make a brief appearance, then are brushed aside. Teachers should make a positive contribution toward the building of character: vision, integrity, selflessness, loyalty, intellectual honesty, sympathy, and conviction are qualities necessary for great speaking. A student who graduates with these attributes will be immune to bribes, graft, influence, poor sportsmanship, and similar traits that at times fill the newspapers.

On another occasion you should talk about the profession of teaching from your side of the desk. A cardinal principle in the ethics of every profession is to recruit new members: just as lawyers and physicians encourage young men and women to follow law or medicine, so should teachers impress their charges with the career of teaching.

Anyone who enjoys teaching can present an account of the advantages of his profession. Thousands of men and women much prefer to be a part of the creative activity of discovering and disseminating information than of any kind of commercial endeavor. Although teachers are tempted to enter the fields of radio, TV, the cinema, the public platform, public relations in industry, and similar occupations, they often, after investigation, decline. Students should know that their teachers were once college men and women, who, with many vocations to choose from, deliberately elected teaching.

The Art of Entertaining.   Only a well-developed sense of humor can keep alive and alert a teacher who is responsible for large classes, faculty committees, discipline problems, reports, and the other score of activities that every teacher assumes. A class needs to provide an outlet for fun along with all of the serious undertakings.

One experienced teacher collects a fund of stories, anecdotes, and incidents as the years go by, some of them concerned with former students, others related to other situations. These stories, scattered through the classroom lecture, help to hold attention and to animate the hour. Other forms of humor are also available. After studying a series of serious poems, bring to class a humorous selection. After a round of serious speeches, take the class to the cafeteria for a simple treat and a round of after-dinner speeches. Some teachers keep the class alive by humorous sallies about various individuals, all done in a spirit of good fun without sarcasm or ridicule. A teacher's jokes or mannerisms may become traditional, and that in itself adds to the fun, if the teacher can laugh at his own foibles. Some teachers are not themselves witty, but enjoy the humorous situations that arise in class. A few teachers have a gift for dramatizing or impersonating situations so as to make them interesting, like the history professor who acted out Gettysburg in the front of the lecture hall.

A sense of humor says something about the poise, balance, and stability of an individual. Few would quarrel with the conclusion arrived at by Charles R. Gruner as a result of an experiment. Two forms of a similar speech, one with appropriate humorous materials added, were delivered to four groups of upperclassmen. The data supported the assumption that a speaker who uses humor in informative speaking is more likely to be perceived by listeners as high in attributes of "character" than one who uses no humor.[2]

Disraeli is invariably thought of as a thoughtful and philosophical speaker associated with such broad themes as parliamentary reform, foreign policy, and conservative principles, but he was listened to attentively because at any time he might come out with some bit of humor that his audience would not want to miss. The occasional diversion kept all minds riveted on the main arguments of the speech. Yet humor can become a dangerous weapon. If a teacher overdoes humor, he will acquire such a reputation for clowning that few will take him seriously. A teacher should not use humorous themes that are in poor taste. No one expects him to be in the vanguard of permissiveness. He should avoid ridicule and biting sarcasm—these are unfair tactics in the classroom. Most of

[2]"Effect of Humor on Speaker Ethos and Audience Information Gain," *Journal of Communication,* September 1967, pp. 228-233.

these cautions, however, are superfluous; the average teacher can no doubt use more humor in his classroom than he does.

Classroom Discussion Techniques. Words like *informing, persuading, entertaining, impressing* tend to describe the teacher as lecturer. A second thought reveals that these forms of oral discourse also enter into teacher-student dialogue.

An outline for looking at teacher talk and student talk is the *Summary of Categories for Interaction Analysis* devised by Amidon and Flanders:[3]

Teacher Talk

Indirect influence
1. *Accepts feeling:* accepts and clarifies the feeling tone of the students in a nonthreatening manner. Feelings may be positive or negative. Predicting and recalling feelings are included.
2. *Praises or encourages:* praises or encourages student action or behavior. Jokes that release tension, not at the expense of another individual, nodding head or saying "um hm?" or "go on" are included.
3. *Accepts or uses ideas of student:* clarifying, building, or developing ideas or suggestions by a student. (As teacher brings more of his own ideas into play, shift to category 5.)
4. *Asks questions:* asking a question about content or procedure with the intent that a student answer.

Direct influence
5. *Lecturing:* giving facts or opinions about content or procedure; expressing his own idea; asking rhetorical questions.
6. *Giving directions:* directions, commands, or orders with which a student is expected to comply.
7. *Criticizing or justifying authority:* statements intended to change student behavior from nonacceptable to acceptable pattern; bawling someone out: stating why the teacher is doing what he is doing; extreme self-reference.

Student Talk

8. *Student talk—response:* talk by students in response to teacher. Teacher initiates the contact or solicits student statement.
9. *Student talk—initiation:* talk by students, which they initiate. If "calling on" student is only to indicate who may talk next, observer must decide whether student wanted to talk. If he did, use this category.
10. *Silence or confusion:* pauses, short periods of silence, and periods of confusion in which communication cannot be understood by the observer.

E. J. Amidon and N. A. Flanders, *The Role of the Teacher in the Classroom: A Manual for Understanding and Improving Teachers' Classroom Behavior,* p. 12. Used by permission.

Imagine an observer sitting in your class, recording the kind of talk going on at that instant. One would hope that for a good share of the classes much *response* and *initiation* (8s and 9s) would be evident, showing active student participation. Some *Lecturing* and *Giving directions* (5s and 6s) are necessary but even these can be interspersed with *response* and *initiation* to indicate that the students are being allowed in the act.

In preparing an assignment the teacher should consider those questions that will give the students opportunity to demonstrate their mastery of the material. Some questions are directed simply at factual content. Others call for reviews or summaries to bring out classifications or groupings. Others seek to get students to apply what they have learned to different situations. If these situations are close at hand, the answers show the immediate practicality of what has been learned. If these situations look to the future, they suggest a long-time value of what has been learned. Teachers master certain techniques: it is better to ask a question of the entire class, give everyone a chance to reflect upon it, and then call on someone, rather than to call on someone first and then state the question. An atmosphere of commendation for good work should prevail: a teacher may say "That's good" or, perhaps, "I hadn't thought of that; let's try to work it out." A look back helps: "Who was it that brought up the point yesterday that . . .?" or "Has anyone ever . . .?" or "Did you see the article in the paper about . . .?" When the hour is over, a quick question to oneself: "Did most of the students have a chance to react in some way to the assignment?" At his leisure he can ponder other categories suggested in the paragraphs above.

Learn by Study and Teaching

To paraphrase Woodrow Wilson, a teacher, like a president, needs not only all the brains he has but all he can borrow. Professors in graduate departments sometimes criticize teachers who try to manage subjects without proper course preparation. A course is the easiest way to learn a subject, but other avenues are available: reading books, consulting with authorities. The temple of knowledge has many doors, for most of which no keys are necessary.

A fellow student once said, "I do not know whether I can become the best teacher in my field, but I am going to try to be the best-trained teacher." His ideal is well worth recalling. As modern education is organized, the initial part of our training comes from course work, but the one certain and continual way of learning is by our own study and teaching. Many problems of classroom management have to be solved by one's own ingenuity and forthrightness.

At least one paragraph about classroom management should be written by students. I feel sure that some of the high school and college students of my acquaintance would like to write something like the following (this was first published in 1952):

Most teachers treat us as if we were still children. We are told what to study, when to study, and under what conditions. We have to walk by the bell, sit by the bell, and leave by the bell. No one ever asks us how much time we need for a particular assignment. The teachers poke along for most of a semester, then all of them start increasing the assignments. Sometimes we get several tests on the same day. Whenever we are given a test, the teacher stands over us like a chicken hawk, as if we would cheat the minute his back was turned—which we certainly would do, because he treats us like children.

Teachers never put confidence in us. If we are absent, they think we skipped class. If we bring an excuse, they think we forged it. If we say we're ill, they think we're trying to get out of work. If we miss an assignment, they think we're not interested in the class.

We'd like to have some voice in what goes on. We'd like fewer rules and fewer requirements. We'd like a chance to know our teachers better, and we'd like to have them know us better. We believe that if teachers would treat us like future citizens we'd all get along first rate.

After hearing this plea several times, I finally began to believe most of it. I seldom question or pry into anybody's excuses. Our trust in students is probably justified about nine times in ten, and if the tenth student seems not to be learning as much as he should, perhaps he will catch a little enthusiasm from the others before too many weeks have elapsed.

Assignments

Report to the class on one of the following topics:

a. Personality Problems of Adolescence.
b. Some Differences between High School and College Students.
c. Personality Traits of Effective Teachers.
d. A Contrast between the Most Intelligent and Least Intelligent High School Pupils I Have Known.
e. A Contrast between the Most Industrious and Least Industrious High School Pupils I Have Known.
f. Examples Showing How Teachers Have Influenced Students.

In preparing any of the above topics, discuss the problem with your friends. Shop talk about the art of teaching with other students, even those who do not plan to teach, reveals a wide variety of opinions.

Questions for Classroom Discussion

. What methods of discipline were in force in your school, and how effective were they?
. How can a teacher use personal conference to improve student morale?

3. What ways of motivation are available to the teacher of speech? Which one were used by teachers of your acquaintance?

4. Are contests overemphasized as a means of stimulating student output? What has been your experience and observation?

5. Do you agree with the advice, frequently given, that the beginning teacher should be fairly stern and reserved, especially at first, and until he feels fairly well established as a teacher?

6. How can the teacher's *character* contribute to classroom effectiveness? his *background* and *general preparation?* his *specific preparation* for each class?

7. What motivating devices, such as contests, increase the interest of the student?

References

Amidon, E. J., and Flanders, N. A. *The Role of the Teacher in the Classroom: A Manual for Understanding and Improving Teachers' Classroom Behavior* Minneapolis: Paul S. Amidon, 1963.

Coleman, James S. *Adolescents and the Schools.* New York: Basic Books, 1965

Dypka, Jessie B. "The Use of Sociometric Techniques in the Classroom." *University of Michigan School of Education Bulletin.* December, 1950. Techniques to locate individuals who exert the most, or the least, influence in the classroom.

Kelley, Earl C. *In Defense of Youth.* Englewood Cliffs: Prentice-Hall, 1962.

Kenner, Freda. "Motivating Students." *Speech Teacher* November 1969

Kohl, Herbert. *36 Children.* New York: Signet Books, 1967. An extraordinary narrative about the experiences of a Harvard graduate in teaching Alvin Dennis, Pamela, Grace, and thirty-two other ghetto-born children.

Jersild, Arthur T. *Psychology of Adolescence.* 2d ed. New York: Macmillan 1963.

McKinney, Fred. *Psychology of Personal Adjustment.* 3d ed. New York: John Wiley & Sons, 1960. Helpful for its understanding of the problems of adolescence: personality readjustment, personal efficiency, social adjustment emotional stability, and the like.

———. *Counseling for Personal Adjustment in Schools and Colleges.* Boston Houghton Mifflin, 1958.

Metcalf, Marguerite Pearce. "Discipline." *Speech Teacher* November 1969.

Youth in Turmoil. The editors of *Fortune.* New York: Time-Life, 1969.

Teaching of Speech

For a list of texts see the references at the end of Chapter 3.

Part Three
the classroom extended

Interscholastic activities shall be an integral part of the school program, to provide experiences having learning outcomes that contribute to good citizenship. Emphasis is to be on teaching through activities.

To this end only can interscholastic activities be justified.

Adapted from *Manual for Missouri High Schools*

14

directing a play

I don't think the audience noticed it.

George Kelly

These chapters discuss activities, principally in the field of drama and debate, that originate in the classroom and extend to the school stage and platform, and beyond that to competitive exercises with other institutions.

When classroom teachers and administrators engage in serious shop talk, sooner or later they ponder whether the American system of education reaches the brilliant student. Any institution, therefore, that means what it says when it expresses an interest in the superior student, should give powerful support to programs in dramatics, debate, radio and TV, and speech contests and festivals.

Put the question another way: "What is our institution doing to enhance the creativity of students?" Or again: "Are we abetting a cultural lag?" The classroom teacher should be able to come up with answers from his own specialty. And of course he is concerned with the student not only clearly identified as superior, but with those who have a latent or potential talent.

The concern of this chapter is for teachers about to direct their first play. From the viewpoint of preparation and interest, teachers of speech are divided into many groups, three of them especially populous. One group has its primary interest in artistic speech: interpretation, drama and the theater. Its members have been active as participants in plays and contests and have had courses in reading, acting, staging, and directing. Members of the second group have their strong interest in public speaking, debate, and discussion. They are the former high school and college debaters who participated in contests and tournaments, and took advanced courses in rhetoric and public address. In college they were not so likely to be found at play tryouts, but took courses in dramatic production or interpretation to meet fixed requirements.

The third group consists of teachers of English—occasionally of other subjects—who find themselves committed to direct a play despite limited exposure to the theater. The issue: the activity must be carried on under a temporary arrangement or dropped altogether. Many of my colleagues argue that if an activity cannot be done right it should not be done at all. I agree with them although I have observed that one should never underestimate the capacity of intelligent, imaginative, and resourceful people to learn; in the hands of such a teacher all is not completely lost, and if students do not learn everything that has cultural and artistic worth they might at least learn something. All of this assumes that the teacher makes a serious attempt to study the requirements of the theater and is not content simply to direct traffic across the stage.

In the classroom the teacher can assign all kinds of roles to all kinds of students, and can overlook a multitude of mistakes and shortcomings. When he produces a play for a public showing, though he still needs to be charitable of the inadequacies of his young actors, he ought to strive for as finished a product as available talent and his own skill can produce. Mistakes are sure to occur, but the general effect should be of a good, artistic performance. The suggestions that follow are written to this end.

The Nature of Play Directing

Long ago Aristotle listed the ingredients of drama: (1) the plot or story, (2) the characters, (3) the thought, (4) the language, (5) the music, (6) the staging. He also had much to say about *discovery*—the moment in the play when a character sees himself in a new light, or in a new relationship to other characters. Arthur Miller is only one of the moderns who confirms the significance of discovery in great drama. Aristotle had peculiarly relevant observations about tragedy—the nature of the tragic hero, for example—but much of what he says has universal application to all types of drama. To be sure, a good deal of modern drama is non-Aristotelian—the playwright of today takes liberties with old rules, Aristotle's and others, that immobilize and straitjacket his imagination—yet Aristotle's six ingredients stake out the territory that the director must explore. As a starting point, he can do no better than to read Aristotle's relatively brief, ever provocative, *Poetics*.

Selecting a Play

Initially, the six ingredients can be applied to the problem of choosing a play. The play text itself is the heart of the enterprise. With a good choice, much of the work is done; once a poor choice is made, however, the situation is like laying a bridge hand with no top cards or coaching a basketball team with no x-footers. The director needs all the help he can get, and the most substantial elp he is likely to get on his first venture is that which comes from a good ript.

he plot.   Aristotle was standing on solid ground when he stated that the most nportant feature of the play was the plot. Better pick a play in which things appen; young actors are better at presenting a story, with plots and counter-ots, than they are at revealing subtle character disintegrations or redemptions. ction is the key word, with its ups and downs, its discoveries and reversals, its xcitement and its movement. The action of course should be sturdy and ubstantial, well-motivated, meaningful, guided by purpose; this paragraph is no ea for the shallow and superficial. Admittedly, there are scores of good, noughtful, reflective plays—for the time being leave those for experienced rectors and sophisticated audiences.

he characters.   The impact of drama comes from the people in it: their bility to convince, their insights and perspectives, their biases and prejudices, neir hopes and motivations. As you search for a play keep in mind the people in , and the extent to which they grip and absorb you. At the same time reflect pon particular students who might be cast in specific roles.

he thought.   A play has a *spine,* a central theme around which the whole is used (the back of this book, holding the pages together in a sensible order, is so called a *spine*). What is the message of the play? What is the playwright ying to say? What basic idea does Shakespeare convey in *Macbeth?* Bolt in *A an for All Seasons?* Wilde in *The Importance of Being Earnest?* Your analysis the central idea of the play will guide you in, for example, your analysis of tion or your interpretation of a character.

he language.   We say that the dialogue of a play is good or bad, meaning that e language is vivid, colorful, striking, pungent, provocative, in some way emorable—or the opposite. Hence we like *Our Town, Hamlet, Antigone, herit the Wind.* The persistence of Shakespeare on play lists—year after year, nuntry after country, comes in part from the richness, variety, boldness, and nsitivity of his language.

he music.   Not, of course, a feature of every play, but of the utmost gnificance in *Oklahoma, The Mikado,* and other performances of this category. nd not to be overlooked where it occurs incidentally in such plays as *Othello, idsummer Night's Dream.*

he staging.   As you read, you will in your mind's eye visualize sets, lighting, pstumes, makeup. Your play does not go on in black and white, but in living olor.

You have hard, practical questions to answer.[1] Such as:

How many characters? Do you have in mind a small cast, like seven or eight, or large cast, like fifteen or more? Does your cast need to be all boys, or a girls?

How many sets? Do you require a play that has one interior set, or do you hav the facilities to provide for changes?

What costumes? Do you want modern costumes throughout, or are you inte ested in a period play?

What technical problems? Are you prepared to handle complicated staging directing, or lighting problems, or do you need something more simple?

What royalty? Can you pay $50.00 or higher for a single performance, or do yo need something more reasonable?

For further inspiration, refer to lists of most-frequently-produced plays t see what is proving generally interesting and successful. These compilations ar not likely to reveal the newest plays, and sometimes come up with titles c ephemeral value, but they do rank the old friends, the persistent favorites.

Each year, for example, the International Thespian Society tabulates th favorite plays presented by its more than three thousand member schools. Her is a typical list: *Our Town, Arsenic and Old Lace, You Can't Take It With Yo The Miracle Worker, The Diary of Anne Frank, The Night of January 16th, Th Curious Savage, The Sound of Music, Teahouse of the August Moon, Bye By Birdie, Oklahoma, The Music Man, South Pacific, The Wizard of Oz, The Ma Who Came to Dinner, Brigadoon, Harvey, My Fair Lady, My Three Angel Charley's Aunt, I Remember Mama, The Importance of Being Earnest, Cheape by the Dozen, The Glass Menagerie, The King and I, Blithe Spirit,* and sixt others that ten or more high schools liked that season. For the current list, writ the Society (address in Appendix E).

The choice of the colleges that same season, as reported in the *Quarterl Journal of Speech*, was a little different. *Twelfth Night* was far and away th favorite, being reported by thirty-five different college and university campuse Others were: *Antigone, The Taming of the Shrew, Hamlet, Merchant of Venic Importance of Being Earnest* (higher institutions are strong on the classics followed by *Fantasticks, Alice in Wonderland, Oh, Dad, Poor Dad, Music Ma Rashomon, Skin of Our Teeth, Streetcar Named Desire, Waiting for Godo*

---

[1]Katharine Anne Ommanney's *The Stage and the School* contains plays for high schoc production: long plays, one-acts, plays for boys, plays for girls, comedies, serious plays fantasies. Joseph Mersand's *Guide to Play Selection,* and Gail Plummer's *Dramatist Guide to Selection of Plays and Musicals,* are good sources. Publications like *Education Theatre Journal, Dramatics,* and *Players Magazine* list new titles in articles and advertise ments.

Romeo and Juliet, Othello, A Man for All Seasons.

The Educational Theatre Journal regularly records the choices of college and university directors. Alan A. Stambusky's list in the May 1966 issue reported these twenty most frequently produced plays (the asterisk indicates that the play was among the top twenty in the previous five-year period): *The Glass Menagerie, *The Crucible, *Antigone, *Blithe Spirit, *The Importance of Being Earnest, A Midsummer Night's Dream, *Death of a Salesman, *Twelfth Night, *Our Town, A Thurber Carnival, Look Homeward, Angel, J.B., *The Taming of the Shrew, The Miracle Worker, *The Matchmaker, *The Skin of Our Teeth, Romeo and Juliet, The Visit, The Fantasticks, *The Madwoman of Chaillot. A still later list shows a few differences: The Glass Menagerie, A Thurber Carnival, A Man for All Seasons, Oh Dad, Poor Dad, Antigone, The Taming of the Shrew, Macbeth, The Importance of Being Earnest, Romeo and Juliet, Oedipus Rex, A Midsummer Night's Dream, Twelfth Night, Blithe Spirit, The Lady's Not for Burning, The Miracle Worker, The Crucible, The Visit, Royal Gambit, Tartuffe, Six Characters in Search of an Author.

In addition the experimentalists were more than occasionally presenting titles from absurdists and modernists like The Sandbox, Waiting for Godot, The Bald Soprano, The Lesson, Rhinoceros, The Caretaker, Home Free, American Dream.

A principal reason for printing these lists is to serve as an index of what is being produced and as a check-list or memory jogger. Some titles will go out of style but others will be around for decades to come. What is popular in New York and London is quickly available to universities and high schools.

The list of one-act titles is endless, but various play publishers suggested these as popular high-school choices from their catalogs: Sorry, Wrong Number, The Hitch-Hiker, The Devil and Daniel Webster, When Shakespeare's Ladies Meet, Overpraised Season, Agamemnon, Opening Night, The Day After Forever, Happy Journey to Camden and Trenton, Ugly Duckling, Old Lady Shows Her Medals, Antic Spring, Orchids for Margaret, The Cuckoo.

Plays popular at high school festivals, where student actors and their directors scrutinize one another's work carefully, include: The Rainmaker, A Venetian Hour, The Day After Forever, High Window, A Sunny Morning, The Case of the Crushed Petunias, The Birthday of the Infanta, The Romancers, Box and Cox, Mary of Scotland, The Madwoman of Chaillot, Peer Gynt, A Thurber Carnival, The Sandbox, Inherit the Wind, the Zoo Story, Medea, A Man for All Seasons, Impromptu, Angel Street, Hello Out There, The Fantasticks.

Hansel and Gretel, The Children's Story, The Miracle Worker, David and Lisa, Beyond the Fringe, The Chairs, Markheim, Masque of the Red Death, Noah, Marco Polo, Abraham Lincoln, Feast of Ortolans, American Dream, A Marriage Proposal, The Immovable Gordons, The Pot Boiler, Our Hearts Were Young and Gay, Joint Owners in Spain, Nobody Sleeps, The Glass Menagerie.

The Hungerers, Aria Da Capo, Midsummer Night's Dream, Overtones, Macbeth, Under Milk Wood, Not Far from the Giocanda Tree, Something Unspoken,

The Ugly Duckling, The Rivals, The Way Things Are, Where the Cross is Made, The Storm, The Lady's Not for Burning, The Sister's Tragedy, Queen of France, Luv, The Bald Soprano, The Doctor In Spite of Himself.

The Forced Marriage, The Grass Harp, Not My Cup of Tea, Brewsie and Willie, The Necklace, Anastasia, The Wonder Hat, Gammer Gurton's Needle, The Pot Boiler, Monsieur La Blanc, The Enchanted, Dark of the Moon, The Sandbox, The Little Foxes, Riders to the Sea, Medea, Mrs. McThing, One Day in the Life of Ivan Denisovich, World of Sholem Aleichem.

This mix of the classic and the absurd, the serious and the comic, the new arrivals and the pieces that have been shown at contests for years, the one-act and the cuttings from full-length plays, have one point in common: each won a superior rating at a state or regional festival. In other language, each held something to command the interest of a teacher and a group of students, and, in competition with other groups, to attract special recognition from a critic judge.

How can you secure copies of the plays that seem to have possibilities? Try the extension division of your state university; it may have a play loaning service that will mail you copies of the titles you wish at a nominal service charge. Some titles you will need to purchase from the publishers themselves.

After you make a collection of plays, your next job is to begin your reading and study. Play reading is an art; if you skim a play as you would a novel, you may be disappointed in your entire selection. You need to visualize the finished production with flesh and blood actors. Business, action, costume, setting, and lighting all heighten the lines of the play, so that the result should be more amusing, more exciting, or more inspiring than the lines alone indicate. You will not be able to visualize all of the possibilities of a given scene, since new ideas will come as you work with the play, and actors themselves will have usable suggestions, but with experience you will learn to imagine actors on a stage as you study the play.

You will need to search out the spine and the ways in which each character related to it. You will need to note the little climaxes and the major climax, the actions and subactions. You will need to understand not only the action of the play but also its mood and spirit. Questions about movement, business, lighting, costuming, and interpretation of lines that arise in your mind, before rehearsals begin and after they have started, cannot be properly answered until you have made the major decisions about the drift and intent of the play as a whole. Not until you have read and reread the script will you be able to take it to the cast.

The question of cutting or in other ways doctoring the script will arise at an early stage of your reading. Long, talky scenes require actors of a competence that may not be available to you. You may therefore need to simplify some passages in order to make them manageable. A play with a performance time of much more than two hours and a half needs special qualities to sustain the attention of the average school audience. Read a play scene by scene with the questions in mind: Can this scene be made interesting to the audience of students, friends, and parents that will come to see it? If a scene is mostly talk, ordinarily a problem to the director, then the specific question is: Can this talk be made interesting, by appropriate business, action, or characterization? Can we cut out part of it? Or if that particular scene does not offer much hope, then the question becomes: Does the playwright redeem himself later on by offering better scenes? You may not be prepared to direct a play that is largely philosophical in nature; on the other hand, if the scene has humor, suspense, excitement, or some element of humanness, then the chances are that the audience will find it enjoyable.

The tastes and capacities of the director are bound up in his choice of a play. Some directors like costume productions and fantasies, staging play after play in this category. Others like mysteries and dramas. Still others like farces; and these are not so easy to direct as the beginner imagines. Eventually a director ought to try various types in order to deepen and broaden his grasp.

To find a play with equally good opportunities for girls and boys is a special problem. A group may have several talented girls, and the best available plays, from the director's point of view, may be skimpy on good female parts; he therefore needs either to widen his search or disappoint the girls. The use of alternate casts is a good solution: more students will have an opportunity to participate, and the risk of jeopardizing the production is lessened if a principal becomes ill. Alternate casts, however, almost double the burden of the director.

Analyzing the Play

Books about the art of directing are so helpful and so specific, it is hardly necessary to present a detailed account here describing how a director studies a play and prepares a production book. Nevertheless, hundreds of poor performances offered to the public show what happens when those who direct them have not yet been guided to good sources of study. Your first task, therefore, should be to get a collection of good books and read them.[2]

Many excellent titles are available. As a student at the University of Iowa I was introduced early to *Fundamentals of Directing* by Alexander Dean, the late distinguished professor of play directing at Yale. My scouts told me that only genuine Yale students could secure the mimeographed syllabus used in his classes, but a good friend was able to smuggle out a copy (without too much difficulty, I suspect) for five dollars. In 1933 one could buy, for five dollars, fifty pounds of hamburger; I include this statement just to get the reader straight on his values. But Abe Lincoln never read his Blackstone or Euclid more faithfully than I read Alexander Dean. My printed copy shows that even in 1953 the book had gone through eleven printings. Directors still like it. A revision is Alexander Dean and Lawrence Carra, *Fundamentals of Play Directing*. Another fine title is *Modern Theatre Practice* by Hubert C. Heffner, Samuel Selden, and Hunton D. Sellman; a fourth edition was published in 1959. The omnibus volume, John Gassner, *Producing the Play* with *The New Scene Technicians' Handbook* by Philip Barber, makes interesting and helpful reading. Gassner writes partly in autobiographical vein, like many authors writing about the theater, and draws upon his own experiences with distinguished plays, actors, playwrights. Supplementary chapters by other authors (for example, Harold Clurman) are illuminating; and there are chapters analyzing specific plays which are especially helpful if you know the plays or will read them. F. Curtis Canfield offers detailed and specific guidance in *The Craft of Play Directing*. The high school teacher will find a

Here again, play companies come to the help of the beginner by providin₉ production aids, giving pictures of other presentations of the play, and a worl₍ of suggestions about movement, action, costuming, lighting, staging, and produc₋ tion. Books about play production—consult the list at the end of the chapter— give helpful suggestions about the preparation of a production book if yo₍ cannot find one readymade. These are useful, but even if you have someon₍ else's production book, you will want to make adaptations of it to your ow₎ situation.

One prepares a production book by securing two copies of a play an₍ detaching their leaves from the bindings, then making a scrap book out of ₍ bookkeeper's ledger, and pasting one page of the play on each right-hand pag₍ One then reads the play as many times as necessary, in order to get it well i₎ mind; not only to understand the plot and the characterizations but also t₍ search out the atmosphere of the play and its message or theme. One also rea₍ whatever accessories are available, such as suggestions by the author or othe₎ directors; one may also make decisions about cutting the play, or revising it t₍ make it more suitable or timely. People who write plays often do not have wis₍ ideas about staging them, so directors invariably feel free to make changes. Yo₍ should make preliminary diagrams showing the setting of the stage, so you wi₎ see where to place the chairs, the sofa, the table, the dresser, and of course th₍ doors and windows. You need to diagram stage movement and make notes abo₍ stage business, off-stage sound effects, lighting cues. You need also to stud₍ entrances and exits: certain scenes in the play are sure to gain addition₍ dramatic effect from a well-located entrance or exit. Consult any text o₍ directing for further suggestions.[3]

When planning individual scenes, consider which part of the stage is to ₍ utilized. Conventionally the stage is divided into six (sometimes nine or mor₍ acting areas: up right, up center, up left, down right, down center, and dow₍ left. These directions are designed for the convenience of the actor; it is *his* le₍

---

hundred disaster-averting ideas in W. David Sievers, *Directing for the Theatre*. H. ₍ Albright, William P. Halstead, and Lee Mitchell, *Principles of Theatre Art*, is clea₍ and specific. The second edition is an extensive revision of the first, and, like th₍ first, is liberally illustrated with drawings and photographs. See the references at the en₍ of this chapter for additional titles.

[3] Hundreds of production books have been prepared as a part of the requirements f₍ advanced degrees; you will find many in the libraries of institutions that have gradua₍ programs in theater. These books analyze the play, discuss problems involved an₍ solutions reached; they are usually illustrated with photographs, sketches, costum₍ charts, and light plots. The plays chosen are usually those that are significant in theate₍ history. More accessible is Toby Cole and Helen Krich Chinoy (eds.), *Directors o₍ Directing*. See the chapters by Tyrone Guthrie and Harold Clurman, and the productio₍ plans by Stanislavski, Reinhardt, Meyerhold, Jessner, Kazan, Clurman. Canfield, *Th₍ Craft of Play Direction*, mentioned in the preceding footnote, has suggestions abo₍ blocking out and interpreting scenes from *The Doctor's Dilemma* and *Winterset*. Beck ₍ al., *Play Production in the High School*, has a sample page from a prompt script (p. 3₍

ʊu are talking about, as *he* faces the audience. *Up* means away from the
ʌdience, and *down* means toward the audience. If an actor were standing in the
ɔnter of the stage, facing the footlights, and you, as director, asked him to
ove *up left*, he would move *back*, and toward *his* left. Obviously some areas of
e stage are more emphatic than others.

Suppose you have two men on stage, the hero and the villain, and you decide
  play their scene in the *down center* area. You need to visualize further how
ey are to stand: face to face? side by side? one farther up stage than the other?
ɪd are they to stand there, hands at sides, or is movement to be provided for
em? Beginning directors usually leave an actor short on movement—unless
ey go to the other extreme and provide movement that is purposeless—and the
tor therefore feels uncomfortable.

Albright, Halstead, and Mitchell have an excellent discussion in Chapter 9,
ʌovement and Gesture," illustrated by full-page figures showing position,
trances, movement, facings, gesturing, and the like. They speak of *inherent*
ovement, rooted in the plot, prescribed by the dramatist (such as a duelling or
ɪting scene) and of *imposed* movement (such as those worked out by the
rector to give a scene balance or variety, or to relieve or heighten tension). The
w director needs a good deal of guidance in both categories, especially the
tter. If the script says, "Maid enters, bringing tea service," he can figure this
ıt and perhaps also devise special touches to heighten the effect of *this* maid in
is situation. But if the script contains a long passage of dialogue in which the
rticipants steadily display more and more antagonism, he will have to invent
e gesture and the movement to heighten and point up the increasing hostility.
ead this and other chapters on movement, and other aspects, and you will find
ur own imagination and creativity being given a considerable lift.

Another important concept to the director is *business*, the actions and
tivities of the characters. Dropping a handkerchief, writing a letter, listening at
keyhole, hiding a present, mending a sock, ringing a bell, are all examples of
siness. Like movement, business has different purposes and functions, includ-
ʒ telling the story of the play, suggesting a state of mind, creating atmosphere
 mood, and the like. Directors are ingenious about inventing business where
ne is provided by the playwright, in order to enhance interest in the play.
ɪur preliminary study of the play should suggest possibilities for business, and
 you rehearse other ideas will occur to you. All movement and business should
ve a definite purpose—it should not be inserted at random—and this purpose
ɔuld be related to the plot, the mood, the theme, the characterization.

All of these ideas should be noted in your book at the appropriate pages.
ɪen later you meet your actors you can tell them where to stand, and suggest
 relevant movement and business. In your book you will also note, on the
ɪnk pages, at the appropriate points, comments like "Warn John" or "Warn
gler" a few moments ahead of the spot where John actually is to enter, or the
gler is actually to blow a call. Later you will hand your book, or a copy of it,

to your stage manager, and he will use it as a guide to make sure that actor
enter when they should, and that sound effects are produced on time. A directo
usually takes pains with his books, compiling them in permanent form as a par
of his library.

Every play brings with it problems of staging and lighting. Your productio
may be as simple or as elaborate as your skill or the physical equipment of th
stage permits. If your stage has only a conventionalized interior set, you ma
want to repaint your set or redesign it by constructing additional flats, so tha
spectators will not again see the set which has for so long been hallowed in thei
memory. If your stage has only the traditional footlights and border lights, yo
may introduce new effects by installing simple floodlights or spotlights. Teache
who have not had courses in stage craft, scenic design, or stage lighting wi
receive considerable help from such books as A. S. Gillette's *An Introduction r
Scenic Design* (New York, 1957), and his *Stage Scenery: Its Construction an
Rigging* (New York, 1959), both of which are eminently clear and eminentl
authoritative; Herbert Hake, *Here's How* (New York, 1958), is useful for i
many drawings and its lucid explanations; and from other titles at the end of th
chapter.

Conducting Tryouts

Meanwhile you have made an announcement of tryouts for the play, and ha
put copies in the library so that those interested may read it. The tryout sessio
themselves take the better part of a week's spare time. Those who sign up ma
have a preliminary session with the director, in which he reads the pla
explaining its problems and possibilities. Eventually each student trying o
should have an opportunity to read one or more parts to you. Nothing qui
takes the place of actual reading of the lines. A director may think he h
students hand-picked for all the roles, but he may find in actual tryouts th
other students read the lines better.

Tryouts consist not only of solo readings, but also of groups worki
together as they appear in the play. Your final choice of *Mary* may be dete
mined in part by the possibilities for her husband *John*; although sizes r
irregular in schools, you would like to have *John* at least as tall as *Mary*. Y
may not have a world of talent to draw from; if you have fifteen girls trying o
you may find that ten of them are not suitable. Among other requirements a
those of clear speech and a strong voice, so that the customers who sit in t
back row of the auditorium will be able to hear the production.

Before the second elimination, after those who clearly do not have possibi
ties have been turned down, give survivors fair warning that acting in a play ca
for hard work. A few of your candidates may have had the idea that acting
entirely glamor, and that they may continue in the cast without breaking in

their work hours, study arrangements, dating conveniences, and the like. The best approach to students whenever a hard or irksome job looms up is to be entirely candid. You never fool anybody by being otherwise, and your frank statement of the difficulties should stiffen the backbones of the waverers. We all feel stirrings of nobility inside us when we face a stiff challenge.

When you decide you have tried the plausible combinations, compile your tentative cast, including names for parts you want to double cast. You may need to look into the academic standing of a few individuals. You will undoubtedly reserve the right to make further substitutions, not releasing the names as final until you have held a few rehearsals. You will also need to select members of your stage crew, who are as important as the actors. After the final elimination, have a conference with each one chosen, to explain the nature of his assignment and its contribution to the production.

The Rehearsal Schedule

The first meeting of the cast and crew is significant. Here you are with the group that will occupy your thoughts for the weeks to come; at this meeting you may try to set a key note for the long series of rehearsals.

One procedure I always followed was to tell the group stories of productions that contained a classic bungle. Theater history is full of these, involving professional groups as well as amateurs. Then I related a series of incidents showing how smart thinking will avoid ridiculous moments on stage. All of this led to a plea to actors and crew members alike to concentrate on their tasks so as to avoid awkward situations. I told the actors, for example, that if some one was late making an entrance, those on stage should improvise lines or business until the later comer arrived. They looked to this opportunity with eagerness. During one of the early rehearsals, in a scene in which a business man was dictating a letter to his secretary, the script called for the entrance of a second man immediately after a few lines had been dictated: on one occasion the second man was late, so the young executive sat there dictating letters until the tardy actor could be rounded up—all of this to the edification of the cast. On another occasion during rehearsal when a door bell failed to ring, two of the girls filled the interval with sprightly and appropriate conversation. The rule soon became established that the actors on the stage meant business; they read their lines with concentration, and let nothing stop a scene except a word from the director himself.

This is only part of the teamwork that has to develop among those taking part in a dramatic enterprise. Crew members have their responsibilities, actors have theirs. On the stage each actor has to maintain certain relationships with every other actor. A is in love with B, is friendly towards C, is suspicious of D, is contemptuous of E but later respects and admires him. These attitudes will be

suggested by the words of the script and in subtle ways not written into th
script. When an actor listens, he is listening to something. When he exits, he i
going somewhere. When he enters, he has come from some where. During hi
absence, something has happened. Certain things are established *solo*, other
ensemble.

Most directors spend the first two or three meetings in group reading an
discussion of the whole play. This period of time is not long enough; th
professionals in the London production of *A Man for All Seasons* spent thre
weeks reading, studying, looking at the play from every conceivable point o
view. Still, we do what we can with the time at hand. We can at least make
beginning, and can refine interpretations as the weeks go on. Seasoned director
say: "Don't lecture to the cast about the play; get the whole group to offe
opinions, ask and answer questions."

Next comes a blocking out of Act I, by which is meant that the actors, book
in hand, read their lines, the director suggesting principal movements an
business. The better part of an afternoon may be necessary to block out the act
and probably the next rehearsal period should be spent in going through the ac
again, adding refinements and making further suggestions. Three rehearsal pe
iods may then be given to Act II, studying the play and blocking it out, an
then, before proceeding to Act III, the cast should be required to memorize Ac
I; and the next rehearsal may be given to Act I, with no use of books, followe
by Acts II and III, with use of books. By the following rehearsal actors shoul
know Act II; and the next rehearsal should be given to Acts I and II, no book
being allowed on the stage. By the next rehearsal Act III should be memorized
(This scheme is only one of many.)

Whether students can memorize their lines this rapidly depends on the lengt
of individual parts and the competence of the actors themselves. At this poin
the strong determination of the director will have to assert itself. He will, o
course, have gone over the rehearsal schedule at the first meeting of the cast, s
that individuals will know what is to be expected of them. Most actors will mee
the director's deadlines if he is firm and persuasive.

A lot of thought and discussion goes on during rehearsals. The student's tas
is not merely to learn lines and to associate certain movements with them, but t
understand why his character is saying what he is saying and doing what he i
doing. The playwright leaves so many questions unanswered; director and actor
have to ferret out the answers. A good director will get more out of an acto
than the actor realized was in him. And often the playwright himself must b
astonished to see what directors and actors together have got out of his play (
statement that certainly can be read in more than one way).

The next week of rehearsal is spent in detailed work on each of the thre
acts. Some scenes will go well, others will prove troublesome. Where the action i
complex, as in a mob scene, the director will need to spend additional time
Love scenes require special attention. Changes in movement and business will b

troduced from time to time and these will need to be incorporated into the rformance. Toward the end of the rehearsal period, the director will give tention to timing, rhythm, breaking up of long scenes, and other details. Two three dress rehearsals should be scheduled.

Although I have suggested a specific rehearsal scheme, you will find as many fferent patterns of rehearsal as there are directors. I realize I have also made at statements about highly debatable points. As to the length of the rehearsal riod, most directors would regard four weeks as too short a time; I found six eeks about right. So much richness of character was developed in the fifth and xth weeks that I was grateful for them. At the same time you are unlikely to ake radical changes after midpoint.

Actors should work with, so far as feasible, the objects they will use in the nal production: the fans, guns, books, dishes, and other hand props that the ay calls for. If a stairway is to be used, or a series of levels, they should be ought into the rehearsal as soon as possible. Hopefully the set will be finished the fourth week. Moreover, technical rehearsals will need to be conducted to periment with lighting effects, and to synchronize light changes with action on e stage. Stand-ins can be used instead of the actual cast. The makeup commit- e may be given an opportunity to practice, not only to facilitate their training, t also to get actors accustomed to seeing one another in mustaches, wigs, and her adornments. Your stage crew needs to drill on changing furniture between ts, and doing whatever other changes are necessary, so that this can be carried speedily and noiselessly during actual performance. Costumes are introduced one or more dress rehearsals so the actors will get used to them. You need to gure out how to handle curtain calls and to practice them. On occasion you ight introduce a few claques into the auditorium, to supply quantities of bogus ughter, to accustom actors to the technique of waiting for laughs.

Leave no detail to chance. Let there be meticulous preparation, and then, if ed be, brilliant improvisation.

You will discover specific ways in which you can help each actor improve. r example:

must create an illusion. While an actor is on stage he must try actually to present a grandfather, a juvenile, a princess. To this end, as has already been ggested, he must give full concentration to the part. He must not step out of aracter for an instant: if some one forgets a line, he must adapt to the new uation without a flicker of an eyelash. He must supply new dialogue or in me way adapt his speeches to get the play back on the track, without letting e audience see that something is amiss.

must create the illusion of the first time. No matter how many performances r Laurence Olivier gives of *Hamlet,* each evening must see him reading lines as he had never spoken the words before. The spontaneity must still be there.

Suppose the leading man is on stage, sitting in a sofa reading a magazine. The villain enters up left, stealthily, unknown to the hero, and creeps menacingly towards the sofa. The audience knows that at any minute the hero will discover the villain—but the hero must act as if he has no idea the villain is around. If he detects the presence of the villain an instant too soon the effect is ruined. If he even looks or moves as if he suspected the villain would be along soon, the surprise is lost. He must read his magazine with proper concentration: and if the action calls for his making the discovery just as he accidentally looked up at the clock, he must accidentally look at the clock without revealing his foreknowledge that he will see the villain nearby.

He must be an actor while he is listening. It is not enough to be Pierrot while Pierrot is speaking; an actor must be Pierrot while Pierrot is listening. As he listens he may let his countenance be amused, serious, astonished, or whatever mood or emotion is called for. He must not give the impression of woodenly awaiting other speeches so he can inject his own. Fine acting can be done without ever saying a word.

He must be audible. Many beginning actors cannot make themselves heard past the first row. Hence the director at times sits in the worst places in the house, in order to detect any let up in clarity of articulation or volume of voice. Shouting is not wanted, but good projection is.

He must pick up his cues. The *cue* is the last word of the preceding speech. When Sir Anthony says, in *The Rivals,*

> Why, Mrs. Malaprop, in moderation, now, what would you have a woman know?

there should not be a long delay between *know* and Mrs. Malaprop's speech:

> Observe me, Sir Anthony.—I should by no means wish a daughter of mine to be a progeny of learning. . .

which means that if Mrs. Malaprop gets ready to say "Observe me" just as Sir Anthony is saying "know," the natural delay in reflex time will make her speech begin promptly. But if the listener hears

> woman know? (long pause) Observe me, Sir Anthony

and hears other pauses between other speeches, he knows the director has overlooked this bit of technique. *Picking up cues* means that the play is proceeding briskly. (This point is not to be confused with the pause for dramatic effect.) In later rehearsals directors time each act with a stop watch, to detect any tendency to slow the performance.

le must use his eyes properly. Eyes can show affection and tenderness or they an blaze with anger. Beginning actors look down at the stage too much, much s a beginning dancer looks fearfully at his own feet instead of rapturously into he eyes of his partner. In the early rehearsals you can teach actors to keep their aze up, and in later sessions you can show them other ways to use their eyes. ;ive attention to the expression of the whole face; the eyes do not have to carry he entire burden. Some actors are too deadpan, others too grimacing or 1enacing. A good actor has total command of his facial muscles.

The director gives the actors such help as is necessary to build a part. His ecret weapon is the art of asking questions, but he can demonstrate if need be. Ie may show one character how to stand, another how to sit, another how to valk around the room and serve coffee. He is open to suggestions from actors bout changes in action, business, or interpretation, but does not require the tudents to take the lead. The ineffectual director seems satisfied to hold the ook and let the characters work out their interpretations. Some directors who re really not very good actors themselves nevertheless seem able to make nportant suggestions to the members of the cast: the actor takes a suggestion 1at is sound, although poorly executed, and works it up into something onvincing. No one can see the whole play as can the director, so the overall uidance must come from him.

Delegating Responsibilities

xcept for the actual directing, delegate everything possible to other members of 1e group. Give the stage manager a copy of your production book, and make im responsible for seeing that all cues are executed. The prompter holds the fficial text, and supplies lines as needed. Some directors try to do their own age managing, and a few even serve as prompter, but often these tasks can be elegated. To avoid embarrassing situations during the final production, the age manager should work out a check list to include the stage furniture, props be used (including the copy of grandfather's will in the upper right hand rawer of the desk), actors who are to be on the stage when the curtain opens, 1d those who are to be off stage awaiting an early entrance. He should check s list systematically; no one should pull a curtain until this chore is done. On ccasion his methodical, unhurried check will reveal omissions.

Makeup can be handled by a committee almost without assistance from the rector. Pick two or three girls who themselves use cosmetics fairly well, give em a copy of the play, a book about makeup, and a suitable kit. Carl B. Cass, *ake-Up for Stage and Television* (Cincinnati, 1958), is written for amateurs. ichard Corson, *Stage Make-Up* (New York, 1960), is eminently helpful. Let the udent committee make up two or three of the characters about the fourth

week of rehearsal—previously they have practiced on each other—and subm
their effort for your criticism. Eventually they will have worked out a makeu
chart for each character. Costumes can be handled by another committee; me
with it and explain in detail what the play requires, and let it locate the materia
for you. Students are likely to know the resources of the community or th
campus better than you do.[4] Finding furniture for the stage is something yc
may need to undertake yourself. Lighting may be handled by one or two peop
unless the problem becomes complicated, but the final effect cannot be work
out all at once; it is a matter for experimentation. Once a suitable combinatic
of colors, intensity, and location is worked out, properly cued to the action, tl
light crew records it, and thereafter is able to duplicate it.

Your dramatic program may develop talent in unexpected places, if yc
encourage the idea. A freshman of about the four-foot-two, ninety pound si
said he wanted to make a career out of stage lighting. I did not take hi
seriously, but gave him a book and told him to read it. I had forgotten him wh
he came back weeks later and said he had finished it. He had asked his physi
instructor to help with the technical parts. At once I became a believer. I to
the student to the stage, and let him experiment with switches and dimmers
was delighted to have him light the next major production. He gave tl
assignment a world of time and thought. We would experiment together until v
got the effect we wanted, then he would take careful notes so he could duplica
it, time after time, and on cue.

If the director undertakes to handle too many details himself, he will
continually harassed during the final production: the students will look to hi
to make the slightest decision. He should seldom go on stage, except to work o
some matter of direction; cast and crew therefore learn to work out mar
problems themselves. During the production, he should sit out in front,
observe the general effect. He may go back stage after the first curtain in ord
to advise the cast to speak louder or more distinctly—a continuing problem wi
young actors—and to give them a word of encouragement. After all, he does n
want them to think he has gone home.

The concept of delegating responsibility overflows into other departments
the institution. Unless your school has a scene shop, you may have to ta
certain problems to the manual training teacher. The home economics teacl
and her students may help solve a rugged costume problem, and the art clas

[4] "The Property Man has the same peculiarity as the oldest inhabitant—he never rememb
anything; nor will he, no matter how familiar the object, confess that he has ever seer
specimen, or that it is procurable, save by the expense of large quantities of mone
time, difficulty, and danger" (Thomas William Robertson, "Theatrical Types," *Edu
tional Theatre Journal*, October 1965, p. 250). I enjoyed reading this, and recalled th
my committee members used to snitch the most valuable heirlooms from their hom
entirely without parental permission, and lay these treasures on my desk; they were f
too precious to use, and as difficult to get them returned, without embarrassing t
student, as to replace the jewelled dagger in *Topkapi*.

help out with scene-painting problems and advertising posters. In any production enterprise, the cooperation of the janitor takes overriding priority. If you can get him to put his support solidly behind the venture, he will vastly simplify many of your problems.

After delegating responsibility, you should not reassume it. If the student assigned to sound effects is late with an offstage gunshot, don't rebuke him: ask the stage manager what happened. Students soon learn that you look to the stage manager, and therefore respect his authority more. If sound effects is supposed to play a phonograph record at a certain instant, don't hover over him, waiting for that moment to arrive, and then say "Now!" Explain the problem to him, and let him execute it. He will take more pride in his work if you leave him in charge. Not all directors, of course, agree with this point of view. Some are happier to do a thing themselves than to ask someone else to do it. They cannot quite delegate responsibility. They can almost delegate it—they can assign someone to a certain task, but they feel they must watch him, and at the last instant they reassign the responsibility to themselves. They should divide the work—and the fun—a little.

Publicizing the Play

Advertising and publicizing the play is of the highest importance. Good advertising starts with the cast and crew; give them a special exhortation to boost the play at all times. Rehearsals may drag, players may lose heart, but loyalty should be unflagging. If someone in the outer world asks, "How is the play going?" their answer should be, "First class; it's a wonderful production." If the question is, "How is the leading lady?" they are to say, promptly, "She's marvelous—very, very good." If he inquires, "How is the director?" they will reply, hopefully, "Positively out of this world. Getting miraculous results." If anyone wants to criticize the play, the actors, or the director, let him wait until after opening night. Up until that time, if the student loses faith himself, let him borrow from the director's supply. Students always need to learn about loyalty, and you may be in need of theirs before your enterprise is over.

The rule of advertising is: Use the best methods that have been tried heretofore, and then devise new media. The trailer is an old device in moving pictures: get your home movie fans to work and show the prospective customers a few scenes from next week's show. You can use an assembly program for this purpose. In publicizing *R.U.R.*, a fantasy about the day when robots will take over the world, one cast thought it necessary to explain what robots are like: not only to arouse the curiosity of students, but also to educate them. The actors worked out an assembly skit in which the director interviewed a couple of beautiful girl robots. They presented a moving picture, made on 8-mm film, showing advance scenes, Hollywood fashion, with Hollywood super-colossal titles. They had robots walking up and down the hall between classes. The resul was a full house every night.

After the Play

Directors usually schedule a postmortem after each run. The work of cast an crew is reviewed in order to get the bugs out before the next performance. Whei the final performance is finished, certain chores need to be looked after, and th sooner these are attended to, the better.

The set should be struck and stored immediately after the last performance that same night, while everybody is around. This procedure means that the stag is available for other uses. Properties should be returned at the earliest opportu nity. As it is more pleasant to borrow props than to return them, this detai should not be allowed to drag on for days after the production. Valuable o fragile articles are less likely to be damaged or lost when speedily returned.

Director's Headaches

On the fine white page on which you write your philosophy of directing, with it aims and ideals, you must add a footnote: prepare yourself for being burned a the stake, sold down the river, blasted into lunar orbit. Despite your bes planning some ridiculous boner may appear, and in front of a thousand wit nesses. Many others that might have happened will have been averted by you well-trained cast and crew, but one dazzler will occur that will out-shin anything in the checkered history of the amateur stage. When someone says t you, "That was certainly a fine production," and you find yourself replying "What night did you see it?" you are at once a full-fledged member of a vas order. When your embarrassment is greater than you can bear, remember tha there was once a professional production of *Cyrano de Bergerac*. In the powerfu fifth act, where Cyrano sits in the park talking to the lost love of his youth Roxane, an occasional falling of leaves to the ground suggests symbolically tha Cyrano is also in the autumn of his life. One night, however, there was tremendous uproar from the audience: the rigging had slipped, and an overhea platform was slowly coming into view; on the platform were two stage hands each with a bucket, methodically tossing out leaves.

Amateur productions present an interminable flow of problems. Student will need to miss rehearsal, despite their best hopes. An epidemic may g through the cast, laying several people low with flu or sore throat. Som characterizations are sure not to develop so rapidly as others. Once a committe of mothers called on a principal to tell him the director was working the cast to long hours. "You're quite right," he said. "If your committee will give me a lis of the mothers who are complaining, I'll see that their boys and girls are relieved of all further responsibilities in connection with the play." No list ever appeared. That director is doubly blessed who has command support from above, loyalty from below.

Opening Night

Finally the great night arrives, and the crowd gathers. You go into the auditorium, to see what the house looks like. Perhaps you see friends and stop to say hello. Eight o'clock arrives, without your knowing. To your amazement the lights dim; the curtains open; the show starts.

After the first act, you go back stage to tell the cast to speak louder and more distinctly, to pick up their cues. "I hope you didn't mind our starting without you," says the stage manager. "We finished the makeup early and everyone was ready, so when eight o'clock came, we made our check and went ahead."

He is standing there, following his list as the set is being changed. Your ninety-pound freshman is adjusting a spot light. Your makeup chairman is brushing a little powder off the ingenue. Your sound effects boy is sitting there with two pistols: he was always afraid that one might jam, and he wanted another handy. Your prompter takes a fresh grip on the page opening act two.

Of course you don't mind. Gridley may fire when ready. Your part of the show is over. Now it belongs to the students.

The Drama Club

Many schools and colleges sponsor a drama club or workshop as an extracurricular activity. The following outline may prove helpful:[5]

Suggestions for a Dramatic Club

I. Purpose:
  A. To stimulate interest in the theater
  B. To develop an appreciation for the theater
  C. To offer an opportunity for activity in dramatics, if such is not provided in the curriculum
II. Suggested procedure:

  A. Organization

[5]From *The Educational Theatre Journal,* March 1950. Adapted from *Speech and Drama, Tentative Guide for High School Teachers,* New Mexico State Board of Education.

    1. Formation of the organization by students under the counseling and guidance of the teacher
    2. Election of temporary officers at the first meeting
    3. Planning of first meeting so as to accomplish also:
       a. appointment of a constitution committee
       b. discussion of purposes of organization
       c. discussion of time and place of meeting
       d. appointment of program committee to function until permanent committee is provided for under the constitution
    4. Formulation and adoption of constitution as early as possible
    5. Election of permanent officers
    6. Setting up of standards for promotion of members
  B. Program planning
    1. Authorization of a program committee to submit suggestions for activities for the year
    2. Full discussion by the group (A definite theme or goal should be set up towards which the club will work all year.)
    3. Submission of specific plans by the program committee to the group at a later meeting
    4. Appointment of a play-selection committee and other committees
    5. Planning of definite programs for weekly or regular meetings
    6. Consideration of methods of financing activities
       a. production of plays by the group
       b. sponsoring of plays by professional groups
       c. sponsoring of a dramatic artist
       d. sponsoring of dramatic programs from other schools or nearby colleges

III. Suggested activities:
  A. Study of some particular phase of theater
    1. Investigation of international theater
    2. Study of building a role
    3. Study of staging and design
    4. Demonstrations of makeup
    5. Demonstration of the effects of colored lights on colors
  B. Production of skits and one-act plays for group discussion and criticism
  C. Study of new trends in theater
    1. Production of a one-act play in arena-theater style
    2. Experimentation with new types of drama
    3. Experimentation with unit sets
    4. Discussion of changes made to adapt a serious play to musical-comedy technique
  D. Production of a play or public performance
  E. Theater parties with discussion in club meeting later
  F. Trips backstage after attending a college, community, or professional performance
  G. Participation in dramatic festivals
  H. Exchange attendance at dress rehearsals of other groups, followed by critical discussions afterwards

I. Exchange of assembly programs with other schools
J. Cooperation with school clubs in the same area to sponsor dramatic club events or to have joint programs
K. Affiliation with the International Thespian Society

Assignments

1. Work out a production book for a one-act play suitable for presentation in a play festival.
2. Make a list of short plays suitable for classroom, assembly or drama club use.
3. Make a selection of long plays suitable for consideration as one of the major plays of the school year.
4. Make a list of equipment needed for presentation of short plays in the classroom.
5. Make a list of equipment needed for the construction of simple interior and exterior sets.
6. Make a list of equipment needed for the public presentation of long plays.
7. Work out a rehearsal schedule for one of the plays listed under Item 3 above.
8. Make a fifteen-minute report on "My Favorite One-Act Play." Tell briefly the plot of the play, and discuss any special features that make it especially suitable for classroom use, assembly, evening program, television, contest or festival.

Questions for Classroom Discussion

1. What standards should be kept in mind in choosing a play? Are there special requirements for the opening play of the season? Should the play be chosen by the director or by a committee?
2. Should members of the cast and crew be selected by the director or a committee? Do you approve of limiting tryouts only to students who are scholastically acceptable?
3. How can rehearsals be scheduled in a high school largely served by school busses departing promptly at the end of the last period?
4. What are some of the common faults of amateur productions? How can these be avoided?
5. How would you plan a budget for a production in a school which has no reserve funds, and which uses profits for such nondramatic purposes as financing the school annual or the senior trip? What advantages can you see in a system in which the budget is controlled by the drama department, or by the director, with profits going to the general improvement of the dramatic program?
6. What are the short-term and long-term benefits of participation in dramatic activities?

References

Elementary School

Ervin, Jean C. "Bibliography of Dramatics in the Elementary School." *Speech Teacher* November 1954.

Garrison, Geraldine. "Bibliography of Puppetry for the Elementary School." *Speech Teacher* November 1954.

Children's Theater and Creative Drama

Crosscup, Richard. *Children and Dramatics*. New York: Scribner, 1966.

Davis, Jed H., and Watkins, Mary Jane Larson. *Children's Theatre: Play Production for the Child Audience*. New York: Harper & Row, 1960.

McCaslin, Nellie. *Creative Dramatics in the Classroom*. New York: David McKay, 1968.

Siks, Geraldine B. *Children's Literature for Dramatization: An Anthology*. New York: Harper & Row, 1964.

Siks, Geraldine B., and Dunnington, Hazel B. *Children's Theatre and Creative Dramatics*. Seattle: University of Washington Press, 1961.

Viola, Ann. "Drama With and For Children: An Interpretation of Terms." *Speech Teacher* November 1956.

Ward, Winifred. *Playmaking With Children*. 2d ed. New York: Appleton-Century-Crofts, 1957.

Secondary School

Barnes, Grace, and Sutcliffe, Mary Jean. *On Stage, Everyone*. New York: Macmillan, 1961.

Beck, Roy A.; Buys, William E.; Fleishhacker, Daniel; and Grandstaff, Russell J.; *Play Production in the High School*. Skokie, Ill.: National Textbook Corporation, 1968.

Cass, Carl B. *Make-Up for Stage and Television*. Cincinnati: International Thespian Society, 1958.

Evans, Dina Rees. "Lab in Human Behavior." *NEA Journal* September 1951. Ways in which drama contributes to the development of personality.

International Thespian Society, College Hill Station, Cincinnati, O. 45224, issues bulletins about aspects of high school dramatics, makeup, lighting, design, staging, choosing plays, etc. Write for a list.

McNess, Wilma. "An Orientation Course in Creative Skills for First-Year Junior High School Students." *Speech Teacher* March 1953.

National Association of Secondary School Principals. "The Arts in the Comprehensive School." *The Bulletin* September 1962.

Ommanney, Katherine Anne. *The Stage and the School.* 3d ed. New York: McGraw-Hill, 1960.

Perry, Charlotte. "Selecting the Play for a High School Cast." *Dramatics* January 1963. Filled with suggestions of recommended titles.

Pritner, Calvin, ed. *A Selective and Annotated Bibliography for the Secondary School Theatre Teacher and Student.* Washington: American Educational Theatre Association, 1967. This office continually issues new publications; write for a list.

Secondary School Theatre Conference. *A Course Guide in the Theatre Arts at the Secondary School Level.* rev. ed. Washington: American Educational Theatre Association, 1968. A revision of the popular course of study published in 1963.

Southworth, Jan. "An Evening With Shakespeare." *Dramatics* April 1963. Describes the highlights of an evening of scenes from *Julius Caesar, Macbeth, Merchant of Venice,* and others.

Of General Interest

Abrams, Dolores M., ed. *Theatre in the Junior College.* Washington: American Educational Theatre Association, 1965.

Albright, H. Darkes. *Working Up a Part.* 2d ed. New York: Houghton Mifflin, 1959.

Albright, H. Darkes; Halstead, William P.; and Mitchell, Lee. *Principles of Theatre Art.* 2d ed. Boston: Houghton Mifflin, 1968.

American Educational Theatre Association publishes various bulletins. Write for a list.

Arnott, Peter D. *Introduction to the Greek Theatre.* Bloomington: Indiana University Press, 1963.

—— *Plays Without People: Puppetry and Serious Drama.* Bloomington: Indiana University Press, 1964.

Bailey, Howard. *The ABC's of Play Producing.* New York: David McKay, 1954.

Barton, Lucy. *Historic Costume for the Stage.* Boston: Walter Baker, 1961.

Blunt, Jerry. *The Composite Art of Acting.* New York: Macmillan, 1966.

Boleslavsky, Richard. *Acting: The First Lesson.* New York: Theatre Arts, 1933.

Bowman, Wayne. *Modern Theatre Lighting.* New York: Harper & Brothers, 1957.

Brockett, Oscar G. *The Theatre, An Introduction.* 2d ed. New York: Holt, Rinehart & Winston, 1969.

Burris-Meyer, Harold, and Cole, Edward. *Scenery for the Theatre.* Boston: Little, Brown, 1966.

Busfield, Roger M. *The Playwright's Art: Stage, Radio, Television and Motion Pictures.* New York: Harper & Brothers, 1958.

Canfield, F. Curtis. *The Craft of Play Directing.* New York: Holt, Rinehart & Winston, 1963.

Cole, Toby, and Chinoy, Helen Krich, eds. *Directors on Directing.* Indianapolis: Bobbs-Merrill, 1963.

Corson, Richard. *Stage Makeup.* 3d ed. New York: Appleton-Century-Crofts, 1960.

Currie, Fergus G. "Arena Staging on a Shoestring." *Speech Teacher* November 1956.

Dean, Alexander, and Carra, Lawrence. *Fundamentals of Play Directing.* rev. ed. New York: Holt, Rinehart, & Winston, 1965.

Elkind, Samuel. "Principles of Learning: Their Application to Rehearsal." *Speech Teacher* January 1956.

Esslin, Martin. *The Theatre of the Absurd.* New York: Doubleday, 1961.

Gassner, John, and Allen, Ralph G., eds. *Theatre and Drama in the Making.* Boston: Houghton Mifflin, 1964.

Gassner, John. *The Theatre in Our Times.* New York: Crown, 1954.

Gassner, John. *Producing the Play,* with Philip Barber, *The New Scene Technician's Handbook.* rev. ed. New York: Holt, Rinehart, & Winston, 1953.

Gillette, A. S. *An Introduction to Scenic Design.* New York: Harper & Row, 1957.

———. *Stage Scenery: Its Construction and Rigging.* New York: Harper & Row, 1959.

Gunkle, George. "A Way of Talking About Acting." *Speech Teacher* November 1966.

Hake, Herbert. *Here's How: A Guide to Economy in Stagecraft.* New York: Samuel French, 1958.

Heffner, Hubert C.; Selden, Samuel; and Sellman, H. D. *Modern Theatre Practice.* 4th ed. New York: Appleton-Century-Crofts, 1959.

Hewitt, Barnard; Foster, J. F.; and Wolle, M. S. *Play Production: Theory and Practice.* Chicago: Lippincott, 1952.

Macgowan, Kenneth. "The Vital Principle in Playwriting." *Educational Theatre Journal* March 1951.

Macgowan, Kenneth, and McInitz, William. *The Living Stage: A History of the World Theatre.* Englewood Cliffs: Prentice-Hall, 1955.

McCalmon, George. "Theatre," in "The Field of Speech: A Symposium." *Today's Speech* January 1957.

Mersand, Joseph. *Guide to Play Selection.* 2d ed. New York: Appleton-Century-Crofts, 1958.

Nicoll, Allardyce. *The Development of the Theatre.* 4th ed. New York: Harcourt Brace, 1958.

Plummer, Gail. *The Business of Show Business.* New York: Harper & Row, 1961.

———. *Dramatists' Guide to Selection of Plays and Musicals.* Dubuque: William C. Brown, 1963.

Selden, Samuel. *First Steps in Acting.* 2d ed. New York: Appleton-Century-Crofts, 1964.

Selden, Samuel, and Sellman, H. D. *Stage Scenery and Lighting.* 2d ed. New York: Appleton-Century-Crofts, 1959.

Sievers, W. David. *Directing for the Theatre.* Dubuque: William C. Brown, 1965.

Spolin, Viola. *Improvisation for the Theater: A Handbook of Teaching and Directing Techniques.* Evanston: Northwestern University Press, 1963.

Walkup, Fairfax Proudfit. *Dressing the Part: A History of Costume for the Theatre.* rev. ed. New York: Appleton-Century-Crofts, 1950.

Whiting, Frank M. *An Introduction to the Theatre.* 3d ed. New York: Harper & Row, 1969.

The Educational Theatre Journal is indispensable to the director of dramatics. Its news sections inform about what colleges and universities are producing, what conferences are scheduled, what educational theater people are doing. Its frequent articles about Broadway link the educational with the professional stage. Its review section notices new books. It prints articles in which a special play (i.e. by Shaw or Shakespeare) is analyzed. Its topical issues may deal with such subjects as the twentieth-century American theater, or on theater research. Its annual directory contains information about affiliated organizations, regional theater conferences, and associations. It is published by the American Educational Theatre Association (address in Appendix E).

e Educational Theatre Journal (October 1963) for a list of 16-mm. films for use in teaching drama and theater. (Reprints available through AETA or SCA national offices.)

directing debate

*If the decisions of judges are not what they
ought to be, the defeat must be due to the
speakers themselves.*

Aristotle

Debating has competitive and noncompetitive features. Practice sessions with
other institutions, debates in public convocations, and debates before service,
educational, or religious organizations comprise the noncompetitive program.
Debates in leagues and tournaments, with decisions by judges, make up the
competitive schedule. Festivals or clinics in which teams from different institutions take part, striving for "excellent," "superior," and "good" awards include
the principal features of both competitive and noncompetitive programs.

During the year superior members of the debate squad should have opportunity to participate in a competitive or semicompetitive situation so they may
secure expert outside judgment on their performance. Students like to be
associated with competition, or at least they like to be associated with winning;
they like a schedule that has variety, particularly when a possibility arises of
taking trips. They do not like any kind of program in which the same old thing
happens over and over. Competitive activity helps to maintain interest and keep
them at work.

This chapter is primarily concerned with problems arising in selecting a squad
and preparing it to present evidence and argument effectively.

Values of Debate

In an age which is placing high importance on science, teachers are asking anew about the uses of debate. Urging that debate is a proper concern of all good students, A. Craig Baird, one of the distinguished names in the field, writes:

> Frankly, I am prejudiced in favor of this ancient-modern learning by dialectic and controversy. In support of my prejudices, may I quote the recent speeches of three national leaders.
> Dr. James B. Conant, former president of Harvard, spoke before the National Education Association, at Philadelphia, on the topic of the role of education after high school. Said Dr. Conant after analyzing the curriculum, "Above all, it is vital that the spirit of the academic community be such as to foster an interest in current, social, economic, and political problems, and a zest for discussion and debate."
> Senator James William Fulbright . . . spoke on the topic of "American life, its order of values." He demanded that we "test the slogans and shibboleths by free and honest discussion."
> Edmund Muskie, of Maine . . . addressing the Speech Convention in Boston, said that "it is our inescapable conclusion that these collective judgments [of the American people] cannot reflect wisdom, responsibility, and foresight, unless they are subject to the critical analysis and evaluation which are possible only through the process of debate."

Baird calls attention to the vital significance of debate in these words:

> First, liberal or general education is decision-making. The educated man or woman's role, as always, has been that of decision-making. Of all people he or she should see most clearly the proper road and point the way. He is not only to absorb knowledge but to apply it. He is to contemplate, to discuss with himself and others, but to translate his discussion into action. . . .
> Why this emphasis on education as decision-making? Especially in this day of mounting issues, more than ever, these things cannot be shuffled off. As Professor Ralph Perry, of Harvard, put it, "For each problem comes a moment of decision. The choice must be made before it is too late. Otherwise all is meaningless." As we have sped up time, so have we sped up the need for handling these snow-balling problems. Otherwise, as the philosophers say, all is meaningless. Otherwise history passes us by to be manipulated by force or choice.[1]

[1] "Discussion and Debate in the Space Age," *Central States Speech Journal,* Spring 1959, pp. 48-52.

The National High School Question

Since 1927 the Committee on Discussion and Debate Materials of the National University Extension Association has taken the lead in helping secondary schools formulate a question for use during the school year.

The NUEA is a nonprofit corporation whose members come from more than 120 institutions of higher education in the United States, Puerto Rico, and Canada. The Committee on Discussion and Debate Materials is one of its standing committees, operating under broad directives from NUEA. Its permanent office is on the University of Oregon campus. It serves a score or more universities and two-score high school leagues and associations, providing the machinery by which those interested can agree upon a common problem for the national secondary school debate and discussion series. Out of this general problem grow specific questions for discussion and debate and, moreover, a philosophical framework for the discussion of public questions: the curricular validity and integrity of this intellectual exercise. Its sponsorship is an assurance that sound educational goals will prevail.

Over the years, secondary school debaters have had an opportunity to speak in depth in fields such as these:

1965-66: What policy in labor-management relations will best serve the people of the United States?

1967-68: What approaches to combating crime would best serve the people of the United States?

1969-70: What should be the United States military commitment in foreign countries?

Out of each problem area are drawn three debate propositions. Committees make preliminary investigations of each proposed topic, survey available sources of material, examine the opportunities for both affirmative and negative sides, and offer the customary warrants for timeliness, significance, and interest.

The principal publication of the Committee is the *Forensic Quarterly*, edited by Charley A. Leistner and Robert P. Friedman, issued quarterly in April, May, August, and November. The April issue contains an analysis and interpretation of the problem area together with a reading list. Subsequent issues contain articles specially written for high school debaters and discussers. Collectively the four issues are bound in a single volume, *The NUEA Discussion and Debate Handbook,* for library use and permanent reference.

Each year the Committee also sponsors the distribution of thirty or forty additional reference items bearing on the year's problem. These may be books, pamphlets, leaflets, or government documents, some favoring one side, some the other, some furnishing basic exposition necessary for either side. Debate directors can receive announcements of these materials by writing to their state forensic leagues.[2]

Another useful item is the current *Reference Shelf* bearing on the selected question, published by the H. W. Wilson Company. This series, consisting each year of several volumes on controversial topics, includes a volume on the national proposition. Debaters also find useful the *Congressional Digest*, presenting both pros and cons on current issues, and *Current History*, which devotes its summer issues to source materials.

With the increasing popularity of high school debating and the large number of students involved, other handbooks and debaters' aids have been made available. Typically these contain affirmative and negative briefs, excerpted material, and occasionally sample speeches. These materials are generally useful though they need to be used in a way that will contribute to the thinking of the student instead of doing his thinking for him.

The National College Question

Colleges and universities also have national questions for discussion and debate. Each year the directors of forensic activities in colleges and universities submit subjects for the national topic. A committee composed of representatives of the Speech Communication Association, American Forensic Association, Delta Sigma Rho-Tau Kappa Alpha, Pi Kappa Delta, and Phi Rho Pi, is in charge of the study of the nominated questions, and the final selection of the preferred ones. Issues of the *Reference Shelf* and the *Congressional Digest* are prepared and other materials are available, although the operation is not so extensive as at the high school level.

Certain benefits may be noted that come from the use of the agreed upon questions. As most colleges and universities prepare debates on both the college and the high school questions, the problem of scheduling intercollegiate debates is greatly simplified. Some invitational meets and tournaments are held in every part of the country on the national question. A college debate director is likely to receive opportunities to take a team of debaters to another campus and there meet teams from other institutions. By comparing their arguments and techniques with those used by others, the debaters quickly discern what is weak and what is strong.

---

[2]The Director of the national office is Dr. Charley A. Leistner, Room 69, Prince Lucien Campbell Hall, University of Oregon, Eugene 97403. For information about available materials for the school year consult his office or the office of your state high school league.

Many teachers are quick to note, however, that debaters should concern hemselves with a variety of questions. The "same old thing" point is frequently nade. Students can profitably prepare a debate on a different proposition—owering the voting age, or a controversial local issue—and then debate it before highly concerned audience (service club, church group, League of Women 'oters). Each teacher will have to decide for himself, along with his students, vhere to put the emphasis, but he should not overlook this readily available •ption.

Use of Materials

'ollege and high school debaters should have no difficulty finding current naterials. In addition to sources already mentioned, the *Journal of the American 'orensic Association* contains articles on both theory and practice. Its advertis-1g pages list debate texts as well as new publications dealing with the annual uestions. Texts of high school debates, often developed at summer institutes, re also made available each fall.[3] These should be used for the purpose for vhich they are intended: a report of how these debaters developed the issues in single debate. Occasionally students scoop segments of these debates into their wn speeches, without proper credit, which is not only plagiarism, but a variety f plagiarism that will quickly be detected.

Once an argument gets into print, it is subjected to careful scrutiny. Debaters ll over the country will study how they can use it, improve upon it, or attack it. hey will go back to the original documents on which the argument was based: 1e speech, the article, the government report. If statistics are used, they will :study the assumptions or limitations under which they were compiled. In ther words, they will analyze their data as a lawyer preparing a case, an ngineer solving a problem, a legislator about to write a statute: with care, trying) eliminate the bugs, check out the inconsistencies, identify the persuasive rguments, predict the outcome.

Conducting Tryouts

he recruiting of good talent is a problem the director of debating continually ices. Often students do not try out for debate because they do not know about . Ideally debating should begin in the upper elementary and junior high school rades; nearly all experienced directors have freshman as well as varsity squads. eachers of other subjects may help locate good students; speech classes may 1ggest others; publicity through regular school channels may turn up candi-ates. The opportunity to know other students in the school and the possibility f meeting students in other schools are inducements as is the opportunity of

---

'or a list of summer institutes consult the *Journal of the American Forensic Association.*

learning to speak more effectively. Debating may be a stepping stone to law an politics.

By tradition tryouts consist of making a short talk on one side of th question selected. Materials should be made available so that the students wil not lose time in aimless search. After hearing the tryout speeches, you, with th help of whatever faculty committee you ask to advise you, select members fo the squad, keeping usually to multiples of four for convenience in schedulin, practice debates. Students may try out either for the affirmative or negative sid of the question; encourage students to debate both sides. (Many tournaments, i fact, are specifically planned so that each team will debate both sides.) Ofte students do not know which side they favor until they have studied the topi and in the process of making a decision they discuss both affirmative an negative positions.

Preliminary Study of the Question

After the tryouts, the director may schedule meetings at which both sides of th question are discussed. A useful activity is for the squad to prepare a *brief* c outline of both sides of the question. The brief has an introductory par containing definitions and preliminary explanatory matter and a statement c the principal questions, the *issues*. Illustrations of the proper form for a brie may be found in most debate texts. Preparing a brief gives all present a chance t examine both sides of the question, and thus serves to familiarize the studen with the arguments likely to be used. When this task is completed, it will, c course, be only a preliminary brief; the main arguments will be developed i more detail as students gather additional evidence.

Each member of the squad should be taught a method of taking notes, ever one presumably using the same system to facilitate team work later on. . superior method is a card system, each item of evidence being put on a separat 3x5 or larger card. The cards are labeled so they may be filed in a small cabine During a debate each team needs to be prepared to answer arguments offered b the opponents, and often in the order presented by the opponents. As th debater hears these arguments he notes them on his flow sheet and selects fro his card file the necessary evidence to use in reply, so that, when only a fe minutes later he rises to speak, he has materials at hand in a convenient form. they were written on large sheets of paper, several to a page, he could not sele and arrange his rebuttal materials nearly so swiftly.

The sessions devoted to discussion of the question and preparation of th brief can be varied by spending part of the time in short speeches, reports o special aspects of the questions, and impromptu speaking sessions. The proble is twofold: to make the students familiar with the questions and to give the actual speaking practice.

Evidence

Most debates are won on the sheer weight of evidence. Evidence means examples, statistics, quotations from authority, reasons.

Evidence is saying that the amount of world trade increased 11 percent between 1967 and 1968. Evidence is showing that world population is growing at the rate of 2 percent a year, and (predicting) that it will likely double by the year 2006. Evidence is pointing out that crimes of violence have increased in the United States by 57 percent since 1960. Evidence is quoting the Secretary of State on the commitments of the United States in European countries. A team that says "Lots of Americans have been killed in the southeast Pacific"; or that "the extent of infant mortality in the United States is shocking"; or asserts "the post office department is a bankrupt outfit"; is going to look pale and inadequate when compared with itself on the day that it has learned to say, "In the first seven years of the war more than 30,000 United States and allied troops were killed"; "The infant mortality in the United States of 22.1 per 1000 live births is higher than that of half the countries of Europe"; "The postal deficit for the last fiscal year was nearly a billion dollars."

Note however that decisions in debate go to the individuals who can not only amass evidence, but who know how to interpret it, how to construct a valid argument, how to analyze the argument of others. It is not enough to scoop bits and pieces out of handbooks and periodicals; the debater must understand the persuasive process in which he is engaged. Hence students should be taught not only to use evidence, but also to interpret evidence. Any fact is vulnerable to different interpretations. A situation that invariably arises in debating is concerned with *cost*. The figure of $50 billion has frequently been cited as the cost of a decade of astronautics, civilian and military. Those who consider this figure to be reasonable indicate that it is only a fraction of a percent of the G.N.P. Still others compare it with the $12.3 billion annually that Americans spend for liquor, or the $7.9 billion for tobacco. Those who feel that the figure is excessive indicate how it could have been used to feed the hungry, shelter the homeless, educate the ignorant. All of these observations are entirely correct. In my high school debate-directing days, I recall deploring the cost of a single battleship, and calculating how the money could be better used. Kenneth Burke likes to say that nothing is more rhetorical in nature than a deliberation as to what is too much or too little, too early or too late. Debaters continually find themselves on opposite sides of the argument as to whether some course of action costs too much; whether we can afford it. If the issue of cost becomes central, debaters have to resolve it by demonstrating comparative or relative advantages and disadvantages, priorities, etc., just as the individual does when he looks at any price tag. Hence when an opponent introduces evidence into his case, you need to consider how to answer him. You may offer *conflicing evidence* that is more recent or from a better source. You may *interpret his evidence* differently from the way he does. You may *ignore it,* if it does not bear on the central issue.

These possibilities are valid because of the basic nature of debate. Topics chosen resemble problems that arise in life: they are usually matters of policy and, since they look into the future, they cannot be solved precisely one way or another. Debaters should not lose sight of this fundamental principle. How can we answer exactly, for example, the question of missile systems when we do not know when or whether war will come? How can we tell whether to introduce socialized medicine, since we cannot predict the effect of such a plan, five, ten or twenty years from now, upon the medical profession? We can only use our best judgment, weigh the alternatives, and act accordingly. In arriving at this judgment, we use such facts as are available, but a point in the argument always arrives when we have to go beyond the facts and leap into the future.

This idea was firmly impressed on my mind late in my college debating career, and most clearly by a team of high school debaters. These boys had debated together during their last three years in school, and in their senior year had won the state championship without losing the vote of a single judge. I heard this debate, and afterwards asked the boys the recipe for their success. As they discussed their season, they mentioned one thing after another they had learned but one boy finally said something like this: "I believe we knew more about the question than any team we met. We used the most recent evidence on every point. We noticed, as we debated sometimes on the affirmative and sometimes on the negative, that we used many of the same facts on both sides. We interpreted them differently. And we found that the judges were as impressed by our reasoning about the facts as they were by the facts themselves."

I, too, was impressed by the reasoning of this brilliant team. Oliver Wendell Holmes put the same idea in vivid language. A one-story mind, he once wrote, can see simple relationships like obvious groupings and classifications. A two-story mind can see complex relationships like trends and movements. But once in a while a man comes along who interprets his observations in an original manner, formulating hypotheses and generalizations that are bold and striking. That man has a three-story mind, with a penthouse on top.

Debating helps develop this kind of thinking.

Case

The word "case" frequently recurs in debate squad discussions. The case is the principal line of reasoning used to establish a conclusion. The *affirmative case* comprises the chief arguments used to support the debate proposition; the *negative case,* those used to oppose it. The affirmative case is nearly always the more troublesome, because the affirmative is advocating a change in the present

'stem. Affirmative speakers who once advocated woman suffrage, the federal
come tax, the repeal of prohibition, the League of Nations, and universal
ilitary training must have done so with many qualms, although now all are
miliar. Affirmative speakers who once advocated a system of socialized medi-
ne had an equally hard row to hoe; the plan has long been in effect in Great
ritain. Invariably the debate director is satisfied with his negative case long
fore his affirmative case seems convincing. Experience with the national
uestions, however, shows that one side wins about as often as the other.

The researching of a question and the building of affirmative and negative
ses is best managed as a joint enterprise by teacher and students. Each member
 the squad may be assigned an article to read and report on, the teacher using
s judgment as to what kinds of articles to assign, taking advantage of superior
titude or experience wherever he finds it. A series of discussions grounds each
udent in the basic issues of the question. After this point has been attained, the
bater, as he reads further, will see that what he is reading better fits one side
an the other, or supports a point previously discussed, or may even lead to a
odification of a previous conclusion.

I always used the chalkboard a good deal. Two parallel columns of arguments
nerge, one labeled affirmative and the other negative. Roman numerals appear,
olstered by capital letters and Arabic figures. One student, acting as secretary,
eps a copy of what is evolving on the chalkboard; other students keep their
vn sets of notes. Statements are worked over, moved to different parts of the
utline, related bits are combined, duplications are eliminated. Abbreviated
otnotes indicate sources. With a little bit of luck, thought mechanisms will
gin to whirr over the room.

Before long, debaters will see that certain arguments on the affirmative
arply oppose certain arguments on the negative. These suggest the *issues* of the
bate, the high ground that each side will defend. The search is then continued
 accumulate new evidence, or better reasoning, to support the issues. The
sition taken by each team on these issues is its *case*. Individual debaters will
nd to favor one side or the other, but each should see that arguments and
idence support one point of view better than another. When they meet these
sues in actual debate they should have a grasp of the basic assumptions as well
 the supporting reasons.

"Lectures" by the debate director and "reports" by individual debaters have
place, but pointed questions bearing on specific details should feature most
eliminary practice sessions. Arthur N. Kruger has set down a dialogue between
acher and students to illustrate the importance of learning how to support and
 answer arguments.[4]

I contrast this procedure with that used by one of my high school coaches, a
rst-rate school superintendent and a fine friend, who, late one afternoon in the

See: "Directing a Forensic Program" (Chapter 23), *Modern Debate: Its Logic and Strategy.*

basement of the town library, dictated a seven-minute chunk of the speech I wa
to use as the closing affirmative constructive argument. My contribution to th
interscholastic debates that followed was to fend for myself during the fir
three minutes of the constructive case, then swing into the prepared finale. W
were swept out of competition long before the regional tournament.

Still, I do not wish anyone to think that I lost every debate. Two years earlie
our town (pop. 800) had been scheduled to debate against the county seat (po
2400). Neither had ever wasted any affection on the other, and debate was a
good a way to continue the rivalry as any.

The sparring began with the two superintendents, ours offering to host th
debate provided he could select the judges. Later he agreed to let the county se
select one. We chose a former resident of the town and another who was relate
to a local family; that seemed fair enough. The county seat selected a resident c
a third locality, someone we never had heard of; that seemed tricky. The que
tion was that of joining the League of Nations, with us affirming and the count
seat denying. For information we relied largely on broken files of th
Literary Digest, plus interviews with the well-read members of the community
Neither my colleague, a charming girl from the country, nor I had had an
debating experience, but we worked our available resources to the hilt. Th
debate would be held at the Lyric Theater and we expected the place to b
filled. This large hall would tax the strength of my voice, but we could manag
to have the judges seated forward. Our debate coach, one of the loveliest youn
women who ever graced a classroom, thought she would sit next to the thir
judge, just to have a chance to visit with him a little.

One afternoon I read an entertaining account of an experiment involving
man whose stomach had been opened by a gunshot wound. For some reason th
attending surgeon instead of promptly sewing him, used this case as an opportu
nity to observe the digestive function. He would feed him, for example, oatmea
and note the time required for digestion. Roast beef I recall took 3 hours and 4
minutes. Roast pork was the most difficult of all: 4 hours and 40 minutes. Othe
items were also listed.

I rushed the book into the superintendent's office. A German who loved goo
food, he immediately grasped the significance of what I explained to him; sinc
we were obligated to provide the county seat debaters with supper, we shoul
select a meal from this table of digestion. Everybody knew that blood wa
siphoned away from the brain for a period after a meal; very well, we woul
stuff the visitors with selected foods, leading off with roast pork. The superin
tendent's German-born wife could take it from there.

The great day arrived. At the table were the debaters and their coaches. Tw
of our most bewitching classmates, fully in on the plan, waited table. They wer
instructed to make sure that our guests had plenty of the main course and all o
the supplements, such as fried, browned potatoes, and thick, rich German gravy
The visitors rose from the table goggle-eyed. On our part, we ate sparingly, eve
spartanly. We had to hurry to get to the theater on time.

The Lyric was packed. The judges were comfortably seated along the fourth and fifth rows, Miss Lois with the third judge in tow. The chairman opened the debate and introduced the speakers. We of the affirmative did our part real well; Woodrow Wilson at Pueblo could not have been more earnest. The county seat boys spoke like the veterans they were; Henry Cabot Lodge and Hiram Johnson could have done little better. Each speaker was applauded generously. When the debate was over, the audience buzzed excitedly. A contest could hardly be a loser; the decision might go either way. On our side we felt we had countered every argument with something, we had used all the information we had, we had said all we had come to say.

Ushers collected the judges' envelopes and carried them, like banknotes, to the chairman. The buzzing stopped as he opened each envelope and extracted a white slip of paper. He put it on the lectern, to one side; ages later, it seemed, he located another slip, and put it on the other side; the third he placed on top of the first. He still had his own little ceremonial speech to make, thanking one and all, expressing his gratitude that *he* hadn't had to judge the debate, it was that close; and then came the skyrocket: by a vote of 2 to 1, the decision went to the affirmative, the home team. The applause was like thunder, cracking and crackling again and again.

I would like to think that we won the debate on merit, but I must confess grave doubts. In the twenties the selection of judges was a villainous business, and judging itself an occult art. In oratorical contests when I gave Ingersoll's beautiful tribute to Thomas Paine, I was often marked down because Ingersoll was not fit material for school children, and Thomas Paine even worse. College forensics proved to be much more respectably managed. But I graduated, convinced of the fine intellectual challenges offered by sound training in debating. It is no accident that most of a whole generation of speech teachers got their start from extensive participation in college debate. We survived the mediocre judging, and occasionally had the benefit of truly first-class criticism. Now the tournament director must either be prepared to locate competent judges or give up the idea of a tournament. Ballots are becoming more and more complex, but even a good ballot form cannot overcome the handicap of a poor judge. If one team is clearly superior to another, almost any judge can tell the difference, acting on intuition and mother wit if little else. Anyone can judge a horse race if one horse is a length ahead. The trouble comes when debaters are evenly matched.

But to go back to the problem of selecting and arranging arguments on each side of the question. Those who judge debate are interested in seeing whether a good case emerges from each team's discussion. Beginners who have not received proper training sometimes have fair evidence, but a poor case. The debaters do not seem to know how to use their facts to lead to a conclusion.

The case is constantly being modified throughout the debate season. One opponent after another will point up weaknesses that need to be considered. The affirmative case especially undergoes great change between October and May.

Even the negative, however, would find it difficult to win an April debate with November case. The questions picked for nationwide debating have so much substance and such high significance that continued study opens up new possibilities.

Refutation

A debate between two beginning teams that have received inexpert guidance very quickly reveals inexpert training. In such a poorly prepared debate, the first affirmative speech opens with traditional preliminary matter and follows with affirmative arguments. The first negative speech makes no reference whatever to the affirmative speech just heard, but proceeds to the negative argument. The second affirmative speaker continues the affirmative case without reference to the negative speaker. The second negative speaker concludes the negative argument without mention of the affirmative speakers. The four concluding speeches contain some rebuttal material. If the debate is of the cross-examination type, the question and answer periods seem inept and undirected.

In reality the opening speeches are not debate at all; they are a series of unrelated talks. Each speaker had prepared his argument in advance, and did no attempt to make any adjustment to the opponent's speech. Although the first four speeches are referred to as constructive speeches, they should also contain some rebuttal. Sometimes prepared speeches make the debater appear foolish, when he says, "The affirmative may say," when he should say, "The affirmative has said." When these teams have had more experience, they will proceed as follows:

First affirmative: States the question, defines such terms as may be necessary, limits the question to such fields as seem proper, and develops one or two major points in the affirmative case. The reasoning and the evidence are presented convincingly that, when the first speaker has finished, the listener feels that good, solid argument has been advanced.

First negative: Accepts, rejects, or modifies the affirmative definitions as seems advisable. Takes up immediately the major points that the affirmative has presented and refutes them. Takes note of any positions established in cross examination. He may spend a good half of his allotted time attempting to overthrow the affirmative position. Nearly everything he has said up to this point is the result of decisions he made while listening to the first affirmative speaker. He then proceeds to the negative case, and tries to establish one of the major contentions of the negative. By the time he has finished, the listener should feel that there are indeed two sides to the question.

Second affirmative: Spends such time as is necessary in (1) reestablishing the affirmative case, bringing in new evidence if necessary, and refuting the neg-tive's attack against it; (2) overthrowing the negative case as thus far revealed. Spends the rest of his time completing the affirmative case. Spends about a minute at the end in summary, reviewing the affirmative case, and showing wherein the negative attack against it is untenable.

Second negative: (1) Continues the attack upon the affirmative case; (2) reestablishes the negative arguments advanced by his colleague; (3) furthers the negative case; (4) makes a final summary of the debate to date.

During the four rebuttal speeches, debaters concern themselves with the problems of reestablishing their own positions and attacking the opposing positions. Experienced debaters use the plan of putting the two sets of arguments side by side and showing wherein their reasoning is preferable. The closing rebuttal speaker on each side has the important responsibility of summarizing the team's case as it finally stands.

Many speakers have achieved unusual skill in presenting argument. In this country Webster, Calhoun, Clay, Lincoln, Borah, Roosevelt, and Wilson are a few of many whose fame rests in large measure upon skill in political discussion and debate. In Britain such speakers as Burke, Pitt, Gladstone, Disraeli, Lloyd George, and Churchill have shown mastery of the ability to present and refute parliamentary argument.

One of the foremost debaters was Charles James Fox, considered by his contemporaries to be the greatest of the eighteenth century. Nine-tenths of his career was spent on the affirmative, speaking against some established practice. He advocated greater freedom of speech, removal of religious restrictions, the independence of the colonies, the abolition of the slave trade.

Fox's debating talents rested upon many factors worth retelling to debaters. One was that he was fair, honest, generous, unselfish; he had many friends, few enemies. Another was that he took a position in which he strongly believed, even when he had to speak against the government's entrenched majority. He read widely, but he gained most of his information from conversation with those best informed. Undoubtedly facts and reasons gained from personal interview are more timely and up-to-date than those that eventually get into print.

His method of answering an argument is particularly helpful to recount. (1) He would state the opponent's argument as clearly as possible. Often he would make it more forceful than the opponent had. (2) He would show that the argument was an important one, a significant link in a chain. After having clearly stated it and shown its importance, he would then (3) answer it, using all of the argument and evidence at his command. His method stands out in sharp contrast to that of many beginners. The novice is likely to misstate or understate the argument, making it appear less important than it is. Thus if he succeeds in answering it, he appears to have answered only a minor contention. In the act of misstating or understating, he shows an attitude of unfairness, or at least inaccuracy, that listeners will detect. Fox's statement of an opponent's argument was so clear that listeners praised him for it, and were even more impressed when Fox turned the tables and replied to the facts he had just set forth. Sometimes his friends, listening to him state an argument, would say to themselves, "Fox has outdone himself this time: that argument is so good he cannot possibly reply to it"; but he invariably redeemed himself. William Pitt himself said, "Mr. Fox has never been answered."

Persuasiveness

In listening to a debate, a judge often feels that the arguments are equally divided. The evidence for one side seems as convincing as that for the other. Neither team has left a stone unturned. Is there, then, any discernible margin of difference that will warrant a decision?

In life we find ourselves in similar situations. An employer cannot decide which of two men to promote. A shopper cannot decide which of two suits to buy. We consult two doctors, or two lawyers, or two insurance underwriters, and wonder which one is more competent.

In those situations, and in the situation of the two evenly matched debate teams, we eventually give our decision to the person or to the team that is the more credible. We believe certain people more than others; we find them more convincing, more persuasive. Beginning debaters and their directors sometimes overlook this important consideration. A debater should be personable. He should show his good sense, his fairness, his cordiality. A team that rants and raves is less persuasive than a team that reflects good will and a congenial attitude. The act of yielding on one point may put a team in a better position to hold a major contention. It may be wiser to admit that a certain course is dangerous, if it is, and argue that the desirable consequences are worth the risk than to insist that the dangers are trivial.

Attention given to developing a persuasive manner of delivery may be of far-reaching consequence later in life. You are not striving, of course, for glibness, fluency, smoothness, or oiliness; you simply want a frank, open, candid, and cordial presentation of the argument.

Language

Persuasiveness is closely related to the precise use of language. The debater should be as accurate and exact as possible. He should avoid such expressions as "we have proved beyond a shadow of a doubt," because certainty is not possible in advocating a course of action that looks into the unknown future. He should not belittle or ridicule an opponent; speakers in older times used to indulge in abuse, but our knowledge of persuasion today is more profound than theirs.

Experienced debaters try also to avoid jargon. Such phrases as "honorable judges" and "worthy opponents" eventually get trite. Use other adjectives, or none at all. Instead of calling a member of the other team "the first speaker of the negative," or "the speaker who just left the floor," call him by name, or use other phraseology. Avoid over-using technical phrases as "in my constructive speech," and terms such as "case" and "rebuttal."

Generations ago bright students headed for the ministry, the law, or a profession in letters or teaching would be given collections of speeches to be studied as models. Many a young man was presented with a copy of Goodrich's *Select British Eloquence,* or *The World's Great Classics,* or *The Speeches of Thomas Erskine.* The thought was that if the young man read these models assiduously, he would absorb something about the use of language and the structure of argument that he could work over and adapt to his own thinking and speaking. The idea was a solid one, having behind it the endorsement and the practice of hundreds of speakers.

These books have a counterpart in collections of modern speeches and debates. A debate director could profitably spend time improving the language of his debaters; this to be sure is not an exercise for the first meeting of the squad, but may be brought in after case and argument have progressed. Read, for example, passages from American and British speakers to see how they phrased their constructive arguments and their refutation. An excerpt from Gladstone, for instance, slightly reworded, reads like this: "Now, let us try to get at the heart of the argument, which is not very complex although it is extremely interesting." The phrase "heart of the argument" is more appealing than the debater's trite "Now the speaker who just left the floor said—." Gladstone went on to declare that his friends the opponents were tearing the issue into *shreds,* and then, he explained, "they set aside one particular shred . . . with which nothing will ever induce them to part." The word *shred* may be too colorful to suit the preference of some debaters, but the overworked American word *point* has no color at all, and actually little meaning. Still later in the speech Gladstone said: "Is your distinction a real distinction at all? I will, for the sake of argument, and for no other purpose whatever, go with you on this dangerous round of splitting the argument into slices, and I ask you: 'Where will you draw the line?' You draw it [brief explanation]. My proposition is that your line is worthless."[5] If this Gladstonian language seems entirely too Gladstonian, water it down to suit your own taste: "I suggest that your line is too thin to be of use to us this evening."

Study models not to parrot words and phrases but to stimulate thinking about language. Debate has come in for salty criticism by debaters themselves.

These lines come from his well-known speech defending the right of Charles Bradlaugh, a notorious atheist, to a seat in the House of Commons. The speech may be consulted conveniently in Houston Peterson, *A Treasury of the World's Great Speeches,* pp. 560-569.

Diane Soubly, a varsity debater at Wayne State, wrote the Gettysburg Address a a typical debate speech:

Good afternoon, one hundred and ninety-two years ago, according to *Th Oxford History of the American People,* a new nation was formed in the Ne* World. The people who formed that nation had two criteria guiding them liberty and dedication to the proposition of equality of men. Because m: partner and I concur with these criteria, we are resolved that governmen which is of, by, and for the people, should be maintained in the Unite States. To implement this resolution . . .[6]

Tournament Debating

If you plan to enter your team in a tournament, you should secure a copy of it official ballot in order to review standards of judging. The ballot developed ove the years by the American Forensic Association is in wide use. Each debater ca* earn a high score of 25 points and each team 50 points; the decision goes to th team with the higher score.

On such a ballot, one debater may receive a score as follows:

Analysis	.4 (out of 5)
Reasoning and evidence	.4
Organization	.4
Refutation (including cross-examination)	.2
Delivery	.2
Total	.16 (out of 25)

This score would indicate that he was a faithful student of the question but wa weak in defending his position and in delivery (perhaps he spoke too rapidly, o* his words were indistinct, or he showed a lack of conviction). His colleagu* might have received 3-3-3-5-5 for a total of 19, indicating that he did not know so many facts about the question but was more effective in refutation and delivery. The total team score, 16 plus 19, equals 35. If the opponents receivec all 4s and 5s they would amass a total in the 40s, which would give them the decision.

Some tournaments employ a more simple ballot, perhaps consisting only of a sentence as "In my judgment the —— team did the better debating," but the other type of ballot is proving popular because it makes possible a comparison between members of a team and between teams.

[6] Read the complete speech in Ronald H. Carpenter, "Style and Emphasis in Debate," *Journal of the American Forensic Association,* Winter 1969, p. 28. Dr. Carpenter urge debaters to free their style of certain debate formalisms.

AMERICAN FORENSIC ASSOCIATION DEBATE BALLOT

Affirmative_____Negative_____

Check the column on each item which, according to the following scale, best describes your evaluation of the speaker's effectiveness, and indicate the *rank* for each speaker in the space following his name.

1—poor   2—fair   3—adequate   4—good   5—superior

	1st Affirmative 1 2 3 4 5	2d Affirmative 1 2 3 4 5	1st Negative 1 2 3 4 5	2d Negative 1 2 3 4 5
Analysis				
Reasoning and evidence				
Organization				
Refutation*				
Delivery				

Total_____   Total_____   Total_____   Total_____

*If a cross-examination debate, this should incorporate evaluation of the cross-examination.

Team Ratings: AFFIRMATIVE: poor   fair   adequate   good   superior
                 NEGATIVE: poor   fair   adequate   good   superior

COMMENTS: COMMENTS:
1st Aff. (name)_____rank ( )   1st Neg. (name)_____rank ( )

2d Aff. (name)_____rank ( )   2d Neg. (name)_____rank ( )

In my opinion, the better debating was done by the_____.
                                              (affirmative or negative)

_____
(judge's signature and school)

In "A Study of the Criteria Employed by Tournament Debate Judges," Kim Giffin analyzed weightings given by thirty-four judges to items usually considered in judging debates.[7] The composite summary follows:

Item	Weight
1. Selection of logically defensible arguments (case)	19.10%
2. Support of arguments with information (evidence)	17.18
3. Perception of irrelevant or irrational arguments (refutation)	17.00
4. Ability to analyze the topic-area (analysis)	14.78
5. Ability to speak well (delivery)	14.65
6. Ability to organize ideas	8.88
7. Clear and concise phrasing	5.29
8. All other criteria	3.12
Total	100.00%

A director preparing a team for tournament participation should give attention to all aspects of debating. Each team will try to anticipate possible arguments of the opposition, and work out, in advance, ways of meeting them. Each member of the team will give attention to his own presentation. Fairness and accuracy of statement (bold, sweeping generalizations are usually not well received by the judges), an abundance of evidence, a reasonable interpretation of that evidence, an attitude of courtesy to the opponents, a delivery that carries conviction, are standards that each debater should try to attain.

Some teachers will want to host a tournament in their own school. The experience is a valuable one since it gives students an opportunity to learn to manage not only the administrative details that are involved in a contest but also to exercise the courtesies that go with being host. Most state leagues can supply materials about how to run a debate tournament. These should be studied assiduously. An ill-managed tournament is frustrating. Teacher and students should think through every phase, from welcome and registration to criticism sessions and posting of decisions—not forgetting check rooms, food functions, timekeepers, chairmen, guides and other troubleshooters, and, most important of all, expert judges.

How Much Contest Debating?

As with all kinds of extracurricular activity, the teacher must make a basic decision about the *amount* of contest debating. The preparation of a debate can

[7]*Speech Monographs,* March 1959, pp. 69-71.

become so absorbing that the student may find himself spending study time that should go to other kinds of school work. Tournaments are usually held during the weekend, so what with preparation time, driving time, and tournament time, the student will expend a considerable amount of his available Friday-to-Monday energy. As materials become available in late summer, the debating season may turn out to be as long as the football and basketball seasons put together. Even parents who fully appreciate the values of debating realize that their sons and daughters must maintain good classroom grade averages in order to be eligible for admission to college and university. The problem is one for the teacher to consider and discuss with the students concerned.

Cross-Examination Debating

In many tournaments the cross-examination debate is popular. Historically a development of the Oregon plan of debating, it follows this procedure:

1. The first affirmative speaker opens with an eight-minute constructive speech.
2. The second negative speaker questions the first affirmative speaker for three minutes.
3. The first negative speaker follows with an eight minute constructive speech.
4. The first affirmative speaker questions the first negative speaker for three minutes.
5. The second affirmative speaker follows with an eight-minute constructive speech.
6. The first negative speaker questions the second affirmative speaker for three minutes.
7. The second negative speaker follows with an eight-minute constructive speech.
8. The second affirmative speaker questions the second negative speaker for three minutes.

Rebuttal speeches then follow:

. Negative rebuttal by first negative speaker, four minutes.
. Affirmative rebuttal by first affirmative speaker, four minutes
. Negative rebuttal by second negative speaker, four minutes.
. Affirmative rebuttal by second affirmative speaker, four minutes.

With these time limits, the debate lasts sixty minutes. Variations are to cut the length of the constructive speeches to seven or six minutes, and to increase questioning periods from three to four minutes. By reducing time limits, the debate can be adapted to a forty-five- or fifty-minute class period.

The attractive feature of this style of debating is the confrontation during the question-answer period. By common consent, the questioner is given command of the time; he may interrupt his opponent to indicate that he wants briefer

answers. He should attempt to reveal weaknesses in the opposition case that ca
be exploited in refutation. By the same token he may be able to frame question
that bring out the strong points in his own case. The opponent should answe
succinctly and to the point; he should not drag out his answers; he may o
course request that the question be clarified. Both the questioner and hi
opponent should display the utmost courtesy. Ill-mannered questions or re
sponses are certain to be taken note of by the critic and by other listeners.

Preparation for this type of debating will need to be fully as rigorous as fo
conventional types. In order to know what questions to ask, the debaters wil
need to detect the implications of the opponents' case as quickly as it i
unfolded. They do this in any debate, but in the cross-examination type thei
first reactions will take the form of questions rather than statements. Th
opponents in their turn will need to defend their position on the spot at its mos
vulnerable points. Most debaters find this form of debate more demanding, an
will, accordingly, need special guidance during their practice sessions.

The realistic nature of the cross-examination debate will be noted at once
The questioner is behaving much like the lawyer in the courtroom, the salesmar
dealing with an inquiring customer, the speaker during the forum period, the
legislator during committee discussion.[8]

Campus Debating

Although colleges and universities expend a good deal of time and energy ir
debating the national question, since this policy facilitates their scheduling
debates with other institutions at various kinds of invitational tournaments, they
will find it interesting to schedule a campus debate on a current topic. If in some
way students seek to alter a part of the educational program, they can through
the debate type of confrontation air views on both sides of the issue. Ethnic
studies, grading systems, residence hall regulations, censorship of student publications, recreational facilities, are topics that come to mind. An intramura
contest might be organized around a question of campus interest.

Owen Peterson has reviewed some benefits of this type of debating.[9] He
suggests provocative topics:

Resolved, that modern art does not communicate.

Resolved, that college fraternities have outlived their usefulness.

Resolved, that most coeds should not be in college.

---

[8]For a general discussion of cross-examination techniques in law that may be applicable to
debate, see Raymond S. Beard, "Legal Cross-Examination and Academic Debate,'
Journal of the American Forensic Association, Spring 1969, pp. 61-66. A list of do's and
don't's and a sample cross-examination appear in Kruger, *Modern Debate,* Chapter 24.

[9]"Forum Debating," *Speech Teacher,* November 1965. p. 287.

Resolved, that freshmen should not be permitted to bring cars on campus.

Resolved, that Campus Security deserves the respect and support of the student body.

Resolved, that religion has failed to meet the challenge of the twentieth century.

Resolved, that coexistence with communism is impossible.

Resolved, that sororities and fraternities wield too much influence on this campus.

Resolved, that the teaching profession is a haven for the incompetent.

Winning and Losing

Various references in this chapter are made to the idea of "winning" or "losing" contest. Winning is not all-important. Once I sat near a university friend listening to his team debate another. His team was awarded the decision and he spent a moment in thought. Finally he said, "That makes 372 won and 151 lost, or a lifetime average of point seven one one." That statement seemed to put the emphasis exactly where it does not belong. The real purpose of discussion and debating is to familiarize students with public questions, and especially to train them to talk about these questions intelligently. That purpose would seem to be the essence of democracy itself.

The occasional scheduling of decision contests, whether as part of a tournament or not, makes the process more intriguing and stimulating for young people. The pursuit of long-time goals becomes tedious, but the substitution of a short-term goal that is immediately rewarding arouses new incentive. Competitive discussion and debating are rewarding; in any tournament where several teams are entered, certain teams slowly emerge as outstanding, and those students receive great encouragement. Those who do not fare so well often leave with a determination to do better the next year. In life there is a certain amount of winning and losing, and teachers hope that competition at school makes individuals better winners and better losers. Often festivals are scheduled instead of tournaments, so that participants can be given recognition without making necessary the hairline decisions that sometimes appear in formal competition. The important factor is to keep the idea of winning in its proper perspective.

Assignments

. Construct a brief on a current national question.

. Compile a list of suitable references on a current national question.

. Work out a unit in debate, suitable for use in a high school or college class.

4. Work out a plan for the management of a debate squad.

5. Work out a plan for a season's debate program, considering both tournamen and campus debates.

Questions for Classroom Discussion

1. Discuss the advantages and disadvantages of tournament debating.

2. Discuss the pros and cons of a tournament in which each team debates botl sides of the question.

3. Discuss: "Democracy can work successfully only when the majority o individual citizens understand the questions to be decided by their govern ment and are able to recognize how and why they want these questions to b decided" (James P. Warburg, *The West in Crisis,* New York, Doubleday, 1959 p. 28). What is the role of *debate* in democracy?

References

Of General Interest

Baird, A. Craig. "Discussion and Debate in the Space Age." *Central State Speech Journal* Spring 1959.

Bauer, Otto F. *Fundamentals of Debate: Theory and Practice.* Chicago: Scott Foresman, 1966.

Braden, Waldo W. "Notes on Debating in the British Isles." *Quarterly Journal o Speech* October 1958. Describes debating procedures at Cambridge, Dublir London, and elsewhere.

Capp, Glen R., and Capp, Thelma R. *Principles of Argumentation and Debate* Englewood Cliffs: Prentice-Hall, 1965.

Ehninger, Douglas. "Debate as Method: Limitations and Values." *Speec Teacher* September 1966.

Ehninger, Douglas, and Brockriede, Wayne. *Decision by Debate.* New York Dodd, Mead, 1963.

Fearnside, W. Ward, and Holther, William B. *Fallacy: The Counterfeit of Argc ment.* Englewood Cliffs: Prentice-Hall, 1959. Excellent for explanations an examples.

Freeley, Austin J. *Argumentation and Debate: Rational Decision Making.* 2d ec Belmont, Calif.: Wadsworth, 1966.

Huber, Robert B. *Influencing Through Argument.* New York: David McKay 1963.

Kerr, Harry P. *Opinion and Evidence: Cases for Argument and Discussion.* Nev York: Harcourt, Brace & World, 1962.

Kruger, Arthur N. *Modern Debate: Its Logic and Strategy.* New York: McGrav Hill, 1960.

McBurney, James H., and Mills, Glen E. *Argumentation and Debate.* 2d ed. Nev York: Macmillan, 1964.

Miller, Arthur B. *Elements of Deliberative Debating.* Belmont, Calif.: Wadsworth, 1969.

Moulton, Eugene R. *The Dynamics of Debate.* New York: Harcourt, Brace & World, 1966.

Murphy, James J., and Ericson, Jon M. *The Debater's Guide.* Indianapolis: Bobbs-Merrill, 1961.

Musgrave, George M. *Competitive Debate: Rules and Techniques.* 3d ed. New York: H. W. Wilson, 1957.

Newman, Robert P., and Newman, Dale R. *Fundamentals of Argument.* Boston: Houghton Mifflin, 1965.

Peterson, Houston. *A Treasury of the World's Great Speeches.* New York: Simon & Schuster, 1954.

Summers, Harrison B.; Whan, Forest L.; and Rousse, Thomas A. *How to Debate: A Textbook for Beginners.* 3d. ed. New York: H. W. Wilson, 1963.

The Reference Shelf. New York: H. W. Wilson. Pros and cons on the annual N.U.E.A. debate topic.

Thomas, Gordon L. "A Survey of Debate Practices in Michigan High Schools." *Central States Speech Journal* May 1965.

Toulmin, Stephen E. *The Uses of Argument.* Cambridge: Cambridge University Press, 1964.

Ulman, Ruth, ed. *University Debater's Annual.* New York: H. W. Wilson. A well-known series.

For a list of magazines (with addresses) used by debaters, see Appendix D.

Note: The *Journal of the American Forensic Association* publishes occasional verbatim reports of selected debates, which could serve as models for study. It also publishes a calendar of college and university speech meetings.

Strategy Procedures

Capp, Glenn R.; Huber, Robert; and Ewbank, Wayne C. "Duties of Affirmative Speakers: A Symposium." *Speech Teacher* March 1959.

Giffin, Kim, and Megill, Kenneth. "Stock Issues in Tournament Debates." *Central States Speech Journal* Autumn 1960.

Kruger, Arthur N. "Logic and Strategy in Developing the Debate Case." *Speech Teacher* March 1954.

Nebergall, Roger E. "The Negative Counterplan." *Speech Teacher* September 1957.

Peterson, Owen. "Forum Debating." *Speech Teacher* November 1965.

Thompson, Wayne N. "In Answer to the First Affirmative." *Proceedings of the 17th Annual Summer Speech Conference.* Ann Arbor: University of Michigan, 1957.

———. "The Effect of a Counterplan upon the Burden of Proof." *Central States Speech Journal* Autumn 1962.

planning the
assembly program

*On the whole the last week had not been
quite as awful as he had expected.*

Evelyn Waugh

The place of the assembly program on the high school calendar is well established. Its purposes are significant: to develop school spirit, to present educational and cultural themes, to offer recreation, to demonstrate and motivate the work of classes, to serve as public relations between school and community. The assignment of organizing and directing it is often made to a teacher who has been attached to the school system long enough to appreciate its resources. Since few special courses dealing with assembly programs are available, the teacher has to amplify his own experience. The purpose of this chapter is to offer suggestions.

Make a Year's Calendar

Making a calendar for the year gives a first look at the size of the job. No one can sit down in August and work out a complete program; special opportunities arise later on that can be utilized. A well-known person arrives in town on Tuesday, for example, and is persuaded to address the school on Wednesday. A university glee club goes on tour and writes the school in February that it will be available for an engagement in March. Windfalls like these can be presented without rehearsal. Nevertheless, chart a tentative schedule; you will want other

369

teachers to plan programs for you, and if you book your colleagues in advance, they can make adequate preparation. In your planning you may have the help of a committee of teachers and students.

If your institution has an assembly every week, you may have thirty or more programs to plan. Some of them may be traditional such as an installation or honors assembly. Still others may be routinely scheduled: the opening assembly, largely official; pep assemblies, scheduled with an eye to the sports calendar; any traditional assembly. With a full calendar, you can better resist the appeals of pressure groups or those whose ideas are not well thought out. Planning a year ahead may seem unnecessarily farsighted, but most institutions must look two, three, or five years into the future. A colleague may have special reason for wanting to contribute to an assembly the following year instead of this year. The school or the community may have an anniversary coming up in two or three years, or you may want to observe national events like the bicentennial of the Declaration of Independence.

Popular Types of Programs

Following are types of assemblies that students seem to like.

Holidays. A year's program could be built around holidays, anniversaries, and other special days if it were wise to do so. Labor Day, Columbus Day, Armistice Day, Halloween, Thanksgiving, Navy Day, King's, Washington's, and Lincoln's birthdays, and Memorial Day are only a few. Yet many teachers find it difficult to locate original materials for special programs. Sometimes a one-act play is suitable. *When the Chimes Rang* fits the Christmas season. Another solution would be to have a number of events on each program. A Thanksgiving assembly, for example, might feature selections by the glee clubs, a solo, a short talk, a simple dramatization or pageant.

One school worked out an original theme for the East season. Along with well-chosen Easter music appeared a series of three talks: one by a minister, one by a priest, and one by a rabbi. The Protestant and Catholic speakers told what the Easter season meant to their faiths; the rabbi reviewed the observance of Passover, which comes at that season of the year. The assembly attracted favorable attention throughout the community. Note that in some communities this or other kinds of religious programs might be unacceptable.

Speakers. A good speech constitutes one of the best programs. Not all speakers, however, can capture the enthusiasm of the assembly audience, which includes a wide range of ages and interests, from freshmen to parents and teachers. If a good speaker is available, schedule him. Some speakers especially like to talk to high school audiences.

Home talent or hobby shows. The home talent or vaudeville show is an entertaining assembly. Have a tryout at which you invite prospective dancers, singers, magicians, comedians, instrumental soloists, and hobbyists to give a sample of what they can do. From this tryout, select a well-rounded bill. Serve it up with a master of ceremonies and an orchestra in the pit, and your assembly hour will pass enjoyably. Arrange special rehearsal for timing, to avoid delays between the individual items. A soloist might perform in front of the curtain while the scenery is being changed behind it. Choose a variety of individual numbers so as to please a variety of tastes. Give special attention to the opening number, to get the program off to a good start, and to the closing number, to set the mood with which the program ends.

One-act plays. A one-act play running thirty or forty minutes is about the right length for an assembly program. Considering that the audience consists of students of different ages, select a play with good plot: comedy, mystery, or drama. This type of program may require two weeks to prepare, but if your speech class or drama club has a play at hand, it can be made available for assembly presentation.

Traditional assemblies. Most schools have developed traditions over the years in connection with assemblies. One school has a program each spring at which the new officers of the various clubs and honor societies are installed. Each outgoing officer relays the emblem of his authority to his successor. Another school has an assembly to award the year's honors. Each activity and each subject matter field is represented. Outstanding students in commercial subjects, art, language, social studies, mathematics, science, English, speech, agriculture, home economics, industrial arts, and so on are given recognition for having made the best grades, written the best essay, or completed some other project. Letters or certificates may be presented. Winners of scholarships are announced. Special awards, like those for the most popular boy or girl, or for the boy or girl who has contributed most to the school, are handed out. Some of the honors may have been won earlier in the year but are included in the special program. The school song is played by the band; the students take a pledge of allegiance. Sometimes the traditional assembly is conducted by the outgoing class in honor of the juniors.

If the school does not have an honors assembly, the faculty or student government may consider instituting one. For at least 25 percent of the students, high school represents the end of the road so far as formal training is concerned. The high school diploma is the last they will receive. The assembly can symbolize a part of their educational experience.

Demonstration by science classes. Much that is magical and mystifying occurs in experiments conducted daily in science classes. Students normally become familiar with only one science; a program like this may interest them in other sciences. Chemistry and physics may have the most spectacular experiments to contribute, but botany, biology, and general science may also plan stunts or demonstrations.

This type of assembly is not limited to science classes. Almost any subject matter field has materials of interest if someone digs them out. Demonstrations by agriculture or vocational classes, or skits or pageants by Latin classes, have entertaining and instructive possibilities. English classes have unlimited resources, from business correspondence to *Macbeth*. Overdoing these programs may make assembly too much like school, but a few deserve a place on the schedule.

Music assemblies. Programs can be developed from the musical talent of the school. Glee clubs, orchestras, bands, a cappella choirs, and vocal and instrumental quartets contribute an important part in the year's processing of assemblies. A musical offering should have variety: it should strike a balance between the serious and the popular, and should intersperse solo performances among group numbers. Musical numbers may be contributed by outside organizations, principally vocal or instrumental groups representing colleges or universities. Institutions like to get their name before prospective graduates, and students benefit by hearing older visitors.

Debate, open forum assemblies. A debate on a lively subject with an audience vote makes a good program. The debate may be of the conventional type, although a popular form is the cross-question debate. Panel discussions or student forums may be substituted for formal debate. Discussions of this type seem welcome when the qeustion is an urgent issue. Call it a teach-in if you like.

Exchange assemblies. An idea not sufficiently exploited is that of exchanging assemblies with other schools. Work out the arrangements in advance so that both schools can prepare adequately.

Contest assemblies. The possibilities of contests have been suggested in other chapters. An assembly is a good place to conduct the finals of speaking, declamation, acting, or poetry reading contests.

Athletic honor assemblies. The school's athletes may be given a place on the assembly schedule. The year's records may be reviewed and awards presented. Or the assembly may take the form of a demonstration or wrestling, boxing, tumbling, fencing, and other sports.

National Library Week suggests an opportunity to talk about books. Recognition can be extended to the winners of the best essays or the best speeches on the value of a personal library, or other topic.

Pageants. Occasionally a school has a faculty member experienced in writing pageants. A pageant about the early days of the community, or other historical event, may be an impressive spectacle. It requires extensive rehearsal and preparation, but has the advantage that successive scenes are presented by different groups, so that no one group has too much to learn.

Faculty assemblies. At some schools the faculty regularly puts on a show for the students. It may be a full-length play, the receipts going to a cherished project. At other schools it is a vaudeville show, musical comedy, variety show, or minstrel. If the faculty has a regular evening performance, excerpts from it may be presented at assembly; or if it is not that elaborate it may be presented as an assembly instead of as a full-dress evening show.

Programs with a central theme. From Doris Niles, speech instructor at Will Rogers High School, Tulsa, comes this suggestion: Do not merely present a succession of talent numbers—weave them into a theme. Students in speech classes, she adds, are imaginative in creating and planning these. The central theme for a Christmas Talent Assembly, for example, was: "Exclusive Showing of Fabulous Imported Children's Gifts from Marcum Niemus's Fifth Floor Toy Bazaar." An assembly for the annual American Education Week program featured speech students on "Better Human Relations Through Sharpened Tools of Thinking," with vignettes on tools of thinking entitled "Accurate Maps," "Adequate Maps," "So Far as I Know," "Up to a Point," "The What Index," "The When Index," and other items from general semantics.

The assembly program at Will Rogers High School has become, under Miss Niles's direction, an important part of high school life. The school year opens with a Student Council Welcome Assembly. Preparation begins in May with many parts assigned then. After a traditional assembly ritual, are welcoming speeches from the council, the principal, and the class presidents. Responses are made by sophomore leaders who have won these roles on a competitive basis. Foreign exchange students, introduced by their hosts are also welcomed. The hour gets the school off to a good start and gives new students a sense of belonging.

For Will Rogers' thirtieth anniversary, students built a program around the theme of "shapes" which they called "The Shape of Things." As a part of the opening ceremony, a huge cut out of the number 30 was dropped from the grid, the stage being lighted to show only the 30. Thus the shape of the 30 set the stage for other shapes. In "Animal Shapes" the performers dressed to suggest animals in the songs used. "Motley Shapes" was a spoof on Shakespeare but with classical ballet, harp, and piano numbers included. Other acts were entitled "Mod Shapes," "Lunar Shapes," and the finale, "The Shape of Things to Come." Three hundred and fifty students took part in the program.[1]

[1] I express my deep appreciation to Doris Niles for these and other materials.

Showmanship Is Important

The assembly program should be produced with showmanship. A part of this showmanship is to begin on time. As soon as the audience convenes, start the show; that in itself eliminates a certain amount of audience restlessness. If there are several parts, see that one part follows another without delay. If the curtains have to be drawn to change the scenery, have the changes executed speedily; otherwise, plan a specialty number in front of the curtain to mask the delay. Fast-moving, well-timed programs take organization, but are worth the effort. Another aspect of assembly showmanship is to advertise the program by intriguing posters.

Speakers, musicals, and educational demonstrations are all good, but too many of any one kind become wearisome. Students even become tired of entertainment; serious or inspirational programs have an important place. Sometimes variation needs to be introduced even in the same forty-five minute period.

Public Relations and the Assembly

A faculty may give thought to the possibility of making the work of the school better known in the community. Parents do not like to visit classes, feeling that they will be conspicuous. Only a concerted visitors' day will get response from fathers and mothers. Many do not know the teachers of their children.

One reason why athletic events attract attention is that they appeal to adults. Alumni who cheered for Tigers or Wildcats when in school come again to see the team play. Public music recitals and dramatic performances have the same important function. They present an opportunity for fathers, mothers, and friends to see what the school is doing. Homecoming has a similar purpose, though the occasion is often overshadowed by a football game; a teacher of speech may well schedule a homecoming of his own, inviting for a special assembly program those who have studied with him in past years. A number of teachers have inaugurated this plan of a homecoming of former speech students, debaters, and members of play casts and crews.

The assembly can be a powerful factor in the life of the community. Few schools have exploited the potentialities of this opportunity. If the auditorium has seats to accommodate fifty or a hundred patrons in addition to the students, a way may be devised to secure visitors on assembly days. The project will need attention to publicity as well as to rehearsal, but the result will be worth the effort.

Assignments

1. Construct a schedule of assembly programs for the academic year.
2. Draw up detailed plans for one of the following assemblies:
   a. Columbus day.
   b. Armistice day.
   c. Thanksgiving.
   d. Lincoln's birthday.
   e. Washington's birthday.
   f. Memorial day.
   g. An athletic honor assembly.
   h. An academic honor assembly.
   i. A panel discussion on a current topic.
   j. A vaudeville or home-talent show.
   k. Recognition day.
   l. An assembly featuring the work of one department: home economics, shop, history, English, science, etc.
   m. An assembly featuring a country: Canada, Mexico, France, Germany, Spain, Russia, China, Japan, India, etc.
   n. A TV variety show.

Question for Classroom Discussion

1. Consider the time spent in the preparation and presentation of assembly programs. Can you justify this activity educationally?

References

Blackburn, Mary. "The Speech Teacher and the High School Assembly Program." *Quarterly Journal of Speech* February 1947. Specific suggestions for the assembly hour.

Niles, Doris. "The Beginning Speech Teacher as Director of the High School Assembly." *Speech Teacher* November 1961.

Ogilvie, Mardel. "Assemblies in the Elementary School." *Speech Teacher* March 1956.

—— Chapter 15. *Teaching Speech in the High School.* New York: Appleton-Century-Crofts, 1961.

Skinner, Theodore. "Suggestions for the High School Assembly." *Quarterly Journal of Speech* December 1947. General principles and suggestions for assembly programs.

Thompson, Nellie Zetta. *Vitalized Assemblies: 200 Programs for All Occasions.* New York: E.P. Dutton, 1952.

Weirich, Dorothy Q. "Participating in Community Affairs." *Speech Teacher* November 1969. This article does not discuss assembly programs as such but does suggest a variety of programs in which students can appear before community audiences.

contests and festivals

*I have begun several things many times
and I have often succeeded at last. . . . Though I
sit down now, the time will come when you
will hear me.*

Benjamin Disraeli (1837)

At last I have climbed the greasy pole.

Benjamin Disraeli (1868)

*'Twas I that beat the bush,
The bird to others flew.*

George Wither

An important part of the program in high school and college is participation in speech and drama activities. These provide intense and relevant experience not always possible in the classroom. Group activity contests in debating have already been discussed. This chapter will concern itself with other events.

The rationale for contest and festival participation is compounded out of *motivation, reinforcement,* and *excellence.* Motivation as a part of the learning process has already been mentioned. The contest, the festival, the tournament offer immediate opportunity to study, practice, and rehearse. Reinforcement is also a part of the learning process. The decisions of the judge or critic are quickly announced. Strengths and weaknesses are promptly identified. Both the good and the not-so-good are made aware of opportunities for improvement. Whether the rewards are in the form of rankings (first, second) or in the form of ratings (superior, excellent), the competitive factor is keen enough to make the effort worthwhile. Excellence becomes the standard around which students and teachers rally. Hopefully everyone profits from the experience so that next time he will do better. The slogan of the Wisconsin High School Forensic Association has long been: "Not to defeat each other, but to pace one another on the road to excellence."

Contests may be outlets for both the superior student as well as the novice. In them he gets an opportunity to compare his talent to that of the best students from other institutions. He is exposed to judgments from teachers whose backgrounds and experiences differ from those of his own teachers.

Admittedly the competitive feature has disadvantages. Overly ambitious teachers may exploit a few talented students and not allow the activity to proceed on as broad a base as it should. When too much emphasis is placed on winning and on the accumulation of awards, the school suffers. Aside from these complaints, the feeling may also persist among student and faculty that too much emphasis is placed on competition. The move toward free universities, noncredit courses, Pass-Fail grading, are trends that each teacher will have to study at his own institution.

As repeatedly urged in this book, teachers should exploit the learning features of contests and minimize the competitive aspects. Extrinsic motivation usually produces little effect on the learning process. Alexander A. Schneiders notes that these stimuli may cause a temporary spurt in learning or studying but cannot sustain an ongoing process such as learning for any length of time. "Only such things as the value of an education, realization of future goals, intellectual interest, and personal satisfaction will sustain the learning process," he observes.[1]

So, as ever, we need balance and proportion. Competition is a striking feature of business and professional life. On every side are awards: Nobel, Bancroft, speaker-of-the-year, halls of fame, conference titles, Olympic games, belts, honorary offices and degrees, distinguished alumni. Might as well learn that a few win, the rest lose; no matter how good, someone else is better; don't look now, someone might be gaining. A lesson emerges: every life, no matter how glorious, tastes its disappointments (Lincoln, Wilson, Churchill). The real test is to be able to set to one side both the excitement of winning and the misery of defeat and, clutching the lesson-strenuously-learned, move on to other tasks.

The classroom teacher is the leading edge of the competitive enterprise. He has to live with his students whether they win or lose. And really there is no good way to console a young loser; I have been exposed to the efforts of experts. It always seemed to me as a contestant that anything one could learn by losing he could learn just as well by winning. Nor did there seem to be any glory quite like winning. I grew up in a time when contestants spoke to full auditori-

---

[1] *Adolescents and the Challenge of Maturity: A Guide for Parents and Teachers*, p. 154. *See also:* Chapter 11, "Helping Adolescents in School, at Work, and at Play."

ums and when the winners were the talk of the town. What I did learn was that the world forgets both wins and losses as, sooner or later, you do yourself.

Contests certainly teach the value of *careful, disciplined preparation and rehearsal.* The student must research with accuracy and thoroughness. Nothing must be left to chance. Contests also reward the virtues of *imagination* and *creativity.* The student with the different approach, the new insight, the bold touch, will likely succeed where others falter. If he can combine these qualities with sense and judgment, he will avoid the reaction, "It's fine if you happen to like it," and hear the other reaction, "It's truly fine."

Effective communication is the key test. "Self-conscious display of voice, gesture, or any other speech technique is the fatal error," say the teachers who prepare the West Virginia Interscholastic Forensic League *Newsletter.*[2] "The final test is the ability of the speaker to make the audience forget this is a contest," say, repeatedly, the teachers who advise Nebraska contestants.[3] Speech activities "create a more responsible citizen by offering realistic situations of judicious listening, intelligent speaking, and mature patterns of behavior; [they develop] leadership abilities . . . [and] appreciation of excellence," say the directors of Wyoming contests.[4]

Original Public Address

In this activity the student prepares an original speech on a timely subject. Most tournaments state that the central theme should be persuasive in nature, but critics have come to expect that the purpose should be to intensify a belief already held by most people rather than to win listeners over to a different belief. Critics also look for supporting evidence, thus warranting that the speech has a logical as well as an emotional content.

Standard length for this event is ten minutes, although on this point the rules of the specific contest need to be consulted. Special penalties may be assessed if the contestant speaks overtime. Not more than one hundred words or so may be quoted (again, see the rules of the specific contest), and what is quoted must be clearly cited. Memorization is usually mandatory; if the contestant departs from the prepared script he must still not exceed the time limit. A manuscript of the speech must be deposited with the tournament committee on or before a specified date; this rule reduces the temptation to plagiarize.

Some tournaments call this event "Contemporary Public Address" and allow minimum notes. All in all the rules are clearly set forth so that each contestant will be doing about the same thing.

October 1966, p.7.
Thirty-Second Annual Yearbook, Nebraska School Activities Association, p. 31.
Handbook of the Wyoming Speech Association and the Wyoming High School Activities Association, p. 2.

Choice of topic is highly important. The following are selected from contest programs. Each one represents an actual entry, though not necessarily a winner. Obviously these titles have been worded with care; some suggest a particular topic and point of view, whereas others may be developed in several ways:[5]

Death on the Installment Plan
Don't Drop the Dropout
The Draft—Why Pick Me?
The Pressure of Population
Accident Care
Parents Without Partners
The Unknown Soldier Speaks
The Great American Tragedy
The Warfare State of Mind
The Nature of Prejudice
Let's Listen to Jazz
Vietnam—Now Where?
The Rights of Man
The Silent Scream
Crime—A Minority Report
What Has America Ever Done for Anyone?
America's Full Cultural Heritage
Late for a Date
Survival of the Safest
The Muslim Menace
Where is the Good Samaritan?
Remains to Be Seen
The Tragedy of Hypocrisy
Man and the Machine
I Protest the Protesters
Dead on Arrival
The Rights of Protest
Police Brutality—Fact or Fiction

Once the central theme associated with the topic has been formulated, the student proceeds to read widely, looking for examples, statistics, and other forms of support. Read fifty winning selections, and invariably you will see in the introductions, in the conclusions, and in the main parts of the speeches striking and vivid materials that came from research. The student may have

---

[5]Most of these titles come from materials of the Wisconsin High School Forensic Association, the Minnesota State High School League, the Illinois High School Association, the Interstate Oratorical Association, the Ohio High School Speech League.

particularly good luck interviewing authorities. Often a combination of specific incidents, followed by an umbrella of statistics, is potent. The incidents dramatize the problem and the statistics show that the instances are truly representative.

As the contestant proceeds with his research, he will make decisions about the structure of the oration. One major area may be the statement of the *problem*, with its subdivisions. Another may be the *solution*. Contest directors agree that speakers handle the problem part better than the solution part (as do professors, Congressmen, editors, other groups of adults).[6]

The *composition* of the oration is expected to rise above the commonplace. Colorful phrases or striking imagery will help catch the judges' attention. The *opening* should arouse interest, and the progression of ideas should be logical. Special attention needs to be given to the *conclusion*—here the contest may be won or lost. As the student prepares his subject he will be on the alert for materials that seem eminently suited for opening and closing parts. Actually he should be encouraged to develop a *design* more imaginative than the usual deductive arrangement.[7]

Again, the student should consult the materials prepared by the contest director. The instructions prepared by the Iowa High School Forensic League for the use of its critic judges well illustrate the high standard of original speaking that is sought:

Each critic shall . . . consider such factors as vital and stimulating ideas, soundness of thinking, excellence of structure, adequacy and concreteness of developmental or supporting details, excellence of language, pronunciation, and articulation, and general effectiveness as a persuasive and/or inspirational speaker whose speaking gives prominence to imaginative and emotional elements. ("Soundness of thinking and weight of content are supplemented by a degree of eloquence in delivery by a speaker who is stirred, aroused, and challenged by his subject and audience.")[8]

Interpretative Oratory

In this activity, also called *oratorical declamation* or *significant public address*, the student selects a speech by someone else, cuts it to the prescribed

---

[6] *See:* James L. Golden, "Achieving Excellence in the College Oration," *Speech Teacher,* September 1965, pp. 184-192.

[7] *See:* Loren Reid, *First Principles of Public Speaking,* Chapter 21, which discusses a variety of speech designs. In the Appendix is also a speech with a striking design, "Six Reasons for Drinking," by Dr. Monk Bryan—the reasons *for* drinking actually being understated reasons for *not* drinking.

[8] *University of Iowa Extension Bulletin,* No. 837 (1966-67), p. 30.

length—eight or ten minutes—memorizes and delivers it. He is not supposed to impersonate the speaker, but rather to give his own interpretation of that speaker's ideas.

Here the problem is to select a speech that the student himself likes and can identify with. Unless the contest director specifies otherwise, the student has two broad fields of choice:

1. He can select one of the classics from a standard anthology; for example a cutting from Lincoln or Churchill. "Toussaint l'Ouverture" by Wendell Phillips is a favorite.

2. He can select a speech by a contemporary, for example, "I Have a Dream" by Martin Luther King. He may have a better chance of success by choosing a recent speech, as he may find subject matter more suited to his own interests. Several state associations require this category of material. The Illinois High School Association, for instance, recommends "that the material be pertinent to current problems" and suggests looking in *Vital Speeches* or *Winning Orations of the Interstate Oratorical Association.* Another source of timely and accurate texts is *Representative American Speeches.* See the collections listed at the end of Chapter 4.

In some contests the student is required to spend two minutes or so at the beginning describing the situation out of which the speech grew. Under what circumstances, for example, did Kennedy give his address to the Houston ministers or Johnson his final speech to Congress? The contestant should review the circumstances under which the speech was given: not only the general tone (what was the mood of the nation in January 1961, at inaugural time) but the specific details (where was the "I Have a Dream" speech given, what was the composition of the audience). He needs to know the obvious meanings (*extenuate,* in the "Liberty or Death" speech) and the hidden meanings ("the brave men, living and dead, who fought here" were for the most part young men white, black, and red). Avoiding singsong and monotone, he should interpret the selection as he would any bit of impressive, evocative material—with sincerity and taste.

The Colorado State Speech League asks its critics to look for the following items in judging its "Interpretation of Oratory event:[9]

1. *Content.* Did the interpreter select and arrange the material effectively?
2. *Appreciation of background.* Did the student give evidence of understanding the framework in which the oratory was presented, i.e., social forces orator's relation to these forces, the speaking situation, and the immediate and lasting effect of the oratory?

---

[9] *Handbook of Speech and Drama Activities,* 4th ed., p. 58.

3. *Unique aspects.* Did the chosen orator make an impact on thought or produce action? Did the student discover and make clear the unique features of organization, language, and style of the orator?

4. *Delivery.* Did the student employ delivery appropriate to the two skills involved—public speaking and interpretation? Was his speaking direct and communicative? Did the facial, bodily, and vocal suggestion enhance rather than detract from the interpretation?

5. *Total effectiveness.* The total impression of the material, interpretation and speaker upon you, the critic.

The American Forensic Association has formulated a "Code for Contests in Oratory" in cooperation with various organizations that sponsor such contests, including the Americal Legion, Optimist International, National Forensic League, and others. With respect to oratory, the Code states: (1) a significant single idea, the original work of the student, with limitation on quoted material; (2) reasonable latitude for the student to advance his own convictions—"creative thought reflecting the speaker's beliefs and experience"; (3) distinction in composition—responsible ideas, incisive analysis, unaffected dignity of expression; (4) straightforward, communicative presentation. With respect to the form of the contest, the Code urges opportunity for individual criticism of each speaker, to enhance the learning value of the contest. With respect to judges, the Code insists upon a competence that derives from speech education or from professional experience in speaking: "competent criticism should be a right of the participants." Judges should receive a reasonable honorarium plus expenses.

Extemporaneous Speaking

The favorite among the individual speaking events (and mine personally), extemporaneous speaking is the most interesting both for participants and listeners.

The procedure is fairly well standardized. In autumn or winter students are given a list of magazines to read. *Time, Newsweek, U.S. News and World Report, National Observer,* and *Scholastic* are usually found on the lists. The topic area may be broadly stated ("any general topic on political or foreign affairs") or narrowly defined ("world events of current significance" or "the American economy"). From this general field, the director prepares a list of thirty to fifty topics for individual speeches. High school teachers may be invited to send a list of topics which the director will mull over, edit, and rephrase.

An hour before the scheduled time for the event, contestants will begin to draw topics. Each student will draw three slips, select one, and retire to an assigned room for an hour's study and reflection. Ordinarily he may take notes and other materials into the room. At eight-minute intervals (assuming the speeches are to be eight minutes in length) the other students will draw. In a few leagues the contest is actually impromptu, as the student draws three topics, selects one, and begins to speak at once.

Much depends on the luck of the draw. As a contestant in the Iowa regional contest, I was required to prepare for fifty listed topics. Knowing I could draw once, and then if I did not like the topic, draw once more, I prepared on only forty-nine. As I did not care much for the first topic I did draw, I prepared to draw again; my teacher, with true adult caution, reminded me of the hazard of making the second, final, choice. It could have been sudden death, but the slip had typed on it "Iowa's Resources," one of my favorites, and I won standing up. The fates have their own devices in these matters which they are pretty careful not to reveal to grownups.

In essence the task of the student, in the weeks preceding the contest, is to prepare himself to speak on every conceivable topic that might come within the assigned field. As he reads each issue of the suggested magazines he asks himself, "What topics do these articles suggest?" Of course there is a good deal of continued reading from week to week on the same general topic, so he ends up with a list of manageable length. He then begins to gather additional materials on each of his topics, going as far afield as he wishes. Eventually he will end up with a series of outlines and fragments of outlines. Well before the contest date he will have rehearsal sessions with his teacher, who will improvise a list of topics and let the student draw three and select one. This can go on at a mature level and prove intellectually useful.

The Ohio High School Speech League, which embraces more than three hundred high schools, is host to more than five hundred students in its state forensic finals. For the extemporaneous speaking finals, the director prepares a lengthy list of topics. The following illustrate the variety of thoughtful topics that the students prepare themselves to speak on:[10]

Are the chances of all-out war increasing?
Will the war in Asia spread?
Is the Negro making progress in the United States today?
What will the rising Negro vote mean in the South?
Is inflation a serious threat?
Can "White" Rhodesia survive?
Can United States prosperity continue?
Should there be a four-year term for congressmen?
Is world communism in trouble?
What are the chances of helping troubled India?
Should we try to stop the flight to the suburbs?
Will medicare work?
Is the present business boom really an American miracle?
Is the United States becoming tougher about foreign aid?

[10]Courtesy of Kathryn Schoen, executive director of the League.

How vulnerable is Red China?
What water shortage problems plague the world today?
What water pollution problems are under attack in the United States?
What is Red China's potential for war?
What activities of the Ku Klux Klan are evident today?
What progress is being made in civil rights?
What is the evidence of growing federal control over our lives?
How is the United States faring in the space race?
What are the strengths and weaknesses of the defense of the United States?
Why is Laos becoming a trouble spot?
What potential for war does the Soviet Union possess in missiles and men?
What are the problems in our balance of payment situation?
Are teenagers any worse than those of previous generations?
Does the United States itself face a population problem?
What changes are taking place in Catholicism?
What can be done about death on the highway?
What trends can be observed in United States foreign policy?
What problems in Indonesia are mounting?
Why is the population explosion the most dangerous explosion of all?
What are signs of increasing cooperation between Catholics and Protestants?
What are the continuing obstacles to friendly relations between Arabs and Israelis?

These topics were designed for high school competition, but can be used by university students as well. They can be grouped under broader subject areas, which would correspond to the student's general preparation, but he is cautioned always to speak to the topic exactly as worded, and not to caress it with soothing platitudes.

The speeches that result should be truly extemporaneous, possessing genuine spontaneity. Canned material does not seem to fool experienced critics. They have visceral reactions to all-purpose introductions, wide-angle illustrations, and round-the-world conclusions that partly fit a number of subjects but do not exactly fit the issue before the house. They are not to be taken in by transparent short-cuts, but are equally prompt to recognize honest effort.

To add to the extemporaneous nature of the contest, some leagues (Wisconsin, South Dakota, Illinois among others) ask a judge or other designated listener to pose questions to the speaker after he has finished his prepared remarks. College tournament directors have also utilized this feature.

For a list of magazines (with addresses) commonly used, see Appendix D.

Radio and Television Speaking

This event takes various forms. In some tournaments the material used is news, reported and interpreted; in others it is straight news announcing, sometimes with commercials; in others it is expository or persuasive speaking. Basically the purpose is to give the student experience in the use of a microphone, either in the radio or the television situation; beyond that to develop expertise in managing the assigned kinds of broadcasting material.

If the event is one in news reporting and interpretation, the student may prepare his script in advance and mail it to the contest director, though in some tournaments the script must be prepared on the day of the contest, using items that have come in over the wire services. Timing is most exact—4 minutes 45 seconds to 5 minutes 15 seconds—the contestant being required either to keep an eye on the studio clock or watch flash cards. If the material is broadcast over television, the student is invited to use visual aids, following precise requirements about size and color supplied by the contest director. Clothing and grooming also become important. The student is specifically asked to be his own natural self and not to attempt to impersonate Walter Cronkite or David Brinkley. One interesting event is expository speaking, in which each participant presents a how-to-do-it theme on topics such as "Developing a Character in a Play" or "Problems in Lunar Exploration."[11]

Whatever the event, the student is required to give his presentation a proper format: suitable opening and closing remarks, identification of the performer, transitions between items and before and after commercials. The event should strike a professional note. The script should indicate what the studio announcer will say by lead-in; in fact, it should be of broadcast quality and in broadcast style. Again and again directors stress the importance of good communication in this situation, as in others: they urge sincerity, naturalness, objectivity, directness.

Other Speaking Events

Tournament directors continually experiment with new forms, with the purpose of stimulating all aspects of the speech program, and beyond that, of developing the many kinds of student talent found in the institution. Some are:

Informative public speaking: five to seven minute speeches expository in nature presented from notes rather than from a manuscript.

After dinner speaking: five to seven minute speeches entertaining in nature. Material must be original; the humor must be in good taste; some directors advise that it have an undertone of seriousness. (As this last quality is not invariably recommended, consult the specifications of the contest being en-

[11]*See: University of Iowa Extension Bulletin, 1966-67,* No. 837, pp. 36-37.

tered.) Most agree that the speech should not be a series of unrelated jokes, nor a vaudeville, nor an "acted-out" performance. Jokes and stories may be told, however, with or without dialect, and with some suggestion of character. What is generally sought is an entertaining speech with a theme, appropriate to the speaker and to the situation. The contest is a form of public speaking, not a form of interpretation or impersonation.

Four-minute speech: A contest in persuasive speaking. Many tournaments have some kind of short speech event.

Sales talk: A contest in effective selling. The student describes his product or service, creates a desire for it, skillfully manages the question of cost, and tells the listener how and where to make the purchase.

Donald W. Klopf surveyed 210 college tournaments and found that 23 different types of individual events were held. High school leagues sponsor almost as many.[12] Contest directors, by frequently consulting their clientele, can keep their programs steadily under appraisal and thus keep abreast of student interest and curriculum changes.

Memorized Declamation

In one form or other, the memorized declamation is an event in most high school contests. (Colleges and universities prefer prose and poetry reading events, the student reading from the printed page; high schools like these events also, but often in addition to the memorized declamation.) Separate contests may be conducted for serious and for humorous selections, or they may be mixed in a single event. Time limits have gradually been shortened over the years: eight minutes has become the usual length.

Before starting preparation, teacher and students should review the contest rules. The time limit is firmly fixed, with penalties for overtime. Certain selections may be forbidden, either because they are trite or because they won the previous year. Sometimes a participant is prohibited from using the same selection a second year.

Chances for success may be markedly enhanced or diminished by the choice of selections. The best source of material is a short story, a novel, an informal essay, a narrative poem. Freshness is desirable, and literary value should be high. Experienced teachers, as they read new books, are on the lookout for possible

---

[12]*See:* Donald W. Klopf and Stanley G. Rives, *Individual Speaking Contests: Preparation for Participation,* p. 74. Good for suggestions, samples from student performances, lists of references. *See also:* Klopf, "Practices in Intercollegiate Speech Tournaments," *Journal of the American Forensic Association,* May 1964, pp. 48-52.

cuttings for declamations. Your judges are certain to be people who have heard many events, and although one delights in hearing an old (not too old) piece, he will applaud the choice of something recent and sparkling.

Buried in older sources, however, may be an eight-minute cutting that most have overlooked. The Wisconsin High School Forensic Association each year provides its teachers with a list of contemporary selections that participants have liked. The list below will give an idea of the range and variety available:[13]

Humorous Selections

Androcles and the Lion, Eileen Johnson
Among the Spirits, Mark Twain
Ask That Man, Robert Benchley
The Biter Bit, from *The Green Fairy Book,* Andrew Lang (ed.)
The Boy's Camp Business, Robert Benchley
Captain Future, Block That Kick, S. J. Perelman
Captain John Smith, Will Cuppy
Charles, Shirley Jackson
A Dangerous Guy Indeed, Damon Runyon
The Deacon's Medicine, Ruth McEnery Stuart
The Departure of Emma Inch, James Thurber
Dr. Arbuthnot's Academy, Frank Sullivan
Father's Finest Hour, Vera Foss Bradshaw
The Goat and I, Robert Ruark
Good Old Fashioned Christmas, Robert Benchley
Hamlet Sees a Ghost, Richard Armour
Henry VIII, Will Cuppy
Hour Of Letdown, E. B. White
Insert Flap "A" and Throw Away, S. J. Perelman
Lady Godiva, Will Cuppy
Last Day, Robert Benchley
The Leaking Sandwich, Frank Sullivan
A Mad Tea-Party, Lewis Carroll
More Alarms at Night, James Thurber
Museum Fleet, Robert Benchley
My Father and the Indians, Lewis Meyers
A Mysterious Visit, Mark Twain
Paul Revere's Ride, Robert Benchley
Penrod, Booth Tarkington
Please Don't Eat the Daisies, Jean Kerr
Restless Nights, Benjamin Jacobsen

[13]From the 1969-70 list.

The Sneaker Crisis, Shirley Jackson
Summer Shirtings, Robert Benchley
Trouble in the Early Morning, Benjamin Jacobsen
Two Letters—Both Open, E. B. White
Uncle Edith's Ghost Story, Robert Benchley
Women Have No Sense of Humor, Robert Thomas Allen
Weekend With the Angels, E. B. White
Why Not Worry, Frank Sullivan

Serious Selections

Abe Lincoln Grows Up, Carl Sandburg
After Twenty Years, O. Henry
Brown of Calaveras, Bret Harte
The Charivari, Zona Gale
Clerical Error, James Gould Cozzens
Come Dance With Me in Ireland, Shirley Jackson
The Crisis, Arthur Gordon
A Day's Pleasure, Hamlin Garland
The Drummer Boy of Shiloh, Ray Bradbury
Elevator Boy in the Wrong Building, Margaret Lee Runbeck
Freedom, E. B. White
The Furnished Room, O. Henry
Grandpa, Jeff Rackham
Go Seeker, Throughout the Land, Thomas Wolfe
The Highway, Ray Bradbury
The Kid Learns, William Faulkner
The Lake, Ray Bradbury
The Last Bullett, MacKinlay Kantor
The Last Leaf, O. Henry
Like Mother Used to Make, Shirley Jackson
The Lost Soul, Ben Hecht
The Lottery Ticket, Anton Chekhov
Magic Morning in Massachusetts, May Wallace
Married Children, Dorothy Canfield
Men of Iron, Guy Endore
Miss Brill, Kathryn Mansfield
Mother in Manville, Marjorie Kinnan Rawlings
The Necklace, Guy de Maupassant
Nothing Ever Happens, Dorothy Canfield
Of Missing Persons, Jack Finney
The Old Man, Daphne du Maurier
The Old Man's Boy, Robert Ruark
Oliver Twist, Charles Dickens

The Outcasts of Poker Flat, Bret Harte
Portrait of My Son as a Young Man, Elizabeth Middleton
The Secret, Steve Allen
The Sniper, Liam O'Flaherty
"The Story of Hok Lee and the Dwarfs" from *The Green Fairy Book,*
    Andrew Lang (ed.)
Survival, Grandin F. Smith
Then Came the Legions, MacKinlay Kantor
These Good Children, Gladys Cluff
The Third Day After Christmas, William Saroyan
Three Days to See, Helen Keller
Toast to Captain Jerk, Russell Maloney
The Tree, Dylan Thomas
The Water of Life, Jacob and Wilhelm Grimm

Actually the Wisconsin teachers strongly recommend that students do *not* use these titles, but instead prepare their own extracts. The list is printed here merely as a general guide to the kinds of things that may be used. Many other state associations prepare lists of titles; consult your regional or state director. Catalogs of declamations are also available; these are wholly candid in indicating prize-winning selections.

Preparing the Selection

Once the student has decided on his selection, he needs to make a preliminary cutting of his excerpt, spending considerable time in reading it aloud. He should read it to others to see if his excerpt holds together. Is the plot clear? Are the characters distinct and readily identifiable? Is the excerpt within the time limits? All these questions need to be answered before the extract is committed to memory.

So that the student will understand the selection, he should read about the author, study the entire text from which the cutting came, search the meaning of words and allusions, and in other ways make himself master of the material. As his teacher, you should urge him to discuss the selection. Who is the main character of the piece? Why does he react to this character or to that event as he does? You should pry into idea, tone, feeling.

Generally the student will need to prepare an introduction in which he identifies author, selection, and scene. He may also need brief, internal transitions to clarify his abridgement.

Practicing the Selection

At rehearsal period, matters of voice, posture, gesture, pausing and other details of timing, and suggestions of entrances and exits will need to be worked out.

Usually the rules forbid chairs, tables, or any kind of props. Judges are likely to disapprove of movements, actions, transitions, facial expressions, that seem mechanical, routine, unmotivated. You should have at hand the judges' criteria. Here, slightly modified, is an outline of the principles that Wisconsin judges are requested to consider:[14]

Memorized Declamation Critique Sheet

The judge [should give consideration] to these factors:

1. The contestant's understanding of the author's meaning and intent.
2. Evidence of the contestant's comprehending the intellectual content of the material.
3. Evidence of his being sensitive to the emotional content.
4. The believability of the characters, if the selection is a story.
5. The contestant's responsiveness to the ideas in the selection as he communicates them.
6. Communication which gives the author's meaning to the listeners and does not call attention to itself.

Ohio judges have these instructions before them at contest time:[15]

Dramatic and humorous interpretation aim at recreating the characters in the story presented and suggesting them with restraint to the audience.

Selections ... must be cuttings from novels, published short stories, or plays. Adaptations may be for the purpose of continuity only. They should be judged for their appropriateness as contest material and their suitability to the particular contestant using them. The use of good literature should be noted favorably and the pieces devoid of literary merit graded lower.

Each selection must be memorized and should be presented without the use of physical objects, properties, or costumes. ...

This is a contest in oral interpretation, not solo acting. Although gestures and pantomime are not barred, they should be used with restraint. The contestants should be graded on poise, quality and use of voice ... and especially the ability to interpret characters correctly and consistently. Narrative should be vivid and animated.

The final test of good interpretation is the ability to create an atmosphere for the listener so that he is carried away to the time and place of the story being unfolded.

Interpretation Contests, Festivals

Local, regional, and state interpretation contests and festivals can serve as a stimulating experience both for high school and college students. As with all

[14]Individual critique sheet of the Wisconsin High School Forensic Association.
[15]Ballot of the Ohio High School Speech League (revised, 1970).

such events, students invariably enjoy participating in different surroundings, laying their best efforts alongside those of students from other schools, and profiting by the suggestions of other teachers.

Basically the events are poetry and prose reading. Prose reading may be termed declamation, and may have two divisions: serious and humorous. *Serious declamation* is usually a dramatic selection (contests for memorized speeches are so named and so limited). The rules of the particular contest will specify whether the material is to be memorized or not.

Specific time limits are laid down and enforced; usually eight to ten minutes is allotted. Often the contestant is required to identify his selection and in other ways orient his reader, and if so, this part of his program is included in the time limit. Generally he is allowed to select his own material. At times he must choose from an approved list; on rare occasions he is confronted with a short list of selections *not* approved (such as "Tell-Tale Heart" or "Sorry, Wrong Number").

Contest directors clearly specify that the selection must have literary merit. The contestant is told that his function is one of interpreter, not impersonator or actor. He must understand the author's point of view and the circumstances under which the selection was written. Unless contest rules particularly require memorization, he is expected to read from the printed page but must not let the manuscript interfere with his presentation.[16]

Play Festivals and Contests

Participation in an invitational or regional play festival is a highly motivating, culturally profitable activity. The event may be for one-act plays, or cuttings from longer plays, or both; operettas or other musical productions are generally not eligible. As a strict time limit—usually thirty minutes—must be adhered to, proper cutting is essential.

Emphasis is placed on characterization and line reading. Costumes can be as ingenious as desired, but elaborate stage settings are impractical. Ordinarily the host school will provide standard large pieces, such as sofas or tables, but will not undertake to provide unusual items. As director of a festival, I once unexpectedly had to provide one cast with two grand pianos. Experiences like this are vividly remembered when one writes the rules for the following year.

---

[16] Materials sent out by state high school activities leagues often contain lists of titles for prose and poetry reading. For example, see *Music and Speech Handbook for Contests and Festivals,* North Dakota High School Activities Association; *Contest Handbook,* Wisconsin High School Forensic Association.

Elaborate lighting effects may also lead to complications. Each director will of course arrange for hand props.

Serious or dramatic pieces usually go better than comedies. Audiences are often of modest size, so not many people are around to laugh. Although size of cast is seldom regulated, critics find it difficult to appraise and critique large numbers of performers. Even so, plays calling for from ten to fifteen people are not a rarity at festivals. The selection of a play should be guided by these factors: literary merit, quality of the dialogue, theme or message, good story line, well-motivated characters. The play must have genuine quality and must be adapted to the capabilities of the cast.

If the chosen play is subject to royalty, the competing school is responsible for making financial arrangements.

Duet acting is a special event found in many festivals and contests. It is shorter in length, usually ten minutes, and basically consists of a cutting in which two actors develop the plot. (Occasionally there is more than one scene, in which instance the actor may portray more than one character.) An introduction is required, presented by one or both members. Stage furniture is strictly limited—consult the procedures of the particular festival—and makeup and properties may be eliminated altogether from the competition.

Organization of Contests and Tournaments

Teachers who wish to organize contests, festivals, tournaments, and similar events can locate detailed suggestions in the materials prepared by various associations. Reference to these suggestions will lessen the possibility of over-looking an important element. Balloting, methods of advancing and eliminating, procedures for ranking, recommendations of judges, have evolved from long practice and should be consulted.

The *Handbook of Speech and Drama Activities,* published by the Colorado State Speech League, University of Colorado, Boulder, has sections on "How to Organize a Speech Meet" and "How to Organize a Drama Festival." The *Contest Handbook,* published by the Wisconsin High School Forensic Association, University Extension Department of Speech, Madison, has sections on planning and conducting drama, debate, and speech contests. The *Speech Bulletin* of the South Dakota High School Activities Association, University of South Dakota, Vermilion, contains suggestions about debate tournaments and individual events. These three are typical of many. Your state association may have similar materials, and if the event you are planning is preliminary to a regional meeting, you will need to follow the established procedures for your state. In general these and other sources contain sample ballots, suggestions for judges, criteria

for evaluation, methods of determining the best performances, and other problems that arise in connection with a speech event.

Assignments

1. Collect ballots or score sheets for one or more of the individual events
described in this chapter, as assigned by the instructor.
2. Prepare detailed instructions for running an intramural speech event on your
campus (or other tournament assigned by the instructor.)

References

Buys, William E.; Cobin, Martin; Hunsinger, Paul; Miller, Melvin H.; and Scott
Robert L. *Contest Speaking Manual.* Edited by William E. Buys. Skokie, III.:
National Textbook, 1964. Chapters on oral interpretation of prose and
poetry, extemporaneous speaking, serious and humorous dramatic inter
pretation.

Buys, William E., ed. *The Contest Speaking Series.* Skokie, III.: National Text
book, 1965-69. Among the individual titles in this series are: Roy A. Beck
Group Reading: Readers Theatre; William E. Buys, *Extemporaneous Speaking,*
Martin Cobin, *Humorous Dramatic Interpretation* and *Serious Dramatic Inter
pretation;* Paul Hunsinger, *Oral Prose and Poetry;* Melvin H. Miller, *Specia*
Occasion Speeches; Robert L. Scott, *Oratory;* Roy V. Wood, *Strategie*
Debate.

Gehring, Mary Louise. "The High School Oration: Fundamentals." *Speech*
Teacher March 1953.

Golden, James L. "Achieving Excellence in the College Oration." *Speech Teach*
er September 1965.

Klopf, Donald W. "Practices in Intercollegiate Speech Tournaments." *Journal o*
the American Forensic Association May 1964.

Klopf, Donald W., and Rives, Stanley G. *Individual Speaking Contests: Prepara*
tion for Participation. Minneapolis: Burgess, 1964. Chapters on origina
oratory, extemporaneous speaking, oral interpretation of prose and poetry
after-dinner speaking, impromptu speaking, salesmanship, declamation, etc

Schneiders, Alexander A. *Adolescents and the Challenge of Maturity: A Guia*
for Parents and Teachers. Milwaukee: Bruce Publishing, 1965.

Winning Orations of the Interstate Oratorical Association, Detroit: Interstat
Oratorical Association. Issued annually.

Part Four
the profession of teaching

Captain Mitty stood up and strapped on his huge Webley-Vickers automatic. "It's forty kilometers through hell, sir," said the sergeant. Mitty finished one brandy. "After all," he said softly, "what isn't?"

James Thurber, *The Secret Life of Walter Mitty*

finding new sources of ideas

The self-taught man seldom knows anything accurately, and he does not know a tenth as much as he could have known if he had worked under teachers, and besides, he brags.

Mark Twain

An advantage of teaching is the opportunity to broaden your education. As you work with classes and activities day after day, you become a more serious student of your field. You learn from other teachers who have a specialized training in their subject and who come from other colleges or universities. Because of the enthusiasm of your friends you may develop new interests in music, art, literature, current affairs.

You will find that students look to you for advice outside of the syllabus. They expect you to be aware of new ideas and methods. They ask about new plays on Broadway, or inquire what can be done to help a cousin who has a speech defect. At election time they want to know where you stand. They ask your opinion about a speech they heard over TV or radio. They wonder what the Soviet Union or Red China is going to do. After a few score questions you will enlarge your concept of your role as a teacher.

Newspapers

As a college student you may not have read a daily paper; as a teacher you will need to find time. If you have never read the New York *Times* regularly, you should write for a rate card and subscribe to the Sunday edition for three to six months to see what a great newspaper is like. Its material on art, music, TV films, and the theater is related to the work of your courses, and you may find yourself taking clippings to class to show students what "the *Times* says." Among teachers of public speaking it is famous for texts of important speeches and state papers. Its book review section appraises new fiction and nonfiction. Its weekly summary reviews the news. To keep abreast of daily events you may also read one of the outstanding papers in your section, such as the St. Louis *Post-Dispatch,* the *Christian Science Monitor,* the Kansas City *Star,* the San Francisco *Chronicle,* the Des Moines *Register,* the Atlanta *Constitution,* the New Orleans *Times-Picayune.* If you are interested in business and professional speaking you should read occasional issues of the *Wall Street Journal.* If you want to familiarize yourself with the British viewpoint, try a subscription to the Manchester *Guardian* or the weekly London *Observer.*

Magazines

Newsmagazines are useful for gaining perspective. *Time* and *Newsweek* keep the reader informed about events over the world. *U.S. News and World Report* is helpful for teachers as it has a keen interest in the nation's schools and colleges. Its interpretations of the selective service act, its reports on school enrollments, its comments and predictions about things to come, its think pieces on the changing cost of living, are authoritative. It is probably quoted more frequently in debate tournaments than any other weekly magazine. Also useful are *Current History, Fortune, Life, Look.*

A teacher should avoid subscribing to too many serials, but may want to see *Harper's,* the *Atlantic,* the *New Yorker,* or *Sports Illustrated* for special articles. An occasional hour spent in the library scanning current periodicals may locate articles you will want to tell your class about. A teacher needs to learn to skim popular offerings ("some books are to be tasted . . . some few to be chewed and digested") in order to select without being overwhelmed. The *Reader's Digest* catches most of the good articles and may be useful for that reason. You need to read the *Digest* in self-defense, since frequently students base speeches upon its articles. Your reading, however, should not consist entirely of newsmagazines and digests, as you put yourself at the mercy of somebody's editorial policy. You may adopt a bias without reasoning the matter. For a corrective, try *New Republic, New Statesman,* or *Spectator.*

A teacher should get his ideas from many sources. You should maintain the same attitude of thoughtful appraisal as a reader that you encourage in your students as listeners.

Professional Journals

Two educational journals will be useful to every classroom teacher. *The Speech Teacher,* founded in 1952, prints articles covering every subject in the speech syllabus. It is primarily designed to meet the needs of teachers in elementary and secondary schools, though its content is also of interest to the college or university teacher. Another publication of the Speech Communication Association is the *Quarterly Journal of Speech,* often mentioned in these pages.

Those whose interest is drama have a number of publications from which to choose. *Players Magazine, Dramatics,* and *The Educational Theatre Journal* are chiefly interested in educational theater. *Players Magazine* has departments such as those dealing with technical problems, costuming, high school theater, and children's theater. It has an extensive review department of new plays, and lists the current productions of schools and colleges throughout the country. *Dramatics* carries articles on acting, directing, and production problems, and has departments dealing with children's drama, radio, cinema, and the high school stage. It gives attention to new plays, and prints lists of frequently produced plays. Both *Players Magazine* and *Dramatics* carry reports on the professional stage. *The Educational Theatre Journal* is primarily aimed at the college and university level, but its articles on high school dramatics are good. The American Educational Theatre Association, its publisher, has compiled a variety of teaching aids for classroom use. The *Journal of the American Forensic Association* has been mentioned in Chapter 15. *The Journal of Communication,* published by the International Communication Association, has authoritative articles in the field of communication theory. For a list of other publications and of state and regional speech journals, see the *Annual Directory* of the Speech Communication Association.

Other publications of interest to teachers are the *Journal of Speech and Hearing Disorders* and the *Journal of Speech and Hearing Research,* published by the American Speech and Hearing Association, and *Speech Monographs,* published by the Speech Communication Association. The primary concern of these journals is to report new research.

Special Events

Make an effort to attend outstanding lectures, plays, musicals, ballets, concerts, and political events. You cannot teach from books alone; you need to collect examples and instances from life itself. A beginning teacher is indeed fortunate if he finds himself a member of a lively, energetic staff or department where others are interested in social, cultural, and political happenings as well as in their own study, research, and teaching.

Participation in Associations

Most teachers feel a need to discuss their professional problems with others. Shop talk in a teachers' room is mostly concerned with personalities: outstanding classroom performances, for example. Shop talk at state and district teachers' meetings discusses larger problems of the profession. Every teacher also needs a still different sort of shop talk: the exchange of ideas related to his own specialty. Accordingly, when a group of speech teachers gets together, an occasion arises for a large-scale interchange of experiences. Such occasions are sponsored by state, regional, and national speech associations.

The opportunity to exchange ideas is not the only reason for affiliating with a learned society. An equally important reason is that these professional associations are responsible for most of the development of speech in this country. State and regional speech associations contribute much to their sections of the country. The Speech Communication Association has for more than fifty years represented the interests of the general teacher of speech at all levels of instruction. The American Speech and Hearing Association, the American Educational Theatre Association, and the Committee on Discussion and Debate Materials of the National University Extension Association, have for years served the fields indicated by their titles. The American Forensic Association and the International Communication Association forward the interests of those specialties.

State Associations

The speech associations of the individual states are primarily concerned with sponsoring an annual meeting, though they also make recommendations about the curriculum and the accreditation of teachers of speech. The programs are usually planned to cover a wide range of interests and specialties.

Generalizations about the contributions of state associations are difficult. One association, in the space of five years, drew up a constitution; appointed committees; formulated a course of study; made recommendations, later officially adopted, about courses to be required for licensing teachers; aided institutions of higher learning to secure approval for new courses; started a newsletter; was instrumental in inviting regional and national associations to meet in the state; sponsored three meetings a year in different sections, bringing to some of them speakers from the outside.

Many state associations conveniently meet at the time of the annual convention of the State Teachers Association, so that the high school teacher will automatically be informed about time and place. College teachers, however, are also active in state meetings. The *Directory* of the Speech Communication Association lists the dates of state meetings and the officials of the associations.

Regional Associations

Regional associations meet at various cities in their respective areas.[1] The Speech Association of the Eastern States usually meets in New York, though it has met in Boston, Washington, and Syracuse. The Central States Speech Association has met in Columbus, Madison, Columbia, Oklahoma City, Terre Haute, Detroit, Milwaukee, Minneapolis, St. Louis, and Chicago. The Southern Speech Association has met in Cincinnati, Birmingham, Gainesville, Houston, Nashville, Atlanta, Baton Rouge, Chattanooga, Jackson, and Waco. The Western Speech Association has met in Salt Lake City, Los Angeles, San Francisco, Santa Barbara, Seattle, Denver, San Diego, and San Jose. The New England Speech Association meets in Boston. The Pacific Speech Association has met in Honolulu, Hilo, and Wailuku.

The Central States Speech Association held its first convention at Iowa City in 1933; Alan H. Monroe was the first president, and Charles R. Layton the first secretary. The following year the Association met at Northwestern University; Harry G. Barnes served as president. The third convention was not held until 1937, at Madison, Wisconsin. The membership continued to be divided on the issue of the need for the central region organization since the national association met every other year at Chicago. The Madison group, still somewhat divided, elected Layton as president and Loren Reid as secretary, and voted to meet in 1938 at Columbia, Missouri. This fourth convention, however, proved highly successful, largely because of the imaginative planning of a local committee headed by Wesley A. Wiksell, and attracted a group of three hundred. Because of World War II, no conventions were held between 1942 and 1947, when the ninth convention was scheduled at Columbia. The official publication is the *Central States Speech Journal,* started in 1949. In 1969 the Association had approximately twelve hundred individual and three hundred library members.[2]

[1] The information about the various associations and societies mentioned in this chapter was gathered from their executive secretaries and other sources. For further information, write the organization at the address given in Appendix E. Students interested in the history of these and other speech and theater associations should not overlook the chapters in Karl R. Wallace (ed.), *History of Speech Education in America.*

[2] Regrettably the history of the Association has not been written. The information above comes from *Quarterly Journal of Speech* "News and Notes" sections and from abbreviated archives. My "numbering" of the conventions is partly, but not wholly, arbitrary; I omit "meetings" held at the time of the national conventions as not actually being "conventions"—i.e. the luncheon meeting at the Hotel Clinton, New York, 1937. With this numbering the 1968 convention was the 30th, the 1973 convention the 35th, although 40 years had elapsed since the first, Iowa City, convention in 1933.

The Western Speech Association was founded in November, 1929. Its membership in 1969 was 1,150, and the circulation of *Western Speech* exceeded 1,500. Sustaining membership includes also a subscription to the *Southern Speech Journal*. Since September 1969, the Association has been housed in its permanent home on the campus of Washington State University at Pullman.

The New England Speech Association was founded in 1940. Its membership in 1969 was 350. Membership dues include both the convention fee and the *Newsletter*. At its annual convention are sectional meetings in rhetoric, theater, oral interpretation, mass communications, communication disorders, and speech education. Often the program includes a workshop for high school teachers.

The Southern Speech Association was founded in 1930, and has a membership of more than one thousand. Its publication is *Southern Speech Journal;* it issued also a *History of the Southern Speech Association* by Dallas Dickey, as a part of its silver anniversary activities. Sustaining membership includes the *Southern Speech Journal* and *Western Speech.*

The Speech Association of the Eastern States held its first meeting in 1910. In writing about this meeting, John Henry Frizzell, last survivor of the founders, stated: " . . . only six or seven of those present were chiefly concerned with public speaking, and the elocutionists and expressionists ganged up on us to give us a bad time." The annual convention of the Association is held early in April, usually in New York City. Publications include *Today's Speech,* an annual directory and a quarterly *Newsletter.* All areas of speech are represented in the Association. Current membership is twelve hundred.

The Pacific Speech Association was founded in 1948. Its current membership is 165. Its annual programs, held in Hawaii, often feature a mainland speaker. It makes an annual award to a speaker-of-the-year. It publishes *Pacific Speech.*

Regional groups have a unique opportunity to work with educational agencies on problems arising out of licensing and accrediting. One group was particularly active in formulating requirements for the teaching major in speech. Regional associations stress, however, their annual convention programs, trying to represent all interests and specialties. Especially in the years when the national association is meeting in a distant part of the country, conventions of the regional group have a special importance. Attendance ranges from two hundred to twelve hundred.

The National Forensic League

The National Forensic League was founded in 1925 as an honor society for high school students interested in speaking. Its original roster of twenty-four chapters has since grown to more than nineteen hundred. Over the years more than 280,000 students have become members.

District and national tournaments and student congresses enable the student to compete against students from other schools in his state and from other states. Its publication, *The Rostrum,* features articles on debating and achievements of its chapters and members. Among its famous members are Lyndon Johnson and Hubert Humphrey: they earned their membership by their own student achievement.

The International Thespian Society

The International Thespian Society is a nonprofit educational organization devoted to the advancement and improvement of theater arts in secondary schools. The Society was founded in 1920 under the name of the National Thespian Society and was incorporated in 1968. Through the organization of troupes in secondary schools, the Society works with teachers and administrators to educate students in the performing arts and related subjects, to advance standards in all phases of theater arts and to create an active and intelligent interest in theater.

Nonsecret and nonsocial, the Society is both a recognition and service organization with 3,206 affiliated secondary schools. Student membership is contingent upon the individual's having met the qualifications and standards of the Society and its respective troupes.

National Collegiate Players

National Collegiate Players was founded in 1922 to serve as a college unit in national movements for the betterment of the drama, and to recognize worthy individual and group efforts in drama on college and university campuses. It has seventy active chapters, and approximately eleven thousand living members. Its publication is *Players Magazine.*

Associate Collegiate Players

Associate Collegiate Players, formerly Junior Collegiate Players, was founded in 1949 by National Collegiate Players as an honorary association in two year colleges. Its purpose is to recognize individual and group achievement in the creative arts of the theater and serves to stimulate an interest in the educational theater, to develop appreciation of the best plays, and to promote higher standards in production. It has nine active chapters.

Zeta Phi Eta

Zeta Phi Eta was founded in 1893 for women interested in drama and other speech arts. It has twenty-eight campus chapters of women engaged in different fields of speech arts and sciences, and twenty-three alumnae chapters. Its national publication is *The Cameo.*

Phi Rho Pi

Phi Rho Pi, the national junior college forensic society, was founded in 1928 at Grand Rapids Junior College, Michigan. It has more than one hundred active chapters. Its purpose is to promote interest "in the several forms of public speech." A national convention featuring a speech tournament climaxes the annual program. Junior colleges with an active speech program are eligible to join.

Phi Beta

Phi Beta, national women's professional fraternity of music and speech, was founded in 1912. It has thirty-one collegiate and thirty alumnae chapters. Its objectives are: to promote the highest standards in music and speech; to develop the highest type of womanhood; to advance members intellectually and socially; to live a life of service; to give professional aid to worthy members and nonmembers; to foster college spirit and loyalty to their chosen campuses; to encourage scholarship and performance; to pursue ethical standards of professional achievement.

Alpha Psi Omega, Delta Psi Omega

Alpha Psi Omega, national dramatic honorary fraternity for senior colleges and universities, was founded in 1925. Delta Psi Omega, national dramatic honorary fraternity for junior colleges, was founded in 1929. The purpose of both societies is to provide recognition for students who have distinguished themselves in dramatic productions. Both are open to men and women. Delta Psi Omega has 245 chapters, Alpha Psi Omega 423, with a total membership of 56,150. The national publication is *The Playbill*.

Delta Sigma Rho-Tau Kappa Alpha

These two forensic honor societies were merged in 1963, each having had a distinguished history of more than half a century. The organization has more than two hundred chapters, with more than twenty thousand alumni. It sponsors regional and national contests in debate, persuasive speaking, extemporaneous speaking, and a congress. It encourages the development of courses in these fields, and promotes high standards for tournaments and congresses. Each year it selects a superior public speaker—distinguished for effective, intelligent, and responsible speaking on significant public questions—as Speaker-of-the-Year. The national publication is the *Speaker Gavel*.

National Association of Dramatic and Speech Arts

The National Association of Dramatic and Speech Arts, founded in 1936, is a professional affiliation of teachers, students, technicians, and craftsmen of the theater communicative arts and allied areas of interest. Its purpose is twofold: to encourage the establishment and conduct of programs in theater and communicative arts at member institutions, and to provide preprofessional and professional experience for students of these schools who have an interest in or special recommendations for professional work in speech and drama.

The Speech Communication Association

The Speech Communication Association (formerly Speech Association of America) is the national organization for teachers of speech. Founded in 1914, it has a membership of more than seven thousand in all states of the union and many foreign countries. Its principal publications are *The Quarterly Journal of Speech, Speech Monographs, The Speech Teacher* and its bimonthly news bulletin, *Spectra.* It sponsors the publication of various bulletins and brochures. National headquarters are located at the Statler Hilton Hotel, New York City, 10001.

The association is an "Associated Organization" of the National Education Association and a constituent member of the American Council on Education. Membership is open to any person interested in promoting the purposes of the association. Among its members are elementary and secondary school teachers, speech clinicians, college and university teachers, students, and administrators. It embraces such areas as public speaking, communication, debate, discussion, interpretation, drama, technical theater, phonetics, linguistics, speech science, speech correction, audiology, speech education, radio, and television. In 1965, it inaugurated its Golden Anniversary prize fund awards for scholarly publication. The James A. Winans award goes each year to distinguished scholarship in rhetoric and public address. Since 1935, the association has operated a national placement service for its members.

All members are listed in the *Directory:* name, address, college or university attended, degrees, and major and minor interests. The *Directory* is consulted by many people for reasons too numerous to list. Some one may wish to learn who is at a particular institution; seeing your name there, he may conclude that the course is in the hands of one who has a professional interest, who reads the official publications, and in other ways is kept informed about current developments. If no name appears for your institution, he can not tell whether speech is taught except by writing a letter to the officials of that school.

Many of the scholarly activities of the association are carried on through the divisions and their elected officers. Members are invited to affiliate themselves with one or more of these groups. They meet at the time of the national convention, and issue newsletters containing short articles, teaching suggestions, mention of new and forthcoming publications, and items about the activities of members. Readers of this book would likely be most interested in the speech education division, as well as those dealing with their own individual specialties.

An outstanding event of the year is the annual convention of the Speech Communication Association and other groups that meet with it. The growth of interest in this nationwide meeting is phenomenal. Sixty people attended the first convention in 1915; fifteen years later the number had increased to 508; the 1,000 mark was passed in 1939; subsequent conventions have been attended by more than 2,000. A part of the reason for increased attendance lies in the fact that these meetings are a focal point for other organizations as well as for the Speech Association. The Committee on Discussion and Debate Materials usually convenes at this time, as do the American Forensic Association and the International Communication Association. The traditional time of meeting is during the week between Christmas and New Year's. The meetings are unparalleled opportunities for renewing acquaintances with fellow students from graduate school days, former teachers, and colleagues. Famous personalities of the profession, including officers, editors, and writers of textbooks, often appear on the programs and are at hand for interview or conference. Outstanding speakers from educational, governmental, and industrial fields are scheduled for addresses.

Conventions are good sources of new ideas because scholars devise procedures or state new points of view which are often tried out in a seminar. Receiving encouragement, they bring them to a convention in the form of a paper. Later the scholar may be invited to prepare the paper for a journal. This process may take months; he may feel that he does not want to go into print until further research has been done. Even after he writes his article it may not be printed for a year. A convention goer and avid convention shoptalker who hears these papers presented can thus keep ahead of the journals. He may even pick up suggestions, hints, or bits of counsel useful to him but hardly significant enough to get into print. In fact, in this whole discussion the term "new idea" must be treated modestly. Nothing on the order of Halley's comet is here visualized. Most scholars are happy just to be able to turn on a little five-watt glow somewhere.

Graduate Study

A good source of new ideas is courses offered by the graduate departments of speech. Our profession, which in 1930 had nine departments qualified to offer advanced degrees, forty years later had one hundred fifty departments that conferred master's degrees, including more than fifty that conferred the doctorate. No statistics have been kept on the total number of students or the number of courses, but the growth has been proportional.

A complete list of the graduate departments of speech appears as Appendix C in this volume.

Continue to Learn

Unless a teacher keeps abreast of developments in his field, his ideas will become outmoded. One who goes into education as a lifetime field of endeavor may expect to have a professional career of forty-five or fifty years. Suppose, like Rip Van Winkle, he has been dozing for twenty years, and has awakened just recently. In 1932 declamation contests were still prominent in the high schools; now they occur only rarely, usually as part of tournament programs. In 1932 the deemphasis of judged debates was beginning; now expert judging and critiquing is demanded on campuses and in high schools. Formerly, play contests were the rule; now festivals are also popular. Previously, homework was assigned in abundance; now supervised study is felt to be more efficient. Flexible scheduling now used in many schools omits compulsory supervised study. The classroom is more permissive; counseling is more indirect. The curriculum has become broader with more "general science," "general history," and "general education" courses. Radio was known to the school of 1932, but TV not at all. Only a few schools in 1932 had disc recording equipment; wire recorders came and went; tape recorders, portable videotape recorders, and other sophisticated devices are now within reach. Many universities now have TV installations of professional quality, and teach film as well. Courses in discussion are increasingly more prominent. Behavioral studies abound; "communication" is part of many course and departmental titles. The little theater and the arena style of presentation are well known to contemporary directors. Interpretation courses are on the increase, and readers theater and chamber theater have been introduced. The speech correctionist of 1932 is now a speech and hearing specialist. Language disorders are also a matter of concern. Even Aristotle has loosed his grasp on rhetorical study.

The old truths about teaching are as sound today as ever, but out on the fringes many things change. Five years out of touch bring marks of obsolescence upon a teacher, ten years label him as one with old ideas, and after twenty years he too can hear the sounds of Hendrik Hudson's crew bowling at nine pins in the Kaatskills. As long as a teacher is active in the classroom he needs to keep up-to-date his fund of information—about speech, about education, about things in general.

Assignments

1. Once installed in the classroom, you are likely to be asked to make suggestions for books to be added to the school library. Other teachers or school patrons will ask you to recommend a good book to help them with a specific problem. The information will need to be complete so that the book can be secured: author, title, publisher, price. Therefore, make a list of books and periodicals suitable for inclusion in a high school or departmental library.
2. Report on the purpose, scope, style, and content of the professional journals mentioned in the chapter, as assigned by your instructor.
3. Report on the program of a state, regional, or national speech convention; if this is not practicable, consult the summaries and critiques of conventions found in the *Quarterly Journal of Speech* or the *Educational Theatre Journal* for the current year.
4. Launch a study of the various associations with which teachers, or schools, may become affiliated. Secure materials from such honor societies as National Thespians, National Forensic League, Delta Sigma Rho-Tau Kappa Alpha, Pi Delta Kappa. Secure materials about the American Educational Theatre Association, the American Speech and Hearing Association, the Speech Communication Association, the International Communication Association, the American Forensic Association, the National Education Association, the American Association of University Professors, the American Council on Education, the American Council of Learned Societies. For addresses, see Appendix E.

References

Auer, J. Jeffery. *An Introduction to Research in Speech.* New York: Harper & Row, 1959.

Bormann, Ernest G. *Theory and Research in the Communicative Arts.* New York: Holt, Rinehart & Winston, 1965.

Morris, William. ed. *Effective College Teaching: The Quest for Relevance.* Washington: American Council on Education, 1970.

Norton, L. E. "Speech and Speech Related Honorary Organizations." *Speech Teacher* November 1968.

Santiago, Florence M. *Inexpensive or Free Materials Useful for Teaching Speech.* Ann Arbor: Braun-Brumfield, 1959.

"Teacher Evaluation: Toward Improving Research." *Junior College Research Review* January 2 1970.

Wallace, Karl R. ed. *History of Speech Education in America.* New York: Appleton-Century-Crofts, 1954.

Wichelns, Herbert A., and Houchins, Thomas D. *A History of the Speech Association of the Eastern States, 1909-1969.* Jamaica, N.Y.: Speech Association of the Eastern States, 1969. Reprinted from *Today's Speech* May 1969

Sources Frequently Consulted

This is a good place to set down the references most frequently used. Anyone building a course, compiling a list of references, preparing a lecture, or writing an article or a dissertation should know about the following:

The card catalog of your university library. Your university may also contain catalogs of books in other institutions, as for example the British Museum or the Library of Congress.

Guides to periodical literature. The *Readers' Guide to Periodical Literature* is a complete cumulative index to articles published in more than a hundred selected periodicals. *Poole's Index* covers, with its supplements, periodicals from 1802 to 1906. The *Education Index* covers the educational field, including, since 1929, the *Quarterly Journal of Speech.* Before 1929, *QJS* was indexed in the *Readers' Guide.* The *International Index* contains a selected list of learned journals, including the *Educational Theatre Journal.*

The United States Catalog and its supplement, *The Cumulative Book Index,* together comprise a list of books printed in the English language.

Speech Monographs annually lists all titles of theses and dissertations, in speech, drama, and speech pathology, classified according to the institutions granting the degrees. A combined *Index* of these titles for the years 1902-1944 appears in *Monographs* for 1945. Drama titles appear annually in the *Educational Theatre Journal.* Since 1951 the annual June issues of *Speech Monographs* have listed titles of proposed doctoral dissertations. *See also* Giles Wilkeson Gray, "Doctoral Dissertations in Areas Contiguous to Speech," *Speech Monographs,* November 1957.

Abstracts of theses and dissertations. For some years these were compiled by Clyde W. Dow of Michigan State University and issued in mimeographed form. Since 1946 they have appeared annually in *Speech Monographs.* As an experimental venture, SAA published, in 1954, a pamphlet containing abstracts of masters' theses for the preceding year, continuing in *Monographs* the publication of abstracts of doctoral dissertations. Beginning in 1955, the annual June issue has contained abstracts of doctoral dissertations; abstracting of master's theses has been discontinued. *Note:* in 1970, the bibliographic features which appeared in *Speech Monographs* were incorporated into the *Bibliographic Annual* in *Speech Communication.*

Index to the Table of Contents of the Quarterly Journal of Speech, Speech Monographs, and *Speech Teacher.* This is brought up to date about every two years by SCA.

Index to the Quarterly Journal of Speech, 1915-1954. Compiled by Giles W. Gray. More complete for the years covered than the bulletin described just above.

Bibliography of Speech Education. Compiled by Lester Thonssen and Elizabeth Fatherson, was published in 1939 and includes titles of books, theses, monographs, and periodicals in speech, drama, and speech pathology. The *Supplement,* compiled by Lester Thonssen, Mary Margaret Robb, and Dorothea Thonssen, brings the compilation down to 1950.

The Index and Table of Contents of Southern Speech Journal, 1935-1965, Western Speech Journal, 1937-1965, Central States Speech Journal,

1949-1965, and *Today's Speech, 1953-1965,* indexes those regional publications. In 1970, indexes to SCA and regional journals were combined into a new index and table of contents.

Psychological Abstracts; Physiological Abstracts; Index Medicus. These publications contain abstracts on the fields suggested by the titles. Much material here for researchers in speech science, psychology of speech, speech correction and pathology.

Bibliography on Theatre and Drama in American Colleges and Universities. This publication appeared as the November 1949 issue of *Speech Monographs.*

Bibliography in Rhetoric and Public Address. This annual compilation is a project of SCA. It first appeared in the *Quarterly Journal of Speech* in April 1948, and April 1949. Since 1950 the lists have appeared annually in the June issue of *Monographs.*

Rhetoric and Public Address: A Bibliography 1947-1961. Compiled by James W. Cleary and Frederick W. Haberman. Madison: University of Wisconsin Press, 1964.

A Bibliographical Guide to Research in Speech and Dramatic Art. Compiled by Oscar G. Brockett, Samuel L. Becker, and Donald C. Bryant. Chicago: Scott, Foresman, 1963.

Bibliography of Speech and Theatre in the South. Published annually in the *Southern Speech Journal.*

Bibliography of Experimental Studies in Oral Communication. Published annually as the winter issue of the *North Carolina Journal of Speech.* Chapel Hill, N.C.

Spectra. This bimonthly publication of SCA is invaluable and indispensable. Every issue is filled with reports of current and possible future developments.

Higher Education and National Affairs. This bulletin, published by the American Council on Education about forty times a year, contains timely information on all aspects of higher education. Every department should have access to it.

Academe. This bulletin, published five times a year by the American Association of University Professors, focuses on chapter and other professional interests. The special reports, such as "Project to Improve College Teaching" (February 1970), are valuable.

Speech Abstracts. California State College. Long Beach, Calif. 90801. Abstracts of current scholarship in the field of speech communication, published annually.

on planning
a teaching career

Students often enter the profession of teaching speech without fully knowing either its requirements or its rewards. This chapter will start with the problem of the individual contemplating a speech major. It will consider choice of courses; participation in activities; finding the first position; writing a letter of application; being interviewed; weighing salary and opportunities; doing additional graduate study; building a specialty; finding a better position; weighing high school versus college teaching; and teaching versus administration.

Choice of Courses

The best policy of choosing courses for the major is well established: students are advised to build on the broadest possible foundation. They may come into a speech department with decided preferences: they want to specialize in television, or drama, or debating, or one or two other fields. Public speaking enthusiasts may shun dramatics; prospective speech clinicians may avoid interpretation; dramatists may bypass debating. Every adviser meets these strong preferences.

The reason for building on a broad foundation is easy to discover. The new high school teacher is asked to teach a variety of courses. He cannot spend his whole day directing debating or teaching communication theory. He may need to teach courses to different grades, which in itself calls for well-rounded training. If his first position is at the college level, he will have no ready opportunity to specialize. Even, however, if each specialty could be pursued intensely, the student would profit by broad undergraduate training. One is a better director of dramatics, for example, if he also understands voice and articulation, oral interpretation, and public speaking.

Most vacancies listed with agencies call for teachers who can teach more than one specialty. The successful applicant is often the versatile person. For a while the school profits by his versatility; as he gains experience, he will have opportunities to specialize, partly because of increase in enrollment, partly because of resignations.

Undergraduates who plan to study toward advanced degrees are particularly advised to secure a broad background. For one reason, they will be competing for assistantships or teaching fellowships, most of which require teaching duties, usually the first course. If, for example, an applicant's experience has been entirely in drama, he will not be as attractive as a candidate who has had a broader range of studies. The first course invariably has a substantial amount of discussion and speechmaking in it; drama, if any, is likely to be limited to improvisation or role-playing. Perhaps a more serious reason is that a graduate department likes to take a prominent part in developing a student's specialty, regardless of what it is. If he comes to the department already having had beginning, intermediate, and advanced courses in that specialty, the department has less opportunity to expose him to the thinking of its own professors in that specialty.

Broad training includes more than courses in speech. Economics, political science, art, literature, psychology, physical and natural science, language, and history are all invaluable. Zoology and psychology are helpful to the speech clinician. The director of dramatics and the teacher of radio and TV need as much art, music, and literature as they can get. Discussion, debating, and public speaking are fortified by history, government, sociology, economics. Phonetics builds profitably upon language study. Graduate degrees also often require a reading knowledge of French or German, or a proficiency in statistics.

The foregoing needs to be read against the background of a steadily increasing specialization in teaching and learning. The broad background of tomorrow will be considerably limited compared to the broad background of yesterday.

Participation in Activities

Students should participate in appropriate extracurricular activities. No substitute can be found for the experience gained by one who has been an actor, a stage manager, a debater, a speaker in a contest. If an appointing officer hesitates to hire teachers who have had no teaching experience, he might feel better about one who has taken part in extracurricular activities. If you have directed a one-act play you know a little about teaching. If you have been on a debate team, taking part in its tryouts, rehearsals, criticism sessions, and tournaments, sometimes judging and often being judged, you can undertake the management of a class with greater confidence.

In addition to participating, you should also often be a listener. If you have attended fifteeen or twenty plays and debates, you have subtly improved your standards. Listening to public speeches is of great value. Every campus has distinguished visitors during the year, and the information they bring will enlarge your horizon. You cannot profitably teach speechmaking exclusively out of a text; you need to complement its information with personal observation. You also need to make speeches. Even if the audience is small, you gain from the practice. The experience of making the unimportant talks helps with the important ones.

A similar argument can be made for readers theater, TV, discussion, clinical demonstrations, campus conferences, and tournaments.

Four Levels of Planning

Every individual in academic life needs to involve himself in four levels of planning.

Subsistence level. In this day-to-day category, the academic is concerned with the lesser fragments of the educational venture: this afternoon's appointment, tomorrow's assignment or lesson plan, day after tomorrow's rehearsal or performance.

Survival level. Here his endeavor is to survive the term or the year. He must rearrange his daily routine in order to prepare term papers or convention speeches, participate in or plan tournaments and festivals, select texts or submit budget requests.

Career level. At this level he makes decisions which alter or change his academic environment. While in the midst of undergraduate activities, the student makes plans to go to graduate school or to secure a teaching position. He changes orbit; he leaves one gravitational system and enters another.

Excellence level. Finally established in what he thinks is to be his specialty, he plans to develop it more thoroughly. He embarks on long-range programs of study, research, writing. He tries new approaches, rethinks old concepts.

Finding Your First Position

The appointing season begins in October or November, after classes have started and the general business concerned with the beginning of a new term has been completed. It reaches a peak in April or May and continues through the summer, to the opening of the school year.

The principal or department chairman will know at the outset of a new school year that some members of his staff are not to return. Some are on one-year appointment only; others have previously informed him that they are retiring, going on leave, going to graduate school, getting married, or committed to other plans. From his advance information he will seek to fill certain vacancies early, in order to get first choice of the available candidates.

Most of his staff, however, will not know until the spring whether they desire to be reappointed. About May 1 (practice varies), staff members are supposed to notify him if they do not wish to be reappointed. The principal may be able to anticipate some moves, and will encourage applications and conduct interviews. He will therefore be able to make firm offers during April and May.

Budget decisions often delay certain categories of appointments. The situation may be frozen until after a bond issue election, a legislative session, a fund drive. Hopefully these decisions are made before the prime, early spring season for interviewing candidates.

Scores of good appointments in the speech area will, however, be made during the summer. These will not normally be open to teachers who have already signed contracts or who are committed by professional ethics not to resign after May 1 (or the agreed-upon date), but will be open to others.

The undergraduate or graduate student whose work towards a degree seems to be proceeding on schedule needs to take steps towards finding a position some months before the degree is actually conferred. Following are definite steps which can be taken.

You should let your professors know that you are interested in a position. Invariably your teachers hear of opportunities, but may not automatically think of you. You will need to request their permission to use their names as references, and these interviews with them will give you a chance to learn about possible vacancies.

You may enroll in the placement service operated by your college. The help of this agency will be invaluable if you want to teach in the region where your college is located. When a college agency learns of a position, it makes a canvass of its registrants, sometimes calling upon the professors for nominations. If you are the choice of the agency and the professor, your enrollment will make it easy for the college to put you in touch with the institution having a vacancy.

Enrollment involves four steps: paying a modest fee, from five to ten dollars; filling forms with details of education and experience; depositing application pictures; securing references.

The latter two require special comment. Your picture should be the best you can possibly get. An application picture is different from a gift photo. It is formal though not solemn or stiff. It should reflect an individual of maturity, judgment, good sense, friendliness, intelligence, and other qualities desirable in a teacher. It is folly to give specific advice. When the market is tight, applicants almost intuitively avoid extremes of dress. If you can visualize your picture being scrutinized by a department chairman, superintendent, or board member, you will know what kind of picture to submit.

Some controversy has arisen over the notion of submitting a picture. Those who oppose it argue that a picture makes possible a subtle kind of racial discrimination. Against this must be set the obvious fact that the interest in employing qualified members of minority groups is sharply increasing. Moreover, many appointing officers do not have the funds to call applicants in for personal interviews. In these instances a picture seems to be helpful, although everybody should know that, given a mix of twenty unlabeled pictures, no one could successfully sort out the respectable types from the criminal types.

References are highly important. With permission, submit the names of the teachers who can best speak of your work. The advice to ask a person's permission to use his name as a reference is not given perfunctorily. He may take the opportunity to ask you to supply specific career details that he might otherwise overlook. A letter from your high school superintendent will be useful if he has kept up with your college career; his name may be recognized by other superintendents who read your application. As the years go by, however, add new references to your folder and delete the old ones. Those who wrote about you at the time you graduated were not able to say anything about your career as a teacher: at best they could say only that you were promising. A letter that describes you as "full of promise" seems musty after five years, when your promise has reached a degree of fulfillment.

Many new teachers like to teach in their hometowns, or on the campus where they received a degree. This gives a continuity to their life that it might not have if they taught elsewhere. Others react favorably to the stimulus that comes from teaching in a different part of the country, where they can make a fresh start, entirely on their own. You are, therefore, not in the same school system or the same department as some of your former teachers. If a person knew where he was going to spend most of his life, he would know better how to make these choices. A Nebraskan who accepted a position in Ohio just for kicks and then decided after all to return to Nebraska would soon discover that all his fine Ohio acquaintances were gradually fading from his memory. Propinquity nourishes professional growth just as it does social acquaintance; out of sight is out of mind. Many well-known professors are associated primarily with a single institution (Brigance and Wabash, for example). This is more than a statistical accident. The institution recognizes the professor's worth, and by various kinds of financial, library, and laboratory assistance manages to keep him happy where he is.

After enrolling in your college placement service, you may also enroll in the placement bureau operated by the Speech Communication Association. This professional service is provided at cost for members of this organization, and will, in the course of a single season, inform you about vacancies that your own college agency will never learn about. You may ask your college to forward a set of your credentials to the Association office, thus making it unnecessary to secure additional references, though you will need to fill out the Association's special enrollment form. Ordinarily you will receive monthly lists of vacancies during the busy part of the placement season, so that you may write a letter of application to each school in which you are interested. As you are not required to pay a commission, the few dollars' enrollment fee is indeed trifling should you learn of a desirable position through the Association.[1]

Writing a Letter of Application

Writing a letter of application is an important step in securing a position. An agency may notify you that a high school has an opening for one who can teach speech and English, direct debating, and direct one major play a year. You may be told that a master's degree is not required for this opening, and that experience is desirable, but not necessary. Apparently either a man or a woman is acceptable. Your application should include the following materials:

I. The letter proper.
   A. How you learned about the vacancy.
   B. What you are now doing.
   C. Your qualifications.
   D. Names of others who can speak of your work.
   E. Your willingness to supply further information.
II. An outline, on another page, of your education and experience.
   A. Degrees.

---

[1] For information, write the Executive Secretary, Speech Communication Association, Statler Hilton Hotel, New York, N.Y. 10001.

B. Experience.
C. Special recognition or honors.
D. Organization memberships.
E. Personal data.

A letter illustrating this information would read as follows:

April 4, 1972

Superintendent R. J. Gabriel
Osceola Public Schools
Osceola, Maine

Dear Superintendent Gabriel:

This sentence shows you are applying through an authorized channel.

I have just learned through the office of the Speech Communication Association that you have a vacancy in speech and English in your school.

Your present work.

I am now a student at Sanskrit College, with a major in speech and a minor in English. By the time I receive my B.S. degree in June I will have completed forty-two semester hours in these two fields, including voice and articulation, public speaking and debating, discussion, communication theory, dramatic production, English and American literature, English language and composition. I have been a member of the college debating team for two years, and last year assisted with the direction of the freshman squad. I am also a member of the Sanskrit campus dramatic organization, and have been active both in acting and staging one-act plays and major productions. You will find

Mention your outline.

these courses and activities listed in detail on the accompanying sheet.

Note experience helpful to a prospective teacher.

In addition to my school work, I have had other experiences which will help me as a teacher. I spent two summers as a playground director in my hometown, being in full charge of athletic and dramatic events. I also spent a summer as counsellor in a boy scout camp. I have, of course, also had the courses in education required for a certificate, including a course in practice teaching.

For further information I should like to refer you to Professor A. G. Jones, chairman of the Department of

These references are selected to fit this particular appointment: English, speech dramatics, debating.

English: Professor R. B. Heller, chairman of the Department of Speech; Professor Henry Noell, director of dramatics; and Professor Georgia Williams, director of debating. My credentials are on file in the national office of the Speech Communication Association and are being forwarded to you.

Where the superintendent can find out more about the candidate.

Appointing officers like to feel you are strongly interested.

I am indeed interested in your vacancy and will be glad to give you any additional information that will be helpful.

Yours very sincerely,

/s/ Leon Miller.

The outline might appear similar to this:

Education and Experience of

LEON MILLER
1314 Broadside Avenue
Sanskrit, Missouri

I.   Education:
Graduate, Sanskrit High School, June, 1968.
B.S. in Education, Sanskrit College, to be awarded in June, 1972.

Courses: speech ⎫
            English ⎬   Give a complete list.
            education ⎭

II. Experience:
Practice teacher, Hokane High School, 3 weeks, 1972.
Practice teacher, Sanskrit High School, 3 weeks, 1971.
Playground director, Tulane, Missouri, summers, 1969, 1970.
Counselor, Lo-Hi-Lo Camp, Musak, Missouri, summer, 1968.

III. Activities:
Stage manager, *Hadrian VII,* major production, 1971.
Leading role of Henry in *Henry Comes Home,* major production, 1971.
Varsity debater, 1970-1972. Participated in eight intercollegiate debates; directed freshman squad, 1971.
Selected as outstanding debater, Valley invitational tournament, 1972.
President, senior class, 1972.

IV. Organizations:
Sigma Pi Alpha, scholastic honorary.
Speech Communication Association.

V.   Personal data:
   Age, 21; health, excellent; height, 5'10"; weight, 170; marital status, single.

The letter should be expertly typewritten; if necessary get someone to type your letter for you. The plan of having a letter plus a separate outline has proved highly successful. Putting personal data at the bottom of the outline is a good way to handle a group of facts that appear awkward in a letter. As a part of your application, include a picture.

Note also that the letter does not raise any problems or ask any questions. After the appointing officer has shown some interest in *you*, you may appropriately ask about salary, courses to be taught, housing conditions, and the like. Otherwise good letters are weakened by questions asked at the wrong moment. A candidate who brings up many problems in his initial letter seems to suggest a teacher who will continually be running to his superior's office whenever he hits a snag. Your questions are important, and need an answer, but you can bring them up later. A good opportunity may arise during the personal interview.

A candidate's insistence upon what are (at the moment) nonessentials loom up out of proportion particularly in a telegram. Consider the following:

VERY INTERESTED IN POSITION OUTLINED. CREDENTIALS EN-ROUTE. PLEASE NOTIFY IF APPOINTMENT MAY BE MADE FOR TWO YEARS.

To the candidate the inquiry about two years seems paramount, but as yet he is not hired even for one year. Why not word the second sentence as follows:

APPRECIATE YOUR INQUIRY. GLAD TO SUPPLY ADDITIONAL INFORMATION DESIRED.

When the appointing officer shows interest, *then* is the time to talk about the future of the position.

Another example reads like this:

JUST LEARNED OF YOUR VACANCY. CREDENTIALS AVAILABLE PLACEMENT OFFICE BLANK UNIVERSITY. IF ACCEPTABLE WIRE ON FURNISHED HOUSING AND OPPORTUNITY SUMMER EMPLOYMENT.

This telegram raises various problems: the candidate seems obviously more concerned about his own convenience than he is about getting the position. "Furnished housing" and "opportunity summer employment" are matters of the highest importance, but they can advantageously be discussed after the prospective employer begins to show an encouraging attitude. Furthermore, the telegram is too aggressive in one way and not enterprising enough in another. Here is a suggested revision:

JUST LEARNED OF YOUR VACANCY. CREDENTIALS FROM PLACE
MENT OFFICE BLANK UNIVERSITY GOING FORWARD TODAY. VERY
MUCH INTERESTED IN POSITION.

Some university placement agencies will mail credentials only by request of a
prospective employer; in that event the candidate may have to word his telegram
differently.

Although the sample letter illustrates the kinds of information that are useful
to include, it may or may not be suitable for you to follow. Write your letter in
your own style. The imaginary Leon Miller is well qualified: he has the range of
courses and extracurricular activities that superintendents wish in all beginners.
He avoids the mistake of apologizing for his lack of formal teaching experience
but sets forth the semiteaching activities that he does have. Two or three items
in his letter will appeal to the superintendent. Being a playground director is not
highly significant, but the fact that Miller was rehired shows that his work was
satisfactory. His selection as an outstanding debater, his presidency of the senior
class, and his membership in a scholastic honorary are evidence of leadership. His
membership in the Speech Communication Association shows that he is taking a
professional interest in his career.

Five years later Leon Miller will write a different sort of letter. His play
ground experience, his summer as a scout executive, his practice teaching, and
his class presidency will likely be deleted. For them he will substitute his formal
teaching experience; he will mention the more unusual of his achievements as a
teacher; he will have become a member of educational organizations; he may
have had an article published; he may be an officer in a state or regional
association; he may have appeared on a convention program. He may have a
master's degree to add to the list. In addition to his own experience as a debater
and actor, he will make note of the plays he has directed, or the record of his
debate team. He will also have other names to add to his list of references.

Some teaching assignments that may have seemed like chores take on a new
light when they become part of an application. Thus "Speech survey, three
hundred and fifty students" took long hours one fall, but in a letter of
application shows initiative and imagination. "Member of faculty committee on
discipline" consumed many sessions, but now it describes a person familiar with
various phases of the program. Your references may not write eloquently about
you, but your talent and enterprise show up in various ways on your *record;* by
slow degrees your record itself may become impressive.

Readers of earlier editions of this book have written asking whether a letter
of application should contain a statement about church preference. Church and
state should be kept separate, they sometimes argue. A candidate might preju
dice himself by identifying himself with one denomination or sect. I happen to
disagree but the decision is, after all, in the hands of the applicant. Part of the

legacy of John F. Kennedy, both from his campaign and from the thousand days of his presidency, was to eliminate a great deal of religious prejudice in this country. Actually many departments and schools are trying to recruit from various ethnic backgrounds, just as they try to recruit from different college and university backgrounds. Exceptions exist; sometimes one meets a prejudice that is as striking as a redwood. In some quarters, for example, a person is not considered really educated unless he holds a diploma from an Ivy League school. Harvard has educated presidents, but so also have Stanford, the Kansas City School of Law, the United States Military Academy, Southwest Texas State Teachers, and Whittier.

Being Interviewed

You will have opportunity to take part in interviews before your teaching career has advanced far. Since the offer of a position will hinge largely on the impression you make, you need to reassure yourself about what an interview is, and especially what it is not.

An interview is not an examination; you are not likely to be quizzed on course work. You will not have to plan a speech program for the institution, though you may be invited to make informal suggestions. You will not be dealt with discourteously; if you are, be grateful that you were forewarned and seek your future elsewhere. You may not be asked any significant questions at all.

The interviewer is trying to determine what kind of person you really are. He knows the details of your record and has letters about you. The interview therefore becomes a conversation such as you might have with an older friend. One candidate sprained her ankle just before an interview, and thus handicapped, hobbled in to talk to the superintendent. By coincidence he had just sprained his ankle, so the two had a pleasant visit about sprains, ending by his offering a contract. This topic of conversation was as good as any; since her references were good and her academic record was excellent, the superintendent simply wanted to talk informally.

You may not make a favorable impression and still get the position. Experienced administrators know that the interview has limitations, and tends to favor the easy conversationalist as opposed to the reserved person. The interview reveals little about industry, cooperativeness, resourcefulness, or even skill in teaching. A candidate was once recommended to a department chairman with the warning that the candidate was not talkative. The chairman was not a talkative person either, so the two spent most of the time in silence. After a pause the chairman said, "I think we'll get along fine," and offered the position.

The question of salary is sometimes awkward. If the appointing officer offers a salary, you may accept or decline on the spot. If you have proposals that seem more attractive, you may explore the salary question further, hoping that he can give you a better contract. If you need time for reflection, you may ask for time to think the matter over. If you are invited to name a figure, remember that administrators are not likely to put a higher value on your services than you put on them yourself. After a teacher is appointed he will not ordinarily seek out his superiors and ask for a raise; accordingly, he should make the best arrangement he can at the outset.

Interviews are by no means perfunctory. If it becomes apparent that the conversation is going against you, or that at best you will receive a delayed decision, you may have to present some fresh arguments. One candidate reported that her interview began satisfactorily but struck a snag halfway through. Apparently the superintendent could not decide whether he wanted his new teacher to teach a schedule primarily in English or in speech. This candidate promptly pointed out that she had thirty-five undergraduate hours in each field and felt qualified to teach either schedule. That information put a new light on the matter; the superintendent agreed to give her the position, saying that he could hire her now and make the other decision later.

Salaries

Teachers like to know about salaries being paid. In many communities the board of education has worked out a scale. Teachers of similar preparation and experience usually receive identical salaries, regardless of the subject they teach. Tables I, II, and III have been adapted from actual scales supplied the author by superintendents of schools. If you are interested in knowing the salary scale prevailing in a specific city, you may be able to secure a copy of that schedule along with other provisions regulating the appointment of teachers by writing the superintendent.

Opportunities in the teaching profession should generally increase even though lean years occasionally appear. A larger percentage of students will finish high school and college. As the curriculum is liberalized and modernized, more pupils will find it possible to stay in school. Those who receive college training themselves will want similar training for their children: a college tradition, once established in a family, is likely to continue.

Those who are concerned about the financial aspects of teaching should be reminded that teachers often augment their incomes with summer jobs, by lecturing and counseling, by writing articles and textbooks. Social security or annuities enable a teacher to retire with a supplementary income. Starting salaries of teachers are often as good as starting salaries in other fields. The salaries of young professors are not so far behind those of young lawyers or young physicians as they were a decade ago. Yet teachers' salaries are not nearly

Table I   Midwestern City, Population 20,000[2]

Years exp.	Bachelor's degree	Bachelor's degree plus 15 hours	Master's degree	Master's degree plus 30 hours
1	$5,600	$5,768	$5,992	$6,216
2	5,768	5,936	6,216	6,440
3	5,936	6,160	6,440	6,664
4	6,160	6,384	6,720	6,944
5	6,384	6,664	7,000	7,224
6	6,664	6,944	7,336	7,560
7	6,944	7,280	7,728	7,952
8	7,280	7,616	8,176	8,400
9	7,616	7,952	8,512	8,736
10	7,840	8,176	8,736	8,960

as high as they should be. Every teacher owes it to his profession to do what he can, in cooperation with his colleagues, both to raise standards and salaries.

Financial rewards, then, are not the principal reason for entering teaching, or any other business or profession. Abundant evidence exists to show that young people are seeking, not the top dollar, but more durable satisfactions. The basic reason for teaching speech is to serve the human race. When one ponders the awesome fact that babies are born knowing nothing about communication except to yell and scream when they are hurt, scared, or hungry, one can reflect that a big job is to be done and we should get on with it.

[2] The tables are representative of about fifty salary schedules collected by the author of this book. The actual figures themselves will quickly be out of date; the tables are included to show that most school systems operate on a fixed salary schedule, with regular annual increments, and that increments are based largely on two factors: length of experience and amount of college training. Some schools provide for merit increases for superior teachers and extra compensation for directing debate and dramatics or supervising a clinic.

A good way to get a picture of college and university speech salaries is to consult the placement service bulletin issued by the Speech Communication Association. In 1969-70 college instructors were being paid less than beginning teachers in the best high schools, although the opportunity that college and university instructors have of studying towards an advanced degree while teaching is an important advantage. Ceilings for university salaries are higher than for the best high school position. In 1967-68 full professors were being paid average salaries of from $14,000 to $18,000, with top salaries on some campuses in excess of $25,000. For later figures for the teaching profession as a whole, see the annual reports in the *AAUP* Bulletin. Between 1958 and 1970 the average increase has been 6 to 8 percent a year—approximately 100 percent increase in ten years.

Table II   Southern City, Population 75,000[3]

Years exp.	Bachelor's degree	Master's degree	Doctoral degree
0	$6,100	$6,771	$7,991
1	6,283	6,954	8,174
2	6,466	7,137	8,357
3	6,649	7,320	8,540
4	6,893	7,564	8,784
5	7,076	7,747	8,967
6	7,259	7,930	9,150
7	7,442	8,113	9,333
8	7,625	8,296	9,516
9	7,869	8,540	9,760
10	8,052	8,723	9,943

Table III   Eastern City, Population 53,000

Years exp.	Bachelor's degree	Master's degree	Doctoral degree
0	$6,500	$6,750	$ 8,000
1	6,600	6,900	8,300
2	6,700	7,050	8,600
3	6,800	7,200	8,900
4	6,900	7,350	9,200
5	7,000	7,500	9,500
6	7,100	7,650	9,800
7	7,200	7,800	10,100
8	7,300	7,950	10,400
9	7,400	8,100	10,700
10	7,500	8,250	11,000

[3]This school system also has salary schedules for those with fifteen hours past a bachelor degree, fifteen hours past a master's degree, thirty hours past a master's degree. Salary paid are for those entering the system with the number of years' experience indicated.

Additional Graduate Study

The question of type and amount of graduate study confronts every teacher. Positions in many institutions are closed to those who do not hold a master's degree. The letter of the rule is often broken, as the scarcity of teachers from time to time makes it necessary for administrators to waive qualifications and restrictions, but the spirit of the rule is in effect. A study of typical scales shows that increments to the starting salary are based upon the two factors of experience and degrees.

Distinguished departments offering graduate degrees may be found in all parts of the country; the list is given in Appendix C. Larger departments offer strong programs in all aspects of speech, but most departments have a specialty. You should study the catalogs of the institutions that seem attractive, and correspond with the chairmen of the respective departments of speech.

A graduate student should select his school carefully and complete his study at that institution until he receives his degree. A student who takes one summer at one school and another summer elsewhere, following the mirage of "taking the courses I can use" or "getting different points of view" is placing himself under a handicap. Most institutions will not accept credits toward a master's degree from another graduate school, and others may not accept more than about six semester hours. An organized program of thirty or more hours, taken at one institution and culminating in a master's degree, is more saleable than the same number of hours chosen haphazardly from four or five different institutions. The reason is that there is no simple way of appraising the work done by an academic gypsy. One who has a master's degree fits into the hiring and promotion schemes of high schools and colleges. The booklets issued by boards of education defining policies of appointing, promoting, and retiring teachers do not seem to contain a section explaining what to do about people who, instead of earning a master's degree, have spent their time attending miscellaneous short courses, festivals, little theaters, playhouses, and overseas seminars. Any department chairman would advise teachers as follows: pick a good graduate school and a field of specialization, work out a program of studies leading to a degree; and stick to the program until it is finished. Take a year off, if your finances permit; an academic year, plus a summer, should more than suffice for a master's degree if one has good undergraduate preparation. If finances do not permit continuous attendance, plan to do graduate study in successive summers. After you receive your degree, you may go vagabonding in search of different points of view.

---

slightly higher schedule is paid those who have had their experience within the system. If a teacher is under contract and is inducted into the military, he is given up to four years' credit for military service.

Study towards a graduate degree brings you again to the attention of those seeking candidates for vacancies. Your degree shows that you have brought your training up to date and that you have the combination of breadth and specialization that systematic graduate study offers. A department and an institution have placed a stamp of approval upon your scholarship and teaching capabilities.

Building a Specialty

Along the way, a teacher begins to specialize. The initial nudge may come from an increase in enrollment or a change in the teaching staff; the senior teacher has an opportunity to turn over a part of his work to someone else.

One whose bent is toward behavioral speech finds himself in psychology, sociology, statistics, computer methodology, and similar fields; he works with experimental projects and problems. The director of dramatics finds his interest in literature, art, music. His problems are building sets, working out light plots, planning scenes, designing costumes. The teacher of public speaking and debating reaches into economics, political science, sociology, and history; he must keep up with current developments. Each of these specialties has a different orientation and a different appeal. At the college level, other specialties appear: interpretation, phonetics, rhetoric, speech education, general semantics, linguistics, discussion, scenic design, stage lighting, playwriting, children's theater, TV and radio, speech pathology and audiology.

A specialty is developed through books and periodicals. Until a teacher learns to use the library—frequently, copiously, and intelligently—he cannot begin to approach his peak. For a teacher a personal library is desirable. A collection on some topic gains increasingly in value, partly because of the nature of the collection, partly because books quickly go out of print and accordingly become scarce. Many items in your collection may cost you nothing to acquire; a collection of speech syllabi covering the last twenty-five years could have been acquired practically for the postage. Used books are as good as new, provided they are in readable condition. By spending time in secondhand book stores, and by consulting the lists issued by such firms as Goodspeed, Heffer, Blackwell, Allen, or Barnes and Noble, you can get out-of-print copies. Addresses of these and many other leading booksellers may be found in any book review periodical.

Whether or not you can afford to collect books, you will find interest and profit in clippings. One teacher has folders of speakers in animated poses, invaluable material for illustrating gesture. Another collects pictures of faces, useful for makeup and characterization. After observing fifty different kinds of beards and mustaches, or seventy-five different kinds of noses, students get a better idea of what can happen to the human face. Another collects playbills of Broadway productions. You may also collect parliamentary law oddities and entanglements, pictures of rooms (for stage sets), cartoons about speakers, jokes about speechmaking, reproductions of great paintings, pictures of costumes. A folder of magazine covers like those appearing on the *New Yorker* may be useful for an hour of impromptu speaking.

You cannot, of course, depend upon books alone. An interesting way to forward your specialty is to attend conferences and conventions. Debate clinics and one-act play festivals are familiar. The annual conventions of such associations as the American Speech and Hearing Association, the American Educational Theatre Association, the American Forensic Association, the International Communication Association, the Speech Communication Association and the regional speech associations have diversified programs, well-known panels of specialists, and large audiences. Eventually a teacher becomes known as a director of debating, a play producer, a scene designer, an expert in verse choirs or pageantry, a speech educationist, and his word in that specialty begins to carry weight.

Improving as a Teacher

The beginner who earnestly wishes to improve in the classroom should avail himself of one extremely useful device: the teacher evaluation questionnaire, filled out by his own students. A sample of such a questionnaire that has been used in various institutions, and that has undergone some modification at the University of Missouri, is given on the following page. In administering this questionnaire, consider these suggestions:

1. Give it in class; it requires only about twenty minutes.

2. Convince the students that their papers will not be identified. Ask a student to collect them and hand them to the departmental secretary.

3. The last week of the semester is a good time. Avoid, however, giving it too soon before or after an especially desirable or undesirable feature of the course.

Suggestions for the interpretation of the questionnaire:

1. Transfer all the checks from an entire class to a master copy (assuming you do not have computer facilities).

2. Find the median check for each scale by counting half the number of checks from either end. This best represents the opinion of the class.

3. Put special effort into improving those checks that seem to be below par. Repeat the questionnaire with a new group next time you give the course.[4]

---

[4]This form is a revision of one that appeared in *Toward Better Teaching in College,* edited by Elmer Ellis, University of Missouri Bulletin, Arts and Science Series, Number 8, May 1, 1954, pp. 78-84. Used by permission of the University of Missouri. I am indebted to Robert S. Daniel, Department of Psychology, University of Missouri, Columbia, for these suggestions. Factor analyses run independently by him and by Charles J. Krauskopf, Department of Psychology, indicate that three fundamental teacher qualities are being tapped: structuring the course, mastering the subject, and ability to motivate.

Course and Teacher Evaluation

The purpose of this rating scale is to permit you to grade your instructor and the course. Your opinions should be marked on the answer sheet in the manner you have used for class examinations [standard optical scanning form for machine scoring].

Part A

The purpose of this part is to assist your instructor in the improvement of his or her teaching ability. You are being asked to evaluate the teaching you have had this semester in the same careful, thoughtful manner that you expect the teacher to use in evaluating your work. Please follow these procedures:

1. For each of the 18 teacher traits shown below, mark the answer sheet with the opinion which most closely agrees with your own feeling.

2. Read the trait level and all descriptions before answering.

3. In general the middle description applies to the average teacher at this institution. Thus answers A and B are above average, C is average, and D and E are below average, in your opinion.

4. Evaluate each trait separately, without considering other traits or your general opinion of the instructor.

1. Organization of Class Meetings
   A. exceptionally well organized
   B. good organization
   C. satisfactory organization
   D. poorly organized
   E. noticeable lack of organization

2. Teacher's Interest in the Subject
   A. intensely interested
   B. very strongly interested
   C. strongly interested
   D. mildly interested
   E. seems to be uninterested

3. How Interesting are the Class Meetings?
   A. high level of interest maintained
   B. somewhat interesting
   C. mildly interesting

    D. neutral in interest
    E. usually dull

4. Attention to Physical Conditions (light, heat, ventilation)
    A. active attention to comfort of students
    B. usually corrects difficulties
    C. some concern for comfort
    D. infrequent concern
    E. indifferent to comfort

5. Knowledge of Subject Matter
    A. knows everything he should know
    B. is quite knowledgeable
    C. broad and thorough knowledge
    D. more than adequate
    E. adequate for routine classroom use

6. Clearness of Explanations
    A. meaning always clear to me: explanation complete
    B. meaning is usually clear
    C. meaning sometimes unclear
    D. meaning frequently unclear
    E. explanations usually unclear

7. Freshness of Presentation
    A. fresh, lively, up-to-date
    B. usually but not always lively
    C. lively about half the time
    D. more often dull than not
    E. follows a stale routine

8. Class Discussion
    A. always highly valuable
    B. usually highly valuable
    C. often of some value
    D. sometimes worthwhile
    E. usually a waste of time

9. Feeling between Teacher and Class
    A. strong atmosphere of mutual good will
    B. most of class friendly with teacher
    C. good relations with half of class
    D. some friendliness with class
    E. teacher and class are indifferent to each other

10. Self-confidence
    A. admirable self-confidence

    B. better than average
    C. good self-confidence
    D. usually but not always self-confident
    E. disturbing lack of confidence

11. Tolerance
    A. frequently encourages students to think for themselves
    B. sometimes does so
    C. respects student opinion
    D. tolerates student opinion
    E. unconcerned about opinion

12. Is the Teacher Helpful and Easy to Talk to?
    A. friendly and eager to be helpful
    B. available and helpful
    C. helpful when student pushes
    D. sometimes difficult to get help
    E. usually difficult to get help

13. Does the Teacher Talk in an Understandable Way?
    A. I can always follow
    B. I can usually follow
    C. is occasionally too advanced
    D. usually too advanced
    E. regularly too advanced

14. Stimulus to Thinking
    A. provokes much discussion outside of class
    B. students frequently talk about class material
    C. occasionally talk about class material
    D. a few projects have stirred up out-of-class discussion
    E. I rarely think of the material beyond class or study periods

15. Fairness of Grading
    A. careful and just in grading
    B. in general is fair and just
    C. probably what I deserve
    D. grades are sometimes unfair
    E. grading standards seem to be ambiguous or whimsical

16. Use of Examination as a Learning Device
    A. goes over exams carefully to help students improve
    B. review of exams is helpful
    C. is usually but not always helpful
    D. sometimes helpful
    E. students are left uncertain of mistakes

17. Major Objectives of the Course
    A. clearly explained and made obvious throughout the course
    B. explained at start of semester
    C. implied but not stated
    D. objectives are vague to me
    E. objectives unknown to me

18. A General Rating of the Teacher
    A. one of the best
    B. well above average
    C. good
    D. fair
    E. poor

19. In Order to Improve Teaching, This Teacher Should: [Mark as many items as you think are pertinent.]
    A. speak more loudly
    B. speak more clearly
    C. speak with less monotony
    D. use more familiar words
    E. talk more slowly

20. In Order to Improve Teaching, This Teacher Should: [Mark as many items as you think are pertinent.]
    A. make chalkboard writing more legible
    B. leave material on the board longer
    C. be more prompt in starting or ending class
    D. improve personal appearance
    E. eliminate annoying mannerisms

21. The Teacher's Effectiveness Would Be Increased By: [Mark as many items as you think are pertinent.]
    A. more effective use of visual aids
    B. more frequent quizzes or exams
    C. less frequent quizzes or exams
    D. less emphasis on rote memorization for exams

Part B

The teacher will use items 22 through 41 to list specific features of the course about which he wishes student opinion. Items might be a unit on parliamentary procedure, exercise material for improving articulation, field trip to Lyric Theater, oral interpretation contest, term paper, one or more of the texts used, etc.]

Please mark your answers in terms of how you profited from the various project (or items). If you felt the project was highly enjoyable and intellectually stimulating, mark it A or B; if you could take it or leave it, mark it C; if you feel it ought to be revised or replaced, answer D or E.

[Items 22 through 41 follow.]

Part C

Summing up. Please write answers to the following questions on the back of your answer sheet.

42. Do you think the credit in this course is about right, too much, or too little for the amount of work required?

43. What aspect of this course have you liked LEAST?

44. What aspect of this course have you liked MOST?

45. What other suggestions can you make for the improvement of this course?

Scores of articles have been written on the improvement of teaching, and various scales have been devised. Below are items that reveal the student's concept of the ideal instructor:[5]

He stirs up and holds your interest in every class.
His lectures are well-organized.
He treats his students with respect.
He understands his students well.
He can make even the dullest topic extremely interesting.
He is composed and at ease while lecturing.
He is always willing to discuss a student's grades.
He has a good review session before an exam.
He has a sense of humor.
He is enthusiastic about his subject.
He discusses the exams after grading.

Neutral items are:
He gives surprise quizzes.
He doesn't care if students come to class or not.
He lists lots of material for outside reading.
He is strict with attendance.

[5] John Digman, "An Investigation of the Student Concept of Ideal Instructor," in Thomas Fujimura and Elizabeth Carr, eds., *Excellence in Teaching: Informal Talks to Faculty Members.* Used by permission of the University of Hawaii.

These items characterize teachers most removed from the student's ideal:
He makes you feel as though you are stupid for asking questions.
He criticizes students before the entire class.
He has a difficult time getting material over to the class.
He lectures in a machine-gun fashion, which is difficult to follow.
He is easily upset.

You may properly ask yourself whether the use of student evaluation forms will help you to improve as a teacher. The most systematic study comes from the University of Nebraska, where eight staff members used and analyzed evaluation forms over a period of seven years. The report of the experience of this staff contains phrases like "substantial and consistent gains" and "continued improvement."[6]

Finding a Better Position

As a teacher's career unfolds, he comes to crossroads at which he must make decisions. The first, of course, is whether or not to continue teaching. Teaching has its difficulties: it requires five to seven years of college study and a long apprenticeship. Gaining anything but a nominal raise is not simple, and securing a new position calls for a combination of talent and good fortune. At times teachers do not see the intangible rewards that the books promised; instead their work seems dull and routinized. When a teacher begins to feel like a square peg in a round hole, he should turn in another direction.

It is true that campus and classroom have been troubled. Many professors, weary of the daily confrontation, seek other intellectual outlets. Many students who as freshmen had planned to teach, decided as seniors that they preferred other careers. The new breed of student, impatient, critical, seeking relevance and meaningfulness, needs instruction from a new breed of professor. Obviously this new type of professor should be recruited in part from the new type of student.

Social restlessness is deep and profound. Centuries old, it has recently surfaced on the formerly insulated American campus. It will present industry and business with new problems. The man who left the kitchen because of the heat was startled to discover that the parlor was ablaze. The chief rule to follow in making a vocational decision is to do the thing you are equipped to do and that you enjoy doing.

[6] Leroy Laase, "The Measurement of Instruction in Speech," *Speech Teacher,* January 1958. The article contains the evaluation form as constructed and validated by the Nebraska staff. This form has items specifically designed for speech classes: "Value of oral performances assigned," "Value of instructor's criticisms," "Ability to demonstrate principles and skills," "Ability to develop desired skills in students."

High School versus College

The second crossroad is high school versus college teaching. No one answer fits all individuals. Many high school teachers eloquently defend high school teaching against all comers. Their argument runs like this: the high school age is more open, free, volatile, exciting, and impressive than the college age. High school students are full of appreciation; their enthusiasm and energy are boundless; they can absorb almost anything the teacher has the skill and patience to present to them. These same students, in college, will have more outside allegiances—more activities, dates, social events; they will require a greater output from the teacher for the same amount of applause. A high school instructor may be a better classroom teacher than his college equivalent: he must present his material with more variety and enthusiasm, or he will lose the interest of his charges altogether. He may not be so good a researcher, and he may oversimplify but, the argument runs, he teaches more effectively. He is less likely to lecture, by the hour, from notes. Furthermore high school teachers point out that salaries paid high school teachers are often higher than those paid college instructors, at least at the lower ranks. This statement will not bear up universally, but good teachers in large cities enjoy stipends that put them beyond the temptation of a college position at an instructor's salary.

Unless a teacher makes a change early in his career from high school to college, he will likely not make it at all. One reason is that he may have to take an immediate cut in salary, which in itself will discourage the move; the advantage of a higher salary ceiling will not be apparent for some years. The other reason is difficult to explain. Some individuals, after teaching in a high school for many years, are unable to adjust their vocabulary and teaching methods to older students. In the college situation they may be too authoritarian, formalized, or patronizing. This may be a prejudice rather than a fact, but college administrators hesitate to consider for a college position a high school teacher who has lost touch with the college age. Accepting the prejudice at its current value, the high school teacher should make the change early so that he may capitalize on his teaching experience without giving grounds for the impression that he cannot adapt to the new situation.

One who plans a career as a college teacher must make provision for earning master's and doctor's degrees. Little prosperity is in sight for a university instructor without the doctorate. Larger universities will appoint him to a rank no higher than instructor, and will deny him tenure. Smaller colleges may appoint him to higher ranks and on permanent tenure, but even smaller colleges prefer the Ph.D. holder. Securing a doctorate is a task comparable to securing a law or medical degree; it involves at least three academic years of study beyond the baccalaureate. It also requires maintaining a good scholastic record and writing an acceptable dissertation. Most students who are today pursuing the advanced degree are doing so by virtue of a part time teaching fellowship, which pays a nominal stipend for the school year, and allows the holder to take a three-fourths program of graduate study. A married student can finance study only if he has some additional help, such as a loan or a wifely paycheck.

College teaching is a different kind of life from high school teaching. A college teacher has twelve or so hours of classes a week instead of twenty-five or more. He has more individual conferences with students, and more faculty committee assignments. He must spend far more time in preparation. So far as salary is concerned, the average salary of college and university teachers is higher than that of the average high school teacher, and the top college salary is possibly double the top high school salary, although income tax deductions and variations in cost of living found among communities of different sizes and sections of the country make comparisons difficult.

The decision of whether to enter college teaching is therefore a complex one, and should be discussed with those who best know all of the specific factors involved. In this, as in any other decision, the teacher should take the long view, and ask himself where he wants to be ten or twenty years from now.

Teaching versus Administration

The third crossroad the teacher may reach early in his career presents the choice of whether to continue as a classroom teacher or enter administrative work.

As with most decisions, this one is likely to present itself as a choice between two specific positions: one teaching, and one administrative. Administrators receive higher salaries than teachers; they correspondingly have greater responsibilities, or at least more perplexing kinds of responsibility. They deal with more kinds of situations, and more kinds of people.

The temperament and attitudes which originally led one into teaching are likely to make him hesitate to accept an administrative assignment. Presumably he went into teaching rather than, for example, into business because he liked working with young people and with ideas, and did not want a life of meeting payrolls, managing employees, and adjusting complaints. A school administrator has some of the responsibilities of a businessman: he also has a payroll to meet, employees to manage, and complaints to adjust. Like the businessman, he is concerned with maintaining good public relations. Nevertheless there is no reason why the teacher should not consider this new vocational choice as carefully as he reviewed the pros and cons that first led him to teaching.

One distinction between teaching and administration is that administration is concerned with a wider variety of activity. A high school administrator's day is filled with conferences with students, teachers, patrons, city officials, school suppliers, lawyers, ministers, doctors, architects, editors, and nearly every other conceivable business and profession. That is because the talents of the whole community go into the creating, maintaining, and expanding of its school program. Moreover, he gives a good deal of his thought and planning to the study and improvement of the school: he needs to know what is being done poorly, what new projects need to be undertaken. He solves a variety of problems: in one morning he may discuss everything from school luncheons to a new building. A college administrator's day is equally busy. He must handle a wide variety of student and instructor problems. His is the decision largely responsible for the hiring of new teachers. He does a fair amount of speechmaking and presiding. If a teacher feels he can handle projects as these, and can take all kinds of problems in his stride, he may consider an administrative future.

An administrator's tenure has an uncertainty that a professor's does not. He may become involved in political controversy. Commenting on his dismissal by the regents, a president of the University of California said: "I left the presidency as I entered it—fired with enthusiasm."

Learned Societies and Associations

From time to time this text has mentioned various associations and organizations, and their usefulness to teacher and student. Looking at teaching as a *career,* one needs to give serious thought to lending his support to the large number of dedicated men and women who strive for the continued betterment of the profession. These are not idle words. *Lending support* should mean, to the beginner, at least these things; joining associations (at least five?) and paying dues (at least one hundred dollars a year?); attending annual meetings or conventions, and reading professional journals. This is a minimum, just-barely-respectable, doing-your-share-and-no-more effort, as you will see when you become a full-fledged member of your profession and become genuinely interested in it *as* a profession.

Learned and professional societies that serve the interests of our community of scholars have already been described. Another organization, professional in nature, about which beginning teachers should be informed, is the *American Council on Education.* This is an organization of organizations; SCA is, for example, one of the members of the Council. When a problem arises that affects education generally, the Council provides the machinery by which the point of view of education can be formulated. Regular meetings held in Washington bring together representatives of universities, colleges, teachers colleges, junior colleges, technological schools, selected private and secondary schools, national educational associations such as SCA and others. With other representatives of SCA, I attended a meeting at which military training was discussed. At the meeting were also representatives of history, psychology, English, and other learned societies; presidents and deans of colleges and universities; officials from library groups, and so on. If a draft law had been hastily written and enacted, college enrollments would have been drastically reduced to the detriment of the colleges and to national welfare itself. Conferences are also held on instruction and evaluation, the education of women, the federal income tax, and a host of other vital subjects.

New teachers who start their careers in high schools will quickly learn about the *National Education Association.* Many schools pride themselves on a 100 percent enrollment, and the beginner may find himself joining almost automatically. His money will be well spent. NEA has given thought to the raising of teacher salaries; its research studies are among the finest. It has helped secure more favorable tax interpretations for deductions spent in professional development. It has countless projects to improve teaching as such. Among its many successes are the securing of educational benefits for veterans under various GI bills and the National Defense Education Act. In the 89th Congress the NEA was influential in helping to formulate, refine, and expedite passage of the administration's 1.3 billion dollar measure to strengthen elementary and secondary schools. Founded in 1857, now in its second century, NEA's purpose is "to elevate the character and advance the interests of the profession of teaching and to promote the cause of popular education in the United States." SCA is a department within NEA.

New college instructors will find their attention being directed to the *American Association of University Professors.* It was founded in 1915 with a charter membership of 867. Nearly every college campus has a local chapter.

AAUP has had a long history of championing the improvement of academic tenure. If a professor on permanent tenure is summarily or unfairly dismissed, AAUP intercedes in his behalf with his superiors. More recently AAUP has also launched a strong effort to improve teaching salaries. In 1957 it endorsed the recommendation of the President's Committee on Education Beyond the High School that academic salaries be doubled within the next decade, and it has adopted a formal program to carry out this goal. Its Committee Z now has rated every college and university from AA (the top) to F, as to whether its salary scale is unduly low relative to the scales maintained by comparative institutions. Where this deficiency is found to exist, those in authority will know that the situation has been called to public attention and will face a frank challenge. AAUP continually puts before the Tax Court evidence that research, travel to conduct research, attendance at learned conventions, and service on committees related to academic life are an integral part of the academic world, and that expenses in connection with these activities are fairly and properly deductible. These enterprises help to raise the economic status of the profession.

The strong advice of this book to any reader who is serious about his teaching career is to affiliate actively with a choice of associations such as the aforementioned so that they may continue to work for the profession of teaching.

Looking Ahead

A teacher's career thus may unfold in many directions. For an alert and enterprising person, the future holds intriguing possibilities. This chapter suggests a few of them, so that the beginning teacher will have an idea of where he is headed. Everything rests upon doing a good job in the classroom, and from there building out into the community and into the profession. In a service station is a sign addressed to the employees. "Would you like to be the president of this corporation?" it reads. "If so, right here is a good place to start." A similar opportunity may exist in your own classroom.

Let us put the matter another way. Imagine one who has gone to colleges and universities for seven long years and has amassed more than two hundred semester hours of credit. Imagine also that he has dipped into a specialty deeply enough to write a dissertation about it; and that, moreover, he has attained ten years of teaching experience. Certainly he has reached the summit of wisdom! If, however, you would ask such a person a candid question as to how much he uses all of that formal education, he would probably reply that from 60 to 90 percent of what he now teaches he has learned since graduate school days. Lawyers and physicians of equal training and experience would tell you much the same story. "In medical college," a physician might say, "I learned the fundamentals, of course; but most of my methods of treatment I have acquired since I took my last degree."

We all hope that the attainment of your last degree gives you a firm grasp of the fundamentals of your field. All degrees, however, are awarded at a ceremony called *commencement*. A long road stretches out ahead of you, as it does ahead of the rest of us.

Assignments

1. Collect salary schedules from school systems or from your state teachers association and compare with those printed in this text.
2. Consult the *Bulletin* of the American Association of University Professors for salary schedules, news items about salary trends, reports of professional surveys. Note: the *Bulletin* contains listings of positions open and positions sought.
3. Study current editions of the *SAA Teacher Placement Bulletin*. Review for yourself the kinds of qualifications most in demand, kinds of positions open, types of institutions seeking new staff.

References

Anapol, Malthon M. "A Survey of Graduate Study in Speech." *Speech Teacher* November 1967.

Conant, James Bryant. *The Citadel of Learning.* New Haven: Yale University Press, 1956.

Castle, William E. "Employment Opportunities in Speech Pathology and Audiology: Fact and Prophecy." *Central States Speech Journal* February 1967.

Eubank, Wayne C. "Improving Speech Training." *Western Speech* January 1951.

Fujimura, Thomas, and Carr, Elizabeth. eds. *Excellence in Teaching: Informal Talks to Faculty Members.* Honolulu: University of Hawaii, 1957.

Giffin, Kim, and Blubaugh, Jon A. "A Survey of Salary Conditions in Speech Departments in American Colleges, Universities, and Junior Colleges." *Speech Teacher* March 1964.

Haberman, Frederick W.; Work, William; White, Melvin R.; Castle, William E.; and Breitenfeld, Frederick, Jr. "Employment Opportunities in My Field." *Central States Speech Journal* February 1967.

McCroskey, James C., and Jackson, Ted R. *A Survey of Graduate Assistant Opportunities in Speech Communication.* East Lansing: Department of Speech, Michigan State University, 1968.

Roberts, Mary M. "Choosing the Time and Place for Graduate Study." *Speech Teacher* January 1966.

Thomas, Gordon L. "Graduate Degree Practices in Speech." *Speech Teacher* November 1968.

Tucker, Raymond K. "The Speech Teacher in American Industry." *Speech Teacher* September 1960.

From the Superintendent of Documents, Washington, D. C. 20402, you may secure a copy of the *Occupational Outlook Handbook,* issued from time to time (1966-67 issue, BLS Bulletin 1450, $5.00). *Reprints* from selected chapters are also available: 1450-78, Speech Pathologist, Audiologist (.05 cents); 1450-111, Radio and Television Broadcasting Occupations, (.10 cents); 1450-83, Teacher; College Professor (.10 cents); 1450-56, Drama Teacher (.10 cents).

The Research Division of the National Education Association issues periodic *Research Reports* on salary schedules. Consult your reference library for recent issues, or write the Association office (address in the Appendix).

U.S. News and World Report is alert to academic and financial changes in the educational scene. It reports enrollments, curriculum developments, salaries offered university graduates in various fields, legislation affecting students and institutions, federal grants, and the like.

20

the lost art of studying

If Socrates was the perfect teacher, the reason is that he was the perfect student. His suspicion of the Sophists was based upon the fact that their primary desire was not to learn. They preferred to lecture.

Mark Van Doren

This chapter is addressed to those who sit in front of a teacher's desk and to those who stand behind it. Anyone who wishes to improve the capacity of his pupils to learn, or to enhance his own effectiveness as a teacher, should ever seek better ways of studying.

Look first to the younger students. In a day when college freshmen are better prepared than ever, administrators and professors can still say, "Many graduates of public high schools do not do well in our institutions." They argue that many youngsters have lost the art of studying. They even imply that they never learned the art of studying.

The criticism is heard so frequently that it cannot be ignored. High school graduates with poorly developed study habits do land on college campuses. Here is a state university currently offering instruction to twenty thousand students. Next year it may be twenty-one thousand, and in ten years thirty thousand. As financial support is not increasing so rapidly, classes are bound to become larger. It will be difficult to instruct each young man and woman well. Many students will get lost. Those who get lost first will be those who have not fully acquired the art of study. Any teacher who looks ahead quickly sees he will have an increasing responsibility to discuss methods of studying.

Contrasts are painful, but look into the career of a South Carolina youngster getting ready to enter Yale. He is pale and gaunt and in only fair health; years before he had had to quit school altogether because of illness. At the preparatory school he is now attending, lessons are long and arduous. Early and late, students huddle over their books. This boy leaves Moses Waddell's school and finds himself in a Yale classroom, a little overawed as he clutches his slate in his hand. An instructor comes in, writes a problem on the board, and young John C. Calhoun bends over his slate. When he looks up from his work, he sees that he is the first to complete the problem. At once he feels that he will succeed at Yale; and he ended, of course, with a diploma and a Phi Beta Kappa key.

Across the ocean, two decades later, a boy in his early teens was absorbed in his studies at Eton College. He read widely in the classics, in mathematics, in history, in literature. He was active in a debating society. The notebooks he filled as a youngster may still be seen in the British Museum. In due course he turned up at Oxford, continued his labors as a student, filled new scores of notebooks, debated at Oxford Union, and in his final year presented himself to his teachers for the exacting competitions in classics and in mathematics. William E. Gladstone won the top prize in both fields—the famous "double first"—entered the House of Commons soon after graduation, and, four times prime minister, became one of the eminent political figures of the nineteenth century.

Gladstone knew Aristotle's *Rhetoric* as well as any graduate student in the country today, and had as firm a grasp of rhetorical theory as many professors of rhetoric. Looking through his student notebooks, one wonders where one would turn now to find similar rugged, systematic, ordered study. Meanwhile his shrewd and imaginative opponent, Disraeli, was carrying on *his* program of individual studies, taking notes that embodied *his* reflections. Sixty-five years later the young Churchill, too stupid in Latin and Greek to enter any university at all, was nevertheless, as a cavalryman, reading history, philosophy, literature, and science during the long India afternoons. All of these careers illustrate the art of study.

Hundreds of young men and women today are intently at their books. Cross any college or university campus at night, and you can see lights burning in libraries and laboratories. Some students working their way through school finish outside duties at nine or ten in the evening, return to their dormitory rooms, and study until an even later hour. But where there are hundreds, there should be thousands.

Students entering Oxford, Cambridge, Manchester, London, and other British institutions seek no orientation, no general studies, no freshman-sophomore requirements; these they have had in high school. At the university of his choice each student goes to the proper adviser. "What do you wish to study?" inquires the adviser. "Nineteenth century French literature," replies the student. Or perhaps his answer is even more specialized.

This is no brief for the British system of education as opposed to ours. In this country about one person in forty is now attending a college or university. In Great Britain the ratio is about one in eight hundred. So the British universities operate with a select group, a severe limitation that appalls many of their own reformers. Students assume intellectual responsibilities with a minimum of guidance. They must be *students* in every sense. The tutors guide as much as instruct. Critics of the British system who also understand the American system say that at the graduate level the American does as well as his English counterpart; the American delays his specializing but eventually catches up, and then his more diffuse background operates to his advantage. This paragraph could be footnoted with exceptions, but compared with the English, we seem to delay our interest in the art of study, and sometimes we lose it altogether.

A teacher, therefore, who has students on the way to still higher education, should take the trouble to teach his charges how to study his course. He should demonstrate to them methods of reading understandingly, note taking, review, writing examinations. He will naturally concern himself with the effectiveness with which his students manage ideas. When his John C. Calhouns go to Yale to work their first assigned problems, they should be able to see that they are doing as well as others in the room. A college teacher often also needs to give students suggestions about how to study his course: tried methods, for example, of reviewing, of applying and interpreting, of researching.

What of those students we call *teachers, instructors, professors?* Some do well, some poorly, at the job of continuing their studying. Some keep up with the field, some fall behind. Look at the professional record of a middle-aged professor of Sanskrit. In three years he has written one short article. And this despite the fact that he has few administrative duties; in no civic, religious, or professional circle is he active; he is only fairly diligent as a classroom teacher. This man of promise has discontinued being a student. At the high school level, look at the record of a teacher of European Geography. Her classroom methods and procedures have altered about as little as the beaches at Normandy. She too, is no longer a student. High school teachers may not be expected to publish but they are expected to grow with the times.

As Josiah Royce said, studying (or as he put it, *thinking*) "is like loving and dying. Each of us must do it himself." And each of us must do it.

Behavior in the Classroom

It might be helpful to review for your students aspects of good studentship to be improved in the classroom. Ask them a few pointed questions:

1. *Taking notes.* Do you take notes in classes? Do you have a good, substantial notebook for that purpose? Do you work hard at taking notes—i.e. do you try to get as much of value as you can? Do you trust little to memory? Do you set

things down accurately? If you miss a point, do you ask a question? Do you watch the spelling of names or technical terms?

2. *Seating.* Given a choice, do you pick a seat where you can see and hear easily?

3. *Attendance.* Do you cut classes? seek duties that get you excused from class? arrive late?

4. *Participation.* Do you chatter with other students during a lecture, or do you converse with yourself, through revery or doodling? Do you take part in discussion? Do you try to avoid being called on? Are you nervous and fearful when the teacher begins to call on individuals for fear he might light on you? Does your fear discourage you from volunteering information you well know?

5. *Attitude.* Do you give every teacher a fair chance to present his material? Or do you handicap yourself by prejudices or preconceptions about him and his topic? Do you find yourself enjoying all your courses? most of them? a few? not any?

A single deficiency in these items could handicap seriously a student's effectiveness. Recall, for example, the student who does not have a notebook, or who keeps forgetting it; he continually borrows sheets and scraps of paper from his associates. To believe that he faithfully preserves and files these scraps places unbearable strain on the teacher's imagination. Recall also the student whose notes are sketchy; as the teacher utters his deathless wisdom the student is apparently saying to himself "Yes, I'll remember this." That places unbearable strain on the student's memory.

You may conduct a quiet survey along these lines:

I neglect certain courses because of lack of interest:
1. Never
2. Rarely
3. Occasionally
4. Almost always
5. Always

It is possible for me to concentrate on my studies:
1. Under almost any conditions
2. When everything is quiet and I am alone
3. After a relatively long warm-up period
4. Only when intensely interested in the material
5. Under practically no conditions

Choose the statement which best describes how you organize your time:
1. I am usually able to do a little more than is required of me in my courses.
2. I am never behind with my regular assignments in my courses.

3. I have all that I can do to keep up with the amount of work required in my courses.

4. I frequently do not have time to do the minimum amount of work required in my courses.

5. I never seem to have time to do the minimum amount of work required in my courses.[1]

While the teacher is discussing these aspects, he may quietly review his own systems of study.

Behavior in Doing Homework

Find an opportune moment to illustrate one or more of the following essentials of the art of study:

1. *Environment.* Treatises on methods of studying often contain pictures of a student trying to prepare his lesson in a room that has pinups on the wall, distracting objects on the desk, and a radio or TV in the corner. Securing a proper environment for study does not mean simply to remove the pinups, take the love letters or fishing lures off the desk, or turn off the radio. A study should be a room, or a corner of a room, that says, loudly and clearly, "When I sit in this chair, I study." At hand are a dictionary, a thesaurus, a *World's Almanac,* a *Table of Square and Cube Roots,* or whatever reference works the student has; pencils, pens, ink, paper, and other items; drawers or boxes in which to corral notes, assignments, themes in progress, and the like. If you do not have a room of your own, then you need to make use of a library; you will then have to carry more things with you so that you can study efficiently.

Students should associate with others who are studying. The atmosphere of a study should suggest reflection. It is easier to keep at your required reading if others around you are busy with theirs. It is easier to keep at your homework in your study at home if your friends are also lashed in for the night, doing their homework in their homes. Why is it that the college student, who at vacation takes many books home with him, gets little accomplished? Because the members of his family are doing everything but studying; because home no longer seems to be a place for homework; because other college students, home on vacation, have abandoned and forsaken assignments. It therefore becomes easier to do laundry, repair clothes, read newspapers, watch TV, plan parties. The home environment is now a nonstudy environment.

---

[1]*See:* the complete article by Parviz Chahbazi, "Analysis of Cornell Orientation Inventory Items on Study Habits," *Journal of Experimental Education,* December 1958, p. 141.

2. *Time.* Just as one requires a place to study, so also does one need a time. No better way has ever been devised for finding time for study than the schedule. Make a plan for a day, or a week. Compile a list of things to do. Unless a person gives himself instructions in the morning to do certain things during the day, says one educator, he is likely to lose the day. If one has a class at eight o'clock on Monday, and another at ten, he should regularly schedule studying for the intervening hour at nine. Schedules should be freely abandoned, temporarily, for cause, but by and large they help us chart our scholarly lives. "During spring vacation I will positively do this paper, or term report." *That* is the directive one gives oneself, in advance. If, later, someone comes forward with a proposal to go fishing, one can then say, "No, I've already planned to write a paper."

So, work out a schedule for yourself. These two hours on Monday afternoon are reserved for speech pathology. Those two hours on Tuesday evening are set aside for rhetorical theory or dramatic literature. You will profit by the nudge it gives you to order your scholarly existence.

3. *Motivation.* A schedule provides you with a motivation to study at a specific time. A scholar must also find other ways of motivating himself to study when he is not under the pressure of a deadline. Nearly everybody can study a required assignment thirty minutes or an hour before the class meets. Nearly anybody can buckle down to the writing of a term paper the night before it is due—can stay up all night if necessary. Nearly everybody is capable of long, persistent, organized study in preparation for final examinations. But what about the quiet hours and the quiet days before the deadline makes itself felt? Where then are habits of study?

A professor of my acquaintance, who at times finds himself too fatigued to study in the evening, motivates himself in this way: "Although I am weary, I will tackle this project and give fifteen minutes to it. If at the end of that time I am still fatigued, I will abandon it." So he forces himself to give the venture a fifteen-minute trial; and then, more often than not, he finds he has stimulated his alertness, and he may stay at his deak until midnight.

Fatigue is easily substituted for inertia or lack of interest. Every high school or college student has had the experience of spending all day Saturday decorating a gymnasium for a dance. With other members of the committee he has worked up to the last minute before the dance begins. Every muscle in his body aches. He has lost interest in the dance; he would like to go to his room and sleep. But advance commitments have been made. Somewhere else on the campus is his date, eagerly making preparations for the evening. To cancel the date would be a painful ordeal indeed. So he forces himself to clean up and dress. Once the dance begins, he finds he is no longer weary. He has somewhere found a second wind. Actually he may go strong until midnight or one o'clock, and then stay up for an hour or two longer.

Study, itself, at times becomes absorbing. The professor who worked out the "fifteen-minute trial" saw that a little determination might see him through the fatigue-period until the interest-period began to take over.

Another professor has on his desk a list of things to do when he doesn't feel like doing anything. This list includes simple chores like cleaning out the files, bringing his scrap book up to date, arranging his color slides. These tasks revive his interest in materials so that when he has finished he may have a new idea or inspiration.

Still another professor uses a secretary as a starter or prodder. To get himself under way on a new productive period, he hires a secretary or a part-time typist. He tells her that he will have work for her at two o'clock Monday afternoon. This forces him to get busy and do some advance writing. Having engaged her services, he needs to keep her busy, which motivates him to keep at his study and research.

Once you become absorbed in a task, you forget your weariness. Everybody knows this is true during final examination week. It is also true during other weeks of the year.

4. *Compulsion.* Compulsion is a ten-letter word that we should respect more than we do. We have discussed methods in the preceding paragraphs whereby one can motivate himself to do more than he otherwise might. Compulsion is motivation with its belt tightened. *Option* becomes *necessity; should* turns to *must.*

A high school student may say to himself, "I do not have to take this fourth year of English, but I will make myself take it because I need it." He knows that once he enrolls in the course, the compulsive forces of the classroom will keep him at his objective. A college student will say, "I do not need to take this additional course in public speaking, but I will make myself take it because I need it." Again, the compulsive forces of the classroom will lead him to forego his momentary worries about anxiety and apprehension. Another student may say, "It is hard for me to get up in the morning, so I will enroll in this eight o'clock section, which will make me get up and get the day started."

A teacher may, similarly, decide to undertake or to resume graduate study. The achievement of graduate degrees is expensive, time-consuming, and self-disciplining. Once, however, the teacher makes the decision and enrolls, the compulsive forces of the school will keep him at his labors.

Opportunities confront all of us to put ourselves under the discipline of this ten-letter word. Compulsion may be almost as important to the scholar as motivation.

5. *Momentum.* How difficult it is to overcome inertia—to change a habit, to reverse a direction, or, in simple words, *to get started.* A graduate student knows that in order to obtain a Ph.D. he will have to demonstrate a reading knowledge of German. He knows that he should get some books or records or

flash cards, audit a course, engage a tutor, or maybe all of these. Each of these things seems simple, but actually any of them represents a major reorganization of time. Hence it is not easy to take the first step and actually develop momentum.

On occasion one meets an individual, who must be bolted together better than most, who seems not to have this problem. He holds the road well and corners nicely. With him an idea is followed immediately by its execution. Or he may calmly ride herd on several projects, all at the same time. For most people, however, the problem is to overcome inertia, to get on with the job, to develop momentum. Once one gets started on an improved habit of study, however, momentum will help keep it going. *Thinking* about getting started, though, is not the same as *actually* getting started. The only mistake the hare made was to say, once too often, "After I get started, it won't take long."

The quarterback, the president of the firm, the general of an army corps, all know the value of a sustained drive. Momentum is also of incalculable value to the student.

6. *Writing.* Those who have not read Professor Hardin Craig's "How to Be a Productive Scholar Without any Time to Work" should locate this sensible, provocative piece. It circulated among his friends at the University of Missouri and elsewhere before finally appearing in print. Among several bits of advice, he urges students to write well, and in good form from the start. "It is surprising how quickly such work builds up on the basis of a few minutes or an hour or two at a time." Have some work to occupy spare time at home as well as at the office or the library. "If you will thus integrate your intellectual life with your professional and domestic life, you can snap your fingers at the foundations."[2]

The Art of Reading

A better source of information than the library may exist, but I have failed to find it. (I am not now thinking about the laboratory or Mother Nature's great school.) Before anyone can start a line of thought, scientific or artistic, he should know what has been done before. He should develop an affection for books. "Only hold a book before my nose," declared Socrates, "and you may lead me all around Attica." Emerson called books "a resource against calamity." And Dr.

[2]Hardin Craig, "How to Be a Productive Scholar Without any Time to Work," *American Scholar,* Winter 1965-66, pp. 126-127. Craig, a Shakespearian scholar, taught at the University of Iowa, Stanford University, University of North Carolina, and elsewhere before he started many years of teaching and writing at the University of Missouri in 1949.

Oliver Wendell Holmes declared, optimistically, that even the foolish book "is a kind of leaky boat on a sea of wisdom; some of the wisdom will get in anyhow."

The beginning teacher should fortify himself with armfuls of books. If the nature of poetry is his theme, read widely about it. If parliamentary procedure is the order of the day, read about each motion in a variety of texts.

The card catalog talks in eloquent language to all students if they will listen. Suppose you want a good book on William Pitt, the great war minister who founded the British empire and was one of the influential speakers of the middle eighteenth century. Suppose you want to make a ten-minute oral report in which you summarize the principal events in Pitt's dynamic career. You therefore need to consult sources that give you a broad perspective. You need something new, concise, broad-based. In the card catalog you find a dozen entries. One says, "Don't take me—I'm dated 1812." Usually old books are less authentic than recent researches of scholars. Another says, "Don't take me—I'm in two volumes." That entry might be fine for someone else, but you want the broad outlines, not the cabinet intrigues. Another says, "I'm written in French," and another, "Reread my title—*The Love Letters of William Pitt.*" But you find one, written two years ago, which the card says is 250 pages long: this is where to start.

This description will seem far-fetched only to the novice. Yet, every teacher of experience has had students come bearing books that had little usefulness for the purpose in mind.

Once a student gets the proper book he *needs to learn how to study it.* Suppose he has been assigned to read a certain Chapter 13. The procedure of most students seems to be to open the book to Chapter 13, begin by reading paragraph one, then paragraph two, then paragraph three. But since psychologists tell us that the mind has the capacity to organize and mobilize ideas if given a chance, a better suggestion is to turn to Chapter 13, and turn the pages slowly, picking up a key phrase or two on each page as you turn it. You might begin, for example, by reading the center and side headings. When you have finished your stint of turning the pages, you have an idea of what the chapter is about. *Then* give the chapter a detailed reading.

Look at a specific Chapter 13 which has the brief title "Entertaining." As it is found in a public speaking textbook, its purpose is to tell how to introduce humor, or other entertaining devices, into a speech. As you turn the pages, these headings leap out:

Types of Humor
Understatement
Overstatement
Irony
Ridicule

Satire
Puns and Plays on Words

Types of Stimulation
The Striking
The Antagonistic
The Problematical
The Unusual
The Familiar

In two minutes you know the plan of the chapter. Your mind is now equipped with a few pegs on which to hang ideas. You flip the pages again, to get the main headings better in mind. This time you also catch names like Mark Twain, Will Rogers, Bob Hope, and others. Now you are ready to go back to the beginning and read the chapter carefully. Now you have a mental map of the territory you are to cover.

Some books, unfortunately, do not respond well to this sort of procedure. Their basic organization is so wobbly that the chapters are confusing rather than enlightening. In those instances the student needs not only to read but to sort out and interpret. But almost any chapter is easier studied if you precede your reading by a preview or two.

This advice is as useful to teachers as it is to students. We need to learn how to rapidly discover the general nature of a book. We need to learn to see at once the devices that suggest the mood and tone and fullness of treatment of a book, the caliber of its scholarship; and, most of all, its value to us right now. Once we locate the right book, *then* we can bear down on it with all our mental resources.

Tell your students also that they need to learn *how to remember what they read.* We are all inherently smarter than we think we are. But our internal combustion engines waste too much power. Pressure blows past our loose rings and our leaky valves.

Here again the remedy is a simple one, but we need to remind our students and ourselves of it. The secret is to be *mentally active while studying.* Discuss with your friends the ideas you read, as Fox and Burke did. Put your fleeting thoughts down in a journal, as Sheridan and Disraeli did. Take copious notes, as Gladstone did. With the most majestic intentions in the world you can curl up with a good, exciting textbook in an overstuffed chair at eight o'clock in the evening. At eight-thirty you are weary, and at nine you are sound asleep. You were not mentally active enough. Leave the stuffed chair and sit at a desk; write marginal notes; prepare an outline of what you are reading; stop and think about it. Look up words, ferret out allusions, refresh your memory of historical or literary events. "A Ph.D. should not be a cento," says the book. Whatever does *cento* mean? and how is it pronounced?

Literature on the art of studying is extensive. These suggestions are partly concerned with the importance of showing the student how to motivate himself for study, how to select and read books effectively, and how to remember what is read. We can expose students to continental masses of material through lectures, demonstrations, class discussions, assignments. If we can take the second step, and get the student to think for himself, and explore for himself, we can tap a lusher source of intellectual activity. Though he may forget the facts to which we exposed him, he can develop a habit of study to serve him all his life. The art of teaching will take a student a long way, but the art of studying will take him farther. The art of studying will take the teacher a long way, too. As an eminent physicist explained, he had to learn his subject three times because new discoveries made obsolete his old information. Yet whereas it took him twelve years to earn his first Ph.D., the second time he mastered his completely new subject in five, and the third time in two. "I am," he said, "an educated man, because I have learned how to study."[3]

Assignments

1. Evolve a discussion on "How Study Habits can be Improved." The discussion may be started by role playing, with members of the class enacting different types of students, by the presentation of a real or fictitious case, or by a formally constituted panel of symposium.

2. Give reports from selected chapters in the references below.

Questions for Classroom Discussion

1. To what extent is a study schedule practicable for a high school student? a university student? Report on any enlightening short-time or long-time experiences you have had with self-imposed schedules.

2. What methods of note-taking are commendable? What are the advantages and disadvantages of bound notebooks, loose-leaf notebooks, file cards?

3. Do you have different systems of note-taking in different subjects and with different instructors? What are some of the useful differences?

4. Is it true that when a student has extra responsibilities his study habits become more efficient?

References

Armstrong, W. H. *Studying is Hard Work.* 2d ed. New York: Harper & Row, 1967.

Cole, Luella. *Student's Guide.* 4th ed. New York: Holt, Rinehart, & Winston, 1960.

Flesch, R. F., et al. *How You Can Be a Better Student.* New York: Sterling, 1957.

[3]Gerald W. Johnson, "The Conquest of Inner Space," *Virginia Quarterly Review,* Spring 1959.

Gilbert, Doris W. *Study in Depth.* Englewood Cliffs, N.J.: Prentice-Hall, 1966.

Morgan, Clifford T., and Deese, James. *How to Study.* New York: McGraw-Hill, 1957.

Newman, S. E. "Student vs. Instructor Design of Study Methods." *Journal of Educational Psychology* October 1957.

Simpson, Ray H. "Speech Teachers and Self-Evaluation." *Speech Teacher* September 1964. This study by a professor of educational psychology lists seventeen procedures that can be used by teachers to improve their own instruction. The five most popular: comparative check on your efficiency by using two different teaching approaches; discussions or seminars by instructors teaching a particular course; visiting a colleague's classes; open-ended written appraisals by students; self-constructed questionnaires or checklists filled out by your own students. Speech instructors are a little above the average in use of and desire to use self-evaluation procedures (physical education, home economics, and education are just above speech; biological sciences, music, and social sciences just below).

Spaney, E., and Jennings, L. A. *Art of Studying.* Chicago: Lippincott, 1958.

Toynbee, Arnold J. "Why and How I Work." *Saturday Review* April 5, 1969, p. 22. Offers five pieces of advice to anyone who undertakes a substantial problem in research: 1. Don't plunge in precipitately; give yourself time to see your subject or your problem as a whole. 2. Act as soon as you feel your mind is ripe for taking action; to wait too long may be even worse than to plunge in too soon. 3. Write regularly, day in and day out; don't wait until you are in the mood. 4. Don't waste odd pieces of time. 5. Look ahead; have an agenda stretching years ahead of you.

Voeks, Virginia. *On Becoming an Educated Person.* Philadelphia: Saunders, 1957.

Weigard, George, and Blake, Walter S. *College Orientation: A Study Skills Manual.* Englewood Cliffs, N. J.: Prentice-Hall, 1955.

Xavier, Sister Mary. "Developing the Scholar Through Effective Methods of Study." *School Journal* December 1955.

Note: Material on the art of study is limitless. Consult the card catalog of your public, college, or university library. And a few minutes with the *Education Index* will quickly expose you to a hundred titles.

Part Five
appendixes

Effort generates creative force.

Sir Winston Churchill

appendix **a**

sentences for testing voice and articulation

Ask each student to read the following sentences clearly, distinctly, and conversationally. As he reads a sentence, listen especially for the sound indicated at the left of the sentence. The symbols are those of the International Phonetic Alphabet. Those who are not familiar with this alphabet should note that one or two letters in each sentence are printed in italics as a way of suggesting the way that symbol is pronounced.

If the reading of the sentences does not also give you an adequate idea of the student's voice, you may ask him to read supplementary material.

The numbers correspond to those used on the Survey Form in Appendix B. Use the Survey Form to record whatever defective sounds are discovered, and for other notes and comments.

For further directions, see Chapter 3.

1.	[p]	Paul looked u*p* at the ripest plum on the tree.
2.	[b]	Bob was *b*arely able to carry the books.
3.	[t]	Tell the *t*eacher the boys are fighting.
4.	[d]	Don't sen*d* the letter to the old address.
5.	[k]	The *c*lass brought a sack of candy to the circus.
6.	[g]	The bi*g* man is lagging behind the man with the gun.
7.	[s]	Some of the ball bat*s* are missing.
8.	[z]	The *z*eal of the players was amazing.
9.	[f]	Frank was laughing at the gira*f*fe.
10.	[v]	Vera and the other wi*v*es are leaving.
11.	[ʃ]	She put a*sh*es instead of sugar in the mash.
12.	[ʒ]	He had a vision of a new garage painted a*z*ure.

13. [θ]   Bo*th* of the thin men were affected by ether.
14. [ð]   Ei*th*er breathe in this way or give up swimming.
15. [h]   Henry *h*eard that it was bad to inhale.

16. [m]   The *m*an attempted to move his right arm.
17. [n]   No one knew what happened i*n* the ninth inning.
18. [ŋ]   Ri*ng* out the old, the chorus sang.

19. [l]   Leo heard the be*l*l tolling in the loft.
20. [r]   The writer drove over the *r*oad himself.
21. [w]   Will fixes the *w*agons in the winter.
22. [ʍ]   The *wh*ite foxes howl when he whistles.
23. [j]   Yesterday *y*ou argued for the union.
26. [i]   We f*ee*l that the reed needs adjusting.
27. [ɪ]   He d*i*d not intend to hit the little boy.
28. [ɛ]   In S*e*ptember Ned received a pen and pencil set.
29. [æ]   He received a b*a*d gash in the back.
30. [ɑ]   F*a*ther arrived on a calm day in October.
31. [ɔ]   He s*aw* a lawyer before he bought the loft.
32. [ʊ]   He t*oo*k as good a look as he could.
33. [u]   Two pairs of b*oo*ts were found under the stool.
34. [ʌ]   He l*o*ved his sons very much.
35. [ə]   Among the items was the editor's sof*a*.
36. [ɝ, ɜ]   Myrtle f*ir*mly believed the fur was mink.*
37. [ɚ]   He is a bett*er* sailor than any of the others.

38. [eɪ]   Make a new d*a*te two weeks later.
39. [ou]   The *o*ld man told a long, sad story.
40. [ju]   A f*ew* more feuds will give the law a cue.
41. [aɪ]   I said fix the t*i*re, not the fire.
42. [au]   No houses are built in the d*ow*n town district.
43. [ɔɪ]   After much t*oi*l the men brought in the oil well.

*The symbol [ɜ] represents the vowel sound in *fur* as spoken by those who do not pronounce their *r*'s.

appendix

a survey form
for voice and articulation

Name. . . . . Sex. . . . . Age. . . . . .

Home address. . . . . Phone. . . . . Date. . . . . .

ARTICULATION (Check defective sounds)

Stop-plosives	*Fricatives*	*Nasals*	*Semi-vowels*
1. p	7. s	16. m	19. l
2. b	8. z	17. n	20. r
3. t	9. f	18. ŋ	21. w
4. d	10. v		22. ʍ
5. k	11. ʃ		23. j
6. g	12. ʒ		
	13. θ		*Affricates*
	14. ð		24. tʃ
	15. h		25. dʒ

Vowels				*Diphthongs*	
26. i	30. ɑ	34. ʌ	38. eɪ	41. aɪ
27. ɪ	31. ɔ	35. ə	39. oʊ	42. aʊ
28. ɛ	32. ʊ	36. ɝ, ɜ	40. ju	43. ɔɪ
29. æ	33. u	37. ɚ		

General indistinctness. . . . . Foreign accent. . . . . Regional dialect. . . . .

VOICE (Check appropriate terms)

Quality: Breathy . . . .   Harsh, husky . . . .   Hoarse . . . . . .
         Muffled . . . . . .   Nasal . . . .   Denasal . . . . . .
         Thin . . . .   Infantile . . . .   Other . . . .
Pitch: Monotonous . . . . .   Sing-song . . . . . .   High . . . . . .   Low . . . .
Loudness: Weak . . . .   Too loud . . . .
Rate, duration: Too fast . . . .   Too slow . . . .

GENERAL RATING:

Articulation:

1: Needs special clinical
    help . . . . ☐
2: Below average . . . . ☐
3: Average . . . . ☐
4: Better than average . . . . ☐
5: Unusually clear and
    distinct . . . . ☐

Voice:

1: Needs special clinical
    help . . . . ☐
2: Below average . . . . ☐
3: Average . . . . ☐
4: Better than average . . . . ☐
5: Expressive, unusually
    pleasing . . . . ☐

SPECIAL COMMENTS:

Name of observer . . . .

appendix C
graduate departments of speech

Alabama
    Alabama, University of, University   35486
    Alabama College, Montevallo   35115
    Auburn University, Auburn   35683

Arizona
    Arizona, University of, Tucson   85702
    Arizona State University, Tempe   85281

Arkansas
    Arkansas, University of, Fayetteville   72701

California
    California, University of, Berkeley   94720
    California, University of, Davis   95616
    California State College, Fullerton   92631
    California State College, Hayward   94542
    California State College, Long Beach   98081
    California State College, Los Angeles   90052
    Chico State College, Chico   95926
    Fresno State College, Fresno   93721
    George Pepperdine College, Los Angeles   90052
    Humboldt State College, Arcata   95521
    Loyola University, Los Angeles   90045
    Mills College, Oakland   94615

Occidental College, Los Angeles   90052
Pacific, University of the, Stockton   95202
Redlands, University of, Redlands   92373
Sacramento State College, Sacramento   95801
San Diego State College, San Diego   92101
San Francisco Valley State College, Northridge   94101
San Jose State College, San Jose   95113
Southern California, University of, Los Angeles   90052
Stanford University, Palo Alto   94305
Stanislaus State, Turlock   95380
Whittier College, Whittier   90605

Colorado
Adams State College, Alamosa   81101
Colorado, University of, Boulder   80301
Colorado State University, Fort Collins   80521
Denver, University of, Denver   80202
University of Northern Colorado, Greeley   80631
Western State College of Colorado, Gunnison   81230

Connecticut
Connecticut, University of, Storrs   06268
Southern Connecticut State College, New Haven   06510
Yale University, New Haven   06510

Delaware
Delaware, University of, Newark   19711

District of Columbia
American University   20016
Catholic University of America   20013
Gallaudet College   20002
George Washington University   20013
Seventh Day Adventist Theological Seminary   20013
Washington Theological Seminary   20013

Florida
Florida, University of, Gainesville   32601
Florida State University, Tallahassee   32301
Miami, University of, Coral Gables   33134
Southern Florida, University of, Tampa   33606

Georgia
Emory University, Atlanta   30327
Georgia, University of, Athens   30601

Hawaii
Hawaii, University of, Honolulu   96813

Idaho

Idaho, University of, Moscow   83843
Idaho State University, Pocatello   83201

Illinois

Art Institute of Chicago, Chicago   60607
Bradley University, Peoria   61601
Columbia College, Chicago   60607
Eastern Illinois University, Charleston   61920
Illinois, University of, Urbana   61801
Illinois State University, Normal   61761
Northern Illinois University, De Kalb   60115
Northwestern University, Evanston   60204
Rockford College, Rockford   61101
Southern Illinois University, Carbondale   62901
Western Illinois University, Macomb   61455

Indiana

Ball State Teachers College, Muncie   47302
Ball State University, Muncie   47306
DePauw University, Greencastle   46135
Indiana State Teachers College, Terre Haute   47808
Indiana University, Bloomington   47401
Notre Dame, University of, South Bend   46624
Purdue University, Lafayette   47904

Iowa

Grinnell College, Grinnell   50112
Iowa, University of, Iowa City   52240
Iowa State College, Cedar Falls   50613
Northern Iowa, University of, Cedar Falls   50613

Kansas

Fort Hays Kansas State College, Hays   67601
Kansas, University of, Lawrence   66044
Kansas State College of Pittsburg, Pittsburg   66762
Kansas State Teachers College, Emporia   66801
Kansas State University, Manhattan   66502
Wichita State University, Wichita   67202

Kentucky

Bellarmine College, Louisville   40205
Kentucky, University of, Lexington   40507
Murray State University, Murray   42071
Western Kentucky University, Bowling Green   42101

Louisiana

Louisiana Polytechnical Institute, Ruston   71270

Louisiana State University, Baton Rouge   70821
Louisiana State University, New Orleans   70122
Northeast Louisiana State College, Monroe   71201
Northwestern State College of Louisiana, Natchitoches   71457
Tulane University, New Orleans   70113

Maine
Maine, University of, Orono   04473

Maryland
Johns Hopkins University, Baltimore   21233
Maryland, University of, College Park   20740

Massachusetts
Amherst College, Amherst   01002
Boston University, Boston   02109
Emerson College, Boston   02109
Massachusetts, University of, Amherst   01002
Mount Holyoke College, South Hadley   01075
Smith College, Northampton   01060
Staley College, Boston   02109
Taft University, Medford   02155

Michigan
Andrews University, Berrien Springs   49104
Central Michigan University, Mt. Pleasant   48858
Michigan, University of, Ann Arbor   45106
Michigan State University, East Lansing   48823
Northern Michigan University, Marquette   49855
Wayne State University, Detroit   48233
Western Michigan University, Kalamazoo   49001

Minnesota
Macalester College, St. Paul   55101
Mankato State College, Mankato   56001
Minnesota, University of, Minneapolis   55401
Moorhead State College, Moorhead   56560
St. Cloud State College, St. Cloud   56301

Mississippi
Mississippi, University of, University   38677
Mississippi College, Clinton   39056
Mississippi State College for Women, Columbus   39701
Southern Mississippi, University of, Hattiesburg   39401

Missouri
Central Missouri State College, Warrensburg   64093
Kansas City, University of, Kansas City   64108

Missouri, University of, Columbia   65201
Missouri, University of, Kansas City   64108
Missouri, University of, St. Louis   63133
St. Louis University, St. Louis   63108
Southeast Missouri State College, Cape Girardeau   63701
Southwest Missouri State College, Springfield   65802

Montana
Eastern Montana State College, Billings   59101
Montana, University of, Missoula   59801
Montana State University, Bozeman   59715

Nebraska
Kearney State College, Kearney   68847
Nebraska, University of, Lincoln   68501
Nebraska, University of, Omaha   68101

New Jersey
Paterson State College, Wayne   07473

New Mexico
Eastern New Mexico University, Portales   88130
New Mexico, University of, Albuquerque   88310
New Mexico Highlands University, Las Vegas   87101
New Mexico State College, State College   88070
New Mexico State University, University Park   88070

New York
Adelphi University, Garden City   11530
Columbia University, Teachers College, New York   10027
Cornell University, Ithaca   14850
Fordham University, New York   10023
Hofstra University, Hempstead   11550
Ithaca College, Ithaca   14850
New York, City University of, Brooklyn College, Brooklyn   11210
New York, City University of, City College, New York   10031
New York, City University of, Hunter College, New York   10021
New York, City University of, Lehman College, Bronx   10468
New York, City University of, Queens College, Flushing   11367
New York, State University of, Albany   12203
New York, State University of, Buffalo   14214
New York, State University of, Cortland   13045
New York University, New York   10003
Syracuse University, Syracuse   13201

North Carolina
North Carolina, University of, Chapel Hill   27514
North Carolina, University of, Greensboro   27412

North Dakota
Minot State College, Minot   58701
North Dakota, University of, Grand Forks   58201
North Dakota State University, Fargo   58101

Ohio
Akron, University of, Akron   44309
Bowling Green State University, Bowling Green   43402
Case Western Reserve University, Cleveland   44106
Cincinnati, University of, Cincinnati   45220
Kent State University, Kent   44240
Miami University, Oxford   45056
Ohio State University, Columbus   43216
Ohio University, Athens   45701
Ohio Wesleyan University, Delaware   43015
Western Reserve University, Cleveland   44101
Xavier University, Cincinnati   45202

Oklahoma
Northwest State College of Oklahoma, Alva   73717
Oklahoma, University of, Norman   73069
Oklahoma State University, Stillwater   74074
Tulsa, University of, Tulsa   74101

Oregon
Oregon, University of, Eugene   97401
Pacific, College of the, Newberg   97132
Pacific University, Forest Grove   97116
Pacific University of Oregon, Portland   97207
Portland, University of, Portland   97208

Pennsylvania
Bloomsburg State College, Bloomsburg   17815
Carnegie Institute of Technology, Pittsburgh   15219
Carnegie Mellon University, Pittsburgh   15213
Pennsylvania State University, University Park   16801
Pittsburgh, University of, Pittsburgh   15219
Temple University, Philadelphia   19104
Villanova University, Villanova   19085

Rhode Island
Rhode Island, University of, Kingston   02881

South Carolina
Bob Jones University, Greenville   29602

South Dakota
South Dakota, University of, Vermillion   57069
South Dakota State University, Brookings   57006

Tennessee
Memphis State University, Memphis   38111
Tennessee, University of, Knoxville   37901
Tennessee Agricultural and Industrial State University, Nashville   37202
Vanderbilt University, Nashville   37202

Texas
Abilene Christian College, Abilene   79604
Baylor University, Waco   76703
East Texas State College, Commerce   75428
Hardin-Simmons University, Abilene   79604
Houston, University of, Houston   77002
North Texas State University, Denton   76203
Our Lady of the Lake College, San Antonio   78207
Southern Methodist University, Dallas   75221
Southwestern University, Georgetown   78626
Stephen F. Austin State College, Nacogdoches   75961
Sul Ross State College, Alpine   79830
Texas, University of, Austin   78710
Texas, University of, El Paso   79999
Texas Christian University, Fort Worth   76101
Texas Technological College, Lubbock   79408
Texas Women's University, Denton   76201
West Texas State College, Canyon   79015

Utah
Brigham Young University, Provo   84601
Utah, University of, Salt Lake City   84101
Utah State University, Logan   84321

Vermont
Vermont, University of, Burlington   05401

Virginia
Richmond Professional Institute, Richmond   23219
Virginia, University of, Charlottesville   22901
Virginia Commonwealth University, Richmond   23220

Washington
Central Washington State College, Ellensburg   98926
Eastern Washington State College, Cheney   99004

Pacific Lutheran University, Tacoma   98447
Washington, University of, Seattle   98101
Washington State University, Pullman   99163

West Virginia
Marshall University, Huntington   25701
West Virginia University, Morgantown   26505

Wisconsin
Marquette University, Milwaukee   53202
Wisconsin, University of, Madison   53703
Wisconsin, University of, Milwaukee   53211
Wisconsin State University, Eau Claire   54701
Wisconsin State University, Oshkosh   54901
Wisconsin State University, River Falls   54022
Wisconsin State University, Stevens Point   54181
Wisconsin State University, Superior   54880

Wyoming
Wyoming, University of, Laramie   82070

appendix d

addresses of publishers and firms supplying production aids

In addition to the following suggested list, the reader should consult such publications as: *Quarterly Journal of Speech, Speech Teacher, Educational Theatre Journal, Players Magazine, Dramatics, Theatre Arts Monthly* for ads of manufacturers, distributors, and publishers. The *Annual Directory* of the Speech Communication Association also carries names and addresses of relevant firms.

The mention of a company in this book does not constitute an endorsement.

Many universities, through their Extension Division or other agencies, operate a film and filmstrip renting service. The catalogs of these universities describe the available films of many different companies. Rental fees are nominal. Catalogs issued by the Visual Aids Divisions of the University of Missouri, Columbia, and the University of Illinois, Urbana, are typical of this type of service. Some state universities or state activity associations operate rental libraries for plays.

Production Aids

Nearly every large city has a firm that supplies costumes and other items for stage and screen. In addition to those companies listed below, consult the *Yellow Pages* and the theater publications named above.

Costumes

Brooks-Van Horn Costume Co., 232 N. 11 St., Philadelphia, Pa. 19107
Dazian's, Inc., 400 N. Wells St., Chicago, Ill. 60610

Eaves Costume Co., 151 W. 46 St., New York 10036
Manhattan Costume Co., Inc., 614 W. 51 St., New York 10019

Lighting, Stage Equipment

Century Lighting, 521 W. 43 St., New York 10036
General Electric, 60 Washington Ave., Schenectady, N.Y. 12305
Hub Electric Co., Inc., 2255 W. Grand Ave., Chicago, Ill. 60612
Kliegl Bros. Universal Electric Stage Lighting Co., Inc., 32-32 48 Ave., Long
    Island City, N.Y. 11101
Kliegl Bros. Western Corp., 4726 Melrose Ave., Los Angeles, Calif. 90029
Charles H. Stewart and Co., 608 Clarendon Ave., P.O. Box 187, Somerville, Mass.
    02114

Visual, Auditory

Bogen Communication Division, Box 500, Paramus, N.J. 07652
Caedmon Records, 505 Eighth Ave., New York 10018
Coronet Films, 65 E. South Water St., Chicago, Ill. 60601
Decca Records, 445 Park Ave., New York 10022
Encyclopedia Britannica Educational Corp., 425 N. Michigan Ave., Chicago, Ill.
    60611
Ideal Pictures, 1010 Church St., Evanston, Ill. 60201
Listening Library, 1 Park Ave., Old Greenwich, Conn. 06870
A. J. Nystrom and Co., 3333 Elston Ave., Chicago, Ill. 60618

Publishers

Abingdon Press, 201 Eighth Ave. S., Nashville, Tenn. 37203
Addison-Wesley Publishing Co., Reading, Mass. 01867
Allyn and Bacon, Inc., 470 Atlantic Ave., Boston, Mass. 02210
American Book Co., 450 W. 33 St., New York 10001
Amidon Press, now Association for Productive Teaching, 5408 Chicago Ave. S.,
    Minneapolis, Minn. 55417
AMS Press, Inc., 56 E. 13 St., New York 10003
Appleton-Century-Crofts, 440 Park Ave. S., New York 10016
Artcraft Press, Standard Publishing Co., Hannibal, Mo. 63401

Baker's Plays, 100 Summer St., Boston, Mass. 02110
A. S. Barnes and Co., Forsgate Drive, Cranbury, N.J. 08512
Barnes and Noble, Inc., 105 Fifth Ave., New York 10003
Basic Books, Inc., 404 Park Ave. S., New York 10016
Beacon Press, 25 Beacon St., Boston, Mass. 02108
Benjamin Blom, Inc., 4 W. Mount Eden Ave., Bronx, N.Y. 10452
Bobbs-Merrill Co., Inc., 4300 W. 62 St., Indianapolis, Ind. 46268

Brooklyn College Press, Brooklyn, N.Y. 11210
William C. Brown Co., 135 S. Locust St., Dubuque, Ia. 52001
Burgess Publishing Co., 426 S. Sixth St., Minneapolis, Minn. 55415

Chandler Publishing Co., 124 Spear St., San Francisco, Calif. 94105
City News Publishing Co., 1 Wolf's Lane, Pelham, N.Y. 10803
Columbia University Press, 440 W. 110 St., New York 10025
Crown Publishers, Inc., 419 Park Ave. S., New York 10016

DBS Publications, Inc., 150 W. 52 St., New York 10019
T. S. Denison & Co., Inc., 5100 W. 82 St., Minneapolis, Minn. 55431
Dickenson Publishing Co., Inc., 1651 Ventura Blvd., Suite 215 G, Encino, Calif.
    91316
Diplomatic Press, Inc., 11 W. 42 St., New York 10036
Dodd, Mead & Co., 79 Madison Ave., New York 10016
Doubleday & Co., Inc. Garden City, N.Y. 11530
Dramatic Publishing Co., 86 E. Randolph St., Chicago, Ill. 60601
Dramatists Play Service, Inc., 440 Park Ave., S., New York 10016
E. P. Dutton & Co., 201 Park Ave. S., New York 10003

Fearon Publishers, 2165 Park Blvd., Palo Alto, Calif. 94306
Samuel French, Inc., 25 W. 45 St., New York 10036
Funk & Wagnalls, 380 Madison Ave., New York 10017

Ginn and Co., Statler Bldg., Back Bay P.O. 191, Boston, Mass. 02117

Hafner Publishing Co., 260 Heights Rd., Darien, Conn. 06820
Harcourt Brace Jovanovich, 757 Third Ave., New York 10017
Harper & Row, 49 E. 33 St., New York 10016
Hastings House, Inc., 10 E. 40 St., New York 10016
D. C. Heath & Co., 125 Spring St., Lexington, Mass. 02173
Holbrook Press, Inc., 470 Atlantic Ave., Boston, Mass. 02210
Holt, Rinehart & Winston, Inc., 383 Madison Ave., New York 10017
Houghton Mifflin Co., 2 Park St., Boston, Mass. 02107

Indiana University Press, Tenth & Morton Sts., Bloomington, Ind. 47401
Institute of Modern Languages, 1666 Connecticut Ave. N.W., Washington, D.C.
    20009
Interstate Oratorical Association, Wayne State University, 694 Putnam, Detroit,
    Mich. 48202

Johnson Reprint Corp., 111 Fifth Ave., New York 10003

Alfred A. Knopf, Inc., 201 E. 50 St., New York 10022

J. B. Lippincott Co., E. Washington Sq., Philadelphia, Pa. 19105
Little, Brown & Co., 34 Beacon St., Boston, Mass. 02106
Louisiana State University Press, Baton Rouge, La. 70803
Lyons & Carnahan, 407 E. 25 St., Chicago, Ill. 60616

McGraw-Hill Book Co., 330 W. 42 St., New York 10036
David McKay Co., Inc., 750 Third Ave., New York 10017

The Macmillan Co., 866 Third Ave., New York 10022

Charles E. Merrill Publishing Co., 1300 Alum Creek Dr., Columbus, Ohio 43216

National Textbook Co., 8259 Niles Center Rd., Skokie, Ill. 60076

Odyssey Press, 55 Fifth Ave., New York 10003

Oxford University Press, 200 Madison Ave., New York 10016

Penguin Books, Inc., 7110 Ambassador Rd., Baltimore, Md. 21207

Plays, Inc., 8 Arlington St., Boston, Mass. 02116

Prentice-Hall, Inc., Englewood Cliffs, N.J. 07632

Random House, Inc., 201 E. 50 St., New York 10022

Ronald Press Co., 79 Madison Ave., New York 10016

Russell and Russell, 122 E. 42 St., New York 10017

Science Research Associates, Inc., 259 E. Erie St., Chicago, Ill. 60611

Charles Scribner's Sons, 597 Fifth Ave., New York 10017

Scott, Foresman and Co., 1900 E. Lake Ave., Glenview, Ill. 60025

Simon & Schuster, Inc., 630 Fifth Ave., New York 10020

Southern Illinois University Press, Carbondale, Ill. 62901

Spartan Books, 432 Park Ave. S., New York 10016

Sterling Publishing Co., Inc., 419 Park Ave. S., New York 10016

Superintendent of Documents, Government Printing Office, Washington, D. C., 20402

University of California Press, 2223 Fulton St., Berkeley, Calif. 94720

University of Chicago Press, 5750 Ellis Ave., Chicago, Ill. 60637

University of Illinois Press, Urbana, Ill. 61801

University Press of Kansas, 366 Watson, Lawrence, Kansas 66044

University of Missouri Press, Swallow Hall, Columbia, Mo. 65201

University of Washington Press, Seattle, Wash. 98105

University of Wisconsin Press, Box 1397, Madison, Wis. 53701

Van Nostrand Reinhold Co., 450 W. 33 St., New York 10001

Wadsworth Publishing Co., Inc., Belmont, Calif. 94002

World Publishing Co., 110 E. 59 St., New York 10022

Note: If you need an address not given here, try the order department of your public library or consult *Literary Market Place,* published annually by R. R. Bowker Co.

Periodicals

Congressional Digest, 3231 P St. N.W., Washington, D.C. 20007

Current History, 1822 Ludlow St., Philadelphia, Pa. 19103

Newsweek, 444 Madison Avenue, New York 10022

Senior Scholastic, 50 W. 44 St., New York 10036

Time, Time & Life Bldg., Rockefeller Center, New York 10020

U.S. News and World Report, 2300 N St. N.W., Washington, D.C. 20037

appendix e
regional and national associations

Regional

The address given below is that of the Executive Secretary. As these addresses are likely to change with the election of each new Executive Secretary, the *Directory* of the Speech Communication Association should be consulted for the current year.

Central States Speech Association, Department of Speech, University of Michigan, Ann Arbor, Mich. 48104

Speech Association of the Eastern States, Department of Speech, St. John's University, Jamaica, N.Y. 11432

New England Speech Association, Department of Speech, University of Massachusetts, Amherst, Mass. 01002

Pacific Speech Association, Department of Speech, University of Hawaii, Honolulu, Hawaii 96822

Southern Speech Association, Department of Speech, Wake Forest University, Winston-Salem, N.C. 27109

Western Speech Association, Department of Speech, Washington State University, Pullman, Wash. 99163

National

American Association of University Professors, One Dupont Circle N.W., Washington, D.C. 20036

American Council on Education, 1785 Massachusetts Ave. N.W., Washington, D.C. 20036

471

American Council of Learned Societies, 1219 Sixteenth St. N. W., Washington,
D. C. 20036

American Educational Theatre Association, 726 Jackson Pl. N.W., Washington,
D.C. 20566

American Forensic Association, Department of Speech, Ohio State University,
Columbus, Ohio 43210

American Speech and Hearing Association, 9030 Old Georgetown Rd., Washington, D.C. 20014

International Communication Association, General Motors Institute, Flint, Mich.
48502

Committee on Discussion and Debate Materials, National University Extension
Association, 68 Prince Lucien Campbell Hall, University of Oregon, Eugene,
Ore. 97403

National Association of Educational Broadcasters, 1346 Connecticut Ave. N.W.,
Washington, D.C. 20036

National Council of Teachers of English, 508 S. Sixth St., Champaign, Ill. 61820

National Education Association, 1201 Sixteenth St. N.W., Washington, D.C.
20036

Speech Communication Association, Statler Hilton Hotel, New York 10001

Related

As with regional offices, the addresses below are periodically subject to change.
Consult the current *Directory* of the Speech Communication Association.

Alpha Psi Omega-Delta Psi Omega, Department of Speech, Eastern Illinois
University, Charleston, Ill. 61920

Delta Sigma Rho-Tau Kappa Alpha, Department of Speech, Butler University,
Indianapolis, Ind. 46207

International Thespian Society, Cincinnati, Ohio 45224

National Association of Dramatic and Speech Arts, Department of Speech, Fort
Valley State College, Fort Valley, Ga. 31030

National Collegiate Players, 4645 E. Granada Rd., Phoenix, Ariz. 85008

National Forensic League, Ripon, Wis. 54971

International Thespian Society, College Hill Station, Cincinnati, Ohio 45224

Phi Beta, 4950 W. Walton St., Chicago, Ill. 60651

Phi Rho Pi, 3214 25 St., Lubbock, Tex. 79410

Pi Kappa Delta, Department of Speech, Bradley University, Peoria, Ill. 61606

Sigma Epsilon, Department of Speech, University of Utah, Salt Lake City, Utah
84112

Zeta Phi Eta, Box 1236, Seattle, Wash. 98111

index